The Wilder Shores of Gastronomy

Hair Soup.

Wants Stuffing.

Welsh Rabbit.

Stilt-on.

Cow Heel.

A Cornish woman, receiving the words "Smothered in Onions" *literally*, secured a tame rabbit to a corner of her pantry, and continued covering it with the edible *roots*, till she had raised a *cairn* above its breathless corpse!

The Wilder Shores of Gastronomy

Twenty Years of the Best Food Writing from the Journal *Petits Propos Culinaires*

Edited by ALAN DAVIDSON
with HELEN SABERI

Foreword by Harold McGee

TEN SPEED PRESS
Berkeley | Toronto

Royalties from this book will go in full to the Sophie Coe Memorial Prize Fund (see page x).

Distributed in Australia by Simon & Schuster Australia, in Canada by Ten Speed Press Canada, in New Zealand by Southern Publishers Group, in South Africa by Real Books, in Southeast Asia by Berkeley Books, and in the United Kingdom and Europe by Airlift Book Company.

Ten Speed Press
P.O. Box 7123
Berkeley, California 94707
www.tenspeed.com

Design by Nancy Austin
Frontispiece illustration from *The Epicure's Almanac* (How and Parsons, London, 1842)

Library of Congress Cataloging-in-Publication Data

The wilder shores of gastronomy : twenty years of the best food writing from the journal Petits propos culinaires / edited by Alan Davidson with Helen Saberi.
p. cm.
ISBN 1-58008-417-6
1. Food writers. I. Davidson, Alan, 1924- II. Saberi, Helen. III. Petits propos culinaires.
TX649.A1 W543 2002
641.5--dc21

2002012313

1 2 3 4 5 6 7 8 9 10 — 06 05 04 03 02

Printed in Canada

CONTENTS

ACKNOWLEDGMENTS

We, the Editors, wish to thank in the first place the contributors who have readily, indeed enthusiastically, made their contributions available for the present book. We have succeeded in contacting virtually all the authors of the essays (or, in a few instances, their executors) and take this opportunity to invite the three or four whom we have been unable to reach to furnish addresses so that they too can be given a formal request for permission and, we confidently hope, will be able to send positive responses to match all the others.

We also thank those who have been responsible for editing and producing *PPC,* thus making this anthology possible; and in particular Jane Davidson whose involvement in these processes, all the way from *PPC 1* to *PPC 63* (the latest issue represented here), has been so close and so fruitful.

So much for the 20th century. But in this context we wish to salute Tom Jaine for enthusiastically taking *PPC* into the new century and new millennium, and congratulate him on the issues which he has published since early 2000.

We are grateful to Kirsty Melville, the Publisher, and to all concerned at Ten Speed Press, for their enthusiastic reception of what must have seemed like an eccentric book proposal, and for producing such a handsome volume to house our anthology. In particular we thank Aaron Wehner, the Commissioning Editor, for the lively and good humoured way in which he has conducted the ramified and high-speed correspondence with ourselves which was necessary; and to Nancy Austin for a lovely design. Thanks also go to Jacinta Monniere for her work creating a typescript, and to Sharon Silva and Harriet Jaine for their proof reading labours.

ANNOUNCEMENT

The Publisher and Editors are happy to announce that all royalties from this book will go directly and in their entirety to the Sophie Coe Memorial Prize Fund.

Sophie Coe was a food historian and author of great distinction, whose numerous major contributions to *PPC* and to the Oxford Symposia on Food attracted wide attention and admiration, even before her ground-breaking book *America's First Cuisines* was published in 1994, shortly before her death in the same year. Soon afterwards her husband, Professor Michael Coe, endowed an annual prize to commemorate his wife. The prize was to be £1000, awarded for an essay, article, paper or self-contained part of a book, on a food history subject. Michael Coe asked the Oxford Symposium to help arrange administration of the Fund, the appointment of judges annually, and the prize-giving ceremony. The Fund was registered as a charity, with a Board of Trustees, and the first annual prize was awarded in 1995. In several years it has been possible to make subsidiary awards; and on two occasions since 1995 Michael Coe has made generous contributions to increase the size of the Fund.

Since those managing the Fund, and the judges of the numerous annual entries, all carry out their tasks on a voluntary basis, administration of the Fund is virtually cost free. So the royalties from the present book are almost 100-percent available for prize money to promote good work in the field of food history.

FOREWORD

BY HAROLD MCGEE

It's about time! For nearly 25 years, a little British magazine called *Petits Propos Culinaires* has been publishing some of the most interesting food writing in the world. But most food lovers have never had the chance to read a word of *PPC*. Here at last is a sampler for American readers. If you enjoy it, good news: there's a lot more where this came from, and you can get a fresh helping every four months. *PPC* delivers.

PPC is nothing like the standard glossy food magazines. It's small, a little over 5 by 7 inches, barely 100 pages long, bound in a matte cover whose striking design changes with each issue, sparsely illustrated in black and white, free of advertisements. Each issue includes several substantial articles, reviews of notable food books from all over the world, and a section of "Notes & Queries" in which correspondents share observations, ideas, questions, and disagreements. Many contributors are professional food writers, but many are not, and no one is paid. In the pages of *PPC*, all contributors are amateurs—lovers of their subject—who write not to complete an editor's assignment and earn a fee, but to share their own personal enthusiasm. The results are refreshingly unpredictable and yet satisfyingly meaty, a unusual combination encouraged by the founding publishers' very unglossy editorial policy. "We have no wish to produce a homogenized publication," they announced, and contributions "should all be based on genuine knowledge, or should be intended to elicit such knowledge or to promote research."

The founding publishers were Alan and Jane Davidson. Turn the page to read Alan's own account of how, after a full career in the diplomatic service, he and Jane came to create *PPC* and then Prospect Books, the publisher of dozens of unusual and important volumes; how Alan unwittingly initiated the Oxford Symposia on food history, then semi-wittingly undertook what would become the 21-year labor of writing the masterful *Oxford Companion to Food*. Thanks to their astonishing and inspiring energy, curiosity, open-mindedness, and generosity, the Davidsons' house in Chelsea came to mark the gastronomical world's Prime Meridian, where dispatches were received from explorers near and far, collected and organized into issues of *PPC*, and dispersed to food lovers across the globe.

When *PPC*'s explorers are on the lookout, they can spot uncharted shores of gastronomy in just about any place and time. This anthology includes reports from the Middle East, Bengal, Thailand, tropical China, Japan, Africa, and Scandinavia, as well as from Europe and the United States.

There are articles on cooking in the Bronze Age and on car and motorcycle engines. There are appreciations of such exotica as cow udder, termite, viper, loon, and salad garnishes meant to impersonate caterpillars. Anglophiles will enjoy the pieces on puddings various, Yule-doos and chacky-pigs, and Denby Dale pies. There's a philosophical rumination on the art of the tapas-eating *tapeador*, and instructions for making a handy kitchen utensil from a coat hanger, copper pipe, and plastic straw. And a few dozen other items besides.

PPC is published in Britain, but it's also where I first encountered some of my favorite American writers. Here in *The Wilder Shores* Samuel P. Arnold, Denver restaurateur and chronicler of life along the Santa Fe Trail, reports on the clever processing, scary cooking, and tasty eating of rattlesnakes, complete with recipe and a commentary by Ogden Nash. Philip and Mary Hyman, independent scholars who have lived in Paris for 30 years, investigate the disappearance of the original pepper—long pepper, used even before black—and describe the checkered career of the French escargot and the surprising reasons for its recent comeback. And Charles Perry, newspaper reporter and a scholar of Middle Eastern languages, rots balls of barley dough on his Los Angeles porch until they turn black, white, green, and red, and discovers that these medieval Arab condiments were the flavor equivalents of soy sauce and blue cheese.

The Wilder Shores of Gastronomy is a delightful sampling of *PPC*s past. Meanwhile Alan and Jane Davidson have turned over the editing and publishing to Tom Jaine, who continues in their spirit, with the benefit of their advice, and with equally impressive energy. In a world filled with predictable and ephemeral food writing, *PPC* remains a rare source of substance and surprise. Gastronomers of the world—enjoy!

INTRODUCTION

Since readers may be both excited and puzzled by the promise of a journey to 'the wilder shores of gastronomy', there is a need for some prior explanation of when and how the vehicle which will take them there came into being.

The birth of *Petits Propos Culinaires* (and of Prospect Books, its publisher) was a haphazard affair. Sure, one could have demonstrated by logical argument the desirability of creating some sort of journal on food history; but what precipitated the birth was not a rational discussion but a freakish conjunction of circumstances.

In 1975 my wife (hereafter Jane) and I returned to London from Laos, simultaneously shedding our past diplomatic career (we needed only a day or so to wriggle out of that carapace) and preparing to be writers instead—indeed two partly written books were in our baggage when we landed at Heathrow. At that time it was still seafood, seafood, seafood for me and translating Alexandre Dumas' *Grand Dictionnaire de Cuisine* for Jane. A kindly warning given to us that activities of this sort were unlikely to bring more than slight financial rewards proved to be true. Jane Grigson, who gave the warning, also provided a partial remedy. She helped tide us over by propelling me into the arms of Time/Life Books, whose huge Good Cook series of 30 or more volumes was just starting, with Richard Olney as mastermind. I was embraced as a consultant, first on seafood and then on just about everything else.

It was brilliant of Time/Life to have Richard set the stamp of his creative mind on the series (and to have his artist's hands photographed in volume after volume as he did the hands-on work in their kitchen). But they didn't want him to go (as we would now say) over the top; so they ensured that there was a counterweight, in the form of the massive bureaucracy at their headquarters in Alexandria, Virginia, and the equally massive rule book which they had compiled for the project. In requiring slavish conformity to these rules they drove Richard, not infrequently, into a state of enraged frustration. This frustration became especially acute, in 1979, over the rule that no recipe could be reproduced in the books unless it had first been published elsewhere. It emerged almost at the outset that there were certain recipes which, as Richard saw it and as any sensible person would agree, just had to be in, but which could not be found in a satisfactory form in any existing publication.

When we visited him one day and heard him inveighing against this petty rule and describing its dire consequences, a solution mysteriously took shape, like a piece of ectoplasm, over the lunch table. It seemed that Richard could only be rescued from his impasse by the creation of a new journal to serve as the vehicle for rapid publication of a few recipes which could then be transferred to Good Cook volumes. So we went into creation mode.

The shape and substance of the new journal was largely determined by the views which Elizabeth David had already formed about what the world needed in this particular field of endeavour. We were all willing listeners. She was as enthusiastic as we were for helping the Royal National Lifeboat Institution. So the first issue of the journal was to benefit that good cause. I and Jane, backed by Elizabeth, Richard, Jill Norman, and our family, were to be its editors and publishers. The name of the journal was to be *Petits Propos Culinaires,* devised by a French neighbour to match our two requirements: to sound modest and to make a friendly little bow to France.

So it all happened, swiftly and successfully; and Richard had his recipe sources available in time; see the fourth and eleventh items in the reproduction of the inaugural table of contents, facing page.

Many years later we paid a posthumous tribute to Richard, in *PPC 62*, and headed it 'Farewell, Nathan d'Aulnay, farewell, Tante Ursule'—the two pseudonyms which we invented for him, so that Time/Life would not be aware of the ruse.

By no means all of those who presided over the birth of *PPC* expected the infant to survive for more than one or two issues. However, it did and it was soon peering over the side of its crib and looking to see what other activities it might perform. Within a year one lateral jump had taken us into book publishing and another had produced the prototype of what subsequently became the annual Oxford Symposium on Food. Of both, more anon. First, a look at the post-natal care of our offspring.

We were wondering, of course, at the crèche stage and while the first issue was being distributed, whether we had succeeded in establishing it on a firm basis. Well, our optimistic answer was 'yes', although others, more experienced in the ways of the world and the financial aspects of publishing, might have said 'no, not really'. Indeed, at a meeting held in December of 1981 in Santa Barbara, California, to set up the American Institute of Wine and Food and its journal, I quickly but belatedly learned the conventional wisdom about what must be done first in such a situation: namely deciding how many millions of dollars have to be raised in advance of any activity, and appointing a firm of fund-raisers to attend to this. It was fortunate that I was unaware of these requirements when Prospect Books was founded, otherwise nothing would have happened. We naively thought that if the ten partners each put

CONTENTS

The table of contents from PPC 1.

the same amount into the kitty we ought to be able to manage. And, given the financial situation of Partner Six, our youngest daughter (Jennifer), we reckoned that this amount had to be £5.

Of course we needed premises. So we allocated part of a broom cupboard under the stairs in our house, plus a small table in an adjacent room and a box of file cards. That seemed to be sufficient and indeed was for quite a while. There were no utility bills, as the presence of this cuckoo in our nest (as it subsequently turned out to be) did not make any measurable difference to our consumption of electricity and most of the phone calls were to people I enjoyed chatting with anyway.

By the time we needed to pay the printers for the first issue of *PPC* more than enough revenues had come in from subscribers. Had we stumbled on the secret of a no-capital-needed enterprise? So it seemed, especially as we had one enormous advantage: contributors to *PPC*, then and thereafter, did not expect to be paid—they were making their contributions because of their interest and enthusiasm. In this connection there was another factor which greatly facilitated our work. Throughout the two decades, believe it or not, we hardly ever had to solicit any material and we hardly ever had to decline anything. By some magical process there was a gentle rain from the heavens of suitable material, always ensuring that the next issue would have a sufficiency of items, but not leaving us with an embarrassing surplus.

Here it is timely to consider whether the performance of *PPC* itself (forgetting the books and the Symposia) over the next two decades matched our stated intentions. These had been set out in an editorial in the first issue, most of which follows.

> To preface this booklet with a statement of 'editorial policy' would risk tingeing with formality or even pretentiousness a publication which is meant to be informal and modest.
>
> Yet there are some things which we should tell readers and prospective contributors. One is that we are glad that the contents of this first issue are varied, not only in content but also in style; and that we want to continue thus. We have no wish to produce a homogenized publication, to cast the contributions in set moulds or to define with untoward nicety what aspects of our subjects—food, cookery and cookery books—should be treated, and what balance maintained between them.
>
> If we have followed any principle in selecting and presenting our material, it is this; that it should all be based on genuine knowledge, or should be intended to elicit such knowledge or to promote research. Our pages are equally open to those who have done their homework, whether in the library or in the kitchen, and are offering the results; and to those embarking on work, or half-way through it, who are still at the stage of posing questions.

These ambitions were realised. As time went by, we found that we had genuinely created a new forum in which those interested in food history and cookery could come together, even if separated by thousands of miles. One might have expected such a forum to be an offshoot of studies in academe. But in those days there was no place in academic studies for food history and hardly anyone was working on the subject in an academic framework. Just about all the useful and interesting work was being done by amateurs, dotted around the world, and something was needed to connect them up. *PPC*, which has now chalked up well over a million words on food history and related matters, certainly has helped to meet this need and will, we hope, go on doing so.

The fact that *PPC* was a pioneering enterprise, meeting a real need in the real world, gave it a dynamism and élan which soon led to it, in turn, producing offspring.

The Books

There is now a long list of book titles to the credit of Prospect Books, over 60. Many fall into the categories which interested us in those early years: facsimile reprints of early cookery books; bibliographies; authentic studies of lesser-known cuisines; and the *Proceedings of the Oxford Symposia on Food.* Within two years we had published something in each category, starting in 1980 with Sri Owen's *Indonesian Food and Cookery,* which to all appearances propelled us into book publishing by our desire to give her earlier book on the subject, then going out of print, a prolonged life in expanded form.

Yet, was there not an earlier catalyst for this expansion of our activities? Our third book, *Traditional Recipes of Laos,* was essentially a facsimile edition of manuscript recipe notebooks compiled by the late royal chef in the then Kingdom of Laos. We took pleasure in telling other publishers that we were doing this, and in observing their amazement—amazement which we compounded by remarking that the manuscript was not in ordinary Lao script but in a special and antique palace script which even Lao people could not read with complete ease. We might also have mentioned that the notebooks were of that maddening French type whose pages are completely covered with a close grid of pale blue lines and that it had taken three Lao people (by coincidence immured at what was just the right time for us in a London hospital for tropical diseases, where they were being rid of a rare parasite) three weeks and several pots of whiting-out liquid and many very fine brushes to efface all traces of the blue lines. To be fair, we should then have explained that the recipes were accompanied by a lavish apparatus of explanations, and many beautiful drawings by the Lao artist Soun Vannithone. Also, the cover (again by Soun and reproduced in part above) was brilliant.

Even so, the venture looked risky, especially as we had to plan a print run of 2500. There were two favourable factors. There was no other competing book on the subject. Then there were Lao refugees scattered all around the world, wishing to preserve their culinary traditions, and people helping them who wished to know about their cuisine. I like to think that there was also a third factor; that our seemingly lunatic enterprise had heavenly support. Before leaving Laos in 1975, we had paid a visit to the royal chef's widow in the royal capital, Luang Prabang. Our purpose had simply been to thank her for the use of some of her late husband's recipes in a book I had written and published, *Fish and Fish Dishes of Laos*. But she told us to our astonishment that it had been her husband's dying wish that his recipes should be published and the revenues used to repair the shelter of a certain statue of the Buddha in Luang Prabang. It became clear that she saw us as the people who could bring this about.

I stammered something to the effect that we would see what we could do when we returned to the outside world. In return I received one of those unmistakeable 'you-are-the-man' looks from her clear eyes as she pronounced with great distinctness words which were translated for us as: 'If you succeed, then the soul of my dear husband will at last rest in peace.'

Well, that seemed to settle it. If the soul of Phia Sing could only rest in peace when we had seen to the publication of his book, we would see to it—which we eventually did, there being no other applicants for the honor. In retrospect we can see that the fate in store for us, to become publishers, was being determined there and then in that small room in Luang Prabang.

Mindful of the purpose for which Phia Sing had wished revenues from his book to be devoted, and of our inability to carry out his wish, we visited his eldest son, working in a shoe shop in Paris, and secured his agreement that the purpose should mutate into helping Lao refugees in Britain. (For another example of what seemed like heavenly intervention on behalf of our book programme, see the Pineapple Tart item on page 499).

The Oxford Symposia

By 1981 *PPC* had hatched another chick, the first full-scale Oxford Symposium on Food, first in a series that became an annual event from 1983 onwards. As always with the offspring of *PPC*, this series did not come into being because it was planned (although, again as always, a logical case could have been made for setting it up) but as an unexpected side effect of my being at St Antony's College as an Alistair Horne Fellow, to study from the historical point of view a subject described as 'Science in the Kitchen'. I was quietly attending to this, when it suddenly emerged that I was too quiet and unobtrusive in my activities to suit the ideas of the wily, mould-braking Dean, the very man who had audaciously endorsed my proposal to study culinary topics under the heading of history, namely Dr Theodore Zeldin. He it was who took me unawares one afternoon and pointedly enquired: 'Alan, how do you propose to make manifest to the other members of the college your presence here and the reasons for it?' I was nonplussed, and asked how this could be done. He replied, with characteristic economy of words: 'You must hold a seminar.' So I did, and the seminar was duly inscribed on the programme of the University (who, oddly, classified Science in the Kitchen under 'Sociology, sub-division Labour Relations'). Theodore was encouraged by the fact that nearly a dozen people turned up for this seminar, and bade me hold another. Again, I obliged, this time taking the history of cookery books as my theme and thereby attracting more than two dozen people, including Elizabeth David and Richard Olney. It was these two seminars which blossomed into the first full-scale Symposium in 1981.

The flavour of these events, or at least of their more exotic features, was well brought out by a writer who posed the question: where else in the world could one:

- observe an Emeritus Professor of Physics conducting unsuccessful experiments on cooking in a vacuum?
- watch and listen to a Spanish lady performing an exorcism over a huge and hugely flaming bowl of brandy?
- eat a dish prepared by Jane Grigson and hear her speak on caul fat in a Japanese seminar room?
- hear from an impassioned Bulgarian that the earliest known surviving loaf of bread has been found by archaeologists in Bulgaria?

Some of the papers embodied in the long series of Symposium documents, published by Prospect Books, have become famous for exemplifying the idiosyncratic nature of the events. An outstanding example was the paper at the 1987 Symposium, by Robert Chenciner and Emile Salvanov, on 'Little Known Aspects of North East Caucasian Mountain Ram and Other Dishes'. Other notable papers have explained how pink tea is made in Afghanistan; described medieval Near Eastern rotted condiments; and given a detailed description of feasting with the Buriats of southern Siberia.

Most of those present at the 1981 Symposium were *PPC* subscribers, since they were the only group of people we could readily reach with an announcement. So the fact that this event was organised by *PPC* in collaboration with the college was fully apparent at that time. In subsequent years the parental role of *PPC* has been less obvious. Of course, once offspring have reached the age of 21 (as have the Symposia), they can paddle their own canoes without parents in attendance. However, it is significant that in 1987 the most acute, witty and sympathetic observer ever of an Oxford Symposium, namely Dan Hofstadter, perceived very clearly the organic connection and proclaimed it in the pages of the *New Yorker*, for whom he wrote 30,000 words on the Symposia, of which they printed 10,000. The whole experience impelled him to acquire a complete set of *PPC*, after which he wrote:

> I glanced at some letters to the editor. "After collecting notes on all aspects of rhubarb off and on for thirty years," one man wrote, "I have recently tried to draw them all together in the hope of, possibly, producing a book on that plant." A lady correspondent volunteered the information that her husband had "just returned from Kuching, bringing with him . . . a vacuum-sealed bag of Dew Honey nutmeg . . . The identification on the bag is in Arabic, Chinese, and Bahasa . . . The picture of the nutmeg is remarkably close to that used by Mrs Beeton in her note on the spice" . . . Clearly these people were not cranks but benign fanatics, and engaging ones at that. I went on to a few of the articles; they were unexpectedly compelling, and were edited with unobtrusive mastery. . . . Over and over, in various understated or implicit ways, food was considered in its metaphorical aspect, as an index of human character.

Naturally, given this organic relationship and community of interests, many *PPC* subscribers continue to attend the Symposia, and many Symposiasts continue to contribute to or read *PPC*. Sophie Coe contributed some of the most important and substantial essays to *PPC* and was likewise a major contributor to the Symposia. This conjunction made it especially appropriate for the Symposium to become the venue for the annual presentation of the Sophie Coe Memorial Prize and subsidiary awards (see page x). This suits everybody.

The Oxford Symposia typically bring together 150 to 200 people, all with some special interest in food—food professionals, food historians, food writers, chefs and people simply interested in the subject. Although some academics have come, and very welcome they have been, the atmosphere and procedures have been quite different from formal academic meetings. Until very recently, the rule was that anyone could submit a paper and it would automatically be accepted for circulation and discussion.

The Oxford Companion to Food

All the activities consisting in or stemming from *PPC* could be said to be largely the result of happenstance. They may have sailed with a favourable tide, but sailing was unplanned. However, there is one tale more to tell. From 1979 to 1998 I was writing *The Oxford Companion to Food.* My part in founding *PPC* and its offspring had its (unplanned) reward. I discovered that the international network of *PPC* subscribers, Prospect Books authors and Symposiasts which had come into being was an unrivalled resource for the sort of specialised information which I needed, and which now reposes within the covers of that book.

Alan and Jane Davidson

announce with great pleasure

the safe delivery of

The Oxford Companion to Food

to the Oxford University Press

at 1055 on Tuesday 21 July

The above announcement was sent out recently by your Editors. They might have added:

Days overdue: 5674
Weight on delivery: 3 oz

The recorded weight was for the version on a 100 Mb zip disk – the weight of the hard copy was of course much more, around 10.5 kg. Word count, by the way, was 1,025,000.

One or two recipients of the message thought that 'delivery' equalled 'birth' and that the book was actually published already. Not so; 'delivery' meant simply delivery to the publisher. Publication may be in the autumn (fall) of 1999.

The birth announcement of The Oxford Companion to Food, *from* PPC 59.

It is right to conclude with a vote of thanks to all these people, whose existence and activity were a sine qua non for *PPC* and its offspring, as well as, incidentally, my own book. What phrase can describe them collectively? I like Dan Hofstadter's 'BENIGN FANATICS, AND ENGAGING ONES'. And their heterogeneous and unorganised nature was well conveyed by Sophie Coe when she referred to 'THE AMORPHOUS RANKS OF FOOD HISTORIANS'. We are all in their debt for the illumination they have brought to their subject, penetrating even its most obscure nooks and crannies. Long live the amorphous ranks of benign fanatics!

* * * *

The Editors of *PPC* took pains to ensure that their contributors were not hampered by house-style instructions such as would be appropriate for a more formal publication. They encouraged all authors to speak with their natural voices, including points of spelling (where they could choose between American or British English), punctuation, abbreviations etc. The Editors of the present anthology have maintained this policy in the interest of preserving the feel of the individual pieces as they appeared in *PPC*.

I.

Scoops and Distant Beachheads

The pages of *PPC* have been packed with scoops ever since the first issue. What greater scoop could there be than the first publication of two hitherto unpublished essays by Elizabeth David? However, here we give a narrower interpretation to the term. A scoop is a scoop if it contains new information on a baffling subject or one which had previously not been treated in any publication. A scoop is a super-scoop if it incorporates information which other authors and publishers would have dearly liked to secure for themselves.

Such a super-scoop was the essay on red (or pink) peppercorns. Diligent Alexandra Hicks, realising that all or anyway most of the chefs who were building this then trendy item into their menus did not know what these peppercorns were, took it on herself to enlighten everybody about them. She set to work to establish definitely their botanical identity, which came as a surprise to most people, and to describe their characteristics and qualities, including the minor but remarkable fact that sometimes they make some birds tipsy. It would be good to think that, because *PPC* published her essay, everyone in the food and restaurant industries now knows the truth. Of course they don't. Many more decades will have passed before Alexandra's revelations have become common knowledge. This does not diminish her feat, but merely serves as one more illustration of how slowly new pieces of knowledge are absorbed by the population.

'Manifold Absurdity' was a slightly different sort of scoop. On the wilder shores of California a book about cooking on car engines had been published, and noticed in *PPC* two years previously. What Rose Arnold and her collaborators did was to give the subject some new and deep practical research. She is to be commended for giving very exact information about the equipment that was used and the way her experiments were conducted.

'A Spicy Mystery', another scoop of the red peppercorn type, was the first scoop for which a pre-condition was the establishment of a new world-wide international organisation. I refer of course to INTERSPI. Since very little has been published about this organisation, which prefers to work behind the scenes, the spicy mystery item has been furnished with a short explanation.

It seems unlikely that anyone besides Esther Balogh, for many years a teacher of Home Economics at a Nigerian university, had ever explored the mushroom-eating of the Yoruba people. But Esther was game for anything and relished the opportunity to conduct this study. Petite, Hungarian and indefatigable, she gained the affection of all at the Oxford Symposia on food whenever she managed to make the journey from Ile Ife to Oxford.

A similar spirit of deep and relentless research enabled Audrey Levy and the others who worked on the subject to unveil at long last the origins of Summer Pudding. Lynda Brown had previously posed the question in *PPC 18.* Those familiar with the long lapse of time which often occurs between publication of a query in *PPC* and the appearance of a satisfactory answer will not be surprised to learn that for this subject the lapse of time was almost 15 years.

Scoops of yet another kind are provided by authors who have travelled in distant parts and brought back revelations about foodways encountered on their journeys. An example is the essay on Chicken Yassa by Eva Gillies, who used to spend four months of the year with her husband, a medical entomologist, in a camp of thatched mud huts on the river Gambia. Chris Hilton, for his part, lived and worked in Hong Kong but took pleasure in exploring the foods and cookery of people in remote parts of China, always with both eyes open for things quaint, such as Tea Soup.

Connections between food and art have bobbed up frequently in *PPC*. Gillian Riley, a designer and author with a special interest in this connection, contributed to *PPC 50* a perceptive short essay about a painting by Velasquez. It illustrates very well what new insights can be generated when a food historian examines a painting which has food in it.

Red Peppercorns—*What* They Really *Are*

ALEXANDRA HICKS

After green peppercorns had their day, it was the turn of red (or pink) ones to attract attention and to serve as a sort of symbolic spice for nouvelle cuisine.

Despite the lack of curiosity with which most people greet a new phenomenon of this sort, some questions were raised about the pink peppercorn, such as: 'What is it?' In PPC 9 *Dorothy Whallon volunteered, under Notes and Queries, what were the generally accepted answers. They were the berries of* Schinus molle, *the 'California pepper tree'; or they could be* Xanthoxylum piperitum, *'Szechwan peppercorns'.*

Meanwhile, however, Alexandra Hicks had been doing some deep research on the subject and came up with a different finding, which created something of a furore in the gourmet world of North America. National newspapers and periodicals were quick to seize on the point that in certain circumstances the berries identified by her as being those which are sold as red or pink peppercorns could intoxicate birds and discomfort human beings.

We took pleasure in printing this article, which was the fullest expression of her findings to date to be published, and which has at the end, for good measure, an Appendix on the California pepper tree to which Dorothy Whallon and others have referred in this context.

As we went to press with the article we received a message from the author stating that the US Food and Drug Administration, whose interest in the matter she had been trying to stimulate, finally ran their own tests on the product, confirmed her findings and suspended importation of the red peppercorns.

Red peppercorns, the so-called darlings of the nouvelle cuisine, and nouvelle cuisine itself, both imports from France, are currently hailed as the new and exciting innovations on the gastronomic scene. But are they really that new and exciting? Exciting—yes, but new—not really. Red peppercorns, introduced to us by the French Fancy Food Trade and hailed by them as 'the food fancy of the 1980s' are as ancient as the native Indians of South America and nouvelle cuisine, today's great 'new cooking', in part, is as old as Classical Rome and the Orient. The cookbooks attributed to Apicius, a Roman cook, written in the first century A.D. are full of the sauces that nouvelle cuisine prides itself in, and the texture and glamorous presentation that is such an exciting part of nouvelle cuisine has always been part of Oriental cooking.

It is little wonder that red peppercorns have created such excitement—they are ideal for enhancing both the flavour and presentation of today's great cuisine. What other spice do we have that has such a lovely bright red colour, and such a wonderful crisp texture? Besides, it is also unique in its flavor and imparts a new dimension to anything to which it is added. It is, indeed, exciting and glamorous.

One wonders, though, how a new spice can become so popular and cause such excitement among gourmets and still remain not properly identified. Some still maintain they are true red peppercorns (*Piper nigrum*) of the pepper family (Piperaceae), although many now acknowledge that they are not and attribute their origin to the Mountain Ash (*Sorbus acuparia*) or some other totally incorrect source such as the ornamental Sweet Pepperbush (*Clethra alnifolia*). Since it is not any of these, what then is this mysterious fancy food seasoning that is causing such a sensation in gourmet cooking?

Surprisingly, they are the berries of a very common shrub that also grows here in the U.S. In fact, it is so common in Florida that it is considered to be a pest. This shrub, *Schinus terebinthifolius* Raddi, is a species of trees which is indigenous to South America and specifically to Brazil where it is known as Aroreira. Some other common names are Brazilian pepper tree, Christmas-berry, and Florida holly. The name Brazilian pepper tree probably originated by association with the related *Schinus molle* (commonly known as California or Peruvian pepper tree) which is indigenous to Peru. The somewhat larger-sized, purplish-red berries of the Peruvian pepper tree have long been used by the natives and later by industry as a pepper substitute or adulterant. By comparison, the use of the Brazilian pepper berries, in spite of its common name, as a condiment or spice is very recent. On the French island of Reunion, *Schinus terebinthifolius* is commonly known as Poivrier, Sorbier and Incense. Other than Brazilian pepper tree, the other common names are shared by other plants and are not appropriately applied to *Schinus terebinthifolius.* The generic name *Schinus* (properly pronounced sky-nus but more frequently pronounced shy-nus) is the Greek word for the mastic tree and the species name *terebinthifolius* is from the Latin 'terebinth' for turpentine and 'folium' for leaf and refers to the pungent turpentine-like odor of the crushed leaf.

It is a low-branching, bushy shrub with attractive, glossy evergreen foliage that is resinous and aromatic. It is fast growing and in some parts of the world reaches tree proportions of some 40 feet. Masses of ivory-white flowers are succeeded by small, resinous, single-seeded berries which are glossy, juicy and green, eventually turning a clear bright red. The seeds are very distinctive—lumpy with much resin, and with an outstanding ridge around the circumference. They are not truly round but slightly compressed on opposite sides. Upon ripening the berries become very dry, losing their fleshiness almost entirely and

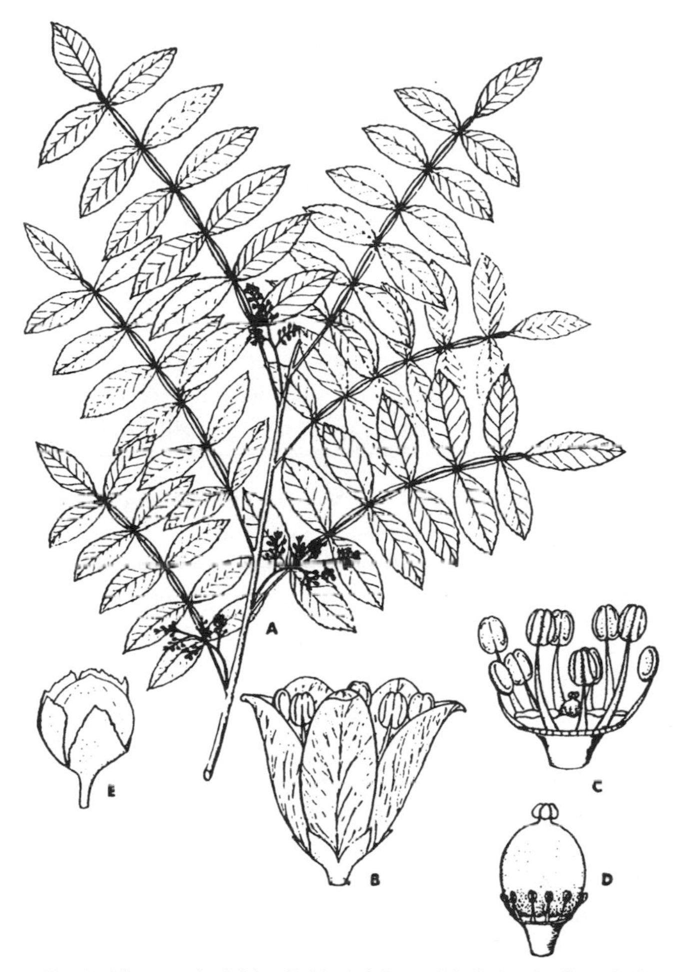

Fig. 7. *Schinus terebinthifolius* Raddi: A, habit (×½); B, functionally male flower (×12); C, id., calyx and corolla removed (×12); D, functionally female flower, calyx and corolla removed (×12); E, fruit with exocarp peeling (×3½). A after *Dusén 14324* (MO), Brazil; B-C after *Macedo 3375* (MO), Brazil; D after *Bertoni 3467* (MO), Argentina; E after *Lindman A1437* (MO), Brazil.

These drawings of Schinus terebinthifolius *appear in 'Flora of Panama',* Annals of the Missouri botanical garden, *Vol. 54, No. 3, 1967, published by the Missouri botanical garden and Washington University Press, St. Louis, Missouri 63110.*

leaving only a seed surrounded by a dry pericarp (skin). The flavor is one of a slight sweetness at first, rapidly becoming peppery (with a hint of menthol), and pungent.

The panicles of bright red berries look very attractive against the dark green foliage, and it was this decorative quality which prompted the export of the plant from Brazil in the late 1800s. Its introduction to the United States took place in the 1890s and later, in the mid-1920s, writer-horticulturist Henry Nehrling reported with enthusiasm and excitement of a new 'effective and ornate berry-bearing shrub'. He marvelled at the dense masses of scarlet berries, most brilliant at Christmas time, and lamented that, 'at present only a limited number are growing in our south Florida gardens'. He then added, 'I predict a great future for this beautiful shrub', and concluded: 'It ought to be in every garden in Florida.'

If Nehrling was alive today, he would be astounded to learn that this tropical ornamental has so invaded Florida that it is the subject of an intensive eradication program; that it has also made its way to many other tropical and sub-tropical areas and, furthermore, that certain regions of the world are taking its decorative values from the garden to the table and capitalizing on its gastronomic values!

It appears that the introduction of *Schinus terebinthifolius* to other tropical and sub-tropical regions began prior to its introduction to the United States. In 1884 it was introduced to Perideniya Gardens in Ceylon. It rapidly spread throughout Mediterranean Europe, southern Asia, both North Africa and South Africa and has overrun islands like Norfolk and Reunion. In Reunion today it is to be found throughout the entire island with the heaviest concentrations being found in the wetland areas.

Recently entrepreneurs, such as Monsieur Boquere, initiated the export of the berries of this shrub from Reunion to Europe under the name of 'Baies Roses de Bourbon'. You will not find this name in any botanical encyclopaedia or dictionary—it simply means red berries of Bourbon (Bourbon being the former name of Reunion). The berries are harvested there during their winter period (May through August) and shipped to France where they are processed (freeze-dried, canned in brine, pickled in vinegar or packed in oil), for further export under the name of Red or Pink Peppercorns. These, then, are what we find on the shelves of gourmet food shops or have served to us in gourmet restaurants.

The names red peppercorns and pink peppercorns are very misleading and inappropriate since they are not true peppercorns, nor in the very least related to them. Species found in the true pepper family (Piperaceae) include *Piper nigrum*—our black, white and green peppercorns are all products of this species. The difference between these three types of pepper lies in the different stages of harvesting and different methods of processing. The true pepper is a vine which produces spikes of berries which are green when first formed. These green immature berries when processed by packing them fresh in Cryovac™, freeze-drying or packing in brine, give us the green peppercorns of commerce. On ripening the berries turn yellow and then finally orange-red. For the production of black pepper the spike of berries is not picked until at least one of the berries has reached complete maturity (orange-red in color). The berries on the whole are still green but more mature than those harvested for the production of green peppercorns. These greenish berries are then spread out either on mats or directly on concrete slabs and dried under direct sunlight. The drying process takes approximately two weeks and during this dehydration the berries turn brown at first and then become black and wrinkled assuming the look of the black peppercorn with which we are all familiar. For the production of white pepper, the spike is allowed to ripen almost completely before harvesting. This ensures that most of the 'corns' (the seeds inside the berries) have reached full maturity. This is very important because for the production of white pepper, the orange-red skin is removed, leaving the seed core alone to supply pungency. This seed core, which is cream to greyish-white in color, is our white peppercorn of commerce, and although it has less flavor than the black peppercorn it appears to have a longer staying power. It is interesting that ripe red berries will not make good black pepper, and that immature green berries will not make good white pepper. So, although true red pepper berries do exist in their fresh state, they do not exist in a processed form and are not found as such in commerce. The exception would be to find them and purchase them fresh in areas where they are grown. Perhaps someone will soon come up with a method of processing the ripe red berries of *Piper nigrum* so that we could, indeed, have real red peppercorns.

There are some 2,000 other species that belong to the pepper family (Piperaceae) but Brazilian pepper (*Schinus terebinthifolus*) is not any of them. It belongs to the Sumac family (Anacardiaceae) and is closely related to species such as poison ivy (*Toxicodendrum radicans*). As a matter of fact, it is interesting to note that, like poison ivy, it can cause severe allergenic reactions, affecting many people in ways similar to poison ivy poisoning.

Dr Julia Morton, Director, Morton Collectanea, University of Miami, who has done extensive research on Brazilian pepper, reports that in Florida, an overall, fine, itching body rash frequently accompanied by reddening and swelling of the face and eyelids, is commonly experienced by those who cut down these shrubs or even single branches while they are in bloom, and that gardeners who regularly trim their Brazilian pepper hedges acquire persistent rash and, in some, running sores. Children who eat more than a few unripe or ripe berries experience digestive upsets and vomiting, and those who squeeze a quantity of the berries at play are afflicted with a rash and swelling of the hands, arms and face.

She also reports that birds that feed excessively on the ripe berries become intoxicated and unable to fly!

Dr Helen A. Lloyd of the National Heart, Lung and Blood Institute in Bethesda, Maryland, who has investigated and reported on the chemical constituents of the ripe berries, suffered violent headaches, swollen eyelids, shortness of breath, chest pains and other discomforts while preparing extracts for study.

The studies performed by Dr Lloyd and her colleagues revealed large concentrations of nine volatile monoterpene hydrocarbons in the fruits and consider these a probable cause of irritation arising from exposure of crushed fruits. Over fifty other components, in lesser amounts, were also identified as present—these included triterpene alcohols, sesquiterpenes and ketones.

The seeds, leaves and bark yield an essential oil which is composed mainly of phellandrene and of a dark-green, aromatic fatty oil. This essential oil is potentially desirable as a flavouring agent by the food industry and as an aromatic ingredient by the perfume industry.

In its native Brazil this shrub has considerable medicinal uses. Crushed, dried leaves are applied as antiseptic poultices on ulcers and decoctions of the leaves or fruits are used to bathe wounds and sores. In homeopathy, it is regarded as a remedy for gout, arthritic pain, strained tendons, intestinal weakness, diarrhoea, hemoptysis, tumours, etc.

In Florida the shrub is a favourite of bee-keepers and bees, and vast quantities of a medium-amber, slightly peppery honey is obtained from the nectar-laden blossoms.

Bees, of course, ensure good fertilization of the blossoms which in turn ensures good production of berries, and this Florida certainly has. It does seem ironic that we, here in the United States, should be paying such exorbitant prices (anywhere from $50.00 to $100.00 per pound) for berries that are being imported from the island of Reunion when these same red berries glisten on shrubs found growing in our own country. Instead of planning eradication programs (the shrub is literally choking out native vegetation), perhaps Florida should hire a good entrepreneur who could turn their Brazilian pepper into a profit.

Appendix: a note on the Peruvian or California pepper tree *(Schinus molle)*

The Peruvian pepper tree (*Schinus molle*) is an interesting tree from the point of view of this article because although its berries are not the berries of the so-called red peppercorns, they could easily be so. In point of fact, unlike its sister, the Brazilian pepper tree, which has just recently made the gastronomic scene with its berries (the so-called red peppercorns), the berries of the Peruvian pepper tree have been used as a pepper substitute for hundreds of years.

Like its close relative, the Brazilian pepper tree (*Schinus terebinthifolius*), the Peruvian pepper tree (*Schinus molle*) (sometimes also known as California pepper tree or mastic tree) is a member of the Sumac family (Anacardiaceae). It is indigenous to the Peruvian Andes and its specific name *molle* is from Mulli, the Peruvian name of *S. molle,* not from the Latin molle, meaning soft, as is sometimes surmised.

It is a fast growing, evergreen tree (20' to 50' in height) with graceful, pendulous branches and compound leaves and is possibly the most commonly grown ornamental tree in southern and central California. It should be familiar to all movie fans as its artistic beauty makes it a tree much favored by movie producers. Panicles of yellowish-white, tiny flowers produce coral-red berries ripening further to purplish-red and then to brownish-red berries. These berries are about the size of true peppercorns, being somewhat larger in size than those of the Brazilian pepper tree berries. The distinctive single seed is enclosed by a very lumpy and resinous bony kernel. When ripe the berry has on the surface a little sweetness (although not as sweet as the Brazilian) which is at first tasty and pleasant but beyond that it is bitter and pungent with a terebinthine aftertaste (the terebinthine being much more pronounced than the Brazilian).

The tree seems to have been and still is of great importance to the Inca who called it the 'Tree of Life' and dedicated it to their deities. They concocted intoxicating drinks from the berries and used other parts of the tree medicinally.

It appears that *Schinus molle* was unknown outside of South America in pre-Columbian days. It was introduced into Mexico sometime in the early 1540s and later made its way from Mexico to California. Clusius, the great Flemish botanist, described the tree in 1579 (it had made its appearance in Europe before its introduction to California) and Gerard, writing in England in 1596, stated that it was then growing in the garden of the King of Spain, in Madrid. Gerard was successful in obtaining a seed from there but was not successful in growing the tree to maturity in the harsher climate of London. However, it subsequently became very widespread in Spain, Italy, on the French Riveria,

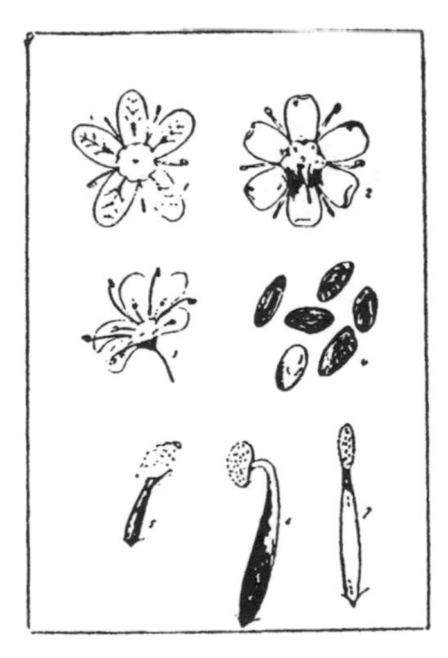

Some details of the 'California pepper tree' are shown above, from Maximo Martinzez, Las plantas mas utiles que existen en la republica Mexicana, *Mexico, 1928. On the following page, to illustrate the other plant from which the pink peppercorn does* not *come, we show the 'Szechwan pepper plant', from Blanco,* Flore de Filipinas Noves, *1877–80.*

and other sub-tropical regions around the world. In California today it is so widespread that it is literally considered to be a pest and, like the Brazilian pepper tree in Florida, it is the subject of eradication programs.

The introduction of this tree to so many areas around the world was due to its ornamental value as a landscape plant. Hooker, an English botanist, writing of this species, said: 'The fruits of Schinus are sugary and edible but they are certainly so ornamental that it would be a pity to eat them if other provisions are to be had.'

However, it is very well documented that Peruvian pepper berries have been eaten for a long time. Ruiz, in his book 'Travels of Ruiz, Pavon and Dombey in Peru and Chile' (1777–78), writes: 'In Peru, even the most intelligent people are persuaded that the fruit of this tree is the true pepper of the East and that it is because they do not know how to prepare it that it is not as much esteemed. Because of the slight taste and resemblance in size and odor that the seeds of the molle have to the grains of the true pepper, some after roasting them, mix them with the latter, with great harm to their health; For this they should continue with these harmful mixtures, for from them originate the vicho or mal del valle and terrible hemorrhoids.'

Eaten in quantity, the berries do indeed cause intestinal inflammation and hemorrhoids. In spite of this, the dried, roasted berries are still used as a substitute for or as an adulterant of black pepper in North Africa, South Africa, Greece and Latin America. The berries are also much used in Greece, Mexico, Chile and Peru for certain intoxicating beverages.

In addition, steam distillation of the berries and leaves yields a volatile oil. The main constituents of this oil include phellandrene, pinene, carvacrol, ethyl phenol, camphene, limonene, and a new sesquiterpene spathulene. It is these principals that are responsible for its warm-spicy, woody-peppery flavor. The oil is used as a substitute for black pepper, as an agent in flavoring compositions and in pharmaceutical products.

Manifold Absurdity

ROSE ARNOLD
(DRIVING MGA AND COOKING ON SCIMITAR)

ILLUSTRATIONS BY WILLY FINDLATER
(DRIVER-CHEF, CATERHAM SUPER 7)

PPC 33 *carried a review by Alan Davidson of* Manifold Destiny *('The One! The Only! Guide to Cooking on Your Car Engine!') by Chris Maynard and Bill Scheller, published by Villard Books, New York, 1989.*

Inspired by the review and undaunted by its warnings about the need for a conversion table, a group of dedicated cater drivers in the south of Scotland contrived to buy two copies of the book, which accounted for 1990, and to put its message into practice on a couple of occasions during the summer of 1991.

I suppose it has to be said that, despite our triumph when we managed to get hold of copies of *Manifold Destiny,* and the 'brilliantly sustained'[1] wit it contains, we didn't use this bible as a very close guide, especially with regard to time. I am no expert in engines, but it seems to me that those in American cars must be very different than ours. Maynard and Scheller seemed able to find 'a reasonable amount of heat' at various places under their hoods; under our bonnets there were cold places (ambient temperature), vaguely warm places, where for example pre-cooked rice or mushrooms could be kept warm without further cooking (perhaps 30–45 degrees), and the exhaust manifolds, which were VERY HOT INDEED. Maynard and Scheller also found it possible to balance or wedge food between bonnet and engine; we didn't. Either the food was wired on, or it fell off. This meant that we did not need to practise the famous *Manifold Destiny* Cone Test:

> Before you put any food on the injector housing, make a cone of aluminium foil about four or five inches high. Put it on the housing and shut the hood. Now lift the cone and see how much the cone has been flattened. Too much? You'll have to cook flat food . . . Not very? Then wad some additional foil and place it atop your packages of food . . . [p 24]

We assumed at first, you see, that what applied to fuel injectors would apply to other types of engine—but such is not the case. Wiring the food onto a VERY HOT exhaust manifold also creates problems about turning the food packages. But about one thing *MD* is absolutely right: it would be impossible to cook on car engines without aluminium foil.

Our first venture took place in May. On a balmy, verdant evening, a small convoy drove from New Lanark to Traquair in the Borders, and thence over the hills to Moffat in Dumfriesshire, finishing off with a blast up the A74 and alongside the Clyde back to Lanark. It was a distance of some 130 miles. Now there were those of us who argued that this was too long a run, and that the food would be overcooked. Nonsense, said the other point of view, *MD* talks of hours of cooking, after all, and it's fun to drive in convoy around the countryside. We were, perhaps I should say, a 1979 Reliant Scimitar convertible, a 1990 Caterham Super Seven (the Lotus Seven of *The Prisoner* fame . . .) and a 1976 Harley Davidson Sportster motorcycle recently imported from the States. There was also a 1957 MGA around, but it proved impossible to cook on owing to the peculiar arrangement whereby its inlet valves are placed above the exhaust manifold: one could only cook something of approximately the size of a pencil on it, and nothing came to mind. Although we later tried to bake apples on the MG by wedging them between the engine-block and a hot-water pipe, they did no more than get mildly warmish. Evidently the potential of the car for cooking was not considered in Abingdon, back in the 1950s.

As we drove around the by-roads of the Lowlands, an increasingly delicious aroma floated around and behind us. People walking dogs turned and watched us out of sight; even sheep reacted. Gradually, though, this mouth-watering smell began to change. It became more like the smell of food wrapped in foil and left on a solid electric plate at full blast for rather a long time: nasty. We stopped in Moffat for fuel, ice creams, and readjustments of food packages. Moffat has a wide and picturesque main street, and the vehicles looked rather fine lined up in the evening sunshine. We took photos. A small crowd of teenagers lounged up, chiefly to admire the Harley, remarking that they were going to have one of them in a year or so. Suddenly their nostrils started to quiver. 'Mister,' said one of them to the Caterham's driver, 'what's that smell? What's that smell, Mister? It's Minging[2]!!' Well, it was irresistible, really. I looked the lad straight in the eye and explained that we were cooking our dinners, which were wired onto our engines. He gave me a look of withering contempt, the sort teenagers use for adults whom they suspect of humour, and waited for the Caterham's answer. He took pity, and explained that he had unfortunately hit a bird back up the road, which had splattered and immolated itself on the engine. The boys went away perfectly satisfied.

Needless to say, by the time we got back, the food was a write-off, a carbonised, charred mass. At least, that cooked on the car engines was, but there was a glorious exception: the Quartet of Quail Harley Cooked were quite magnificent. They, together with contributions from the Caterham's larder, and a side of smoked salmon from a participant who hadn't made the starting grid that evening, saved us from going to bed hungry.

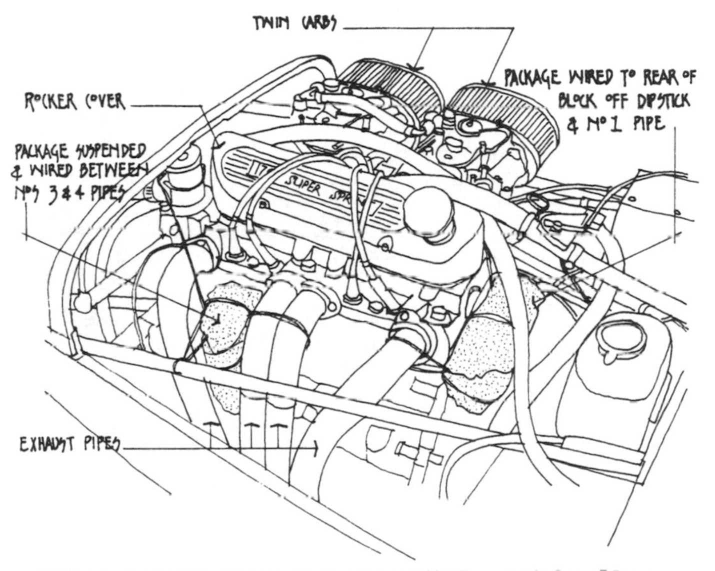

MODIFIED CATERHAM 1700 cc SUPER SPRINT ENGINE : 150 BHP : 3750 miles

And there the story rested for a while. Keith Floyd did it in Australia, and fed the result to a passing dog.[3] We thought that this absolved us from further efforts and went back to having picnics as the civilised do. But none of us likes to fail, so a second trip was arranged for early September. Again the weather was kind, so we could have the car hoods down, but this time we were going to be sensible. We knocked a hundred miles off the route, for a start. A mere 30 miles' round trip, and we were sitting down to an entirely edible, even worthwhile meal. Only the baked apples previously mentioned needed a boost in the oven before we consumed them. This time there was a second Reliant Scimitar, and the Harley rested on his laurels and went sailing instead.

The recipes which follow are as supplied by the driver-chefs involved. Perhaps before readers embark on any of them, they should consider that, far from using otherwise redundant heat on a necessary journey, we went out and burned fuel specially for the purpose. Which is a waste of fossil fuels and an unnecessary pollution of the environment. It might be greener (though less fun) to stay at home and poach salmon in the dishwasher.

QUARTET OF QUAIL, HARLEY COOKED

Lightly brush quail with olive oil, season, and wrap in two parcels, each with two quail placed end-to-end. Foil should be triple-layered. A garnish of kumquats was considered for alliterative reasons, but discarded.

In order to cook this dish, the rear exhaust pipe heatshield must be removed to allow an even temperature gradient. The parcels are tucked between the cylinder fins and the exhaust balance pipe, one parcel to each of the two cylinders. No retaining wire is necessary as the fit is very snug. (Careful use of a carpenter's rule in Safeway had confirmed that the quails would fit the space—the Harley is ridden by a Quantity Surveyor.) Juices spilt onto the exhaust 'ensured that the bike had a pleasant odour for a long time afterwards'.

Ride the bike for 130 miles or thereabouts over varied country roads.

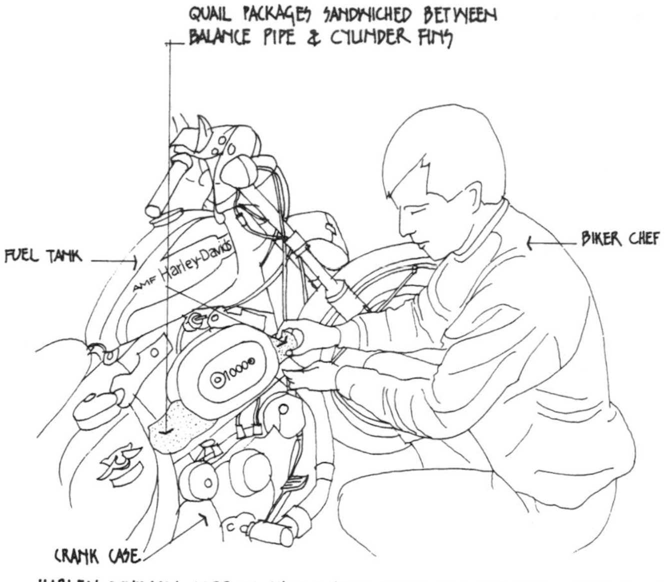

SALMON TAMWORTH PERRY-SMITH

Prepare as for Salmon in Pastry with Herb Sauce (Jane Grigson, *Fish Cookery,* p 223), but replace pastry with triple-wrapped foil.

Wire onto a hot exhaust manifold (eg after driving from Lanark to Biggar) of a Reliant Scimitar with a small air-filter, and drive approximately 15 miles.

Scimitar Spiced Pork

2 pork fillets cut into 1 cm dice
bunch of syboes (spring onions)
2 onions
100 g button mushrooms
1 green capsicum
a piece of fresh ginger root

Marinade the pork overnight in a mixture of sesame oil and dark soy sauce. Next day, prepare syboes and mushrooms; slice onions and capsicum; cut the ginger into julienne strips and blanch to taste. Drain the meat, then stir-fry briefly, adding the vegetables for the last minute of cooking. Season and commit to triple-layered foil, with the added precaution of a pad of foil on the side of the package destined to sit on the manifold. The package should be about 12 cm by 20, and can be tightly wrapped. If desired, it can be cooled and refrigerated at this point.

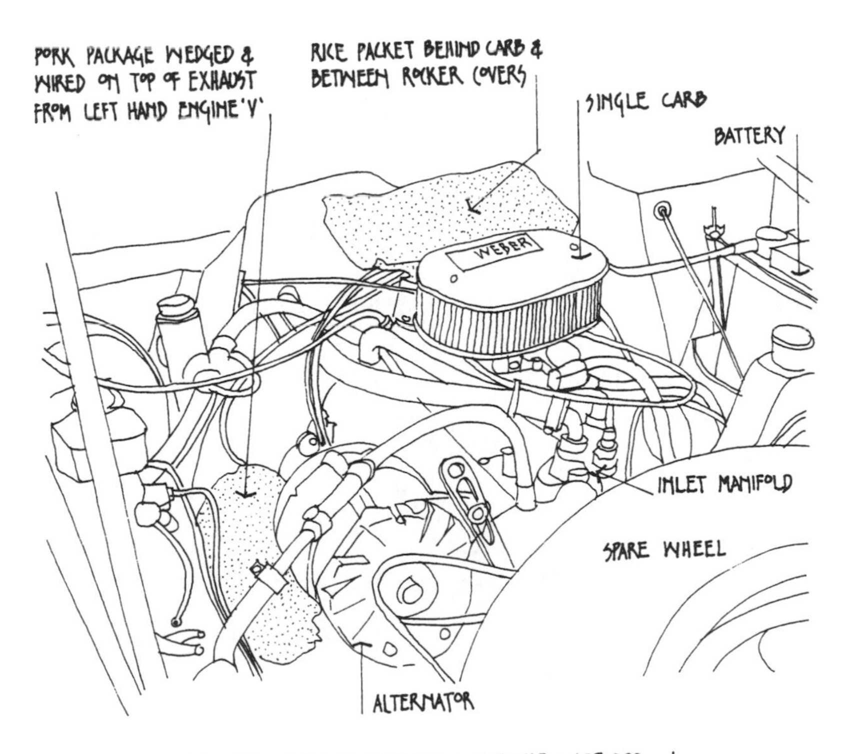

The Scimitar GTC has a Ford 2.8 litre V-6 engine, but in order to cook on it a reduced-size K&N air filter has to be fitted, otherwise there is no room for the food. This is a super engine to cook on. Because it has a V formation, there are exhaust manifolds on either side of the block, both of which can be used for cooking. Then there are warm spaces on top of the air-filter and in a special little plate-warming space right at the back, nearest the dashboard. Wire the food into position, and drive for 30 miles at speeds varying from 25 to as fast as you can.

Four from Seven

4 red peppers, blanched
1 red chilli
6 cloves of garlic
8 dried apricots plus 2 oz chopped
1 onion
4 oz chopped mushrooms plus 4 whole ones
2 oz chopped tomato
3 oz chopped nuts
1 tbs olive oil
salt, pepper
oregano
tomato purée

Stuff peppers architecturally and wrap in two packages of 15 layers of foil. Bind with wire coathangers, leaving hooks free. Suspend one parcel between the exhaust pipes of a Caterham Super Seven, hanging from the oil-cooling pipes, and clamp the other to the 4th cylinder. This is the only position which will not vaporise the foil. Drive as dynamically as possible around country roads for 30 miles.

Notes and Acknowledgments

1. Alan Davidson in *PPC 33,* p 50.
2. Forceful dialect epithet meaning 'stinking'.
3. *Floyd on Oz* by Keith Floyd, Michael Joseph, 1991, p 209—'Carpet Bag Steaks a la Toyota'.

We are grateful to the other New Lanark Cleikum members who contributed to this venture: John Macmillan (Harley Davidson), Steve Kay (Scimitar GTE), Jim Arnold (Scimitar GTC, MGA), June Findlater (sympathy, derision and wonderful puddings)

A Spicy Mystery

OR with Soap on Our Hands and Foam at Our Mouths . . .

HELEN J SABERI,
WITH ANISSA HELOU AND ESTEBAN POMBO-VILLAR
AND DRAWINGS BY SOUN VANNITHONE
STAR WITNESS: CLAUDIA RODEN
COORDINATOR AND LIBRARIAN: ALAN DAVIDSON

In PPC 47, the then newly formed international organization INTERSPI, the young sister of INTERPOL, but dedicated to intercontinental investigations of mystery spices (or spicy mysteries), scored its first triumph in (more or less) identifying a spice which had eluded the attention of all previous English-language cataloguers of spices.

Detective Saberi (daughter of a former Chief Inspector of Police in the City of York, author of Noshe Djan: Afghan Food and Cookery, *and now co-author of* Trifle *with Alan Davidson) inaugurated the enquiry, as she explains in this report (sequential in construction, to expose her modus operandi), but found that the scale of the operation called for international cooperation. The co-investigators whom she enlisted are named above. They were shrewdly chosen. Anissa Helou was working on her book* Lebanese Cuisine *(published in 1994). Dr Pombo-Villar, who runs his part of INTERSPI from a base in Switzerland, is a chemist with a particular interest in spices.*

Each of the authors speaks in turn. Detective Saberi then invites the Project Coordinator to review the somewhat perplexing results of the enquiry and to indicate the course of the further investigations which the whole team believe must be made. All help to this end will be welcome.

Helen J Saberi Speaks

Some time ago I volunteered to try out a few of the Lebanese recipes being prepared by my friend Anissa Helou for her forthcoming book.

One of the recipes I tried was for *ma'amoul,* which are small, round or oval, pastries prepared all over the Middle East especially at Easter time. They are usually made with semolina flour and stuffed with nuts such as pistachio, walnuts or dates. At the same time I thought I should write up about *ma'amoul* pastries for *The Oxford Companion to Food* [then under construction, for publication in 1999]. For more information I looked them up in one of my favourite books, Claudia Roden's *A New Book of Middle Eastern Food,* which I always find is full of interesting information. Claudia's recipe was a little different from Anissa's but the basic concept was the same—little pastries stuffed with a nut or date filling.

Claudia also described *karabij.* They sounded very similar to *ma'amoul* except that they are served with or bathed in a white 'cream' with a very distinctive flavour, called *naatiffe.* This sounded just my cup of tea—a lovely rich, nutty pastry served with what sounded like a delicious cream. Claudia described how to make *naatiffe.* 'Pulverize or grind the dried white branch of Bois de Panama . . .'

Hey, Wait a Minute— Bois de Panama? What's That?

I'd never heard of it. Claudia gave the Arabic name, *'erh halawa,* which means 'soul of the sweet', and gives a short description: 'Bois de Panama [also called *saponaria*] is a pale dry wood which, when boiled in water, produces a thick white foam. It is used to make the cream called *naatiffe* for *karabij.*'

I was intrigued and I asked Anissa whether she had more information. She explained on the same lines as Claudia, but said that in the Lebanon, at least, *karabij* are finger-shaped pastries (Claudia Roden describes them as round) and that she knew bois de Panama as *shersh al halaweh,* which means 'vein or root of sweetness' (*halaweh* meaning sweetness—it is the same word as the English halva). She said that in some of her Lebanese cookery books it is referred to as *saponaria* or soapwort but that she was unsure as to its real identity or English translation. After drawing a blank in her Arabic dictionary she had asked a friend to look up saponaria/soapwort/bois de Panama in Bean's dictionary of trees and shrubs, where it is stated that *Saponaria* (*officinalis*) and soapwort are the same plant, a wild flower . . . But Bean said nothing about bois de Panama.

My husband looked up soapwort in our English-Arabic dictionary, and found two meanings: (1) *Al Saboonnia Al Makhzanniah* (preserved soap?) and (2) *'Erq al halawa* (which he understood to mean root or vein of sweetness—cf Anissa's information above).

Anissa went on to explain that *karabij* with *naatiffe* cream were a speciality of Aleppo, as the Arabic name *karabij Halab* (Halab meaning Aleppo) indicates, and that she would bring me some bois de Panama to see and perhaps test and try out.

While waiting for this, I looked up *karabij* and *naatiffe* in Arto der Haroutunian's book, *Patisserie of the Eastern Mediterranean.* He wrote:

> Natife is the Syrian-Arabic name for bois de Panama, which is also sometimes called 'halva wood' because it is used in the commercial sugar and sesame seed–based halvas. *Karabij* is a small semolina-based pastry filled with walnuts or pistachios. There is nothing spectacular about the pastry, but the cream [i.e. *naatiffe*] is out of this world—a unique experience!

Also, I took some of my test batch of *ma'amoul* to Alan Davidson for tasting and mentioned the bois de Panama to him. He had his usual bookworm reaction, instantly starting to look it up in dozens of reference books, but especially in *Cornucopia,* our 'bible' for the botany of food plants. There he found *Saponaria officinalis,* which is soapwort, also known as 'bouncing bet'; but no mention of bois de Panama. On the other hand, he did discover a very explicit and detailed entry for the mystery product in the *Dictionnaire Encyclopédique de l'Epicerie* by Albert Seigneurie (Paris, 1898):

> PANAMA, bois de. On donne ce nom à une sorte de bois fourni par un arbre qui croît en quantité sur l'Isthme de Panama, le *Quillaja saponaria.* On enlève à cet arbre son écorce en la débitant en pièces longues de 80 centimètres environ et larges de 10 à 15. Cette écorce est ensuite mise en paquets et exportée en Europe et dans les diverses contrées qui l'emploient.
>
> L'écorce de Panama, pulverisée et mêlée à l'eau, fait mousser celle-ci comme le savon. Elle a la propriété de détacher et de dégraisser les étoffes de soie et de laine. Le bois de Panama, lorsqu'on le brise, produit des éternuements comme le poivre ou les épices. Ils sont produits par de fines aiguilles cristallines qui s'échappent de la cassure et agissent mécaniquement sur la membrane nazale. La substance qui produit l'effet utile est une matière piquante qui est unie à de la chlorophylle et à une matière grasse sucrée.
>
> L'Epicerie débite couremment du bois de Panama et divers articles à base d'extraits de ce bois qui ont le même emploi: la panamine, l'extrait de Panama, le savon de Panama, etc., etc.
>
> Elle se pourvoit de ses divers articles chez les fabricants ou les négociants en droguerie.

Anissa then brought some bois de Panama for us to see. To me they just looked like a lot of dried twigs (see illustration on page 31), not like the bark to which Seigneurie referred! and she also brought instructions for me to test making the *naatiffe* cream. I must confess my heart sank when she explained what I was supposed to do with the twigs. Quite daunting, and it was with great relief that I heard a few days later that she had herself done the testing.

Meanwhile, no stones were being left unturned:

- Alan in his quest for the true botanical identity had despatched one sample to Dr Pombo-Villar in Basle and another to Harold McGee, the food scientist in Palo Alto (a colleague of whom bore that sample away but has not been heard of since).
- Claudia Roden gave oral testimony to the effect that in her family in Cairo no grand family celebration would be considered complete unless *naatiffe* cream were served; but that they counted it as a Syrian speciality (her family came originally from Aleppo) rather than an Egyptian one; and that the whiteness of the cream symbolized purity.
- Anissa and I were looking up soapwort in herbals. The description seemed to fit. There was a lot of information about soapwort's cleaning properties, including use as a shampoo and medicinal uses (but no mention of its use in cooking).

By now I had a new worry. Reference books referred to soapwort's saponin content being toxic. So we decided to double-check on this in *A Modern Herbal* by Mrs Grieve, who we knew had a passage on soapwort. What we now discovered when we turned the relevant page was that she described not just one but three items (all of which contained saponin), any one of which might be what we were looking for:

(1) Soapwort, *Saponaria officinalis.* Habitat: Central and Southern Europe. Also known as Soaproot. Bouncing Bet. Latherwort. Fuller's Herb. Bruisewort. Crow Soap, Sweet Betty. Wild Sweet William.

(2) Soapwort root, Egyptian, *Gypsophila struthium* (the mention of 'Egyptian' threw us off track for a while, as did a reference I found to Gypsophila being used as a soap in Afghanistan in *Notes on the Products of Western Afghanistan and of North-Eastern Persia,* 1890, by Aitchison);

(3) Soap tree, *Quillaja saponaria,* also known as soap bark, Panama Bark and Cullay. Habitat Peru and Chile, and cultivated in Northern Hindustan.

Panama bark, despite its distant habitat, sounded a very good possibility but we noticed that in none of the three references was any mention made of the Middle East, nor of culinary uses . . . We weren't exactly getting nowhere but we wondered whether we were, so to speak, barking up the wrong tree.

Then came the letter from Dr Esteban Pombo-Villar in which he announced that 'the mystery of bois de Panama is solved'.

* * * *

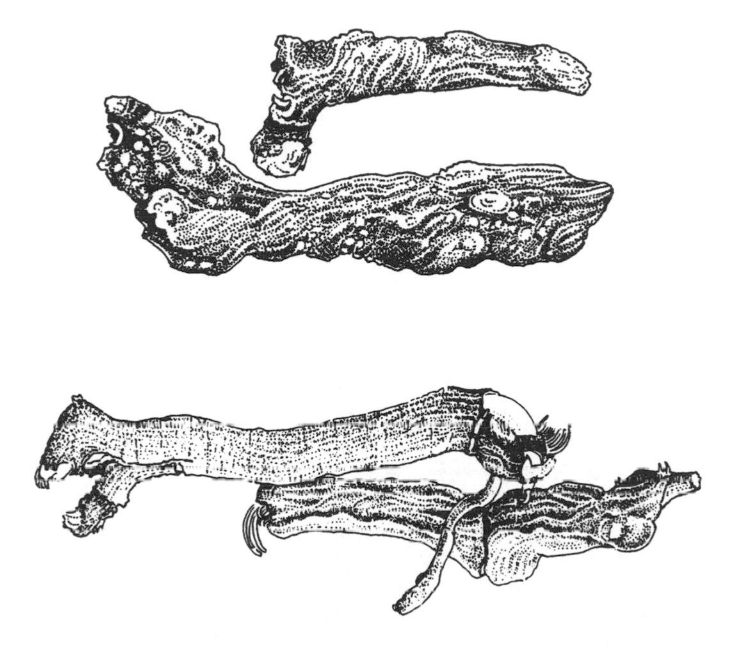

Evidence in the Case. The drawings by Soun Vannithone show two pairs of specimens of material supplied to Anissa Helou as, perhaps, the mysterious 'bois de Panama'. The lower pair are certainly roots, probably of Saponaria officinalis, *soapwort. The upper pair were at first thought to be the rolled inner bark of the tree* Quillaja saponaria, *but close inspection of their outer surface (all that is visible in the drawings) suggest that they too may be roots, although the appearance of their interior is ambiguous. More news is promised when the specimens have been subjected to expert examination at the Royal Botanic Gardens, Kew.*

Dr Esteban Pombo-Villar's Letter

The mystery of 'bois de Panama' is solved. Initially I had only been able to find references to Panama Bark, and therefore thought that the wood referred to was a variant of 'bois de Bahama' to which several of my XIXth century chemistry books had references. It was when I looked at *Fenaroli's Handbook of Flavour Ingredients*[1] that I came across the reference for 'bois de Panama' as a foreign name for *Quillaja* or Panama bark, the bark of a perennial South American tree called *Quillaja saponaria* Molina. It is known by many synonyms: soap bark, quillay bark, China bark, Murillo bark, Seifenholz, saponaria. This member of the Rosaceae family was taken to India and Indonesia, particularly northern Hindustan where it is mainly grown to prepare tinctures and extracts for use in shampoos and beverages. Fenaroli's book gives the organoleptic properties as 'bittersweet aromatic flavour', but points out that the bark extracts are mainly used for their foaming and detergent properties. In shampoos, many references are made to its mildness and the fact that it does not induce seborrhea.[2] It has very low long-term toxicity,[3] making it safe in beverages and foods. The soaplike fraction, known as quillaja saponins, consists of quillaic acid (whose structure is illustrated below) and several complex sugars attached to it. The quillaic acid structure was determined among others by a group of Swiss scientists at the ETH in Zurich, under the direction of the legendary Ruzicka[4] whose famous art collection now hangs in the Kunstmuseum of that city. As a recent development, several groups have been using quillaja saponins to enhance the body's response to vaccination, as a so-called adjuvant, which could make vaccinations much more effective. This is under trial for a variety of vaccines, including an experimental AIDS vaccine.[5] Quillaja saponins have an emulsifying effect that has found use in photographic developers, and other chemical and pharmaceutical applications; among the more exotic perhaps is its use as emulsifier for rocket fuels.[6] Unfortunately I have not found any South American recipe calling for 'bois de Panama' but perhaps with its identification you can now find something.

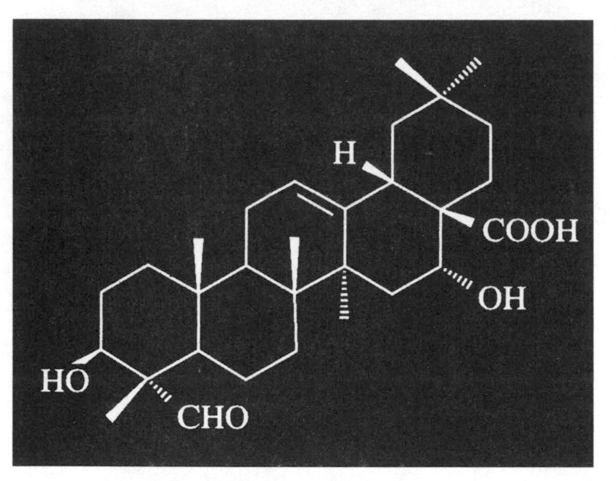

Woods as spices are certainly rare nowadays. A traditional ingredient for a type of marzipan known as Zürileckerli is ground sandalwood. Some time ago in Zurich, looking for ground sandalwood I went to a beautiful shop called Schwarzenbach, in the old town, where the windows are full of all sorts of dried fruits, coloured sugar drops, dried pulses and noodles. They did not have the sandalwood, which they only stock around Christmas time, but some twigs in a jar attracted my attention. The shop attendant said that they were called Süssholz, or sweet wood, and told me people liked to chew it or to make it into a tea. After some enquiring, it turned out to be *Glycyrriza glabra,* from whose roots a decoction is made and concentrated—licorice. According to Brockhaus, the roots were used by Indians, Babylonians, Egyptians and Romans for medicinal purposes, especially for colds. But I guess the European children must have enjoyed chewing on the twigs as much as we did when we were given sugar cane to munch on. Having tried both, I prefer sugar cane as it is juicier; but both have a rather unpleasant and no doubt unhealthy grinding effect on the teeth! Interestingly, the sweet substance of *Glycyrriza glabra,* known as Glycyrrhizine, is fifty times sweeter than cane sugar (saccharose), but most is found in the roots of the plant. I wonder how much of it is actually in the wood. Anyway, it is a similar type of compound to the quillaja saponins, but obviously different in flavour.

It makes me wonder how many other barks and woods are still in use today. Cinnamon, of course, is one. But how often are flavourings like wild black cherry bark used? According to the Merck Index, the dried stem bark of the north American wild black cherry, *Prunus serotina* Ehrh., is used in flavouring foods, but it does not say which. As with quillaja, I would like to find traditional recipes using woods as flavourings.

PS I am indebted to Dr B. Huegi for help with the searching of databases.

* * * *

Anissa Continues the Story . . .

In his letter Esteban focuses on the bark of *Quillaja saponaria,* which is what Fenaroli, his main source, refers to. Fine; but the 'bois de Panama' we had in front of us looked like dried roots or 'twigs', reddish brown in colour with a creamy white core. This fitted Mrs Grieve's description of the dried roots of soapwort (*Saponaria officinalis*) more than any description of the bark of *Quillaja saponaria.* Moreover, when I asked our Librarian to let me have a look at a rare FAO publication which gives botanical identifications for all Arabic food plant terms, I found that according to this *'erq* (or *'erh,* or *shersh*) *al halaweh* (i e the Arabic term corresponding to bois de Panama) is *Saponaria officinalis.* Puzzle!

Luckily, I received more 'bois de Panama' from Beirut and this new batch, at which I am gazing as I write, does look like an inner bark (although it is neither dark nor very tough, as Mrs Grieve describes it, but softer than the 'roots' and paler). Most of the pieces are thick spliced bits of outer and inner bark. There are a few twig-like pieces but not many. The outer bark has the same texture as the outer surface of the dried roots (see drawings).

In the Lebanon the two types are sold separately and according to my mother one is known as *baladi* (local) and the other as *gharbi* (foreign). Unfortunately my mother, who brought both types, the roots and the inner bark, could not remember which was which, nor where the foreign type was imported from but she was quite sure the local one was considered to be superior.

The recipe for *natef* (my spelling) I give in my forthcoming book is based on one in Ibrahim Mouzannar's *La Cuisine Libanaise.* And another, slightly different, from George Rayes's *L'Art Culinaire Libanais.* Having studied these sources, I tell readers of my book to peel and grind the bois de Panama. This is a difficult and time-consuming operation, as peeling the roots is rather hard work (the bark less so) and grinding either type is nearly impossible. The bois de Panama is too hard to be pulverized in a food processor and unless you have a sturdy mortar and heavy pestle you might have to resort to a meat cleaver as I did. Unfortunately it was only after the manuscript of my book was delivered that I was told by two professional Lebanese sweet-makers in London that there was no need to peel or grind the bois de Panama; instead they boil it whole to produce the liquid which is the basis of *natef.*

The recipe given below takes account of this information and is therefore infinitely easier to carry out than the one in the book. In fact it will seem quite easy to you as you read it. Please bear in mind that the simplicity has been achieved by great efforts—what in retrospect seem like two weeks of unremitting experiment on my part with batch after batch of white sudsy stuff. And it is only fair to add that in the Lebanon people rarely make *natef* at home; it is normally bought with *ḳarabeege* (my spelling) from sweet shops or, more often, eaten at a sweet shop or in a restaurant. This little piece of information perhaps carries a message for you!

* * * *

Natef
(bois de Panama mousse)

These quantities make about 1.5 litres (54 fl oz).

60 g (2 oz) bois de Panama
600 ml (22 fl oz) water
sugar syrup (quantity as in the sub-recipe below, or to taste)

Rinse the bois de Panama under cold water to get rid of the grit, then put it together with the water in a large saucepan. Place over a medium heat and bring to the boil. Watch it as it is about to boil as it will make quite a froth. If you leave it boiling too hard the froth may spill over, in which case reduce the heat, to bring the froth down. Cover the pan and leave to simmer on a low heat for about 2 hours. The liquid should reduce to a quarter of the initial amount, or about 150 ml (5 fl oz).

While the bois de Panama solution is boiling, prepare the sugar syrup as in the recipe below and keep it warm.

Strain the reduced liquid into a large mixing bowl and leave to cool before whisking it until it becomes very foamy, brilliant white and somewhat shiny. If you are doing this by hand it will take rather a long time and you might need someone to take the *relève,* or else use an electric beater which will relieve your arm and considerably shorten the whisking time.

Gradually add the warm sugar syrup to the frothy bois de Panama solution and fold it in well until you have a white elastic mousse. Leave to cool before refrigerating. Serve as a dip with *Karabeeje* (pistachio nut fingers).

Ater
(sugar syrup)

These quantities make about 350 ml (12 fl oz)

350 g (12 oz) white granulated or golden caster sugar
100 ml (3.5 fl oz) water
1 teaspoon lemon juice
1 tablespoon rosewater
1 tablespoon orange blossom water

Put the sugar and water in a saucepan and place over a medium heat. Bring to the boil, occasionally stirring the mixture. Leave to boil for 3 minutes or until it reaches a temperature of 130° (250°F). Then stir in the lemon juice, rose and orange blossom water and boil for a few seconds.

Turn off the heat and keep it warm and ready to use with the *natef.*

* * * *

Helen Next Describes the Tasting

Anissa brought three samples of *naatiffe* for Alan and me to taste: one made with the roots; one made with the bark; and one sample made by a Lebanese restaurant. Interested and fascinated though I was, I must admit that I tasted rather gingerly because I could not dispel from my mind the references to its toxic qualities and the warning in *Herbs* (by Roger Phillips and Nicky Foy) that '. . . taken internally in large doses, soapwort may cause muscular paralysis and should only be taken under the guidance of a medical practitioner.' Anissa assured me that she had eaten a whole bowl of *naatiffe* without ill effect. Alan was enjoying the tasting (he likes the pastries which you dunk in the *naatiffe*) until I pointed out that the risk of toxic shock from saponin was surely less than that of salmonella poisoning from the restaurant sample, which we agreed seemed to have the addition of whisked egg whites. (Anissa had already told us that some people do add egg white; and indeed that people who have no bois de Panama may make *naatiffe* with just whisked egg white and sugar syrup.)

Anissa's samples all looked very frothy, even soapy. All the samples had a bittersweet, almondy taste but the bark version tasted rather more bitter than the root version. Anissa said that the restaurant version with the egg whites looked something like the *naatiffe* she knew—a brilliant white, smooth, mousse-like cream with a distinctive taste, but she somehow felt that it was still not quite right. So off she went to visit another professional Lebanese sweet-maker, Kamal Moudallal, to see if he could shed any more light on the matter. There she learned that where she had gone wrong was that she had not whisked the bois de Panama solution enough and her sugar syrup was too thin. The sweetmaker's *naatiffe* was just as it should be: a glossy, elastic mousse-like brilliant white cream with a bittersweet taste.

So far, so good. But Kamal Moudallal's senior colleague then made a comment which put us back into a lather of perplexity. He blandly informed us that *'bois de Panama' is the root of a plant which grows in the Lebanon, Syria and Jordan'*. Heavens, we thought, he's telling us that bois de Panama and soapwort are one and the same thing! And he ought to know.

At this point we felt that our powers of detection were exhausted and that we had better wash all this soapy gook off our hands and ask the Coordinator of this INTERSPI enquiry to scrutinise our findings.

* * * *

Alan Draws Conclusions

When I met the two detectives at INTERSPI headquarters (in a hidden garden courtyard in Chelsea) and assessed all their information and clues, I found that certain conclusions leaped at once to my mind.

- We are dealing with two things which have similar properties. One is bark from a tall (60 feet) Central or South American tree (of Chile, says *Hortus Third,* and cultivated in the deep south of the USA). The other is the root of a flowering plant (3 or 4 feet high) of the Near East and Europe etc (naturalized in North America).
- The one which is entitled to the name 'bois de Panama' is, clearly, the indigenous American one, the inner bark of *Quillaja saponaria.*
- But few botanists are skilled confectioners, and vice versa. A confectioner in or from the Near East is hardly likely to make a botanical distinction between two products which look like each other and which have similar effects. He will tend to call both by the same name.
- If addressing other Arabs, he will use the Arabic name.

- But if addressing a non-Arab, the confectioner's choice will lie between a French name which has international currency and sounds romantic, and an English name which sounds like a laundry term and is off-putting. He is likely to prefer the first.
- Hence the confusion. The use of the name 'bois de Panama' has been extended, in certain contexts, to include soapwort.

But . . . the above must be treated as a hypothesis. The process of verification should include, belatedly, submission of our samples to the authorities at the Royal Botanic Gardens, Kew, so that we can be sure that what we have is what we think we have.

And we need to establish how far back in time the making of *naatiffe* can be traced in the Lebanon and Syria, and what evidence can be mustered to show whether the material originally used for this purpose was genuine bois de Panama or soapwort root.

In addition, it would be good to know how it came about that a French name is used for the dried bark of *Quillaja saponaria.* The tree does not grow in a francophone part of the world. Is the explanation that French was a current language in the Lebanon and Syria and that the product was used there more than anywhere else? Or is it possible that, as suggested by Helen's husband, we have here a relic of French involvement in the early stages (up to 1889) of constructing the Panama Canal?

Finally, I have a conclusion which I regard as definite, not a mere hypothesis. Let me state it thus, and let the detectives rejoice to see it stated:

This document is now
the LOCUS CLASSICUS on
bois de Panama.

* * * *

Some of the books consulted by Helen and Anissa

Bean, W. J. et al, *Trees and Shrubs Hardy in the British Isles,* 8th edn, 4 vols, 1970–80

Culpeper, *Complete Herbal,* 1826 edn (from original work of 17th century)

FAO (Food and Agriculture Organisation of the United Nations), terminology Bulletin 25/2 (Arabic food plant names), Rome, 1983

Grieve, Mrs M., *A Modern Herbal,* 1931

Haroutunian, Arto der, *Patisserie of the Eastern Mediterranean,* 1988

Helou, Anissa, *Lebanese Cuisine*, 1994

Hortus Third, 1976

Michael, Pamela, *All Good Things Around Us,* 1980

Mouzannar, Ibrahim, *La Cuisine Libanaise,* 1983

Page, Mary, *The Gardener's Book of Herbs* [date missing in our copy]

Phillips, Roger & Foy, Nicky, *Herbs,* 1990

Rayes, Georges N, *l'Art Culinaire Libanais,* 1957

Roden, Claudia, *A New Book of Middle Eastern Food,* 1986

Seigneurie, Albert, *Dictionnaire Encyclopédique de l' Epicerie,* Paris, 1898

Esteban's Notes and References

1. T. E. Furia and N. Bellanca (eds), *Fenaroli's Handbook of Flavour Ingredients,* CRC Press, Cleveland, 1971, p. 208.
2. G. Andermann, C. Andermann and P. Masson, 'Absence d'effet sébogénétique d'un shampooing à base de saponines au bois de Panama', *Pharmaceutica Acta Helvetica 1981*, 56, 194.
3. J. J. Drake, K. R. Butterworth, I. F. Guant, J. Hooson, J. G. Evans, S. D. Gangolli, 'Long-term toxicity study of quillaia extract in rats', *Food Chem. Toxicol.* 1982, *20,* 15.
4. L. Ruzicka, B. Bischof, E. C. Taylor, A. Meyer, O. Jeger, 'Über Zusammenhänge zwischen Gypsogenin, Hederagenin und Quillajasäeure', *Coll. Czech. Chem. Commun.* 1950, *15,* 893.
5. J. Glanz, 'Adjuvant rejuvenates vaccine Science', *Research and Development,* January 1993, *35,* 53, and C. R. Kensil, M. J. Newman, R. T. Coughlin, D. J. Marciani, 'Novel Adjuvants from *Quillaja saponaria* Molina', *AIDS Res. Rev.* 1993, *3,* 379.
6. J. Guillard, 'Qu'est-ce que le bois de Panama?, *Revue Forestière Française,* 1978, *30,* 78.

A Spicy Mystery, Part Two:

Now with the Help of the INTERSPI Team

The first installment of this saga of detection, published in *PPC 47,* has already attracted the comments printed below. The time is not ripe for drawing conclusions, because the experts at Kew have still to identify the pieces of *bois de Panama* which Anissa Helou and I submitted to them recently; and, who knows, their identification may well blow away many of the soap bubbles generated in the early phases of the enquiry.

First off the mark was Phil Iddison, writing from London and then sending a postscript from Al Ain in the UAE, whither he had been transferred while in the middle of his research.

The Gypsophila/Helva Connection **from Phil Iddison**

I had thought there was a connection between soapwort and candy floss. I was wrong on this point, the connection was between soapwort/gypsophila/ fullers herb (*Gypsopohila arrosta*) and Turkish helva and is described by Evelyn Lyle Kalças in *Food from the Fields*. She describes a liquid being prepared from the large white fleshy root. The root, dried for storage and sale, becomes dark brown. The liquid creates a good lather when shaken and in fact the root is also used to make a soap. The liquid is used in the preparation of helva.

True soapwort root (*Saponaria officinalis*) is poisonous although the leaves and stems yield a soapy sap which is used both as a soap for fine textiles and as a medicinal herb usually taken externally.

At lunchtime today I went to Books for Cooks to top up on books on Arabian cuisine in preparation for going to the UAE. I selected *Food for the Vegetarian, Traditional Lebanese Recipes* by Aida Karaoglan (Interlink Books, New York, 1992) as it looked to be authentic and original. On the train home practically the first page I looked at had a recipe for *natef* which satisfied your description [over the phone] of this. Furthermore a prime ingredient was *'bois de Panama'*. *Bois de Panama* is called *halawa* wood and is described as 'a 3 ounce piece of white root'. By soaking and boiling this ground root a thick foaming liquid is produced to make the *natef*.

By now I think we have too many coincidences:

(1) 'Bois de Panama' is a white root, so is gypsophila. The active ingredient in the roots of *Gypsophila* spp. is saponin.

(2) Both are associated with *helva, halawa* in Arabic.

(3) The root is used as the base of a soapy/foaming liquid.

(4) Both are associated with sweet dishes.

(5) Both references come from the Middle East.

I would therefore make a tentative identification of *'bois de Panama'* as *Gypsophila arrosta,* but have no idea as to how it came by its rather exotic French name; perhaps a good French dictionary would help!

A Postscript from the UAE **from Phil Iddison**

Further to my letter of 25 July and speculation that *'bois de Panama'* is *Gypsophila arrosta,* I have found that, as mentioned by Evelyn Lyle Kalças, the 'extract of halawa root' is a common ingredient of the halawa or helva on sale in the UAE. I send herewith a label [not reproduced] from a sample purchased at the local Al Ain co-op. There were five brands on offer and all included this particular ingredient. It was described differently on other brands, as *cheleh halawa* on French language lists of ingredients and as halawa yeast on others. This latter description seems to be a reference to the lightening effect of the saponin. The specimen sent is manufactured in the UAE but there were also Lebanese and Saudi brands.

The confection is quite light; I cannot be sure whether this is the result of the saponin component of the halawa root extract. Any nutty flavour from the halawa root is of course, in this confection, completely masked by the tahina and sugar flavours. As I do not have any of the books with me yet I am unable to check helva recipes for this ingredient.

Have not yet located a traditional spice stall where I could ask for halawa root to see if it is available and what it would look like in this part of the world. Most spices are prepackaged now in the supermarkets. There are some interesting items from Sri Lanka which I will be investigating in due course.

By the way, one Turkish way to eat helva is with bread, *ekmek*. It is not as strange as it sounds when you consider the ingredients, and a good way to enjoy the flavour as the texture can be quite cloying if eaten neat.

Notes on the Uses of Soapwort **from Patience Gray**

I was deep in the Spice Mystery with detectives so sympathetic; they also made me laugh, the atmosphere surrounding this enthusiasm was so delightful—then came an interruption. When I hastened back to it, fluttering the pages to find my place, I caught sight of Spigolizzi's roof and wondered what on earth is that doing in *PPC 47.* That was a delightful surprise for later!

I am longing to hear Kew's verdict. Botanically *Saponaria officinalis* has a 'rhizome' with dependant rootlets, rather than a 'root'. Soun's bottom drawing reflects this (horizontal growth).

In the last war Lady Featherstonehaugh at Uppark, South Harting, under the Sussex Downs began using this plant as detergent for restoring her ancient tapestries. Their true colours returned after immersion in the soapy liquid. She was so successful that she was besieged by other Ladies from great houses with faded tapestries. She guarded the 'secret' of the process; only the miraculous results reached the press. This lovely house, where Nelson's Emma was once a dairymaid and her mother the housekeeper, was burnt down a few years ago. The plant is common in Britain. Leaves as well as roots were used (as I recall). Some references follow.

Paul Schauenberg and Ferdinand Paris, *Guides des Plantes medicinales,* in the series 'Les Guides du Naturaliste', Delachaux et Niestlé (Neuchatel, 1969), which I use, says it occurs throughout Europe, Asia and North America. A general comment is: '*Feuilles et racines* peuvent s'employer pour la lessive (détergents).' They also note:

APPLICATIONS: Le rhizome (Radix Saponariae) est utilisé en décoction lors d'affections des voies respiratoires.

PARTIES UTILISEES: Le rhizome.

HISTORIQUE: Tous les médécins de la Grèce antique faisaient un grand usage de la saponaire. [Theophrastus, 372–287 BC, might have something on this . . .)

The section (Chapter XIV) on Plantes à Saponosides begins: On entend par saponosides, sapogénines ou saponines, des hétérosides naturels don't la matière efficace est un composé soluble à l'eau qui la rend moussante comme une eau du savon.

There is a mention of this soapwort used in Tea to assist digestion but nothing about a delicious cream . . .

In the introduction to this section nothing 'toxic' is mentioned!

It also says in this introduction that the 'lather' effect can be obtained by other substances such as starch but that the 'saponosides' produce a finer lather and more durable . . . (This has relevance only if *Saponaria* turns out to have been used for making *natef* [Anissa's spelling].)

My Use of Soapwort — from Mary Wondrausch

Saponaria—this does occur in the wild here, I remember finding a polyptoid type near Cutmill and this was recorded.

I grow it and use it as does my daughter—for 'washing' frail textiles. Now this is the leaves, stems and flowers. I slow boil these in about a quart of water for 5 minutes. The pulp is put in butter muslin. The bath (bathroom) is one eighth full of warm water—in goes the material into the stewing water and we bounce the Saponaria bag gently and lengthily on the cloth—a couple of rinses and out on the line in the shade.

Lady Featherstonehaugh of Uppark was famous for the retexturing of priceless damaged brocades with saponaria and she told me of this some 20 years ago.

I have a pretty large and comprehensive herb garden and this year I have only grown a modest amount of Saponaria as it is so invasive. I like the pretty pink colour and the form is somewhat similar to the old fashion'd phlox.

An Early Turkish Recipe **from Maria Kaneva-Johnson**

I would like to add that all parts of soapwort, *Saponaria officinalis,* are poisonous, the poisonous constituent being *Saponin glycoside* (see Pamela M. North, *Poisonous Plants and Fungi in Colour,* Blandford Press, London, 1967). The use of the plant to produce a soap-like substance when soaked in water has been known since Dioscorides.

I found mention of this plant in an 1838 Turkish cookbook entitled *Dögu' da Tatlıcılık* (Eastern Confectionery) by Friedrich Unger. A direct translation from the Turkish original is as follows:

Plain Semi-Soft Halva

> Cook, stirring, 1 okka (1.283 kg) peeled and crushed *Radíx Saponariae* [his spelling] roots in water. Strain the water and boil again to the right consistency. Discard the roots.
>
> The halva itself is then prepared by adding the extract to a sugar/honey syrup or *pekmez* (clarified, condensed grape juice).
>
> Soapwort is also described in many Balkan phytotherapy books as curative, when used in moderation.

Botanical and Pharmacological Comments from Professor Arthur Tucker

I loved 'A Spicy Mystery' and the concept of INTERSPI. Please enroll me as a member. [Professor Tucker has been enrolled. He is invited to the First Annual Dinner of INTERSPI, in whatever year it is decided to stage this spicy occasion. H.J.S.] I have been identifying mystery herbs from The Herb Society of America and the International Herb Association (previously IHGMA) for many years. I am currently Research Professor in the Department of Agriculture and Natural Resources, Delaware State University, Dover, Delaware 19901–2277, USA.

Quillaia extracts, along with Mohave yucca, are used extensively as foaming agents in root beer and cocktail mixtures and approved by the US

FDA for this purpose (see Albert Y. Leung's *Encyclopedia of Common Natural Ingredients,* John Wiley, 1980). When I first read the article, I immediately consulted M. Salah Ahmed, Gisho Honda, and Wataru Miki's *Herb Drugs and Herbalists in the Middle East* (Institute for the Study of Languages and Cultures of Asia and Africa, Studia Culturae Islamicae No. 8, 1979). However, in Part I, 'Names of Herbalist's Materials', they only list *Gypsophila struthium* and *Saponaria officinalis* as 'ir' ḥalāwa. Maurice M. Iwu's *Handbook of African Medicinal Plants* (CRC Press, 1993) says that *Quillaja saponaria* is cultivated in North Africa with another name of kilaya in both French and Arabic. Iwu also presents a concise discussion of the immunomodulatory activity of quillaia saponins, showing that they actually stimulate the immune system and have shown success in experimental vaccines against protozoal diseases such as malaria, babesiosis, and trypanosomiasis.

Thus, I suppose, the common Arabic name 'ir' ḥalāwa, for foaming agents from *Gypsophila* and *Saponaria* has carried over to *Quillaja.*

And Now Nishalla **from Charles Perry**

For years I wondered about *nishalla,* a sweet that often shows up in Central Asian cookery writings. When I went to Uzbekistan in 1993, I asked about it and all anybody could tell me was that it was an old-fashioned sweet that had just about disappeared from use because people preferred factory-made sweets. It turns out to be a soapwort sweet. Helen Saberi's article put me on the track.

In Tajik (the Persian dialect spoken in Tajikistan and Uzbekistan), this dish is called *nishallå.* In Uighur, the Turkic language spoken in Xinjiang Province, China, the name is *nishala* or *rishalå.* It's *nishalda* in the languages of Kyrgyzstan and Kazakhstan; the form of the word in Uzbek (*nishålda*) shows that the Uzbeks learned of it from their Kazakh or Kyrgyz cousins, and not from their Tajik neighbors, because the dissimilation of *ll* to *id* is not an Uzbek sound change. *Nishalla* does not seem to be made outside this Central Asian area—neither in Iran nor Azerbaijan, nor, to the north, the Tatar country of the middle Volga.

The word has no Persian or Turkic derivation I can find. It looks rather like the Arabic religious phrase *'in sha' Allah* ('God willing').

Russian sources refer to the essential ingredient as 'spiny-leaf' (*koliuche-listnik*) or 'soap root' (*myl' nyi koren'*), which is defined as 'a spiny-leaved, panicled plant of Turkestan'. The Uzbek word for it is either *yetmak* or *bekh.* The latter is the Persian word for 'root', and here, of course, we have struck pay-dirt. Aitchison's *Notes on the Products of Western Afghanistan and North-Eastern Persia* defines *bekh* as 'the root of any shrub; technically applied to the root-stocks of Acanthophyllum macrodon and Gypsophila paniculata.' QED.

For anyone's curiosity, this is the Tajik recipe for *nishalla,* from *Natsional'nye Kukhni Nashikh Narodov* by V. V. Pokhlëbkin (Pishchevaia Promyshlennost', Moscow 1978):

NISHALLO (IE NISHALLA)

1 kilogram sugar
1 liter water
4 egg whites
50 grams soap root
2 teaspoons lemon peel
0.5 teaspoon citric acid
0.5 teaspoon vanilla

Dissolve sugar in 1–1.5 cups water, boil to syrup, carefully skim and cool.

Clean the surface of the root, cut in 0.5 cm pieces, place in a teapot, pour on 1–1.5 cups water and boil thoroughly 20–30 minutes. Then strain the broth through cheesecloth and let cool until just warm.

Whip the egg whites to a froth. Introduce the still-warm soapwort broth in small doses, whipping continuously to make thick beaten egg whites. Beat in the syrup in stages until it forms a syrupy, thick, creamy mass. At the time of testing this, crystals of sugar will be felt. And at this time the syrup must not separate from the beaten whites but form a single white with them. Several minutes before the end of the beating, introduce the citric acid, vanilla and peel into the nishallo.

The measurements are distressingly imprecise; either 1 or 1.5 cups syrup; either 1 or 1.5 cups soap root broth. The only hint we get is the description of *nishallå* as 'a half-liquid sort of *halva* which does not keep long'. In Karim Makhmudov's *Uzbekskie Bliuda,* the syrup is precisely described (0.5 kg sugar, 0.5 liters water) but no measurement is given for the soapwort.

Lemon and vanilla are recent additions to the recipe, needless to say. The way they are called for in Makhmudov's recipe, otherwise identical to the above, have the feeling of an afterthought.

A Spicy Mystery, Part Three:
Bois de Panama, the Verdict from Kew

ANISSA HELOU

The author, who partnered Helen J Saberi and Alan Davidson in preparing earlier reports on the Bois de Panama Mystery (see Parts One and Two) celebrated her promotion in INTERSPI (to be Detective Extraordinary with Multiple Portfolios and Superintendent, Safe Houses, London Area) by writing the third report in the series, the Big One, the one which incorporates the official verdict from the Jodrell Laboratory of the Royal Botanic Gardens, Kew, on the samples of 'bois de Panama' which she had submitted to them. In congratulating Anissa, we must remark that the tale is not yet fully told; as she points out herself, there is more to be done.

What a thrill it was for me to read the opening paragraph of our recent press release!

> INTERSPI, the fastest growing international organisation of 1995, is pleased to announce progress in cracking its first case, the Bois de Panama Mystery.

Yes, progress indeed! The official letter (reproduced on the following page) which we received from the Royal Botanic Gardens, Kew, shows that of the five samples of 'bois de Panama' which I had obtained from the Lebanon none was from *Quillaja saponaria,* the American tree which is the source of the authentic product; all were from the European/Middle Eastern/Central Asian shrubs *Saponaria officinalis* (soapwort) or *Gypsophila paniculata* (baby's breath)—maybe one, maybe the other, says Kew, as they are closely related. In fact, recalling that from my point of view as cook the samples fell into two groups readily distinguishable by the difference in the results they produced, I hypothesise that it may have been a case of some from one shrub and some from the other.

Thus are the frontiers of knowledge pushed back. Yet they must be made to retreat further. We need to know whether the true bois de Panama is ever used nowadays, for culinary purposes, in the Middle East. And, above all, we need to obtain some and to evaluate its culinary properties (better or worse than the soapwort etc?). As a step in this direction I have asked two resourceful friends in Paris to get me the real thing and am confidently expecting to receive two 250 g batches, one from Egypt and the other from Panama.

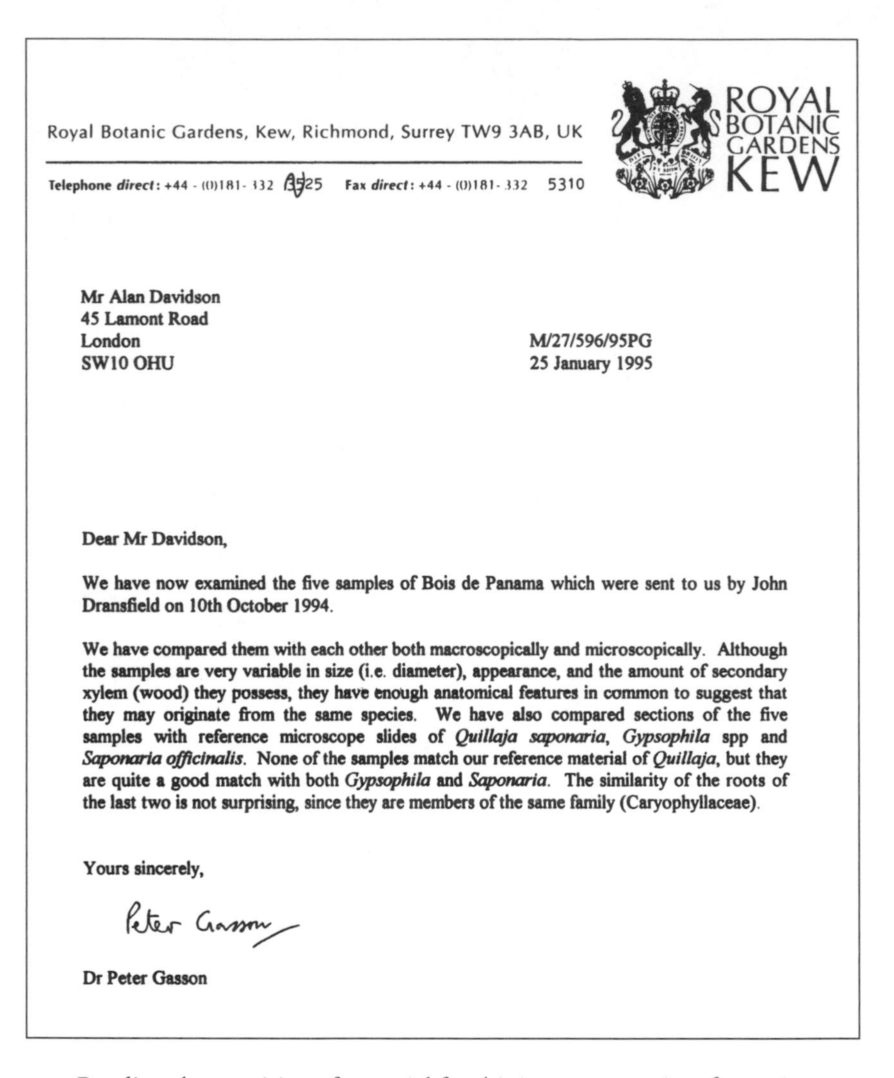

Royal Botanic Gardens, Kew, Richmond, Surrey TW9 3AB, UK

Telephone *direct*: +44 - (0)181 - 332 5525 Fax *direct*: +44 - (0)181 - 332 5310

Mr Alan Davidson
45 Lamont Road
London
SW10 OHU

M/27/596/95PG
25 January 1995

Dear Mr Davidson,

We have now examined the five samples of Bois de Panama which were sent to us by John Dransfield on 10th October 1994.

We have compared them with each other both macroscopically and microscopically. Although the samples are very variable in size (i.e. diameter), appearance, and the amount of secondary xylem (wood) they possess, they have enough anatomical features in common to suggest that they may originate from the same species. We have also compared sections of the five samples with reference microscope slides of *Quillaja saponaria*, *Gypsophila* spp and *Saponaria officinalis*. None of the samples match our reference material of *Quillaja*, but they are quite a good match with both *Gypsophila* and *Saponaria*. The similarity of the roots of the last two is not surprising, since they are members of the same family (Caryophyllaceae).

Yours sincerely,

Peter Gasson

Dr Peter Gasson

Pending the provision of material for this important series of experiments, whether in the end it has to await the Interspi Bois de Panama Expedition to South America or—as I hope—anticipates that major event, we are setting in train some subsidiary experiments. Famed American artist Shirley Jaffe, seated at dinner in Paris with our Librarian, confided in him that she and many other Parisiennes had recently been using Bois de Panama Shampoo. The fashion, it seemed, peaked a while back, but the product is still on sale in a certain pharmacy in the shadow of the legendary Butte de Montmartre. A large bottle was procured, bearing the inscription 'Phytopanama au Bois de Panama 65%'. The product is now being tested by myself and by Detective Superintendent Helen J. Saberi and others. A report will be furnished later.

Other developments in the bois de Panama saga include communications from Donna MacDonald and Alice Arndt, extracts from which follow. We at HQ are particularly excited to hear that Alice, with her friend Lili, has actually started trial plantations of soapwort in Texas. This New World initiative will shortly be matched in the Old World, where recently promoted Laura Mason has been entrusted with the task of establishing trial plantations of Gypsophila at suitable sites on the Yorkshire Moors.

Extract from letter from Donna MacDonald

Reading the two instalments of the INTERSPI adventure prompted me to consult *The Encyclopedia of Herbs and Herbalism* (London, Orbis, 1979). It mentions some alternative names and a source for the English word 'soapwort' and I pass on this information now as it may serve to clarify (or obscure) the issue.

Soapwort (Bouncing Bet) is noted as *Saponaria officinalis* L caryophyllaceae. The entry focuses on the cleansing properties such as have already been discussed and then adds that 'Dioscorides probably knew *Saponaria officinalis* as *Struthion* while in the Middle Ages it was variously called *Herba Phillippi, Sapanaria* or *Herba fullonis*. The latter name indicates that those who fulled cloth (that is the fullers who cleaned and thickened it) used it as a cleaning agent, and from this William Turner in *The Names of Herbes* (1549) called it Soapwort.

There follows a note that it 'must be treated in special ways before it can be used medicinally' but, annoyingly, these special ways are not divulged. The entry observes that it has been used as a fish poison and has been implicated in the poisoning of both animals and man. After hearing of its properties as a diuretic, laxative, cholagogue, choleretic and expectorant, and in the treatment of certain skin conditions, we are told: 'In India the specially prepared rootstock is considered a galactogogue, and elsewhere it has been employed as an expectorant in respiratory complaints.'

Finally, readers are warned to use soapwort only under medical supervision, though it's worth observing that this is very modest by comparison with the encyclopedia's warning about the dangers of deadly nightshade. I suspect if readers take into account all the information which is appearing in *PPC*, they will know more than most medical practitioners on the subject.

Extract from letter from Alice Arndt

I'm very pleased to be a member of the spice intelligence agency. Did I tell you I invited a group of people for a karabij and naatif party? A local Lebanese chef—Lili of Café Lili—made the wonderful karabij and some naatif with the soapwort roots I gave her; these had been sent to me from Saudi Arabia. I also made a naatif dipping cream with powdered soapwort from a health food shop. (They've not allowed to tell me what they're selling it *for*!) I found the powder very irritating to my nose and sinuses, but my naatif was good. Since the roots that Lili used were rather old and dry, she didn't have enough and, beside the difference in flavor, it was interesting to see how her sauce 'wept' after a couple of days while mine stayed emulsified until it was gone. Now both Lili and I have soapwort herbs growing in our gardens.

Meanwhile Charles Perry has sent us what he calls 'another wrinkle in the soapwort issue'. He says, electrifyingly: 'I just examined the recipes for natif in the 10th century *Kitâb al-Tabîkh,* and they are made strictly from eggs and sugar, no root or bark of any kind called for. No recipes for natif at all in the 13th century *Kitâb al-Wusla ila al-Habîb,* nor in the 13th century Spanish book, etc. Curious.'

* * * *

We conclude with two subsequent communications from INTERSPI's Senior Academic Investigator, Professor Arthur Tucker.

First he told us that the great authority P A G M de Smet, in a learned paper published in 1993, had reported that experiments on mice and rats show that if Quillaja bark in one form or another is fed to these animals they come to little or no harm; that reports in secondary sources of systemic poisoning of human beings as a result of ingesting large amounts of quillaja are not supported by primary sources; and that the FAO/WHO Expert Committee on Food Additives (in their 29th Annual Report, 1986) established an acceptable daily intake for quillaja extract of 0–5 mg/kg body weight. He went on to interpret this, having a normal helping of natef would not come anywhere near causing harm to a human being. But remember, they are talking about true quillaja extract, not soapwort!

In the second communication, Professor Tucker drew attention to an old report to the effect that in the mountainous areas of Uzbekistan and Tajikistan (where 'every Uzbek or Tajik child learns of the soaproot plant, since it is a necessary component in the production of a local cotton candy') there has been very serious depletion of the population of this plant. 'Botanists working in the mountains say that shining holes still dot the sloping harvest areas. In fact, there have already been documented cases of livestock falling into the holes and breaking their legs. Shepherds have lodged official protests against the harvesters with the local authorities because of the environmental damage.'

Tucker added: 'It is true that this report is 40 years old, but it is at least possible that in the new Central Asian States the plundering of natural resources which began under Soviet rule is continuing. In that case, we must fear that the survival of soaproot in the region may be under serious threat. Do travellers still notice these large shining holes with animals falling into them? Any up to date information would be greatly appreciated.'

Among the Yoruba Mushroom-Eaters

ESTHER BALOGH

Professor B. A. Oso introduced his inaugural lecture (Oso 1981) with the following story: 'Shortly after obtaining my PhD degree in London some years ago, I returned to Nigeria and paid a visit to my home town. One evening my aunt came to say hello to me. During the course of our conversation, which was of course in the Yoruba language, she suddenly asked me: "Now that people call you doctor despite the fact that you don't work in the hospital, which kind of doctor are you?" I replied that I was an academic doctor of plants and that I obtained my PhD on the study of fungi. Then I explained to her what I meant by fungi. She asked in utter surprise: "Do you mean to say, that the Government of this country has spent such a huge amount of money on you to go to the white-man's land only to study the common ogogo [the name of a popular mushroom]? Look here, although I cannot read or write I know the names of all of the edible mushrooms in this area. Had I known that this academic work is so easy, I would have registered for my own PhD degree."'

The story much amused the audience but it contains a basic truth. Two generations ago food gathering and hunting provided a significant contribution to the feeding of the population, then living in small scattered villages in practically intact forest. Food gatherers everywhere in the world do know well the edible resources of their environment.

The academic knowledge of tropical mushrooms is progressing only very slowly and can't yet replace the practical experience of the native mushroom-eaters.

It is very odd that none of the Nigerian cookery books (six up to now), not even the otherwise very reliable anthropological articles of Bascom (Bascom 1951 a, b), mention that any mushroom is eaten in the country. It is possible that the authors of these books are 'town-dwellers' separated from the tradition, or that they did not trust it. It is also possible that the habit of mushroom eating was never general, but confined to aficionados. This could have been the case in Europe before the introduction of the cultivated French mushroom (*Agaricus bisporus*). Either one eats and likes wild mushrooms or one is horrified by the idea. Many of my Yoruba friends and colleagues (among them food scientists) would never touch wild fungi and have warned me against them. Except for the real connoisseurs mushrooms in Nigeria never represented a prestige food such as beef, goat, and some kinds of fish, and up to now have remained the poor man's food, a kind of meat replacement. To ask somebody whether her family eats mushrooms is almost tantamount to asking: 'Are you so poor, that you can't afford beef?'

I confess that I and my husband like mushrooms and we frequently eat those species which come to the market, but neither of us would dare to try to collect and identify them by their scientific names. (My own academic training is in microbiology but among the fungi I know the yeasts best.)

It is difficult to explain briefly why the identification of tropical mushrooms presents such problems.

Modern taxonomists do not yet quite agree what kind of organisms belong to the 'Kingdom of Fungi'. For example, Margulis and Schwartz (1982) exclude a few groups which were earlier accepted without any doubt. Their 'Kingdom of Fungi' includes lichens which are not organisms but associations of organisms, and also the 'imperfect fungi' which probably all belong to some other groups. 'Mushroom' is not a scientific term, but more or less means a large, edible fungus. In contrast the name 'toadstool' was preserved for inedible or poisonous species; but this distinction has not been consistently maintained, otherwise we would not speak about 'mushroom poisoning'.

Edible Mushrooms in Nigeria

Latin Name	Yoruba Name	Source	
		Oso (1975, 1979, 1981)	*Zoberi* (1973)
Termitomycetes robustus	ogogo	x	x
T clypeatus	tekele	x	x
T manniformis	akurukooro	x	x
T globulus	olubeje	x	x
T microcarpus	oluoran	x	x
T striatus			
Pleurotus tuber-regium	olu-ohu	x	x
P squarosulus	olu-awo	x	x
Volvariola volvacea	origiagbo	x	x
Vesculenta			
Psathyrella atrombonata	wowo	x	
Calvatia cyanthiformis	isoapero	x	x
Auricularia auricula			x
A polytricha			x
Tricholoma lobayonsis			x
Schizophyllum commune	ipekpenelu		x

Note: the 'French mushroom' (*Agaricus bisporus*) is successfully cultivated on General O. Obasanjo's farm near Lagos. This is of good quality and has largely replaced the imported, canned mushrooms.

Mushrooms (in the sense of large fungi) belong to only two phylla of the Kingdom: the Ascomycota and Basidiomycota, both also containing many microscopic species. In the temperate climatic zone all edible species are Basidiomycota (except morels and truffles). In Nigeria all species traditionally eaten belong to the Basidiomycota. According to Margulis and Schwartz (1982) about 100,000 species constitute the Kingdom of Fungi; from these about 25,000 would fall into the category of Basidiomycota, and 'tens of thousands' to Ascomycota.

About 3,000 species of mushrooms were reported from the British Islands. Phillips (1983) lists about 50 species which are actually eaten in Britain, while Christensen (1943) recommends about the same number in the United States. (Some of the species are identical, others closely related.) In the European continental markets, where trade in wild mushrooms is very carefully regulated, about 30–35 species are permitted. There are of course scientific monographs about mushrooms in most of the European languages, and many popular treatments of the edible species. Several cookery books are devoted exclusively to mushroom recipes and almost all general cookery books contain at least a few examples.

There is nothing of this kind in West Africa or, more specifically, in Nigeria. No estimate of any kind can be given of the species occurring in the country, although about 15 edible species are listed in a series of short papers (Alascadura 1967, Oso 1975, 1977 and 1981, Zoberi 1973).

The first thing which strikes us on reading the cumulative list (p 51) is the relative poverty of genera and species. Should we accept that in Nigeria, which extends through several climatic zones from the tropical rain forest to the desert (including some high mountains on the Cameroon border), the number of mushrooms is much smaller than in an average European country? It would be strange—but not impossible. Strange, because tropical floras are generally considered much richer in species than the temperate ones. Could it be—and I offer this as a hypothesis—that the prevalence of termites so much impoverish the oils in organic materials, that only a few species can establish themselves? About a hundred species of termites are listed from Nigeria (Johnson et al 1980). Not all of these build conspicuous mounds, yet they are comparable in destructiveness. Nye, in a series of articles (1954–55) later discussed in an important monograph 'Soils and Land Use in Central Western Nigeria' (ed Smyth and Montgomery 1962), attributed a prominent role to termites in the formation of soils in Western Nigeria. The termites collect and digest all organic material from the soil and leave a sterile layer almost one foot thick just under the surface.

In the light of this theory it can be argued that the termite fungi are the result of adaptation to the very low organic humus content of the termite-infested soils. These species found the organic waste material in the termite nests and survived the presence of termites. We do not know if the termites actually feed on the mycelium of the fungus, but some recent authors cast doubt on the fabulous underground 'mushroom gardens' of the termites. For example Zoberi (1973) wrote: 'The fungi in the fungus garden are not cultivated, they are wild, the nest being their natural habitat.' According to Quimio (1980), the termites do not cultivate these fungi intentionally, but consume them occasionally and propagate them involuntarily—and become powerless to destroy them when the mycelium starts ramifying in the nest.

What is the intention of these termites, and whether they really like these fungi or not, we do not know; but we are lucky that they leave enough of the delicious mushrooms for us. The naming of the Nigerian termite mushrooms is a complicated issue. Alasoadura (1951) lists four, Oso (1975, 1981) six species, which are not yet fully described (named). I believe that the large Termitomycetes I usually buy and enjoy is *T robustus* (in Yoruba, ogogo or ewe). This is also the favorite species of the Yoruba mushroom-eaters. Its season is from August till October, when the rainy season ends. In this period, when you approach Ife on the Ibadan road, women run to your car with baskets full of large caps of this mushroom. I never experienced roadside trade in this mushroom at any other spot. (It is not however infrequent that a certain product or commodity is sold only on one spot along the roads, for example the Ikire-dodo, fried plantain chips with hot paprika at Ikire, which is also on the Ibadan road.)

The only other Nigerian mushroom of which I have personal experience is a *Pleurotus* species. I first encountered this mushroom in a supermarket in Ibadan—nicely packed in plastic bags in a cold counter. Since then, I have seen it several times on roadside stalls in dried form. I believe that it is a variant of *Pleurotus squarsulus.* It differs from the description given by Zoberi (1973) in only one respect; the cap is not 'whitish', but absolutely snow-white. The species grows on decaying wood, and on rotting banana stems (as I observed in our own garden). It is possible that the specimens in the shop are from experiments in cultivation, but I do not yet have definite proof of this; the printed packing does not give exact information. The mushroom keeps well in fresh state, and is probably available all the year round.

This would be the place to list the poisonous fungi of Nigeria and point out those features which make it possible to distinguish them from the edible species. In spite of the occasional reports of alleged mushroom poisoning in Nigerian newspapers, we know only one case which is well investigated. The *Nigerian Weekly Star* reported on 25 July 1977, that 12 people died within 72 hours in Eziodu in the Imo State after collecting and eating mushrooms (Oso 1981). Professor Oso, a few weeks later, visited the hospital where the victims were treated and collected some mushrooms from the site. He is of the opinion that the mushroom was *Amanita phalloides* and the poisoning was caused by an amatoxin. (Strictly speaking *A phalloides* contains the related phallotoxins, and it is several other *Amanita* species which have amatoxins. Both groups of toxins are small cyclic peptides made up from either seven or eight amino acids [Litten 1975].) As far as we know only the *Amanita* genus and the related *Galerina* contain these kinds of deadly peptide toxins responsible for 95% of the serious mushroom poisonings in Europe and in North America. All other mushrooms which are reportedly poisonous (but rarely deadly) have different hallucinogenic compounds (mostly modified amino acids) which interfere with the neuro-transmitters in the central nervous system (Schultes 1970). In Central Asia and in ancient Mexico mushrooms (*Amanita muscaroides, Psilocybe aztecorum* and other species) were used in magical-religious rituals. There is no report about the occurrence of mushrooms containing hallucinogenic toxins in Nigeria. (The Ifa divination of the Yoruba is a very sober ritual based on a chance event followed by the recitation of a sequence of traditional verses by the babalawo. The supplicant himself is requested to choose the relevant verse. The system is similar in principle to the Chinese 'I Ching'.) As we shall see, the Yoruba 'magical medicine' uses certain mushrooms but in an entirely different way.

Returning to *Termitomycetes robustus,* as this is available only for a few weeks, and very perishable, I usually preserve a lot in the form of duxelles (Grigson 1975). The only difference is that I do not slice the mushroom too fine and I do not 'go on cooking over a good heat until the mixture is dry but not browned or burnt'. My duxelles contains more butter (and some water) and keeps the original taste well. My impression is that the taste of *Termitomycetes* mushrooms is closest to the European cep (*Boletus* spp). While the volatile compounds of mushrooms are described (see summaries in Straten and Maarse 1983) we can't yet replace the organoleptic assessment with a chemical test.

The Yorubas also preserve much of the ogogo either by drying in their clay cooking pots on open fires or by smoking above fires. As these mushrooms are available in the last weeks of the rainy season, sun drying is impossible. I have never witnessed the Yoruba method of pot drying and smoking, but I have occasionally seen dried termite mushrooms on sale at roadside markets. Encouraged by this, I tried the smoking myself and I am pleased with the result. Large, whole *Termitomycetes* mushrooms take eight hours to dry in low temperature smoke. I never heard of any mushrooms being smoke-dried in Europe, but I should like to recommend to those readers who have the opportunity, to try it. I use the smoke-dried mushroom to flavour soups.

My extensive inquiries from mushroom-sellers did not provide many new recipes on mushroom cooking (except for the hints found in Professor Oso's papers). All informants agreed that mushrooms are used in stews, supplementing or replacing meat. In the appendix, following the oldest Yoruba cookery book (originally published in 1934), I have tried to reconstruct a mushroom-meat stew. I myself adapted the European tradition of mushroom cooking (Grigson 1975, Phillips 1983) to the Nigerian mushrooms. In the appendix I also give variants of two Hungarian recipes originally used for the wild relative (*Agaricus campestris*) of the cultivated French mushroom, and for the fairy-ring mushroom (*Marasmius oreades*). For the olu-awo (*Pleurotus* sp), with its rather chewy texture, only the first of these is applicable.

No discussion of the use of mushrooms among the Yorubas can be complete without at least a brief mention of their role in magical medicine. We must first clarify the meaning of the term 'magical medicine' (Maclean 1974, Boszormenyi 1983). Magical medicine is not a form of 'herbalism', using drugs obtained from plants in treatment of identified diseases. Most of the cases dealt with in magical medicines are not diseases, nor even symptoms, but 'conditions' such as bad luck in business, in love, in social interaction. There are magical medicines (a) to act with impurity, (b) to achieve good and fast sales in the market, (c) to take something by spiritual force, (d) to frighten people, (c) to cause people to love (appoint, promote) you, (f) to improve memory, e g in examinations, (g) to command acts to damage an enemy's house, (h) to improve the power of your own curses and repel those against you, and (i) to make your yams grow well and your trees bear plenty of fruits. These and other similar 'medicines' intermingle with others which can be taken for (or directed against) a group of symptoms of different diseases.

At least one third of the procedures are remedies connected with sexual life. There are medicines to win the love of a girl, or to compel a woman to run away, and have sexual dealings with you. For your success you can choose medicine to stiffen the penis, or to have more semen, or generally to help to 'devirgin' a girl. Against your competitors you can invoke 'magun' or you can buy medicines against it, if you believe that somebody tried to apply 'magun' against you. There are a few medicines against unfaithful women, but most of those applicable to women are to ensure fertility.

Professor Oso carefully collected the Yoruba mythology amd magical medicine of mushrooms (Oso 1975, 1977, 1981). I mention here only a few characteristic examples and refer readers to the original articles for details.

Termitomycetes microcarpus is a fungus with small fruiting bodies that grow in groups spreading over large areas. According to Yoruba myths a woman whose name was Oran went to god Oronmila and asked to have many children. She was requested to make a sacrifice and soon started to have issue, mushrooms of this species. Unfortunately Oran did not heed the further advice of Oranmila to make a second sacrifice to enable the mushrooms to change to real children, so the people soon discovered that these mushrooms are good to eat and started collecting them. The myth explains the Yoruba name of the mushroom: 'oluoran'.

Termitomycetes microcarpus is used in magical medicine as a charm against bad luck. To prepare this charm about 200 fruiting bodies are pulverised after being roasted in a clay pot together with ripe bananas, papaya, salt and some herbal ingredients. The preparation is collected on a piece of white cloth and magical verses are recited over it. It is then tied with a thread and hung above the door of the trader's shop. It is believed that this medicine will promote sales by drawing into the shop buyers as numerous as the mushroom caps used in the preparation.

Hunters prepare a magical preparation from *Termitomycetes globulus* caps by chewing them with seven seeds of meleguetta pepper (*Aframomum melegueta*) and a leaf of *Phyllanthus floribundus*. When this is spat on the palm and rubbed on the bow and arrows (or gun) with some incantations, the hunted game becomes drowsy and easy to kill. Different genera of 'stinkhorns' are also used by hunters to make a charm which allegedly makes them invisible in case of danger.

Some mushrooms (*Termitomycetes robustus* and the puffball *Calvatia cyanthiformis*) are roasted with other ingredients and mixed with a local black soap and then used as a rinse against discharges of women. An oral medicine is made from *Termitomycetes microcarpus* with squash, leaves of *Cassia alata* and other ingredients for treatment of gonorrhea.

Another example of oral medicine is made from *Termitomycetes robustus* against the most feared 'disease' of Yoruba men, the so-called 'magun' (or 'maagun') affecting unfaithful men. The symptoms, if the condition really exists, resemble a heart-attack or stroke (Elewude 1979) and are supposed to be deadly if no counter-magic is done in time.

There are numerous preventative, premonitory and curative medicines. According to Professor Oso, *Termitomycetes robustus* caps with *Loranthus* (a mistletoe) leaves, corns of Guinea pepper, pork meat, lime juice and Schweppes, when mixed in a proper way, give an effective curative medicine.

I selected my examples to show that, when magical medicine is taken orally, an effort is usually made to improve its palatability by the addition of spices and regular food ingredients. The preparation methods also include some techniques used in the kitchen. The effectiveness is not supposed to come from any chemical compound or from the common techniques but from certain magical actions. When the belief in magic falters, some of the 'medicines' become food and beverages. The very same process happened in Europe.

* * * *

Yoruba Mushroom and Meat Stew

6 cubes of meat
9 large mushrooms
1 large onion
2 large tomatoes
fresh or dried chilli peppers, to taste
salt to taste
oil for frying

Wash the meat and put it into a clay pot on an open fire. Add salt and cover the pot. Stir the meat until quite dry, then remove it and wash the pot.

Meanwhile chop and grind the chilli peppers, slice the tomatoes and the carefully washed mushrooms. Put back the meat into the pot and fry 5 minutes in oil. Add the rest of the ingredients and cover with water. When the mixture has become thick, serve it with plain boiled rice or pounded yam.

Hungarian Paprika-Stew of Mushrooms

500 g fresh mushrooms
2 onions, finely chopped
2–3 tsp ground paprika (medium hot)
2–3 tbsp sour cream
salt to taste
lard for frying

Wash the mushrooms, slice them, and braise them in a little lard with the onion. When all the juices have been absorbed, add the salt and paprika, stir in the sour cream and bring to a boil.

Note that if you are using *Termitomycetes* or *Pleurotus* mushrooms, then after dissolving the paprika you must add a little water and cook till the mushrooms are soft enough—the sour cream is added later, as the final step.

This dish is served with Hungarian or Italian forms of pasta or with plain rice.

Breaded Fried Mushrooms

choice large mushrooms
flour
1 beaten egg
bread crumbs
lard for frying

Clean the mushrooms very carefully and cut off the greater part of the stems (which can be used later in soups). Drain and dry thoroughly. Dip the caps first in flour, then in egg and finally in bread crumbs and fry in hot fat.

Serve immediately with mayonnaise, tartare sauce, lemon wedges and/or any green salad in season. If it is a main course, plain rice is also served.

References

Alasoadura S. O. (1967): 'Studies of higher fungi of Nigeria. I. The genus *Termitomycetes* Helm': *J. West Afr. Sci. Assoc.,* 12: 139–146.

Anthonio H. O. and M. Isoun (1982): *Nigerian Cookbook:* Macmillan, London.

Bascom W. F. (1951): 'Yoruba food' in *Africa,* 21: 125–131.

Boszormenyi Z. (1983): 'Witchcraft, pseudo-science and the progress of science', parts I–III: mimeographed paper of 166 pp, Inst. Of Ecology, Univ. of Ife, Ile-Ife.

Christensen C. M. (1972): *Common edible mushrooms:* Univ. of Minnesota Press, Minneapolis.

Elewude, J. A. (1979): 'Magun-a means of causing sudden death used in Nigeria', in *African medicinal plants,* Sofowora A. (ed): Univ. of Ife Press, Ile-Ife.

Grigson, J. (1982): *The Mushroom Feast:* Penguin, Harmondsworth.

Johnson R. A. et al (1980): 'A check list of Nigerian termites (Isoptera) with brief notes on their biology and distribution', in *Nigerian Field,* 45: 50–64.

Litten W. (1975): 'The most poisonous mushrooms', in *Sci. Amer.* 232 (3): 90–101.

Maclean U. (1974): *Magical medicine* (a Nigerian case-study): Penguin, Harmondsworth.

Margulis D. and K. V. Schwartz (1982): *Five Kingdoms:* Freeman, San Francisco.

Mars J. A. and E. M. Tooleyo (1979): *The Kudeti book of Yoruba cookery:* CSS Bookshop, Lagos.

Oso B. A. (1975): 'Mushrooms and the Yoruba people of Nigeria', in *Mycologia* 67: 311–319.

Oso B. A. (1977): 'Mushrooms in Yoruba mythology and medical practice', in *Economic Botany,* 31: 367–371.

Oso B. A. (1981): 'Fungi and mankind' (inaugural lecture): mimeographed paper of 40 pp, Univ. of Ibadan, Ibadan.

Phillips R. (1983): *Wild Food:* Pan Books, London.

Quimo T. H. (1980): 'Termite mushrooms, anyone?' in *Mushroom Newsletter for the Tropics,* 1: 14–16.

Schultes R. E. (1970): 'The botanical and chemical distribution of hallucinogens', in *Ann. Rev. Plant Physiol.,* 21: 571–598.

Smyth A. J. and R. R. Montgomery (1962): *Soils and land use in Central Western Nigeria:* Government Printer, Ibadan.

Straten van S. and H. Maarse (eds) (1983): *Volatile Compounds in Food:* TNO, Zeist.

Zoberi, M. H. (1973): 'Some edible mushrooms from Nigeria', in *Nigerian Field,* 38: 81–90.

Summer Pudding

This turned out to be one of those subjects which run and run, attracting comments from many contributors. So far as PPC *is concerned the subject began in* PPC 18 *when Lynda Brown posed the question: How old is summer pudding? Her enquiry is reprinted here and followed by five contributions from other readers. Most of these appeared in Notes and Queries, but the fourth of them is in effect a whole essay by Audrey Levy.*

How Old Is Summer Pudding? **from Lynda Brown**

This question occurred to me whilst I was writing a piece on desserts recently. I had assumed that something so quintessentially English must be very old indeed. But that doesn't seem to be the case. Indeed my initial enquiries seemed, much to my surprise, to be pointing towards an origin in the early 20th century.

A friend's mother-in-law, in her 80s, has a recipe in a gas cookery book dating from the late 1920s, and remembers it well from 'tennis parties in the thirties'. Recipes also exist, so I'm told, for Queen of Summer Pudding made with sponge cake instead of bread (note also 'Summer Pudding in the Florentine Style', *Jane Grigson's Fruit Book,* p 402). Mrs David hints at the problem in *Summer Cooking* when she notes that authentic recipes are rare. Neither Dorothy Hartley nor Florence White has it, Mrs Leyel, in *The Gentle Art of Cookery* (1925), does and says that it is 'probably known to everyone'.

On this basis, I had been thinking that it might have started in those early gas and electricity cookbooks (even though it needs no cooking), which would have accounted for its initial spread; and that it subsequently became one of those recipes which are handed down from mother to daughter.

However, a new light has been thrown on the question by Tom Jackson of Ilkley, who has kindly been helping me out on this one and sent me a recipe for 'Hydropathic Pudding' taken from *Cassell's Shilling Cookery* (1916), adding that the contents of that book come wholly or mainly from the earlier Cassell's *Dictionary of Cooking.* The 1916 recipe is plainly our Summer Pudding. But in an undated (? c 1895) edition of the *Dictionary of Cooking* there is no Hydropathic Pudding, and the recipe given for Summer Pudding, although related to the dish we know, is different.

Prompted by Tom Jackson, I saw that I should have paid more attention to two other references. Sheila Hutchins gives a recipe for Summer Pudding (or Sussex or Hydropathic Pudding) in *English Recipes* (1967), p 349. And

Lizzie Boyd (in *British Cookery,* 1976, p 401) says that 'Summer Pudding . . . Also known as Hydropathic Pudding' was a sweet 'designed in the 18th century for patients not allowed the then fashionable pastry desserts'.

The latter reference is particularly interesting, since it takes us back to the 18th century. No specific reference is given, unfortunately (and the item is not indexed under Pudding but only under Compotes and Other Fruit Desserts). Alan Davidson then stepped in and did a search for me. The recipe does not occur in *The Lady's Companion* (edition of 1753), which contains the largest compilation of pudding recipes of the century. Nor is it given by Mrs Mary Cole (edn of 1789), or Mrs MacIver (edn of 1789), or Richard Briggs (edn of 1794), or Mrs Mason (edn of 1801), or John Macdonald (edn of 1812), or Dr Kitchiner (edn of 1823), or Mrs Dalgairns (edn of 1829), or Mrs Rundell (edns of 1807, 1847, 1864), or Eliza Acton (edn of 1853), or . . . well, the list is a long one, stretching up to Theodore Garrett's monumental *Encyclopaedia of Practical Cookery* (c 1895) and leaves one wondering how the recipe could have been an 18th century one if all these authors had nothing to say about it! Incidentally, neither did Parson Woodforde. Am I presuming too much, but he would have, wouldn't he?

However, Alan Davidson turned up one 19th century recipe, in the 3rd edition of *A Year's Cookery* by Phillis Browne (undated, but the flyleaf of the copy consulted has an inscription for Christmas 1885). This is word for word the same as that later printed in *Cassell's Dictionary of Cooking,* and is reproduced on the next page, since it could, I suppose, turn out to be the earliest published recipe.

So, my one question has turned into several: when and how did Hydropathic Pudding originate; when and how did it turn into Summer Pudding; what was responsible for its spread (I cannot believe that it was only those taking the waters, or that they were in a fit state to spot a culinary winner when they saw one); and why is there still a scarcity of authentic recipes?

Looked at another way, maybe this is all nonsense, mere conjectural roly-poly. Maybe Summer Pudding never was *that* popular, and its reputation in the pages of the few cookbooks which give it based chiefly on a fleeting vogue among the surburbanite elite of the Home Counties and the fanciful and nostalgic culinary imagination of writers. Mind you, I still like it, and I have to say that it intrigues me as much now as when I first set out on this unfinished hike, asking myself the seemingly simple question: 'How old is Summer Pudding?' At least we now know that it will celebrate its hundredth birthday, if this has not already passed, in 1985.

Phillis Browne's Recipe

2. Make hydropathic red currant pudding for dinner to-morrow. *Hydropathic Pudding* may be made with fruit of all kinds, fresh or bottled. If fresh fruit is used, it must be stewed with water and sugar until it is about as much cooked as it would be in a fruit pie. If bottled fruit is used, the syrup only should be boiled with sugar, and the fruit simmered in it for a minute or two. Take some stale bread. Cut a round piece the size of half-a-crown and lay it at the bottom of a basin, and arrange around it strips or fingers of bread about half an inch wide, remembering to leave a space the width of the finger between the strips. When the fruit is ready, and while it is still hot, put it in a spoonful at a time, so as not to displace the bread, and, as a further means to this end, put the heavier part of the fruit—the pulp and skin and stones, if there are any—at the bottom of the mould, and the juice last of all. Cover the top entirely with stale bread cut into very small dice; lay a plate on the pudding, put a weight on the plate, preserving the juice that rises above the plate, and set the pudding in a cool place till wanted. If it is well pressed down it will turn out in a shape, and will be found an excellent pudding. This dish is thus named because it is served at the hydropathic establishments as a substitute for fruit pies and tarts, as pastry is not considered wholesome. In cold weather it will turn out if it is made three or four hours before it is wanted, but in warm weather it needs to be made overnight.

Summer Pudding — from Two Contributors in PPC 60

AUDREY LEVY wrote to us recently to say that she had identified an early reference in print to Summer Pudding. This took the form of a recipe for making it in an (undated) edition/impression of May Little's *A Year's Dinners*, evidently published early in the century. Audrey Levy asked whether we could furnish a date of publication, and wondered whether the same recipe occurred in the 1st edition of the book. We were able to tell her, after reference to Elizabeth Driver's *Bibliography of Cookery Books published in Britain 1874–1914* (Prospect Books, London, 1989), that several major libraries have dated the 1st edition at 1910; that several subsequent editions were published by Harrods (without a date until the 1930s); and that such evidence as there is suggests that a long time elapsed before the text of the 1st edition was revised. We have not yet been able to consult the 1st edition, but note that copies are held by the British Library, The National Library of Scotland and the Bodleian at Oxford (so the task is not of unsurmountable difficulty). We note also that George Newnes published another work by May Little, called *The Little Book of Puddings*, undated but estimated to have come out in 1912.

HELEN J SABERI has meanwhile had the good fortune to locate at a school jumble sale a rare volume which contains an even earlier reference by name to Summer Pudding. The book, remarkably, was published in Calcutta in 1904, and was the work of a British woman missionary, Miss E S Poynter.

The earliest reference in the *OED* is to a catering book of 1933. Helen Saberi therefore visited the OED in Oxford to tell them of this latest discovery and of some other pre-1933 references she had noted. She is not sure whether the rare volume published in Calcutta, given the fact that its recipe (see below) is rather different from what would now be called Summer Pudding, would be a suitable citation. However, the *OED* seemed very glad to have it and will also be taking into account the other early references noted by Helen Saberi—plus of course the one described by Audrey Levy. This would yield the following sequence:

1904	Miss E S Poynter, "What" and "How", Calcutta
c 1911	L. Sykes, *An Olio of Proved Recipes and Domestic Wrinkles* (7th edition), Manchester (see below for her recipe too).
c 1912	May Little, as described by Audrey Levy
1917	Florence Petty, *The "Pudding Lady's" Recipe Book*, London.

Two Very Early Recipes for 'Summer Pudding'

First comes the 1904 item:

No. 505. Summer Pudding.

Two oz. breadcrumbs, 2 oz. butter, 2 eggs, sugar and fruit. Stew any fruit with sugar, add 1/3 cupful water. Rub through a sieve, add 2 oz breadcrumbs, 2 oz. butter and 2 eggs. Bake 1/2 hour. Good hot or cold.

Next, the item of c. 1911:

263 Summer Pudding.

Stew any kind of fruit in season with sugar. Butter a basin, line it with bread and butter 1/4 inch thick without crusts; put in a layer of the stewed fruit and bread and butter alternately, pouring the juice in last of all, just sufficient to soak through the bread; press down tight with a plate. When cold turn out, and serve with custard round or whipped cream.

That there is some public interest in this question was demonstrated during a recent edition of Derek Cooper's famous *Food Programme*. The panel of experts correctly identified Summer Pudding as a new name for the 19th century Hydropathic Pudding, and correctly supposed that the use of the new name extended back at least into the 1920s, but did not have at their disposal the specific earlier references listed above. Another coup for *PPC*! Thank you, Audrey Levy and Helen Saberi.

Niggertoes, the Pope's Nose and Summer Pudding
from Elizabeth Driver in PPC 61

In *PPC 60* Karen Hess reported the common use of the term 'niggertoe' for brazil nuts in the southern United States in the 1920s. She will probably be surprised to learn that we used the same name for the nut in our family, in the 1950s, far north of her hometown of St. Louis, in Toronto, Canada, with no sense that it might cause offence— perhaps we can be excused as I am almost certain that as a child at that time I had never seen a real person with black skin.

I was, however, aware of the prejudice behind the name for the roast turkey's tail, the 'pope's nose', having asked probing questions of my parents at the dinner table about its meaning.

On a lighter note, I am submitting another reference for Summer Pudding from a well-known English author (as opposed to the more indirect Calcutta source, E S Poynter): S Beaty-Pownall's *Sweets (Part I)*. I own the third edition, London, 1904 (Driver 65.3). On page 106 she gives her recipe for Summer Pudding, the classic version, and also a variation of the recipe that she says is known as Dr Johnson's pudding. Readers will see from the reproduction of her recipe (following page) that she concludes with the comment: 'These puddings go by many names, such as Hydropathic, Rhode Island, Wakefield, &c.'

The first edition of *Sweets (Part I)* was published in 1901 and copies are held at the National Library of Scotland, Edinburgh, the Bodleian Library, Oxford, and the Cookery and Food Association, London. Perhaps someone living closer to these libraries than I do now could confirm the inclusion of the recipe in the 1901 edition and report his or her findings to the *OED*. Mrs Beaty-Pownall was Departmental Editor of 'Housewife and Cuisine' in the *Queen* newspaper, which leads me to suggest that scanning that newspaper and other women's journals might well reveal references to Summer Pudding earlier than the one in *Sweets (Part I)*.

Summer Pudding

Line a well-buttered plain china mould, or basin, with bread as for Apple Charlotte, pressing it well into the mould, then pour in sufficient hot stewed fruit of any kind to fill the basin, fit a round of bread on top, turn a plate over it, and let it stand till next day, when it can be turned out and served with cream, or a thin custard. Any rich-coloured fruit does for this, whether of one or many kinds. A variation of this, known as "Dr. Johnson's pudding," may be recommended: Slice thinly about 10 oz. of bread, and have about a pound of hot stewed rhubarb, then put these in alternate layers into a rather deep dish, finishing with the fruit (mind the dish is only three-quarters full), and put it aside till cold. When served pour on to it from half to three-quarters of a pint of more or less rich custard. These puddings go by many names, such as Hydropathic, Rhode Island, Wakefield, &c.

Het of Atworth's Purple Mountain

AUDREY LEVY

This essay took the subject about as far as the combined resources of our readers could take it but does seem to leave scope for further research, eg into the processes by which summer pudding mutated from Hydropathic, Rhode Island and Wakefield pudding. However, although it is here followed by a short note from Professor Jack Lang, it has not attracted further information which would change its conclusions. Here is another instance of PPC *providing what has become the Locus Classicus on a culinary question to which there had previously been no clear answer.*

Het of Atworth's Purple Mountain is, so to speak, the pinnacle of English Summer Puddings. Its glorious purple emanates entirely from black currants. Neither raspberries nor redcurrants may intrude. Moreover, instead of the customary bread, stale spongecakes line the pudding bowl. Yes, the spongecakes must be stale, otherwise they vie with seaweed for sliminess. (Spongecakes can be artificially dried in a cool oven or microwave.)

Here is the recipe. You will see that I give ingredients for a proper egg custard (optional). Het used this egg custard, but I cannot deduce from her recipe how she administered it. I therefore suggest that the custard could be handed round in a jug.

HET'S PURPLE MOUNTAIN

Ingredients

2 lb (1 kg) blackcurrants
1 tablespoon water
9 oz (250 g) caster sugar or to taste
8–10 stale spongecakes
½ pint (300 ml) double cream

Equipment

fork
colander
large thick-based saucepan, with lid (I use a Le Creuset 24 cm pan)
long wooden spoon
tablespoon
large pastry board
serrated breadknife
2 pint pudding basin (1200 ml)
ladle
large soup-plate
small plate to fit top of pudding basin
weights—4 lb or 2 kilos
flexible metal spatula
large circular serving dish, with slightly upcurving edges, to catch juice (my dish is about 12" (300 cm) in diameter)

For optional egg custard
1/2 pint (300 ml) milk
2 oz (60 g) white loaf sugar
1/2 teaspoon proper vanilla essence
2 egg yolks

Method

Remove stalks from blackcurrants. I use a fork. Check that no small stalks remain. Wash currants, if necessary, in a colander. Put currants in a large heavy saucepan. Add a tablespoon of water. Bring gently to the boil. Lower heat to very low, put on lid and simmer. After about two minutes check to see fruit is not sticking. Then in about three minutes more lift the lid and stir carefully with a wooden spoon. The currants should be cooked: they glisten magically and the aroma is quite rapturous. There should be plenty of juice. Add the sugar whilst the fruit is hot and stir in tenderly.

Now take a large pastry board, and, with a serrated breadknife, cut the spongecakes in half horizontally. Then cut each half into two triangles. Rinse the pudding-basin and leave damp. Fit the triangles into the bowl, with the crusts outside. Arrange about three triangles at the base, adding small bits of sponge so there are no gaps. Fit more triangles around the side of the basin, the apex of each triangle pointing downwards. This may be a little fiddly. Again use odd bits of sponge so that there are no gaps. Slowly and carefully ladle the blackcurrants and juice into the lined pudding bowl. Cover the assembly with more triangles of spongecake; again the apexes should face inward. Fill any gaps. Put the pudding bowl in a large soup-plate. Pour a little more black-currant juice over the top of the pudding and reserve the unused sugared juice and currants. Place a plate on the surface of the mixture. On top of the plate, place heavy weights of about four pounds or two kilos. Put the basin and soup-plate in a cool place (the refrigerator if possible). Leave several hours, preferably overnight. Two to three days is an improvement.

When ready to serve, lift off weights and small plate. The top will be flat now. Remove bowl from soup-plate wiping the bottom of the bowl. Ease the pudding by putting a metal spatula between the pudding and the sides of the bowl. (Het used a round-ended flexible knife.) Centre the serving-plate over the pudding-bowl. Holding the plate and bowl firmly, invert the basin and put the plate on a table. Tap the bowl and carefully lift up. The Purple Mountain should be revealed. If any white sponge should be visible pour over some reserved juice. The mountain is now ready to be capped with lightly whipped double cream. The cream should be whisked until it just stands up. Then it is spooned gently over the top of the mountain, but not smoothed out, so that it falls like snow on a mountain peak. The remaining reserved juice, unwhipped cream and the custard can be put into jugs and handed round as desired.

Three Criteria for Today's Summer Pudding

Het's Purple Mountain conforms to the three criteria essential for today's Summer Pudding:

(1) the summer fruit;

(2) the farinaceous support—in Het's case spongecake;

(3) the shape derived from making in a traditional pudding-basin.

(1) THE SUMMER FRUIT. Het used only one summer fruit, the blackcurrant. Margaret Costa tells of a Summer Pudding made exclusively with blackcurrants: it is called a 'Top Hat'. For me the name conjures up shades of Fred Astaire. However, the fashion today is for a medley of fruits, especially all colours of currants and raspberries. Yet Ruth Lowinski warns: 'Don't spoil the flavour of the raspberries by adding redcurrants to them.'

(2) FARINACEOUS SUPPORT. Het used stale spongecakes, though in today's recipe slices of bread are advocated. Yet the efficacy of bread which has undergone the Chorley Wood Process is dubious. Jane Grigson wisely suggests 'good bread'. A 1912 edition of Mrs Beeton describes an embryonic Summer Pudding called Fruit Pudding. Rather snootily, the recipe states: 'For a plain pudding, stale bread may be used instead of the cake.' The 1960 edition uses: '12 individual spongecakes (approx.).' Bee Nilson suggests bread or spongecakes. Interestingly, some recipes, like Het's, pour the fruit and juice into the lined bowl. But several recipes layer the fruit and sponge or bread.

(3) THE PUDDING-BASIN SHAPE. The pudding-basin shape is delightful, derived as it is from the basin developed to steam winter puddings. Not all named Summer Puddings conform to the pudding-basin shape. Mrs Martineau (1927) employs 'a deep dish or better still a silver souffle dish'. I think the turned-out pudding sitting vertically on a plate can be more spectacular.

Some Thoughts on the Use of the Word 'Summer'

I cannot discover the original date of Het's Purple Mountain, but unlike mince pies, which have a long lineage, that of named Summer Puddings is relatively short. In fact as recently as 1993, John Ayto, in his *Diner's Dictionary,* declares that 'it was not actually recorded by name until the 1930s'. However, more up-to-date research, especially by Helen Saberi, discovered a named Summer Pudding as early as 1904; see *PPC 60.* She also notes Florence Petty in 1917. Now, due to the indications of Liz Driver in Canada (see *PPC 61*), a named Summer Pudding has been discovered in the 1901 first edition of the delightful little 'Queen' Cookery books. Actually, it is in their Series VI, Sweets Part 1. The editor, Mrs S. Beaty-Pownall, uses bread and hot stewed fruit. She also alludes to a 'Dr. Johnson's Pudding' with stewed rhubarb. She says further that 'these puddings go by many names such as Hydropathic, Rhode Island, Wakefield &c.'

Nevertheless, the flurry of interest in Summer Puddings appears to belong to the 1930s. By the end of that decade, the dish was so well established that Marguerite Patten was able to include a Wartime recipe in her *We'll Eat Again.* The ingredients used were (extraordinarily) rhubarb and prunes (soaked overnight). More temperately, in a 1942 collection of 122 recipes, called 'The Kitchen Front', selected by the Ministry of Food, the named Summer Pudding recipe simply tells one to 'stew enough fruit'. Today, the Summer Pudding appears to be 'de rigueur' in most popular compendia of British cooking, and it even appears on the shelves of supermarkets.

Prototypes of the Summer Pudding

Although the appearance of the Summer Pudding on the culinary firmament is relatively recent, there are prototypes. In a really charming little book on Old Sussex Recipes, well researched by its compiler, Jan Kendall, a date of 1891 or earlier may be given to *Mrs. Maple's Pudding:*

> Line a pudding basin tightly with stale bread, putting a piece at the bottom. Have ready any kind of fruit, stewed and sweetened, and pour into the basin. Cut a piece of bread to fit the top and press down with a saucer.

It is interesting to note that Jan Kendall's grandmother was a cook at Hatfield House.

In Lady Clark of Tillypronie's wonderful cookery book, there is a *Malvern Pudding.* This has the same format of today's Summer Puddings, but uses a pie dish. Apricots, apples or raspberries and currants are the suggested fruit. Lady Clark's book was published in 1909; however, the recipes appear to have been collected in Victorian times. It is noteworthy that Dorothy Hartley also writes about a Malvern Pudding, but this is 'a fruit and hasty pudding mixture' and is baked for 20 minutes.

However, Dorothy Hartley does describe a Summer Pudding, though she states that it was called Hydropathic Pudding, 'because it was served in nursing-homes, where pastry was not permitted'. Actually, according to the *OED,* the word hydropathic appears first in 1843 and refers to a 'water cure'. The name Hydropathic Pudding was still used in the first half of the reign of George V. Florence Jack has an excellent recipe, which could be a carbon copy of today's Summer Pudding recipes. She uses bread, a basin and one summer fruit, namely redcurrants, but she writes that raspberries and black-currants can be used in the same way.

Nevertheless, neither the Hydropathic nor the Summer Puddings could be concocted without the pudding basin. For boiling a pudding, the precursor of the basin was the pudding-cloth, dated by C. Anne Wilson as early 17th century. But it would be palpably useless for Summer Pudding shaping; as would the intricate moulds that abound in, say, Mrs A. B. Marshall's cookery book. Furthermore, as a name, hydropathic is severely clinical. How much more charming and evocative is the English word summer, so favoured in both prose and poetry! In Jane Austen's *Emma,* an English summer view is described: 'It was a sweet view—sweet to the eye and the mind, English verdure, English culture, English comfort, seen under sun bright, without being oppressive.'

Indeed, there is something peculiarly British about the Summer Pudding and especially something particularly English. Alice Wooledge Salmon asks: 'Why should the British, blessed with black, red or white currants that coincide with raspberries, be the only nation to enjoy one of the world's best desserts?' And John Ayto affirms that the Summer Pudding is 'now regarded as a traditional, almost quintessential, English midsummer dessert'.

Conclusion

It is doubtful whether the name hydropathic could afford much inspiration, but that the Summer Pudding could capture such eulogies is startling. 'This wonderful pudding', declares Elizabeth David. Mrs Leyel extols: 'Though simple and inexpensive, this is one of the most delicious puddings for a hot day.' And Jeremy Round alerts us to the fact that: 'Summer Pudding is this month's [July's] biggest treat.'

Shakespeare bemoans that 'Summer's lease hath all too short a date'. For summer berries and currants the season is also very short, often marred by rain. I think it is the fleeting moments that these fruit appear which add to the magic and excitement of Summer puddings. As soon as there are sufficient blackcurrants we, as if going to 'catch a falling star', rush out to pick or buy them for Het's lovely pudding. For with its glorious purple capped by the snowy cream, Het's Purple Mountain is surely one of the most beguiling of Summer Puddings.

Bibliography

Austen, Jane: *Emma* (ed. R. W. Chapman). OUP, 3rd edn, 1934. (The novel was first published in 1816.)

Ayto, John: *The Diner's Dictionary:* OUP, 1993.

Beaty-Pownall, Mrs S.: The 'Queen' Cookery Books, No. 6, Sweets, Part 1, London, Horace Cox, 1901.

Beeton, Mrs: *Mrs. Beeton's Book of Household Management:* Ward, Lock, edn of 1912.

Beeton, Mrs: *Mrs. Beeton's Book of Cookery & Household Management:* Ward, Lock, 1960.

Clark, Lady: *The Cookery Book of Lady Clark of Tillypronie:* Southover Press, 1944 (1st edn was published in 1909).

Costa, Margaret: *The Four Seasons Cookbook:* Cookery Book Club, 1st edn, 1970.

David, Elizabeth: *Summer Cooking:* Penguin Books 1965. (The 1st edn was in 1955.)

Grigson, Jane: *English Food:* Macmillan London, 1979. (The 1st edn was published in 1974.)

Hartley, Dorothy: *Food in England:* Macdonald & Jane's, 1975. This book was first published in 1954.

Jack, Florence B.: *Cookery for Every Household:* T.C. E.C. Jack, 1924 edn. Had first been published in 1914.

Kendell, Jan (ed.): *Old Sussex Recipes:* 1982.

Leyel, Mrs C. F.: *Puddings:* George Routledge & sons, undated.

Lowinski, Ruth: *Food for Pleasure:* Rupert Hart-Davis, 1950.

Martineau, Mrs Philip: *Caviare to Candy:* Richard Cobden-Sanderson, 1st edn, 1927.

Ministry of Food: *The Kitchen Front:* 1942.

Oxford Book of English Verse: OUP, 1939 (for quotations from Shakespeare & John Donne).

Shorter Oxford English Dictionary: 2nd edn, 1936.

Round, Jeremy: *The Independent Cook:* Barrie & Jenkins, 1988.

Saberi, Helen: in 'Notes and Queries' in *PPC 60.*

Salmon, Alice Wooledge & Hugo Dunn Meynell: *The Wine & Food Society Menu Book:* Heinemann, 1983.

Wilson, C. Anne: *Food & Drink in Britain,* Cookery Book Club, 1973.

Summer Pudding **from Jack Lang in PPC 63**

In response to the article on Summer Pudding in *PPC 62,* similar early recipes are:

- *Warne's Model Cookery* by Mary Jewry, about 1880 (my edition is the New Edition of 1887): called Malvern Pudding. See below.
- *Sweet Dishes* by Wyvern, author of *Culinary Jottings from Madras* (1881), recommends plantains and raspberries, or mangoes and pineapple.

I suspect, however, the derivation is different from that given in your article and it is derived from the old style of Charlotte, a bread case filled with fruit compote, traditionally apples, then baked, and dating from the late 18th century. I have not been able to find any exact references, but *Cook and Housewife's Manual,* Meg Dods, (4th Edition 1829), under 'A French Fruit Pudding' says that 'any kind of ripe fruit may be used instead of apples', and elsewhere suggests a compote of raspberries and redcurrants.

Rowley Leigh published an article on the history of Summer Pudding in the Sunday Times in July 1998.

Cherries give a particular stickiness to the juice; those who add blackcurrants to raspberries and redcurrants, are of course, heathens.

MALVERN PUDDING.

TIME, TEN OR TWELVE MINUTES.

2015. Some slices of stale bread; one pint and a half of currants; half a pint of raspberries; four ounces of sugar; some whipped cream.

Dip a pudding-basin into cold water, and line it with rounds of rather stale bread; stew the currants and raspberries with the sugar for ten or twelve minutes after they are hot, fill the basin with the fruit, and cover it over with rounds of bread, put a plate on it with a weight, and set it in a cold place until the next day. Then turn it very carefully out, cover it with whipped cream, and pour round it a little of the currant and raspberry juice.

Chicken Yassa

Eva Gillies

'First catch your chickens' I reminded myself; and indeed it seemed we would have to before matters could proceed further. Not that anyone seemed very worried: Ramu, our hostess, was still placidly dispensing tea and fruit juices; Ndey and Jabo sprawled in easy-chairs, gossiping; the normally remote and elegant Mariama lay on her back on the cool tiled floor, playing delightedly with a new baby. 'My daughters will catch the chickens for us when they get back from school' said Ramu comfortably.

No West African housewife would dream of cooking for guests single-handed. What are relatives, friends and neighbours for? The excuse for tonight's party was, in any case, to teach me how to make Chicken Yassa; but Ndey and Jabo and Mariama had been drawn in too by the prospect of a long sociable afternoon in which gossip and cool drinks and the leisurely preparation of food would merge insensibly into the party itself. Meanwhile, the chickens still squawked and scrabbled in the yard outside. There was no hurry; our menfolk were not expected until much later.

The fowls were duly caught in the end, killed and plucked and jointed before being left to macerate for an hour or so in a marinade of lime-juice, chopped onions and hot red chilli peppers fresh from Ramu's garden. By the time the men arrived, the stew was bubbling gently in the big iron *kalero*—the all-purpose cooking-pot of Senegambia whose name (derived from *caldeiro*) shows its Portuguese origin. The kitchen and verandah had been washed down, the whole house sweetened with incense in little clay fire-pots, and we ourselves were decked out in our best *grands boubous,* the long wide-sleeved gowns that have, over the last few years, spread from Senegal to the whole of the West African coast.

Mariama, her baby safely asleep on a young sister's back, was vigorously whisking egg-yolks. 'You know this sauce? I learnt it in Dakar when I was there. You make it with eggs and oil, they call it mayonnaise. Oh, you know it? Well, it's very good with Chicken Yassa, you'll see.'

I had previously eaten Chicken Yassa in London (they have a Senegalese chef at the Africa Centre in Covent Garden); *Yassa de poisson* I had met at the seaside restaurant of the Hotel Diarama in Dakar. Both establishments served the dish with rice, and nowadays I usually do so myself; all the same, Mariama's idea of mayonnaise (mopped up with crusty white bread, Ndey's contribution to the feast) turned out to be surprisingly good. West African cooks are fond of innovating in this way, of adopting exotic ingredients and preparations and combining them with an established classic dish; and Dakar, to which the French brought not merely their own cooking but also an avidly intelligent interest in local gastronomic possibilities, has always been a centre for culinary experiment.

Ramu's cook-in and the ensuing dinner-party were in fact taking place some two hundred miles from Dakar as the crow flies, at the experimental rice-growing station of Sapu on the south bank of the river Gambia. The river gives its name to a narrow slice of English-speaking independent republic, unaccountably wedged into the middle of Senegal—a country three hundred miles long and nowhere more than thirty miles wide, an economically absurd and humanly charming piece of national flotsam, left behind on the West African coast by the receding tide of colonialism. The Gambia is a proud member of the Commonwealth as well as of the United Nations; for the rest, it quietly gets on with its day-to-day business of growing groundnuts, rice and millet and (on the coast) a few tropical fruits and vegetables. During the cooler part of the dry season (November to March) it also extends a mildly profitable hospitality to German and Scandinavian tourists.

During the rains, the local mosquitoes flourish, and so does malaria. My husband, a medical entomologist, finds it essential to spend four months there every year, observing and recording his quarry's behaviour in their natural habitat. We spend our summers, therefore, in a camp of thatched mud huts on the river bank, some three miles downstream from Sapu, where Ramu's and Ndey's and Mariama's husbands work. Shopping trips to the capital are few and far between; the supply of imported goods is in any case largely a matter of luck. All of which provides an extra incentive—if one were needed—for exploring a native cuisine which relies largely on more or less local ingredients.

Such exploration seems, in colonial days, to have been less usual in British than in French West Africa. In The Gambia and the Gold Coast, Nigeria and Sierra Leone and British Cameroons alike, bachelor District Officers, themselves fresh from the rigours of public-school refectory and College hall, hired male cook-stewards-men who came to pride themselves on the esoteric skills their craft demanded, but who regarded the preparation of African foods as 'women's work' and therefore beneath them. A huge Saturday luncheon curry with its complement of 'small small tings'—some two dozen side-dishes of sliced banana, onion, tomato, sweet pepper, coconut and other relishes, both fresh and fried, plus several sorts of bottled chutney—the whole washed down with copious cold beer: such was, until quite recently, the zenith of expatriate gastronomy in English-speaking West Africa. Later, wives began to come out, and with them such delights as English biscuits and tinned Brussels sprouts: there are still a few white housewives in the big cities who hardly know what an African market looks like.

Meanwhile, however, a more robust tradition of good food was growing up among the Creole and Aku communities—that extraordinary network of prosperous, largely Christian 'old West Coast families' that have, over the last century or so, provided half a dozen countries with a lively and progressive professional class. Many of the Akus came originally from Nigeria; the Creole heartland was always Sierra Leone. But members of these communities travelled extensively, intermarried, settled in new places; their women, wealthier and more leisured than their tribal sisters and always eager to learn, must have swapped recipes and ingredients with enthusiasm. It was they who combined Bennechin Rice and Groundnut Chop from the north, Akara and Palaver Sauce from the south, into one recognizable regional cuisine. They took readily to certain imported ingredients, and to new skills such as baking; unlike the white expatriate housewives, they positively *enjoyed* haggling in local markets. And if, by bad luck, they really could not lay their hands on some such essential ingredient as palm oil, they grumbled volubly—and made their Palaver Sauce with groundnut oil and tinned tomato purée instead! Between them, these women created a varied and characteristic culinary tradition, heartier and less subtle perhaps than the Senegalese, but rich and satisfying and infinitely adaptable.

The third great influence upon West African food has been that of the Lebanese. Most major cities have a flourishing Lebanese business community, living and eating in comfortably traditional style, growing herbs and salad greens in sheltered minuscule gardens, lovingly making the daily yoghurt from powdered milk. It is often a Lebanese who starts the first restaurant in town, closely followed by a French-trained Senegalese chef.

And what, meanwhile, of the bachelor District Officer and his steward? The D.O. has, naturally, long since gone home to England; the steward, if he has not retired or gone into business, is working for a diplomat, or perhaps for the representative of some UN aid agency, and has probably had to adapt to the rule of an exigent and gastronomically ambitious mistress. For the traditional expatriate housewife with her array of tinned vegetables is also rapidly becoming a period figure. Outside diplomatic circles, few of the new young wives employ a steward. You are likelier to find them (clad in some modish version of local dress) jostling and bargaining among the other women in the markets; inquiring diligently after ethnic foods; deploring the rarity of cookery-books in a region where cooking has never been the kind of thing anybody expected to learn from books . . . And, if they are lucky, they end up, as I did in Ramu's kitchen, learning to make Chicken Yassa from a party of West African cooks.

Chicken Yassa

(4 to 6 portions)

1 chicken, cut up into serving portions
1 cup wine vinegar
1/2 cup lime juice (lemon juice may be substituted)
salt and freshly-ground black pepper
2 fresh chillies, de-seeded and ground in a mortar
2 cloves garlic, crushed in a mortar with the chillies
4 medium onions, sliced thin
1/2 cup groundnut oil (any other tasteless oil may be substituted)

Combine the vinegar, lime-juice, salt, pepper, chillies and garlic into a marinade, and leave the chicken pieces in it for one hour at least. Then take them out and wipe them with oil. Grill them for a few minutes until they are brown on all sides; then place them in a large saucepan with a little more oil and about half the marinade. Stew gently until the liquid is almost consumed; then add the onions, and continue cooking for another half hour or so. Serve with rice.

The same process can also be very successfully used with any firm-fleshed white fish, cut into thick steaks; though in this case three quarters of an hour's marinading will be enough.

'The Ultimate Anchovy' and Tea Soup:

Brief Notes on the Foods of the Dong People of Guangxi Province, South China

CHRIS HILTON

Guangxi is one of China's poorer provinces, although that is all changing nowadays, with new-found prosperity from the burgeoning Pearl River Delta finding its way steadily upstream into the drainage basin of the West River, which is the local name for the Pearl, and which takes in most of Guangxi.

Guangxi is also home to several non-Chinese National Minorities, many of whom migrated southwards as much as a thousand years ago to escape increasingly bitter conflicts with land-hungry Han Chinese invaders from the north.

The major Nationality in Guangxi are the Chuang, related, linguistically at least, to the Thais; and in fact Guangxi's full title is 'The Guangxi Chuang Autonomous Region', with the Chuang people having, on paper anyway, a substantial say in their own internal affairs.

As well as the Chuang there are a million or more representatives of other National Minorities scattered throughout Guangxi and its neighbouring provinces: Guizhou, Yunnan, and, to a lesser extent, Guangdong and Hunan. Perhaps the most colourful of these hilltribes, as they are sometimes called, are the Yao, whose women wear astonishingly intricately embroidered clothes which an expert can 'read' for the wearer's family tree and history. The Miao also go in for elaborate textiles, although in their case starch-resist indigo-dyed batik is the decoration of tradition.

The Dong number around 170,000, most of whom live in San Jiang County in the North of Guangxi, near the border with Guizhou, and, while textiles are important to them as well, it is their architecture which has made them famous: their amazing 'wind and rain' bridges, their drum-towers, and their houses—all of them massive free-standing timber structures built without nails and measured up by line of sight.

Like most of the other Nationalities of Southern China, and Thailand, Burma and Laos, come to that, the Dong for preference eat glutinous or sticky rice, which comes in several forms. The everyday staple is white, but there are brown, red, black and even purple varieties. Glutinous rice is becoming easier to find outside South East Asia, especially the white version, and as well as being delicious, with a delightful nutty flavour and a unique *al dente* texture, it is simplicity itself to cook and eat; more about that later.

According to legend, during their journeyings south the Dong were often forced up into the mountains for long periods; so long that the foodstuffs which they had brought with them often underwent a lactic acid fermentation and went sour. There was nothing else to eat, so necessity became a virtue, and nowadays, with fresh food in relatively plentiful supply, the Dong still pride themselves on their 'sour things', not just because they taste good, but because they say they are unique to their cultural heritage.

Fermentations of various kinds play an enormously important role in the production and preservation of foodstuffs in Asia and, generally speaking, one of two things happen as a result: perishable foods are preserved; and indigestible, sometimes even potentially toxic foods are rendered more wholesome and palatable. The first of these is probably the more important to the Dong.

Life in the hills of Guangxi is hard, as it is for the vast majority of China's teeming, and growing, population, but in most years the Dong are able to produce enough to feed themselves without recourse to famine foods. The only real problem is that it all gets produced in a rush, so to speak. As in olden-day Europe, or anywhere else before the advent of refrigeration, summer, the rainy season, usually means plenty of everything, while winter, the dry, means shortage: but in their flight into the mountains the Dong learned how to control the organisms of decay and today apply that knowledge so that summer's plenty lasts through the average winter too. There are still very few deep-freezers in San Jiang county.

One of the great bounties of the rainy season in Guangxi is fish, not just from the almost innumerable streams and rivers, but from the paddy fields as well, and this fish is laid down as *Ba Som,* literally 'sour fish'. Every family will have at least one tub of this working at any time, and most make it like this:

Ba Som

Take a wooden tub, approximately 1 metre deep, by 1 metre long, by 1/2 metre wide. Line it with large bamboo leaves, fresh or dried (the species was said not to be important). Take plenty of fish (any kind will do), gut them, but otherwise leave them whole. Spread a generous layer of rock salt in the bottom of the tub, cover this with a 2 cm layer of cooked glutinous rice and a layer of fish. Salt this, then repeat, alternating rice, fish and salt until the tub is full or the fish used up. Seal over with more bamboo leaves, then weight everything down with a stone from the river-bed small enough to fit the opening of the tub, but as heavy as possible. Leave for at least *six* months!

Obviously there is great skill and judgment at work here: too much salt and no fermentation will take place; too little and fermentation will rapidly become putrefaction.

When it has been made properly though, a 30 year old *Ba Som* is what a publicist, using a turn of phrase which has become almost omnipresent in the world of publicity blurbs, would describe as 'possibly the ultimate anchovy'. It is quite salty, but with the mellowness of a well-cured Parma ham for instance. It is undeniably fishy, but its freshwater origins mean that it does not have the rankness of so many commercial anchovies. What it does have though is a distinct sourness.

It is not very attractive to look at, being a sort of sullen purplish grey, but a sample of vintage 1980 literally melted in the mouth, with all the bones, scales and other hard parts collapsing as though they had been pressure-cooked; perhaps a fair description of 13 years under that stone.

Exactly the same method is applied to any type of surplus meat: pork, duck, goose, 'beef' (which of course means water-buffalo) and any kind of game.

Ba Som is an obligatory component of the great Dong traditional meal, *Yau Cha,* literally 'oil tea'.

Tea grows wild all over the mountains of South China, and a century or so ago, tea seed oil was a major export of Guangxi, being sent as far away as the USA. Today the trade is showing signs of revival, with tea oil being touted as a possibly less harmful cooking medium than some other oils. Certainly many of the hilltribes have used little else for generations, and the Dong have turned its use into a ritual; not as refined as the Japanese tea ceremony perhaps, but a ritual nonetheless. It's one which goes like this.

Yau Cha

Gather a group of family and friends together. Set up a large wok on a trivet over a wood fire. When the wok is hot, ladle in 2 cups of tea oil. When the oil is hot, but not smoking, fry a bowl or two of peanuts in it until they are well browned (small nuts seem to be preferred). Drain and set aside the nuts and then fry, very quickly, glutinous rice which has been prepared 24 hours in advance by being boiled and spread out to dry. Fry until it puffs, but do *not* brown it. Set the rice aside and remove all but a very small amount of oil from the wok.

In this, fry one handful of large-leaf black tea for a few seconds. (The Dong use wild tea, but a reasonable substitute can be had be mixing equal quantities of a green tea like *Shui Sin* with a black tea like *Pu Erh,* plus a spoonful or so of *Lapsang Souchong.* The important thing is that the tea should have large leaves.) After a few seconds, certainly never more than a minute, ladle in boiling water and simmer for a few minutes. Add a generous amount of salt, strain out the tea leaves. Save them for re-use later.

The serving ritual is in 5 parts: for each person, put into a small rice-bowl a spoonful of nuts, some of the puffed rice and some chopped chives. Fill up with the tea soup. When that bowl has been consumed, refill it with the same mixture, plus slices of steamed glutinous rice-flour cake. Refill a third time with the original mixture, plus cooked greens. The fourth filling is the same as the third, but includes plain, non-glutinous rice; while the fifth and final bowl is also the same as the first but with slices of steamed sweet glutinous cake instead of the chopped chives.

Everyone *must* have at least one bowl of each of the five courses, but having had the one, may wait out that course by putting a chopstick on the bowl. Any bowl not bearing a chopstick will automatically be refilled.

It is permitted to use two chopsticks when eating *Yau Cha,* but the Dong prefer to demonstrate their dexterity by using just one. This is not an easy skill to acquire.

While all this is being consumed, the cook is brewing up more tea, using the original leaves, which often, once they have been well-stewed, find their way into the soup with the vegetables in bowls 3 or 4.

The meal is served either sitting round the open fireplace or hearthstone in the centre of the main room of the house, or at a low table nearby, and it is always accompanied by as many other dishes as are available. *Ba Som* is a must, as is stir-fried pork, often with chillies and garlic. Stir-fried vegetables are always served, and so are a wide selection of 'sour things'; pickled vegetables like bamboo shots, shallots, garlic cloves, cucumbers, radishes, green papaya, peppers, ginger root and so on. Often there are preserved eggs, spiced offal, stewed chicken's feet and plenty more glutinous rice to ensure that no-one goes home hungry.

The beverage of choice is a home-distilled glutinous rice wine with a robust Saké-like flavour and a sherry-weight punch of about 20% alcohol. The Dong tend to drink this out of their bowls, between courses, in single draughts.

While perhaps a Dong meal is not that easily reproduced in a Western kitchen, there are a few dishes that can be made anywhere, starting with glutinous rice, if you can find it.

Glutinous (Sticky) Rice

Measure out the same sort of quantities as you would for ordinary rice, but start 24 hours ahead. Wash the rice and leave to soak at least overnight in plenty of clean water. When you are ready, line a colander with a double layer of cheesecloth, pour in the rice, fold the cloth over it and steam, covered, for about 30 minutes. Tip it out into a warmed serving dish and it's ready to eat. The great thing is that cooking times are virtually irrelevant, the only rule of thumb being that the longer the soaking, the shorter the steaming needs to be. To eat, gather up a golf-ball sized lump, roll it into a convenient shape and use it for dipping-up gravy, sauce etc.

A Dong dish with which to try the above is:

Yue Sheng (Chinese) or Ba Saag (Dong)

Take any fleshy freshwater fish, preferably Grass Carp, fillet it and slice the fillets into mouth-sized pieces. Lay these on paper for a while to absorb moisture, rub them with tea oil (or a good, delicate olive oil), place in a bowl, salt them and pour on half a cup of mild white vinegar (Chinese white rice vinegar, if available). After a while the vinegar will have 'cooked' the fish, which should then be served up on a bed of rice vermicelli, garnished with crushed deep-fried Chinese yellow beans (garbanzos will do), deep fried peanuts, chillies, chives and a good drizzle of sesame oil. This is delicious, especially if well-chilled, and even better if made with fresh lime juice rather than the vinegar, although this is *not* authentic as the Dong do not use limes.

Finally, I give a recipe for a 'sour thing':

Sour Ginger

Combine together, to taste, sliced, scraped fresh young ginger-root, crushed chillies, and salt. Pack into a jar, seal tightly, and store for at least one month. Before using, add just a little sweet rice wine.

What Was the Old Woman Doing?

OR *What Velasquez Was Really Showing Us*

GILLIAN RILEY

The author is a designer, with a special interest in food and art. Her books in this field include The Dutch Table *and* Impressionist Picnics. *The essay reproduced below was published in the summer of 1995.*

Many readers of *PPC* must have enjoyed the recent exhibition at the National Gallery in London, 'Spanish still life from Velasquez to Goya', both for its visual pleasures and for all the detailed information about food and drink of the period. A recent correspondence in the *Times Literary Supplement* raised the subject of the old woman cooking eggs in the painting by Velasquez in the National Gallery of Scotland in Edinburgh.

Perplexed and distressed at the suggestion by Alejandro Oliveros that the old woman in the Velasquez painting might be attempting to poach her eggs in acidulated water, I turned to Spain's leading food historians, Alicia Rios and Manuel Martinez Llopis, for comfort and enlightenment. They expounded to me the honourable role of the fried egg in the gastronomy of Spain. The old woman is instructing the boy in the art of frying eggs, one of the basic skills of olive oil cookery. They can be prepared *'sin puntilla, con puntilla, y abuñuelados'*, with or without a crisp, golden, lacey edging to the white, or deep fried at a very high heat. This last is a high-risk procedure which would indeed produce a shower of 'sputtering sparks', and has been known to destroy many a kitchen. The non-lace treatment, however, uses oil at a low temperature, where careful basting would give a gently rounded, opaque egg, without splashes. My sources explained that the old woman is flicking moderately hot oil around the edges of the eggs with a wooden spoon to achieve a lacey frill, like that on the skirts of a *traje de Sevillana.*

Cookery books of the period make no mention at all of methods of poaching eggs, a technique that is quite alien to the spirit of Spanish cooking. It is hard to imagine Velasquez choosing to illustrate any other way of preparing eggs, though an equally respectable alternative might have been Don Quixote's Saturday night supper of *'duelos y quebrantos',* 'lamentation and mourning', which may have been bacon and eggs, or a more sophisticated version of eggs scrambled with *tocino* and *chorizos,* the ingredients of which are lovingly recorded by Meléndez in one of his kitchen still lives.

So back to the National Gallery for eyeball to eyeball scrutiny of the Velasquez eggs. They yield some helpful clues: the depth of liquid in the shallow earthenware cooking pot is just right for frying, but too shallow for poaching, which demands enough liquid for the eggs to float, rather than glide over the base of the vessel as in frying.

The drawing by Soun is a partial representation of the painting by Velasquez, showing those features which are discussed here. It is based on the excellent reproduction in the catalogue of the National Gallery exhibition to which Gillian Riley refers.

The bright glow of hot red coals at the bottom left of the base of the pot will produce a heat ideal for the *puntilla* method. The eggs themselves are nice and fresh, the firm part of the whites have just set, and the old woman is flicking hot oil over the outer, liquid part, the critical point and moment of high drama in the operation. If the oil gets too hot the lacey frill will brown before the yolk is perfectly cooked, still slightly liquid, so to adjust the heat she can either add another egg to cool things down, or the boy can add a slug of oil, for oil it is, from the flask in his left hand. She looks intently at him, about to speak, or having just uttered some oracular pronouncement about the process.

The splatters which Velasquez is reproached for not portraying would, in this gentle mode of frying, have been virtually invisible droplets of oil, but are implied by the fact that the woman's right sleeve is not rolled up, but protects the hand which wields the wooden spoon.

She would have known, empirically, that cooking with vinegar and water in a lead-glazed vessel would have had unpleasant results, but the brass pan on the left by the storage jar whose neck supports the dish of coals, would have been used for the slow cooking of stews with wine or vinegar or the preparation of *escabeches*.

The humble, improvised nature of the cooking arrangements—a shallow earthenware dish sitting snugly in a pot of coals perched on the neck of a big storage jar, proclaims one of the glories of the fried egg in Spanish cuisine, the perfect fall-back position for an unexpected guest, rapid, a sustaining and an honourable offering of skills and nutrition, the perfect fast food, with still a legitimate place on restaurant menus.

This painting gains in significance when seen alongside the two other *bodgegones* in the series, *Christ in the House of Martha and Mary* and *The Waterseller,* produced by the young Velasquez between 1616 and 1620, here together at the National Gallery for the first time since they left his studio. They are so often described as vehicles for Velasquez' skills in rendering low life and humble domestic objects, but the paintings go much further than that. Between them they illustrate three fundamental aspects of the gastronomy of Spain: an aromatic, garlic-based sauce pounded in a mortar, simple ingredients cooked with skill and precision in olive oil, and the paramount importance of fresh, cooling drinks—non-alcoholic, regenerative, soothing, stimulating, that preceded the turgid brews of hot tea, coffee and cocoa that were later to prove so addictive.

Velasquez is also saying something about youth and old age: in all three paintings the elder person looks directly at the younger, profound words are being spoken. But the unresponsive, sulky creatures avoid eye-contact, look shiftily away, scowl, behaving exactly as one would expect. We all know that in a few years the lad in the painting will be telling his wife that she will never be capable of cooking eggs like his grandmother . . .

A smart young painter who knows it all is here commenting on the tedium of received wisdom, the tragedy of non-communication between generations and the power of his own skills. In this context the eggs are not mere accessories to a kitchen scene, they are crucial—and fried.

2.
Culinary History

Culinary history can produce some lengthy and important essays, but it can also produce shorter and sometimes lighter pieces of writing. In this section we present examples of both, and have covered a huge span of time, from the Bronze Age to 20th century trifles and the current enthusiasm in Japan and Hawaii for the surprising dish called Curry Rice.

The first item serves to exemplify the importance of archaeology in the history of food and also provides a vivid account of the experimental reconstruction of a bronze age cooking technique. This took place in a field in County Cork in 1993, an event in which the editors of *PPC* took an active and pleasurable part.

The foodways of the Western world have often been perceived as stemming from classical antiquity. Classic Greece and Rome have been seen as the sources to which we must look for the origin of many features of our cuisines. Recently food historians have been placing greater emphasis on the role of the Arab world and the part played by countries of the Near and the Middle East, long ago. We preface Claudia Roden's major essay on early Arab cookery with an indication of the context in which she composed it in 1980, and draw attention to the remarkable new book to which her research and her enthusiasm for the subject have now led. Anne Wilson's essay on the Saracen Connection was explicitly connected to that of Claudia Roden, which it followed almost at once. The story of how Anne Wilson came to be interested in this field of study is described in the preface to her essay.

Moving forward to the later medieval period we present one part of a remarkable survey by the leading Dutch food historian, Joop Witteveen, of how what he calls 'the Great Birds' were cooked and eaten in Europe at that time. The part we have selected deals with the heron, and follows similar descriptions on how swans and cranes were consumed. The author subsequently added a bonus section on peacocks. To have the whole series available one needs to have copies of *PPC 24, 25, 26* and *32.*

The 17th century affords us a look at the work of Caroline Davidson in preparation for restoring a historic English kitchen of that period. The essay shows clearly the wide scope of research required for a project of this kind. In part two of her essay (not reproduced here) Caroline described how she organised the acquisition or re-creation of all the pieces of kitchen equipment which would have been in the original kitchen 300 years previously, thus completing the restoration which the Victoria and Albert Museum had commissioned her to do.

The Yule-doos, Pop-ladies and Pig-hogs described by Peter Brears seem to date from a somewhat later period, perhaps the 18th century onwards, but their real origin, if it could be traced, may be earlier. Peter's essay gives us a glimpse of popular festival foods such as rarely appeared in cookery books although they had some importance and significance for people in communities where old traditions were maintained.

Where the true origins of something have not been established, folklore is quick to fill the gap with an entertaining or dramatic legend. However, Helen Saberi, writing her essay on the history of the trifle, did not have to contend with myths but simply with a gap in the literature. No one had previously traced the origins of this famous British sweet and festive dish, nor explained how it evolved over the centuries; and there was no legend about it. The way was clear to expound its true history.

Finally, we learn from Keiko Ohnuma 'How the British version of an Indian dish turned Japanese'. Here is an example of another frequent phenomenon, the migration of a dish from one cuisine to another and perhaps to a third, in a manner which changes it so much that it would hardly be recognised in its region of origin.

An Experiment in Bronze Age Cooking:

The Fulacht Fiadh, Castlemary 1993

DIARMUID A Ó DRISCEOIL

The mastermind of the experiment here described and the author of this essay is a teacher who lives and works in County Cork in Ireland. He has a special interest in archaeological matters, and particularly in the fulachta fiadh, which were the subject of his thesis (1980) for an MA degree at University College Cork, and on which he has since published learned articles in Antiquity, *237, 62, 1988, and in* Burnt Offerings, *sub-titled 'International Contributions to Burnt Mound Archaeology'. These and other relevant references are listed at the end of the essay.*

Lá Bealtaine, the Celtic Mayday, seemed appropriate for the gathering. Archaeologists, food historians, cookery writers, musicians and members of the local Cloyne Literary and Historical Society, with a retinue of children and dogs, assembled in a valley on Castlemary Estate on the east side of Cork Harbour. A stream flows westwards along the bottom of the valley and large spreads of burnt stone and blackened earth were visible in the ploughed fields on the far side of the stream.

An anonymous scribe, writing in the 12th century, describes two warriors making camp for the night in a similar location:

> *And Caoilte and Finnachaidh go down to the stream to wash their hands. 'This is a cooking place,' said Finnachaidh, 'and it is a long time since it was made.'*
>
> *'That is true', said Caoilte, '. . . and it is not to be worked without water.'* (Hyde 1916, 339, 345)

Five hundred years later, in the early 17th century, Geoffrey Keating, the most famous scholar of his time, wrote that

> *These sites are today in Ireland burnt to blackness, and these are now called Fulacht Fian by the peasantry.* (ed Dinneen 1908, 326–9)

The Rev R. Smiddy, a 19th-century antiquarian, was familiar with this term and wrote:

> *The name folach fiadh is well known to the country people, and they bestow it on a heap of burnt stones, of which, as a rule, they know neither the origin nor the use.* (1873, 52)

The 20th-century assembly in Castlemary was ranged about a water-filled pit, 1.5 metres long, 1 metre wide and 75 cm deep. This had been lined with timber planks. Nearby blazed two fires. The smaller covered a large sandstone slab; the larger had many pieces of stone layered between its burning timbers. Joints of venison and lamb lay wrapped in bundles of straw.

The aim was to cook (with satisfactory results!) in a manner suggested by the excavated features of ancient Irish cooking places and occasionally described in early Irish literature, and thereby to produce debris like that spread through the ploughed soil on the far side of the stream.

'Fulacht fiadh' is the term, from the Irish language, used in Ireland to describe one of these ancient cooking places. 'Fulacht fia' and 'fulacht fian' are also used. These terms may be somewhat awkwardly translated as 'cooking place of the wild' or '. . . of the deer' or '. . . of a roving band of hunters/warriors'. In Britain such sites are generally called 'burnt mounds'.

The sites survive as relatively small grass-covered mounds of burnt and broken stone, ash and charcoal. They vary in size from a few metres in diameter to over 20 metres in some cases. The height of the mounds varies also, but most are between 1 and 2 metres high. The 'classic' fulacht fiadh is horseshoe-shaped in plan, i.e. two horns or arms of the mound incompletely enclose a shallow area or depression. About half of the known examples are of this shape, which is exemplified in the impressionistic drawing reproduced on page 93.

With very few exceptions, fulachta fiadh (plural) are located in wet or marshy areas, by streams or quite close to springs. They also tend to occur in closely spaced groups. Over 4,500 examples have been identified in Ireland, making them one of the most numerous archaeological monument types. The majority of these occur in the southern parts of the country. Similar monuments are also known in Britain and they may also be present on the European mainland.

The central feature of the fulacht fiadh is the trough or pit. Excavation usually locates this in that part of the site enclosed by mound material. Dimensions again vary, but a typical trough would be 1.5 to 2 metres long, 1 metre wide and 75 cm deep. Such a trough would have been capable of holding up to 500 litres of water. As the sites are located in damp situations, where the watertable is close to the surface, the troughs will fill 'automatically' from the surrounding water-laden ground. The troughs were frequently lined. Stone slabs would have formed the floor and sides where such material was readily available, where elsewhere split oak planks would have been used. Wooden dug-out troughs and unlined examples are also known, however. The presumed function of the lining was to prevent the trough sides from crumbling, rather than rendering it watertight; this latter function would not have been necessary except in a rare dry location.

Another important feature of the sites is the hearth. This usually lies quite close to the trough and generally within the enclosing mound. Some hearths were roughly paved, others were delineated by settings of stones, while the humbler examples reveal themselves to the archaeologist as spreads of fire-reddened soil. The quantities of stone necessary for heating the water were fired here before transfer to the trough.

The mound, usually the only overground indicator of a site, is an accumulation of debris from the trough and hearth. The burnt and cracked stones from the bottom of the trough and the ash and charcoal from the hearth were cleared after each use of the site and deposited outside the central working area. With prolonged use quite a sizable deposit would have built up. Re-heating of stones would of course diminish the apparent length of use of a site. It has been shown that harder igneous rocks such as basalt or gabbro can be reheated over 20 times, whereas softer rock types such as limestone may survive only one heating and immersion in water. This suggests that fulachta fiadh, were they to occur in areas of igneous rock, could be less than 1/20th the size of a similarly used site in an area of limestone. This may explain the apparent paucity of sites in northeastern Ireland where igneous rock types are dominant.

Small finds from excavated sites are rare. Sherds of pottery, stone or metal weapons or implements, items of decoration or ornament do not usually feature. A site at Fahee South in County Clare in western Ireland did produce some faunal remains. Domesticated cattle, red deer and horse were represented in the small sample and suggested that the users of that site relied on a combination of domestic and hunted animals for meat. No other of the 30 or so excavated sites in Ireland or Britain produced such evidence.

Until relatively recently accurate dating of fulachta fiadh was not feasible. In the absence of diagnostic pottery, flint or metalwork it was not possible to associate the sites chronologically with other monument types. Even relative dating was not possible. For these reasons the sites, though known in not inconsiderable numbers, were, with a few honourable exceptions, largely ignored by archaeologists. The increasing availability of accurate Radiocarbon or C14 dates changed this unfortunate neglect. Nearly all the 20 or so dated sites in Ireland fall between 1,500 BC and 500 BC, a period known as the middle and later Bronze Age. This is a period in Irish prehistory for which we have relatively little archaeological information. The great number of fulachta fiadh now being identified, coupled with an accurate dating, has the potential to fill large gaps in our understanding of settlement patterns and of the culture and economy of the period. On a more specific level a satisfactory function has to be established for the different features of the sites.

In Ireland, fulachta fiadh have traditionally been interpreted as cooking places. This has been largely based on descriptions in early Irish literature, though the physical archaeological evidence, tradition, and the meaning of the term 'fulacht' also support such an interpretation. The most frequently quoted account is that of Geoffrey Keating who, in the early 17th century, wrote a history of Ireland. Then, and indeed still today, many prominent field antiquities were attributed to the Fianna, a mythical, pseudohistorical army much given to hunting and the outdoor life and about whom a great body of literature was composed in the medieval period. In his discussion of this band of roving warriors and hunters Keating writes:

> From Bealtaine until Samhain, the Fianna were obliged to depend solely on the products of their hunting and of the chase as maintenance and wages from the kings of Ireland; thus, they were to have the flesh for food, and the skins of the wild animals as pay. But they took only one meal in the day-and-night, and that was in the afternoon. And it was their custom to send their attendants about noon with whatever they had killed in the morning's hunt to an appointed hill, having wood and moorland in the neighbourhood, and to kindle raging fires thereon, and put into them a large number of emery stones; and to dig two pits in the yellow clay of the moorland, and put some of the meat on spits to roast before the fire; and to bind another portion of it with súgáns (twisted straw ropes) in dry bundles, and set it to boil in the larger of the two pits, and keep plying them with stones that were in the fire, making them seethe often until they were cooked. And these fires were so large that their sites are today in Ireland burnt to blackness, and these are now called Fulacht Fian by the peasantry.
>
> As to the Fian, when they assembled on the hill on which was the fire, each of them stripped off, and tied his shirt round his waist, and they ranged themselves around the second pit we have mentioned above, bathing their hair and washing their limbs, and removing their sweat, and then exercising their joints and muscles, thus ridding themselves of their fatigue . . . (ed Dinneen 1908, 326–9)

It is interesting that Keating regarded washing and bathing as a function of the site, though this took place in a second pit.

A similar, though eminently more entertaining, account comes from another Irish language text 'The Romance of Mis and Dubh Ruis'. The manuscript from which it comes dates to 1769, but the tale itself may be some centuries older. Dubh Ruis goes to rescue a woman called Mis, the daughter of a king. She is living in the mountains of southwestern Ireland and is insane. Her body is completely covered in hair and she lives like a wild animal. Dubh Ruis plans to intercept her:

When he reached the mountain he sat where he thought she might pass and he spread his cloak on the ground and spread his gold and silver around its edges. He lay on the cloak and took up his harp. He opened his trews and bared himself for he thought that if he could lie with her it would be a good way to bring her to sanity again. Not long after that she came to where he was on hearing the harp-music and she stood there in all her wildness listening and looking at him and waiting.

'Are you not a person?' she said.

'Yes,' he said.

'What is this?' she said, putting her hand on the harp.

'A harp,' he said.

'Ho,' she said, 'I remember the harp. My father used to play one. Play it for me.'

'I will,' he said, 'but please do not harm me.'

'I will not,' she said.

She saw the gold and silver and said: 'What is this?'

'Gold and silver,' he said.

'I remember,' she said, 'my father used to have gold.'

She glanced again at him and saw his playful members and said:

'What are these?', pointing to his bag or testicles. And he told her.

'What is this?' she said, pointing to the other thing she saw.

'That is my magic wand.'

'I do not remember that,' she said. 'My father did not have anything like that. A magic wand,' she said, 'What tricks can it do?'

'Sit near me and I will do the trick for you.'

'I will,' she said, 'but stay with me.'

'I will,' he said and he lay with her.

'Ha,' she said, 'that was a good trick. Do it again.'

'I will,' he said, 'but I will play the harp first.'

'Don't bother with the harp,' she said, 'but do the trick.'

'Well,' he said, 'I would like some food first, I am hungry.'

'I will get you a deer,' she said . . .

She was not long gone from him when she returned carrying a deer under her arm. She was about to tear it apart and eat it as it was when Dubh Ruis said to her:

'Wait until I slaughter the deer and boil the meat.'

With that he cut the deer's throat and skinned it. Then he made a large fire of dead wood from the forest and he gathered a heap of granite stones, and put them in the fire, he made a pit, square all round, in the ground, and he filled it with water. He cut up his meat and wrapped it in marsh grass,

> with a well turned straw rope around it, and he put it in the hole. He was supplying and continuously putting the well-reddened, long-heated stones in the water, and he kept it constantly boiling until his meat was cooked . . .
>
> He then took her to the hole in which was the cold broth with the fat of the deer melted on it, and he put her standing in it, and he took a piece of the deer's skin and he rubbed and massaged the joints of her body and all her bones, and he took to smearing her, rubbing her and spreading her with the grease of the deer and with the broth until he had cleaned much of her, and until he brought streams of sweat out of her like that. (O Cuív 1954)

Bathing again figures prominently in this account. Should this surprise us? At a time when washing and bathing were not as readily enjoyed as they are today in the developed world, surely the opportunity presented by a large quantity of hot water would not have been ignored. The melted fat and ash would have served as a basic soap to cleanse the skin.

These two accounts are the most detailed in the early literature. While the information they provide is illuminating, one must be aware that they date to a period at least 2,000 years after that suggested by C14 dating for the fulachta fiadh known to archaeology. Neither passage presents itself as a description of normal contemporary practice and though the Irish literary tradition, both written and oral, is very ancient and doubtless has roots in prehistoric times, one cannot use its archaism or conservatism to explain away this apparent 2,000 year gap. Nonetheless, experiments based on such descriptions are valid, test the feasibility of the suggested cooking method, and on Mayday 1993 attracted a curious and interested group to Castlemary.

By the stream the large fire burned fiercely. It had been set long and narrow and while the flames moved slowly from the windward end the stones were heated through and fell, as the timber turned to ember and ash, to lie glowing on the ground. Myrtle Allen, the doyenne of Irish cooking and food writing, describes what followed:

> Joints of lamb and wild venison were covered with bay leaves, wild garlic and rosemary, wrapped in hay or straw, and were tied into parcels. After an hour about 20 stones were shovelled out of the fire and placed most spectacularly into the cold water.
>
> There was a great hissing and rumbling, a spout of steam shot up into the air, and, when big stones went in, the ground vibrated. It took about 20 minutes for the water to boil and then the meat was put in. Looking into the trough I understood the full meaning of the word seething. Here and there the surface broke with slow bubbles while the whole area of water gave off a dense steam. Similar, but yet very different to the little pot that simmers on top of a modern cooker, this was on a massive scale.

A hearth-stone had been set between the stream and the fire, a thick rough slab of sandstone about two feet in diameter, slightly raised. On top of it another fire was lit and more sticks were placed all around it and were also set alight. Families with children began to gather, picnic baskets were unpacked . . .

Later the musicians arrived. All the time helpers watched over the cooking pit, adding more hot stones whenever the bubbles faltered, and sometimes throwing out cooled stones. The meat would take two hours to cook.

Meanwhile, the hot hearth-stone was swept ready for use. We thought oatcakes would be appropriate, so my guess at the prehistoric version was a mixture of Macroom ground (not rolled) oats, with a little butter rubbed

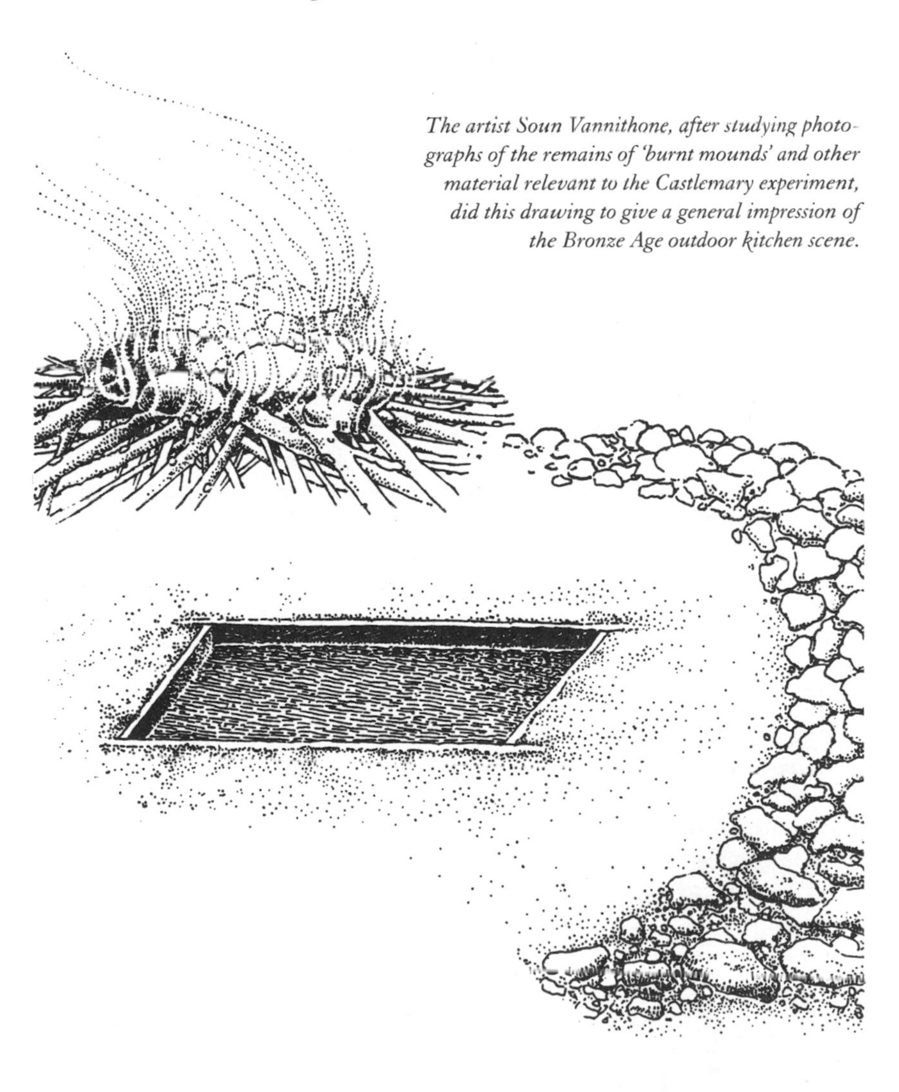

The artist Soun Vannithone, after studying photographs of the remains of 'burnt mounds' and other material relevant to the Castlemary experiment, did this drawing to give a general impression of the Bronze Age outdoor kitchen scene.

> through, salted and moistened with milk. We flattened pieces in our hands and threw them on the stone. We turned them, they swelled up, and they were definitely edible. Steaks and scraps of venison were next for the griddle, they were delicious. Finally the joints were taken from the murky water, unwrapped, carved up, and tasted by all. They were perfectly cooked, very tender, with no taint of ash or anything other than herbs and meat. A little sauce could have brought them up to restaurant standards. (*The Irish Times,* 15 May, 1993)

The experiment was successful but a doubt lingered. Why the apparently troublesome and lengthy boiling, when cooking smaller pieces on a stone griddle or roasting on a spit would appear more sensible? The collection of large quantities of fuel and stone, the lighting and maintenance of large fires followed by a period of tending the trough is time consuming. However, the size of the trough allows the cooking of many pieces at one time, and for that boiling is a satisfactory method. Boiling in this manner may take more time in initial preparation than open roasting or broiling, but it requires far less time in attention and tending. If the water were to be used subsequently for washing or bathing, the effort would be further rewarded. This does perhaps emphasise a use of the sites in communal, ceremonial or even ritual cooking rather than in everyday food preparation for small groups.

Cooking with hot stones is a practice common to many cultures and ages. The fulacht fiadh, however, is evidence of a particular use of the principle on a large scale. It is, in the present state of knowledge, unique to Ireland and Britain. What conditions, social, economic or otherwise, in the Bronze Age, led to the practices suggested by fulachta fiadh or burnt mounds? Why did the activity apparently die out after a thousand years or so? These wider questions await further archaeological enquiry.

The Castlemary experiment showed that the provision of large quantities of cooked meat, though quite feasible, need not have been the only function of the sites. Bathing was not attempted on this occasion but the diverse and lively gathering did experience a unique event and perhaps sampled an ancient atmosphere, recreated with spectacular visual and sound effects and seasoned with woodsmoke and the lingering scents of wild garlic, rosemary and bay.

References and Works Consulted

1. Barfield, L. & M. Hodder, 'Burnt mounds as saunas, and the prehistory of bathing', *Antiquity,* Vol 61 (1987), pp 370–9.
2. Buckley, V., 'Experiments using a reconstructed fulacht with a variety of rock types: implications for the petro-morphology of fulachta fiadh', in Buckley, V. (ed), *Burnt Offerings* (Dublin, 1990), pp 170–2.

3. Dinneen, D. S. (ed), *The History of Ireland. Foras Feasa or Eirinn* by G. Keating, Vol 2 (London, 1908).
4. Hedges, J. W., 'Excavation of two Orcadian burnt mounds at Liddle and Beaquoy', *Proceedings of the Society of Antiquaries of Scotland,* Vol 106 (1974–5), pp 39–98.
5. Hyde, D. (ed), 'The Cooking of the Great Queen', *Celtic Review,* Vol 10 (1916), pp 335–50.
6. Lucas, A. T., 'Washing and Bathing in Ancient Ireland', *Journal of the Royal Society of Antiquaries of Ireland,* Vol 95 (1965), pp 65–114.
7. O Cuív, B. (ed), 'The Romance of Mis and Dubh Ruis', *Celtica,* Vol 2 (1954), pp 325–33.
8. Ó Drisceoil, D. A., 'Burnt mounds: cooking or bathing', *Antiquity,* Vol 62 (1988), pp 671–80.
9. Ó Drisceoil, D. A., 'Fulachta fiadh: the value of early Irish literature', in V. Buckley (ed), *Burnt Offerings* (Dublin, 1990), pp 157–64.
10. O Kelly, M. J., 'Excavations and experiments in ancient Irish cooking-places', *Journal of the Royal Society of Antiquaries of Ireland,* Vol 84 (1954).

Early Arab Cooking and Cookery Manuscripts

CLAUDIA RODEN

Claudia Roden, author of A Book of Middle Eastern Food *(new edition Knopf, 2000), was led in her researches for it to examine the surviving evidence about Arab Cooking in the pre-Islamic period and the era of the Moslem Empire.*

Learned articles by Professor A J Arberry and Professor Maxime Rodinson (see references 2, 4, 5, and 7) formed the basis on which she prepared a talk delivered to the Symposium on Cookery Books held at Saint Antony's College, Oxford, on 31 May 1980.

The present essay is a slightly elaborated version of the notes she used in giving her talk. We printed it in the belief that it was an important contribution to an era of research in which much work remained to be done—work which could be expected to cast fresh light on the origins of European cuisines of the Renaissance and later. Now, more than 20 years later, we are happy to announce that much progress has been made and that the key documents which Claudia Roden was using have now been published in English, with other, and new, relevant essays in the book Medieval Arab Cookery. *This was edited by Charles Perry, himself a contributor, and published by Prospect Books, Devon, in 2001.*

Very few cookery books are published in Arabic these days and they generally feature European foods. No one in the Middle East would go and look in a book to learn how to make a local dish. The explanation is that ways of preparing food are passed down in the family and jealously kept among closest friends. The written word is not much trusted in matters of the kitchen; a person who writes is not thought of as able to cook and it is always assumed that you can only learn by watching.

But in the past, as early as the 8th century, writings on food were abundant and popular. So much so that the scientist Salih b. Abd al-Quddus, who was to be executed as a heretic, complained bitterly: 'We live amongst animals who roam in search of pastures without seeking to understand. If we write about fish and vegetables we are invested in their eyes with great merit, but truly scientific subjects are for them painful and boring.'[1]

In the Abbassid Period, from the 9th to the12th century, the Golden Age of Islam, when Baghdad was the capital of the Islamic Empire, culinary literature proliferated and reached the level of an art. There were two parallel trends. One, the result of the interest in food of the Abbassid upper classes, written by them or for them, was a princely activity devoted to the refinement of pleasure and to setting high standards of taste and savoir vivre for the élite. The other was the development of a branch of medicine, dietetics; and this was the work of doctors concerned with health.

Gastronomy was especially esteemed in this rich period of Arab history when the search for the most delicious combinations of food, according to increasingly subtle criteria, formed the preoccupation of a distinguished society of gourmets.

The banquets at the royal courts of the Caliphs of Baghdad were proverbial for their variety and lavishness. The Caliphs commissioned people to invent dishes, to write poems about foods and to sing their praise at gatherings which became legendary. Mas'udi describes one such event at the court of Mustakfi, the Caliph who was blinded and deposed in 946, in his *Meadows of Gold*. I quote from Professor Arberry's translation:[2]

> One day Mustakfi said: 'It is my desire that we should assemble on such and such a day, and converse together about the different varieties of food, and the poetry that has been composed on this subject.' Those present agreed; and on the day prescribed Mustakfi joined the party, and bade every man produce what he had prepared. Thereupon one member of the circle spoke up: 'O Commander of the Faithful, I have some verses by Ibn al-Mu'tazz in which the poet describes a tray containing bowls of Kamakh.'

Ibn al-Mu'tazz too had been a tragic prince who ruled for one day only and was put to death in 908. The poem, concerning a tray of hors d'oeuvre, described the different elements in an ardent and sensuous manner. Others followed with long poems to the glory of many delicacies in terms of ecstatic love.

Poets, astrologers, astronomers, scholars, princes and even caliphs took pleasure in writing about food. Many manuals of cookery and collections of recipes were written, most of which have unfortunately been lost. They are often referred to in works of the period and an Arab bibliography of the 10th century listed more than ten important cookery books.[3]

Two works which have survived, and to which I now turn, have received special attention.

The Baghdad Cookery Book of 1226

In 1934 the Iraqi scholar, Dr Daoud Chelebi, discovered 2 manuscripts written in Baghdad in the year 1226 by a certain Muhammad ibn al Hassan ibn Muhammad ibn Al-Karim al Katib at Baghdadi, otherwise completely unknown. Dr Chelebi published it in Mosul with the title *Kitab al Tabikh* (Cookery Book). The late Professor A.J. Arberry translated it into English and included it in his article in *Islamic Culture* in 1939.[2]

In the preface, after the obligatory praises to God and some remarks on the importance of good wholesome eating, the author says he wrote the book for his own use and for those interested in 'the art of cooking'. He talks of the different pleasures and subscribes 'to the doctrine of the pre-excellence of the pleasure of eating above all other pleasures'. He has general advice about the necessity of keeping nails trimmed and pots clean, of rubbing copper pans bright with brick dust, potash, saffron and citron leaves, and on such things as the value of using fresh and strongly scented spices ground very fine.

There follow 160 recipes, divided into 10 chapters, which include 'sour dishes', some of which are sweetened with sugar, syrup, honey or date juice; and milk dishes with 'Persian' milk which is actually curdled milk or yoghourt. The 'plain dishes' are not at all plain. The 'fried' or 'dry' dishes do not have much broth or sauce. The 'simple' and 'sweet' dishes are not puddings but meat dishes. Those grouped under 'harissa' are of meats cooked with meal. There are fresh and salted fish dishes and recipes for fish caught in the lake of Van in Armenia. And there are recipes for sauces, relishes and savouries, vegetable pickles and salads, desserts, pastries and sweetmeats.

The recipes are remarkable in their variety and in the imaginative combination of a wide range of ingredients including apples, prunes, quinces and currants, almonds and pistachios with vegetables and meats. Their delicate flavouring is the result of the subtle blending of herbs and spices, roots, resins and essences of flowers. Their preparation requires skill and patience, and their presentation calls for taste and artfulness. They are all perfectly explained and precise, but although they often give quantities of spices and aromatics they do not usually give measures when dealing with main ingredients. A certain knowledge and experience on the part of the cook are assumed.

The two recipes appended to this article illustrate the general style and the detail of information. A translation of each recipe is given in italics, followed by my suggested quantities for the ingredients and such further directions as a cook making the dishes today might need. I have selected these two recipes for my present purpose; but there are many others which are equally explicit, delicious and feasible to follow in a modern kitchen—more than seven centuries after they were written.

The Second of the Surviving Early Works

Another culinary work, the *Kitab al wusla ila l-habib fi wasfi t-tayyibati wat-tib* (Book of the bond with the friend, or description of good dishes and perfumes), exists in at least 10 handwritten copies, each with minor variations and additions. One manuscript, reproduced in part on page 100, is in the British Library (shelfmark Or. 6388). Others are in Aleppo, Damascus, Cairo and Mosul.

Professor Rodinson describes and analyses the manuscripts at length[4] but unfortunately circumstance prevented him from giving a full translation of the recipes.

The true origin, date and authorship of the original manuscript are uncertain; but it is very likely that it dates from before 1261 in the Ayyoubid period in Syria, and that it was written by someone close to the courts because of the many references to the Sultan, his cooks and the royal kitchens. It may have been a Prince or a grandson of Safadin and great-nephew of Saladin, or the historian Kamalad-din Ibn al-Adim or the poet and historian Ibn al-Jazzar.

It is in two parts, one of which is on table manners, while the other contains the recipes. A chapter is devoted to perfumes and incense, another to drinks and juices. There are 74 recipes for cooking chicken and recipes for fried and roast meats as well as omelettes and stews. Vegetables, rice, wheat, fruit and yoghourt dishes are featured; and there is a chapter on desserts and pastries.

Comparisons with Arab Food of Today

I was lucky to have discovered Professor Arberry's translation and Maxime Rodinson's study at the start of my research for *A Book of Middle Eastern Food,* so that I was able to compare the recipes with those of the Arab world today and to appreciate the extent to which they had spread whilst remaining faithful to their origins.

The favourite meat is still lamb; the favourite vegetables are still courgettes and aubergines, leeks, cauliflower and cabbage, colocasi, cucumber, spinach, onion and garlic; and the favourite fruits remain oranges, dates, grapes, apricots, apples, pomegranates and melon. Rice and wheat, lentils, pine nuts, almonds, pistachios and vine leaves are still employed. But that is not surprising, for all these things grow there. What is extraordinary is that after eight or nine hundred years the marriage of ingredients continues in the same way. Rice is still coupled with lentils or chick-peas, chicken with nuts, and meat with fruit. Lamb, cut into little cubes or rolled into balls, is cooked with yoghourt or stewed with vegetables or with fruits such as quinces, apricots or prunes. And everyone still loves the delicate combinations of flavour which are produced with cinnamon, cumin and coriander, ginger, saffron and mastic, mint, nutmeg, cloves, cardamom and garlic; they still use orange flower water and they still love to colour things yellow and red.

Some of Al Baghdadi's recipes for stews could be word for word instructions for an Iranian 'khoresh' or a Moroccan 'tagine' of today; and we still make in my family many of the dishes described in the *Wusla.* As for the methods; grinding fine, rolling into balls or oblongs, pounding in the mortar,

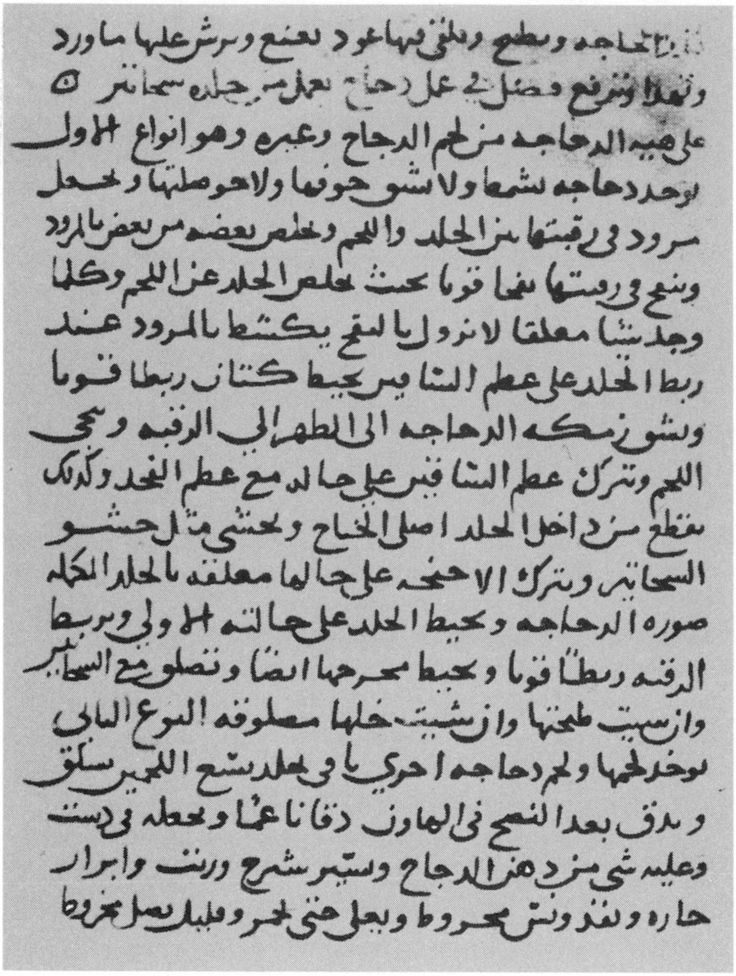

This is a reproduction of a page of the Kitab al Wusla, *the early Arabic cookery manuscript to which Claudia Roden refers on page 98. This section of the manuscript deals with a chicken dish which is remarkably close to some modern recipes. The chicken is completely emptied, its flesh chopped finely and spiced, and the mixture then replaced inside the empty skin.*
(Reproduced by kind permission of the British Library.)

simmering long in broth, cutting up in lozenges, bathing in syrup—every touch and movement required are those employed today. As in the past, milk puddings are thickened with ground rice and cornflour or semolina; and the same honeyed pastries filled with chopped nuts are the usual fare of vendors in the street, to be kept preciously in boxes for festive occasions or the much appreciated visit of an unexpected guest.

Arab Influence on European Cuisines

In the last few years I have become increasingly aware of the debt owed by early European cookery to the Arab tradition. I have come across recipes here and there in old English and French cookery books which are almost identical to those featured in the Islamic manuscripts. They make use of ground almonds or milk of almonds, of the same mixtures of spices and aromatics and the whole range of dried fruits and nuts which the Crusaders brought back, and which were part of the early trade with the Levant. At the enchanting medieval banquet given by Lorna Sass (author of *To The King's Taste,* Richard II's book of feasts and recipes, and *To The Queen's Taste*), which Audrey Ellison helped to prepare in London in 1978, I felt that I was the guest who was the most familiar with the dishes.

It is interesting to discover the background of this court cuisine which has over the centuries filtered down to the masses and influenced countries further afield than those conquered by the armies of Islam. Maxime Rodinson has made an admirable study of the conditions which forged it and the society in which it found expression in his 'Récherches sur les Documents Arabes Rélatifs à la Cuisine'.[4] In what follows I have also made use of the information he gives in the entry 'Ghidha' in the Encyclopedia of Islam.[5]

Pre-Islamic Arab Food

Before Islam the food of the Arabs combined ingredients of agricultural and pastoral origin. Preparation was elementary—the Bedouin diet consisted of bread and dates; of mutton, with some goat and camel meat, and the milk of these animals; with the occasional game and wild berries found in the desert.

The settled agricultural populations ate chicory, beets, gourds, courgettes, marrow, cucumber, leeks, onions and garlic, olives, palm hearts, broad beans, lemons, pomegranates and grapes. A gruel called harira was made of dried barley meal to which water, butter or fat was added, and flour was cooked in milk.

The favourite dishes of the prophet was *tharid,* bread crumbled in a broth of meat and vegetables, and *hays,* a mixture of dates, butter and milk.

Spices were hardly used in the early days even though the Arabs were engaged in transporting them to Europe. They obtained too high a price on the Roman market to be used locally.

Changes in the Muslim Empire

In the Arab Empire which after 750 became the Muslim Empire, the food in the various occupied countries naturally continued to be the same as it had been before they were conquered. At first the Arab conquerors were austere and puritanical and not much concerned with food, but they gradually came to adopt the foods of the countries which they governed, adding some of their own tastes and practices to the developing repertoire of Arab court cuisine.

Although differences between countries remained, the Muslim conquest created a relatively coherent cultural era, and the rich and highly placed everywhere were eager to adopt the fashionable trends.

Under the new empire there were thus many changes which affected food habits. Here are five important ones.

The Spread of Food Products

Products which had formerly been grown only in one part of the area now spread throughout it. Rice is a good example. It originated in India and was grown in Syria, Iraq and Iran before Islam. Now it spread as a crop all over the Arab world and became a popular food as far away as Spain (although it did not quite take the place of wheat which was everywhere a commodity traded on a large scale). Sugar, introduced to Iran from India shortly before the Muslim conquest, spread after this through the whole of the Mediterranean.

Large Scale Transport

This brought food from one part of the Empire to another; truffles from the desert, olive oil from Syria, dates from Iraq, coffee from Arabia. Later, a wide range of ingredients was introduced from places outside the Empire. Spices such as pepper, ginger, cinnamon, cloves, cardamom, cumin, coriander, betel, music, mastic and nutmeg were brought from China, India and Africa. In the 12th century, dried and salted fish, honey and hazelnuts came from Russia and the Slav countries, cheese from Sicily and Crete, wine, chestnuts and saffron from the south of France.

Increased Travel

Cooks from parts renowned for their food were employed in distant regions. In the Middle Ages, Egyptian cuisine and cooks had a high reputation. So did the cooks of Bolu in Turkey. And there were massive migrations, with immigrants introducing their traditional dishes into their new habitat.

Bigger and Better Kitchens

The rulers had huge, well equipped and well stocked kitchens, staffed by numerous cooks and their assistants, in which all types of dishes could be attempted.

The Elite in Baghdad

By the 10th century there was a new prosperous élite in Baghdad which aspired to refinement and had strict rules in this matter. Their quest for the grand, the exotic and the unusual led them to the adoption of the cuisines of foreigners whose civilizations enjoyed in their eyes a certain prestige for the power and glory which they had formerly enjoyed. Hence the vogue for Iranian dishes, and later the fashion for things Turkish. The European influence began to be evident in the period of the Crusades ('Franc' dishes appear in the second of the manuscripts we are considering.)

Characteristics of the New Court Cuisine

The cookery manuals naturally dealt with the new cuisine which was constantly developing in the kitchens of the courts, and which was much discussed. It had not been handed down from the past and therefore needed to be recorded.

What was the style of this princely cuisine? The following features characterised it.

1. *It used expensive ingredients which only a few could afford.*

   Some of these were rare and came from far, such as spices; others were newly grown on Arab soil, such as rice and sugar. Chicken and lamb were used; and so were locally grown vegetables, but the more common ones such as okra, beans and figs were not.

   Everyone knew which were the foods of the poor and which of the rich. (Proverbs, songs and popular literature express this awareness.) Meat and rice were for the rich; lentils, beans, burghul and honey for the poor. Although these latter foods retained their popularity, they were stigmatised in a book by al Jahiz as the food of misers and were almost ignored in the manuscripts we have mentioned. When simple local dishes were included, they were glamourized; for example, the melted down lamb's-tail fat which was perfumed with a variety of aromatics as well as with quince and apple and dried coriander, aniseed, onion, cinnamon and mastic, and which was coloured red and yellow. Bedouin dishes with dates were made grand by replacing the stones with blanched almonds. Traditional peasant dishes with wheat and lentils were enriched with meat and delicately spiced.

2. *Techniques were elaborate and sophisticated.*

   Methods of preserving with salt and vinegar, lemon juice and mustard were inherited from the ancient East and classical civilizations. Fruit was crystallized in honey. Smoke drying was said in Egypt to be a Greek process. (In the past they had dried meat by hanging thin strips in the open or preserved it by burying it in fat.)

3. *The grander dishes were Iranian.*

   Their origins are revealed in the Arab repertoire today by their names ending in -ak and -aj. Techniques of cooking and elegant ways were adopted from conquered Iran which had been the most prestigious civilization in the area.

4. *Koranic prohibitions were observed.*

   Koranic regulations and prohibitions advised by the pious specialists on religious questions were followed. No pork was used and no wine.

5. *Newly acquired tastes became fashionable.*

   The taste for highly spiced foods and sweet things appeared at a more advanced stage of Muslim civilization; it was simply a continuation of the tastes of classical antiquity. So was the taste for sweet and sour which came via Iran.

6. *Visual appeal was important.*

   Saffron and turmeric were used for colour, and much care was taken to give delight in presentation. Counterfeit dishes such as mock brains and an omelette in a bottle were devised as pleasant surprises.

7. *Complexity was valued.*

   Complexity in flavour was valued for its own sake, quite apart from the actual flavour itself. Aromatics were used in tiny quantities but in a great number and a variety of combinations. All the spices already mentioned were combined with herbs such as parsley, mint, rue, thyme, lavender, mallow, purslane, bay and tarragon. Poppy and sesame seeds, fenugreek, rose petals and rose buds were used. The result was delicate and subtle, and, if we go by the tastes handed down, not too strong or too hot.

   Complexity in form was also esteemed. Confections which required skill, application and time were well considered, especially if they were small and delicately shaped. Vegetables were hollowed out and stuffed, tiny pies were filled, elegant little parcels were made with wrappings of pastries or leaves.

The Place of Dietetics and Medical Books

Dietetics were at the same time a branch of medicine and a form of culinary literature.

Anecdotes of the period depict doctors sitting at the tables of Caliphs to advise them on what was good for them. (Maimonides sat for al-Malik al Afdal.)

The educated classes paid a great deal of attention to dietetic precepts so that this science was of great importance. It stemmed for the most part from the scientific medicine systematised by the Greeks and was based on the theory of humours, from which had been deduced all kinds of conclusions on the nature of each food and its suitability to one or another human temperament.[6] It incorporated local popular ideas such as the one that dates cause ophthalmia but are good for childbirth, and penetrated deeply among the masses.

Arab books on dietetics preceded medical books, and all the early books of medicine contained a long chapter enumerating, usually in alphabetical order, the attributes and faults of each food from the point of view of bodily and spiritual well-being. They also gave recipes, which were much like those which went round the courts, and accompanied them by critical advice on what was good for the liver and the heart.

Their Legacy

Some of these books were translated into Latin and had a considerable influence on European dietetics and medicine (as did old Greek texts) until well into the 18th century. Maxime Rodinson demonstrated this in a paper for the *Accademia Italiana della Cucina* in 1967 on the spice trade and the oriental influence on European cooking.[7]

In the 12th or 13th century a book of Arab dietetics was translated into Latin in Venice by a certain Jambobinus of Cremona who called it 'Liber di Coquina'. This translation was one of the earliest 'cookery books' of Medieval Europe.[8] The original author was Ibn Jazla, a doctor of Baghdad who died in the year 1100. Jambobinus used 83 of his recipes and kept their Arab names. Many of these were to reappear in other Latin cookery books and later in Italian, French and English translations where their origin remains detectable by their names, the oriental ingredients and the way the method is described.

Ibn Jazla was not the only source of Arab recipes in European cookery books. Much later, in the early 16th century, Andrea Alpago, a Venetian doctor and scholar who had spent 30 years in the Orient, translated the works of the Arab doctor and philosopher Avicenna who was born in 980. He added parts of other Arab books on dietetics as glossaries to each volume.[9]

The Decline

Arab culinary literature faded with the decline of this brilliant civilization and of the Abbassid dynasty which was marked by the fall of Baghdad in 1258 at the hands of the Mongols. Gastronomy continued to have its enthusiasts but with the growth of religious puritanism, they became more discreet. Its authors were no longer the aristocratic arbiters of taste but obscure people who painstakingly recorded recipes for their own use and the instruction of their servants.

References

1. Finkel, J., *King Mutton,* 1932, page 130; taken from *Tiraz al majalis* by Jafaji, page 176. See the essay cited in reference 4 for details.
2. Arberry, Professor A.J., 'A Baghdad Cookery Book', in *Islamic Culture* 13 (1939), (British Library shelfmark p.p. 978 fb), pages 21–47 and 189–214.
3. This bibliography, entitled *Fihrist,* was the work of Ibn al-Nadim, and was written in the year 988. An English translation by B. Dodge, entitled *The Fihrist of Ibn al-Nadim, a 10th century Survey of Muslim Culture,* was published by the Columbia University Press in 1979.
4. Rodinson, Professor Maxime, 'Récherches sur les Documents Arabes Rélatifs à la Cuisine', in the *Revue des Etudes Islamiques,* 1949, (British Library shelfmark p.p. 3807 dab), pages 95–165.
5. Rodinson, Professor Maxime, the entry 'Ghidha' in the *Encyclopaedia of Islam,* volume 2, fascicule 39, pages 1057–1072. Published by Brill, Leiden, 1965.
6. For a good survey of this subject, focussed on but not confined to writings in Elizabethan England, see Dr Jane O'Hara May's book, *Elizabethan Dyetary of Health,* Coronado Press (Box 3232, Lawrence, Kansas 66044, U.S.A.), 1977.
7. Rodinson, Professor Maxime, Venezia: 'Il Commercio delle Spezie e le Influenze Orientali sulla Cucina Europea', being a contribution to Il Primo Convegno dell' Accademia Italiana della Cucina, held in May 1967 in Venice: subsequently published in the Atti of the conference, 1968: pages 19–38.
8. It constitutes part of a manuscript which is in the Bibliothèque Nationale in Paris and which includes one other treatise on cookery besides material on agriculture.
9. As for reference 7: page 27.

Recipes from the Baghdad Cookery Book of 1226

RUTABIYA

Cut red meat into small, long thin slices: melt fresh tail, and throw out the sediment, then put the meat into the oil [i.e. rendered fat], adding half a dirham of salt and the same quantity of fine brayed [ground] dry coriander. Stir until browned. Then cover with lukewarm water, and when boiling, skim. Put in a handful of almonds and pistachios, peeled and ground coarsely, and colour with a little saffron. Throw in a fine-ground cumin, coriander, cinnamon and mastic, about 2½ dirhams in all. Take red meat as required, mince fine and make into long cabobs [meat rolls], placing inside each a peeled, sweet almond: put into the saucepan. Take sugar candy dates, or Medina dates, as required: extract the stone from the bottom with a needle, and put in its place a peeled sweet almond. When the meat is cooked and the liquor all evaporated so that only the oils remain, garnish with these dates. Sprinkle with about 10 dirhams of scented sugar, and a danaq of camphor: spray with a little rose water. Wipe the sides of the saucepan with a clean rag, and leave to settle over the fire for an hour: then remove.

This dish of meat (almost always lamb) and dates derives its inspiration from traditional Bedouin Arab food and its sophistication from ancient Persian ways.

Suggested quantities for 4 to 6 people

1 lb lean lamb, cubed
2 tablespoons oil
salt and black pepper
1 teaspoon ground coriander
2 oz blanched almonds or pistachio nuts, chopped
¼ teaspoon saffron (optional)
1 teaspoon ground cumin
1 teaspoon ground cinnamon
¼ teaspoon pulverized mastic (optional)
1 lb minced lamb, beef, or veal
¼ lb whole blanched almonds (to stuff the meat rolls and dates)
½ lb dried dates
1 teaspoon sugar (optional)
[leave out camphor]
1 teaspoon rose water

The preparation of this dish requires time and patience, especially in making the stuffed cabobs so that they do not come apart during the cooking.

But the results are well worth the effort. Cooking time should be 50 to 60 minutes, not counting the further hour during which the dish is to be kept hot while 'settling'. In practice the 'settling' seems to be an unnecessary refinement, if the garnish of stuffed dates is added 5 minutes before the end of the cooking, which I myself recommend.

Mishmishiya

A meat stew with apricots is named after the fruit.

> Cut fat meat small, put into the saucepan with a little salt, and cover with water. Boil and remove the scum. Cut up onions, wash, and throw in on top of the meat. Add seasonings, coriander, cumin, mastic, cinnamon, pepper and ginger, well ground. Take dry apricots, soak in hot water, then wash and put in a separate saucepan, and boil lightly: take out, wipe in the hands, and strain through a sieve. Take the juice, and add it to the saucepan to form a broth. Take sweet almonds, grind fine, moisten with a little apricot juice and throw in. Some colour with a trifle of saffron. Spray the saucepan with a little rose water, wipe its sides with a clean rag, and leave to settle over the fire: then remove.

Suggested quantities for 6 people

2 lb lean lamb, cubed
salt
1–2 onions, finely chopped
1/2–1 teaspoon ground coriander
1/2–1 teaspoon ground cumin
1/4 teaspoon pulverized mastic (optional)
1/4–1/2 teaspoon ground cinnamon
black pepper
1/4 teaspoon ground ginger
1/2 lb dried apricots, soaked and passed through a food mill
2 oz ground almonds
1/4 teaspoon saffron (optional)
1 teaspoon rose water

The stew requires about 1 1/2 hours of gentle cooking, preferably on an asbestos mat. Leave out the mastic and saffron if you wish—I do not think they are at all necessary.

The Saracen Connection: *Arab* Cuisine and the Mediaeval *West*

C ANNE WILSON

C Anne Wilson was for many years a librarian at the Brotherton Library of the University of Leeds. This library acquired two important collections of early cookery books. Attending to these gave Anne what became a lifelong interest in food history and led to the publication of her well known book Food and Drink in Britain *(first published by Constable in 1973). When she wrote the present essay she had been doing research into the French influence on English cookery from the 14th century onwards (see* PPC 2 *and* 4*). She then turned to consideration of how the foodstuffs and cuisine of the Saracens (as they were known to the medieval western world) influenced European cuisines. It is this latter topic which she explored in the present essay which appeared in two parts in* PPC 7 *and* 8*. It is the first part which we reproduce here. Anne Wilson's work in this field can be regarded as complementary to that of Claudia Roden (see the preceding essay). Both essays had a seminal influence on the development of food history studies.*

The experience of the Crusaders at the eastern end of the Mediterranean was to have considerable impact on the diet of western Europe. The Europeans who settled in the kingdom of 'Outremer' remained there for generations, enjoying a much higher standard of physical comfort than was available to most of their cousins in the West. Antioch was occupied by the Franks and their allies 1098–1268, Jerusalem 1099–1187, Tripoli 1109–1289, Acre 1189–1291; and even the 'County of Edessa' on the edge of ancient Babylonia was held for nearly 50 years. When they were not actually fighting over the holy places, the Franks lived on harmonious terms with the Saracens.

'For we who were occidentals have now become orientals,' wrote Fulcher of Chartres. 'He who was a Roman or a Frank has in this land been made into Galilean or a Palestinian. He who was of Rheims or Chartres has now become a citizen of Tyre or Antioch. We have already forgotten the places of our birth; already these are unknown to many of us, or not mentioned any more. Some already possess homes or households by inheritance. Some have taken wives not only of their own people, but Syrians or Armenians or even Saracens who have obtained the grace of baptism . . . People use the eloquence and idioms of diverse languages in conversing back and forth. Words of different languages have become common property . . . Our relatives and parents join us from time to time . . . Those who were poor in the occident, God makes rich in this land.'[1]

The Franks could therefore afford to indulge in Saracen cuisine at its best. Those who did eventually return to their former homes included members of the nobility or even royal families, like Eleanor of Aquitaine and her estranged husband Louis VII of France, who had responsibilities and properties in the West too great to be abandoned. They were the people best able to afford exotic ingredients of the type called for in Arab court cookery, and the introduction of Saracen-inspired dishes in the West began in noble and royal households.

The special nature of Saracen cuisine was due to the cultivation and use of some food plants that were little known, or even unknown in northwest Europe. These included sugar (a complete novelty to the Crusaders, who encountered and sucked upon the 'honey-cane', as they called it, while they were marching through the Syrian hinterland from Antioch to Jerusalem in 1099[2]); almonds and pistachios; rice; dried fruits, especially dates; citrus fruits and pomegranates; roses (in the form of rosewater, much used in Arabic medicine and food); and spinach. The Saracens also had access to a wider range of imported spices from India and the Far East than had hitherto reached the Westerners. In addition to those already well-known in royal and noble circles in western Europe, such as pepper, ginger and cinnamon, they used zedoary and galingale, mastic, cubebs, cloves, nutmegs and mace. All these were to be incorporated into western cookery before the end of the middle ages.[3]

The Baghdad cookery book of 1226[4] gives extensive examples of the types of dishes that many Crusaders may have been lucky enough to enjoy in the Saracen lands. Some of them may not have been totally strange to the newcomers. Both western European and eastern Arabic cookery had developed under the influence of Greek dietetics. Spicy meat stews existed in both cuisines; and spices did reach the West by overland trade routes through southern Russia and central Europe, and increasingly after the end of the eighth century by the Mediterranean sea-route. The West had thick cereal pottages, based on wheat for the wealthy (and more usually on barley, rye or oats for others), and honey as a sweetener. We do know that the sixth-century dietetic cookery-book of the Greek physician Anthimus was a guide for cooks in the West for some hundreds of years: several copies of the tenth, eleventh and twelfth centuries still exist, scattered around various European libraries. Apicius' Roman cookery book also survived in more than one version, and here too were to be found a number of recipes deriving from Greek dietetic cookery. Sadly, what we do not know is how a great feast was served at, say, the court of Charlemagne, and what sort of dishes were set before the emperor and his guests.[5]

The western European cookery books which we do have, from the thirteenth century onwards, show the influence of Saracen cuisine in many ways. By the time they were written, the new Saracen foodstuffs had become more easily obtainable in the West. Contacts between Saracen and European had increased there, too—in the Norman kingdom of Sicily, where Greeks, 'Latins' and Arabs created a shared culture; and in northern Spain (after 1085 when the Christians won back Toledo). Such crops as sugar, rice, citrus fruits, pomegranates and saffron were already being grown in the Arab West. Rice and the fruits were taken into cultivation in northern Italy. Saffron was eventually grown as far north as England, e.g. around Saffron Walden.

Saracen recipes became known in the West partly by direct translation, as in the *Liber de Coquina*. It is interesting to see that recipes such as *Limonia, sumacho, romania* (from Arabic *rumman:* pomegranates), which comprised chicken meat cooked with lemon, sumach and pomegranate juice respectively, still appear under their Arab names in the fifteenth century Italian translation of that book.[6] It is perhaps even more interesting to try to trace the influence of the trends, ideas and ingredients of Saracen cookery in the French and English recipe books from the late thirteenth century onwards.

Frying Before Boiling

First there is the matter of methods. In the Baghdad cookery book, the second and third chapters contain many recipes in which meat is cut up and browned or fried in fat before being boiled with a variety of vegetables and seasonings. This culinary idea was adopted by the French; it appears in several recipes in the earliest *Viandier* text (late thirteenth century), and even more often in the later texts. The English took to it less readily, but when they did practise it, they recognized its origins. In the *bruet of Sarcynesse,* beef 'beaten all to pieces' is breaded and fried in 'fresh grease' and then boiled in wine with sugar and powder of cloves, thus combining the method with some typical Saracen ingredients.[7]

Sweet-Sour Sauce

The sweet-sour sauce came from the Greek tradition and was already known in the West. Anthimus finished his stewed beef by adding to the stock vinegar and honey, with heads of leeks and herbs, followed by a further addition of spices.[8] But the Saracens created many varied sweet-sour sauces in which to cook their meat. The sweet element could be supplied by sugar, sugar-syrup, honey, date-juice or ripe grapes; the sour might be vinegar, pomegranate-juice, sour apple-juice, the juice of Seville-type oranges, lemons or citrons, and a selection of oriental spices was usually added.

In France the idea is translated into a northern version, again called *bruet Sarassinois* or *Saraginee.* The earliest recipes show it to have been made with sugar, which nearly always appears in recipes labelled 'Saracen', wine and verjuice (the sharp fruit vinegar produced in the north from unripe grapes or apples), and spiced with cinnamon and cloves. English sweet-sour sauce was acquired at two removes from the Saracens, and differs from the French *bruet* in including onions as well as spices and sometimes dried fruits.[9] But although it appears in the English books under the menu-French name *egerdouce,* the 'siryp' of sugar, wine and vinegar in the *Forme of Cury* recipe (no. 133) is clearly Saracenic ('syrup' is the westernised form of the Arabic *sharāb*).

COLOURING: WHITE, GREEN

A delight in the colour of foods was another aspect of Saracen cuisine which appealed to the Franks: rice gleaming white or made golden with saffron; eggs dyed vermilion, and sauces of the same hue; sweetmeats confected from pistachios or saffron-stained ground almonds. A poem recited before Mustakfi, Caliph of Baghdad 944–946, describes rice (*aruzza*) in these fulsome words:

> O glorious *aruzza*! What a boon . . .
> Purer than snow that hath been furrowed twice
> By handiwork of wind and frosted ice;
> Set out in ordered strips upon the dish,
> White as the whitest milk that heart could wish,
> Its brilliance dazzles the beholding eye
> As if the moon ere even shone in sky;
> While sugar sprinkled upon every side
> Flashes and gleams, like light personified.[10]

Food of such snowy whiteness was a novelty for the western Europeans. The frumenties and pottages available to them at home were no sort of equivalent to the Saracens' white dishes made with chicken-meat and almonds, rice and refined sugar; and these were the recipes which they took back to the West under the name of *blanc mange.* Other thick, pale-coloured pottages, such as *mawmeny* and *blanc dessors,* have the same basic ingredients, are enriched with Saracenic spices, almonds and dried fruits, and obviously derive from Arab cookery. But the western forms are further enriched with non-Saracenic wine.

Another novel pottage was the green version of blancmange which appears in the Baghdad cookery book under the name *fustaqīya,* from the Arab word which has given us 'pistachio'.[11] Concocted from cooked chicken breasts teased into threads, combined with equal quantities both of sugar and of the pounded nuts, it is clearly a dish which closely parallels the almond blancmange in the recipes adopted in the West (not to be found in the Baghdad book, perhaps because it was so commonplace among the Saracens). But the pistachio version was not transferred to the European cookery books, and in fact green pistachios almost never appear there. Even in the Saracen recipes, they are much rarer than almonds, which may reflect personal tastes, or perhaps some difficulties in cultivating the trees. In the West, almonds became by far the most commonly used nuts in the cuisine of the great households for which the cookery books were compiled, with pine kernels a poor second.

Colouring: Yellow and Red

Despite the pleasure the Saracens took in shining white rice, red and yellow foodstuffs may have appealed to them even more, for these carried the magic colours of alchemy. While much of the Arabs' alchemical lore had come to them from the Greeks, some had travelled along the trade routes from distant China. There, in the hands of Taoist masters, alchemy had developed along somewhat different lines. When they tried to make alchemical gold from sulphur and cinnabar (alias vermilion, the brilliant red mineral sulphide of mercury also used as a dye), they did so with the aim of transferring the longevity of gold to human beings. The most dedicated Taoists even consumed small quantities of cinnabar and other minerals, thus shortening their own lives. But since the minerals trapped in their bodies actually helped to preserve them from decay, that was taken as a proof that their search for an alchemical elixir of life had already achieved some success. Those who were not willing to risk eating the minerals were recommended to prolong their lives by consuming their food from vessels made of alchemical gold.[12]

The Arabs reinterpreted this view of the elixir; and while their alchemists were still striving to transmute base metals and minerals into gold, their physicians were recommending real gold as the medicine that would lengthen the span of human life. They urged their patients to swallow shavings of the precious metal along with food (and rumours to that effect may have lain behind the massacre of two or three thousand prisoners in 1191, during the third Crusade, by Crusaders who burned the corpses in the hope of picking up a fortune out of the ashes[13]).

In the 'chemia' of the Greeks, great stress was laid upon the importance of golden colour as a vital property of gold, and that idea too appears to have passed into Arab dietetics. It would account for the special popularity of saffron as a food colouring, well attested in the recipes of the Baghdad cookery book. The same theme of goldenness was expressed in the garnish of the 'eyes of eggs' (yolks) allowed to set over the hot cooked ingredients of several meat dishes.[14]

Sauces were served in yellow and red dishes (the colours of gold and cinnabar) at the court of the Caliph of Baghdad at least as early as the end of the ninth century. Vermilioned eggs, still a symbol of resurrection and immortality in Greece today, are mentioned in an Arabic poem by Kushajim (915–967), and they too represented the sulphur and cinnabar of alchemical gold, and thus the elixir of life.[15]

Recipes for red foodstuffs in the Baghdad cookery book are rarer than for golden saffroned dishes, but a few can be found there. *Ribasīyah* was made from mutton cooked in a sauce of red-currant juice (distant forebear of our lamb with red-currant jelly). *Kamakh* was a savoury relish, sometimes coloured with dried red rose-petals, and sometimes perhaps with vermilion itself. Another relish, *milh mutayyab,* was either yellowed with saffron, or 'may also be coloured with sumach-juice or vermilion'. This does sound as though the idea of adding cinnabar to foodstuffs had reached the Saracens from China.[16]

In the West coloured foods became very popular. Saffron was put into the dishes of the French and English mediaeval cookery books perhaps even more readily than into those of the Baghdad book. A red colour was achieved with Indian sandalwood, which came West on the spice ships along with pepper and other Indian spices; or with alkanet, derived from the roots of a south European borage. It could also be created from rosehips (a western variant on the Saracens' dried red rose-petals, and more readily available since the scarlet hips of wild roses would have served). *Sawse Sarzyne* in the *Forme of Cury* (no. 84) was made from rosehips pounded in a mortar with blanched fried almonds, red wine, sugar and spice-powder, thickened with rice flour and further reddened with alkenet. All these ingredients (except the wine) were typically Saracenic, and the dish could be enriched with cooked capon teased into threads, so that it became another coloured version of blancmange.

Saffron had been used in the West since Roman times, though perhaps only intermittently. But the Westerners do seem to have seen red as a typically Saracenic food colour. Later they favoured it for their winter dishes, to make them glow warmly on the board. As for the elixir of life, that quest too passed over to Europe via Arabic Spain. But Latin scholars reinterpreted it once more in medical terms, and the notion that yellow and red foodstuffs might carry some of its properties faded away.

Almonds

Most of the culinary uses which the Saracens found for almonds were transferred to western cookery. 'Take a portion of sweet almonds, peel, grind fine, stir in water, and add to the saucepan, making a broth as desired of the milk of almond', says the recipe in the Baghdad cookery book with the Persian name *isfidbaja,* which means 'white gruel'.[17] The almond milk was added to a stew of pieces of mutton, with spices, onions and chick-peas.

In the West, almond milk was frequently called for in the recipe books of the nobility. The ground almonds were drawn through a strainer with wine, broth or water; and the thicker forms of almond cream and almond butter were also made. Both almond milk and almond butter were especially in demand on the Church's fasting days, when the consumption of animal milk and butter was prohibited. Ground almonds thickened blancmange and similar standing pottages, and they were an ingredient of marzipan.

Marzipan

Marzipan was once thought to have been invented, or at least to have acquired its name, in Italy. But the chapter on *halwa* (cake) in the Baghdad cookery book soon shows us that its origins are to be sought in lands further east. In it several recipes appear that are clearly for confections of marzipan type. They are made with either ground almonds or ground pistachios together with varying proportions of sugar, honey, sugar syrup, sometimes with the addition of a little oil and wheat starch; they are scented with rosewater, and in the case of the almond pastes are further coloured with saffron.[18]

There is some evidence that in thirteenth-century France, the nobility enjoyed pistachio marzipan.[19] But by far the most usual type in the West was that made from almonds. The last of the Baghdad cookery book's *halwa* recipes has the sugar and almond paste thickened with cornstarch, and set in carved wooden moulds in the shapes of fishes, loaves, cocks, lambs, etc. Here must be the inspiration for the 'sotelties', cunningly constructed marzipan and sugar-paste figures forming little scenes, that were presented at the end of each course of a great feast in mediaeval western Europe.

The name of the confection in its various forms—French *massepain,* Italian *marzapana,* Spanish *mazapana*—has been a puzzle. 'Pain' or 'pana,' it is thought, means bread. But what about 'maza' or 'masse'? I would suggest that it arose from the experience of the Franks and other Westerners in Outremer. They encountered Saracen food and also Saracen alchemy, and may have been aware of the echoes of the alchemical elixir of life in the dietary of the Arabs. The Saracen name for the art was *alkhimia.* But the Franks called it by a Greek word, *maza* (Latinised as *massa*), which had earlier been a term for the bronze used in some of the experiments.[20] For the Franks, the delicious golden pastes of sugar, ground almonds and saffron may well have seemed magical creations, brought into being by the alchemy of the Saracen cooks, and thus earning the name of *maza pana*—alchemical bread.

Endoring

Another novelty for the Westerners in Outremer was the citrus fruits, especially the oranges and lemons whose juice and pulp went into some of the sweet-sour sauces. The bitter oranges of the period could not be eaten raw with pleasure, so their culinary use approximated to that of lemons. But one recipe in the Baghdad cookery book shows that the Saracens enjoyed counterfeit oranges instead, in a dish entitled *nāranjīya* (from *naranj,* the Persian word for orange). Finely minced red meat, seasoned and spiced, was made into balls the size of oranges which were cooked through. They were then dipped into egg yolks beaten with a little saffron and put to cook again, the process being repeated three times. Shortly before serving they were sprinkled with chopped sweet almonds, and with real orange and lemon juice.[21]

Here we have another example of golden food from Saracen lands which passed into western culture. The recipe was taken over and adapted by the Franks, as was the whole idea of 'endoring' food for special feasts. Rounded rissoles of the type in the *nāranjīya* recipe were endored with egg yolks and saffron and served under the name *pommes d'orenge;* and sometimes they were greened by adding chopped parsley or other greenstuff to the egg yolks (making them simply *pommes*). *Pommes d'orenge* were also confected in England, where they were endored and roasted on little hazelwood spits that were tied to a longer spit. Whole chickens were endored too, to be served with endored *pommes* of stuffing.

Oranges and Lemons

Real oranges and lemons did have a role in western cookery, though at first it was a small one. In France bitter orange juice was eaten as a sauce, or mixed into other sauces in place of verjuice (approximately the same usage as in Arab cookery); while the peels were candied and consumed as sweetmeats. In Italy, according to the *Libro della Cucina,* orange or lemon juice also went into pork pies and stand pies of such oily fish as eels, lampreys, trout and even squids.[22] The Italians were able to cultivate citrus fruits in certain parts of their country, even as far north as Lake Garda, so to them they were not perhaps quite such a luxury as to their northern neighbours. North-west Europe had to import oranges and lemons from Spain and Portugal, and for a long time they remained very expensive in relation to other foodstuffs. The candying of the skins ensured that as little as possible was wasted.

The art of candying first developed in the West in that part of the Iberian peninsula which was under Arab rule, since there both sugar and citrus fruits were available. Orange and lemon peels, candied either wet, in syrup, or dry, were exported to northern France and England where they were known as 'succade'. Once sugar became a little more plentiful in northern Europe, not only were orange peels candied in the wealthier households, but also a number of home-grown roots and herbs, such as eringo and angelica. The art of candying which thus developed reached its apogee in the sixteenth and seventeenth centuries; for this was an area of food preservation where the impact of Saracen influence was felt very gradually over some hundreds of years.

[Editor's note: This article was to be concluded in a subsequent issue of *PPC*. To round off this first part, Anne Wilson supplied a pertinent recipe from the Baghdad cookery book of 1226. The italicised version is a straightforward translation of the original. What follows is an interpretation for use today.]

Almond or Pistachio Paste from the Baghdad Cookery Book of 1226

Makshufa

Take equal parts of sugar, almonds (or pistachios), honey, and sesame-oil. Grind the sugar and almonds and mix together. Add saffron to colour, mixed with rose-water. Put the sesame-oil into a basin, and boil until fragrant: then drop in the honey, and stir until the scum appears. Add the sugar and almonds, stirring all the time over a slow fire until almost set: then remove.

Ingredients

4 oz sugar
4 oz ground almonds or pistachios
4 oz honey
very little saffron steeped in 2 tablespoons of rose-water
sesame oil

Mix sugar and ground almonds/pistachios, and add rosewater with saffron. Heat honey in large basin over boiling water, and stir in 2 tablespoons of oil (if sesame oil is not obtainable, ground nut oil may be used, but the final flavour will be slightly different). Add other ingredients gradually to honey in basin, constantly stirring and keeping water simmering beneath. If too stiff, add a little more oil. (The recipe implies 4 oz unrefined sesame oil, but this was probably reduced when boiled 'until fragrant', and it is best to proceed carefully, adding not much at a time.)

References

1. Fulcher of Chartres, *A history of the expedition to Jerusalem, 1095–1127,* trans. F.R. Ryan and ed. H.S. Fink, 1973, pp. 271–2.
2. *Ibid.,* pp. 130–1.
3. Mastic, a resin from the lentisk, a tree of the same genus as the pistachio, was never very much used in the West, though it is listed with other spices in later mss. Of Taillevent's *Viandier* (ed. J. Pichon and G. Vicaire, 1892, p. 96; 250).

4. 'A Baghdad Cookery Book, (1226)', trans. and ed. A.J. Arberry, *Islamic Culture,* 13 (1939), hereafter referred to as BCB.
5. Charlemagne 'rarely gave banquets and these only on high feast days, but then he would invite a great number of guests. His main meal of the day was served in four courses, in addition to the roast meat which his hunters used to bring in on spits, and which he enjoyed more than any other food.' Einhard the Frank, *The Life of Charlemagne,* c. 830, trans. L. Thorpe, Folio Society, 1970, p. 64.
6. *PPC 6* (1980), p. 24; *Libro della cucina,* ed. F. Zambrini, 1863, pp. 44–5. In the English recipe for a similar dish (Warner, R., ed., *Antiquitates culinariae,* 1791, Ancient cookery III, p. 84) the name is changed to *garnade* (from 'pomme garnade' = pomegranate).
7. Warner, op cit., Ancient cookery II, recipe no. 54. For Viandier texts, see 'The French connection, part 1', *PPC 2* (1979), pp. 10 f.
8. Anthimus, *De observatione ciborum,* ed. E. Liechtenhan, 1963, p. 4.
9. The onions may be due to confusion with a rather similarly-named French recipe, the *soringue.* The origin of this name is uncertain. It may derive from Anthimus' 'sodinga' (= a cooking vessel: Anthimus, p. 4.) The sauce contains wine and vinegar, but is unsweetened.
10. BCB, intro., p. 27.
11. BCB, p. 197. For western blancmange, see *PPC 4* (1980), p. 17.
12. Davis, L.T., 'An ancient Chinese treatise on alchemy . . . about 142 A.D.', *Isis,* 18 (1932), pp. 210–26. For the fullest up-to-date account of Chinese alchemy, see relevant volumes of Needham, J., *Science and Civilisation in China,* 1954–.
13. Heer, F., *The Medieval World,* trans. J. Sondheimer, N.Y., 1963, p. 136. The idea of eating gold shavings was adopted in the West from Arabic medicine in the thirteenth century, and is mentioned by several writers including Arnald of Villanova.
14. BCB, p. 39, etc.
15. BCB, intro., p. 21; 23.
16. BCB, intro., p. 21; 38; 207–8. It is just possible that the name 'vermilion' was also applied to some red vegetable dye that would have been less dangerous than cinnabar with its mercury content.
17. BCB, p. 46. Almonds themselves are symbols of the Creator and of life in the pre-Islamic religions of the Middle East, which may partly explain why the Arabs favoured them so much as a foodstuff.
18. BCB, pp. 210–2.
19. Mead, W.E., *The English Medieval Feast,* 1931, p. 164, quoting Le Grand d'Aussy, *La vie privée des françois d'autrefois,* ed. de Roquefort, vol. 2, p. 317. I have not had the chance to verify this reference.
20. Berthelot, M.P., *Collection des anciens alchimistes grecs,* 1887–8, vol. 1, p. 209.
21. BCB, p. 190.
22. *The Goodman of Paris,* ed. E. Power, 1928, p. 288; 307; *Libro della cucina,* pp. 63–8. In France and England, orange peels were at first candied with honey. *Goodman,* pp. 207–8.

On Swans, Cranes and Herons:

Part 3, Herons

JOOP WITTEVEEN

The author, who has been an eminent food historian in the Netherlands for three decades or more, has tackled one important subject after another during this period, often sharing the fruits of his work with PPC *or the Oxford Symposium on Food. His astonishingly precise chronicle of the progress of the potato northwards through the Netherlands from the 16th till the 20th century, and its corresponding infiltra tion of early Dutch cookery books earned him at Oxford the nickname 'Mr Potato'. Recently, in 1998, he and his partner Bart Cuperus published* Bibliotheca Gastronomica, *a monumental two-volume bibliography of 'books on food and drink printed in the Netherlands and Belgium up to 1960', recently also on CD-ROM, and much connected material in various languages.*

In contrast to cranes, which are migratory birds, most herons (*Ardea cinerea* L.) remain in their habitat all through the year.

Herons usually breed together in large numbers in so-called colonies or heronries. They build their nests in high trees in areas abounding in water and fish. In former times, they often shared the territory with cormorants, egrets, night herons and bitterns. In the Middle Ages, all these birds, except the cormorant, were eaten by the nobility at festive meals. The cormorant was considered fit to be consumed by the lower ranks of society only.

The habitats where all these birds used to breed together in large numbers have disappeared from Western Europe. One would have to go to the riverine woods of Yugoslavia, along the rivers Drava and Danube at the Hungarian border, to find nearly all the species of birds which, in the Middle Ages, were hunted for food.

Heron Hunting

The practice of hunting herons had been described in 1235 by Emperor Frederick II of Hohenstaufenin his book *De arte venandi cum avibus* ('The Art of Falconry'). In this book, the emperor explained how the falcon or goshawk was trained to hawk herons—an unusual prey for wild falcons and hawks. To train the falcon, domesticated herons were used, taken out of the nest when young and fed with fish by men. According to the emperor, it was simple to domesticate the young herons, as they opened their beaks wide immediately to receive food when they were approached. In this way, they became accustomed to men. As soon as the young heron was able to fly, it was suitable for the training of falcons.

First, the tame heron was tied up with a bait fixed on its back, on which the falcon had to swoop down. Having accomplished this, the falcon was given the bait to eat. The second step was to teach the falcon to swoop down on a flying heron. A well-trained falcon could recognize a flying heron from a far distance and rush towards it, approaching it from behind and above, to swoop down on it and drop to the ground with its prey. The falconer then killed the heron and the falcon received a piece of it as a reward.[104]

In a similar way, falcons were trained to hawk cranes. It should be noted that each falcon was trained to hawk one specific species of bird.

Hawking, already known as early as the 8th century, remained in vogue until the middle of the 17th century. King Louis XIII of France (1610–43) was a great devotee of hawking. He owned a falcon court that was divided in eight departments, one of which was designated for heron-hawking. This department consisted of a falconer, twelve falcons, four greyhounds and sixteen servants. His successor, Louis XIV (1643–1715), also used to hawk in the early years of his reign and paid an annual sum of 10,000 francs for maintenance and protection of the heronries, including the famous heronry at Fontainebleau.[105] However, he soon ceased to allocate money for this purpose.

Falconry was pursued by the nobility throughout Western Europe and was once held in high esteem. It was not unusual for members of the nobility to have their portraits painted, depicting them with their favourite falcon, to show their attachment to the falcon and falconry.

Heron Harvest

In the Netherlands numerous data have been preserved about the heron. The 13th century Dutch poet Maerlant mentions two species of herons, a white one and a grey one. The grey heron tasted best and had the healthiest meat. The fat of this heron was expensive because it was used as a medicine against gout. The white heron must have been the egret, *Egretta garzetta,* a rather small variety. Recipes for egret can be found in the 14th and 15th century English cookery books.[106]

As early as the 13th century famous heronries existed in the Netherlands at Berkenrode, near Haarlem and in the Bijlmermeer, near Amsterdam.[107] In the 14th century heronries are mentioned in the vicinity of Gouda, the Gouda Forest and the Zevenhuizen Forest. The latter forest existed till about 1700 and was famous. In 1651 this forest was 750 metres long and 350 metres wide,

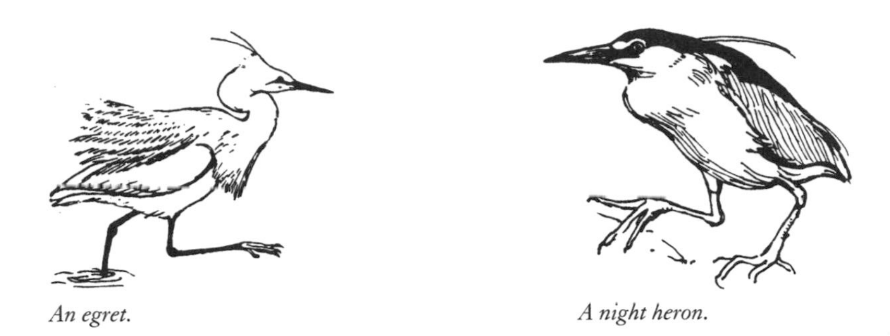

An egret. *A night heron.*

in all about 75 acres. In this heronry herons as well as cormorants, night herons and spoonbills[108] used to breed. All these birds were eaten, but the grey heron was most appreciated. Physicians, however, believed that the heron was strong-scented and unwholesome. They advised that it should be eaten only when young.[109] This advice was in accordance with the public belief of how herons should be eaten.

When the young herons were fully developed and about to leave the nest, the owner of the heronry shook them out of their nests. The young birds, still unable to fly, tumbled to the ground and were easily caught. Cormorants and night herons were given a similar treatment, after which the young birds were sold by the proprietor. The herons and night herons were meant for the tables of the rich, the cormorant for the commoners.

In 1357, as many as 564 herons and 2000 night herons from the Gouda Forest[110] were sold.

In the 17th century, the shaking down of the young birds in the Zevenhuizen Forest was a curiosity that attracted many spectators, natives as well as foreigners. Famous spectators were, for example, the English biologists John Ray and Francis Willoughby in 1663:

A young heron.

> We made a by-journey to Sevenhuys . . . to see a remarkable grove, where in time of year, several sorts of wild fowl build and breed. We observed there in great numbers cormorants . . . spoonbills, quacks [night herons] . . . and . . . herons. Each sort of fowl hath its own quarters. When the young are ripe, they who farm the grove, with an iron hook fastened to the end of a long pole, lay hold on the bough on which the nest is built, and shake the young ones out, and sometimes nest and all down to the ground . . . This place is rented for 3000 guilders per annum . . . only for the birds and grass.[111]

In 1668, the Emperor's commissioner from Vienna visited the Zevenhuizen Forest. On the day of his visit, 400 to 500 herons and cormorants were shaken out of their nests. The shaking at that time was practised twice a week during the breeding season. The number of breeding birds had by then lessened. Twenty years earlier about 800 birds could be collected in one day. The decrease was attributed to the dying off of the trees, caused by the excrement of the birds.[112]

The young birds were transported to the Dutch cities and sold at the markets. A publication dating from 1627 shows that during the reign of James I (1603-25), two shiploads of these birds, but not including cormorants, were exported to England annually.[113]

In the first half of the 17th century the heronry of Berkenrode, which had then been in existence for over 400 years, had been the hawking ground of the Dutch Stadholders, the princes Maurice and Frederick-Henry. At that time the heronry counted a thousand couples of herons.[114]

In a heronry, the breeding season started in late February and early March, but not all herons hatched at the same time. Consequently, edible herons were available from early May until the end of July. Household accounts of the Bishop of Utrecht dating from 1377–8[115] and those of the Count of Holland, William of Bavaria, dating from 1401,[116] show that in the Netherlands herons were eaten in these months only. Herons were not only eaten at banquets but were a daily fare on the days when meat was allowed: Sunday, Monday, Tuesday and Thursday. At this time of year other game birds weren't yet available; herons were the first game after the winter season.

The Preparation of Herons

The Netherlands

From the Northern Netherlands, no heron recipes have survived. The first known recipe originated in the Southern Netherlands and dates back to the second half of the 15th century. The heron was basted with fat during the roasting and the sauce was made with wine, spices and drippings.[117]

An early 16th century recipe was more detailed. The heron was roasted with its feet left on, and if the bird contained not enough fat of its own, it had to be basted. The sauce was made in the usual way: roasted bread was soaked in wine and vinegar and drawn through a strainer, then diluted with wine and vinegar and spiced with pepper. Then the drippings were added and cooked until the sauce thickened.[118] Instead of pepper, a mixture of cinnamon, ginger, saffron and grains of Paradise was sometimes used.[119]

The Sensible Cook, published in Amsterdam in 1667, noted that herons and swans were household foodstuff, but no recipes were mentioned.[120]

Herons were also kept in captivity and fattened, as practised by the monks of the Abbey of Egmond near Alkmaar in 1566/7.[121]

France

In France, about 1300, the heron was hung for two or three days before its preparation.[122] It was then plucked and cut open from head to shoulders to let it bleed. The blood wasn't used for the sauce but thrown away. Subsequently, the heron, with its wings, leg and neck still on it, was put into boiling water. (Whether or not the bird was boiled, and if so, for how long is not recorded.) At this point, the wings were cut off and the heron was spitted and roasted. It was eaten with fine-grained salt only.[123] Until after 1500 the heron as well as the crane was prepared and consumed thus.[124]

At the end of the 14th century a more complicated way of preparing was practised. The heron was prepared as described above and after the roasting the bird was 'gilded', that is coated with egg yolks beaten with pulverized saffron, and roasted a little while longer until the coating turned golden brown. Sometimes the gilding was green, due to the use of parsley, spinach or sorrel instead of saffron. The leaves were pounded in a mortar and drawn through a strainer with the beaten egg yolks.[125] The yellow or green gilded heron was eaten with fine-grained salt[126] or with a *sauce cameline.*[127] In winter, this sauce was served cooked. During the summer it was served cold and uncooked.[128]

About 1400, the well-to-do burghers of Paris had the heron served in the second course of the meal.[129]

By the end of the 15th century, the heron was basted with lard during the roasting,[130] which was also customary in the Southern Netherlands.

From the 16th and the first half of the 17th century no French cookery books or recipe collections have survived. To find data on the preparation of herons as well as cranes, we have to search elsewhere. As sciences were then beginning to develop, we should best turn to books on natural history. Around the middle of the 16th century, the first books describing birds, fishes and other animals appeared in print. These books were shaped after the somewhat older herbals, which described mainly edible and medicinal plants. The books about birds and fishes also described mostly edible species and they often contained observations on the gastronomic qualities of the animals.

The best known French 16th century bird book was written in 1555 by Pierre Belon and called *History of the nature of birds.*[131] Belon treated all birds which were edible as well as a few which then weren't, such as the parrot and the turkey. However, it was not long before the turkey ranked high as a bird to be eaten during festive meals.

According to Belon, the heron was foodstuff fit for kings, and this was why the French nobility took pains to be able to eat herons, preferably young ones. The heron was thought to be much more delicate than the crane.[132]

As for the preparation, Belon remarked that the heron, like all birds, should be larded before roasting and then set aside to cool, since roasted meat eaten cold was considered healthier, whereas boiled meat was to be eaten hot. The French thought it to be a sign of bad taste when no sauce was served with a roasted bird.[133]

The carving of the birds had to be executed at the dinner table. To be a good carver, Belon stated, was one of the qualities of a nobleman. In some nations, however, notably in Florence, the carving was done in the kitchen rather than at the dinner table, and the bird was served cut into pieces.[134]

At the elaborate and sumptuous banquet offered by the Bishop of Liège in 1557 on the occasion of his accession to office, roasted herons and cranes were served in the first course. Roasted swans were served in the second course, as was customary in France. In the third course, roasted wild swans were served and once again, roasted crane. Furthermore, there were crane and heron pies, covered with gold leaf and decorated with the necks and heads, wings and tails of the cranes and herons. The birds, carrying banners, looked as if they were still alive and sitting on the pies. The big roasted birds which were served cold carried banners too, and their long legs were covered with gold leaf.[135]

As mentioned before, Louis XIII was a devotee of hawking and the young Louis XIV enjoyed hawking as well. It is therefore hardly surprising to find a heron recipe in La Varenne's *Le Cuisinier François* (1651):

> Pluck it and empty it; next you search for the six bitter [areas] on its body, and for a seventh one, which is on the inside; bind the legs along the thighs and blanch it over the fire, and lard it and wrap a buttered piece of paper around its neck, and roast it then, and when done, serve it.[136]

The heron was served without sauce in the second course. To make the presentation of a roast platter more appealing, La Varenne advised decorating the platter with flowers.[137]

In France between 1650 and 1670, the heron, along with the crane and the swan, disappeared from the menu of the king and the nobility.[138] In the same period, hawking ceased to be a favourite sport, and a few years after the beginning of his reign, in 1661, Louis XIV stopped the allocation of funds for the maintenance and protection of the heronry at Fontainebleau.[139]

England

The 14th century English recipes for heron were the same as for crane: 'Cranes and herons shall be larded with lard of swine, roasted and eaten with ginger.'[140]

The sauce was made of roasted bread, soaked in vinegar, ginger, galingale and the blood of the heron or the crane. The blood was used to colour the sauce and to thicken it. Very dark roasted bread was sometimes used instead of blood.[141]

In the 15th century, the heron and the crane were roasted in the same way as in the previous century, and the sauce, too, is similar: mustard, vinegar and ginger powder,[142] or a *sauce cameline.*[143] These sauces were given only in autumn and winter. In summer, the young herons were served without a sauce, just sprinkled with salt and ginger powder.[144] Herons were a part of the second course of the meal[145] and sometimes part of the first one.[146]

Carving was done as follow: 'Unlace them, break off the pinnions, neck and beak, than raise the legs and let the feet be on still, than the wings.'[147]

At the end of the 16th century and at the beginning of the 17th century, the nobility still ate herons. In 1605 the Lords of the Privy Council of the King ate them every Wednesday in September and October in the Star Chamber, during their meetings.[148] The sauce for herons was the Galandine, which was also served with cranes.[149] Herons were now also cooked in pies:

> Trusse them, and parboyle them but upon one side. Season them with Pepper, Salt and Ginger. Put them in deepe coffins with store of Butter and let the heads hang out for a show.[150]

Italy

In Italy, we find the earliest recipe for heron in the cookery book of Maestro Martino, written in the middle of the 15th century. Martino worked as a cook for the Patriarch of Aquileia. This city is located amidst the lagoons north-east of Venice, a region abounding in water and an excellent habitat for herons and other waterfowl. Maestro Martino stuffed the herons—as well as swans, cranes, storks, wild geese and ducks—with garlic or onions before he roasted them before the fire.[151]

Messisbugo, head of the household of the reigning d'Este family in Ferrara, stated in 1549 that the heron was suitable to be served at festive occasions.[152] The environment of Ferrara, at that time very watery and a perfect habitat for herons, was in 1598 reclaimed by Dutch engineers.[153]

Germany

The southern part of Germany was unfit for herons to breed and in the cookery books published in that part of Germany, recipes for herons are lacking. The heron was only mentioned in the book of Marx Rumpoldt (1581), cook of the bishop of Mainz. Without giving recipes he noted that the heron should be prepared in the same way as other big birds such as the swan, bustard and turkey.[154]

However, Frantz de Rontzier (1598), living at the court in Wolffenbuttel near Braunschweig in northern Germany, gave four recipes. He began his chapter on herons with the lapidary line: 'The taste of a heron is almost equal to fish.' His recipes were more advanced than the French and the English ones of that time. He used fewer spices, no cinnamon, only pepper or a combination of pepper and mace, ginger, or cloves. For basting, butter and olive oil were suggested.

De Rontzier soaked the cleaned heron in water overnight. On the following morning he washed it in vinegar brought to a boil. It was then ready for further preparation. The four recipes are as follows:

1. Put the butter and pepper in the inside of the heron and roast it; when it has browned, wrap it in thin slices of lard, sprinkled with pepper; let it roast until done and before serving sprinkle it with salt and pepper.

2. Stick cloves in the outside of the heron, roast it and baste it with butter; cook onions in wine and draw them through a cloth, add pepper and mace and pour it over the heron. If there should be too much sauce, boil it down by laying coals under the dripping pan.

3. Lard the heron with small pieces of lard and roast it; cook the drippings with wine vinegar and pepper and pour it over the heron; when it is served, sprinkle with salt and pepper.

4. Roast the heron and baste it with olive oil and when it is done, add pepper and ginger to the drippings. When the heron is served, pour the sauce over it and sprinkle with salt and pepper.[155]

De Rontzier also made heron pies, and just as in the Netherlands, he decorated them with the head, wings and tail of the bird. In the same way he decorated peacock, turkey, and pheasant pies, but he left swan pies undecorated.

Sometimes he stuffed the heron's skin with cotton and shaped it like a living bird and placed it on top of the pie. The legs and bill were gilded or silvered and a gilded apple, or flowers, or a wax figuring were put in its beak. On some occasions the heron was made to spit fire.[156]

* * * *

Swans, cranes and herons were not the only great birds eaten in Europe from the Middle Ages to the Renaissance; there was also the peacock. I hope to write about this bird before long, and also, as foreshadowed in the earlier parts of the present essay, to make some general comments on all these great birds, connecting the cooking and eating of them to the notions of chivalry prevalent at the time.

References

104. Wood and Fyfe, *op cit* (ref 53), p 318.

105. De Swaen, A.E.H., *De valkerij in de Nederlanden*, Zutphen, 1937, pp 18–19.

106. Verwijs, *op cit* (ref 78), vol I, p 180, lines 307–9, and p 181, lines 320–1.

107. De Swaen, *op cit,* p 27.

108. Brouwer, *op cit* (ref 50), pp 18–19.

109. Merula, Paulus, *Placaten ende Ordinancien op't stuck van de Wildernissen in Orde ghestelt,* 's-Gravenhage, 1605, p. 40.

110. Brouwer, *op cit,* pp 37–8.

111. Ray, John, *Travels through the Low Countries, Germany, Italy and France,* 2nd edn, London, 1738, vol I, p 33.

112. 'Briefwisseling tusschen de Gebroeders van der Goes, 1659–1673', in *Werken van het Historisch Genootschap,* series 3, vol X, Utrecht, 1899, p 447.

113. Brouwer, *op cit,* pp 18–19.

114. De Swaen, *op cit,* p 27.

115. Vermeulen, J. P., 'De Bischoppelijke Rekening van 1377–1378', in *Codex Diplomaticus Neerlandicus,* 2nd series, vol II, pt 1, Utrecht, 1853, pp 252–470.

116. 'Keukenrekening der Grafelijkheid van Holland en Zeeland, 1401', in *Kroniek van het Historisch Genootschap,* 2nd series, year 8, Utrecht, 1852, pp 126–49.

117. Keukenboek, *op cit* (ref 37), p 4.

118. *Een Notabel Boecxken Van Cokeryen, op cit* (ref 38), p 21.

119. Cockx-Indestege, *op cit* (ref 100), pp 165, 173, 177.

120. *De Verstandige Kock,* Amsterdam, 1667, fol 2 recto.

121. Henrik van Wyn, *Huiszittend Leeven,* vol I, Amsterdam, 1804, pp 387–9.

122. Baudet, *op cit* (ref 77), p. 80.

123. Aebischer, *op cit* (ref 17), p 90; Lozinski, *op cit* (ref 7), p 183; Brereton and Ferrier, *op cit* (ref 2), p 228.

124. Pichon and vicaire, *op cit* (ref 3), pp 19, 90, 186.

125. *Ibid,* pp 13, 17, 90; Brereton and Ferrier, *op cit* (ref 2), p 228.

126. Pichon and Vicaire, *op cit* (ref 3), p 186.

127. *Ibid,* p 90.

128. Brereton and Ferrier, *op cit* (ref 2), p 258.

129. *Ibid,* p 179.

130. Pichon and Vicaire, *op cit* (ref 3), p 186.
131. Belon, *op cit* (ref 82), p 132.
132. *Ibid,* p 190.
133. *Ibid,* p 53.
134. *Ibid,* p 52.
135. De Casteau, *op cit* (ref 4), pp 147–53. Léo Moulin, one of the editors of Casteau, translated the *Ouverture de Cuisine* into modern French. In the first course of the Banquet of 1557 were served, among other dishes, 'Grue rostie en olives' and 'Craemsvogel rosty'. Moulin translated the Dutch word 'craemsvogel' as 'grue' (crane), but the correct translation is 'grive' (thrust).
136. Flandrin, J. L. and Hyman, Philip and Mary (ed), *Le Cuisinier François,* Montalba, Paris, 1983, p 165.
137. *Ibid,* pp 158–9.
138. Wheaton, *op cit* (ref 83), p. 103,
139. De Swaen, *op cit,* pp 18–19.
140. Hieatt and Butler, *op cit* (ref 1), pp 62, 131; Warner, *op cit* (ref 1), p 37.
141. Hieatt and Butler, *op cit* (ref 1), p 85.
142. Austin, *op cit* (ref 1), p 116.
143. *The Book of Kervynge, op cit* (ref 88).
144. *Ibid.*
145. Hieatt and Butler, *op cit* (ref 1), p 39; Austin, *op cit* (ref 1), pp 59, 61, 63, 68; *The Book of Kervynge, op cit* (ref 88); A. W., *A Book of Cookrye, op cit* (ref 94), fol 2 recto; Thomas Dawson, *The good huswifes Jewell* (1596), reprinted by Theatrum Orbis Terrarum, Amsterdam, 1977, fol 1 verso.
146. Austin, *op cit* (ref 1), pp 57, 62, 69.
147. *The Book of Kervynge, op cit.*
148. Simon, André L., *op cit* (ref 32), pp 65–7.
149. A. W., *op cit,* fol 4 recto.
150. Murrell, John, *A new Booke of Cookery* (1615), reprinted by Theatrum Orbis Terrarium, Amsterdam, 1972, p 30.
151. Faccioli, *op cit* (ref 73), vol I, Maestro Martino, p 120.
152. *Ibid,* vol I, Cristoforo Messisburgo, p 267.
153. Slicher van Bath, B.H., *Agrarische Geschiedenis van West-Europa,* Het Spectrum, Utrecht/Antwerpen, 1960, p 221.
154. Rumpoldt, *op cit* (ref 5), fol LXX recto.
155. De Rontzier, *op cit* (ref 49), p 195.
156. *Ibid,* pp 305-19, 327–8.

Historic Kitchen Restoration: The Example of Ham House

CAROLINE DAVIDSON

Recently, an increasing number of houses open to the public have allowed their visitors to go below stairs and to see, for the first time, the domestic offices which served the grander rooms above. Ham House, an elegant 17th century country house on the banks of the Thames just west of Richmond Park, was about to do the same in 1982, when the work described by the author was under way. Ham House had a whole labyrinth of domestic offices in its basement area. During the 1670s and 1680s (when the house was enjoying its greatest prosperity, under Elizabeth, Countess of Dysart, and her second husband, the Duke of Lauderdale) these included a kitchen, two larders, a scullery, dairy, bake-house and still-house, four cellars for beer and wine, the Usher of the Hall's Office, the servants' hall and a laundry. In this article Caroline Davidson describes how she set about restoring the most important domestic offices of all: the kitchen.

One of the most exciting aspects of restoring the kitchen at Ham House has been the discovery of new, unexpected sources of information revealing what it contained in the 1670s and 80s and how it functioned.

When I first started work on the project, I had only two sets of clues. The first set lay in the kitchen itself. During the course of its long life, it had acquired many fitments. Some were clearly quite modern, like the Edwardian servants' bells and the imposing iron range in the fireplace stamped 'Dobbie Forbes and Co. Lambeth 1947', with its separate iron boiler jutting into the room. But the others looked as if they might be much earlier. The table standing on a platform in the middle of the room was so large and archaic in appearance that it must have been built with the house in 1610. The same applied to the thick dresser boards running along the wall opposite the fireplace: for they stood on a platform very similar to the table. However, both table and dresser boards had been altered in the late 18th or early 19th centuries by the addition of large drawers and the table had clearly been given a new top. The four shelves in the kitchen had been put up at different dates. Two matching shelves above the dresser boards had carved supports almost identical to the shelves in the staircase leading to Elizabeth's private bathroom, making it easy to date them to the 1670s. But the plainer shelf below them had a wooden support typical of the late 18th and early 19th century and the high

Ham House today, drawn by the Laotian artist Soun. The kitchen is behind the semi-basement window, bottom right.

shelf running along the wall to the left of the door rested upon factory-made, late Victorian or Edwardian metal brackets. The rather nondescript cupboards built round the corner opposite the door to waist height at first appeared (from their handles) to be Edwardian. But inspection of the panelling and inside joinery suggested that they had been put in at the end of the 18th century, along with the mantel piece above the range.

The second set of clues consisted of three inventories made in 1677, 1679 and 1683, listing the contents of the domestic offices, of which the kitchen was by far the most important (if importance is judged by the number of entries!). These inventories show that the kitchen at Ham was at the forefront of technological progress in cooking methods. Entries for a coal basket and an iron grate with a sliding cheek, for example, prove that food was being cooked over a coal-burning 'open' range, rather than an open hearth burning wood or peat. This arrangement was about a century ahead of its time: Thomas Robinson is usually credited with having 'invented' the open range with his patent of 1780. The listing of a jack with three chains is another indication that the kitchen was avant-garde, since the turning of spits by mechanical means was still a great novelty in 17th-century England. The six stewing pans listed in 1677 and seven stewing dishes listed in 1683 are also significant, since they suggest that there must have been a stewing stove in the kitchen. Stewing stoves were an innovation, seldom to be found in grand kitchens until the mid-18th century, and even then unusual.

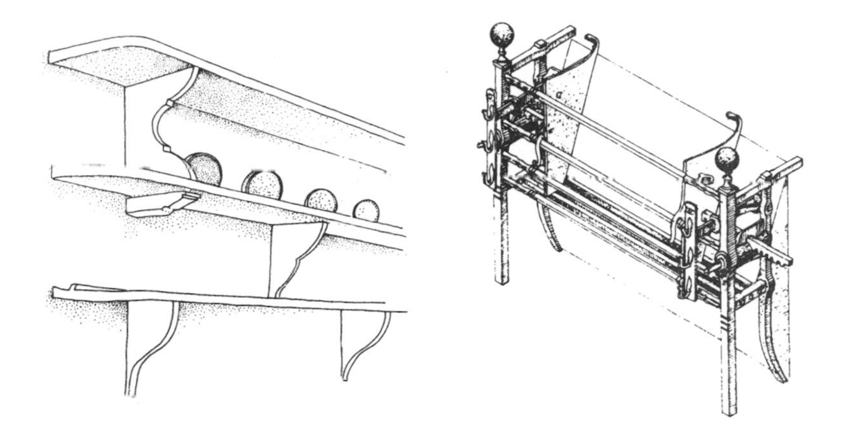

Above left, the kitchen shelves (p. 129). Above right, a drawing from The Kitchen Catalogue, *Castle Museum, York, showing sliding cheeks (p. 130) on an early 18th-century range. Below, part of a satirical broadsheet (1757, against the French and their foods) shows a stewing stove (p. 130).*

Although the inventories readily reveal what cooking technology was in use at Ham during the 1670s and 80s, they tell us less about the actual utensils in the kitchen. This is partly because they are so inconsistent. Examples:

- The coal basket which I mentioned earlier is listed in the inventory for 1677 but not in the later ones. One wonders why not. Was the coal basket new in 1677 but so battered and black two years later that it wasn't worth putting down? Or was a servant replenishing it with fresh supplies of coal, delivered by a Thames barge, when the persons making the later inventories happened to be in the kitchen?
- A rowling pin appears in 1683. Was this a new acquisition? Or had it been omitted accidentally from the previous inventories? Perhaps it had migrated from another domestic office, like the bake-house?
- Is the fish kettle and false bottom enumerated in 1679 the same as the fish pan and cover listed in 1683, or had the first been replaced by the second? And how did they differ from the large carp pan with false bottom listed in 1683?

A computer would have been useful in sorting out these differences and chasing kitchen objects which had been misplaced in other domestic offices (rather than my cumbersome card index file, burned with a web of cross-references), but I doubt whether even it would be able to draw up a definitive list of contents.

The inventories are also less informative than I would wish because so few items are described in detail. Entries like 'one stone mortar with wooden pestle' and 'twelve brass larding pins' and 'one leather chair' are helpful because they say what the objects were made of, but many of the entries are tantalizingly brief. If there was more detail about the 12 patteits listed in 1683, for example, it might be possible to guess what they were. (Something to do with pastry perhaps?)

However, the main deficiency of the inventories as a source of information is that they are woefully incomplete. As anybody who has ever tried to make an inventory of his or her possessions knows, it is a time-consuming, tedious business. It is terribly easy to leave something out because it is so familiar or to omit it because it seems trivial or valueless. This is precisely what happened at Ham. All inexpensive objects such as small wooden utensils, glass, ceramics, cleaning materials etc. were omitted from the inventories.

To take account of this, I started to compile a new inventory of all objects that *would* have been in the kitchen at Ham during the 1670s and 80s. I started off by reading in a fresh light all the 17th-century cookery books and manuscripts that I could find. I was now less interested in learning about gastronomy of the period than in spotting references to kitchen utensils in the recipes and noting their context. The results were quite interesting. For one thing I discovered the universality of the pipkin, a small pot or pan, with or without a lid, generally made of earthenware, which came in different shapes and sizes (pipkins seem to have been used interchangeably with dishes, flat pans, stewing pans and skillets). The pipkin was most commonly used for boiling and stewing, but also as a temporary storage vessel ('let the broth stand in an earthen pot or pipkin, till it be cold') and as a bain-marie (one way of cooking salmon was to put it and some liquid into a large pipkin with a cover and immerse this in a kettle of 'seething' water). For another, I found out that most 17th-century cooks employed several more means of straining food than I had realized: they used coarse or fine lawn cloths, hair sieves, jelly bags, strainers made out of tiffany or cushion canvas, and both earthen and metal cullenders. They beat egg whites with birch whisks, boiled puddings in napkins or 'double cloths' and emptied utensils with wooden spatulas. To see whether boiled pippins (apples) were tender they tried to prick a rush through them. Or, if no rush was to hand, a bodkin was used instead. This was a short, pointed instrument made out of wood, bone or ivory, with an eye at one end which women also used for piercing holes in cloth, drawing tape or cord through hems, and fastening their hair.

The more recipes I read, the more details I picked up. I hadn't known, for example, that 17th-century cooks used so much paper. Pasties were often put on paper before baking and almond biscuits baked on 'paper plates'. Nor had I known that the nobility and gentry could afford a certain amount of glass in their kitchens. But they must have done, for their recipes call for turning raspberry cakes (made in pewter moulds, incidentally) onto glasses; serving white leach cream in glasses; laying cooked plums on a glass dish; storing conserves of violets in a glass vessel; drying boiled oranges on glass plates in a stove; and so on.

Finally, I had been under the illusion that the skillet, a metal cooking utensil with three or four feet and a long handle, was a standard kind of kitchen pot. But in fact it was almost always called for in recipes for preserving food and therefore belonged more to the still-room than to the kitchen.

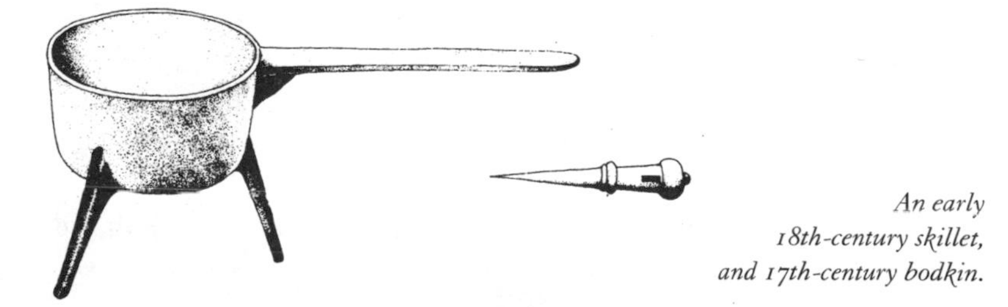

An early 18th-century skillet, and 17th-century bodkin.

To supplement the new inventory of 'extras' that I was compiling, I also went through other late 17th-century inventories to see whether they might be fuller than those at Ham House. But this proved a rather fruitless exercise. For even when I found a good inventory of the right date, the household concerned was not usually comparable. (The contents of a farmer's kitchen in Scotland are not altogether relevant to the task of establishing what was in an aristocratic, wealthy kitchen near London.) Household account books, by contrast, were very useful. If one reads through every entry of household expenditure over a given period, one is almost bound to come up with new kitchen finds. For example, after going through the household account book of Sarah Fell of Swarthmoor Hall, Cumberland, which covers the years 1673–8, my eyes were opened to all sorts of new possibilities. If she was recording the purchase of large quantities of earthen pots, wooden trenchers and dishes, and lesser numbers of baskets, porringers and meat piggins, the same thing may well have been bought at Ham. If the paper sold to Swarthmoor Hall was brown, and if the servants' aprons were green and blue, surely the same could have been true of Ham? And as Sarah Fell's accounts make plain that her house was kept clean with soap, ashes and sand, and her hearths coloured red or white, surely these humble cleaning materials should be represented at Ham House too?

It was just at the point when the number of items in the new inventory had overtaken the number on the official list collated from the three inventories (facing page), and when I feared that I might be in danger of overcrowding the kitchen with objects which wouldn't have been there in the 1670s and 80s that I had a stroke of unbelievable luck.

This was the discovery of the 17th-century manuscript archives from Ham House, carefully catalogued and conserved in the strong room of the Buckminster Park estate office near Grantham, Lincolnshire. I had written to the descendants of Elizabeth, Countes of Dysart, by her first husband, Sir Lionel Tollemache, to see if they had any family papers in their possession which might be relevant. A helpful letter soon came back from Major General Sir Humphry Tollemache saying that his son, Mr Lyonel Tollemache, had consulted the index to the family archives and found 'a dozen or so references which would seem to be worth following up'. Mr and Mrs Tollemache then very kindly invited me to spend couple of days looking at the archives at Buckminster Park and I set off in a mood of cautious optimism. Little did I expect the treasure trove which awaited me. For the archives are astonishingly full, and so comprehensive in their scope that, if properly analyzed (preferably with the help of a computer), they would present an almost complete picture of life at Ham during the 17th century. Further, as they do not

The 'official' list of objects in the kitchen at Ham House collated from the inventories of 1677, 1679 and 1683

1 tin APPLE ROASTER
1 coal BASKET
1 copper BASKET
1 copper BASIN
1 pair of BELLOWS
1 flour BOX
1 spice BOX
2 iron CANDLESTICKS
3 CHAIRS
1 leather CHAIR
2 CLEAVERS
2 COLANDERS (at least one of which is brass)
1 COPPER TO BOIL MEAT
iron serving DISHES
4 brass DISHES for servants' meat
2 copper DISHES for meat
2 tin DREDGING BOXES (i.e. DREDGERS)
4 DRESSER-BOARDS
1 FENDER
1 fire FORK
1 flesh or beef FORK
1 FORM
1 iron GRATE with sliding cheek
1 tin GRATER
2 GRIDIRONS
1 JACK with three chains
1 brass water KETTLE
1 fish KETTLE and false bottom
2 chopping KNIVES
3 mincing KNIVES
1 brass basting LADLE
1 brass LADLE
12 brass LARDING PINS
1 brass MORTAR with an iron pestle
2 marble MORTARS with pestles
1 stone MORTAR with wooden pestle
1 brass PAIL
1 PAIRING SHOVEL (?)
1 large carp PAN and cover, with false bottom
2 iron dripping PANS
3 frying PANS
9 saucePANS
6 stewing PANS
4 PATTYPANS with 3 covers and 2 sets of PATYPANS
12 PATTEITS (?)
2 pastry PEELS
2 POT HOOKS
5 brass POTS and 4 covers
1 pair iron RACKS (i.e. jack racks)
2 iron RINGS
1 ROWLING PIN
2 SHELVES
1 fire SHOVEL
2 SKIMMERS
6 SPITS
9 lark SPITS
1 brass SPOON
1 iron STAND
1 TOASTING IRON
TONGS
1 wooden TRAY
9 iron TRIVETS
TUBS (1 for rinsing and 1 for salt and 1 for flour)

break off in 1700, detailed pictures could be drawn for the 18th, 19th and 20th centuries too.

For the purpose of kitchen restoration at Ham, the archives have been a godsend. Some of the material, although fascinating for other reasons, has limited relevance, serving rather as corroborative background information than as a source of new discoveries. Such are the account books recording purchases of food and drink, including 12 volumes of detailed weekly expenditure on food from 1661 to 1697. These show exactly what foodstuffs were being consumed at Ham at every period of the year, the quantities bought, the cost, and in some instances who was providing them. These are complemented by 10 volumes of household stock books containing weekly notes of the quantities of 'food received, used and remaining' for the years 1663–90. Together with the gardening account books which show what was being grown in the garden and greenhouse for kitchen use, they provide a full picture of what was being processed in the kitchen. No great surprises, but much detail otherwise unavailable and all reassuringly consonant with assumptions which I had been making on the basis of less direct evidence.

The same applies to the most desirable item in the archives: a booklet written in a single hand entitled 'Receipts of Cookery' and probably compiled by Elizabeth's mother, Catharine Bruce, in the 1630s or 40s. In searching for 17th-century cookery manuscripts I had never expected to find one that actually belonged to Ham House!

But the prize item is the set of account books of general household expenditure from 1630 onwards, including five volumes of detailed weekly accounts of general domestic expenditure from 1661 to 1683. These books record all the mundane, everyday objects and materials that were bought for the house in order to keep it going (as opposed to luxuries like furniture, paintings, books, textiles and clothes, all of which are recorded in other account books, or objects bought for particular members of the household). From these books of general household expenditure, I found entries proving that the following items were bought in the 1670s and 80s, either certainly or probably for the kitchen:

2 Baskets
2 Basons
1 Beer can (wooden)
2 Beer glasses
2 Bottles
1 Bowl (hand)
2 Brooms
4 Brushes
1 Butter seal
2 Cabbage nets
1 Chafing dish
1 (Drinking) cup or pot
4 Earthen pans
12 Gally pots and wings
6 Glasses
1 Glazing iron

Kitchen paper (one quire at a time)
2 Ladles (wooden)
1 Mop
1 Mouse trap
1 Mug
1 Mustard pot
2 Porengers
2 Piggins
5 Pipkins
1 Platter (wooden)
8 Pots
3 Pots for pickles
24 Preserving glasses
1 Rubbing brush
2 Saucepans
1 Sieve (made out of hair)
1 Silibub pot
2 Skillet frames
1 Spoon (wooden)
18 Tea cups and pot
8 Thirkens (for pottage)
4 Tinder boxes
12 Trenchers (wooden)
1 Whisk

This mass of information has removed many of the question marks which had been hanging over kitchen ephemera. It is now possible to state with confidence that all of these humble objects should be represented in the restored kitchen.

Finally, some of the bills which have been preserved throw new light on the history of the kitchen itself.

- A bricklayer's bill for 1673, which shows that he set up a 'standing sink' in the kitchen and made up a wall at the kitchen door, suggests that the passage from the kitchen to the courtyard was added to the house at this date.
- A carpenter's bills for 1672–4 indicate that he made '2 planks for the kitching jake' (presumably shelves for the jack to sit on) and cedar tables for the two cooks.† He also shored up the kitchen 'mantle tree' because 'yt was burnt' and constructed some sort of wooden horse on a pulley for drying things in the kitchen.
- A mason's bill of November 1674 for some new ironwork 'about ye stove in ye kitchen' supports the view which I had already formed that there must have been a stewing stove in the kitchen.

So much for establishing what fixtures, fitments and objects filled the kitchen three centuries ago. But what about their physical appearance? Provision had been made for the purchase of a certain number of antique items and to commission craftspeople to make replicas of everything else. But if I was to recommend the purchase of 17th-century items, I had to be sure that what I was recommending was genuine and 'right'; and in order to commission craftspeople to make replicas I had to be able to explain exactly what the objects looked like and how they had originally been made.

In short, the detective work was not complete, but it had entered a new phase: procurement. I hope to describe my adventures in this field in a later article.

† Lists survive of the servants employed in 1668, 1669 and between 1689 and 1698, with dates of appointment shown and wages. In 1668 there were 10 men servants and 10 women servants. The cook was a man and earned £20 a year, the same rate as the steward and the page. In 1669 there were 9 men and 11 women. The cook was now a woman and, in keeping with her lower status, earned £10 a year. Whether the pair of cooks employed in 1672–4 were both women or both men or one of each is not stated.

Yule-Doos, Pop-Ladies and Pig-Hogs

PETER BREARS

Peter Brears is very much a Yorkshireman and a Leodiensian, meaning someone belonging to Leeds. His family has lived there for some 200 years, he was trained at the Leeds College of Art, and was director of Leeds City Museums from 1979 to 1994. Earlier he had been in charge of the food and kitchen exhibits in the Castle Museum at York. He is well known as a food historian with specialised, perhaps unique, knowledge of the north of England, and has published among other works Traditional Food in Yorkshire. *He is also a consultant for museums and historic houses and has worked for bodies such as Historic Royal Palaces, The National Trust, English Heritage, a number of noble households, and museums. He is very much at home, as this essay demonstrates, with popular foods—'popular' in the sense of plebeian, of the people.*

If you look into the window of virtually any baker's shop between Berwick in the north-east of England and Penzance in the south-west during December, you can guarantee that its display will include a pile of standardised small round mince pies, and some equally standardised iced Christmas cakes. The identical items may be found in almost every home, while a search through the popular recipe books published over the past 150 years will confirm that these are *the* traditional items of Christmas bakery.

In 1891 Mrs Alice B. Gomme, one of the great pioneers of English folklore studies, questioned this apparent uniformity. In a letter published in *Notes & Queries* she requested 'particulars of any cakes made . . . now or in previous years, either for special purposes and customs, or such as are peculiar to certain towns and villages, and commemorative of special events'.[1] The response was so good that the editors could not find sufficient space to publish the replies, although they did pass them on to Mrs Gomme. Next year she repeated her request, asking particularly 'Is there no place in the North where a yule-doo is still made? Would G.K. kindly give me some more information about these? Would it be possible to obtain one of these now?'[2] As she had discovered, a large number of regional yule cakes, Christmas cakes and mince pies were still being made in a great variety of shapes and sizes. In this paper we will look at just a few of these, the yule-doos, the pop-ladies, and the pig-hogs.

Yule-Doos

In 1777 John Brand's *Popular Antiquities* had recorded that the yule-doo was 'a kind of Baby or little Image of Paste, which our Bakers used formerly to bake at this Season, and present it to their Customers'.[3] This earliest reference to the yule-doo gives the impression that it was already a thing of the past, but in fact it was still alive and thriving in the popular traditions of Northumberland and County Durham,

In a scene in Robson's *Pitmans Courtship* of 1849, the pitman promises his lady love that they will set up a shop to sell

> Spice hunters, pickshafts, farthing candles,
> Wax dollies, wi' red leather shoes
> Chalky pussy-cats, fine curly greens,
> Paper kites, penny pies and hull-doos

while Brockett states in 1924 that 'these little images of paste, studded with currants [are] baked for children at Christmas, probably intended for the virgin and child'.[4] About this time it was customary in the mining communities for each hewer, who actually dug the coal out of its underground seam, to give a yule-doo to his putter, the man or boy who pushed the full tubs away to the 'flat' ready for haulage to the shaft, and then returned with the empty tubs ready for filling. If he failed to provide this gift, the hewer could expect to find that his clothes had been impounded when he came to the end of his shift.

One of Mrs. Gomme's informants, Miss Jessie Barker of Hexham House, Hexham, was able to tell her of the yule-doo customs at Harbottle. Here, in this Coquetdale village on the fringe of the Cheviot hills, she had been told

> by a native that an old woman in the village always made them a cake at Christmas time—a woman for the girls & a man for the boys. She simply cut them out with a knife. The mother of my informant remembers the children coming round for their Hogmaney, singing.
>
> Get up awd wife, & shake your feathers,
> Don't think we are beggers
> We are children come to play
> Please give us our Hogmanay.
>
> I had a little poke
> I filled it full of glesses
> If you don't give me my Hogmanay
> I'll kiss all your lasses.

Up the water & down the water
The water gave a plump,
If you don't give us a whole cake
Give us a good lump.

To most people in England, Hogmanay has decidedly Scottish implications, but throughout Cumberland, Westmoreland, Northumberland and North Yorkshire this title was given both to New Year's Eve, and to the gifts of small cakes, pie or spice bread and cheese which children begged for at the doors of friends and neighbours on this day. This tradition survived into the early 20th century in places such as Chester-le-Street in County Durham. As Peggy Hutchinson remembered in the 1930s, the young lads there used to call at all the surrounding farmhouses for their yule-doos, but in her day they only gave them to the children who regularly came to the farm for milk. These were made up in the form of the Christ Child, and were of quite a different recipe to the local Yule cakes.[5] Similarly there are memories of yule-doos being baked in north Northumberland in the 1940s, but they were rapidly falling out of use about this time.[6]

Although one Northumbrian description says that yule-doos might be made of gingerbread, most indicate that, as their name suggests, they were usually made from a fruited dough, similar to that used for yule loaves. A County Durham source states that they had a sweetened yeast-raised dough, enriched with currants, sultanas, and lemon peel.[7] No well-provenanced recipes appear to have survived, but perhaps they were similar to this example from Bolton Mill given by Peggy Hutchinson in her *Old English Cookery,* page 84.

Curranty Doo

1 lb dough, which has risen once and been knocked back
2 oz lard
2 oz sugar
6 oz currants

Spread the dough flat on the pastry board, spread the lard over it in little bits, then sprinkle with the sugar and currants before working it to distribute the lard, sugar and currants. Roll out thinly, cut to shape, and allow to rise in a warm place until doubled in size before baking at 220° C (425° F) gas mark 7 for around 20 minutes.

One yule-doo seen in 1986 appeared to have been made from an ordinary local scone recipe, rather like the following:[8]

YULE-DOO

3 oz lard
1 lb flour
3 tsp baking powder
1 tsp salt
3 oz sugar
2 oz currants
milk & water to mix

Rub the lard into the flour, add the baking powder, salt, sugar and currants. Mix well, adding the milk and water. Roll out, cut to shape, and bake for 15 minutes at 220° C (425° F) gas mark 6.

As to the shape of the yule-doos, the extant written descriptions are of 'a baby', 'made like a doll', 'a woman for the girls & a man for the boys', and 'flat, cut out with head, arms and body, arms as if touched in front, currant eyes'. An anonymous drawing in Mrs Gomme's cookery manuscripts shows just such a cake. Measuring 8 inches (203 mm) in length, it takes the form of an oval cake which has been knife-cut to form two arms which are folded across the body exactly as in the above description, the head decorated with currant eyes etc. Presumably this had been collected from an informant sometime in the early 1890s. Given the pose etc, it is almost certainly the only authentic representation of a yule-doo (rather than being one of the Pop-ladies described below). In 1986, while spending the New Year at Beamish, in County Durham, I was able to draw a yule-doo (shown below right) apparently made in the traditional manner. It was one of a number which had been made that year by Mr Athur Reay of Consett, a member of an old Teesdale family, for presentation to each of his relations. Made of a scone mixture, it was cut out in the form of a man, with arms and legs,

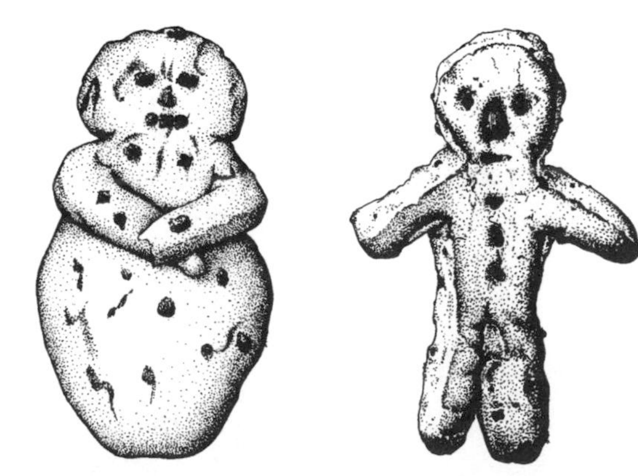

The cake on the left, recorded in a drawing sent to Mrs Gomme in the 1890s, has its arms folded in the typical pose of the Yule-doos of Northumberland and County Durham. The cake on the right is described in the text above.

currant eyes, and a nose cut from a glacé cherry. Although they have not been regularly made by the past generation or two, it was good to see that the tradition had not died out completely.

Popladys

On returning towards London from the country, 'S.P.' of Kilburn found a bed for the night of December 31st, 1819, in the town of St Albans.[9] Early next morning, on New Year's Day, he was woken 'by a confused noise of boys and girls in the street, crying for sale "Popladys! Popladys!". Enquiring at breakfast time the meaning of those words, I was informed, that it was a very ancient practice in that town, to cry and sell in the streets and in the Baker's shops on New Year's Day, a species of cake or bun, called Poplady, one of which was brought to me. It was a plain cake, like the Cross buns sold on Good Friday; but instead of being circular was long and narrow, rudely resembling the human figure, with two dried raisins or currants stuck in to mark the eyes and another to represent the mouth, the lower part being formed like the outer case of an Egyptian mummy'. He was unable to discover the origin of these cakes, but suggested that they might be a local variety of yule cake, representing the infant Christ or the Virgin Mary, or perhaps the legendary Pope Joan.

About the same time, Thomas Weedon Kent, who had been born in St Albans in 1806, observed 'the shop of Mrs Osborn, the chief pastry-cook in the town, whose window [near the Market Cross] was filled each 6th of January with Twelfth-cakes [and] on the first day of each year, 'pop ladies', curiously shaped buns crudely resembling the female figure with two currants for eyes'. He too could find nothing of their origin, but considered that they could be representations of the Virgin Mary, which received the jeering name of 'Pope's Ladies' at the time of the Puritans.[10]

This plain cake with currant eyes is the last of the St Albans Popladys, and is now preserved in the Museum of St Albans.

A further suggested origin for Popladys appeared in the columns of *Notes & Queries* in 1873,[11] where Henry W. Hedfrey stated that:

> When I lived at St. Albans these buns were made and sold on lady-day in each year, and not on the 1st of January. The story which I was told was that a noble lady and her attendants were travelling on the road to St. Albans'

(the great north road passes through this town) when they were benighted and lost their way. Lights in the Clock-Tower, at the top of the hill, enabled them at length to reach the monastery in safety, and the lady, in gratitude, gave a sum of money to provide an annual distribution, on Lady Day, of cakes, in the shape of ladies, to the poor of the neighbourhood. As this bounty was distributed by the monks, the "Pope Ladies" probably thus acquired their name. I cannot vouch for the accuracy of the above story, but I only give it as it was told to me.

This story may well be apocryphal, but it provides some useful clues regarding the probable origin of these cakes. Lady-shaped cakes representing Our Lady would make very appropriate charitable gifts of food to the poor on Lady Day, particularly in pre-Reformation England, and it is easy to imagine such a custom being transferred to the Christmas period when the traditional celebrations of Lady Day were suppressed, as smacking of popery. The prefix 'pop' probably has nothing whatsoever to do with the Pope. This word has a number of obsolete meanings, including those of 'puppet', 'doll', or 'a term of endearment for a girl or woman', these being related to the French *popine,* a pretty little woman, or today's 'poppet'. It would therefore appear from the above description that the popladys might be lady-shaped cakes originally made on Lady Day to commemorate Our Lady, only becoming associated with Christmas and New Year at a later date.

One thing that is certain, is that the St Albans' bakers of the 1890s had no idea where or how these cakes originally came to be made there every New Year's Day. In letters dated March 18th and April 8th, 1892, in Mrs Gomme's manuscripts, Mr [Emance?] writes that he now encloses:[12]

> 3 Pope-ladies, they are all made one size only on the first day of the year . . . The usual price of Popeladies is one penny each but making a small quantity specially I must charge you 2d each and postage 3d . . .
>
> I cannot give you any information as to the origin of the Pop-ladies, they were always made in the form of those I sent you, & with currants, they are made without moulds & marked with four cuts from a knife to represent arms and legs . . .

In 1896 the *Church Times* recorded that the seasonal demand for Popladys was already in decline, and over the following half century they seem to have almost entirely disappeared from local popular memory.[13] However, one example was preserved in the St Albans Museum, where it still survives today. Measuring 5¼ ins in length, it bears a great similarity to a yule-doo, although the arms are not folded as with its northern counterpart.

Pig-Hogs

A third variety of cake, also sold on New Year's Day, was the pig-hog. It had already gone out of use by the 1890s, and there are no references to it in any of the major sources. It does not even appear in Joseph Wrights' comprehensive *English Dialect Dictionary.*

Fortunately Miss Mary B. Morris of Dudley Villa, Bexley Heath, recorded details of them in a letter to Mrs Gomme dated November 16th, 1891:

> There was formerly (within my memory) a cake sold on January 1st, in my native Colchester, which was known by the name of a 'Pig-Hog'—It was in texture like a bun, but was eight or 9 inches long & about half the width, tapering at the ends,—On the top of it was a little lump of a sort of heavy dough, which was white & not like the rest, of the ordinary colour of a bun.
>
> I have never been able to find out the origin nor the meaning of the custom—but in my childhood days it would not have been New Year's Day without 'Pig-Hogs' which were sold in all bakers' & confectioners shops . . .
>
> P.S. I believe the Custom has quite fallen into desuetude.

This custom was also followed in some parts of Cornwall, as George C. Boase of 15 Queen Anne's Gate, London SW, reported in *Notes & Queries* in 1878:[14]

> It is customary for each household to make a batch of currant cakes on Christmas Eve. These cakes are made in the ordinary manner and coloured with a decoration of saffron, as is the custom in those parts. On these occasions the peculiarity of the cakes is that a small portion of the dough in the centre of the top of each is pulled up and made into a form which resembles a very small cake on top of a large one, and this centrepiece is specially called 'the Christmas'. Each person in the house has his or her special cake, and every one ought to taste a small piece of every other person's cake. Similar cakes are also bestowed on the hangers-on of the establishment, such as laundresses, sempstresses, charwomen &c. and even some individuals who are in receipt of weekly charity call as a matter of course for their Christmas cakes. The cakes must not be cut until Christmas Day, it being unlucky to cut them sooner.

Pigs of quite a different kind were eaten at Christmas-time in Leicestershire. Instead of being a variety of yule-cake, they were a type of mince-pie, baked as a unique pig-shaped pasty, in contrast to the more usual covered round tart which is universally made today. On December 29th (1891?), Mrs C. C. Bell of Epworth, near Doncaster, wrote to Mrs Gomme, with the information that a 'pig' would be sent off to her within the next day or so. It would be made by Miss Hanbury, just like those which were still made and eaten at her home at Welby Grange, Melton Mowbray, Leicestershire, except that one of its principal ingredients, pig's lights, boiled and chopped small, would be omitted, since this 'is a delicacy beyond us here':

> In regard to shape & general appearance, however, your pig should be thoroughly orthodox . . . We had no precise ritual for these feasts, but we ate the pig with a . . . sense of something about the act beyond the mere gustatory satisfaction derived from it. Why they were so shaped and called, and why proper to be eaten, then we did not of course know nor could any one have told us, but it was known to be an old custom without which Christmas would be shorn of its due observance . . .

Dorothy Hartley found that they were still being made in Leicestershire, probably up to the 1940s or '50s, and she provides a drawing of one in her encyclopaedic *Food in England.*[15] It takes the form of an elongated triangular pasty, with pointed ears and a tail protruding from the base of the three joints. This shape is of considerable antiquity, Thomas Dawson recommending that pastry should be 'cut in three corner waies' filled, closed, and baked to make pasties as early as 1596.[16] The fact that Dorothy Hartley refers to them as 'Chacky Pigs' is of no real significance, since 'Jack, Jack' is the traditional call used to bring pigs back to the sty in the evening throughout the north Midlands, where 'Jacky-pigs' are just as common as 'Moo-cows'.[17] It is most probable that these Leicestershire 'Chacky-Pigs' are just a localised form of the Christmas mince-pie, their shape being derived from an early form of pasty, simply but ingeniously converted into a pig-like form both to suggest their contents, and to make them more interesting for the children.

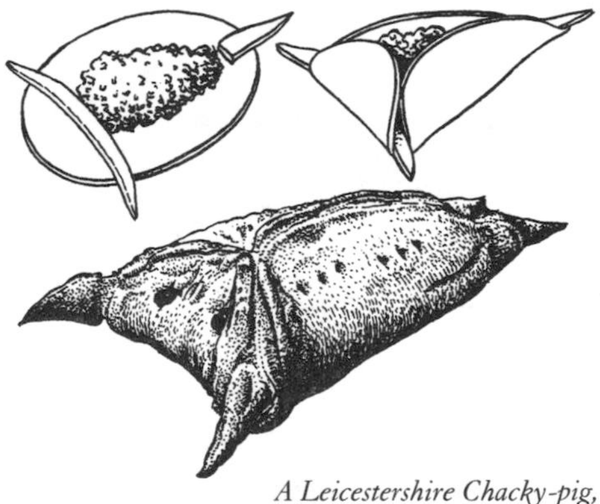

A Leicestershire Chacky-pig, showing its method of construction.

The various human-shaped cakes described in this paper probably represent the final flowering of a once much more widespread Christmas tradition of baking cakes to represent either the Christ-child or the Virgin Mary. The 'pigs', meanwhile, had pig-like shapes, and perhaps included pig-meat in their contents, the pig being widely recognised as a source of good, cheap food and hence of general domestic well-being. The symbolism of other cakes is much more difficult to interpret. Why, for example, did the inhabitants of Llantwit Major make their Christmas 'finger cakes' in the form of a hand with a little bird on the back?[18] Perhaps we will never know, but we must still be extremely grateful to the folklore collectors of late Victorian and Edwardian Britain who had the foresight and energy to record at least some of these fast-disappearing traditional cakes. But for them, we might still believe that the British Christmas was only celebrated by those rather boring iced cakes and diminutive minced pies which dominate the scene today.

Notes

1. *Notes & Queries* 7th Series XII (1891), 388.
2. *Notes & Queries* 8th Series I (1892), 254.
3. Brand, J., *Observations on Popular Antiquities* (1777), 163.
4. Brockett, J. T., *Glossary of North Country Words in Use* (Newcastle upon Tyne 1825).
5. Hutchinson, P., *Old English Cookery* (1973), 84.
6. See 'M.G.M.'s letter in *The St. Albans Review* 7th Jan, 1980.
7. See Wright, J., *The English Dialect Dictionary* (edn of 1923) VI, 593, for these and similar references. Similarly a correspondent to *Notes & Queries* 7th Series XII, 492, says: '"doos" are flat cakes some six to twelve inches long, roughly cut to the shape of a human figure, raisins being inserted for the eyes and nose. The arms are usually crossed in front; the feet are not usually shown.'
8. Hutchinson, *op cit,* 71.
9. *Gentleman's Magazine* CX (1820), 15.
10. *Transactons of St. Albans and Herts. Architectural and Archaeological Society* (1929), 24.
11. *Notes & Queries* 4th Series XI (1873), 341 and 412.
12. This, and other similar quotations in this paper, is taken from the manuscript letters referring to 'Cakes Local & Feasten' sent to Mrs (later lady) Gomme from 1891 to the 1930s. Now in private ownership, they were the subject of an article, 'A Treasury of Cakes', in *PPC 35* (1990), pp. 50–56.
13. *St Albans Review* 27th Dec, 1979.
14. *Notes & Queries* 5th Series X (1878), 493.
15. Hartley, D., *Food in England* (1954), 121.
16. Dawson, R., *The Good Huswifes Jewell* pt II (1596), 31.
17. Wright, J., *The English Dialect Dictionary* (edn of 1923) III, 340.
18. *Notes & Queries* 4th Series IX (1872), 175.

Acknowledgments

I wish to acknowledge the great help I have received from Mr John Gall of Beamish in researching the Yule-doos, and from Mr Sam Mullins of St Albans for providing a photograph and additional information regarding the Popladys.

Whims and Fancies of a Trifle-Lover

OR *'An Idle Tale, a Thing of No Importance'*

HELEN J SABERI

The sub-title of this essay is quite inappropriate, as the author herself demonstrates. One of the great paradoxes of culinary terminology is that what many people see as Britain's supreme contribution to the dessert tables of the world, for children and adults alike, to wit the trifle, should bear a name which suggests that it is of no consequence. This, surely, is carrying much too far the British tradition of playing down the merits of things British. In the present essay, Helen Saberi gives this confection the lustre which is its due—not so much because of the distinguished and intricate ancestry which belongs to it, but mainly because of its excellence in the form in which we know it today. In cottage and castle alike this plebeian yet aristocratic, complex yet simple, creation achieves a degree of satisfaction for human appetites and an aesthetic and emotional impact which stand unrivalled on the tablecloth.

The fondness of British people for trifles was demonstrated by the eagerness with which PPC *readers commented (favourably or critically—those who believe that a trifle should never contain jelly took the opportunity to express their view) or sent additional information. All this was built into the book of which the present author and Alan Davidson were co-authors:* Trifle, *Prospect Books, Devon, 2001. The essay was the basis for the book, but the latter was considerably expanded and room was found for a citation, for the benefit of the no-jelly school of thought, of a mid-18th century recipe (by Hannah Glasse 1760) which did include jelly, thus demolishing any argument that its inclusion is unhistorical.*

PPC 50 is a special edition, calling for a note of festivity, a celebration and a party dish. And the summer season invites something light and frothy. So what better than Britain's great party dish, the trifle?

Trifles offer a rare combination of sensual and intellectual pleasures. How many times have I dipped my spoon into one and experienced in succession the light frothy cream, the smooth velvety custard, the tangy fruit mingling with the bouquet of wine (or sherry or liqueur), and perhaps a touch of almondy crunchiness from ratafias or macaroons, and lastly the sweet, soft but crumbly texture of the sponge or sponge fingers. Mmm, the very thought sets me off. But this literal dipping of the spoon can be matched on the intellectual side by delving into the successive layers of the history of the trifle, with a pleasure almost as intense.

Actually, the present occasion is the first time I have done any historical delving intro trifles, but I am a veteran of many spoon-dipping episodes, for I have made trifle many, many times over many, many years and always with real enjoyment—a trifle with its carousel of flavours, colours and textures is so easy to make, and the ingredients are never a trouble to find, whichever of the different types one is making.

Different types? Yes, I know that *The New Shorter Oxford English Dictionary* defines the current meaning of trifle quite precisely:

> Now a dessert of sponge cake (esp. flavoured with sherry or spirit) with custard, jelly, fruit, whipped cream etc.

But in fact variations on the trifle theme—all delicious—seem to me to be just about as infinite as the stars in the sky. And don't overlook the last word of the *NSOED* definition. That little 'etc' covers a multitude of things (yes, 'hundreds and thousands' one might say, if tempted by a play on words), to which I come later on.

The same entry in the *NSOED* tells us that originally, in the late 16th century, the culinary meaning of the word trifle was 'a dish composed of cream boiled with various ingredients'. (That sounds to me close to what we call a fool, in which nowadays a fruit purée and cream are combined. Indeed Florio, in his dictionary of 1598,[1] bracketed the two terms when he wrote: 'a kinde of clouted cream called a foole or a trifle'.)

As for the derivation of the word itself, Webster says that it comes from the Middle English *trufle* which in turn came from the Old French *trufe* (or *trufle*) meaning something of little importance, a fit subject for mockery, or, as in my sub-title, 'an idle tale, a thing of no importance'.

All this fits in with the theory,[2] which appeals strongly to me, that trifles evolved from or alongside the dishes called fools—another name indicating something of little importance or a jokey nature. This will become clear if we look at some of the recipes from the distant past.

The first of these is also the first known recipe entitled trifle. It comes from *The Good Huswife's Iewell* [ie Jewel] (1596) by T. Dawson—a reference which I owe among many other things to Anne Wilson:[3]

A Trifle

> Take a pinte of thicke Crème, and season it with Sugar and Ginger, and Rosewater, so stirre it as you would then have it, and make it luke warme in a dish on a Chafingdish and coals, and after put it into a silver piece or bowle, and so serve it to the boorde.

At the time when Dawson wrote, a fool often contained no fruit, so his recipe, so far as I can see, could just as well have been headed 'A Fool'.

The next recipe on my list, which comes from the little known book by Jos Cooper (1654),[4] is in fact entitled 'To make a Foole'. But when I saw this recipe I thought to myself: this sounds more like a trifle than a fool. Just the other way round! Cooper's introduction of bread under the cream and his use of eggs brings us much closer to the modern idea of what a trifle is.

> Slice a Manchet [loaf of fine bread] very thin and lay it in the bottom of a dish; and wet them with Sack; boyle Creame, with Eggs, and three of foure blades of Mace; season it with Rosewater and Sugar, stir it well together to prevent curdling; then pour it on the Bread and let it coole; then serve it up to the Table.

Hannah Woolley, in *The Lady's Closet* (1672)[5] provides the next development. She added rennet, producing a 'set' rather than a liquid confection.

To Make a Trifle

> Take Sweet Cream, season it with Rosewater and Sugar, and a little whole Mace, let it boil a while, then take it off, and let it cool, and when it is lukewarm put it into such little Dishes or Bowls as you mean to serve it in; then put in a little Runnet, and stir it together; when you serve it in, strew on some French Comfits.

Robert May, in *The Accomplisht Cook* (1685)[6] followed suit.

To Make a Triffel

> Take a quart of the best and thickest cream, set it on the fire in a clean skillet, and put to it whole mace, cinnamon, and sugar, boil it well in the cream before you put in the sugar; then your cream being well boiled, pour it into a fine silver piece or dish, and take out the spices, let it cool till it be no more than blood-warm, then put in a spoonful of good runnet, and set it well together being cold scrape sugar on it, and trim the dish sides finely.

And so did Mrs Mary Eales (1718),[7] the self-proclaimed Confectioner to the late Queen Anne. Her trifle is similar to May's, except that she added orange flower water, whereas he had used cinnamon and mace; and she says specifically, after the rennet had been put in, 'let it stand 'till it comes like cheese'. This instruction gives us a very clear idea of the consistency.

Our next author, Hannah Glasse, helpfully illustrates for us the connection between Trifle and three related dishes. In the first edition (1747) of *The Art of Cookery Made Plain and Easy,* her recipe for the first of these, Floating

Island, is quite a full and colourful one—and of her own composition, so far as the sleuths who have traced her sources have found out.[8] I love what she says in this about having any colours you fancy and about the effect of having lighted candles around the dish. In this same edition, she also has three recipes for the second and related item, a hedgehog, which I will come to explain later. However, to get back to the point, in the 4th edition (1751), the Floating Island was joined by a shorter recipe for Trifle:

To Make a Trifle

> Cover the bottom of your dish or bowl with Naples biscuits broke in pieces, mackeroons broke in halves, and ratafia cakes; just wet them all through with sack, then make a good boiled custard, not too thick, and when cold pour it over it, then put a syllabub over that. You may garnish it with ratifia cakes, currant jelly, and flowers, and strew different coloured nonpareils over it.[9]

This is where the third related dish, Syllabub (for which Hannah Glasse also gives separate recipes) makes its appearance as part of the trifle.

Syllabubs, which also date back to Elizabethan times, were originally a drink with a foamy head.[10] Sweetened spiced white wine, cider or fruit juice was placed in a jug and the cow was milked directly into it. The origin of the word 'syllabub' is obscure. Some say it means a 'bubbly' drink made with Sill or Sille—wine from the Champagne regions of France (although fizzy champagne had not been invented at this time). Others say that the first part of the name is due to the drink being silly, in the sense of innocent, light-hearted. Whatever the correct version is, I like the second and would even add that perhaps this alcoholic drink made people a bit silly—this all fits in with the theme of trifles, fools etc.

Meanwhile, north of the Border, Elizabeth Cleland published in 1755[11] an engagingly Scottish recipe for trifle, into the text of which I have inserted explanations of Scottish terms which she used.

To Make a Trifle

> Cover your ashet [platter, from the French assiette] with Spunge Biscuits; then pour over them a Mutchkin [a Scottish measure, about 3/4 of an imperial pint, 0.43 litre] of Malaga, or white Wine, then a yellow Cream [which is made with cream, egg yolks, cinnamon, orange rind, and eaten cold]; then lay on it Heaps of coloured Sweetmeats; roast six or seven Apples, and rub them through a Search [sieve/strainer]; put a little Sugar to then, and mix them with four Eggs, the White only, and wipe [whip] them up very high, and put this by Spoonfuls over the rest, but let a little of the Cream and Sweet-meats be seen. Raise it up as high as you can so send it to the Table.

Back in England, I notice that Martha Bradley, whose *The British Housewife* (c 1758) may soon come to be seen as the finest English cookery book of the 18th century,[12] has a good trifle in her repertoire. However, although I like Martha Bradley's recipe, I do find that the one given by Elizabeth Raffald in 1772[13] reads better; it has those extra touches which we all recognise when we see them, which give us a 'real feel' for how a dish is made.

To Make a Trifle

> PUT three large macaroons in the middle of your dish, pour as much white wine over them as they will drink, then take a quart of cream, put in as much sugar as will make it sweet, rub your sugar upon the rind of a lemon to fetch out the essence, put your cream into a pot, mill it to a strong froth, lay as much froth upon a sieve as will fill the dish you intend to put your trifle in, put the remainder of your cream into a tossing pan, with a stick of cinnamon, the yolks of four eggs well beat, and sugar to your taste, set them over a gentle fire, stir it one way till it is thick, then take it off the fire, pour it upon your macaroons, when it is cold put on your frothed cream, lay round it different coloured sweetmeats, and small shot comfits in, and figures or flowers.

Comfits, from Old French confit (preserved), as Karen Hess (1981, see Note 2) tells us, 'were small fruits, bits of aromatic root or rind, or seeds, preserved with a sugar coating. Caraway comfits were especially popular.' Harlequin comfits, specified in some old recipes, are interpreted by Catherine Brown (1985)[14] as meaning hundreds and thousands.

We have already seen one attractive Scottish recipe for trifle (Mrs Cleland), and in the 19th century we soon come to another, that of Mistress Margaret Dods (1829).[15] In fact she gives two: one for 'an elegant trifle' which is indeed elegant and suitably impressive but she also has a much simpler trifle, called gooseberry or apple trifle (which sounds to me more like a fool—the ancient convergence between the two dishes lives on!).

The trifle tradition continues to be strong in Scotland, which seems to be where the engaging alternative name 'whim-wham' has been put to use, eg by Sir Walter Scott in *The Bride of Lammermoor* and Mrs Dalgairns (1829).[16] But Ireland is an equally powerful stronghold of trifles—every family has its own treasured recipe, or so Myrtle Allen (1977)[17] implies, in giving her own family favourite, prefaced by these charming observations.

> I once heard three men arguing about how to make the one-and-only, authentic trifle. Each man's grandmother had made the trifle of his life, and each made it differently.

One of them had a Drogheda granny who made trifle with sponge cakes spread with raspberry jam, topped with tinned pears and moistened with pear juice. These were covered with a layer of custard and another of cream. No decorations, no sherry.

An East Cork granny, belonging to the second man, dissolved jelly in the juice of tinned peaches or pears and poured this with sherry over sponge cakes. She put the fruit between the layers and topped the lot with whipped cream. She used no custard or decorations.

The third man's rather grand Yorkshire granny put ratafia biscuits, macaroons and sponge cakes in layers in the bowl. She moistened them with sherry, fruit juice and lemon curd. Custard and sometimes cream topped the bowl, and crystallised violets and roses were used for decoration.

Another point about Scotland, which is probably just as true of Ireland, is that there has been considerable enthusiasm there for a high alcoholic content. But there are also, as one would expect, Scottish books which assume that trifle eaters are all teetotal.[18] I noticed with amusement that Michael Smith in *A Cook's Tour of Britain*[19] vaguely remembers that there was a Church trifle which had alcohol and Chapel trifle which did not. This leads me to introduce you to yet another relative of the trifle, the tipsy cake, which is perhaps the most alcoholic of the trifle's relations, a bit like a tipsy uncle or aunt taking illicit nips at a family party.

Eliza Acton, the greatest English cookery writer of the 19th century, gives a really good range of trifles—beautifully written recipes—which include one item with an interesting pair of alternative titles:[20]

Tipsy Cake, or Brandy Trifle

The old-fashioned mode of preparing this dish was to soak a light sponge or Savoy cake in as much good French brandy as it could absorb; then, to stick it full of blanched almonds cut into whole-length spikes, and to pour a rich cold boiled custard round it. It is more usual now to pour white wine over the cake, or a mixture of wine and brandy; with this the juice of half a lemon is sometimes mixed.

To confuse matters further we then have the tipsy hedgehog . . . oops! Sorry, I mean hedgehog tipsy cake. Hannah Glasse had a recipe for hedgehog cake and so did Mrs Cleland but Florence White, *Good Things in England* (1932)[21] gives an 18th century recipe for a hedgehog tipsy cake. Her instructions tell one to cut the cake to look like the body of a hedgehog, fining off one end to represent the head and the nose; to pile syllabub all around this; and finally to put some redcurrant jelly just in front of the hedgehog to look as if he is eating it.

I'm not sure whether the tipsy hedgehog crossed the Atlantic, but the tipsy parson certainly did. Esther Aresty in *The Delectable Past* (1964)[22] tells us that in America tipsy cake also goes under the name of tipsy parson. Yes, the trifle found a ready welcome in the USA, and also in other overseas English-speaking countries (including Australia, New Zealand[23] and anglophone Canada). Mrs Mary Randolph's trifle recipe of 1824[24] was famous; and it was an American writer, Oliver Wendell Holmes (1861) who wrote of: 'That most wonderful object of domestic art called trifle . . . with its charming confusion of cream and cake and almonds and jam and jelly and wine and cinnamon and froth.'[25]

Finally, what happened to the trifle when it sailed overseas to non-English-speaking countries? It wasn't allowed to land in many ports (it got into France only as 'Bagatelle', the name chosen by the baffled French translator of the English authors Colllingwood and Woollams to head their recipe for this item, evidently incomprehensible to the French, although they seem to have had no difficulty with Iles Flottantes/Floating Islands[26]); but the open-minded Italians gave it an entry visa and promptly turned it into Zuppa Inglese. Sheila Hutchins in *English Recipes* (1967)[27] tells us that 'The curious dish known as Zuppa Inglese or English Soup has in fact nothing to do with soup but is really a tipsy cake. It may have passed into the Italian repertoire from the English families who wintered in Florence, such as the Brownings, the Duke and Duchess of Teck and "Ouida".' (I would be interested to hear any other theories on this point, and also to know when Zuppa Inglese first appeared in print in Italy.)[28]

Travelling further eastwards, the trifle became embedded in the standard menu of the social circle of Anglo India in the days of the Raj. E. M. Forster in *A Passage to India* (1924) makes this clear:

> And sure enough they did drive away from the club in a few minutes, and they did dress, and to dinner came Miss Derek and the McBrydes, and the menu as: Julienne soup full of bullety bottled peas, pseudo-cottage bread, fish full of branching bones, pretending to be plaice, more bottled peas with the cutlets, trifle, sardines on toast: the menu of Anglo-India . . .[29]

It is interesting that during the 19th century some English cookery writers offered recipes for an 'Indian trifle'. And I see that Jennifer Brennan in her *Curries and Bugles* (1990),[30] gives her Anglo-Indian trifle the presumably Scottish title 'Tipsy Laird Cake' which at least helps to fill out the increasingly inebriated landscape (parsons, lairds, hedgehogs—tipsy the whole lot of them!).

Some food writers have strong views about what are legitimate ingredients or decorations for trifles. So far as the main ingredients are concerned, there are some who would banish fruit and others who would not admit jelly, just to take two examples. But passions run high, also on decorations. Thus Meg Dods (1829) wouldn't have comfits (vulgar), Mrs Beeton tactfully tells her readers that 'small coloured comfits [are] considered rather old fashioned'.[31] Jane Grigson in *English Food* (1974) advised against glacé cherries in her Whim-wham as 'out of style', and in the same book, but this time in the Trifle recipe, asked of her readers: 'Try and avoid the brassy effect of angelica and glacé cherries.'[32] Prohibitions of this sort are common enough, but I wouldn't make any myself. I am very taken with Hannah Glasse's philosophy and quote words used by her in the Floating Island recipe: 'you may make it of as many different colours as you Fancy and according to what Jellies and Giams, or Sweetmeats you have . . . but that is as you fancy'.

So, if you fancy 'strewing comfits according to your fancy' on your trifles, do. Thinking about the trifles I used to make in Afghanistan, I realise that they were always traditional English ones (without the alcohol for my Muslim guests, I hasten to add), but it did occur to me while writing this essay that for this festive occasion I should link this essentially western dish with the east (as many of the original recipes did) by using flavourings such as orange flower water and crystallised ginger. So I have.

Now I must go and make the final pre-publication prototype of the *PPC* Celebration Trifle (recipe follows)—pass me the hundreds and thousands and the orange flower water please!

Trifle, based on an illustration in Mrs Beeton, 1861.

PPC Celebration Trifle

3 1/2 oz (100 g) boudoir biscuits (see PPC 49*) or sponge fingers*
strawberry jam
1/4 pint (5 fl oz: 140 ml) Cointreau or sweet sherry
9 oz (250 g) halved strawberries, reserving a few for decoration
1 strawberry or orange jelly
6 macaroons, lightly crushed

for the custard
1 pint (20 fl oz: 565 ml) double cream
2 tbs sugar
6 egg yolks
2 tsp cornflour
1 tsp vanilla essence (optional)

for the syllabub
1 lemon
3 tbs sweet or dry white wine
2 tsp orange flower water
3 oz (90 g) caster sugar
1/2 pint (10 fl oz: 280 ml) double cream

Sandwich the boudoir biscuits together with the jam in twos and lay in the bottom of a glass bowl (preferably a decorative one). Sprinkle over the Cointreau or the sherry and allow it to soak into the biscuits. Cover with the strawberries.

Make the jelly with just under 1 pint water and pour over the biscuits and fruit. The jelly should soak into the sponges but I prefer it not to come above the biscuits. Sprinkle the crushed macaroons on top and leave to set in a cool place.

Now make the custard. Heat the double cream in a saucepan. Blend the egg yolks, sugar and cornflour together in a basin and, when the cream is hot, pour it over this mixture, stirring constantly. Return the mixture to the saucepan and stir continuously over a low heat until the custard thickens. Then remove it from the heat and allow it to cool a little. (If it starts to curdle, whisk vigorously until it is restored.) When sufficiently cool, pour it over the now set boudoir biscuits, fruit and jelly. Once again, allow to cool and set completely before adding the syllabub.

Now make the syllabub. Grate the rind of the lemon. Then squeeze out the juice from the lemon, and soak the rind in the juice for a couple of hours. Whip the cream until stiff. Add the sugar, wine and orange flower water to the lemon juice and then gently mix everything together to make a light frothy cream. Spread this syllabub over the custard.

Decorate according to your fancy with the strawberries, hundreds and thousands, silver dragées (little silver balls, can be bought in packets from any shop selling cake decorations), toasted flaked almonds, angelica or, for that extra eastern flavour, crystallised ginger.

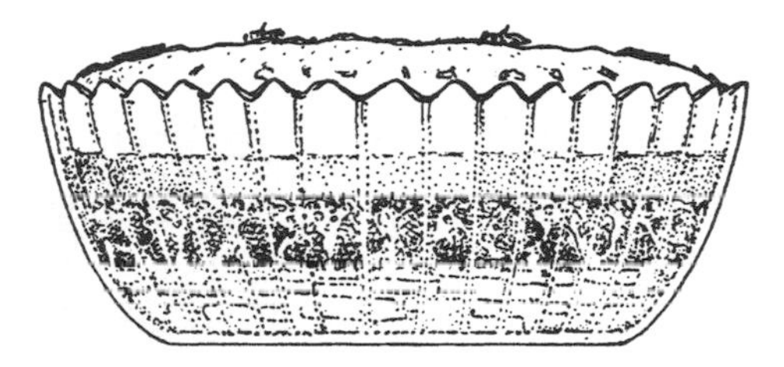

This diagrammatic drawing by Soun of the Celebration Trifle shows the four layers. From the bottom upwards they are: (1) the soaked sponge biscuits and jam; (2) the fruit and crushed macaroons; (3) the custard; and (4) the whipped cream with decorations on top. The drawing is more schematic than the reality. In practice the two lower layers (plus the jelly which invades them) tend to mix together; and the dividing line between them and the custard is irregular, whereas that between the custard and whipped cream higher up is as clear as the drawing suggests.

Notes and References

1. John Florio, *First Fruites. Also a perfect induction to the Italian, and English tongues,* London, 1578 (reprinted, Theatrum Orbis Terrarum, Amsterdam, 1969).
2. The theory has been given what is perhaps its clearest expression by Karen Hess in her edition (Columbia University Press, New York, 1981) of a very important pair of 17th century cookery manuscripts (under the title *Martha Washington's Booke of Cookery*). See especially page 132 where, with characteristic thoroughness, she traces the original meaning of fool, explains what sort of clotted cream Florio (see Note 1) was referring to, shows how fools passed from the custardy dish indicated by Florio to a mixture of custard and fruit purée and cream, while trifle took its separate path of evolution, the one I have tried to sketch out here.
3. Thomas Dawson, *The Good Huswifes Jewell,* Parts 1 and 2, London, 1596, 1597 (reprinted as a single volume, Theatrum Orbis Terrarum, Amsterdam, 1977). The trifle recipe occurs in Part 1, on the verso of the leaf numbered 23. I was led to this by C. Anne Wilson, *Food & Drink in Britain,* London, 1973.
4. Jos Cooper; see the essay 'Joseph Cooper, Chief Cook to Charles I' by Louise A. Richardson and J. R. Isabell in *PPC 18.* I wonder whether this recipe of Cooper's may not be among the ancestral versions of what is now well known as Bread and Butter Pudding (which is, come to think of it, another distant relative of the trifle—but following this trail would take us into completely new terrain).
5. Hannah Wooley, *The Queen-like Closet:* 5th edition, London, 1684.
6. Robert May, *The Accomplisht Cook,* edition of 1685, reprinted in facsimile with much explanatory material by Prospect Books, Devon, 1994.

7. Mrs Mary Eales, *Mrs. Mary Eales's Receipts,* London 1718 (and facsimile reprint from the edition of 1733, Prospect Books, London, 1985).

8. A Lady [Hannah Glasse], *The Art of Cookery Made Plain and Easy,* London, 1747. This has most recently been reprinted in facsimile in 1995 (by Prospect Books, Devon) with the full text of the two essays by Jennifer Stead and one by Priscilla Bain which track down the sources from which hundreds of the recipes were copied. These essays originally appeared in *PPC 13, 14* and *23.*

9. Hannah Glasse adds a little note at the end of this recipe explaining that 'non pareils' are bought at the confectioners. They were in fact a kind of comfit. It was fashionable in the 18th century for theatregoers to buy non pareils and eat them in the theatre. Exact size and composition seem to have varied.

10. For general remarks about the syllabubs and related items such as fools, with a trifle thrown in for good measure see the 1969 booklet by Elizabeth David called *Syllabubs and Fruit Fools,* conveniently reprinted in: Elizabeth David, *An Omelette and a Glass of Wine,* Robert Hale, London, 1984.

11. Elizabeth Cleland, *A New and Easy Method of Cookery,* Edinburgh, 1755.

12. Martha Bradley, *The British Housewife.* (For the likely date of publication see Cooks Books, *The Grosvenor Catalogue,* Rottingdean, 1995, page 31, citing a newspaper clipping pasted into one of the numerous blank leaves added to a copy of Dr Kitchiner's *The Cook's Oracle.*)

13. Elizabeth Raffald, *The Experienced English Housekeeper,* 3rd edition, London 1773.

14. Catherine Brown, *Scottish Cookery,* Richard Drew, Glasgow, 1985.

15. Mistress Margaret (Meg) Dods of the Cleikum Inn, St Ronan's, *The Cook and Housewife's Manual,* Edinburgh 1826. There is a useful note about this book and its real author (Mrs Isobel Johnston, wife of an Edinburgh publisher and friend of Sir Walter Scott) in Catherine Brown's book cited in Note 14.

16. Mrs Dalgairns, *Practice of Cookery,* 2nd edition, Edinburgh, 1829. The information about Sir Walter Scott and Whim wham comes from Marian McNeill, *The Scots Kitchen,* Glasgow, 1929.

17. Myrtle Allen, *The Ballymaloe Cookbook,* 3rd edition, Gill and Macmillan, Dublin, 1987.

18. See, for example, *Tried Favourites* by Mrs E. W. Kirk, the 26th edition of 1948; this proudly records that over 730,000 copies had already been sold—so the teetotal trifles can't have been much of a handicap in marketing it.

19. The Women's Institute and Michael Smith, *A Cook's Tour of Britain,* Willow Books, London, 1984.

Mention of a tour of Britain reminds me to say that I have not overlooked Wales. However, Bobby Freeman (*First Catch Your Peacock—A Book of Welsh Food,* 1980) says that so far as the Welsh are concerned the trifle is something which has reached them, if at all, in a downward direction from the English occupants of the *plas* (ie mansion, big house). She gives one recipe for a Trifle with Jelly which is documented as having been made in Wales—but without any suggestion that it represents an indigenous tradition.

20. Eliza Acton, *Modern Cookery for Private Families,* revised and enlarged edition, London, 1860.

21. Florence White, *Good Things in England,* originally published 1932, Cookery Book Club edition, 1968.
22. Esther Aresty, *The Delectable Past,* New York, 1964.
23. New Zealand provides a good example, just one among many, of how the trifle can be adapted overseas to use different ingredients. David Burton, in *Two Hundred Years of New Zealand Food and Cookery* (Reed, Wellington, 1982) gives a recipe for Green and Gold Trifle, using feijoa fruits and blossom ends.
24. Mrs Mary Randolph, *The Virginia Housewife* (ed Karen Hess), University of South Carolina Press, Columbia, 1984.
25. Oliver Wendell Holmes, quoted by Catherine Brown (*op cit,* Note 14).
26. The ease with which this translation can be made in either direction masks differences between the French and English dishes. Mary Norwak, in *English Puddings* (London, Batsford, 1981) points to these differences, while thinking it possible that the two versions have a common ancestry. The bit about the translators of Collingwood and Woollams comes from Elizabeth David (*op cit,* Note 10), who also remarked on how they transformed Gooseberry Fool into a 'wild whirl of summer gaiety and greenery', *Folie de groseilles verte.*

    On French bafflement over the trifle, I ought to add that the illustrious Jules Gouffé (in *Le Livre de Pâtisserie,* 1873) included a chapter on foreign confections, in which we find quite a full and plausible recipe under the English title 'Trifle', which he translates as 'Mousse à l'Anglaise'.
27. Sheila Hutchins, *English Recipes and Others from Scotland, Wales and Ireland as they appeared in Eighteenth and Nineteenth Century Cookery Books,* Methuen, London, 1967.
28. As this essay went to press, I learned from Françoise Sabban that there are indeed other theories about the circumstances in which *Zuppa Inglese* acquired its name; and that use of the name (but applied to something rather different from what it denotes today) goes back to the mid 16th century. Such a wealth of information has she supplied that the only solution will be to print it as a separate item in *PPC 51,* thus shifting the spotlight from trifle to its mysterious Italian relation.
29. E.M. Forster. I owe this reference to Brigid Allen, *Food, An Oxford Anthology,* Oxford University Press, 1994.
30. Jennifer Brennan, *Curries and Bugles,* Viking, London, 1990 (and later as a Penguin paperback).
31. Mrs Isabella Beeton, *Mrs Beeton's Book of Household Management,* first published in book form London 1861, facsimile reprint by Chancellor Press, London, 1982.
32. Jane Grigson, *English Food,* Macmillan, London, 1974. I notice, however, that in the Whim-wham recipe in the same book she actually recommended angelica (while only mildly deploring glacé cherries as 'out of style').

Curry Rice: Gaijin Gold

How the British Version of an Indian Dish Turned Japanese

KEIKO OHNUMA

When sending this essay the author told us that she wrote it for Professor Rachel Laudan at the University of Hawaii, and that it represented her 'first foray into food writing'. She described herself as a business journalist from San Francisco, spending a year at the University on a fellowship aimed at training journalists to cover Asia. When she heard of Rachel Laudan's pioneering course on food history, she immediately decided that she should study this, since food was essential to the proper study of Asia. She added that one of the guest speakers at the course pointed out pertinently that 'the Chinese didn't need missionaries, they disseminated their culture by opening restaurants'.

A steaming, pungent, mud-yellow sludge poured over rice on a plate: What could seem more out of place than Japan's favorite lunch fare, 'curry rice'? Chunks of carrot, potato and stew meat tumble undistinguishably from the communal vat, streaking diners' plates an appalling ochre. Japanese food historian Elizabeth Andoh recalls being sickened by such first impressions of the national cuisine: 'dreadful curry rice with a terrible smell which nauseated me' and 'funny fish things that scared me'.[1]

Small wonder if the dish is rarely mentioned in their cookbooks or restaurant menus abroad. Yet, overlook it as they may, there can be no question the Japanese love their *kare raisu*. Every train station and shopping district has its hole-in-the-wall curry rice stand, and most Japanese eat the dish as often as Americans do pizza. A survey conducted in the early 1980s found curry rice among the top three home-cooked favorites year round, along with *tonkatsu* (pork cutlets) and *yasai itame* (vegetable stir-fry).[2] Curry is especially popular with children, who voted it the best meal served by the national school lunch program in January 1982.[3]

Strange as the sloppy concoction may appear to an observer schooled in the 'first principle [of Japanese food] . . . that the ingredients should retain their natural appearance and taste as much as possible',[4] curry rice fulfills like few other foods the age-old Japanese tradition of cheap, sustaining fare to fuel the hard-working masses on quantities of rice and beer.

* * * *

Warm, hearty, soothing winter gruel: What could signal the comforts of home to me more succinctly than these cubed potatoes, these hearty chunks of beef piled shamelessly thick on the plate—a friendly introduction to all the Irish, Portuguese, North African, Spanish and plain American stews I would encounter?

It's no accident if the humble *kare* of my childhood helped forge a gastronomic sympathy for Europe: Japan's curry stew originated in Britain and has remained essentially unchanged since it was brought to Japan on board British ships during the rapid opening to the West during the Meiji era (1868–1912). The earliest Japanese recipes for curry appear not long after England gained access to Japanese ports in 1868, around the time of the first cookbooks.

Coming from Britain, these feature pre-mixed curry powder, a relatively mild British concoction that was originally packaged and sold by the East India Company, whose ships plied the spice route. Among the early versions, *Seiyo Ryori Tsu* ('The Western Cooking Expert') of 1872 described a curry stew nearly like the home-cooked *kare raisu* of today: beef or chicken heated in a roux of flour, curry powder and stock, sweetened with apple, and stewed for several hours.[5] Add a dash of cream, and this is scarcely distinguishable from the Curried Fowl recipe that appeared in the first (1861) edition of the British cooking classic by Mrs Isabella Beeton, which called for chopped onions, apple and chicken fried in butter and cooked in a stock containing flour and curry powder; cream and lemon juice were added just before serving in a ring of rice.[6]

Imported verbatim from the British, Japanese curry has nonetheless—like all foreign foods and ideas—evolved according to cultural idiosyncrasies. Presentation is one important difference: although *kare raisu* is always served on Western plates with Western utensils (usually a spoon), '[a] significant factor . . . is the fact that the rice is not totally covered with the curry stew,' according to historian Andoh, '[a]lthough it gets mixed later,' Even fast-food curry chains keep the stew to one side of the plate. 'The pure white rice is important to the Japanese',[7] Andoh notes. Tradition also dictates the addition of pickled vegetables (*fukujinzuke*) on the side, without which a Japanese meal would appear 'incomplete'.[8]

Mild as the spice mix may have been, it is a wonder the lean, vegetarian Japanese would take to a taste so foreign to anything in their own cuisine. Some might credit the extraordinary atmosphere of the times for the sudden fascination with things Western, such as deep-fried pork cutlets (*tonkatsu*), potato croquettes (*korokke*) and hashed beef (*hayashi*) rice—all of which have become enduring favorites.

Japanese food historian Lucy Seligman notes that many of the *yoshoku,* or Western, dishes dating from the Meiji and Taisho (1912–26) eras go well with rice.[9] They also happen to draw heavily on the new foods being introduced to supplement the spartan Japanese diet of rice, fish and pickles—foods such as Irish potatoes, tomatoes, onions, eggs, chicken, butter, beef and pork, many of which the Japanese would not eat willingly until the modern era.[10] But of all the *yoshoku* dishes, none begs for the accompaniment of rice—or sake—with quite the urgency of *kare.*

One story from curry history illustrates this happy pairing. The backwards name 'curry rice' (over the original 'rice curry') is credited to the pioneering American schoolteacher Dr William S. Clark, one of dozens of Western technical experts hired by Sapporo Agricultural College (now Hokkaido University) in 1877–8 to help settle the wilderness of Japan's northern island. Clark reportedly served curry to encourage more rice-eating among his charges, who supplemented their diet with wheat and millet.[11] Since all rice had to be imported to the snowy hinterland, the story presupposes an influx of rice that the boys would be encouraged to eat.

Over the next three decades, the Japanese military latched onto *kare raisu* for much the same reasons. The strong flavors proved an ideal way to use up leftovers in a cheap, easy, substantial meal that incorporated vegetables, rice and meat on one plate. With its lingering image of luxury and progress, *yoshoku* dishes like curry rice became so trendy during the Taisho era that the army used it to draw conscripts. The convenience, price and heartiness also made the dish a favorite in rural areas at harvest time.[12]

One suspects that the same qualities made curry stews an ideal shipboard food for Japanese steamship lines traveling to Europe. It was on board such a ship in 1930 that Osaka merchant Kazuma Kobayashi tasted the dish and begged the chef for the recipe. When he opened the Hankyu Department Store in Osaka a few years later, Kobayashi put *kare raisu* on the menu, winning thousands of converts. By 1938, when he expanded the cafeteria, Hankyu could serve 45,000 customers a day. Their top choice? Curry rice, shrimp fry and cutlets.[13]

Ask Japanese today why they are so fond of curry rice—a rude, sloppy meal out of keeping with their aesthetic—and they can't pin down the attraction beyond convenience, bulk and price. 'It's the cheapest lunch, everyone likes it, it has both potatoes and meat', my mother said of the quick spread of *kare* from the cities to the countryside after World War II. 'But it's never *gochiso* [feast food for guests].'[14]

Indeed, the dish is more akin to Japanese 'comfort food'. The fact that it is eaten hot and in quantity places it firmly within a meal structure dating back over 350 years, in which rice and miso soup form the staple—the only foods eaten hot and in quantity—while side dishes of fish, meat, vegetables and pickles (*okazu*) are offered sparingly, at room temperature, as relish.[15] A curry recipe published in a magazine in 1905 marks the evolution from soup + rice to stew: It directed the making of a plain miso soup with bits of meat, thickened slightly with flour, flavored with curry powder and poured over rice.[16] Even as late as the 1940s, home cooks who couldn't bother with chicken bones and beef broth simply cooked curry in *katsuobushi,* the ubiquitous Japanese fish stock that forms the base of nearly all soups, sauces and stews.[17]

In short, a typical warm gruel composed of rice, soup and bits of pickles and meat, at once familiar and foreign, *kare*'s closeted image reflects Japan's schizoid sense of its own culture. On the other hand, we have the carefully cut and lovingly arranged platters of sushi, the artfully composed place settings and serene kimono-class hostess—all triggers of a minimalist aesthetic that Westerners love to photograph and Japanese love to promote. On the other, there is the daily reality of trying to eat lunch in central Tokyo with millions of other office workers, 'an exercise of considerable logistical proportions', according to one observer. 'The custom of carrying a box lunch prepared at home is now quite rare . . . The vast majority of office workers flock outside to eat meals that can be ordered and consumed quickly.'[18]

Dinner, the account goes on to note, is often a two-tiered affair, with mother and children eating first, and the hard-working 'salaryman' father returning late to eat alone.[19] As more women go to work outside the home, few have time to devote to the painstaking preparation of traditional Japanese fare. Lucy Seligman cites a popular saying that describes the modern Japanese diet: '*Okaasan yasuma, Haha kitoku*' ('Mother, take a rest, Mother is near death'). The acronym lists popular convenience foods, beginning with omuretsu (omelettes), kare raisu, aisukurimu (ice cream) and sandoicchi (sandwiches).[20]

It is this daily reality that finds salvation in curry rice.

* * * *

None of the aforementioned qualities—rice, warmth or sustenance—could have made curry a household word were it not for technological advances that made the dish accessible to the masses as it brought down the price.

The flour used for thickening was the first hurdle. Japan did not have milling machinery until 1895, and significant flour production began only after 1905.[21] In 1931, the Japanese finally succeeded in duplicating the manufacture of England's C&B (Crosse & Blackwell) curry powder.[22] But the dish really owes its phenomenal postwar success to some singular food processing innovations that turned the packaging of curry rice into a ¥122 billion industry,[23] feeding the fortunes of two of the nation's largest food companies.

S&B Foods Inc and House Foods Corp—both billion-dollar companies that operate US subsidiaries—originally dealt in spices, including curry powder.[24] The instant curry roux they began selling after World War II is still unique to Japan.[25] These suet-like cakes of spices and flour suspended in animal fat put foolproof, home-cooked curry within reach of anyone who could boil water. Resembling fat chocolate bars, scored for easy separation, they embody the ultimate in bachelor cuisine—Japan's answer to bottled spaghetti sauce.

Interestingly, a comparable product introduced in 1927 had failed to generate anywhere near the same response. An enterprising Indian national exiled in Japan, Rass Bihari Boas,[26] began marketing a ready-made Indian-style curry lunch after his marriage to the daughter of Soma Aizo, founder of Nakamuraya confectioners. The company's so-called 'genuine rice curry for the masses' came packaged with rice and stew in separate pouches. Nakamuraya's Indian-style curry apparently failed to capture the niche that has put S&B Curry in supermarkets from Asia to the US West Coast.[27]

In the 1970s, Japan's curry merchants reaped another industrial windfall with the advent of the retortable pouch, a preservation technology embraced in Japan largely for want of alternatives such as freezing. Similar to boil-in-bag meals, hermetically sealed retort pouches hold foods without refrigeration or the damage to texture caused by canning. Retorts have become a way of life in Japan,[28] where they account for some 40 percent of packaged curry sales.[29]

* * * *

Evolving along parallel but separate lines, Western foods have always been more amenable to such industrial experiments than their Japanese counterparts. They are never *gochiso,* as my mother puts it, and thus exempt from culinary laws of purity and perfection. Spaghetti, ramen, pancakes, hamburgers: all make frequent appearances on school lunch menus, company cafeterias, stand-up train station eateries, as well as in the packaged food aisle. Favored by the young, these faddish foods invite a rebellious improvisation that seems to snub its nose at the rigid formality of *kaiseki ryori,* ceremonial Japanese fare that carries all the weight of tradition.

Perhaps nowhere is this irreverent attitude more apparent than in a modern fast-food eatery like curry House Coco Ichibanya, a rapidly growing chain of 300 stores that has opened its first US outlet on Honolulu's Waikiki Beach strip. The restaurant offers curry selections including cheese, banana, frankfurters, fried chicken and squid, all drowning in a soupy brown sauce even more distant from its British ancestor than instant curry roux (though the restaurant's molded take-out trays do include a tiny well for pickles).

Customers can choose from seven levels of spiciness and varying quantities of rice, from the standard 300 grams to 600 grams ('max. for a lady'), 900 grams ('max. for a man'), to the 1300-gram challenge—free to anyone who can wolf down a veritable lake of lumpy mud and nearly three pounds of rice in 20 minutes. How very Japanese!

True to the wording, the Coco chain is popular with men, who take a certain macho pride in ordering their curry extra-spicy, even though *kare raisu* is traditionally so mild as to make Indian or Thai dishes intolerably hot to the average Japanese.

As surely as my childhood love of *kare raisu* formed a bridge of familiarity to chili con carne, chicken cacciatore, Irish beef stew and Moroccan couscous, urban Japanese are venturing beyond Western fare in the 1900s to a new interest in curries from India and Southeast Asia—a fitting reflection of the nation's renewed ambition to regional leadership status.

Meanwhile, across the Pacific, those clever curry roux blocks—like Nissin's cup ramen before them—continue their steady advance across US supermarket shelves.

Footnotes

1. Elizabeth Andoh, interviewed in 'Gochiso-sama!', Spring 1995.
2. Kosege, 1984.
3. Kosege, 1984. The kids' top choices were curry rice (46 percent); *yakisoba,* or chow mein (35 percent); hamburger, and spaghetti with meat sauce. Another survey found children's favorite foods to be hamburger, ramen and curry rice (Higuchi, 1988).
4. De Mente, 1995.
5. Kosege, 1984.
6. Beeton, 1861.
7. Andoh, 1995.
8. Leibenstein, 1983. Also Andoh, as quoted by Seligman, addressing the Culinary Historians of Ann Arbor in February: 'The rules of the game are that a basic Japanese meal consists of rice, miso soup and pickes.' ('Gochiso-sama!', 1995).
9. Seligman, 1994.
10. Lvov, 1975. It wasn't until the Showa era (1912–89) that most Japanese would eat tomatoes, according to Lvov, although the Tokyo government encouraged their cultivation. 'Even in the Taisho Period, people held their noses to avoid the smell of tomatoes, and added sugar to them when eating them to disguise their taste' (p 244). As Seligman notes, tomatoes figure prominently in three favorites of the Meiji era—*kare raisu, omuraisu* and *hayashi* rice—in the form of ketchup (Seligman, 1994).
11. Kosege, 1984.
12. Seligman, 1991.
13. Seligman, 1991.
14. Ohnuma, 1995.

15. Leibenstein, 1983.
16. Kosege, 1984.
17. Ohnuma, 1995.
18. *Japan: An Illustrated Enclopedia,* 1993.
19. *Japan: An Illustrated Encyclopedia,* 1993.
20. Seligman, 1994. The complete list includes omuretsu (omelettes), kare raisu, aisukurimu (ice cream), sandoicchi (sandwich), yakisoba (chow mein), supagetti, medamayki (fried egg), hambagu, hamu-eggu, yakigyoza (potstickers), tosuto (toast), kurimu supu (cream soup). In the 1980s, she writes: 'this multicultural hodgepodge of foods became part of the typical weekly menu in households throughout Japan.'
21. *Japan Year Book, 1946–48.*
22. 'House Foods Guidebook'.
23. House Foods Corp.
24. *Japan Company Handbook.*
25. *Asahi Shimbun Weekly (Aera),* 1992.
26. The name is taken from an article in Japanese, so the transliteration is unclear.
27. *Asahi Shimbun Weekly (Aera),* 1992.
28. Hui, 1992. As well as the difficulties of distribution and display space, freezing may have been unacceptable in Japan because it affects food texture. Retort technology, developed by the US military in the 1950s, never gained favor in this country except for backpacking food and military rations, where retort pouches have completely replaced cans.
29. House Foods Corp, 1995. According to the company, curry roux accounted for ¥74 billion in sales in 1993, retort pouch curry for ¥48.5 billion. The same year, House Foods had 70 percent of the market.

Sources

Andoh, Elizabeth, correspondence dated October 15, 1995.

Asahi Shimbun Weekly (Aera), 'Kare no rutsu tampo' [Investigating the roots of curry], September 8 1992, p 42. Material is credited to food history researcher Yoshiko Yoshida.

Beeton, Isabella, *The Book of Household Management* (London, 1861), facsimile reprint by Farrar, Straus & Giroux, 1969, pp 941–2.

De Mente, Boye Lafayette, *Japan Encyclopedia,* Lincolnwood Ill, Passport Books, 1995, p 146.

"Gochiso-sama!' newsletter, vol 7, no 2 (Spring 1995).

Higuchi, Kiyoyuki, *Omoshiro zatsugaku Nihon shi,* Tokyo, Mikasa Shobo, 1988. Translation by Lucy Seligman.

House Foods Corp, Torrance CA. Correspondence dated October 30 1995.

'House Foods Guidebook and Magazine.' House Foods Corp Marketing Department, Osaka, Japan, 1995–6.

Hui, Y.H., *Encyclopaedia of Food Science & Technology,* vol 4, New York: John Wiley & Sons, 1992, pp 2253–8.

Japan: An Illustrated Encyclopedia, Tokyo, Kodansha, 1993, pp 392–3.

Japan Company Handbook, Tokyo, Toyo Keizai Inc, Autumn 1995, vol 1, p 238 and vol 2, p 148.

The Japan Year Book, 1946-48, Tokyo, Foreign Affairs Association of Japan, 1948, p 373.

Kosege, Keiko, *Nihon yoshoku monogatari* [Tales of Japanese Food], Tokyo, Shinchosa, 1984. Translation by Lucy Seligman.

Leibenstein, Margaret L., 'Japan's Cuisine: A Story of Continuity', *Petits Propos Culinaires 14,* June 1983.

Lvov, Norman Basil, *Japanese Daily Life From the Stone Age to the Present,* New York, Carlton, 1975, pp 244–5.

Ohnuma, Toshi, telephone interview, November 5 1995.

Seligman, Lucy, correspondence dated October 1 1995.

———, 'The History of Japanese Cuisine', *Japan Quarterly,* April-June 1994.

———, 'Out of India', *PHP Intersect,* June 1991.

3.
On Your Plate

In this section 'your plate' is seen as the recipient for either a dish, which would be normal, or an ingredient, which you might be displaying to friends or food historians. The items selected are so disparate that it would have been impossible to put them in any sort of logical order, and we have therefore given them in temporal sequence, from *PPC 4* to *PPC 50*.

When *PPC 4* was being prepared, Caroline Davidson was playing an active role in editorial matters and profited from a stopover in Reykjavik to enlist Sigriđur Thorlacius as a *PPC* author. She had heard from your Editors, following their earlier stay in Reykjavik, about the somewhat mysterious dairy product called skyr, which according to the Icelanders they had met on that earlier occasion, was absolutely unique to Iceland. Now read on.

Right after skyr comes long pepper, a subject which had greatly intrigued Philip and Mary Hyman in Paris when they were studying the changes in the use of spices in French cuisine from earlier medieval until more recent times. In their essay they have commented on the decline in the use of long pepper and have speculated about likely reasons for this. Philip and Mary were, incidentally, the first people to volunteer to become *PPC* agents in a country outside the UK, and they are still filling that role nearly a quarter of a century later.

The olive oil made in Tuscany by Mrs Leslie Zyw was a great favourite of Elizabeth David, who prevailed upon her to contribute the next piece, a charming account of how her olive oil is produced.

An alternative to olive oil which many people enjoy is one of the several nut oils which can be had, especially from France and especially from Berry.

Jane Grigson's essay about these includes a recipe of her choice. It was Jane, a supporter of *PPC* from the very first issue until her untimely death in 1990, who proposed that the arrangements for subscribing to *PPC* should include provision for life subscriptions. We were attracted by this idea but felt unable to adopt it because of uncertainty about what the distant future might hold.

Now follows a characteristic essay by Elizabeth David, exhibiting two of the skills for which she is renowned. First, her exploration of the names given to the aubergine and of the thinking which lay behind some of the epithets applied to it is a good example of how she could present scholarly explorations in a way which makes for irresistible reading. Secondly, observe her skill in choosing particularly interesting old recipes and in handling them in a manner which preserves the original text but gives today's cook exactly the sort of advice and detail which she or he will need.

Philip and Mary Hyman almost invariably operate as co-authors, for example in the essay on long pepper (page 177); rarely, one of them flies solo. The piece on snails is an example of Philip doing just that, and is also an excellent example of how the sort of research which he and Mary have been doing for decades can bring surprising changes to our perceptions of aspects of culinary history. What, have the French not always been wild about snails?

It was Philip and Mary who introduced Jim Bauman to your Editors, with the result that his extensive research on the galettes des rois found expression in a particularly attractive essay in *PPC 27*, illustrated by the author himself. It would have been great to include further essays by him, which he half-promised to us for the future, saying that he first had to find a way of unpacking his scores of cartons of cookery books into his tiny Parisian apartment. Alas, that time never arrived, for this most accomplished writer and artist died young.

In the same issue, No. 27, there appeared not for the first time in the pages of *PPC*, a major essay by Alicia Rios, the only Spanish food historian with academic qualifications in psychology; a record of studying and practising surrealism; the feat of creating the most harmonious (all white) restaurant ever to grace the streets of Madrid; a facility for stage performances based on culinary matters; and a surprising ability to design and make edible hats. This essay, very slightly abbreviated here, is an outstanding example of how Spanish writing about gastronomy has a different construction, flavour and purpose from similar writings anywhere else. We say 'purpose' because Alicia has consistently striven, by patient analysis, to deconstruct Spanish ways with food into their constituent elements, only to re-combine them in glowing descriptions which make her readers long to be in Spain and enjoying the experiences which can only be fully appreciated on Spanish soil.

The next item, 'The Norwegian Porridge Feud', is furnished with its own little introduction, explaining its origin and pointing out how evanescent the 'current wisdom of the scientists' can sometimes be. Astri Riddervold, incidentally, is an eminent food historian who has specialised in writing books about food conservation which are, like the present essay, as entertaining as they are instructive.

Following the same theme of food conservation, Peter Graham contributes an illuminating essay on stockfish (wind-dried unsalted cod), a commodity which has puzzled many people. Peter lives in France in the Châtaigneraì, and it was there that he has written various books including his classic work on cheese cookery. Here he explores a mystery about stockfish in the Châtaigneraì and tells us what to do with it if we have some.

Laura Mason made her debut as a food historian in *PPC 35* with an essay on some traditional English sweets. She swiftly became the leading authority on this subject and author of an important book, *Sugar Plums and Sherbets*. This was followed by the most comprehensive survey yet made of traditional foods of Britain, in her book with that title (Prospect Books, Devon, 1999). In this she took particular pleasure in describing the extraordinary Denby Dale Pie. The piece which she wrote about it for *PPC 50*, our special anniversary number, is reprinted here.

In the same anniversary number we published a typical piece of writing from Harold McGee, familiar to the world as the leading writer about scientific aspects of food and cookery, and familiar to readers of the present book as the author who kindly agreed to provide the foreword. What he has written about long-cooked eggs is certainly the locus classicus on this subject.

The essay by Rose-Ellen Hope with which this chapter concludes considers camas, an unusual vegetable, in its botanical, historical and folkloric aspects, but above all as food.

Do You Know Skyr?

Sigríður Thorlacius

A visitor to Iceland will soon be offered a dish of skyr for dessert. He will be given a bowl of a soft, white substance, offered sugar and cream to pour over it, and if he is very fortunate, some blueberries to go with it.

What is this, the visitor will ask, and his hosts will give a rambling explanation about the story and making of skyr. For ages this has been a favourite dish and valuable ingredient of the nutrition of the Icelandic people, formerly made on every farm, now produced in huge machines in the dairies.

Origins and History

Skyr is made out of milk, the culture of certain bacteria*, and rennet. When asked about the origin of the dish, we have to admit that we only know from our ancient literature, the Sagas (written in the 11th to 14th centuries), that skyr has been made in Iceland since the first settlers landed there in the 9th century. When archeologists dug up the site where, according to the Saga of Burnt Njall, the farm of Njall should have been, they found remnants of buildings destroyed by fire and among them traces of skyr. This was in 1870–80. The reason why they could find these traces was that, up to modern times, the skyr was stored in big barrels.

We also learn from the Sagas that skyr was not commonly known in Scandinavian countries at that time; whereas a modern expert of nutrition states that certainly skyr was made in Scandinavia and the British Isles in ancient times, but probably disappeared when the growing of grains increased.

Be that as it may, in modern times skyr was not made anywhere in these countries, until a Dane, who had worked in a dairy in Iceland, brought the formula with him to Denmark and started making skyr in a dairy in Jutland with great success.

A personal experience made me wonder about the origins of skyr, but brought me no nearer to a conclusion.

* Editors' notes. According to a paper delivered at the 12th International Dairy Congress at Stockholm in 1949 and not, as far as we can ascertain, superseded, there are three species involved: *Streptococcus thermophilus, Lactobacillus helviticus* and *Lactobacillus bulgaricus.* All occur in other parts of the world. The first is used as a starter for Swiss cheese. The second is one of a group of bacteria which are used in milk fermentation. The third is the high acid-producing lactic acid bacterium of yoghurt.

Many years ago my husband attended a dinner party in New Delhi, given by the late Prime Minister Nehru. The last item on the menu was something called Shrikhand. Great was his surprise when this turned out to be skyr, made and served in exactly the same way as in Iceland. He was told it was a very popular dish in Northern India.

I have since been told that it is also made in the Caucasus and other eastern countries. It is difficult to find facts about the eating habits of people in such far away places. But in the Sagas we have many accounts of Icelanders travelling to the east, to Novgorod and Constantinople, so they might have learned the method there.

The people in Iceland went through great hardships in times past. Famine was more than once brought on by pestilence; volcanic eruptions destroyed animals and spoiled the grazing; a deteriorating climate and many other things led to abject poverty. To mention just one example, one third of the population died of smallpox in 1707–9.

The people had to learn to use all possible resources of nourishment to stay alive. Perhaps the skyr and the whey extracted from it played an important role, not only as food, but also as a means to preserve food.

We are told that cattle and sheep became quite numerous soon after the settlement of Iceland. From that time and up to the 18th century it was customary to keep cows and ewes in the mountains and herd them from the mountain-huts during the summer, to utilize the best grazing. In some parts of the country the custom to take the lambs from the ewes as soon as they could live on grass went on until the beginning of this century. Around and after the great disasters already mentioned, the milk from the ewes became the main source of butter and skyr. At the turn of this century cattle increased again. When the mountain huts were no longer in use, the ewes were herded from the farms and driven home for the milking.

But the ewes only supplied milk during the summer, so during the period when they were the chief source of milk, the skyr could only be made for some months every year and had to be stored for use during the rest of the year. The method of making skyr is the same whether milk from cows or ewes is used, but the taste is different. Few people are now alive who remember the taste of products made with sheep's milk.

Making Skyr

For making good skyr one needs a few spoonfuls from batches already made in order to get the right bacterial growth, which makes the right consistency; but when there was no milk to be had for months, another method had to be found when starting the skyr-making for the summer. Chemically made rennet first came into use here in the 19th century, so the housewives of old had to make their own and found an ingenious method.

One of the last calves born during the summer was slaughtered. Then, before it had any nourishment other than milk, the stomach was carefully cut from the intestines. The openings were tied with string and the stomach hung up to dry. Next summer, just before there was milk enough to permit the making of skyr, the stomach was carefully washed, placed into a bowl and covered with salted water. After 1–2 weeks the rennet was ready to use.

Then small bowls of milk were set out in the fresh air on a bright day and after a while put into a warm spot indoors. Later the housewife selected the bowl in which the milk had curdled to her liking and with that she started the skyr making for the summer.

Skyr is made of skimmed milk. Before separators came into use, every farm had several wooden bowls or troughs made with holes near the bottom, stopped by plugs. After sieving the milk it was poured into these vessels to set and at the right time the plug was removed and the milk poured through the holes, leaving the cream in the vessel. The skimmed milk was then poured into a pot and boiled to kill the undesirable bacteria. Big wooden bowls, carefully scrubbed and dried in the fresh air, were filled from the pot and the milk cooled down to 37°C. There were no thermometers at the farms, so the heat was simply tested with the tip of a finger. For each ten litres of milk a good spoonful of skyr or curdled milk was needed, and only two drops of rennet.

I remember it as a very serious moment when my mother taught me how to make skyr. It was considered something of an art to make a really good skyr and anyone who was so unlucky as to make a batch that was not perfectly bland, and even, felt degraded. So it was a solemn occasion to be taught how to measure the temperature, whip the spoonful of skyr into the right consistency, measure the rennet carefully and stir it slowly, slowly into the milk, before covering the bowl with a lid, and on top of that a clean sheet and a special blanket. The milk must not cool too fast. I never had the experience to start making skyr from curdled milk, as we made skyr all the year round, but knew that it would take a few batches before the right consistency was obtained.

After 1½–2 hours the milk had curdled. A wooden frame to which was tacked a sieve of cotton cloth was put over a barrel, the skyr carefully spooned into the sieve, so that the whey could run out of it into the barrel. After a couple of hours the skyr was ready for eating. In a cool place it kept its freshness for some days and then started getting sour. Some preferred it that way.

Up to the time of modern refrigeration, the farms had to store skyr during the summer for the winter months, when there was less or no milk to be had.

That was done by putting skyr in a barrel, adding cool, boiled milk day by day and scooping the whey from the top. When you had a full barrel soured to the right degree, melted tallow was poured on top and the skyr was safe for several months. The sour skyr was never eaten with sugar and cream, but mixed with porridge (in later times) and eaten with milk.

By the way, sugar of course has only been in daily use for about a hundred years. Before that it was a great luxury, sparingly used.

In former times there were many things which were difficult to obtain, even cotton cloth for the sieves, but the housewives found other materials. They cut the long hairs from the tails of horses and cows, spun them and knitted or sewed sieves. Even rough grass could be used, and later sack-cloth.

Uses of Whey

Now we come to the manifold uses of the whey.

The Sagas tell of great barrels of whey in the larders of the farms. Once a chieftain hid in a barrel of whey and saved his life when his enemies burnt down his farm. Sometimes whey was used to put out fires, so there has been a good supply at hand, which again means that a lot of skyr was made from plenty of milk.

Whey was much sought after as a drink and it had a fixed price in barter between farmers and fishermen. A fisherman who had a drink of whey in his boat neither went thirsty nor starved. To become a really tasty drink the whey had to be stored for a long time, some say two years. In my youth the housewife who had an oak barrel for her whey was greatly envied, as the oak improved the taste, and mixed with water it is a very good drink. The dairies are now putting whey mixed with fruit flavour on the market, hoping to make people use it instead of soft drinks.

As mentioned before, whey was used to preserve food and as such was very important before modern refrigeration.

When the lambs were slaughtered in autumn, practically every home made a lot of liver and blood sausages. The sheeps' heads were singed and boiled, the meat cut from the bones and pressed into forms. These and many other things were put into a barrel of whey and will keep for a year in a cool place. Even some vegetables, edible seaweed, hardboiled eggs were stored in whey or sour skyr. When food was scarce, fishbones, bones from sheeps' heads and other small bones were put into whey for a long time. When they had gone soft they were boiled and eaten.

It improved the taste of a roast to marinate it in whey, a custom long forgotten.

Serving Skyr

But to our own day, plain skyr or skyr mixed with porridge, served with a slice of liver- or blood-sausage and milk, is found by many to be a very satisfying meal and much recommended by nutrition experts.

Today skyr is one of the most popular products of the Icelandic dairies. It is easy to serve, tastes good and is rich in nutritional value. It can be varied by whipping a raw egg into it or mixing it with fruit. A tasty spread for biscuits can be made out of it mixed with finely chopped onion, a little paprika and salt. It goes well instead of cottage-cheese in cheese-cakes. Weight watchers mix it with honey and eat it with skimmed milk.

But to get the full enjoyment out of your first taste of skyr, just sprinkle it with sugar and pour some cream over it and forget about the calories.

References

Baldur Johnsen: *Húsfreyjan:* Reykjavík, 1960.

Gísli Guðmunsson: *Mjólkurfraettir:* Reykjavík, 1918.

Jónas Jónasson: *Íslenskir þjóðhættir:* Reykjavík, 1945.

Hólmfríður Pétursdóttir: 19, júní, Reykjavík, 1960.

Skúli V. Guðjónsson: *Manneldi og heilsurfar í fornöld:* Reykjavík, 1949.

Iceland 874-1974: Reykjavík, 1975.

Bergsveinn Skúlason: verbal information.

Long Pepper: A Short History

PHILIP AND MARY HYMAN

Philip and Mary Hyman, Americans who met in Paris in the 1960s and have lived there ever since, have a long record of achievements in the field of food history, usually but not always French culinary history. When the enormous 25-volume survey of traditional French foods, region by region, was being initiated by the Conseil National des Arts Culinaires, they were invited to take responsibility for the extensive historical content of all the volumes which were to be compiled. This has kept them more than busy for well over a decade and has left them with an unrivalled knowledge of the foods of France. Following this great enterprise, they have been invited to write The Oxford Companion to French Food, *expected in 2005.*

In the third century B.C., Theophrastus wrote that there were two kinds of pepper: black pepper and long pepper. Nearly four hundred years later, Pliny described and gave prices for three: black pepper, which cost 4 deniers a pound; white pepper, which cost 7 deniers a pound; and long pepper, costing 15 deniers a pound. Almost two thousand years later on, two of Pliny's peppers are still with us, but the third—long pepper—seems to have disappeared. This 'disappearance' is a relatively recent phenomenon; it occurred somewhere midway between Pliny and us. In the middle ages, for example, long pepper is still a popular condiment—it is mentioned in all the medieval cookery manuscripts. Still later, Bailey, writing about peppers in 1588, notes that 'long pepper is to be seen in every shop'. But things had changed since Pliny's day, when long pepper cost about four times more than black pepper; a 1607 French book (*Thrésor de Santé*) lists the price of long pepper as only 1 ducat a quintal, whereas black pepper cost 12! Curiously, at about this same time, when one would think that the low price of this spice might indicate its being more readily available and in greater use, it mysteriously begins to disappear from recipe books. Its disappearance was so rapid and so complete that by 1702 a prominent French food writer wrote: 'I have nothing to say about long pepper since it is no longer used with food.' Indeed today, many people (even some authorities) no longer know what long pepper is, and it has become virtually impossible to buy the spice in the west.

The two questions this article will try to answer are, what is long pepper, and why did it disappear? [Those who are curious will find futher interesting comments by Charles Perry and Colin Dence in *PPC 7*.]

The answer to the first question is relatively simple. Long pepper, like black pepper, is a member of the *Piperacea* tribe; it is said to be native to India, and the fruit (the pepper itself) is an elongated, grayish-black, catkin-like spike made up of numerous tiny seeds, all adhering to a central core. Long peppers are picked before they ripen (ripening on the plant is said to lessen their potency), then dried in the sun or in special ovens. There are two varieties of long pepper, which differ primarily in size: the Indian long pepper (*Piper longum*) and the Javanese long pepper (called either *Piper officinarum,* or *Piper chaba,* or *Piper retrofractum!*). The Javanese variety is the longer of the two—up to two and a half inches (6 cm) long and five-sixteenths of an inch (8 mm) thick—and is generally considered the better in quality.

In India, long pepper has been used in cooking since as early as 2000 B.C.; it was being used there even before black pepper, though both spices are native to the same region. Ironically, India is now a major *importer* of long peppers. In 1971–72, India imported over 250 tons of long pepper to supplement its own production. 'Production' may be too strong a word in this case, since one Indian authority says that long peppers are generally still gathered from the wild plants rather than cultivated in an organized fashion. However, India does seem to export some of its own long pepper crop, although when, and if, one encounters long peppers for sale they are probably of the Javanese variety.

It is important to note here that long pepper and black pepper have quite different names in Sanskrit; black pepper was called 'Maricha ushana', or 'hapusha' (modern Hindi 'Kali Mirch') whereas long pepper was called Pippali' (modern Hindi 'Pipli'). It is this second name that gave us our modern word for pepper. For the Greeks, pepper was 'Peperi', which became the Latin 'Piper'. Thus the evolution and origin of the modern word 'pepper' simply go to prove that long pepper was the *first* pepper known in classical times; and it is clear that, when black pepper appeared, it was simply given the name, by extension, of its forerunner. So long pepper was the more ancient of the two spices in Europe as well as in India. Why did it disappear? Black pepper was no rival, since the two spices were used side by side for thousands of years in Europe, as they still are in India. We believe that the explanation is to be found in part by closely examining long pepper itself.

Gerard, writing in 1597, said of long pepper: 'It is in taste sharper and hotter than common black pepper, yet sweeter and of a better taste.' Long pepper's disappearance may not be so much due to the fact that this 'hotness' displeased people, but that another 'hotness' took its place. From its first appearance in the 16th century, authorities began confusing long pepper with the fruits of *Capsicum annuum,* a completely different plant of American origin. This plant exists in many varieties, from the mild green pepper to the hot, red chilli pepper. The latter kind, the ones which concern us here, are not only 'long', but they (like the true long peppers) were sometimes also referred to as Guinea Pepper—adding to the confusion between the two spices. Unlike long pepper, some of the hot varieties of *Capsicum annuum* could be grown in warm European climates. These American hot 'peppers' (which aren't true peppers since they belong to a completely different family of plants), first made their appearance in Europe in the 16th century, strangely coinciding with the period during which the long pepper began to disappear. Could it be that this 'new' American pepper filled the need for a spice that was 'hotter than common black pepper', as Gerard had said, cost less, and was more readily available? We think so. But there is another reason why long pepper may have been so easily replaced by this newcomer; long pepper travelled poorly. Unlike black pepper, which keeps well, long pepper was particularly subject to mold. If the peppers were not thoroughly dried before shipping, the little moisture they contained would suffice for mold to set in. Bailey had warned in 1588 that: 'long pepper is moister than any other kind and it will sooner mold and waxe mustie than any other and so will quickly be woorme eaten and full of holes.' So chilli peppers must have been all the more welcome to merchants (and consumers), plagued by such an easily (and oft) damaged exotic product. Lastly, we would suggest that most European cuisines (unlike those of tropical and subtropical countries) have no requirement for two spices 'hotter than common black pepper', so that once the chilli pepper was made available, there was probably little need or desire to retain its predecessor.

Who knows? It is difficult, if not impossible, to explain why a spice like long pepper disappeared from European kitchens—there are probably answers other than those we have put forward. In any event, it would be a welcome sight to see it more generally available in the west again, so that we today could make our own decision about this spice's merits and demerits.

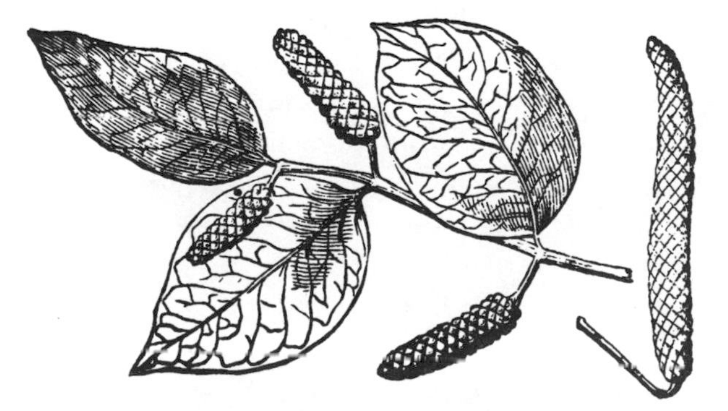

Long pepper, from Gerard's Herbal *(the revised and enlarged edition of 1633).*

Tuscan Cold Pressed Extra Virgin Olive Oil

LESLIE ZYW, WITH AN INTRODUCTION BY ELIZABETH DAVID

Although Tuscany, in Central Italy, has for centuries been renowned for the excellence of its olive oil, the very finest of those oils have seldom found their way into foreign markets. Such oils, in a sense the equivalents of single vineyard wines, have been sold direct from the farmer producers to local people who go to the farm to get their supplies. Today, massive publicity promoting commercially refined, rectified, blended, characterless olive oils and seed oils, combining with the immensely high cost of labour in Italy, threatens the live growers who produce their oil by traditional methods. Many have abandoned the struggle, destroyed their olive trees and replaced them with vines. A few of the more persistent are finding export markets for their oils. I cannot speak for American readers, but for English ones I can with certainty say that information about how to choose these fine oils is almost as much sought after as the oil itself. Again, as with wine, the only certain way to find out which you like and which you don't is by trial and error, and errors come expensive. So it does help if you have a sound idea of what you are looking for and of what the label means—if anything. Is there, for example, a significant difference between an oil labelled cold pressed and one with no reference on the label to pressing method? Is there such a thing as hot pressing and if so what is its effect on the oil? What distinguishes Extra Virgin oil from *Soprafino* Virgin, Fine Virgin and unqualified Virgin? What is the importance of First Pressing as opposed to Second Pressing? Why are some olive oils green and other golden? Why have some a strong smell and taste of the fruit, others little of either? Some oils are much publicised as 'health' foods on the grounds that they have a very low acid content. How does the finest cold pressed virgin olive oil of Tuscany stand in relation to such claims? What about those saturated and unsaturated fats the dieticians are always on about?

In the following article Mrs. Leslie Zyw who, with her husband and son, produces a remarkable olive oil on an estate in the hills of Castagnato Carducci in the province of Livorno, answers all those queries and some others I didn't know I needed to ask. Her account seems to me most enlightening.

ELIZABETH DAVID

The olives are harvested in winter, beginning when they are almost ripe, usually in November. They are taken to a press at a local farm. There they are ground into a paste, flesh, stones and all. This paste is then pressed hydraulically to extract the oil and liquids. These then pass to a centrifugal separator, which yields pure oil on one side and gets rid of water and wastes on the other. That is all. That is how First Pressing, Cold Pressed Olive Oil is made. The residual dryish pulp is then sold to a factory, where it is pressed again with heat and boiling water. It yields a fattier and more acid oil called Olio di Sansa. This is Second Pressing Oil. It is often blended with virgin oils by the big oil merchants to make commercial branded oils, which have a standard flavour (if any) and quality. The point to note is that farm produced, cold pressed olive oil is always First Pressing. It has to be. The facilities for doing a second pressing with heat do not exist in a small press, or *frantoio.*

This woodcut and that on the next page were drawn by Isabella Parasole and carved by Leonardo Norsino for the first edition of Castore Durante's Herbario Novo, *1585.*

Another important factor to bear in mind is that the best oil is classified as Extra Virgin. This means that it must have less than 1% of acidity. Then, in descending order of quality come Soprafino Virgin, Fine Virgin and Virgin. This last can have up to 4% of acidity. Then comes Olio Lampante (lamp oil), which is inferior oil of high acidity. This goes to the refineries for blending with other oils. Unfortunately, these classifications of olive oil are misleading and need to be changed. They classify oil by acidity only, without making it clear whether this is obtained by cold pressing of good, clean olives, or by rectification of inferior oil in a factory.

Another point of importance to understand is that, here in Tuscany, each grower of olives takes his harvest to the press and gets back his own oil. There is no need to go to the communal press, where the quality is, inevitably, average rather than high.

So, when choosing olive oil it is necessary to make sure that it is Cold Pressed. That means that it must also be First Pressing. Then to see that it is classified as Extra Virgin. Finally, to choose an oil that has the grower's name on it, if that is possible. Only in this way can the consumer be sure that the oil is a genuine, natural product and has not been subjected to any heating or chemical processes, which destroy its nutritious qualities.

Real olive oil of this kind does, of course, vary from year to year, like wine. There are also differences of colour, consistency, aroma and flavour from one district to another. As a general rule, however, the finest oil comes from the Tuscan hills. Olive oils can be chosen, tasted and selected, just like

OLIVA DOMESTICA.

wines. The range is enormous. It remains only for the consumer to find an oil that pleases his palate and to buy that.

Olives are green when unripe and purple black when ripe. There are many different varieties of olives grown in Tuscan olive yards and this too influences the character and flavour of the oil.

Table olives grow on different kinds of trees, specially developed to produce large, fleshy olives.

When the olive harvest begins, the first oil coming from the press is often very green, as the olives are less ripe than later on. Some people find this delicious. It is less bland and more piquant than the more mature oil. It also contains more vegetable residue than the oil which is sold later and which has therefore had more time in which to settle. A harvest time treat for the olive pickers is made by toasting bread over a wood fire, rubbing it with garlic and then pouring the fresh green oil over it. This simple food is quite superb. The very green oil becomes less green with time and eventually it looks much the same as the oil pressed later in the harvest.

Unfiltered oil has more and better flavour than filtered oil. But it is turbid and has vegetable residue. This *fondo* is characteristic of the best oil and it is quite harmless. It can easily be used up just by shaking the bottle a little when using the oil.

Olive oil, alas, cannot be produced cheaply. The trees need a lot of costly and laborious attention throughout the whole agricultural year.

In early spring the trees must be pruned. This is highly skilled work, essential to the productivity of the trees. It is done with ladder, secateurs and handsaw; branch by branch and tree by tree, through the whole olive grove. Then the prunings have to be cleared up. The thicker wood is extracted for firewood and the little branches either burnt or minced up by machine to be ploughed into the earth later. Then the land must be manured and ploughed. Olives demand manure with a high nitrate content. This, nowadays, is very expensive indeed. Like all fruit trees, olives have to be sprayed from time to time to guard them against attacks by fungi and insects. This too costs money. Suckers which sprout from the base and branches of the trees must be removed by mattocking and pruning and the fields left completely clear of briars and stones, so that the expensive nylon nets which are laid down before the harvest cannot be ripped or torn. The laying down of these nets is another heavy chore. They have to be sewn together by hand and supported at the sides by stakes, so that the olives cannot escape, even in a high wind. Then the harvest begins. It is a long and labour intensive job; lasting weeks and sometimes months, if the crop is a heavy one. Unfortunately, it has, so far, proved difficult to get much benefit from the use of machines for the harvest on old olive trees in the hills and most olives are therefore still picked by hand. The harvesters climb up ladders placed against the trees and pull the fruit down with their hands; a slow and costly business, as even in a small olive grove it is necessary to employ hired labour to get the job done. Labour costs in Italy are at least as high as they are in Britain. Over and above these burdens, there are high charges for pressing and transport to be paid.

For these reasons good olive oil is expensive. But it is an essential and delicious ingredient of good cooking. Grills, roasts and stews made with herbs and cold pressed oil have a unique and incomparable flavour. Good olive oil should also be added raw and uncooked to all sorts of foods. For salad dressings and for mayonnaise it is exquisite. It can be poured over pasta, over bread and vegetables, or added raw to soups and stews and, indeed, to almost anything one can think of. A little spoonful added to a baby's soup is a valuable addition to his diet. An excellent quick sauce for spaghetti is made by sieving a small quantity of ripe tomatoes and adding to them crushed garlic, salt, pepper and a good dollop of the best oil. Warm all this up, but on no account let it boil. Serve over hot spaghetti with grated Parmesan cheese on top. Salsa verde, or green sauce, is another quick and good olive oil sauce. It consists of finely chopped parsley and garlic, salt, pepper and plenty of olive oil to mix it with. This is excellent with baked potatoes, cold left-over potatoes, anchovies and many other things.

A point of importance follows from all this: the health value of cold pressed olive oil, particularly when eaten uncooked. It must rank as one of the most nutritious foods available to mankind. It is low in saturated fats and rich in unsaturated fats. It is therefore not harmful to people with arterio-sclerotic or coronary disease. It is low in acidity and exceptionally easy to digest by delicate stomachs, by the old and by the very young. It is very mildly laxative and ideally suited to keep the human inside running in a happy and well oiled fashion. In olive growing districts it is traditional to give olive oil against the rheumatism and to benefit the liver, stomach and vascular troubles. Olive oil is, in addition, full of valuable minerals and vitamins, including vitamins A, D and E. These health benefits, it must be emphasised, come mainly from eating cold pressed olive oil *uncooked*. One eats it cooked for gourmet reasons rather than health reasons. The oil is also good used as a liniment and as a sunburn lotion. That is, of course, when it can be spared from the table!

Good olive oil can keep for a long time without spoiling, although it is considered to be at its best in the first year. Certainly it is good to benefit from the fresh oil when it arrives after the harvest.

Glass, steel or tin containers are ideal for olive oil. Plastic is unsuitable for more than a short time. It keeps best when stored in dim light at moderate room temperature. Sunshine, bright light and extremes of heat or cold are all deleterious. Cold will make the oil congeal and too much heat or light can adversely affects its flavour and colour. In a normal kitchen none of these things should present any problems.

The Nut Oils of Berry

JANE GRIGSON

Jane Grigson wrote numerous books and many of her fans would hesitate, with such a lavish display before them, to identify any one book as their favourite. However, we believe that many people would name the pair of books which Jane wrote quite early on: Jane Grigson's Vegetable Book *(1978) and* Jane Grigson's Fruit Book *(1982), the second of which, incidentally, is reviewed by Jane Davidson on page 331. These two books were brilliant concepts, and because they so charmingly combined historical and description material with heaps and heaps of wonderfully good recipes, they have become more or less indispensable references, guaranteed their place on a cook's book shelf 'from here to eternity' (to borrow a suitably sweeping phrase from the world of cinema).*

In the Fruit Book *there is a recipe for Cranberry Tea Bread, in which she mentions the oils which are the subject of this essay, but briefly. She had clearly, as was her wont, done a great deal of research on them, and we were very fortunate in having the essay which reflected this research offered to us by Jane in* PPC 9 *in 1981.*

In the summer of 1980 in France, we saw an advertisement in the local paper for walnut oil 'from the last oil-mill in Berry'. The Berry is tucked into the great bend of the Loire above Orléans, and part of it—the part containing the oil-mill—falls into our department. We set off full of expectations to Noyers-sur-Cher. Such an appropriate address indicated a picturesque old stone mill on the river bank, surrounded by a walnut orchard.

The Huilerie Guénard turned out to be a smart new factory on a four-lane highway, with a shop and office in one corner. There we saw walnut oil, an oil we knew from occasional purchases in England and France, and also hazelnut oil which we had never come across before. Madame Guénard uncorked a bottle for us and we smelled a waft of toasted hazelnuts. Then her husband showed us round the factory, pointing out the old crushing machinery and the new electronic scanner for sorting out the nuts. Three generations of Guénards worked an oil mill at Saint Aignan immediately across the river, until the recent move to Noyers. In the grandfather's time, a donkey turned the stone for the first crushing of the nut: farmers who had brought in their loads of walnuts sat and talked and drank until the oil was ready.

The walnut harvest comes neatly after the vintage, with a restful break in between. Sadly in our country of Loire and Cher it is not what it was. The decline began with the appalling winter of 1880. Then came the passion for walnut furniture. In the last twenty years walnuts dotted about in fields and hedgerows have been sacrificed to the convenience of tractor and combine. Walnuts were never popular too near the house: once when our young daughter had a headache and temperature, our neighbour scolded me for letting her play beneath a walnut tree. Walnut shade is still reckoned to be unhealthy by country people.

Monsieur Guénard's walnuts now come from the Dordogne where they flourish in the warmer climate. He does not buy the expensive thick-shelled nuts that are intended for winter dessert, but the thin-shelled variety that crushes easily. His hazelnuts do not come from France at all, but from Italy, from Avellino behind Vesuvius where Europe's best hazelnuts grow.

We asked if the oils were exported to England. No. Indeed the Guénards had just returned from a fortnight in London, and had had a poor reception from Fortnum's and Harrod's. They were disappointed—and hurt. Their oils are good enough for Fauchon's in Paris after all, which is a far better food shop than anything in Britain.

We took our load of oil back to Trôo and wrote three letters. One to Justin de Blank of the grocery shops, one to Robin Yapp, the Loire and Rhône wine merchant of Mere, in Wiltshire, and one to William Tullberg the mustard maker. They all ordered Guénard oil, and were pleased with the sales. William Tullberg handed the idea over to Taylor and Lake, wine and speciality food importers, who also sell a good green Tuscan olive oil.

Six months after that first visit to Noyers-sur-Cher, I went into the shop at Neal's Yard in Covent Garden and stubbed my toe on a pile of boxes. The French friend with me observed that they were full of Monsieur Guénard's oil, walnut, hazelnut and a new almond oil which is delicate yet full of character (they had been supplied by Taylor and Lake).

These oils are expensive—consider the price of a packet of nuts and you will understand why. They are luxuries by comparison with the unnamed oils of the ordinary grocery. If you use them as a flavouring though, the price seems more affordable. People sometimes add a collection of dubious ingredients with the idea of 'cheering up' a green salad, or make an elaborate sauce for a cooked vegetable: if they were to use a nut oil for a simple vinaigrette, money would be saved and the dish improved simply and elegantly for less money. It is always a good idea to check the quantity of vinaigrette you make for a salad. Most of us make far too much. When the salad is turned there should be no liquid left in the bottom of the bowl, and the leaves should be lightly coated. I find that 2 tablespoons of oil and half a teaspoon of vinegar is about right for a fine healthy summer lettuce. If you watch the quantities, measuring them abstemiously, you will save enough virtuously to buy an occasional bottle of walnut or hazelnut or almond oil.

Other uses for these oils? Try nut vinaigrettes with globe artichokes or Jerusalem artichokes, cooked and sliced. You can chop a few of the appropriate nuts—toast hazelnuts and almonds first—and add them with chopped parsley. Mayonnaise flavoured finally with a small quantity of nut oil is delightful with fish and fish fritters, with cold chicken, too. Walnut oils have their own salads in France, salads that come into their own after Christmas with lamb's lettuce. The vigneron's salad is lamb's lettuce topped with beetroot and hard-boiled egg and dressed with a walnut and oil vinaigrette. In other versions you put lamb's lettuce into a warmed bowl, perhaps with beetroot, when you fry little cubes of bacon or salt pork or bread lightly and not too fast in walnut oil. This is tipped over the salad very hot. The pan is deglazed with cider vinegar or wine vinegar and added sizzling to the bowl. The whole thing is then turned and eaten immediately, as a first course. This old salad is, I suspect, the original of the fashionable warm salads of *nouvelle cuisine* chefs. it is more successful than many of them.

Nut Oil in Cake-Making

My final suggestion is that you use these oils when making cakes (or puddings), substituting them for two thirds of the butter in, say, a pound cake. Quarter of a pound each of sugar, self-raising flour and eggs (this usually means two of medium size), plus a level teaspoon of self-raising powder, 6 tablespoons of nut oil and 2 tablespoons of melted butter. All this mixed together electrically, and a final addition of chopped nuts and a spoonful or two of walnut or hazelnut liqueur or brandy. Oven temperature 350°F (180°C, gas 4) for 45 minutes upwards according to the depth of the tin you bake it in. Good and simple. If the family has a sweet tooth, you can ice the cake adding a little oil to the glacé icing.

A Greek Recipe

Sometimes I substitute nut oil for olive oil when making one of those cakes they serve at breakfast time in Greek hotels. Very good with coffee, and they keep well. In Lent and Advent especially, Greeks leave out the eggs in the following recipe.

Mix together in the order given:

150 ml (1/4 pint) nut oil or olive oil
175 g (6 oz) caster sugar
juice and finely grated zest of a large lemon and a large orange
2 eggs
2 tablespoons walnut or hazelnut liqueur or brandy
350 g (scant 12 oz) self-raising flour
rounded teaspoon cinnamon
60 g (2 oz) each of appropriate nuts, chopped, and candied peel

Use a processor if you like, and add a little extra of one or several of the liquids to make a cake dough. Bake in a deep loaf tin for about an hour, or until cooked through, at 350°F (180°C, gas 4).

Mad, Bad, Despised and Dangerous

Elizabeth David

The attractive proposition that aubergine and auberge might have some connection was recently put to me. It opened up some glorious possibilities. The game had to be resisted. There are already plenty of garblings of the Indian *badinjan* without my weaving an *aubergiste* or a *jardinier de l' auberge* or other such fancy into the rich confusion. So I turned instead to a few remembered cookery book and other references, early and late, to the aubergine, badinjan, berenjena, melanzana, or egg plant. Quite a collection of oddities could be put together. The present one is no more than a beginning.

The first book I turned to was a modern one, Dr. Henri Leclerc's *Les Légumes de France,* undated but circa 1930. Dr. Lerclerc, a physician on General Foch's medical staff during the 1914 war, subsequently produced some entertaining and original works about vegetables and fruit, their origins, their history, and how best to cook them. He was keen on vegetarian diets, but—being possessed of a sense of humour—never over-persuaded. His comments on the derivation of aubergine provide a good example of his touch:

> The word aubergine is among those which must fill with joy the souls of those numerous philologists whose innocent mania it is to claim that every term in the language derives from Sanscrit; without in the least being forced into the tortuous acrobatics which such exercises usually entail, they may elegantly and painlessly prove that *Vatin Gana,* name of the aubergine in Sanscrit, gave birth to the Persian *badingen,* from which the Arabs derived *albadingen,* which via the Spanish *albadingena* became the aubergine.

The Spaniards appear to have accepted *berenjenas,* as they were called in the early Spanish cookery books, without difficulty. In the 1529 edition of *Libro De Guisades Manjares Y Potajes,* Ruperto de Nola[1] for example, gives four recipes for them, including one for *berenjenas en escabeche* and one for *berenjenas espesas,* peeled aubergines cooked in meat broth with onions and pounded almonds, sieved, and made into an egg-thickened custard spiced with nutmeg, cinnamon, cloves, dried coriander 'softened', and Aragonese cheese.

In Italy *berenjenas* had a bad press. They were variously called *mala insana* and *pomi disdegnosi,* and also had some garbled names such as *molegnane moniache* (Cristofaro di Messisburgo, *Libro Novo,* 1557) indicating that they were in some way associated with Armenia, like apricots. Antonio Frugoli, an early seventeenth century steward who wrote a hefty work on the art and practice of stewardship, published in Rome in 1631,[2] calls them *marignani,* and says they are low class food, eaten by Jews. This curious piece of folklore—did it have some relation to the provenance of the plant?—was repeated two and a half centuries later by Pellegrino Artusi in his *Scienza in Cucina,* ca. 1880, asserting that 'forty years ago they were scarcely to be seen in the Florence market, being held base Jewish food'. He calls them *petonciani.* We are almost back to *badinjan.* At what period *petonciani* turned into the modern Italian *melanzane* I have no idea. Probably both names, with local and regional variations coexisted for a long time. Certainly Scappi in 1570 uses both *molignane* and *melanzane;*[3] so does Castore Durante in his *Herbario Novo* of 1585. As for those *pomi disdegnosi* of the fifteenth and sixteenth centuries, a recipe for candying them in the

MELANZANE.

A woodcut of the aubergine from Castore Durante's Herbario Novo, *1585.*

Genoese fashion appeared in Alexis of Piedmont's *De Secreti* published in 1557. In the English translation[4] of this work, done from the French and published in 1558, the recipe was omitted. The translator was probably baffled by those mad, bad, despised, noxious apples. I don't know if candied aubergines were still made in Genoa or anywhere else, but I do remember many years ago in Greece buying, out of curiosity, a tin of aubergine jam, one of those very sweet and heavily syrupy confections you get given in Greece in spoonfuls, as a token of hospitality. The aubergines were tiny little things, and could just as easily have been infant melons or cucumbers as aubergines. The confection was a strange one, but then the aubergine *is* strange, in appearance, in texture and in taste. Its capacity to absorb olive oil, butter or whatever cooking medium is used is also notorious. One way and another, early resistance to this odd fruit is understandable.

The sixteenth century Roman physician Castore Durante, in his *Herbario Novo* mentioned above, said *petronciane* or *melanzane* were really not of a very agreeable taste, they were windy, hard to digest, and not a healthy food. Although they are eaten in Italy like mushrooms, boiled, with oil, salt, and pepper, or boiled in slices and eaten as a salad with oil, pepper and vinegar, or again prepared in a pickle, if you eat them too often they generate melancholy humours, cancer, leprosy, headaches, hardening of the liver and the spleen, and induce long fevers and a bad complexion in the whole person. However, prepared and eaten as he had described 'they are less harmful'. In Germany, says Durante, *melanzane* are called *Dollapffel,* and in Latin *melengena* or *mala insana,* in French *'pomes demoers,* which is to say *pomi d'amore'*. A fine piece of confusion, not helped when you find that Durante also calls tomatoes both *pomi d'oro* and *pomi d'Amor,* but in Latin *aurea mala.* They are a kind of *melanzane,* he says. Some were red as blood when they are ripe, others the colour of gold; some call them *pomi d'etiopia,* Ethiopian apples. They are eaten in the same way as *melanzane,* with pepper, salt, and oil, but they provide little and poor nourishment. Interesting, that reference to tomatoes being known as Ethiopian apples. They must have already been cultivated in Africa some while before Durante, who is supposed to have been one of Pope Sixtus V's physicians, was working on his Herbal.

Perhaps I should also mention that the tomato, like the aubergine, was at one time dubbed *mala insana,* at any rate according to Doctor Leclerc. As for the *pommes d' amour* confusion, that one persisted for quite a while in France. La Quintinye in 1695 mentions *melanzane* or *pommes d'amour* in his list of plants which dislike the cold, others being Indian pepper, summer savory, and the *pomme d'orée.*[5] Evidence of how the French cooked aubergines in the seventeenth and eighteenth centuries is singularly lacking. Doctor Leclerc says they didn't. What the Doctor seems not to have known is that in the Catalan language the aubergine is *albergìnia,* surely an indication that aubergines had crossed the Spanish Catalan frontiers into southern France long before the time they were first launched on the Paris market which, again according to Doctor Leclerc, was not until 1825, when they were introduced by a specialist in *primeurs* called Decouflé, whose business was in the rue de la Santé. Whether by that time European cooks had discovered that the two kinds of *pommes d' amour,* both of the Solanaceae family, had a certain

This woodcut of the tomato plant, like that of the aubergine on page 190, was drawn by Isabella Parasole and carved by Leonardo Norsino for the first edition of Castore Durante's Herbario Novo, *1585.*

affinity for each other, I am none too sure, but what is certain is that in our own times the aubergine began to get submerged in tomato purées and sauces, and modern French recipes became rather repetitious. But Doctor Leclerc offers the following variant of the Turkish *Imam bayeldi,* which has one or two original features, with the tomatoes kept under control . . .

Aubergines a l'Athenienne

Split a dozen aubergines in quarters lengthwise and without completely separating them. Prepare a mixture of vegetables as follows: coarsely shred 5 skinned and deseeded tomatoes, a handful of sorrel and 2 onions; add 6 chopped cloves of garlic and a little fennel, likewise chopped; season with salt, pepper, and cayenne. Stuff the mixture into the quartered aubergines, which you press back into shape and tie with string. Arrange them in a baking dish. Pour over them the juice of 5 lemons and a quarter of a bottle of olive oil. Put into the oven for 35 to 40 minutes, then leave them to cool in their sauce, if possible on ice.

Arrange the aubergines in a vegetable dish and pour the cooking juices over them. This is served cold and as an hors-d'oeuvre.

'In savouring the preparation,' Doctor Lerclerc adds, 'in which so many different flavours have harmonised, it is difficult not to feel compassion for the centuries of ignorance and darkness in which the aubergine, the aubergine with its amethyst skin, confined in dispensaries between the pallid marshmallow and the perfidious hemlock, was reduced to the subaltern and humiliating role of anodine poultice.' This last remark is explained by an earlier paragraph in Doctor Leclerc's essay in which he quotes from Valmont de Bomare's *Dictionnaire raisonné universelle d'histoire naturelle,* 1776. According to Valmont de Bomare the aubergine was used only in the form of anodine and resolvative poultices in the treatment of haemorrhoids, cancers, burns and inflammations. Doctor Castore Durante, who was of the opinion that *mala insana* or *melanzana* could cause cancer, would probably have thought it very proper to use the same offending fruit in its treatment.

* * * *

As I have already mentioned, Bartolomeo Scappi, private cook to Pius V, elected Pope in January 1566, gives a variety of recipes for *melanzane, molignane* or *pomi disdegnosi.* He obviously found them useful for Lenten meals. His briefest recipe provides a good idea of the way Italians at that time cooked most of their vegetables.

Per Friggere Molignane in Giorno Quadragesimale (to fry aubergines in Lent)

> Peel the *molignane,* cut them in slices, & parboil them in water, & let them drain on the work table, & flour them, & fry them in good olive oil, & when they are fried, serve them with pepper & pour orange juice over, or else with a sauce made of verjuice, basil & garlic. They may also be covered with *agliata* made with walnuts, or with *salsa verde,* or with other relishes over.[6]

Scappi's *agliata* is made with 6 ounces of fresh peeled walnuts, 4 ounces of sweet almonds, and 6 cloves of parboiled garlic or 1½ raw ones, all pounded together in the mortar with 4 ounces of crumb of bread softened in meat or fish broth, not too salted. To this mixture is added a quarter ounce of powdered ginger, 'and if the sauce is properly pounded, there is no need to sieve it, but it should be diluted with a little of one of the above mentioned broths'. If the walnuts are dry you soften them in cold water so that you can skin them, 'and with the sauce you may pound a little piece of turnip or cabbage stalk well cooked in meat broth if it is a meat day'.

This sixteenth century Italian sauce is surely of Arab origin, and is curiously like one I have eaten two or three times recently in a London Lebanese restaurant. The walnut mixture is used as a stuffing for unpeeled aubergines split down the centre, baked or stewed until very tender, and served cold as a mézé. Vinegar or lemon juice also appear in the Lebanese version, although so far as I remember there is no ginger, or certainly not in the quantity specified by Scappi for his *agliata.* In fact, a little grated fresh green ginger would be an improvement on that enormous amount of ground dried ginger.

* * * *

My concluding curiosity is a recipe for one of those Levantine *torchi* or pickles which have many devotees, although personally I find them rather too violent. It is the method used in the following Turkish version which strikes me as being of particular interest.

Bàdingan Tùrshussu

> Procure as many egg-plants as are required, take the stalks off, split each one in three or four lengthways, without separating them from the bottom, and scald them; then place them in a wicker-basket one over the other, put a piece of board or a plate over them, over which place an iron weight, and let them remain for eight or ten hours, so as to draw the bitter water from them. Then chop up some parsley and celery, which mix with one or two dozen cloves of garlic, each cut in two; then stuff between each slice of the eggplants

with the ingredients, and tie up each of the egg-plants with the stalks of celery, to prevent the stuffing falling out; then arrange them in a stone jar one over the other, cover them with wine vinegar, place a piece of clean board over, and on the top an iron weight to press it; let it remain for about three weeks: it is then ready for use.[7]

References

1. This work, first published about 1520, was originally written in Catalan and later translated into Castilian Spanish. De Nola was perhaps a Catalan born at Nola near Caserta in southern Italy. He claims to have been cook to Ferdinand, King of Naples, meaning presumably the first Aragonese king of that name, who succeeded in 1468 and died in 1494.
2. *Practica E Scalcaria,* Rome, 1631.
3. Bartolomeo Scappi. *Dell'Arte del Cucinare, Con II Mastrao Di Casa E Trincinte.* Venetia 1643, Combo, pp 103, 189-90. Scappi's great work was first published in 1570 and ran into many editions, no two being quite the same.
4. *The Secrets of the Reverende Maister Alexis of Piedmont.* Translated out of the French into English, by Wyllyam Warde, 1558.
5. Jean de la Quintinye. *Instruction pour les Jardins Fruitiers et Potagers.* 1695 edition, p. 14, but a card inserted in the Royal Horticultural Society's copy of this edition says that the section quoted is not by La Quintinye. The book was first published in 1691, soon after La Quintinye's death.
6. Scappi, *op. cit.,* p. 190.
7. *Turkish Cookery Book, A Collection of Receipts.* Compiled by Turabi Effendi, from the best Turkish authorities. Second edition. London. W. H. Allen & Co. 1884.

Snail Trails

Philip Hyman

Certain foods are standard-bearers of national cuisines, and their very mention immediately calls to mind both a people and a place. Such is the case today with snails and France; yet not only were snails barred from many a French table in the past, but they were viewed with as much disgust and disdain as is common in Anglo-Saxon countries today. Attitudes toward the snail have been everything but consistent in France, and it is the object of this article to look at those attitudes historically to see when and how they changed.

Eating snails is by no means a new thing in France. The presence of great mounds of snail shells around dwelling places in France and elsewhere has led one authority to speak of certain prehistoric sites in terms of a 'civilisation d'escargot' (Barrau 1983, p 91). Archeological evidence cannot tell us who was eating snails, how they were prepared, or whether or not they were part of an 'haute cuisine' or common fare, so we must basically wait until the first snail recipes appear in French towards the end of the Middle Ages before we can begin systematically to follow French attitudes towards this food.

Early Recipes and Attitudes

The first French snail recipe we know of is that given around 1390 by an aging Parisian in a sort of anthology of worldly knowledge he had copied out for his young bride. Under the heading 'Limasson que l'en dit escargolz' he described how snails were eaten: simply boiled and served with bread or, he added, 'some people say that they are better fried in oil with onions or in another sauce after being cooked as described above, and they are eaten with [spice] power, and are for rich people' (*Menagier* 1846, vol 2, p 223). Rich people? Why, then, didn't the King's cook, Taillevent, include them in his recipe book which antedates this one? Perhaps because, as later evidence will show, even when snails were high on the list of 'fancy' foods, they were not to every Frenchman's taste.

Indeed, the next time we encounter snails, an anonymous French author seems to be keeping his distance from them. In a late 15th century edition of the *Grant Kalendrier et compost des Bergiers* (The Shepherd's Calendar), 'an argument involving a gendarme and a woman against a snail' is described.

The woman accuses the snail of eating the leaves off of the grapevines in her vineyard, and going on to eat the leaves off of the trees. 'If you don't stop', she says, 'I'll give you such a beating that they'll hear it all the way to Nantes.' The gendarme then speaks up (to the snail) adding: 'we'll sauce you with pepper and onions and serve you up to some Lombard if you don't move on.' Neither the woman nor the gendarme (both of whom we assume are French because of the reference to Nantes) seems to be interested in eating the snail themselves. Instead they threaten it by evoking what must have been the epitome of the snail eater at the time: 'some Lombard' from across the Alps. In 1507, however, we get another opinion. 'Snails,' wrote Nicolas de la Chesnaye, 'are good and wholesome food and are eaten by nobles and gentlemen alike who hunt after them with joy and pleasure, using specially trained dogs[!] as they do in Italy, and this sort of hunt brings them more pleasure than hunting either partridges or quail' (Chesnaye 1507, f° 69). Hunting snails with pointers? Quite clearly, if snails had experienced a period of eclipse, they were making a spectacular about-face.

This change of attitude is further witnessed by the inclusion of snails in one of the first French cookbooks of the Renaissance, *Le Livre de Cuysine* printed around 1540, and their presence in an elaborate banquet served to visiting Swiss dignitaries eight years later (Vial 1937, pp 125–6). Snails also figured on the list of foods to be furnished to the house of Henri d'Albret, King of Navarre in 1538 (Dartigue 1937, p 416); and in 1550, one of the earliest French books on wine, the *Devis sur la Vigne,* described how snails were served in a meal which, until their appearance at the table, had inspired little enthusiasm from one of the participants. The host laughed at his guest's eagerness to help himself to the snails (Gohory 1550). In his *De re Cibaria* (1560), Bruyerin Champier wrote: 'We eat snails only during Lent because they are so much trouble to prepare.' The rich, he said, 'eat them in pies, or serve them on little silver skewers' (quoted in Le Grand d'Aussy 1815, vol 2, pp 143–4). But the best proof of the snail's popularity, at least up until mid-century, was their inclusion in a little booklet published in 1530, whose title translates as *A Noteworthy Treatise concerning the properties of turtles, snails, frogs, and artichokes* by Estienne Laigue (or Daigue). The author criticized four foods that he felt were all equally bizarre but popular with his contemporaries. Of the four, he was kindest to the snail.

> I know snails are ugly, but not so hideous as turtles, nor so vile, and nothing like as poisonous: I also know that the ancients ate them, but I can't accept people's eating them daily, since other foods are more nourishing and of better substance.

The association of the three animals named by Laigue was no novelty or accident, and is of some importance. Already in the *Menagier de Paris,* the author included his snail recipes immediately after one for frogs; and, in the 16th century French cookbook previously alluded to, the snail preparation, as well as one for frogs, was appended to a recipe for turtles. This association was to be a constant in French cookbooks virtually from then on, no doubt partly because there have always been people, like Laigue, who consider these foods unconventional, but also because all three were, oddly enough, considered 'fish' by the Catholic Church and therefore permitted on meatless days. Indeed, the fact that they were a somewhat special form of 'meat' made them attractive to the guest who so enthusiastically ate them at the dinner described in the *Devis sur la Vigne:* 'I'll pounce upon this dish of amphibious creatures,' he exclaimed, 'since they smell less of fish.'

Eclipse

Despite the clear place of importance attributed to snails in texts prior to 1560, the next 90 years saw the snail's fortune take a dramatic turn for the worse, culminating in a virtual banishment from refined tables for almost 200 years thereafter. The first hint of a problem can be perceived as early as 1606 when Joseph Du Chesne, a native of Gascony and a proud defender of that region's cuisine, wrote:

> In Italy and in Gascony, more is made of snails than in France. In the first two places, snails are considered both appetizing and delicious when well prepared. Indeed, snails are common and frequently eaten there, but in some parts of France people don't even know what they are; they are horrified at the idea that we eat them and cannot stand to see them eaten or even prepared. (Du Chesne 1606, p. 476)

Despite Du Chesne's insistence, we suspect that he may have been exaggerating the situation somewhat since only one year later another author (who was neither Gascon nor Italian) says that snails are 'bien bonnes' and describes several preparations for them (*Thresor* 1607, p 347).

Nevertheless, Du Chesne's remarks foreshadow those of 50 years later when opinions had changed. Nicolas Bonnefons, for example, wrote: 'I am astonished that men are so oddly constituted as to find something desirable in this disgusting food which is nothing more than a gastronomic extravagance. Regardless of how they [snails] are prepared, I can find nothing good to say about eating them. But,' he added prudently, 'since I want this work to be as complete as possible, I must inform the reader as to when they are best eaten . . .' He then went on to describe how to prepare them for cooking, and to give several recipes as well (Bonnefons 1654, pp 344–5).

With the exception of some snail recipes in a treatise ostensibly on Spanish cooking published in *Le Nouveau et parfait Maistre d'Hostel Royal* by Pierre de Lune in 1662, snails were totally absent from all French cookbooks of the 17th century. Their exclusion from La Varenne's *Cuisinier François,* the most popular book of the period, is particularly significant, and shows that Bonnefons' remarks reflected more than a personal opinion; snails were clearly out of fashion by the end of the 17th century. As Jean-Louis Flandrin has pointed out, this was a time when the seasonings most commonly used in the Middle Ages and the Renaissance, spices, were giving way to more 'modern' condiments (Flandrin 1983, pp 66–83). Thus it is not surprising to see some of the more 'exotic' food preferences of a previous generation being condemned along with them. Not only was the seasoning of food to change during the 17th century, but the choice of foods as well, and one of the first to go seems to have been the snail. Interestingly enough, however, frogs and turtles did not suffer a similar exclusion, since almost all of the books that omitted snails included one or two recipes for either frogs, or turtles, or both.

The movement away from snails was accentuated throughout the 18th century. Already in 1713, we read: '[Snails] do not merit a place on our tables, however highly they may have been esteemed by the Greeks and Romans' (Andry 1713, vol 1, p 385). French cookbook authors of all kinds continued to avoid them, although some included an odd recipe, often expressing personal distaste as Bonnefons had done in 1654. In 1758, the anonymous author of the *Traité historique . . . ou le Cuisinier Instruit* wrote:

> [The Romans] gave themselves over to the most outrageous forms of indulgence . . . They would eat the finest foods along with the strangest things. It's not that [snails] are in the least appealing as food, no matter how they are prepared, given the natural repugnance they inspire; but there are still some people who find them excellent, and for them I give the following recipes. (*Traité historique* 1758, vol 2, p 228)

Two recipes followed which no doubt gave little pleasure to the author who had perfunctorily included them.

As the century progressed, the snail seemed to make a timid comeback, appearing in works whose earlier editions had excluded them. Take for example the *Cuisinière Bourgeoise:* this did not include them in either the 1746 first edition, nor in the greatly enlarged 1752 edition, but later, around 1769, one recipe for snails was added. Was this simply a concession to that sneered-upon public of snail lovers previously alluded to by other authors? Or was it a first indication that the snail's fortune was about to change? If we are to judge by the gastronome and historian of French taste, Le Grand D'Aussy, writing in 1782, the former was more likely the case. After describing how snails were highly esteemed in the France of the 16th century he added: 'One still sees them for sale in markets today, something which implies that there must still be people around who eat them' (Le Grand D'Aussy 1815, vol 2, pp 143–4). Hardly a return to favor!

The Comeback

When the 19th century began, no one would have foreseen that snails would experience a dramatic comeback in the course of the next 70 years, nor imagined that this creature, virtually banned from a well-dressed table, would become one of the gastronomic emblems of France—and yet this is exactly what was to happen, albeit by no means overnight.

An illustration from Lovell's Edible Mollusca of Great Britain and Ireland *(1884), showing the 'common garden snail' (above) and the 'apple or vineyard snail' (below).*

Grimod de La Reynière, father of the French gastronomic press, did not mention snails in either his 8 volume *Almanach des Gourmands* (1803–12) or his *Almanach des Amphitryons* (1808). Any thought of eating them was so far from his mind that he didn't even go to the trouble of saying he didn't like them. Not so a contemporary, Cadet de Gassicourt, who in 1809 had a character in a dialogue on the history of cooking exclaim, 'How could they [the Romans] possibly have liked that disgusting reptile [sic!]' (Cadet de Gassicourt 1809, p 205). But the most significant proof of the snail's continued ostracism is found in a survey of Paris' best restaurants published in 1815. The menus from 21 of the city's finest dining places were reproduced, and not a single one served snails (Blanc 1815).

What about people outside of Paris? If we have virtually ignored regional cooking up until now, it is largely because evidence about food in the provinces is lacking. From the 19th century, however, documents survive which make it clear that, if snails were absent from the best Parisian tables in the early part of the century, they occupied a place of honor in several provinces. According to a cookbook published in 1811 in Metz, the Romans' passion for the snail was still alive in the Lorraine: 'We imitate the Romans,' the author wrote, 'and fatten snails for the table, raising them in special enclaves that we call "escargotières". We feed them with herbs and bran until winter comes and they seal themselves up in their shells; this way we can eat them all winter long, when there's too much snow to go hunting for them in the hedgerows' (*Manuel de Cuisine* 1811, pp 147–8). Don't think that our Lorraine gastronome was describing some simple rustic fare—after describing how snails are cooked and seasoned, he specified serving them on special silver or lined-copper platters, destined for the finest tables.

The snail's importance in the eastern provinces of France is a point that will eventually be of great consequence when trying to understand how Parisians finally rediscovered a taste for it later in the century.

One of the first signs that change was in the air is to be found in a gastronomic anthology published in 1828. The unnamed author of one of the articles seemed to plead, for the first time, for greater tolerance on the part of his fellow gourmets, inciting them to make an effort to overcome their prejudice towards the little mollusc.

> Many people are repulsed by snails, without realizing that this animal, when you think about it, is much less disgusting than an oyster, and that if we were to eliminate all foods that are physically repugnant or which we have been taught to think of as ugly, we would deprive ourselves of numerous occasions for gastronomic enjoyment. A true gourmet will taste anything, courageously, without consideration for its appearance, and with total impartiality;

just as a bee will alight upon many a flower before settling on the one it likes best, a gourmet will try all foods, refusing none before deciding which are most worthy of his table. (*Gastronome Français* 1828, pp 141–2)

If change was coming, it is not immediately perceptible by looking at the cookbooks of the period. Carême, the great 'renovator' of the early part of the century, did not mention snails in the works he specifically devoted to cuisine (*Le Cuisinier Parisien,* or *L'Art de la Cuisine au XIXe siècle*); nor did Viard, in his work of 1806, *Le Cuisinier Impérial*, which in many respects served as a sort of transition from the cooking of the 18th to the 19th century in France. Jourdan Lecointe, to whom is attributed a popular book, *Le Cuisinier des Cuisiniers*, did not include snails in the first edition of that work (1833). But when it came time for any of these books to be 'revised', 'enlarged', or 'completed', the snail suddenly made its appearance: as early as 1822, a certain Fouret added new recipes to Viard's book, including a mention on how to prepare snails without giving a detailed recipe (this follows a recipe for frogs); Plumerey, who finished Carême's *L'Art de la Cuisine* in 1844, included four recipes for snails, although he felt the need for a disclaimer:

I know that the dishes I have just described [for snails] will not appeal to certain people, and some will even consider them repugnant, but there are people who like them and will ask their cooks to prepare them . . .

Escargots à la Bourguignonne

That same year, 1844, *Le Cuisinier des Cuisiniers* was revised and enlarged, and for the first time in approximately 300 years, a Parisian cookbook seemed to have unqualified praise for snails. It was the author's habit to include a little comment after almost every recipe; after the one he gave for *Escargots à la Bourguignonne* he exclaimed, in parenthesis, 'succulent!'. It is noteworthy that he included this comment after this particular recipe, saying nothing after the two other preparations he gave for snails, for it is *Escargots à la Bourguignonne,* or snails served in their shells with garlic butter, that was to become the standard preparation for snails served in restaurants. The first mention of this specific preparation is to be found in Borel's 1825 *Nouveau Dictionnaire de Cuisine.* Called *à la bourguignonne*, garlic was not mentioned specifically, but only implicitly in the *fines herbes* which are called for and which could include garlic among other things at that time. Long before this first *bourguignonne* recipe, snails had been served in their shells, but the prevalent way of preparing them was either deep fried, or in a sauce thickened with egg yolks and flavored with lemon called a *sauce poulette*.

Lecointe's preference for the *bourguignonne* preparation, in which he specified the use of garlic, is the first hint that it had, in 19th century eyes at least, something more appealing about it than its rivals. The snail's 'success' may in fact be related to the growing popularity of the *bourguignonne* recipe, served particularly in restaurants, and this for several reasons. It has often been pointed out that the appearance of the snail was unattractive; therefore, a tray filled with shells full of bubbling butter was no doubt a more appealing sight than little snail fritters or whole snails swimming in a white sauce. The taste of the snail was certainly more enhanced (not to say replaced) by the aromatic garlic butter than by the other, milder preparations. What's more, cooks often complained of how time-consuming snails were to prepare. Since snails packed into their shells with garlic butter could be kept for long periods of time, particularly in cold weather, and, for that matter purchased already prepared (neither of which is true for snail fritters or snails *à la poulette*), the *bourguignonne* preparation couldn't help but appeal to restaurant owners. Finally, and here one must alas allow for the unscrupulous chef, nothing was easier to cheat on than snails *à la bourguignonne*, if one is to believe writers at the end of the century who claimed that many a so-called 'Burgundy snail' was nothing more than a bit of twisted calf's lung stuffed into a shell with margarine and garlic.

But let us return to the situation at mid-century and see what other factors were at work in changing the snail's status. In about 1855, a certain Monsieur Duval opened a restaurant with an inexpensive fixed-price menu. Dubbed a *Bouillon*, the term was quickly adopted by imitators and used widely to designate other similar establishments. Duval made a fortune by creating a chain of these restaurants, characterized by low prices for relatively high quality, and *Bouillons* became popular eating places with a wide range of Parisians. At about the very same time, a similar sort of restaurant run by Alsatian immigrants appeared in Paris. Called *Brasseries*, they served beer and at least one Alsatian specialty, sauerkraut, along with a wide range of other foods often very similar to those served in the *Bouillons*. It is to the *Brasseries* that the author of *Paris-Restaurant* seems to be referring when he wrote: 'There have appeared of late some restaurants which we can only call "artistic", where good humor, mutton stew, rabbit gibelotte, and sauerkraut are all to be found in great quantities' (*Paris-Restaurant* 1854, p 27). In 1867, a writer referring to a period ten years earlier described the Brasserie des Martyrs as being 'the haunt of artists and writers, and wit and beer were both plentiful' (Chavatte 1867, p 90). So what does all this have to do with snails?

First of all, these new eating places appeared at exactly the time when all later writers agree that snails made their comeback—the 1850s and '60s. Was this mere coincidence? Insofar as their relationship to the *Brasseries* goes, it should be remembered that snails had long been a specialty not only of Lorraine, but of Alsace. In the late 17th century, when they disappeared from almost all French cookbooks, an Alsatian cookbook written in German gave recipes for them, as did the first Alsatian cookbook in French, *Le Cuisinier du Haut Rhin*, in 1833. What's more, already in the 17th century, Alsatian recipes called for stuffing the snail back into its shell with an aromatic butter, and indeed, if we look at recent Alsatian cookbooks, it quickly becomes apparent that what they call *Escargots à l'alsacienne* is exactly the same thing that everyone else is calling *Escargots à la bourguignonne!*

Another element in the snail's favor was that when the *Brasseries* and *Bouillons* first appeared, oysters enjoyed great popularity. If we recall that snails were considered 'fish', we can understand why snails were frequently compared to oysters. But, since oyster farming was relatively undeveloped in the France of the 1850s, oysters were not cheap, making snails all the more attractive to 'petites bourses'—even as late as 1873, the cheapest oysters still cost 10 times as much as snails. Already in 1859, an Englishman, Peter Lund Simmonds, declared:

> The snail is now a very fashionable article of diet in Paris . . . There are now 50 restaurants, and more than 1,200 private tables in Paris where snails are accepted as a delicacy by from 8,000 to 10,000 consumers. The monthly consumption of the mollusc is estimated at half a million. (Simmonds 1859, p 346)

Eleven years later, J. P. A. De La Porte not only confirmed the chronology of the snail's return to favor, but added some significant details that seem to justify some of our previous conjectures.

> Preparing snails for the table is a recent [sic] phenomenon in France. It was introduced via our Eastern provinces which, being far removed from the sea and therefore deprived of oysters, used snails as substitutes for them . . . Many of my readers might be surprised to learn that snail farms in the Poitou, Burgundy, Champagne, and Provence send about forty-five thousand kilograms of snails to Paris markets every day . . . They are cooked 'à la casserole' with a sauce that is generally quite strong: that which is called 'provençale' enjoys great favor in cabarets. (De La Porte 1870, pp 292–3)

It is worth noting that in 1870 a cabaret was not a nightclub, but what could otherwise have been called a *café, brasserie,* or *bouillon,* depending on its size, location, and clientele. We consider with some stupefaction in the figure of 45,000 kilos (nearly 100,000 pounds) of snails sent daily to Paris. But, even if this figure is suspect, it is undeniable that by 1870 the snail had made a spectacular comeback; all the more interesting because it returned 'through the back door', so to speak, via inexpensive eating places and 'from our Eastern provinces' if we are to believe De La Porte.

Although snails remained a specialty of the *Brasserie/Bouillon* set, they were not to be excluded from nobler gastronomic realms. The chic Restaurant Champeaux on the Place de la Bourse was serving them in 1913, as was the fashionable Café de la Paix restaurant in 1914. This led at least one Englishman to evoke with force and a noticeable dose of prejudice the association alluded to at the very start of this article.

> It has been argued that the national food forms the national character; in proof of which have often been put forward the contrast between the smooth, slippery, volatile character of the soup-, snail- and frog-eating Frenchman and the heavy, stolid, and imperturbable character of our own beef- and pudding-eating countryman. (Hackwood 1911, p 312)

If anything is to be learned from this study of snails in France, it is quite simply that this sort of reasoning is as 'slippery' and 'volatile' as the people it pretends to describe. If indeed 'national' foods exist, their importance can vary from one period to another, and any tendency to generalization based on current tastes is very dangerous business indeed. No permanence can be attributed to taste without thorough investigation even if, perhaps especially if, we are dealing with those that seem to be well established. Neither the availability of a food, nor current attitudes toward it suffice for an understanding of attitudes in the past; hence one must constantly question the stereotypes that cloud our impressions of national food preferences in order to understand the complex relationships that exist between a people and 'their' food.

Sources

This list includes basically only those works we have quoted from directly. We consulted every cookbook printed in French from the 16th to the end of the 18th century, as well as a large number of 19th and 20th century texts. Many of them are cited specifically, but were we to list all of them here, this article would take on a bibliographic dimension that neither time nor space permits. Readers interested in early French cookbooks are referred to George Vicaire's classic *Bibliographie Gastronomique,* first published in Paris in 1890.

Andry, Nicolas (1713). *Traité des alimens de caresme.* Paris: Coignard (2 vols).

Barrau, Jacques (1983). *Les Hommes et leurs ailments.* Paris: Temps Actuels.

Blanc, Honoré (1815). *Le Guide des dîneurs.* Paris: chez les marchands de nouveautés.

Bonnefons, Nicolas de (1654). *Les Délices de la campagne.* Paris: Des Hayes.

Cadet De Gassicourt, Ch.-L (1809). *Cours Gastronomique.* Paris: Capelle et Renand.

Chesnaye, Nicole de la (1507). *La Nef de santé.* Paris: Verard.

Chavatte, Engène (1867). *Restaurateurs et restaurés.* Paris: Chevalier.

Dartigue, Ch. (1937). 'Mélanges et Documents'. *Annales du Midi,* 47:416.

De La Porte, J.-P.-A. (1870). *Hygiène de la table.* Paris: Savy.

Du Chesne, Joseph (1606). *Le Pourtraict de la santé.* Paris: Morel.

Flandrin, Jean-Louis (1983). 'La diversité des goûts et des pratiques alimentaires en Europe du 16e au 18e siècle', in *Revue d'histoire moderne et contemporaine,* 33: 66-83.

Gastronome Français, Le (1828). Paris: Béchet.

Gohory, Jacques (1550). *Devis sur la vigne.* Paris: Sertenas.

Hackwood, F. W. (1911). *Good Cheer.* New York: Sturges and Walton.

Laigue, Estienne (1530). *Singulier traicte contenant la propriete des tortues, escargotz, grenoilles et artichaultz.* Paris: Gaillot du Pre et P. Vidoue.

Le Grand D'Aussy (2nd ed. 1815). *Histoire de la vie privée des français.* Paris: Laurent-Baupré (3 vols).

Manuel de la cuisine ou l'Art d'irriter la gueule par une société des gens de bouche (1811). Metz: Antoine.

Menagier de Paris, Le (1846). Paris: Crapelet (2 vols).

Paris-restaurant (1854). Paris: Taride.

Simmonds, Peter Lund (1859). *The Curiosities of Food.* London: Bentley. [Reprinted in facsimile by Ten Speed Press, 2001.]

Thresor de santé (1607). Lyon: Hugueton.

Traité historique et pratique de la cuisine ou le Cuisinier Instruit (1758). Paris: Bauche (2 vols).

Vial, Eugène (1937). *Institutions et coutumes lyonnaises.* Paris: Brun.

Les Galettes des Rois: The Eating of Fine Art

JAMES BAUMAN

This essay would have been fascinating even if it had consisted of nothing but prose, but the inclusion of illustrations by the author gave it an added and special charm.

The day was cheerless enough, with an icy drizzle discouraging what little business was afoot in the street market. With Christmas and New Year's behind them, few Parisians were in a mood to buy more than a steak and potatoes, some apples and a baguette as they hurried home. I don't remember what I was shopping for when the drizzle turned into a downpour and sheets of rain began sweeping the street; all that mattered was to take cover. From beneath the nearest shop awning I watched the pavement empty, as even the toughest stallkeepers fled their carts for a neighboring doorway.

'Oh regarde, maman . . . qu'elles sont belles, les galettes!' The clear voice came from under a hood near my elbow. I turned to see two little girls and their mother, backs to the storm, their interest taken entirely by a glowing windowful of those singular pastries. And beautiful they were indeed: dozens of golden discs, each one etched with a spinning sunburst, glazed on top and notched at the rim to show off their papery layers of lightness, piled at inviting angles and begging to be eaten. Sunshine on a dreary day.

For over twenty years I have shared in the eating of them (for share them you must) with friends and families and total strangers. Yet every new year they come as a surprise. And they hold a surprise of their own. They are called *les Galettes des Rois,* and the 'Kings' they honor are the three Wise Men come to pay homage to the new-born King of Kings in Bethlehem. They appear around the Feast of Epiphany and they, or their counterparts, are to be had at almost every one of the 38,056 bakeries (at last count) in France.

It is a commonplace to observe that the French consider eating a fine art. Yet visitors seldom fail to notice that *bon appétit* begins with the Gallic pastime of strolling in the national gallery of stalls and shop-windows, contemplating the sheer visual beauty of what you may eat, or may wish to eat, next. No admission charge. Fish, fruit, sausages and salads, *bifteks,* brains and breads; the real stuff of still-life. A new show every day. Your feet are a season ticket.

For me, the bakers' trays are gem-cases, offering garish pink and green fondant figurines, all manner of fruity jewels, deep mysteries of coffee, chocolate and caramel, and in the darkest days of the year, those sunny medallions graven with a profusion of striking patterns and arabesques. All suitable for framing, but slated for demolition.

The hell with the rain. I sought out a stationer's, bought a cheap copybook and a pen, and hurried back to sketch as best I could the *galette* designs to be seen in the six pastry-shops in that street before they could be gobbled out of existence. For the next few weeks I continued to record the themes and variations of this admittedly minor art-form on display all over town, until one day they were nowhere to be seen. It was February 1st.

Adieu les rois!
Jusqu'à douze mois!
Douze mois passé!
Vous les reverrez!

* * * *

A *galette* is a flat, round cake; the word derives from *galet,* a pebble weather-worn to the shape that is perfect for skipping. Buckwheat or maize *crêpes* are also called *galettes* in some regions, as are various cookies. 'Flat as a pancake' is just as graphic in French: *plat comme une galette.* As a cake, it is made of flour, sugar, butter and eggs in infinite variations, or simply of puff pastry. The glowing *galette des rois* found in Paris, Lyon, and generally north of the Loire is fashioned almost exclusively from the latter, the classic *feuilletage.* It may be filled with almond paste or frangipane, but that is a post-war fillip that bumps up the price, and anyway, is properly a *Pithiviers.* The Kings' Cake is thoughtfully made in all sizes: for two or three to enjoy with tea, or for any number in need of an ice-breaker; but most of all, for every family to share in a merry annual ritual.

Were you to buy one of those pretty but plain cakes, take it home and eat it, even pronounce it good, you might still wonder what all the fuss was about. The answer is to experience their consumption in the proper context. Should you be a January dinner guest in a French home, you might take part in a last-course tradition that goes something like this: the warm *galette* is brought to table where its fragrance and beauty are admired briefly before it is cut into the proper number of wedges. A child, usually the youngest, is sent to hide under the table, there to act as oracle. To the summons 'Phoebe' (or 'Apollo') he replies in Latin, 'Domine' (master). As he indicates each portion, the 'master' asks, 'For whom is this piece?' and the child calls out the first name that pops into his head, without regard to age or station, until all are served and begin eating in an air of anticipation. **For someone is about to find the Bean** in his cake and thereby become King (or Queen) of the festivity. To cries of 'Long live the King!' he is duly crowned and must choose his Queen (or King). Whenever he raises his glass, all must cheer *'Le Roi Boit!* [The King Drinks!] *Vive le Roi!'* and drinks his health. Pranks and general merriment ensue, according to the humor of the company or the times.

So it was described from the 16th century onward, and so it was observed almost exactly by an astonished friend this last year in a Brittany farmhouse. However, the Latin interrogatory is rarely heard these days, and champagne has supplanted the hypocras that was served at the table of the Sun King.

But what, you may ask, does this have to do with Epiphany, the manifestation of Christ's divinity, and the Adoration of the Magi? The answer is, virtually nothing. It is a cheerfully pagan rite that can be traced at least as far back as the Saturnalia and Kalends of Roman times, as Bridget Ann Henisch informs us early on in her excellent book, *Cakes and Characters.* The *magister bibendi* (or toastmaster) of these winter revels was chosen by means of a bean (which had served as a voting token earlier for the Greeks). Thus when the church, in 336, decreed December 25th as Christ's birthday, with the clear intention of co-opting these immensely popular holidays, 'twas already the season to be jolly. By the end of the century, Epiphany joined it twelve days later on the liturgical calendar. The Wise Men were soon elevated to Kings, to divest them of any occult connotation. The ancient ritual of bean, cake and kingship, with its powerful, if only vaguely similar, symbolism, was brought into the fold. (The pious always reserved the first piece of cake 'for God', the Virgin, the baby Jesus or the poor, to whom it was given.) But for all its haloed innocence, it remains an unabashedly secular entertainment.

* * * *

The propitious Bean was just that: the fava or European broad bean (similar to the American lima), called *fève* in French. In 1874, some clever baker replaced it with porcelain 'beans' which, despite many a chipped tooth, became all the rage. They evolved into figurines representing the Babe in swaddling clothes, kings, queens, a four-leaf clover . . . even the Concorde jet. Inevitably, plastic *fèves* appeared, but as they tended to melt in the baking, their vogue was mercifully brief. Today these fanciful charms are prized by collectors, but that is another story. Whatever the shape, it is still called *la fève,* and in some parts it is still a real bean.

'Not a family in France was without cake to eat that day' . . . least of all the royal families, all of whom revered Epiphany. For Hugues Capet and St Louis it solemnly served as 'an annual lesson for earthly kings to acknowledge God as the greater and more powerful King than they'. It amused Louis XIV for the court to 'separate' the cake and play at Bean-king. More modestly, the *roi de la fève* reigned in homes rich and poor, where the entire household, servants and strangers alike, participated in the mock-royal lottery. Not even the Revolution (when bakers and their clients were accused of *liberticide* intentions in honoring 'the shades of tyrants') could dethrone the King of the Bean.

Exactly what cake the bean was baked in then remains a mystery. The 13th century *gastel à fève* was a *gâteau,* the generic term for all cakes. Whatever

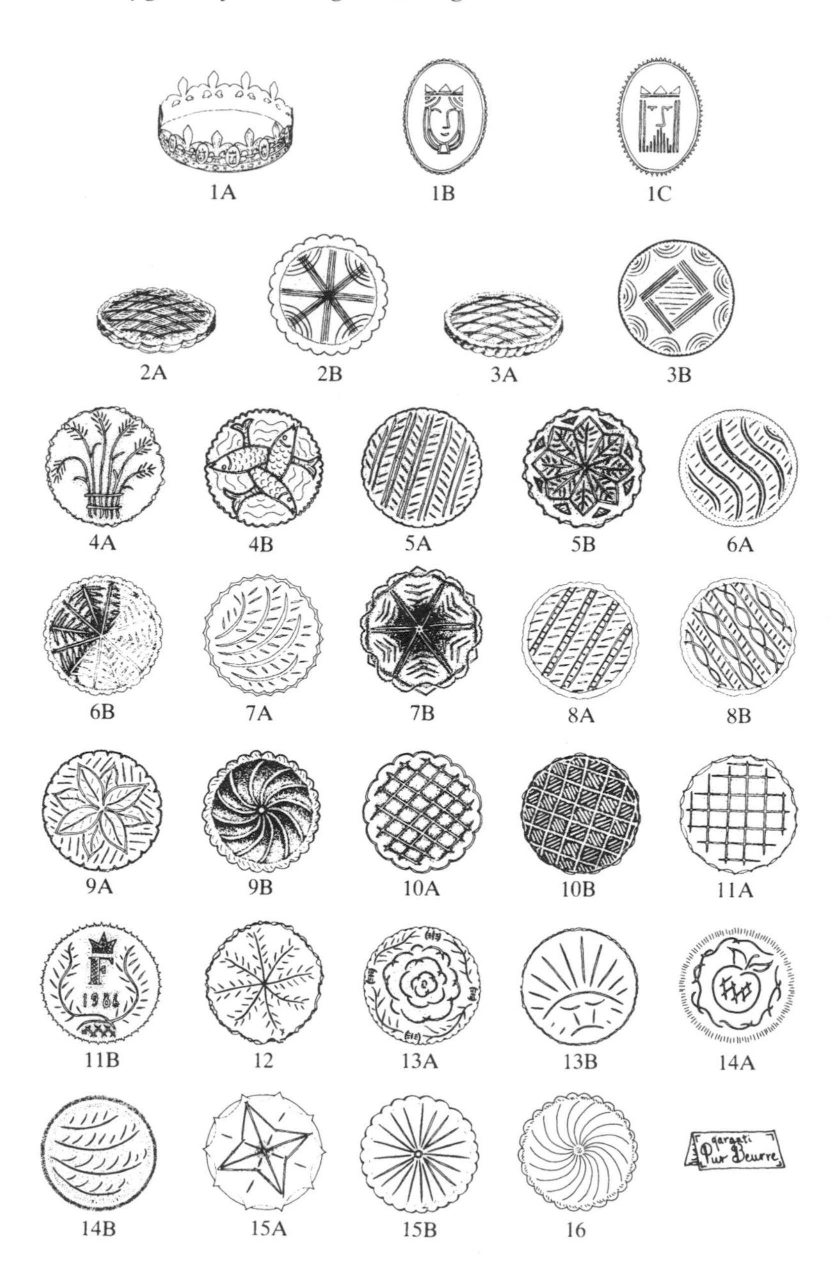

the ancient origins of puff pastry are, 'flaky cakes' (*gasteaux feuillés*) were cited in 1311. My 16th and 18th century sources fail to say whether the Bean Cake was 'flaky' or not, and the 18th century recipes for *galettes feuilletés* fail to mention the bean. The earliest of my authors to pull all together neatly is Carême; his *pâte brisée-demi-feuilletée* was 'particularly employed for *gâteaux des Rois*'. The Parisian *galette* was thus well established by the early 1800s.

In much of France however, the Kings are fêted with entirely different cakes. For the most part they are versions of the sweet brioche, studded with candied fruit (angelica, citron, cherries, etc), ring-shaped (*couronne* aptly means crown in French) and always with the *fève* baked inside. (The *gâteau des rois* of Bordeaux and the *royaume* of Provence are prime examples.) They may also take the shape of a *fleur-de-lys* mold (Alsace) or a cheese *tarte* (Boulogne), and bear such local names as *garfou, norole, fougasse* or *pompe des rois, dreikönigsküche* or simply *le roi-boit.* Another tasty world to explore.

Kings and Queens must have crowns, real or whimsical; in old paintings of the festivity they are gaily regal in wreaths of roses, playing-cards or waffle-wafers. Nowadays a gold or silver paper crown often comes free with a (purchased) *galette.* (In fact, the *galette* itself used to be free, the baker's gift to

The author's gallery of galette *designs appears on the facing page. Here they are identified by their numbers.*

1A, the gold (or silver) paper crown; 1B and 1C, queen and king medallions from the crown.

2A, a variation of the grillwork design (see 10A) from rue Saint Sulpice; 2B, a design from rue du Cherche-Midi.

3A, grillwork, double-stroke variation (Monoprix, by the thousand); 3B, design from rue de Rennes. 4A, wheat-sheaf, Poilâne, rue du Cherche-Midi; 4B, stylized fish design, fairly common.

5A, ladder or stylized wheat design, common; 5B, stylized leaf, fairly common (cf 9A). 6A, ladder variation; 6B, branch or stylized leaf, Mulot, rue Lobineau.

7A, stylized wheat, rue de Buci; 7B, branch or stylized leaf, rue Saint Antoine. 8A, ladder, variation of 5A, rue Poncelet; 8B, ditto, avenue Franklin Roosevelt.

9A, classic leaf design, common; 9B, classic sunburst or pinwheel, very common, rarely counterclockwise (also found on Pithiviers*). 10A, classic grillwork, very common; 10B, 'squared' grillwork variation, rue Poncelet.*

11A, 'squared' grillwork, Fauchon, Place de la Madeleine; 11B, centennial of Fauchon with branches (one meter in diameter, where else but Fauchon!). 12, wheat star, Poilâne again. 13A, rosace with branches, rue Saint Dominique; 13B, sunburst, the morning after.

14A, apple design (filled with apple), avenue Franklin Roosevelt; 14B, stylized wheat, Poilâne again. 15A, star, Poilâne; 15B, straight sunburst, Mulot, rue Lobineau. 16, classic sunburst, simplified. The gallery is rounded off with the customary assurance that pure butter is used.

See also the author's imaginary shop window of various designs on page 215.

his steady customers. No more.) But with shiny paper or foil and scissors, a child will make the best one himself, with an eye toward wearing it, of course.

Every French child can also sing the 'March of the Kings', an air the rest of us know from Bizet's *l'Arlésienne;* the universal affection for the *Fête des Rois* inspired writers from the middle ages to Victor Hugo and de Maupassant; Jordaens' canvas, *Le Roi Boit!* is pure, infectious mirth, and Monet's *galettes* whet the appetite. Thus the celebration has become a part of our common artistic heritage.

* * * *

Happily, this is one tradition that is flourishing; the French Bakers' Confederation gleefully reports that *galettes* sell, well, like hot-cakes throughout the month of January. (They've become yet another excuse for that 20th century ritual, the office-party.) To meet the demand, the larger bakeries use modern techniques: machines that roll out kilometres of *feuilletage,* cutters that make perfect discs, and wicked-looking pinwheels that impress the pattern. However, machine-made pastry is not as 'tender', it often rises lop-sided for want of crimping, and the design is of a sad sameness. Most local bakers prefer to roll, cut and incise their *galettes* by hand. Their respect for traditional methods produces finer pastry and gives them *carte blanche* for creative embellishment.

The plain, flat surface not only invites decoration, it demands it. Once the *feuilletage* is prepared, rolled out 1 cm (3/8") thick and a circle cut from it, the rim is notched at an angle with the back of a knife. This crimping makes the attractive scalloped edge typical of the *galette;* at the same time it keeps the leaves of dough from slipping as they rise. The raw pastry is brushed with egg glaze and the 'artist' etches his design 2–3 mm (1/16") into the surface with the knife-tip. In the oven, the dough puffs up and expands, while the glaze hardens to a golden brown crust and shrinks slightly. As a result, the scoring opens up, the top keeps its shape, the heat penetrates the dough for more even cooking, and the design is thrown into clear relief. Art that serves a very practical purpose.

Kings of any religious persuasion or none whatsoever may be created at any time; all you need are a bean, a crown and a *galette.* Parisians invariably buy them, but they are still baked in many rural homes. You can make your own as well. Three expert and widely available recipe sources are cited at the end of this article, one for the pastry alone, one for the plain *galette* and one for the almond-filled confection.

For those with a taste for rustic authenticity, I provide a fourth reference, a most solid authority on French home cooking, Mme Saint-Ange. Quoting from 'a good old cookery book from the time of Louis XV', she assures us that the classic *galette feuilletée* is properly made of *galette* pastry, a dough not to be confused with even simple puff pastry, despite some similarity. It is easy and relatively quick to make good to eat, and of a tradition 'going back nearly two hundred years' at the time she recorded it, in 1927. (Her book is still in print. Her recipe, in translation, is given below.)

* * * *

THE 'TRADITIONAL' GALETTE DES ROIS OF MME E. SAINT-ANGE

(The translator's glosses and comments, after making the recipe several times, are in parenthesis.)

for 6 to 8 persons: 250 g (1¾ cups) flour; 190 g (7 oz) butter (unsalted); 5 g (1 tsp) salt; 7 g (2 tsp) sugar; ¾ dl (⅓ cup) water; an egg yolk blended with 2 tbsp water, to glaze the galette.

Make a well in the flour, put the slightly softened butter into it. Dissolve the salt and sugar in the water, pour in to the well. With your fingers (or a fork) roughly mix the butter and water, gradually incorporating the flour until you have a rather firm dough. Do not knead. Gather it into a ball, flour lightly, wrap and let rest for ¾ hour in a cool place.

On a floured surface, roll out the dough into a rectangle about 60 x 22 cm (24 x 8"). Fold in thirds and let rest 10 minutes. Repeat this operation twice, always rolling and folding in the opposite direction. After the third 'turn' fold the corners up over the dough to form a round pad. Roll out a disc 1.5 to 2 cm (about ¾") thick. With the back of a knife, notch the rim at intervals, evening out the circle if necessary. With the point of the knife, make a slit in the edge, insert the bean and reseal. If you will want to know where it is later (a nice touch) insert it underneath the dough and mark the spot. Place on an ungreased, unfloured baking sheet. Brush the top with the egg glaze, taking care not to let it drip over the edge. Score with grillwork or any other design, with the tines of a fork (or the point of a knife). Prick through in several places.

Bake in a moderately hot oven (preheated to 230° C, 450°F or Mark 8) 30 to 35 minutes. (For a shinier, sweeter glaze, dust with powdered sugar a few minutes before removing.) Cool on a rack. The *galette* is always served warm; if need be, reheat it to that point.

* * * *

Which brings us back to those magical designs! . . . for sunbursts, stalks of wheat and geometric greenery are evocative indeed. During the dark days of the winter solstice, the ancients regarded these as symbols of regeneration, rebirth and fertility. (As they did the *fève,* once an Egyptian funerary offering, now a seed buried . . . in our *galette.*) Apollo, the sun-god (whose oracle *ephebos* was invoked), would return; the grain would sprout and bring prosperity; the evergreen would never die. Persistent traces of the bean-cake's pagan past? Perhaps, though the baker seems unaware of it; he also turns out variations on ladders and lattices and whatever pretty patterns strike his fancy. Art that is not long.

It was the ephemeral nature of this edible art that prompted me to preserve it in my notebook last year. By month's end I had collected over 30 different designs. Some are traditional and commonly encountered, others unique to one baker. As they are rarely (save one) found on other cakes and seldom appear in cookbooks, I have put them in a little gallery of *galettes* which I would like to share with you (see page 210). My models appeared in bakeries all over Paris, from the most elegant to the more modest, and even in supermarkets. They averaged 22 cm (9") in diameter, but ranged from half that to 1 meter (3') across. My own drawings are fairly faithful to the originals, although I confess to doodling about the edges and playing with the shading. The stacked cakes in the shop-window give an idea of how the scalloped rims should look.

The most common motifs are the sunburst, grillwork, and 'ladders'. The first (a star for some, or a pinwheel) also adorns the *Pithiviers* cake. (It rarely turns the other way, as few bakers are left-handed.) Grillwork and 'ladders' can be infinitely varied: squared, diagonal, wavy; with double strokes, etc. The wheat-sheaf theme is also dear to bakers; and 'ladders' may be an abstraction of it. Leaves or branches lend themselves to geometrical forms as well. But the most striking designs are the original inventions of artistic pastry-makers.

The top shelf of my imaginary pastry-shop window (opposite) holds the wheat-sheaf variations; below it are several sun variations with stacked *galettes.* the bottom shelf offers three very personalized designs: a rosace, a centennial *galette* (1 meter wide!) displayed at Fauchon, and an unusual apple-filled cake.

The *fèves,* of infinite variety, are not seen; they are concealed in the cakes. Nor is the rare, elusive design of the Magi's camel, complete with palm-tree and star; it didn't appear in the shops last January. Maybe next year.

Bid the Kings farewell,
For a twelve-month spell!
When the year is o'er,
You'll see them once more!

References

Carême, Antonin: *Le Pâtissier Royal Parisien:* Paris, 1841 (1st ed 1815).

Castellot, André: *L'Histoire à Table:* Paris, 1972.

Chatillon-Plessis: *La Vie à Table à la Fin due XIX Siècle:* Paris, 1894.

Colombié, Auguste: *Nouvelle Encyclopédie Culinaire:* Meulan, 1906–7.

Gilbert, Philéas: *La Cuisine de Tous les Mois* (3°) Paris, 1925.

[Gilles de Gouberville]: *Un Sire de Gouberville* (the accounts of a Norman country squire from 1553–62): published by Abbé Tollmer, Paris, n.d.

Gouffé, Jules: *Le Livre de Cuisine:* Paris, 1867.

Henisch, Bridget Ann: *Cakes and Characters:* London, Prospect books, 1984.

Larousse, Pierre: *Grand Dictionnaire Universel de XIX Siècle:* Paris, 1866–79.

Lebrault, Armand: *La Table et le Repas:* Paris, 1910 (citing Pasquier, Etienne, *Recherches sur la France,* c 1560).

Le Grand d'Aussy: *Histoire de la Vie Privée des Français:* Paris, 1782.

Montagné, Prosper and Gottschalk, Dr A.: *Larousse Gastronomique:* Paris, 1938.

Root, Waverley: *Food:* New York, 1980.

ALSO

Dictionnaire de l'Académie des Gastronomes: Paris, 1962.

Confédération Nationale de la Boulangerie et Boulangerie-Pâtisserie Françaises, Paris.

Exhibition and Catalogue, *Crèches et Traditions de Noël:* Musée National des Arts et Traditions Populaires, Paris, 1986–7.

Recipe Sources

Beck, Simone and Child, Julia: *Mastering the Art of French Cooking (vol 2):* Knopf, New York, 1970: also London, Penguin, 1978: FOR THE MAKING OF FINE PUFF PASTRY

Healy, Bruce and Bugat, Paul: *Mastering the Art of French Pastry:* Barron's, New York, 1984: FOR THE PASTRY AND THE GALETTE DES ROIS.

Lenôtre, Gaston: *Faites Votre Pâtisserie Comme Lenôtre:* Paris, Flammarion, 1975: also as *Lenôtre's Desserts and Pastries* (translated by Philip and Mary Hyman) Barron's, New York, 1977: FOR THE PASTRY AND THE ALMOND-FILLED GALETTE.

Saint-Ange, Mme E.: *Le Livre de Cuisine:* Paris, Larousse, 1927: FOR A MORE TRADITIONAL VERSION OF THE GALETTE DES ROIS.

El Arte del Tapeo

Alicia Rios

Tapeo is a term used to describe the Spanish tradition of going out before lunch or dinner to mingle with friends while drinking an apéritif, and sharpening the appetite for the main meal ahead by choosing from the myriad of tempting appetizers on offer in the bars throughout Spain.

The art of *tapeo* represents the perfect marriage between food and drink, because, unlike the more well known concept of food supplemented by good wine, in the case of the art of *tapeo,* it is not the wine which lubricates the ingestion of good food, but quite the contrary; it is the food which really acts as an accompaniment to the series of sips of good wine.

Tapeo has a balance of reciprocal stimuli. It could be compared to a kind of eroticism; an eroticism of *tapeo* in which the stimulation is reciprocal.

Geographical Variations

The art of *tapeo* is practised throughout the whole of Spain, but has differing features in each of the regions, not only from the point of view of the ingredients and the culinary techniques used to achieve the maximum stimulation of the taste buds, but also from the aspect of its development as a social practice. The form in which it develops is a rich sociological key.

It could be said that in the northern half of the Spanish peninsula the art of *tapeo* is carried out under the perspective of saving oneself for a definitive meal, in the form of an excuse. In these regions, where the people certainly have strong stomachs, there is a complicity among those who wish to predispose themselves for the enjoyment of the art of *tapeo* by saying things like: 'but we have to have lunch soon!' However they then become embroiled in an almost neverending series of rounds, one after the other, as if the postponed meal was never going to take place. Nevertheless, they subsequently tuck into their lunch as if this prelude had never happened.

The whole phenomenon starts from a very interesting basis in that we can suppose that the practice of the art of *tapeo* serves the purpose of an appetizer, an event previous to the meal which will follow. There is always a certain element of reserve in the mind of the *tapeador* (a person who practices the art of *tapeo*) which can even have moral connotations, as missing a meal carries the risk of destroying a family which can turn into a nightmare as it implicitly includes a loss of respect for the meal under threat from the *tapeo.*

These factors convert the *tapeo* into a sort of surreptitious meal, a stolen ceremony while playing truant from the family dining table. All these problems must be compensated by the art of *tapeo,* which could be seen as a substitute for the vomitorium; the greatest assimilation of the pleasures of eating and drinking, offered by this balance between the food and the drink which plays not only a hedonistic role by being pleasant to the taste, but also has a digestive, or predigestive function. The ultimate essence of the art of *tapeo* is that it allows the possibility of the meal which it precedes.

However in the southern half of the country, and especially in Andalusia, the *tapeador* gives himself over wholeheartedly with no consideration for anything else, apart from the degree of sobriety and politeness appropriate to his own sensitivity. He surrenders himself with the maximum degree of abandon to the custom of 'tipples with *tapas*'.

The whole procedure is dominated by moderation and restraint in the number of participants, in the number of *tapas* and their proportions, and in the route of the '*tapa* crawl'. However although there is this moderation and economy, there is no restriction with respect to the surrender of the spirit to the freedom of expression, to the sheer pleasure of communication, the fluidity of social contact; in the art of *tapeo* it is as important to see as to be seen. There is also a full and virtuous surrender to pleasure with regard to the enjoyment of the surrounding environment; the streets, the situations, the sight of a friend, a handsome boy, a pretty girl, an as yet unknown person who will be brought closer by a glass of wine and a *tapa,* which together diminish the distance between you until a confident proximity is achieved.

General Characteristics

The art of *tapeo* is like a baroque, sybaritic game, as it pleases the five senses by means of the multifarious smells, the friendly pats on the back, the sight of beauty on the streets. It induces states of inspiration and delight, it gives rise to witty banter on trivial topics and the interchange of snippets of juicy gossip. There is a kind of irony and philosophy peculiar to this custom, like a treaty of coexistence accompanied by elegance and a generosity of the spirit developed to the ultimate possibilities. The *tapeo* is a peripatetic art which takes the form of a route: a path paved with chance meetings and random conversations.

The drink stimulates the appetite and aids digestion, and the food palliates the ethylic effects of the drink. The combination of these factors results in a perfect balance which is supported by the concept of physical space, as the *tapeo,* by its very nature, inherently involves a plurality of settings. It is impossible to imagine the art of *tapeo* taking place in a single session with no element of sequence or spacing. However good a particular bar may be, a good *tapeador* could never exhaust his possibilities in any one place. Movement is essential to the creation of the spacing concept and also involves physical exercise which, as well as aiding digestion, is really a trick, as the stimulating effect of the movement consequently leads to more changes of location.

As well as the spacing effect of the various mouthfuls of food and sips of wine, and the physical movement, conversation also forms a fundamental and essential part of the art of *tapeo.* If in the case of other meals conversation may be considered an obstacle or perhaps as an additional factor, verbal communication and the exchange of looks complete the concept of the *tapeo.* At times the *tapeador* has to try very hard to separate himself from his *tapeo* companion when he becomes lost in the pleasures aroused by the focus of his digression. As in a game played with counters, the portions of *tapas* are shared out mysteriously between snatches of conversation. On occasion, albeit rarely, the more voracious *tapeadores* have gone as far as to violate these ritual pauses between bites and sips when one surrenders oneself completely to raising the spirits because the enjoyment of the various different tastes is an inevitable and imperative pleasure for them. These lucubrations, however, are usually only interrupted by a furtive flirtatious compliment directed at an attractive women passing by. The combination of conversation, compliments,—even if only about flowers—the art of peeling prawns and the sharing out of a portion of something is always impregnated with the smell of seafood.

And finally, within the framework of physical aspects, the perfect *tapeador* practises his art standing up, using the following reasoning as his alibi: 'Soon I shall have my lunch sitting down at the table. This is no time for the comforts of luxurious, plush bars.' Standing up at the bar, the *tapeador* can resort only to his elbows for comfort, as he tries to nudge a niche for himself in between the various plates on the wooden or metal bar, to then soak his elbows in pools of wine and vinegar.

These are therefore some of the physiological advantages of the *tapeo,* to which we must add the element of journeying through a series of stages, like the pilgrimage of a penitent in chains; the eternal pharisaism of the Spanish people.

The *tapeo* can turn into a task of great physical effort requiring its exponents to be on top physical form, compensated by the final reward of being able to sit down comfortably to enjoy lunch or dinner. It is fascinating to watch the prawn shells and heads cascade from the height of the bar down to the sawdust covered floor, to see how the different scraps of waste accumulate underfoot like the fruit of the impeccable toil of the eternal *tapeador.*

The Bars and the Landlords

Tapa bars are like guilds. They are to be found concentrated in particular areas and might be situated side by side, but, as we have said before, the attraction of moving and changing places means that the practice is executed on a basis not of one, but of two. There are different options and the bars are frequented to an equal extent by the same clientele.

Another very interesting aspect is the attitude of the landlord. The landlord does not restrict himself just to the preparation and service of the *tapas* and the wine, but attempts to establish a relationship with the *tapeador,* aimed at destroying the various forms of ecstasy sought by his customers: ecstasy in their conversations, alcoholic ecstasy or Sunday afternoon ecstasy, because the *tapeador* is capable of attaining a manner as grim and fierce as that of the landlord himself, who greets the *tapeadores* who come in and go up to the bar by shouting: 'Good morning/evening! What will you have? What is to be, gentlemen?' The shout might consist of an appropriate salutation such as 'Good evening!' or 'Good morning, gentlemen!', immediately followed by a hopefully stimulating proposal, usually proferred in a demanding and imperative tone, e g, 'What will you have?', 'What's it to be?', 'What can I get for you?'. When the customer has made up his mind, which he usually does in a low voice in keeping with that fierce manner which annoys the landlord so much, the landlord, although he has heard the request perfect well, repeats it in a loud booming voice, with all his might, as if it were a sort of public announcement which could embarrass the customers: 'Four dry sherries and a portion of snails!'

The landlord of a bar almost always adheres to a humorous, witty attitude, creating a sort of complicity with his customers. One example of this is the frequent occurrence of antithetical phenomena such as calling *boquerones morcillas,* and vice versa. The regular customer of course understands this code and answers correspondingly, perhaps by asking for a 'Call to Burgos!' if the *morcilla* which he is going to savour happens to come from that city. This kind of repartee illustrates the humour involved in the *tapa* jargon, imposed by the landlords themselves.

This custom also carries the commercial function of avoiding any possible repentance on the part of the customer. This is all said in a tone which is phonetically and musically in keeping with the establishment in question. The giving of a tip gives rise to a few final musical verses, different in each bar: 'Booteeee! Tip! Thank you gentlemen!'

Specialities and Heterogeneity of Tapas

Tapas can be divided into sections according to their different places of origin, and likewise the many kinds of bars can be classified according to their specialities. Later we will look more closely at the culinary criteria within this area of consideration.

Some of the most representative *tapas* come from the area of Castile which offers *montados de carne* which are small pieces of bread with a slice of meat on top such as marinated loin of pork fillets, *chorizos a la plancha*—slices of spicy pork sausage cooked on the griddle, *morcillas*—a kind of black pudding sausage made with blood and rice or onion and served fried, *cazuelas de callos a la madrileña*—the Madrid speciality of tripe casserole, and *patatas bravas*—medium sized chunks of fried potatoes coated in a hot, spicy sauce made from tomatoes and chili peppers.

In Galicia, on the northern coast of Spain, we find a great variety of dishes related to the cephalopod family such as octopus prepared in the typical Galician way and many kinds of shellfish, also the Galician omelette made with potatoes, vegetables and chorizo.

As a prototype of the *tapas* available in Andalusia we could perhaps take the seafood group, which in this region is usually served fried or seasoned with a vinaigrette dressing.

Indeed there is an enormous range of diverse regional specialities, far too many to list here. Furthermore, many *tapas* are to be found nationwide, like for example the inevitable unpeeled prawns or *boquerones* (fresh whitebait) served in vinegar, which are to be found in display on the counters of bars everywhere, not to mention *tortilla española,* Spanish potato omelette.

It is instructive to analyse the treatment of mushrooms, a Mediterranean *tapa* which is also internationally known. Whether they are *champiñones* (*'champis',* cultivated button mushrooms) or *setas* (other mushrooms of conventional mushroom shape, such as *setas de cardo*, *Pleurotus eryngii*, or *níscalos*, *Lactarius sanguifluus* and *L deliciosus*), the procedure used to cook them is almost always the same.

The origin of this culinary technique is probably the Catalan system, which is possibly the oldest in Spain. This is as follows. On the same mountainside where you gather the *rovellóns* (Catalan for *níscalos, i e Lactarius* spp), you make a fire and put a slate griddle rubbed with garlic on top of it. The *rovellóns* are chopped coarsely, without damaging the gills under their caps, put on the griddle and sprinkled with chopped parsley, olive oil and salt. This method of cooking combines various special conditions such as cooking over a low heat with a high degree of moisture loss.

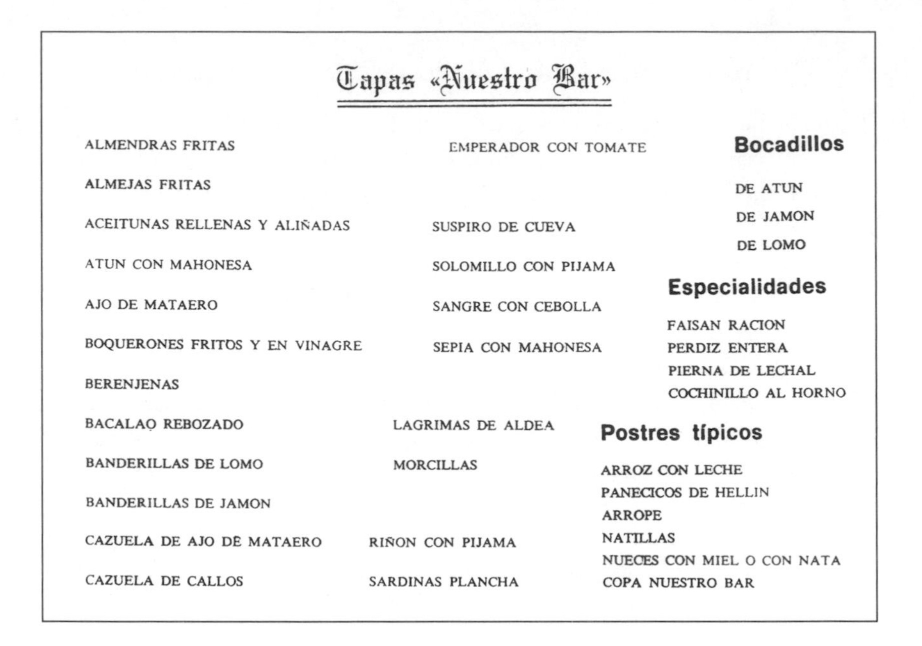

Tapas «Nuestro Bar»

ALMENDRAS FRITAS
ALMEJAS FRITAS
ACEITUNAS RELLENAS Y ALIÑADAS
ATUN CON MAHONESA
AJO DE MATAERO
BOQUERONES FRITOS Y EN VINAGRE
BERENJENAS
BACALAO REBOZADO
BANDERILLAS DE LOMO
BANDERILLAS DE JAMON
CAZUELA DE AJO DE MATAERO
CAZUELA DE CALLOS

EMPERADOR CON TOMATE
SUSPIRO DE CUEVA
SOLOMILLO CON PIJAMA
SANGRE CON CEBOLLA
SEPIA CON MAHONESA
LAGRIMAS DE ALDEA
MORCILLAS
RIÑON CON PIJAMA
SARDINAS PLANCHA

Bocadillos

DE ATUN
DE JAMON
DE LOMO

Especialidades

FAISAN RACION
PERDIZ ENTERA
PIERNA DE LECHAL
COCHINILLO AL HORNO

Postres típicos

ARROZ CON LECHE
PANECICOS DE HELLIN
ARROPE
NATILLAS
NUECES CON MIEL O CON NATA
COPA NUESTRO BAR

Some of the items on the very extensive menu of tapas *at Nuestro Bar in Albacete (Castilla).*

In a bar situation this method is reproduced on a large gas-fired griddle with no worries about moisture loss. The *setas* are thrown onto the intense heat created by the flickering flames under the griddle and are coated with a dubious liquid poured from a small bottle with a perforated cork top. If button mushrooms are being used, then the stalk is removed to leave a wonderful natural receptacle which can be filled again with the flesh of the mushrooms combined with some exquisite mixture, perhaps of minced meat, onion and ham, arousing a thousand pleasurable sensations.

The same procedure is used to prepare swordfish, of which people were formerly rather afraid; its name was consequently sometimes changed to 'emperor fish' to avert this fear and it is nowadays often to be found amongst a selection of *tapas*. If the *champiñon* has a certain French feel to it, the 'emperor fish' is Mediterranean and is today one of the most expensive and also most highly esteemed *tapas*.

The Size and Handling of the Tapa

It does not matter if the ideal *tapa* is somewhat large, but this volume must be distributed in terms of height, and not of surface area. For example the *montado*—a piece of fried *morcilla* on a small slice of bread, speared with a cocktail stick, or perhaps assorted pickles on sticks, can be piled very high because they do not conflict with the requirement for occupying a minimal surface area. This phenomenon has various explanations. Let us consider first the ethical reasons, which are always connected with the respect shown with regard to the meal awaiting in the home. Food with a large surface area is reserved for the more intimate atmosphere of meals enjoyed with the family or friends. There are also various other fundamental reasons. The individualization of the portions is an important factor as it renders cutlery virtually unnecessary. The fork, for example, is only needed to spear the bite-sized morsel, and the use of the knife is not considered correct form, even if only to cut a sausage up into pieces. Cutlery has no place in the art of *tapeo,* belonging to the environment of sit-down meals.

The portion assigned to each *tapeador* should be easily accessible in the game of *tapeo.* The cocktail stick, *palillo,* for example, is fundamental to the art of *tapeo.* This small stick serves the purpose of a small skewer, used in the Spanish version of the shish kebab, known as *pincho moruno.* The Spanish cocktail stick is very short and is not put into the heat. (This is not because it is made of wood; after all, in the Far East chopsticks are used in direct heat.) The Spanish stick is used once and thrown away.

There are two kinds of stick. The flat type is cheaper and of inferior quality, but has the advantage of being more noticeable because of its greater surface area, an important factor when it comes to reckoning up the bill; furthermore, it does not roll away and get lost. This method of keeping track of the number of *tapas* consumed by counting the number of sticks left on the bar is both traditional and also practical, and is used when the stick forms an integral part of the *tapa.* Another use is its function as an instrument to aid consumption, to convey the piece of food to the mouth. The stick as an integral part of the *tapa* bears a perfect relation to its ancestor the *pincho moruno,* or kebab, and can be found fulfilling the following functions: securing a piece of sausage to a slice of bread; used to make a vegetable kebab; or in the typical pickles on sticks, which are usually hot and spicy such as, for example, the *guindilla,* the Spanish chilli pepper.

Some other more exotic variations are aubergines in vinegar seasoned with spices, and the *tapas* formerly known as *toreras* which feature alternate slices of gherkin with red pepper, chilli pepper in vinegar and stuffed olives, all packed tightly onto the support or stick. We could also mention marinated tuna fish accompanied by some other tidbit, such as baked red pepper or perhaps just a dash of mayonnaise. Practically all of the larger individual portions are served with a cocktail stick, the universal Spanish ‘handle’, descended no doubt from the mediaeval spit. Within the group of individual portions which involve a support we can also mention the *montado,* where a piece of bread is sufficient support and is eaten together with the delicacy it carries.

Although all these expedients apparently avoid any need for direct use of the fingers, in the end it is always necessary to resort to the small paper napkin which is an essential element in the art of *tapeo.* The napkin is offered in several ways, starting from the original packaging presented in all kinds of metallic and plastic dispensers, passing through the glass stuffed full of napkins folded into cone shapes, up to the rustic hook on the counter or bar where the napkins are remorselessly nailed and whence they are ruthlessly ripped to eventually end up rolled into little balls, thrown onto the floor and trodden on amongst the piles of shells, stones and cocktail sticks mixed up in the sawdust. Napkins, even though they are used in a hygienic way, are also used compulsively and there is a high degree of wastefulness on the part of the *tapeadores.* This has led to the Spanish *tapa* napkin becoming very thin and economical, although this does not mean it lacks decoration and usually bears a cheeky red or blue border and sometimes the name and address of the establishment as a happy memory.

Tortilla Española, de Patatas Con Cebolla
Spanish omelette (with potatoes and onions)

4 or 5 medium potatoes
1 or 2 medium onions
olive oil
salt
5 or 6 eggs

Peel the potatoes, wash and dry them. Cut them in very thin slices, and dry again. Slice the onions too.

Put six tablespoons of oil in a pan (till its level is around one finger, 2 cm). Heat it. When it is hot, add the onions. Turn them over and, when they are transparent, add the potatoes and salt. The potatoes and onions should just cook gently rather than be fried. Turn them over, so that they don't stick or break up. They can be cooked with a cover on, keeping an eye on them, so that they are done, but not too brown. At this point turn off the heat and drain away all the oil (reserving it for some other cooking).

Beat the eggs, lightly salted, in a bowl. Add the potatoes and leave them to soak for 15 minutes. This way the omelette will be juicy and fluffy.

Clean the pan thoroughly and put some new olive oil in it. Heat this up, then put in the egg mixture, spreading it equally. The temperature has to be very high in the beginning, so that the bottom of the omelette is well cooked. With your right hand, turn the pan frequently so that it acquires a nice rounded shape. To help achieve this, push the edges of the omelette with a spoon. Turn the heat down and allow it to cook.

Take a lid or plate, bigger than the pan itself, put this over the pan and turn the whole thing over. Keep the omelette in the lid or plate while you heat up the pan with some more clean oil. When it is hot, put the omelette back in the pan, uncooked side down. Cook for a while at a high temperature, then turn the heat down to finish the cooking. Shape the edges again with the spoon.

The ideal point is when the omelette is juicy inside. (For picnics it is easier to transport if it is dry. For that, just cook a bit longer at a low temperature.)

It is easier to make two small omelettes than a big one. Remember that any Spanish omelette should be thick—about two fingers or 3–4 cm.

Pinchos Morunos
Moorish skewered meat

half a pork loin or 1/2 kg of lean lamb, or half the quantity of each
2 finely chopped garlic cloves
1 tbsp hot paprika
1 tbsp sweet paprika
1 tbsp oregano
1 tsp ground cumin
salt
4 tbsp olive oil

Cut the meat (free of fat) into fillets of 1 cm, and then into cubes.

Mix the other ingredients in a bowl and put the meat in it, stirring. Leave it to soak for at least four hours; ideally for a whole day.

Insert the bits of meat in the skewers, leaving room at both ends to pick them up (around three or four bits on each stick). Cook them on the spit, griddle, or under the grill, turning them over so that they cook evenly. Eat straight off the skewer, pulling off the meat with your teeth.

Empanadillas de Bonito (o Atún)
Bonito (or tuna) pasties

for the dough
150 g flour } mixed together
1/2 tsp baking powder } mixed together
1 pinch of salt } mixed together
100 g butter
1 small egg, beaten
1 tbsp water or sherry

for the filling
1 small can of bonito (or tuna) in olive oil
1 small can of tomato purée
1 garlic clove, smashed in the mortar with a little salt
1 bay leaf
1 small onion, finely chopped
and also
oil for frying

To prepare the dough, first put the flour on the table in the shape of a volcano. Put the remaining ingredients in the middle. Mix everything carefully. Then knead it, having first floured the table so that it won't stick. The resulting dough has to be delicate and dry, so that it won't stick to your hands and won't absorb oil when you fry it.

To make the filling, first fry the onion in a pan. When it begins to brown, add the tuna cut up in little pieces, and stir. Then add the tomato purée, and remaining ingredients, and let all this stew or fry over a gentle heat. When it is done, set it aside to cool before use (otherwise the heat would soften the pastry).

Roll out the pastry till it is quite thin (but not too thin—it mustn't break while being fried). Cut it in circles with a pastry cutter or a glass. Put a tablespoon of the filling in the middle of each circle.

Paint the edge of each circle with the beaten egg, to seal it, so that it won't open up whilst being fried.

Finally, heat up plenty of oil in a frying pan to around 180°C (smoking point), then fry the pasties in this, on both sides. Eat immediately.

The pasties can also be cooked in the oven. In that case, brush them with beaten egg and cook in a medium oven for 20 minutes.

The Norwegian Porridge Feud

Astri Riddervold and Andreas Ropeid

The authors contributed two papers, concerned with the influence on the Norwegian diet of the natural sciences in the 19th century, to the 5th Ethnological Food Conference in Hungary in 1983. Dr Riddervold subsequently turned much of the same material into a long essay which appeared in Ethnologia Scandinavica *in 1984. The story of the porridge feud is such an interesting one that we wished to publish it in* PPC *and are glad that the authors gave us a free hand to abridge and adapt it for this purpose, and to present it without the copious references given in the 1984 essay, but with the charming illustration by Ingrid Lowzow.*

It is salutary to reflect that, at any given point in the history of the last hundred years and more, people have believed that the current wisdom of the scientists represented a sort of final revelation about what they should eat. We believe that now, do we not? And we may be right to do so. Yet the tale unfolded here, showing how the Norwegian housewife in the third quarter of the 19th century was told that coffee and sugar were beneficial foods and that praise of wholemeal flour was misguided, does make one stop and think: how will the accepted wisdom of the 1980s look in 2100?

During the 19th century the natural sciences—chemistry, biology, medicine, etc—developed rapidly and discoveries were made which have revolutionized people's lives. In some instances the new thinking was in direct conflict with traditional practices.

In Norway such conflict was exemplified by a remarkable event, the 'Porridge Feud'. This broke out in 1864 when the new ideas were introduced into a cookery book, *Fornuftig Madstel* (Sensible Cookery), which was published under the name Clemens Bonifacius (The Gentle Helper), subsequently revealed as the pseudonym of Peter Christen Asbjørnsen. Its content clashed with many Norwegian traditions relating to food and diet, and also the role of women. But it was one aspect of this clash on which attention soon became focussed.

When Norwegian farmers' wives made porridge, they customarily added a certain amount of flour to the porridge when it was cooked and ready to eat; so this extra flour was eaten raw. Asbjørnsen, referring to the natural sciences, attacked the practice, stating that the uncooked flour went right through the body without being used: a loss not only to the farmer's family but also to the economy of the country. He claimed that popular diet and methods of cooking must be changed to accord with the principles of natural science, and that women must learn everything anew.

Eilert Sundt reviewed the book in his periodical *Folkevennen* (the organ of the Association for the Enlightenment of the People). He accorded some praise to the new knowledge in it, and to its style, but criticized it for its derogatory remarks about women and their proficiency, notably in porridge-making. He stated firmly that the 'thousand years old tradition' had taught women what was best and accused Asbjørnsen of writing nonsense.

When the Association held its general meeting in February 1865 Sundt was in his turn attacked. He was accused of having no qualifications to discuss porridge-making, and of denying to the people, by his ignorant intervention, the means of a new and better life. Defending himself, he denounced Asbjørnsen's book in even stronger terms, describing it as a great insult to the people of Norway.

Thus started the conflict which was, and always has been, looked upon as a slightly comic event. But it has never been quite forgotten, and people still wonder why it aroused such passions. In fact, the study of it conducted by Andreas Ropeid, on the basis of contemporary newspapers and periodicals, shows that its underlying causes were complex; and the present essay covers a correspondingly wide field of questions. Just how did the new knowledge influence views on popular diet? How did it affect the position of women, as the persons responsible for this diet? How, indeed, did the Norwegian women perceive themselves and their role as housewives? This last question will involve an examination of 19th century cookery books (on which see Hroar Dege, 'Norwegian Gastronomic Literature', in *PPC 19* and *21*).

With this preamble, we proceed to survey the two protagonists. Both were well-known and highly respected. Asbjørnsen was a forester, fairy-tale collector and author, whose books were well loved by Norwegians then, as they still are today. Sundt was the founder of sociology and ethnology in Norway, who travelled widely in the country to study people's ways and conditions of life. The results of his studies were published in several books.

Both men favoured enlightenment of the people. But their views on the content and method of such enlightenment were quite different.

Sundt fought alone. He needed courage for this, and he had it. He also had a lot of knowledge, but it was not in the field of the natural sciences. Asbjørnsen, on the other hand, had the backing of several learned men, in particular doctors and natural scientists; and at the time, the prestige of natural science was such that it was almost unbelievable that anyone would oppose one of its representatives.

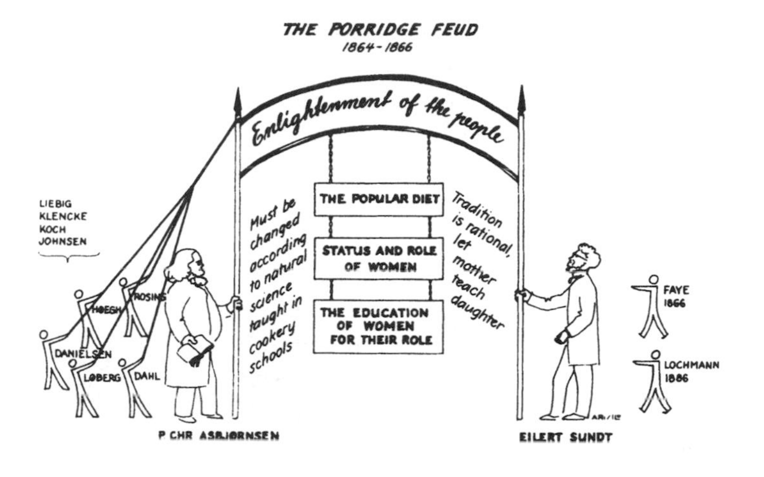

Until the 1830s and 1840s, the representatives of science in Norway had mostly been topographers or, in harmony with the topographical tradition, sociologists. But by the time the Porridge Feud broke out the dominant theme among scientifically inclined members of the upper classes was 'enlightenment of the people', and in this movement it was doctors and natural scientists who had the greatest influence.

Even before the publication of *Fornuftig Madstel,* four Norwegian doctors had published a severe criticism of the Norwegian diet and also of Norwegian women, who were responsible for their family's health. The doctors maintained that women's traditions were old-fashioned and that domestic schools must be established to teach women what they needed to know.

When Asbjørnsen repeated these arguments he referred to foreign publications, particularly German ones, as being the only ones of value on these questions. The effect of this was to bring into the controversy elements of nationalism and ideology. As an anonymous contributor to the newspaper *Morgenbladet* put it in 1867, on the one side was 'the great progressive world culture', but on the other were the traditions of the Norwegian people which 'neither can, nor ought to be, swept away immediately.'

What, then, had 'the great progressive world culture' to say about diet? It is interesting to try to find out what Asbjørnsen had picked up during his studies in Germany (1856–8) and then presented in his book as the scientific truth about diet, tradition and women. There had indeed been a 'progression' in world (meaning West European) culture: from the Middle Ages, when most situations were explained on a religious or magical basis, to the Renaissance, when the writings of classical Greece and Rome served the same purpose, to the 18th century when, as the Norwegian ethnologist Hilmar Stigum put it, the old ideas were exchanged for 'the engineering perception of life'. This perception means that one does not persist in applying traditional solutions but instead asks the question: 'Can this be done better?' The question was posed in many contexts, including such matters as the prevention of scurvy, which proved to be a dietary one.

In the first half of the 19th century, poor diet was thought to be the cause of illness and poverty, and not vice versa. But from the middle of the century came knowledge of bacteria as the cause of diseases, and of the importance of hygiene. Suddenly, it seemed important to give even the simplest domestic actions a scientific explanation: porridge-making, for example.

Meanwhile progress in chemistry and knowledge of the chemical elements had opened up the possibility of discovering what the human body, its foods, and its excretions consist of. A logical and simple conclusion was reached: 'that which the body consists of, it gradually breaks down, and more must be provided. Like replaces like.'

This theory was constructed by the German Justus von Liebig in the 1840s and had wide currency at the time when Asbjørnsen studied in Germany. Another German author, Koch, whose book on 'Foodstuffs' was translated into Norwegian in 1863, put it this way:

> In a period of between 24 and 40 days, or about a month, the entire body, both flesh and skin, nails, hair, yes even the skeleton, has been completely renewed. These decreases and losses must be replaced, partly by foodstuffs and partly by the air which penetrates through the skin and lungs into the body.

Koch refers to Liebig and his doctrine about the two types of loss which the body undergoes:

1. The inner combustion which maintains the body temperature.
2. Secretion and excretion of the used materials.

The lost elements are re-supplied to the body by two types of food:

1. Respiration stuffs which give the body warmth, and
2. Blood-formers which build muscles, bone, nerves, brain.

According to Liebig, the body needs the elements required for renewal in an exact proportion, and each meal should therefore reflect this proportion.

Dr Klencke, another German, presented this doctrine in his chemical cookery book, translated into Norwegian in 1859. Both Koch and Klencke maintained that most people, rich and poor, did not have the remotest idea of these matters. 'Everything must be learned again' was the slogan used by Klencke, Koch and Asbjørnsen.

Liebig's theory also lay behind the negative view of certain of the old foodstuffs, and the positive view of several of the new ones; views which would cause considerable surprise if they were expressed now.

Klencke said, 'Coffee is **not** as many believe just a luxury article, but a really blood forming element.' He based this on coffee's nitrogen content. He described further the positive effects of coffee: it stimulated brain activity, assisted skin secretion, stilled hunger and assisted digestion. Tea and chocolate received the same recommendation as coffee. Tea was 'a real food'.

Still on the theme of new elements in the diet, Koch acknowledged that some people complained about the use of good land to grow sugar beet and potatoes instead of grain. This was because they did not understand that sugar and alcohol were necessities. Moderate use of alcohol was healthy and right. The poor worker who spent money on alcohol should not be reproached, because alcohol would replace the warmth he lacked, besides eking out his poor diet.

Even narcotics such as coca, betel, hash, opium and tobacco earned approval. The anonymous translator of Koch's book referred to the view of the German author Dr Osterlen that such narcotics were a necessity for millions of people, that they made the diet go further, were strength-giving and exhilarating, banished sorrow and created joy and energy. Other authors were content with praising coffee, tea, chocolate, sugar, syrup and to a certain extent alcohol. However all of them said that food which one likes and wishes to eat, is automatically healthy. This view was used to explain that not all the old recipes were useless. Despite ignorance, people had occasionally and instinctively done things correctly.

The opinion of the time with regard to salt requires special mention. There was a growing understanding of the connection between diet and certain diseases such as scurvy, and a suspicion that this was due to a one-sided diet of salt meat and fish. However, this was not taken to mean that salt or salt meat was itself unhealthy, merely that it was nutritionally inferior. The scientists thought that salting drew from 1/3 to 1/2 of the nutrients from the meat and into the brine, and that salt meat thereby lost more of its nourishing value. Klencke maintained that the brine which was thrown away was as nutritious as the meat juices, and that it was therefore an inexcusable and unnecessary waste to salt meat. (It is important to realise that when Klencke and other 'enlighteners' urged people to eat more fresh meat, this was for reasons of economy, not health. In their nutrition tables, fresh meat was shown as having a pure nitrogen content of 3, while salt meat was rated at only 1.5 and coffee scores 2.1.)

On the other hand the scientists of the time had high praise for salt itself: 'Salt is not only the most pleasant and necessary spice, it is also an indispensible requisite for our life, our nutrition and for a healthy mixing of the body juices. Salt constitutes 62% of the solid part of the blood. The body tissues are rich in salt, and all excretions such as sweat, tears, urine, gall contain up to 60% kitchen salt', according to Klencke. Basing himself on the theory that like replaces like, he described how these large amounts of excreted salt must be supplied to the body again in the food.

* * * *

Enough has now been said to indicate what was supposed to be the contribution of 'progressive world culture' to ideas about the Norwegian diet. This contribution was essentially German. It was based on the theories of Liebig, and found expression in the works of Klencke and Koch. Here were the fountain-heads from which Asbjørnsen drew his inspiration and much of his material. But a question arises: was he an out-and-out disciple of the German authors, or did he modify their views to suit Norwegian conditions? The answer is that Asbjørnsen's book is in effect a simplified copy of Klencke's work, and that it is presented as being based on that and on Koch. Asbjørnsen faithfully echoed the German views throughout the first part of his book. With regard to such matters as the defects of traditional diet, the role of women, the need to apply science in the kitchen, and for schools of domestic science, etc, one might just as well read Klencke as Asbjørnsen.

However, when Asbjørnsen came to the subject of new elements in the diet, he modified the German position in some respects. To be sure, he praised coffee in much the same way as the German authors—it was an excellent source of nutrition for old or poor people, especially if taken with sandwiches and sugar. Sugar was a real blessing, and syrup was a healthy and good food. As for salt, Asbjørnsen more or less translated what Klencke had written, adding his own recipe for a nutritious soup made from brine in which meat had been steeped. But on grains he diverged somewhat. It is true that his explanation of how porridge should be made and his passage on the bursting of the carbohydrate grains (and how they would not burst if not cooked) came from Klencke, while his calculations of the loss of 1/6 of the nutritional content when uncooked flour is 'stamped' into porridge were drawn from the notes of the Norwegian translator of Koch's book. However, he gave a strong recommendation in favour of finely sifted flour, especially of barley and oats, arguing that the husks of these cereals were indigestible and even harmful, although the husks of rye could be nutritious if they were finely milled. He labelled as 'prejudice' and 'false' the idea that porridge and bread made of wholemeal flour was nutritious.

Asbjørnsen did not discuss alcohol and narcotics. But he did recommend the use of vegetables and of wild as well as cultivated berries and fruits, citing Genesis 1.29.

To sum up, he followed his German models to a very large extent, largely repeating what they had written, but showing some discrimination in what he took from them and a few minor divergences from them, evidently prompted by his knowledge of his own country and conditions therein.

Bearing in mind that Klencke's chemical cookery book had been translated into Norwegian in 1859, and Koch's book about nutritional elements in 1863, it would be impossible to describe Asbjørnsen's work as truly innovative. Its importance lay in the attention which it directed to the question of porridge-making. Here was a Norwegian making controversial comments about the most important item in the popular Norwegian diet. Here was the spark which lit the fire of the Porridge Feud, which in turn provoked debates on much wider issues. Among these issues was the role of women in Norway, which has already been touched upon (being inseparable from questions of diet) but which we will now examine in more detail.

Women in Norway

One thing must be said about Asbjørnsen's book in this respect. It was highly derogatory, 'a great insult' as his opponent Sundt put it.

In this connection it is interesting to hark back to the four Norwegian doctors who were mentioned above as earlier critics of the Norwegian diet and Norwegian women. One of them had actually made the claim that women in western Norway were at a lower cultural level than their husbands, basing himself on the doctrine that different dimensions of the brain were an index of different cultural levels. But he didn't say anything about how to make porridge, so his claim created no great stir.

However, to revert to our main theme, if wrong diet caused poverty and poor health, and if women controlled the family diet, then the nature and role of women deserved attention; and attention they now received.

Klencke published not only cookery books, but also books about women with such titles as: 'Maiden', 'Wife', 'Mother', 'Housewife'. His aim in these books was 'to explain the female from a natural science point of view'. Since his views on the subject are reflected to some extent in his cookery books, it is worthwhile to look at a summary of them.

> The male by his nature possesses strength of will and character.
> The female inclination is towards the emotions, and subjection to the male.
> Woman is more heart, man intellect.
> The male body represents strength and will, the female beauty and comfort.
> The female's entire nature is not suited to activity in the outer world as is the male's. So her duties and rights with regard to public life are restricted; she functions and lives solely within the family.

Ida Blom, a Norwegian women's history researcher, has investigated the 19th century European opinion of women. Basing her study on the work of the German researcher Grethe Hauser, she shows that Klencke's opinions were, or at least became, the general view about women within the German upper middle-classes. It seems that the origin of this view was Jean Jacques Rousseau's work, *Émile,* book V, where he presented his philosophical view of the future man and woman. Rousseau held that woman is inferior to man, and that women must from childhood be brought up to accept this.

The Swede Ewa Sjögren has shown how science gained prestige during the 19th century with regard to childcare and upbringing. The authors who wrote on the subject changed in the latter half of the century from 'Experienced mother', 'Anonymous', etc, to male experts. And the writers who expressed the new views about diet and nutrition were also males.

What the natural scientists had to say about the upbringing and education of women in the future echoed the views of Rousseau. Women should be taught to use the findings of natural science in their work as housewives. Learning from a mother, mother-in-law or the lady of the house was no longer sufficient. The existing cookery books could no longer be used either. 'Over the entire country, owing to ignorance, foolish cookery book recipes and inherited bad habits when salting, skimming, baking etc, nutritional elements for thousands are daily squandered.'

The introduction to Klencke's cookery book, from which these statements are taken, was written by a Norwegian—the anonymous translator. His presentation gives the impression that the opinions stated were both Klencke's and his own. There is no hint of disagreement between the two. The translator mentions the Danish Professor Schartlig's speech at the opening of the University of Denmark's new chemical laboratory. Schartlig had asserted that 'nothing is done for women's knowledge either in higher or lower circles'. Education in languages and music were lost years, education in housekeeping was what was needed. Now was the time to raise a thoughtless, almost mechanical, work to an inspired activity.

The first part of Klencke's cookery book finishes by presenting the goal for women's upbringing. His main point was that women as well as men must be educated for their work; but, for women, only domestic science was relevant. The natural sciences must come into the kitchen as they had into the factory. Then the dualism in women's life would cease and the gap between spiritual and material activity would be closed. This would in turn lead to the disappearance of that common illness, weak nerves, and women would be prepared to be man's friend and companion, her children's educator and the servants' mistress.

Clearly and simply, we can read here the West European man's opinion of diet and the role of women. This opinion was shared by some Norwegians, but certainly not by all, neither within the middle-class, nor by academics or farmers.

What women thought of all this, and in particular of themselves, is virtually unknown. However, a study of 19th century Norwegian cookery books throws a little light on the matter. If we take 1864, the year in which Asbjørnsen's book was published, as a watershed, and survey the cookery books before and after, we may, in fact will, find that there is a significant difference between them, indicative of changing attitudes.

The books we have examined are of two types. Some are only collections of recipes, with emphasis placed on finer food for social gatherings and on raw materials which were not usual in the Norwegian popular diet (goose, grouse, lobster, oysters with wine sauce, etc) and on food which was time-consuming to prepare. The surnames of the female authors were in many cases of non-Norwegian origin (Thams, Filliong, Bang, Rude, Holmboe).

The other type aimed to be a textbook for housekeeping, not just cookery, and often had a phrase in the title such as 'for town and country', or 'for small and large households', occasionally only 'for small households'.

Of the material examined, all, except for a collection of recipes in verse by parish clerk Allum, were written by women. Most of these cited their own experience as justification for writing a cookery book. From before 1864 seven different authors have been found, who almost all published books of the first type; from after 1864 cookery books by 23 authors.

In the pre-1864 period, *Lærebog I de forskjellige Grene af Huusholdningen* (Textbook of the different branches of housekeeping), written by a vicar's wife, Hanna Winsnes, is supreme. She stressed her own lack of written aid when as a young girl she had to take over housekeeping from her sister who was ill. She related how she asked advice from others, gained experience in various parts of the country, experimented, often failed, but succeeded in the end. She now wished to give other young women the benefit of her knowledge and experience in book form.

What emerged was a really good textbook, educational, encouraging, dotted with such remarks as: 'This is difficult, but you will surely manage.' The recipes were for traditional Norwegian food made from Norwegian raw materials. All types of preserving, both short and long term, were described carefully. This applied to meat, fish, game, vegetables, fruit and berries.

The majority of cookery books after 1864 had the same type of female authors as earlier: Experienced Housewife, Country Vicar's Wife, etc. They still claimed their own experience as justification for publishing a cookery book. However there was one difference: a great many included a chapter about nutrition and this was written by a man (or the introduction stated that the chapter had been checked by an expert).

Then, from the 1890s, a new type of cookery book writer appears, educated female domestic science teachers, who often ran well-reputed housekeeping schools or school kitchens in the towns. They stood on a double platform, with their own experience and their theoretical schooling.

The female authors of these later cookery books adhered to tradition, but they also accepted that tradition was not enough; it was necessary to include the new developments in natural science. Their recipes reflected this attitude.

We can also observe an evolution in the attitudes of Norwegian women generally; and this evolution is seen to be parallel to the changes in the cookery books. Women wanted more education in housekeeping. The question had already been raised by male politicians, and the discussion was lively: should public funds be used for domestic schools for women or not?

Before the problem was solved at the official level, Minna and Fredrik Wetlesen started a school in 1865 at their farm outside Oslo. This was for girls of farming families, with both practical and theoretical education in cookery, dairy work, washing, sewing and general subjects such as Norwegian, arithmetic, history, geography. The course lasted for one or two years. From 1876 public funds were granted for the domestic education of young women throughout the entire country. From 1890 domestic teaching for girls was included as a subject in the primary schools, and from 1950 boys were also taught domestic science.

It was women themselves who solved the problem and formed the pedagogical plan. The main work was carried out by two women's organizations: Norsk Kvinnesaksforening 1887 (The Norwegian Women's Rights Association) and Norske Kvinners Sanitetsforening 1896 (The Norwegian Women's Health Association, NWPHA).

NWPHA's chief aim was that the population of Norway should consist of as many as possible strong, healthy women and men, willing to sacrifice everything for a free and independent Norway. The aim is interesting, seen in relation to our point—women's conception of herself and her duties. It accorded with the view of Sundt rather than that of Asbjørnsen.

It is noteworthy that around 1890 some women pursued studies abroad (at Liège, Glasgow, Edinburgh) in order to become qualified teachers. And it was women who succeeded, in 1891, in persuading the Norwegian Parliament to make a grant for the new teaching.

It is obvious that Asbjørnsen had not managed to take from all the women their belief in their own ability; but the continental attitudes did have some female, as well as male, supporters.

Conclusions

It is difficult to say to what extent Asbjørnsen's cookery book was responsible for the changes in diet during the 19th century. But it is clear that the book had some responsibility, for both the positive and the negative changes. Several of the post-1864 cookery book authors stated that they had read the book, and some transcribed certain paragraphs without stating the source. One author stated that she had learned everything she knew from Klencke and Asbjørnsen, whilst another transcribed his praise of salt.

So it is abundantly clear that many of the female cookery book authors read and used Asbjørnsen's book; and it is reasonable to ascribe to him a share of the credit for positive changes in the diet, for example increasing use of vegetables and fruit, fresh meat and fish.

The negative effect of his book on the diet can be traced quite directly, and these effects were long-term. The use of coffee, sugar, syrup and finely-sifted flour increased. Towards the end of the century doctors complained in medical reports about just these four elements: too much coffee was drunk, too much bread made from finely-sifted flour was eaten with margarine and syrup or sugar, whilst sour milk, flat bread, porridge, butter and cheese seemed almost to have disappeared. This tendency continued far into this century until the war in 1944-45 finally stopped it, at least for some time.

Given the influence exerted by Asbjørnsen's book, and the important role of the Porridge Feud which it provoked, it is amusing to find that on this particular matter his view was disproved only two years after it had been stated. A Norwegian, Dr Faye, started analysing what really happened when porridge, with uncooked flour added, was eaten. Using himself and his assistant as guinea-pigs, he analysed their excrements when, for several days, both of them had been fed solely on porridge of that type. Not a single molecule of starch was found; so, two years after *Fornuftig Madstel* was published, it was known that Asbjørnsen's assertion that the uncooked flour could not be used by the body, was not true. In the course of the next twenty years, many more of the assertions made in 1864 were overturned.

However, the influence of Asbjørnsen's book survived these revelations and proved to be more powerful than the reasoned criticisms which were made of his views. Thus at a natural sciences meeting in 1886 a Norwegian, Professor Lochmann, demolished Asbjørnsen's doctrines and upheld the virtues of the traditional diet. He finished by saying that scientists now recognized the validity of that diet for Norwegians, and realized that they should learn from the collective experience and wisdom underlying it rather than seek to impose ill-considered and potentially harmful changes.

Yet there was no public debate after that meeting. Asbjørnsen's reputation was such that his views continued to enjoy authority. His book with its message that coffee, sugar, syrup and white bread was sensible eating spread all over the country and through the social layers.

Professor Lochmann also showed clearly at the same meeting what was his view of women. The experienced housewife was a physiologist and hygienist without knowing it, often far more advanced than the so-called scientists. Lochmann showed his attitude to women's participation in public affairs when he welcomed a woman as professional participator at this meeting. He concluded by saying: 'To solve the difficult tasks which await modern hygiene, we will scarcely find more active and better help than that which the intelligent women of our time can give.'

Both Asbjørnsen's view and Lochmann's contrary view are to be found in Norwegian culture in at least the following 60–80 years, and they can both be documented, for example in the minutes from parliamentary debates on any matter which concerned women's position in society. So one cannot really say that either side was victorious. But it is still true that our analysis of 19th century cookery books indicates that Norwegian women to a great extent preserved their belief in themselves, their experience and their skill, despite the energetic attempts made in the name of science to foist on to them a conception of themselves as inferior to men.

And it is certainly correct to regard publication of *Fornuftig Madstel* in 1864 as initiating a shift in the history of Norwegian popular diet and also in the history of Norwegian women.

Encounters with the Elusive Stockfish

PETER GRAHAM

Peter Graham lives in France and is the author of Classic Cheese Cookery *(first published by Penguin in 1988), which won the 1988 André Simon Memorial Prize. More recently, his book* Mourjou: The Life and Food of an Auvergne Village *has won great critical acclaim. It was first published by Viking, London, 1998.*

My first encounter with stockfish (wind-dried unsalted cod) came in the mid-seventies, when I sampled that delicious Niçoise speciality, *estocaficada*. It is a dish where the startlingly gamey flavour of stockfish is accentuated by garlic, tomatoes and black olives. Later I came to translate Jacques Médecin's *La Cuisine du Comté de Nice (Cuisine Niçoise,* Penguin), which naturally contains a recipe for *estocaficada,* and began to look more closely at this Ur-food extraordinary. A veritable bundle of calories, vitamins and minerals, wind-dried cod from Norway was much appreciated as a preserve in southern Europe from very early times. The French manuscript of 1392–3 which has been published as *Le Ménagier de Paris* says it could be kept for as long as 12 years: 'Item, quant icelle morue est prise es marces de la mer et l'en veult icelle garder .x. ou .xii. ans, l'en l'effondre et luy oste l'en la teste, et est seichee a l'air et au soleil, et non mye au feu ou a la fumee. Et ce fait, elle est nommee stofix.' The reference books I consulted at the time I translated Médecin said that nowadays stockfish is eaten in Portugal, Spain, the Côte d'Azur and Italy (especially Venice), as well as parts of Africa.

A few years later I moved house to the Châtaigneraie, an area that straddles the Cantal and the Aveyron in the southwest Massif Central. This, I thought, was solely a land of chestnuts (*châtaignes*), cheese, *choux farci,* and good solid charcuterie. As indeed it was; but that was not all. One November day, I went into the superette in my nearest market town, Maurs-la-Jolie. As I stood in front of the vegetable counter, my nostrils were engaged by a curiously insistent and not very pleasant smell which reminded me of the fish food which, as a boy, I used to give our goldfish. There, next to bags of potatoes, was a cluster of stockfish standing upright in a tub like baguettes at the baker's. Just as when I had last encountered them, I caught a split-second image of agonised pain: this optical illusion was caused by the way the gill-bones of the dried and headless fish formed what looked like a screaming mouth. What on earth, I wondered, was the creature doing in the Massif Central?

Friends in the village told me that *estofinado* was a favourite local stockfish dish, eaten from All Saints Day to Easter (the reasons for this 'season' became clear later). Local restaurants apparently vied with each other to produce the best version. I telephoned a warmly recommended restaurant in the village of Almon-les-Junies, near Decazeville, to book a table for the following Sunday, but it was booked out. Eventually I and some friends managed to get a table two Sundays later. When we arrived in Almon, it struck us as odd that such a small village should have a spacious car park, much of which was occupied by large coaches. It turned out that the village had three competing *estofinado* restaurants, and had had to build facilities to cope with the coachloads of old-age pensioners, anciens d'Algérie and hunters' associations whose winter gastronomic outings centred on stockfish.

Our meal began, as almost all restaurant meals do in the Châtaigneraie, with vegetable soup followed by a platter of Auvergne ham and *saucisson sec*. Next came a *bouchée à la reine* (vol-au-vent), a pause, then the *estofinado*. It looked like a steaming bowl of mashed potatoes. But when sampled it revealed its other ingredients: cream, eggs, garlic, parsley and what looked like little wood chips—the stockfish. The flavour was indescribable. Behind the familiar tastes there lurked a flavour that was neither fishy nor meaty nor cheesy, but had overtones of all three—and was excellent. When asked if we wanted more (a tradition with *estofinado*), we rashly beamed and nodded, and another steaming bowl appeared. Little did we know that the *estofinado* was not the *plat de résistance*. It was followed by roast chicken, cheese and *îles flottantes* with *fouace* (a relative of *brioche*).

Later, after taking the advice of an old woman in the village, I tried making *estofinado* myself. She had warned me it was time-consuming and complicated, so I waited till I had a houseful of guests before attempting the dish. The stockfish I bought was extremely hard and planklike. As a joke I laid its tail on one chair and its 'mouth' on another, and took a photograph of my ten-year-old god-daughter sitting on its middle (with a piece of newspaper to protect her clothes from the smell). Its woodlike qualities persisted during the first stage of making the dish, which requires it to be sawn up into sections and soaked in water: as I sawed away, a gentle rain of stockfish dust fell to the floor.

Soaking stockfish is no simple operation like desalting salt cod. It takes anything from six to ten days for the dried fish to reconstitute itself, and it needs to be soaked in running water (or under a dripping tap). If this is impossible, the water it soaks in has to be changed very frequently. This is because stockfish is not salted at all and can go off very quickly. (Hence its consumption during the winter months only. In 1988 the Rodez Chamber of Commerce rashly organised a mammoth stockfish banquet in mid-August as part of a campaign to promote local tourism; 1,500 portions were served, but most were left untouched, as the stockfish had gone off in the heat.)

The locals, who tend to make *estofinado* less frequently now that transport to local restaurants has become easier, used to tie their stockfish to a rock (it remained in one piece because they left a sliver of skin connecting the sections) and put it for a week in an outside cattle trough with spring water trickling into it. The rock was to stop it floating to the surface and thus risk being eaten by dogs or foxes. If they did not have the right kind of cattle trough they might leave the stockfish in a small stream or irrigation channel, after first taking the precaution of tying it up in a bundle of twigs to keep scavengers away. The pre-war French prime minister, Paul Ramadier, who hailed from Decazeville, the small industrial town in the heart of *estofinado* country, reportedly reproduced the cattle trough technique when he lived in Paris by putting his stockfish in the lavatory cistern, thus ensuring that the water it was soaking in got changed several times a day.

My stockfish had swollen considerably after six days of soaking under a trickling tap from a rainwater tank. There was scum on the water—and a stink that defied description (according to people in my village you can always tell from the smell when *estofinado* is being made in someone's house; nowadays many shops sell pre-soaked stockfish for that reason). When the stockfish was cooked (a 45-minute simmer), I embarked on the lengthy task of picking the flesh off the bone. I had nearly finished—neat piles of skin, bones and flesh littered the kitchen table—when my guests returned from a walk. The smell that greeted them as they came in from the bracing Auvergne air prompted various reactions, the mildest of which was 'I'm not eating any of that stuff!' The fact that those same people later ate their words, and indeed clamoured for second and third helpings of *estofinado,* is less a tribute to my cooking than to the extraordinary way the aggressive flavour of stockfish transmogrifies itself, when combined with potatoes, cream, eggs, garlic and parsley, into something delicate and gently aromatic.

I was naturally interested in finding out why stockfish was a traditional dish in the Châtaigneraie. Its presence on the Côte d'Azur was easily explained: for centuries Norwegian sailors had exchanged it for fresh fruit and vegetables. But this far inland? The books I consulted were of little help, apart from revealing that the area of the southern Massif Central where *estofinado* was eaten was larger than I had imagined, stretching as far as Figeac (Lot) to the west and Villefranche-de-Rouergue (Aveyron) to the south. The fact that this area is bisected by the river Lot, which was for a long time navigable from Bordeaux as far as Vieillevie, just before Entraygues, seemed an important clue.

Authors offered various theories about the presence of stockfish in the area, some of them plausible enough, but none supported by hard evidence. It had been brought there, they variously alleged, by North European pilgrims on their way to Santiago de Compostela, by Norwegian merchants who had come to buy wool in Villefranche and Figeac in the late Middle Ages, or by local soldiers who had fought in Louis XIV's campaigns in the Low Countries and picked up the habit of eating stockfish there (it was not explained why they should have brought it back with them).

An enthusiastic local historian (a retired civil servant) told me he had seen evidence of stockfish being introduced to the area in the mid 14th century by a British soldier whose name he pronounced as Robert Kenofflesse (Knowles?), and who at the head of an army of 30,000 troops spent five years unsuccessfully laying siege to the town of Montsalvy, in the hills above Vieillevie. This sounded a promising line of inquiry; such a large number of soldiers tied down for so many years would have had a far greater chance of establishing stockfish in the local diet than the occasional pilgrim or wool merchant.

In 1989, in a chapter entitled 'Un Ilot insolite de consommation du stockfisch: les confins Rouergue-Quercy', in *Alimentation et Régions* (Presses Universitaires de Nancy, 1989) Guy Mergoil contributed by far the most thorough examination so far of the *estofinado* phenomenon in the southern Massif Central. Mergoil quotes yet other 'explanations' for the presence of stockfish, but concludes that it is well-nigh impossible to distinguish myth from reality. However, he goes on to say that since stockfish could be kept for a very long time and has a high nutrition/volume ratio its consumption could easily have been introduced by troops in the Middle Ages, become more widespread with the development of river traffic and trade with northern Europe, and then been boosted in the 19th century as a result of the industrial revolution in and around Decazeville and the arrival of many Spanish immigrant workers. He charts *estofinado*'s gradual transformation from poor peasant fare into a rather expensive dish for special occasions. He supplies no direct evidence that the English introduced stockfish into the area, but simply quotes a cookery writer (Henri Philippon in *Cuisine du Quercy et du Périgord*) who surmises that this was so.

Could my retired civil servant, I wondered, come up with chapter and verse? Unfortunately, when pressed, he was unable to give me the exact references for what he had jotted down. After I had spent a fruitless day in the Archives Départementales du Cantal trying to track down his quote, the trail went dead. All I managed to establish was that the Englishman who allegedly fed his troops on stockfish was not called Knowles but Knolles or

Knollys, that he was one of John of Gaunt's captains, and that he had indeed spent some time in the area during the Hundred Years War (he was known to the French at the time as Canolles).

One or two other mysteries remain. We do not know what form *estofinado* took before the potato's arrival in the area in the mid to late 18th century. But on the analogy of *patranque* (an Auvergnat dish consisting of bread mashed up with cheese), which preceded *truffade* (potato and cheese), it is likely that stockfish was mixed with bread, or at least eaten with bread.

Why is *estofinado* consumed only in an area surrounding one stretch of the upper Lot and not farther down the river? Mergoil suggests that this is because peasants farther downstream had more abundant resources and therefore did not need to rely on dried fish. He also points out that they had much less running water at their disposal for the soaking process. But there is much evidence that when running water was lacking another technique was used—both in France and in Italy—to make the woodlike stockfish fit for human consumption. According to the *Ménagier de Paris,* if the *stofix* was first beaten with a mallet for an hour it then needed to be soaked in warm water for only 12 hours or so, rather than for several days ('Et quant [. . .] l'en la veult mengier, il la couvient batre d'un maillet de boiz bien une heure, et puis mectre tremper en eaue tiede bien .xii. heures ou plus').

Why stockfish is so called also remains a mystery. Both the Old English 'stocc' and the Old High German 'stock' mean 'a stick'. But to what does the stick refer? Most plausibly in my view, it describes the phenomenal stick-like hardness of the fish. Others argue that it got its name because it was habitually beaten with a mallet or stick. Mergoil mentions yet another possible derivation: it was so called because the fish was dried on poles. Any other suggestions from *PPC* readers as to the history and/or etymology of stockfish would be welcome.

How to Make Estofinado

As with many peasant dishes, there are several ways of making *estofinado,* but the basic ingredients vary little. Some say no *estofinado* is complete without walnut oil, either added smoking-hot and in large quantities at the last moment, or used to sauté the stockfish flakes in. Others (including myself) find that the pungency of walnut oil cancels out the subtle stockfish flavour. It also makes an already rich dish much richer. Another addition commonly found in restaurants—but frowned on by the purists—is hard-boiled eggs. They have the effect of spinning out the dish. It is also rumoured that some less scrupulous restaurateurs get round the very high price of stockfish (about

180 francs a kilo) by adding a certain quantity of much cheaper salt cod to their *estofinado.*

Often walnut or another oil is used to 'lubricate' the dish. Mashed potatoes, in the orthodox version, can absorb a vast amount of oil. The following recipe uses diced potatoes instead, which are less absorbent and thus obviate the need for oil on top of the eggs and lashings of cream. Of the many versions of *estofinado* I have tasted, this is the best. The recipe was given to me by Eliette Pons of l'Auberge de la Cascade near the charming little bastide of Villecomtal in the Aveyron (Polissal, 12320 Saint-Félix-de-Lunel: telephone 65.44.61.54: if you want to eat *estofinado,* which is available from November to April, say so when booking).

ESTOFINADO

The quantities are to serve eight people

650 g (1 lb 7 oz) stockfish (unsoaked)
650 g (1 lb 7 oz) potatoes, peeled and cut into very small dice
vegetable oil
80 cl (28 fl oz) single cream
2 large cloves garlic, finely chopped
4 tbsp parsley, finely chopped
4 eggs, beaten
salt, pepper

Saw the stockfish into 15 cm (6") lengths, place in a very large saucepan and soak for six days under a trickling tap (alternatively, change the water twice a day). Rinse, place in salted boiling water and simmer for 45 minutes, skimming from time to time. Sauté the potatoes gently in oil until cooked. Strain the stockfish. As soon as it is cool enough to handle, quickly separate the flesh from the skin and bones (if the stockfish is allowed to cool too much it becomes impossibly sticky). Cut a little of the skin (about one tablespoonful) into very thin strips and add to the fish flakes. Put the potatoes into a large deep fireproof dish or casserole, add the fish and mix together over a very low heat. When very hot but not sizzling, add the cream, garlic and parsley and continue stirring until hot. At the last moment mix in the eggs, stir a little longer (but do not allow the eggs to curdle), add salt and pepper to taste, and serve immediately.

The Denby Dale Pie

OR Une Fiche à Faire Monter les Sourcils

LAURA MASON

The author, familiar to PPC *readers from her essays in (and covers for)* PPC 35 *and* 49, *was engaged for nearly three years in making the UK contribution to the Euroterroirs project, sponsored and financed by the European Community in Brussels. Annexed to the present piece is a suitably serious note which describes the project, and the nature of the fiches (database entries) which are its tangible results, and thus explains why Laura Mason (with help from Catherine Brown on Scottish products) has been compiling hundreds of fiches for British food specialities and is in a position to offer one, and a nicely chosen one, for inspection by* PPC *readers.*

But the purpose of this contribution to PPC 50 *is not just to inform our readers of this massive enterprise; it is, rather, to put the spotlight on what must surely be not only the strangest of the 400 or so British fiches but also the outright winner in any Community-wide competition to identify the product best calculated to strain credulity and boggle minds. Indeed, when a frivolous observer asked the author, some time ago, whether she would not insert into her pile of fiches one which would represent a product that never was and to the attentive reader would seem like something which never could have been, she had to reply that she already had a genuine fiche which would outdo anything which she or anyone else could invent by way of jest.*

We had hoped to show here the commemorative plate issued in 1928 to mark the creation of the Infirmary Pie, but it wasn't going to reproduce well; so instead we offer the measurements of the pie, as inscribed on the plate: 16 feet long, 5 feet wide, 15 inches deep.

The Fiche

Region: Yorkshire and Humberside
Sector: Bakery
Classification: Pie
Name: Denby Dale Pie
Other names:—
Variants: the Denby Dale pie is a huge version of meat and potato pies commonly baked by housewives, butchers and bakers in West Yorkshire and Lancashire.

Description

Dimensions: small individual pies made in the village are roughly 9 cm by 5 cm by 3 cm deep.
Weight: the 1988 pie weighed 9.03 tonnes; the small pies weigh about 175 g.
Form: oblong.
Colour: pale gold pastry on top, covering pale potato layer with browned beef filling.
Flavour: savoury beef.
Composition: figures not available.
Distinctive features: the immense size of the special occasion pies.

History

The Denby Dale Pie is a special occasion pie which is baked once in about every 25 years; the last making took place in 1988, on the bicentenary of the first recorded pie. David Bostwick (1987), discussing the history of these notes that other large pies have been recorded elsewhere in England for special occasions, but it is the huge size which distinguishes the Denby Dale pie. Tradition has it that each time the pie is baked, it is made larger than the last one.

The first Denby Dale pie to be documented was baked in 1788 in celebration of the return to health of King George III. This was followed by: the Victory Pie (1815, to commemorate the Battle of Waterloo); the Repeal of the Corn Laws Pie (1846, to celebrate the removal of the unpopular legislation which kept the price of corn artificially high); the Golden Jubilee Pie (27 August, 1887, intended to celebrate Queen Victoria's Golden Jubilee); the Resurrection Pie (3rd September 1887, to replace the Golden Jubilee Pie which went bad and had to be buried in quicklime); the Repeal of the Corn Laws Jubilee Pie (1896, commemorating that from 50 years earlier); the Infirmary Pie (1928, to raise funds for the local hospital); the Would-Be Coronation Pie (1953, planned but never made because meat was still rationed in the aftermath of the Second World War); the Village Hall Pie (1964, to raise funds for a community hall); and most recently, the Bicentenary Pie (1988, to recall the beginning of the tradition). A local butcher holds the formula for a special seasoning mixture which has been used in the last two pies, and is also put into small pies which are made on a routine basis. The Denby Dale pie was originally filled with meat and game, but after the debacle of 1887, the recipe was changed to one similar to that now used. This is a gigantic version of the common shortcrust pastry and baked. Small versions of such pies are well known in Yorkshire and Lancashire. Fresh beef is always used in the preparation of these, distinguishing them from the cottage pies which utilise leftover meat, and demonstrating a relationship with the similar Lancashire hotpot, a stew of mutton covered with sliced potatoes.

Use

The Denby Dale Pie is only made for special events. Small meat and potato pies are popular for dinner in the industrial areas of west Yorkshire and south Lancashire.

Method

The last Denby Dale Pie to be baked entire was the 1928 one. To satisfy modern hygiene regulations, the pies are now made by producing a stew of beef and potato using the special seasoning, cooking the crust separately, and assembling the pie on site.

On a smaller scale, the method is as follows: *Preparing the meat:* this is always fresh beef, which is cut into pieces of 1–2 cm, and partially cooked with seasoning and liquid (usually water) to produce plenty of gravy; this mixture is placed in the bottom of a pie dish. *Assembly:* the beef mixture is covered with a layer of sliced, lightly seasoned raw potato, which is covered, in turn, with a sheet of shortcrust pastry. *Baking:* for about 45 minutes, at about 190°C.

Production

The Denby Dale Pie is made roughly once every generation. Figures are not available for production of the small pies, but they are popular in their home area, and total production throughout the region must be hundreds of thousands annually.

Number of producers: only the village of Denby Dale, West Yorkshire makes the huge pies. One butcher in the village makes small pies with the special seasoning. Ordinary small meat and potato pies are made by many butchers and bakers in the area.

Area of production: particularly the industrial areas of West Yorkshire and South Lancashire.

Season: Ordinary meat and potato pies are made at any time, but are more popular in winter.

Legal status: none.

Bibliography

Bostwick, D., 1988, 'The Denby Dale Pies in the Folk Life': *Journal of Ethnological Studies:* edited by W. Linnard and published by the Society for Folk Life Studies.

Holmes, P., personal communication September 1994, Upper Denby, West Yorkshire.

Matthews, P., (ed), 1994, *The Guinness Book of Records,* Guinness Publishing.

In Affectionate Remembrance of the

Denby Dale Pie,

WHICH DIED AUGUST 27th, 1887,

AGED THREE DAYS,

And was interred in Quick Lime, with much rejoicing,
in Toby Wood, Sunday, August 28th, 1887

With the Committee's Regrets.

Strong, strong was the smell that compelled us to part,
From a treat to our stomach and a salve to our heart;
Like the last Denby Pie which the crowd did assail,
Its contents a rank mixture, it quickly turned stale.
Though we could not eat, yet we still lingered near,
Till the stench proved too much for our nasals to bear;
So like sensible men the committee did say:
"'Twas best to inter it without further delay."
This mystic pie, so large and rare,
Smell'd awful as a tomb,
But came to show how long a pie,
In Denby Dale could bloom.

THE RESURRECTION PIE.

Undeterred by previous efforts the people of Denby Dale have attempted another pie, which is to be consumed to-day, Saturday. This has been made by the ladies of the village, and is expected to be a success. It consists of 48 stones flour, 98 stones potatoes, a heifer, two calves and two sheep.

This remarkable illustration was reproduced in the article by Mr Bostwick about the history of the Denby Dale Pie (see Bibliography on page 247). He explains just what went wrong with the Golden Jubilee Pie and led to its being buried in quicklime: a blunder on an awe-inspiring scale.

Explanatory Note

THE EUROTERROIRS PROJECT

This project is organised by the Conseil National des Arts Culinaire (CNAC) at 75 Rue Vieille du Temple, 75003 Paris: Laura Mason is co-ordinator and researcher for the UK part of the work.

Euroterroirs is a name which translates very roughly as European regions. The aim is to write database entries (fiches) on selected European regional food specialities. The project is based on a French initiative: similar work has been going on in France for about four years. The total number of entries is projected to be 4,000; it is estimated that Britain will provide about 400 of these.

Criteria for including various foods have been established with a strong emphasis on regional and historic links. The criteria are:

1. History: the food should have a 'traditional' element. Roughly, this is defined as something which as been made for three generations or longer.

2. Geography: preferably, the food should be linked to a region; to really please CNAC, the locality should be included in the actual name of the project.

3. Savoir-faire, or 'knowledge': this means the specific knowledge required for processing the ingredients or manufacturing the product. Again, CNAC prefer this to have a regional link.

4. Marketing: the product should be 'alive', ie still sold. Scale of production is not an issue. It can be measured in kilos or tonnes.

'Catering' foods, in the sense of items sold through restaurants or take-aways are not included.

Two additional categories were proposed. They are not popular with CNAC but may eventually be included. These were:

1. Recently extinct products, now vanished, but which people still alive can remember.

2. 'Emerging' products based on traditional craftsmanship, but adjusted to the demands of today's consumers.

Britain can provide quite a lot for both categories, due to the enormous changes which have taken place within our food industry since the First World War.

The information gathered for this project will initially take the form of a database, but should be published as an encyclopaedia covering the whole EU, plus smaller publications in each country, containing the relevant entries for that state. It may eventually have other applications, notably for use in special naming schemes (similar to appellation contrôlée), promotion of tourism, and rural development.

On Long-Cooked Eggs

Harold McGee

An electric light bulb perched on a cut avocado adorned the cover of PPC 38, *which contained Professor Kurti's major (seven-page) review of Harold McGee's latest book on scientific aspects of cookery,* The Curious Cook *(1990). This essay shows that his curiosity is unabated.*

I'd always thought of hard-cooked eggs as among the most straightforward of dishes to prepare and to understand. An egg is a package of compactly folded proteins dispersed in water; when you heat it, the proteins unfold and bond together into a continuous, solid mass. Well, recently I came across a version of hard-cooked eggs that seemed very much at odds with my simple picture. This version can be described generically as *long*-cooked eggs, *long* meaning anywhere from 6 to 18 hours. Since it only takes 10 or 15 minutes to hard-cook an egg, I assumed that eggs cooked for hours would be very hard indeed. But Claudia Roden and Paula Wolfert report that long-cooked eggs come out with a soft, creamy texture quite unlike that of an ordinary hard-cooked egg. Tom Stobart confirms this, and explains that 'like meat protein, [egg protein] becomes soft again when boiled for several hours'. This was news to me, and an incitement to experiment.

Although Chinese tea eggs are also cooked for few a hours, the long-cooked eggs known today in the Near East, Europe, and North Africa appear to have been discovered as a consequence of the prohibition against cooking on the Sabbath. There is a venerable Jewish tradition of putting together a pot of meat, grains, pulses, and vegetables on Friday to cook slowly in the oven overnight and serve as a hot mid-day meal on the Sabbath. According to the *Encyclopedia Judaica,* the ingredients for this Sabbath stew vary from country to country, as does its name. In Eastern Europe the name is *cholent;* in North Africa *dafina* or *shahine;* and the Hebrew term is *hamin,* which means 'hot'. Eggs are an optional ingredient, and when cooked in such a stew are called *hamindas.*

Paula Wolfert gives a Moroccan recipe for *sefrina,* a beef and chickpea stew with eggs which calls for an initial hour in a hot oven, and then five more at 'lowest setting'. She remarks: 'Eggs cooked for so long a time come out creamy and tan-colored. They really are very good.' Good enough, apparently, to inspire stripped-down recipes for the eggs alone. Claudia Roden calls *beid hamine* 'great favorites of ancient origin', and directs that the eggs be cooked in a pan of water together with the skins of several onions, 'very gently over the lowest heat possible for at least six hours, even overnight'. 'The whites acquire a soft beige color from the onion skins, and the yolks are very creamy and pale yellow. The flavor is delicate and excitingly different from eggs cooked in any other way.' In his *Sephardic Cooking,* Copeland Marks reports having eaten 'Jewish eggs' among Calcutta Baghdadis, in Morocco, Tunisia, Turkey, and Greece. He gives a Spanish version via Salonica, *huevos haminados,* that calls for tea leaves, coffee grounds, and onion skins in the cooking water, as well as a bit of oil and vinegar. The eggs are brought to the boil, then cooked over low heat 'for at least 5 hours, preferably 6'. Marks notes that 'the longer one cooks them at very low heat, the softer they become instead of the reverse'.

Thus the tradition and lore: eggs cooked for a long time at a low temperature develop an unusual color and flavor, and their texture softens. According to Tom Stobart, a full boil will also tenderize egg proteins.

I began my investigation by looking at the effects of prolonged heat *per se* on egg texture. For the sake of comparison, I first made a batch of ordinary hard-cooked eggs (12 minutes just below the boil). Then I cooked several eggs in plain water using an electric skillet with a thermostat that maintains a steady temperature. I monitored the water temperature with a laboratory-quality digital thermometer. After 12 hours at 180° F (85° C), the eggs were as firm as the hard-cooked control, with a dark green layer at the yolk surface. No softening was evident. However, to my surprise the whites had turned light brown throughout, and were detectably richer in flavor.

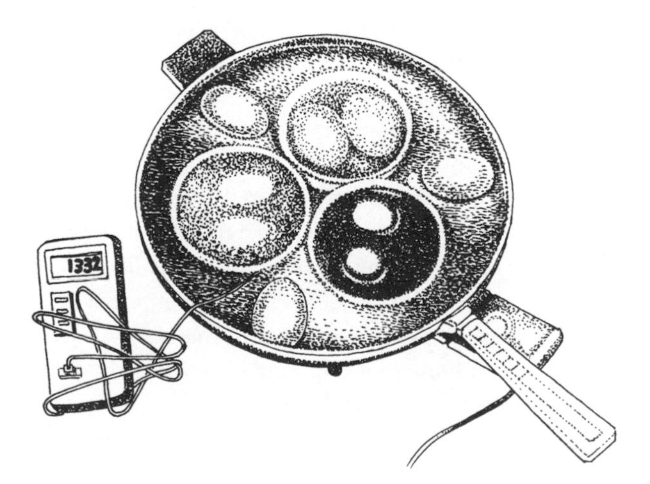

Harold McGee's experimental set-up. Drawn by Soun from a photograph.

Preliminary finding: long-cooking does not automatically produce softer eggs. But it does produce an unusual color and flavor in the white, even in the absence of onion skins and coffee.

In general, the degree to which any protein coagulates depends on both cooking time and cooking temperature. I therefore guessed that the soft texture of long-cooked eggs might be obtainable only at temperatures lower than 180 degrees. My next experiment tested this idea. I cooked separate batches of eggs for 12 hours at three different temperatures, again using the electric skillet and lab thermometer. At 150° F (65° C), the yolk was cohesive and moist but the white—which was still white—not quite solid. At 160° F (71° C), the yolk was still somewhat softer than that of an ordinary hard-cooked egg, while the white was just slightly beige and barely solid. Where the hard-cooked white broke into pieces in the mouth, this one disintegrated into a creamy mass—a very unusual and delightful sensation. The problem, though, was that the egg couldn't be cleanly peeled—the barely coagulated white clung to the inner shell membrane more strongly than it did to itself. At 170° F (77° C), the yolk was all but hard-cooked, the white more distinctly darkened and still relatively tender, but no longer creamy.

Finding: there is only a narrow temperature window, between 160 and 170° F, that produces a melting consistency in the white. Higher cooking temperatures give the ordinary hard-cooked texture. On the other hand, greater heat also deepens the color and flavor of the white, and allows one to peel the egg cleanly.

This result led me to wonder whether the purpose of onion skins and coffee in the cooking water might be to deepen the color and flavor of nicely tender but perforce relatively pale, bland eggs. Alan Davidson called my attention to a recipe which suggested just that. For *Oeufs à la constantinopolitaine* in their *Gentle Art of Cookery,* Mrs Leyel and Miss Hartley prescribe a cooking liquid composed of equal measures of olive oil and Turkish coffee, and a very slow cooking for twelve hours or more. 'After a long time the mixture penetrates the shells, makes the whites of the eggs amber colour, and the yolks the colour of saffron, and gives to them a flavour of chestnuts.' So I next cooked four different batches of eggs in the same skillet for 12 hours at 160° F: one group in plain water in the skillet itself; one group in a small bowl containing water and onion skins; one group in a small bowl filled with freshly made espresso coffee; and one group in a small bowl filled with an espresso-olive oil mixture *à la constantinopolitaine.* Of course the shells took on a range of earthy hues, but once peeled, the onion-skin- and coffee-cooked eggs were indistinguishable from the water-cooked eggs! All had light beige whites. I left one egg in each of the bowls to cook a further 12 hours, for a total of 24, and again found no evidence that color had penetrated the shell and inner membranes. The eggs cooked in oil and coffee did indeed pick up a mildly nutty flavor, those cooked in coffee alone a more distinct coffee note.

So colors in the cooking liquid tint only the shell, but external flavorings can penetrate to the white.

In sum, my experiments did not support the idea that long cooking softens egg proteins. Tough meat does get tenderer as it stews, but this is because its toughness derives from connective tissue that heat gradually dissolves into gelatin. Eggs contain no connective tissue, and their proteins only bond together more and more tightly with prolonged heating. The key to egg texture is cooking temperature. At 160° F (71° C), the proteins barely cohere and the texture is creamy. If an egg gets much hotter than that, it is merely hard-cooked.

To me, the truly remarkable thing about long-cooked eggs is their color and flavor, which develop even in a pan of undoctored water. Why do they become nutty? The same question was posed rather differently during World War II, when American troops in the Pacific complained that their dehydrated eggs were going brown and nasty. The white turns out to contain a small amount of glucose, a quarter of a gram or so per egg, not enough to taste, but enough to react with amino acids to form the brown color and complex flavor characteristic of roasted and toasted foods. Unaccustomed sensations in eggs! (Troop rations were improved by removing the glucose from eggs before dehydration.) The Maillard reaction ordinarily proceeds at a noticeable rate only at temperatures above the boiling point, in the oven and frying pan. Dehydration accelerates the reaction by concentrating the reactants, while long cooking simply gives the slow reaction enough time to manifest itself. And not just in eggs. Apparently the Maillard reaction gave offense long before World War II in certain versions of the Sabbath stew. *The Jewish Encyclopedia* noted in 1903 that from a *cholent* made with meat, potatoes, fat and water, 'the potatoes appear on the table on Saturday glistening with fat, and are of a dark, brownish color. Some even consider them not alone palatable, but an excellent remedy for various ills.'

I imagine that the lore surrounding long-cooked eggs arose from the effort to identify which aspects of the Sabbath stew were essential to its effect on eggs. The dark color could well come from the other stew ingredients, so one should add dyestuffs to the cooking water. And since long cooking tenderizes meat, it could well do the same to eggs. In fact, long cooking pretty much guarantees a deepened color and flavor, but you have to be lucky with your dying coals or low flames to hit the right temperature for a melting consistency. Apparently that happened often enough over the centuries to keep the lore alive.

Here are my suggestions for the Revised Standard Lore On Long-Cooked Eggs. You can get creamy eggs in 40 minutes as long as you keep the temperature close to 170° F (77° C). But they'll peel even more raggedly than the overnight 160° F eggs. If you want to experience the unusual color and flavor of long-cooked eggs, you'll have to give up on creaminess and cook them at 170–180° F for 6 to 12 hours (or, according to Claudia Roden, after an initial boiling, in a pressure cooker for 1½ hours). Onion skins are not necessary unless you want a beautiful shell. Coffee will indeed accentuate the nuttiness.

Sources

Claudia Roden, *A Book of Middle Eastern Food,* 1968, 1972; Vintage, 1974, pp 136–8.

Paula Wolfert, *Couscous and Other Good Food From Morocco,* New York, Harper and Row, 1973, pp 41, 268–9.

Tom Stobart, *The Cook's Encyclopaedia,* 1980; Papermac, 1982, p 152.

Copeland Marks, *Sephardic Cooking,* New York, Donald I. Fine, 1992, pp 37–8.

Encyclopaedia Judaica, Jerusalem, Keter Publishing, 1972 (vol 5, p 490, *s.v.*'Cholent').

Mrs C. F. Leyel and Miss O. Hartley, *The Gentle Art of Cookery,* 1925; Phoenix Edition, 1929, p 232.

The Jewish Encyclopaedia, New York, Funk and Wagnalls, 1903 (vol 4, p 256, *s.v.* 'Cooking').

The Legacy of Western Camas

Rose-Ellen Hope

The author is an authority on food history in the Pacific North-west. Her essay includes detailed descriptions of how camas is prepared and cooked—not easily found anywhere else.

Camas, *Camassia quamash,* a member of the lily family, was a staple food as important as salmon and blackberries for Natives in the Pacific North-west of America. According to Indian legend the camas seed was brought by Silver Grey Fox (Tkope Chikamin Talapus) from the Great Spirit. Then the plant spread from British Columbia to California to Montana. Within the area are nearly twenty geographical sites named after camas (also kamas, lakammas). Yet, today even residents of these towns, mountains, and prairies view camas only as a wild-flower, unaware of its nutritious qualities.

A Chinook word, camas means 'pleasant taste'; but opinion on its flavor varies. Traveling up the Columbia River in October of 1792, Captain Vancouver's staff recorded use of a

> bulbous root, about the size and not unlike crocus, that ate much like mealy potatoes.

The Shoshone guide Sacajawea prepared the root in soups for the explorers Lewis and Clark. The journals of Meriwether Lewis extensively describe the harvest, cookery, and use of camas. He disliked the slimy texture of the uncooked bulb, an opinion shared by modern backpackers. But Lewis's journal entry of September 20, 1805, at Weippe prairie indicates a favorable view of the cooked camas:

> They now set before them . . . several kinds of roots. among these last is one which is round and much like an onion in appearance and sweet to the taste. it is called quamash, and is eaten either in its natural state, or boiled into a kind of soup or made into a cake, which is then called pasheco. after the long abstinence this was a sumptouous treat.

Other members of the expedition likened it to gingerbread. However, by June 11, 1806, his partner Clark had apparently had his fill when he recorded

> this root is palateable but disagrees with us in every shape we have used it. the natives are extremely fond of this root, and present it (to) their visitors as

> a great treat. when we first arrived at the Chopunnish (Nez Perce) last fall at this place our men who were half starved made so free a use of this root it made them all sick for several days after.

Nevertheless the vegetable saved many pioneers from starvation along the Emigrant Road to the Oregon Territory. For David Douglas, a Scottish botanist, camas evoked the taste of baked pears. On November 17, 1826, he remarked:

> On this day with a few hard nuts and roots of *Phalangium Quamash,* I made a good breakfast.

Douglas also called the plant *Scilla esculenta.* Its tendency to cause flatulence, he described as 'blown by strength wind'. A decade later missionary Narcissa Whitman observed:

> The Cammas grows here in abundance and it is the principal resort of the Cayouse and many other tribes, to obtain it of which they are very fond. It resembles an onion in shape and colour, when cooked is very sweet, tastes like figs. This is the chief food of many tribes during the winter.

Others compared the flavor of camas to maple sugar, molasses, quince, jujube and dates. I suspect not just individual variation in taste buds, but the degree to which the carbohydrates are cooked accounts for the diversity of impressions.

Besides carbohydrates the camas root provides protein, fat, vitamins (C, thiamine, and riboflavin), minerals (iron, calcium, magnesium, zinc, potassium, sodium, and a trace of copper), and fiber. In the low-grain diet of northwest Natives camas was an important source of these nutrients.

Natives still celebrate camas at an annual Root Festival. Once occurring at the first appearance of camas blooms, the event now happens at a more fixed time for each tribe from mid-April through May. It is a sacred occasion to praise the abundance of the Creator. For this massive feast not only is payment inappropriate, but thank yous for either the food or the cooking are out of order. Consequently advance information may be given reluctantly to non-Indians who may take advantage of the hospitality, or not honor the religious tone. But all present all welcome.

In the spring the dense blue camas glimmers like a clear lake in the subalpine meadows of the Cascades, Sierras, and Rockies. The flower is also seen in profusion through the Columbia Gorge and some fields along interstate-five highway in Washington and Oregon. The Nature Conservancy preserves thirty-three acres as a Camassia Nature Area at West Linn, Oregon, outside of Portland.

Spring is the first of three camas harvests. Indians traveled great distances, seasonally, to obtain camas. When the shoots are finger high, Indian women accompanied by children pry out camas bulbs with an implement fashioned of a three to four-inch fire-hardened digging stick, usually made of mountain mahogoney, attached to an eight to ten-inch antler from deer or elk. Such a scene inspired Captain Lyman to sketch the Umpqua Squaws from his schooner during the 1850s. A reproduction of the drawing is at the Douglas County, Oregon, Museum in Roseburg. For the Root Festival, held on a Sunday, the bulbs are dug the prior Wednesday. According to Indian lore the ancestral gatherer of camas was Kah Nee Tah. In her honor is named the resort on the Warm Springs Indian Reservation in Central Oregon.

Extreme caution is required to harvest camas in the wild. For growing among the blue (or sometimes white or pink) flowered camas is the cream (or occasionally green) flowered poisonous white camas, *Zigadenus zygidenus,* known as death camas. To assure safety native women devised a labeling system by leaving the blue flowers attached until the last possible moment before cooking. The largest harvest was usually transported home in skin bags. However, decorated woven baskets with a drawstring are in the collection of the Museum of Natural History at the University of Oregon in Eugene. Today, burlap bags are common.

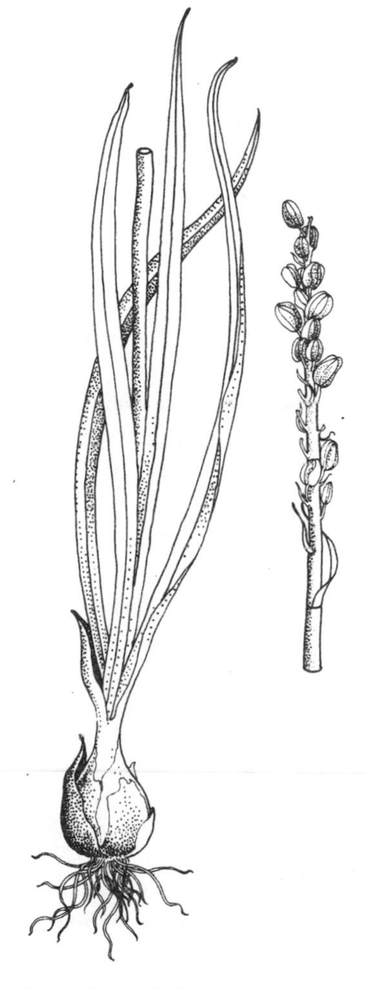

Camas, drawn by Soun. The flower head is shown on the right.

The early crop is best boiled or raw. A favorite Indian beverage consisted of camas boiled down to a molasses-like stage. Often, the root is boiled with salmon. The raw bulb best retains vitamins B and C. However, the gelatinous texture is unappealing to many. The Great Harvest occurs when the seeds ripen, but the blooms are intact during mid-June to July. Digging is more difficult due to the hard, dry ground. The final harvest occurs in autumn. The latter crops are best baked, traditionally in a fire pit. At the Flanagan site near the Willamette River baked camas dating 6,000 years ago was uncovered. Indians call this method barbecue, a word often misunderstood by others. The Nez Perce process required community effort. First a hole three feet deep and ten to fifteen feet across was dug. In the bottom a foot of hardwood was lit under a layer of four to six pound weight smooth stones. When the rocks glowed red, a time often declared by the shaman, the stones were leveled and covered with two to three inches of grass, maple leaves, or ash leaves. On top of this twenty to thirty bushels of peeled white bulbs were piled conically. (Chehalis Indians usually preferred to leave the black peels on during baking.) An additional two to three inches of grass, pine needles, or skunk cabbage and several inches of earth covered the bulbs. Then water was poured over the mass. The Kalapuya layered sticks on top, which were set on fire. After the camas steamed for twelve hours a tantalizing aroma invited the women to test for doneness. While the fire cooled, a portion of the warm, brown meal was eaten. To preserve the rest before spoilage began it was pounded between stones, shaped into one-half to one-inch thick cakes of various shapes, baked another sixty hours, and hung to dry. The Nisqually placed the camas cakes in maple-leaf lined baskets, which they stored in trees. This supply was used by itself or baked with dry coush (*Lomatium cous*) or dry salmon during the next several months. Today, baked camas served at the Root Festival is often supplemented with bulbs frozen from the year before. This may explain the bland taste which I experienced. The flavor also differs according to the type of wood and the mulch. That selection depends on local conditions and availability.

By comparison the early Oregon and California settlers' preparation of camas pie or venison-camas stew seems simple. Of course, the number of cooks was decidedly fewer. Reputedly, Nebraskans still serve the dish, although I am unable to verify this. Late European settlers plowed up camas fields to plant the more familiar wheat or potatoes. Blue camas came to be regarded as a persistent weed. When the natives noticed their camas supply dwindle along with other food sources, fights broke out between farmers and tribes. By 1878 the hungry Bannock Indians found hogs and cattle trampling their camas fields. So they ordered whites off the Big Camas Prairie in Idaho. The Bannock War that ensued is now recalled by historical markers through the area. The battle had precedents in Indian legends of rival tribes fighting over camas. The pioneers were doubly foolish. Not only did they misname the camas prairie 'Kansas Prairie' in the Treaty of Fort Bridges, but their stock died from eating the white camas.

Unlike salmon and blackberries, that became commercial crops, camas must still be gathered or gardened. The danger of fatal white camas is overcome by growing camas. The seeds and bulbs are available from a few companies. (Not to be confused with its Eastern and Southern counterpart: the wild hyacinth, *Camassia esculenta,* which tribes from Pennsylvania to

Minnesota to Texas ate.) The seed is planted in late fall or early spring in moist, sandy soil. Boggy soil and manure prevent its thriving. Camas takes several years to bloom. Yet, once established it provides high density food value, a desirable quality of future food.

It is a rare cookbook, script or printed, that includes a camas recipe. The use of camas still belongs to the oral tradition. One modern exception is Russ Mohney's book *Why Wild Edibles?* that contains interesting combinations of camas with other wild foods. However, they are not historical derivations of either the Indians or pioneers. The Nez Perce of today eat baked camas with sugar and cream. It is known that most new potato recipes adapt to camas. The basic method is to wash, cook, peel, and eat the bulbs. If overcooked, camas turns dark and soggy. If the taste is bland, the texture and nutrition of camas can still be used to advantage in a vegetable or meat pie.

Perhaps one day, visiting Camas Valley, camas will be on the menu or in the produce selection.

References

Beckham, Steve. 1977 *The Indians of Western Oregon: This Land Was Theirs.* Arago Books, Coos Bay, Oregon.

Benson, Eva et al. 1973 'Wild Edible Plants of the Pacific Northwest,' *American Dietectic Association Journal,* Vol. 62, pp. 142–147.

Douglas, David. 1929 *Journal Kept by David Douglas During his Travels in North America 1823–1827.* New York, Antiquarian Press.

Fahey, John. 1965 *Inland Empire,* Seattle, University of Washington Press, pp. 127–128.

Gunther, Erna. 1941 *Ethnobotany of Western Washington,* Seattle, University of Washington Press.

Hilty, Ivy et al. 1980 *Nutritive Food Values of Native Foods of Warm Springs Indians.* Corvallis, Oregon, Oregon State University Extension Service, Circular #809, February.

Kirk, Donald. 1970 *Wild Edible Plants of the Western United States,* Healdsburg, California, Naturegraph.

Madsen, Brigham. 1958 *The Bannock of Idaho,* Caldwell, Idaho, Claxton Printers.

Mohney, Russ. 1975 *Why Wild Edibles?: The Joys of Finding, Fixing, and Tasting West of the Rockies.* Seattle, Pacific Search.

Seaman, N. G. 1967 *Indian Relics of the Pacific Northwest,* Portland, Binford and Mort.

Smith, Harriet L. 1978 *Camas, The Plant That Causes Wars,* Lake Oswego, Oregon, Smith, Smith, & Smith.

Spinden, Herber Joseph. 'The Nez Perce Indians,' *Memoirs of the American Anthropological Association,* Vol. II, part 3.

United States Park and Service. 1975 *Lewis and Clark,* Washington, D.C., U.S. Department of Interior, Government Printing Office.

Welsh, William. 1958 *A Brief History of Camas,* Camas, Washington, Crown Zellerbach Corporation.

4.
Books and Cooks

This section of our anthology is a rich one, covering various themes: what might be called 'literary' items, embodying the views on food of famous novelists such as Chekhov; essays which celebrate the achievements of some of the finest food writers in the 20th century, not with us, alas, in the 21st; some other personal items, linked with particular people; and a bibliographic item which has all the excitement of a detective story.

For some people, the idea of taking breakfast with Jane Austen would represent an experience of surpassing interest and pleasure. For those who dream on these lines, Eileen White, a noted food historian in the north of England, provides a brief about what took place in the breakfast rooms in the houses frequented by her characters.

In fact, not much is known about the actual food eaten for breakfast by Jane Austen's characters. In contrast, Chekhov tells us a great deal about what his characters ate. His work includes some of the most subtle and poetic descriptions of food to be found in the literature of any country. Jean Redwood, our guide in mining this rich vein of gastronomic lore, worked at the British Embassy in Moscow, and it was principally there that she carried out the studies which resulted in this brilliant essay.

Rossini was not an author but a musician. He comes in here because he gave his name to certain dishes, most notably tournedos Rossini (he loved foie gras). Lesley Chamberlain's essay on the subject touches on this, but is more concerned with the link between the composer's creative energy and his appetite. She suggests, surprisingly, that 'Rossini took his food more seriously than he did his art'. The essay is adorned with a sketched self-portrait of Rossini showing what might be called his Falstaffian shape, consonant with one description of him as 'the only great composer to have led a happy life'.

The essay by Chitrita Banerji is an outstanding example of a style of food writing which used to be rare but is now becoming more common, to wit a combination of personal reminiscences with culinary information and recipes. Chitrita is the author of a book in this genre, *Bengali Cooking, Seasons and Festivals.* In the essay presented here she provides us with a charming personal memoir about the perceptions which she developed in childhood and youth of both Hindu and Muslim foodways in this part of the subcontinent. Readers will not wish to skip over any part of this essay, and it is probably unnecessary for us to recommend particularly the last three paragraphs. Still, we do so because they are so stimulating, one might also say electrifying, in opening a window on to some fresh and fundamental thoughts about how we conduct our lives.

Andrew Dalby's essay 'The Wedding Feast of Caranus the Macedonian, by Hippolochus' might be regarded as a scoop. The piece by Hippolochus survives only in the pages of *The Deipnosophists* by Athenaeus. Dating back to the third century BC, it seems to be the earliest surviving text which is devoted exclusively to the description of a banquet; and it has many other features of interest. This is the first article to be written about the text, and the first time when it has been presented on its own.

As we have already explained (page 2), Elizabeth David was one of our founders, who played a key role in starting *PPC* and gave it the impetus which only she could provide, to carry it through its first years. The essay written in celebration of her achievements, concludes with a linked essay about her 'dream kitchen' (complete with illustration).

The tribute to M F K Fisher, like that for Elizabeth David, appeared in *PPC 41*. The two ladies never met, although there were times when they were both near San Francisco and friends sought to bring them together. In fact, their approaches to writing about food differed markedly; but they had this in common: that they were both preeminent in this field, one in England and the other in California. Both had potent links with France as well.

From 'Quarter-Deck to Cooking Pot' brings a new cast of people on stage, and a strong whiff of sea air. With it, for reasons which will be apparent, comes a drawing after a photograph of Millicent Rogers, possibly the most glamorous character ever to appear in our pages. The quartet of recipes from family manuscripts which are appended to the essay would, it seems, not have survived without her good offices. The whole essay is a striking illustration of the persistence of culinary traditions in family circles. Do not miss the description of 'Hell Hound Rogers'.

Next is another example of surprising survival. I had occasion, back in the 1980s, to describe and praise the custom prevailing in Thailand, whereby mourners at a funeral are presented with an elegant little cookery book containing favourite recipes, and sometimes reminiscences, of the departed. Little did I think at that time that I would later be privileged to publish in *PPC 58*, what appears to be the first recorded example, and a royal one too, of this genre. Corresponding with Su-Mei Yu, who had come across the precious item in a street market in Bangkok, about the history of the book and the people concerned and the necessary elucidation of the recipes was one of our most delightful editorial experiences.

We should have liked to reproduce here the celebratory bibliography which appeared in *PPC 38* as a tribute to Jane Grigson, whose writings we so admired. This, the work of Isobel Holland, Lynette Hunter and Geraldine Stoneham, is highly unusual, indeed possibly unique, in that it gives the full bibliographical treatment to a recent cookery author. And it is very long (30 pages), reflecting the large number of books she wrote and their numerous editions; indeed too long to fit into this book comfortably. So instead we print just the introduction which prefaced the bibliography, plus an essay by myself and a review by Jane Davidson of what for many people is Jane Grigson's best loved work, *Jane Grigson's Fruit Book*.

To conclude this section we reprint (necessarily in somewhat condensed form) an essay which constitutes one of the great feats of detection in English culinary history. In 1983, the then forthcoming publication by Prospect Books of a facsimile of the first edition of Hannah Glasse's *The Art of Cookery Made Plain and Easy* prompted Jennifer Stead to make an extensive study of the sources used by Hannah Glasse. This shows that the source on which she drew most heavily was the voluminous but little known book first entitled *The Whole Duty of a Woman* and renamed with effect from its second edition *The Lady's Companion*. The study has also revealed interesting connections between that work and earlier books, and has thrown much light on the manner in which Hannah Glasse set about her task of making cookery 'plain and easy', by judicious adaptation of and additions to the earlier material. (There were also some injudicious touches which produced hilarious results.) The upshot is a wide-ranging survey which for the first time evaluates Hannah Glasse's work on the basis of detailed research; and which at the same time illuminates the whole subject of English cookery books of the 18th century.

Jennifer Stead's essay was a truly pioneering work and many other authors working on the history of English cookery books have declared themselves deeply indebted to her, both for inspiration and for the meticulous information she compiled. It is worth noting that at the time when she wrote there was current a general opinion that the authors of 18th century cookery books all copied each other and that it would be pointless to try and work out relationships between their various collections of recipes. The general opinion now is that it is very definitely worthwhile undertaking such studies, and that it has become clear that the books of certain 18th century authors (for example Richard Bradley and to a large extent Elizabeth Raffald) were truly original, while those of others (including John Farley, the most notorious example) were scissors-and-paste jobs of no intrinsic worth. In the case of John Farley, Detective Fiona Lucraft, avowedly following in the steps of Detective Jennifer Stead, revealed that of the 798 recipes in Farley's book, the *London Art of Cookery,* it was possible to demonstrate that 797 were directly copied from identifiable sources. The identity of the person wielding the scissors and paste was subsequently revealed (by Peter Targett in *PPC 58*) when a record of the payment made to the hack writer Richard Johnson for 'writing' in 1782/3, and proof reading in 1785, and making additions to Farley's *London Art of Cookery* came to light. (The 798th recipe, incidentally, was a short one for Beef Tea, and the Editors of *PPC* offered a reward to anyone who could track down its source. So far this award is unclaimed.)

As will be seen, the extent to which Hannah Glasse's recipes could be traced back to other books was less dramatic, but we should say that another researcher, Priscilla Bain, using a different edition of Hannah Glasse's principal source, was able to find a substantial additional number of 'culinary thefts'. The curious will find this further research in *PPC 23*.

Jennifer Stead's entire essay, including the table showing the sources for many of Hannah Glasse's recipes, was so long that it had to be split between two issues of *PPC, 13* and *14*. What we furnish here is most of Part One and some of the information contained in Part Two.

Breakfast with Jane Austen

Eileen White

The author contributed the chapter on breakfasts, 'First Things First', to Luncheons, Nuncheons, and other Meals; Eating with the Victorians, *papers from the Seventh Leeds Symposium on Food History and Traditions, edited by C Anne Wilson, published in 1994 by Alan Sutton Publishing.*

The Great British Breakfast evokes a picture of the Victorian Age: but it is to be found established by the very beginning of the century, peeping out of the pages of Jane Austen. It is the breakfast of the leisured class, to be sure: but who would not take the chance to be leisurely at a good breakfast table? By Jane Austen's time, it had gained the acknowledged status of a meal—in fact, it was the favourite meal of Mrs. Jennings, to be indulged in when she returned to London with her guests Elinor and Marianne. (*Sense and Sensibility*)

Most of the houses inhabited by Jane Austen's characters had a specially designated Breakfast Room. There was one at Netherfield Hall, another at Northanger Abbey; at Kellynch Hall its chimney smoked when the wind was due north. Edmund took the newcomer, Fanny, to the breakfast room at Mansfield Park to comfort her and write a letter for her, thus beginning their childhood friendship. (*Mansfield Park*) At Longbourn, in a house with five daughters, the breakfast room provided a quiet refuge, and the chance of solitude, after its primary function had been fulfilled. There Jane and Elizabeth Bennet first sought their father when he received the much awaited letter from London, and there they returned to discuss the development of Lydia's marriage. It was also the room where the family assembled to meet the returning prodigal after the wedding; and, as at Mansfield Park, it was a good place to write a letter later in the day. (*Pride and Prejudice*)

Not only was there a special room, but the appearance of the breakfast table could now rival that of the dinner table for display and refinement. General Tilney revealed a patriotic taste at Northanger Abbey:

> The elegance of the breakfast set forced itself on Catherine's notice when they were seated at table; and, luckily, it had been the General's choice. He was enchanted by her approbation of his taste, confessed it to be neat and simple, thought it right to encourage the Manufacture of his country; and for his part, to his uncritical palate, the tea was as well flavoured from the clay of Staffordshire, as from that of Dresden or Sêve. But this was quite an old set,

> purchased two years ago. The manufacture was much improved since that time; he had seen some beautiful specimins when last in town, and had he not been perfectly without vanity of that kind, might have been tempted to order a new set.
>
> (*Northanger Abbey*)

The time of breakfast varied, as it always must, from household to household. Mr and Mrs Gardiner had breakfast at ten o'clock, even on Lydia Bennet's wedding day. (*Pride and Prejudice*) Elinor and Marianne joined the party of friends and relations at Barton Park for a ten o'clock breakfast before the proposed trip to Whitwell. (*Sense and Sensibility*) Their medieval ancestors would have been sitting down to dinner at this time. Elizabeth Bennet received the news of Jane's illness scarcely after she had finished her breakfast; she walked the three miles to Netherfield in time to see the Bingleys still sitting at theirs: so the breakfast period could be lengthy. (*Pride and Prejudice*)

Travellers often needed to take an early breakfast. Fanny's brother, William, and Mr Crawford met at Mansfield Park for an early breakfast before leaving at 9.30. Fanny had an even earlier start when she ended her visit to her parents and returned once more to Mansfield Park: Edmund, having already eaten, came to collect her at eight in the morning, and finding the family had not breakfasted, arranged to have the coach there by 8.30. Even so, Fanny and Susan had to leave without sitting down to the table, 'which by dint of much unusual activity, was quite and completely ready as the carriage drove from the door'. (*Mansfield Park*) On the day Catherine went to Northanger Abbey with the Tilneys, she joined them for breakfast at their Bath lodgings. They only just managed to finish, and get their trunks carried down, by ten o'clock. (*Northanger Abbey*)

Hunters would also eat as soon as possible. When Charles Musgrove invited Captain Wentworth to spend the day shooting with him, they decided to breakfast at Uppercross Hall, where the hours were earlier, rather than at the Cottage, where Charles' wife Mary had a late breakfast. (*Persuasion*) J.E. Austen-Leigh, looking back to the times of his renowned aunt, had some memories of the hunters' breakfast:

> I remember to have heard of only two little things different from modern customs. One was, that on hunting mornings the young men usually took their hasty breakfast in the kitchen. The early hour at which hounds then met may account for this; and probably the custom began, if it did not end, when they were boys; for they hunted at an early age, in a scrambling sort of way, upon any pony or donkey that they could procure, or, in default of such luxuries, on foot.
>
> (*A Memoir*)

A regular breakfast, then, seemed to fall about 9.30 to 10 o'clock. One wonders at what hour Mrs and Miss Bates and Jane Fairfax took their late breakfast. (*Emma*)

The reformed Marianne stated her intention to get up by six in the morning, so as not to waste any time of the day. Even getting up a little later, most of Jane Austen's characters had time for some activity before breakfast, much of which was revealing of their situations and preoccupations. Edward, on his first morning at Barton Cottage with the Dashwoods, had time to go down to the village before breakfast to see to his horses: it enabled him to escape being left alone with Elinor, to whom he could not reveal his engagement. (*Sense and Sensibility*) Marianne, restless in London at not hearing from Mr Willoughby, had no occupation to while away the time, and she wandered about Mrs Jennings' house, avoiding everyone. On another morning, she and Elinor went over the subject of Mr Willoughby several times before breakfast.

For those fortunate in love, however, no time was to be spent apart. Colonel Brandon, a regular visitor to Barton College after the engagement of Elinor and Edward, arrived each morning to join their first tête-à-tête before breakfast, and no doubt he hoped to find Marianne there also. Similarly, Mr Bingley arrived at Longbourn from Netherfield Hall every morning before breakfast after he became engaged to Jane. (*Sense and Sensibility; Pride and Prejudice*)

The would-be lover could use this time for a purpose. Mr Collins revealed the reason for his visit to Mrs Bennet, to learn that her eldest daughter Jane was likely to be engaged soon; and he took even less time to turn his interest from Jane to Elizabeth. (*Pride and Prejudice*) Otherwise, it was a time to sort out affairs or catch up on duties. Edmund, giving in to the temptation to act in the theatricals at Mansfield Park, determined to inform his brother of this before breakfast (if he was up), so that everyone would be in a good humour when they met round the table. (*Mansfield Park*) Emma wrote a necessary letter to Harriet before breakfast. (*Emma*) For the more active, there was time for a walk. John Knightley took his two boys out before breakfast. (*Emma*) A walk was more enjoyable when on holiday: Anne and Henrietta had time to walk by the sea at Lyme before breakfast at their hotel, incidentally setting the scene for Louisa's accident later in the morning. (*Persuasion*)

Breakfast itself was the first coming together of a family or group, and therefore a time to make plans and impart news, over and above the private discussion that went on beforehand. Mrs Dashwood took the opportunity to advise Edward to engage in a profession (*Sense and Sensibility*); and Mrs Clay, the morning after Anne's arrival at Bath, used the meeting at breakfast to ascertain that she was still welcome to stay with the family. (*Persuasion*)

Sir Thomas, having prevented the theatricals at Mansfield Park, informed the company at breakfast of his decision to hold a little ball before William's departure (*Mansfield Park*); and Mr Bennet informed Mrs Bennet and his family of Mr Collins' visit on the very morning of his arrival. (*Pride and Prejudice*) Not all announcements were good: the news of Frank Churchill's sudden departure from Highbury, thus cancelling the ball, came as a dampening finale to Emma's breakfast. (*Emma*)

The only people who had to hurry through breakfast were the travellers; everyone else could talk and read their letters and their newspapers at leisure. Mr Woodhouse observed that it rained for half an hour while they were at breakfast on the morning of Mrs Weston's wedding. (*Emma*) Mrs Jennings spent a 'considerable time' at her breakfast—sometimes no doubt to the impatience of her guest Marianne, whose preoccupations were elsewhere. (*Sense and Sensibility*)

In all this detail, the least we are told by Jane Austen is what her characters ate and drank. It is always character which is important, and details are used to enhance this aspect, not for their own sake. However, some information can be gleaned.

Tea was the established breakfast drink. Edward revealed his ring with a plait of hair in its centre when he reached out to take his tea from Mrs Dashwood, and thus set off Elinor's speculations. (*Sense and Sensibility*) General Tilney's breakfast table was served with tea from his Staffordshire teapot—but he himself divided his attention between his cocoa and his newspaper. (*Northanger Abbey*)

The food can only be inferred, and it rarely seems to concern Jane Austen unless it reveals something of her characters. Several items could be offered on a breakfast table, enough to confuse a nervous guest: Catherine's timidity during her breakfast with the Tilneys was hardly reassured by the General's attentions:

> His anxiety for her comfort—his continuous solicitations that she would eat, and his often-expressed fears of her seeing nothing to her taste—though never in her life before had she beheld half such variety on a breakfast-table—made it impossible for her to forget for a moment that she was a visitor.

Only one item of this variety is revealed on Catherine's return home, when Mrs Morland suspected her daughter had become too sophisticated after her holiday:

> 'Wherever you are you should always be contented, but especially at home, because there you must spend the most of your time. I did not quite like, at breakfast, to hear you talk so much about the French-bread at Northanger.'

> 'I am sure I do not care about the bread. It is all the same to me what I eat.'

As usual, Jane Austen is not commenting on breakfast fare, but on the heroine's preoccupation with Henry Tilney.

Breakfast is also mentioned when it is not eaten. Miss Bates confided that her niece only ate a little bread and butter; but then revealed that Jane's appetite caught up once her spirits improved during the day:

> 'Besides, dear Jane at present—and she really eats nothing—makes such a shocking breakfast, you would be quite frightened if you saw it. I dare not let my mother know how little she eats; so I say one thing, and then I say another, and it passes off. But about the middle of the day she gets hungry, and there is nothing she likes so well as these baked apples, and they are extremely wholesome.'
>
> (*Emma*)

We are given these facts by Jane Austen not for their own sake, but because they reveal something of the mystery around Jane Fairfax.

The greatest hint of the variety offered on the breakfast table from which the individual can choose, pointing towards the normal fare of the end of the nineteenth century, is given by what was left; and even here Jane Austen is telling us more about the characters of the participants than about breakfast at the beginning of the century:

> The ball was over—and the breakfast was soon over too; the last kiss was given, and William was gone. Mr. Crawford had, as he foretold, been very punctual, and short and pleasant had been the meal.
>
> After seeing William to the last moment, Fanny walked back into the breakfast-room with a very saddened heart to grieve over the melancholy change; and there her uncle kindly left her to cry in peace, conceiving perhaps that the deserted chair of each young man might exercise her tender enthusiasm, and that the remaining cold pork bones and mustard in Williams's plate might but divide her feelings with the broken egg-shells in Mr. Crawford's.
>
> (*Mansfield Park*)

Chekhov and Food

JEAN REDWOOD

The author, a graduate in Russian, lived and worked in the British Embassy in Moscow during the late Stalinist and 'Cold War' period. Subsequent journeys, during the 1970s and 1980s, of several months each, to various parts of the Soviet Union enabled her to assess the great changes which had come about in the demand for and supply of consumer goods, especially food. This led to a book on food and cookery in the (then) Soviet Union as a whole (not just Russia).

I have been asked, why Chekhov and not another? Why not Nikolai Gogol, who so often wandered into people's kitchens, peering into simmering saucepans, giving them a stir and tasting the contents, and who took a great interest in preparing food for himself and his guests?

My answer is that Chekhov's interest was of a more general and scientific turn. He went into many a humble kitchen in his capacity as a doctor and in hundreds of peasant huts when he helped to conduct the general census in 1897. He looked with a beady eye at all the cockroaches he saw there, the dirty dish cloths, the ill-managed stoves creating poisonous fumes, and pigs running in and out. 'Man is the dirtiest animal' the artist proclaims in one of the debates in his long story *The House with the Mezzanine* (1895–6).

Chekhov was very conscious of what man lives by; and few of his stories and plays are without some timely reminders, usually slipped in by a seemingly chance and insignificant remark, of prevailing economic factors, of the great 'out-of-doors', of where food comes from, whether it is from the fields or from the slaughterhouse.

The irony of 'rational agronomy' in the dry south steppeland did not escape him when he wrote his long story *Steppe*. 'Here they kill swallows, sparrows, bumblebees, ravens and magpies so that the fruit blossoms should not be damaged; and they fell trees so that they should not impoverish the soil'. This has a familiar ring, as does the chopping down of trees described by Dr Astrov in *Uncle Vanya* and which leads to the drying up of streams and upsets the balance of nature.

The lot of the peasants, who constituted three-quarters of the population in 1897 when Chekhov wrote his long story *Peasants,* was a sad one. Their numbers were increasing at a time when grain was being exported relentlessly, and when they themselves had not enough to eat. By the time Lent

A drawing by Soun of Chekhov, after a contemporary photograph.

came most families were out of flour. In short, the peasant was being squeezed to pay for rapid industrialization.

Chekhov enlarges on the theme of 'upset nature' when traditional pasturage was being changed into wheatlands in his story *The Reed Piper* in 1887. The irony that such changes often produced the opposite effect to that intended is brought out in the story. Here an old shepherd tells a passing bailiff of the gradual disappearance of wild duck and geese, of fish and bees and even birds of prey. The bailiff racks his brains to think of some reply, but can only say: 'but man is getting cleverer and cleverer.' To this the shepherd rightly responds with the question, what good is that, if man loses his strength through the impoverishment of the soil and the cutting down and burning of forests?

In the *Cherry Orchard* (1904) trees are also cut down but for different economic reasons. The owners have neglected it and frittered away time and money. The orchard was once renowned for its beauty and the quantity of cherries produced. But the trees no longer bear and the art of preserving the cherries has been lost.

At the end of the play the orchard is chopped down to make way for building summer datchas for the new commuters on the expanding railways. Here is one illuminating remark made by the theorizing student Trofimov that all Russia will be their orchard, which makes one wonder about possible ensuing devastation and development.

Like many other writers Chekhov found that food and the daily gatherings round the Russian table served as an admirable literary device to bring about dramatic denouements, and he made use of it for creating atmosphere and for showing the social positions, divisions and temperaments of his characters.

Bourgeois snobbery, for instance, is seen in a table scene from *A Boring Story* (1889). Here a professor is deprived of his usual simple Russian fare by his ambitious wife when he becomes Dean of his faculty. His favourite cabbage soup and accompanying savoury pies, goose with apples, bream with buckwheat, are replaced by refined purééd soups and kidneys in Madeira.

On a humbler level, the story *At Christmas-tide* (1900) is about an old couple who cannot read or write and who seek out a scribe in order to write to their daughter whom they haven't heard from for four years. The letter writing takes place in the kitchen of the local tavern where a pork casserole is spluttering on the stove. The atmosphere is stifling and the old woman is distracted by the strange hissing and 'flu, flu' noises emanating from the casserole so that her thoughts are confused and she doesn't say anything of what has been in her heart—that they hadn't enough bread to eat for Christmas and that they had to sell the cow.

Pork was the most commonly eaten meat by the peasants at festival times. In his story *Pecheneg* (1897) a discussion takes place on the question of vegetarianism and Chekhov raises some interesting points. An old man, reputed to like philosophizing, gives a young man a lift from the station, where they had met by chance, and presses him to spend the night at his house. The 'philosopher' is a terrible bore and keeps his guest from sleeping, and moreover treats his wife like a servant and neglects his children's education. He observes the healthy young man, who is a vegetarian, and thinks that maybe it would be a good thing for him too as he is in poor health. Then he wonders what would become of the domestic animals if everyone became a vegetarian, and the young man says they would go back to the woods and live in the wild. 'But what about the pigs?' asks the old man, 'they trample the fields and woods and orchard and uproot everything.' At this insoluble problem they fall silent.

Comic relief is provided by Chekhov's description of many of the foods consumed by characters in his stories. He himself loved good food and was quite critical of what was offered to him on his travels. Overeating, to which Russians were prone, especially at festival time and on special occasions, forms the basis of a number of stories, notably *In the Ravine* (1900) where, in an obscure village, a Deacon had once consumed a whole 4 lb jar of the best non-pressed caviar when attending the funeral of some rich merchant. The

Deacon, we understand, subsequently died. In another story, *Victory Celebration* (1883), the *bliny* (pancakes) were so splendid that it was difficult for the narrator to describe their golden puffiness. They seem to leap into the mouth of their own accord, dripping with hot butter and accompanied by *smetana* (soured cream), caviar and other fishy delights. This is all washed down by a sea of wine and vodka. After this comes fish soup (*ukha*) and partridges with a complicated sauce. But *bliny* are seen to be the 'temptations' leading the eater down the slippery slope.

In contrast to such festivity, Natasha, the joy-stopping wife of Andrei in *The Three Sisters,* puts her husband on a diet of yoghurt, ironically just at Maslenitsa, the week before Lent, when everyone else would normally consume *bliny* and a good deal more in preparation for the great fast which was strictly kept until Easter.

The Siren is perhaps Chekhov's best known food story and is a splendid account of a meal, summoned up in the imagination of a secretary of a local magistrate's court. Certainly the effect on the reader is a desire to bustle off to the kitchen and prepare something. It is a kind of culinary drama amusingly strewn with a few phrases of a legal turn.

In this story Chekhov's little legal clerk Zhilin lets his fancy roam on the consumption of a meal of almost banquet proportions and is so eloquent that he completely disrupts the thoughts of the Chairman of the Legal Committee, who is unable to finish making his assessment of the recent legal proceedings. The other committee members present are also distracted and eventually all disperse at great speed, presumably to their respective dinner tables. The story gradually reaches a culinary crescendo and along the way pies are discussed so caressingly, viewed as temptresses, shameless in their nakedness and so on, that one feels that the clerk is making a plea in court and that the criminals have been transposed into food. However, Chekhov describes all this so subtly that it is better to read the entire story yourself.*

Chekhov's attitude to food is ambivalent. He relished good food but sees danger: satiety can produce complacency; gluttony can lead to illness and decay. He shares our wistfulness when we think of what should be and what

* I have translated this in full in my book to be published in the spring of 1989: *Russian Food—All the Peoples—All the Republics;* published by Oldwicks Press Ltd, 5 Links Avenue, Felixstowe, Suffolk IP11 9HD; distributed in the UK by Spa Books Ltd, PO Box 47, Stevenage, Herts SG2 8UH; hardcover, +£14.95.

Non-Russian readers who would like to read some of the other stories mentioned will find Constance Garnett's translations very good. Though purists say there are some inaccuracies, this is more than made up for, as she has caught the true register of Chekhov and there are no annoying out of place modern turns of phrase slipped in.

is. But, as in real life, so in his stories Chekhov rubs in his lessons with a light hand. His artistic vein leaves 'Doctor Chekhov' far behind. 'Look at yourselves' he says, and forces the reader to do just that in his skillful allusions to nature and man's place in it.

Before I join the ranks of hungry philosophers or stray into unknown paths, perhaps it might be well to finish this article with a glass of Russian tea (without the standard piece of sugar held between the teeth and of which our dentists would disapprove) and perhaps a spoonful or so of gooseberry jam and a delicious little pancake, not so slippery or buttery as the ones described above, but delicate lacy ones made with buckwheat flour. Lacy, like Chekhov's prose, as Tolstoy once described it.

The pancakes are made as follows, Armenian style, with more than a dash of brandy beaten into the yolks.

Arkanj: Bliny, Armenian Style

8 oz (225 g) each of plain flour and buckwheat flour
3 egg yolks
4 tbs brandy
2 tbs castor sugar
4 oz (100 g) butter
pinch of salt

Beat the brandy and egg yolks, gradually sift in the flours and salt and mix to a soft dough. Divide into four pieces, roll these out very thinly, make three incisions in each and fry them in the sizzling butter until golden. Drain and sprinkle with castor sugar.

If you have no buckwheat flour, take ordinary buckwheat and grind it in the coffee grinder.

The above are similar to Ukrainian fried doughnuts, though more rich as they have more yolks to the amount of flour.

Tournedos Rossini

LESLEY CHAMBERLAIN

Lesley Chamberlain is a woman of many parts, whose career as an author and literary critic has embraced two disparate fields of study. She studied Russian and German at Exeter and Oxford, and taught both languages and literature before becoming a journalist in 1977. She worked in Moscow from 1978 to 1979 and then travelled around Eastern Europe.

Lesley is perhaps best known for her book The Food and Cooking of Russia *(1982), which was followed by* The Food and Cooking of Eastern Europe *(1989). Both books are shining examples of what might be called the 'new wave' of food books, providing a wealth of historical background and literary allusions together with excellent and well researched recipes. However, her fame also rests on her philosophical writings, especially those about Nietzsche.*

The life of Rossini was intensely physical. One senses the preoccupation in the way he often reached for the metaphor of food to express an idea at the heart of his creative life, or to avoid talking about it. He might be compared to Tolstoy, another genius of vibrant appetite, except that he took his pleasures without disgust. His sensuality did not trouble him. It made him want to sing.

Yet surely he did not mean food? Not **the** Rossini, embroiled in the kitchen? The appearance of Tournedos Rossini on the menu still makes disbelievers of serious men.

Rossini claimed cheese and pastries inspired him. The truth of such a statement lies somewhere between the literal and the metaphorical. It points to *La gaia scienza,* as Nietzsche called the wisdom which transcends the miserable division of spirit and flesh. Freud called the energy libido and Marcuse argued it was the Erotic force which could save the modern world from the cold creations of the technological mind, which threatened to destroy it. If any composer ever did, Rossini glorified the joyful instinct in his music. Such an artist is rare and will always be needed.

When Stendhal made the comparison, which was to become a classic feature of Rossini appreciation, in the mid nineteenth century, between Mozart and Rossini, Mozart seemed gloomy, inward, and cerebral alongside the spontaneous Italian. The physical nature of Rossini so fascinated Stendhal that he made a study of it. Rossini's doctors preferred to be shocked. They recognised his nervous energy and demanding appetite as the key to his medical history. They described him as hypersensitive with a tendency to manic depression and obesity, and regretted they were too late to warn him off Venus, as they quaintly put it.

How Tournedos Rossini arrived on our menus is a version of Rossini's life, a story involving some of the most lovable characteristics of his life and music.

He was the sort of man who made his preferences known at the table, and liked them gratified. He loved pasta, for instance, and Stilton cheese. His manager Barbaia tried to exploit those desires as a weakness, which gave rise to a story Rossini told in a letter. One day in 1816 Barbaia locked the composer in a room, with only macaroni at intervals, to get him to write the *Otello* overture. Rossini released himself by handing page after page of the same music out of the window. A schoolboy triumph perhaps, but also a victory for art. Did Barbaia not understand him? Rossini, a longtime guest in the impresario's lavish Naples house, was excessively devoted to wine, food and friends, but those joys inspired his music. Barbaia's discipline could only have furthered the development of a hack.

Rossini's creative energy and his appetite were close. Today, happily, we have the music to help us feel the temper of the man. The music expresses satisfaction, and joy, and is the very opposite of music for an occasion; it is beautiful music but it doesn't overvalue itself, being a product of inclination rather than duty; it is as spontaneous and common as laughter, and just as

Pen and ink sketch by Rossini, showing himself (right) and a friend during his stay in Florence.

fragile and liable to dry up abruptly. For long years, from around 1830 until 1842, and from then until 1863, when Rossini was in ill health, it did dry up, as is well known. That was perhaps akin to the mystery of a lost appetite.

Rossini's appetite for food did not diminish with his taste for musical creation. That fact has caused his biographers some embarrassment. Most of them have gone out of their way not to make him seem a glutton. Not wanting to dwell on the subject they point out he was discerning, rather than greedy. He was probably something of both, a fat man, a sort of Falstaff. A few years ago Anthony Burgess described him as the only great composer to have led a happy life. Bloated contentment was not implied, but perhaps appetite was.

The unstrained gaiety of Rossini's music is what is most lovable; and its accessibility doesn't depend on our mood. *Its* moods are immediately inviting; they are warm, sometimes passionate but never truly inward, morbid or intense. Rossini is never pretentious, never afraid of making a fool of himself. When he reached for the metaphor of food he was underlining that lack of pretension.

The characteristics of his muse were traits in his life generally. He was casual and idiosyncratic about things other people regarded as hugely important. His claim that the inspiration for the *Stabat Mater* came from contemplating cheese was typical. 'I am searching for motives and all that comes into my mind is pastries, truffles and such things.' Herbert Weinstock in his biography of Rossini quotes him as saying this while he was composing the work, begun in the early 1830s, but not finished until 1842.

Rossini's music can seem then like an invitation to dinner. He is there, jovial and informed, giving his guests the lead in taking copious second helpings and spilling his wine. The example of enjoyment borders on abandon. If the comparison is apt, it is because, as Rousseau, the patron saint of honest living, pointed out, those who are overly restrained at the table are likely to be false, and Rossini was never that.

Rossini took his food more seriously than he did his art, which didn't need his attention to flourish. He was so interested in what he ate and so attached to the dishes of his Italian childhood that he had his favourite Bologna sausage and pasta sent by post to him in France, of all countries.

Paris though leapt to attention at the merest hint of Rossini's whims. The young composer's fondness for food earned him a reputation even before he arrived in 1823, and a contemporary play marking his entrance into French society, *Rossini in Paris, or The Dinner,* gave him a retinue of *bouffe* characters, one called Biftekini. In subsequent years, during intermittent stays in France, Rossini became a friend of the celebrated chef Carême and a well-known figure in cafés and restaurants.

This was the time of his life when he became immortally associated with classic recipes. The tournedos were named after him because he so liked the *foie gras* with which they were served. But it is a pity Rossini's gastronomic reputation is so bound up with Paris. He deserves the name in his own right.

The happiest years of his life in France and Italy were spent with Olympe Pelissier, who eventually became his second wife. They were also that time of illness and anguish, in which he composed little. She kept him company, and nursed him, until he died in 1868. Their Parisian life became famous for its musical and gastronomic soirées, out of which the *Petite Messe Solennelle* was born.

Weinstock records the pleasure Rossini took not only in eating but in shopping for his suppers with his wife, and preparing their meals, during that middle life. The composer would breakfast with restrained relish on two boiled eggs and a glass of bordeaux and then he would be seen in the early mornings browsing about his favourite Parisian shops. Amongst them was a grocer's whose imported Italian delicacies Rossini knew so well he had to chide the owner one day for trying to pass off Roman pasta as Bolognese.

Far from home, Rossini resorted to making his own pasta with a special piece of equipment. The tube unfortunately recalled the medical treatment he had to endure all those years in France. That illness, the very opposite of appetite, was the other great accident of Rossini's physical life. Weinstock's descriptions of catheters surpass the worst impedimenta in Molière, and poor Rossini became very involved with the technicalities of his body, even considered studying medicine, to try to restore his flesh to health. No one can escape the closeness of the kitchen and the operating room on certain occasions, and Rossini is a good example of a man tempted by the fiddliness of both, a bodily satisfaction. Both tubes were shown to visitors.

Olympe nursed Rossini through terrible bladder troubles and psychic pain in those years in Italy and in France, where they returned permanently in 1855. As early as 1840 she announced that having lost so much else they now lived to eat, and did so 'religiously'. La Pelissier shared with her husband the greatest sensual pleasure he could still enjoy. (It is no coincidence that such a man should find his happiness with a former courtesan, rather than the beautiful, temperamental Spanish soprano, who was his first wife, Isabella Colbran.) He felt he owed her a tribute. What emerged in 1863, however, was more than a personal gift. The *Little Solemn Mass* was unique and prescient devotional music, which sounded as if it had been written in a quiet moment after supper. Worldly ease, iconoclasm, and down-to-earth joy never deserted its author.

This triumphant, mysterious composition, his first since the *Stabat Mater,* marked Rossini's enduring earthly happiness, and he compared it with food.

Lest his final musical savouring of the world be misunderstood the 71 year old composer scribbled a note to God in which he said he was unsure whether the music was sacred or sacrilegious. It was scored for twelve voices. The number made Rossini think of a group of men and women enjoying an intimate supper. But then he thought again and compared his composition to the Last Supper. It was a last bold, irreverent idea about the value of his music, for which two explanations suggest themselves today: one, that Rossini felt the enjoyment of food to be potentially transcendent, in the same way some men think of sexual pleasure; the other, that he so intensely relished earthly pleasures that the energy of consumption itself amounted to devotion.

Of Food, Prejudice and Discovery

Chitrita Banerji

Here, Chitrita Banerji has provided us with a charming personal memoir about the perceptions which she developed in childhood and youth of both Hindu and Muslim foodways.

The defining experience of my life has been close encounters with communities that were the opposite of mine but had existed in close contiguity for centuries. The daughter of a family deeply rooted in the Indian province of West Bengal, I happened to form many close friendships in school with girls whose families originally came from East Bengal, the province that became East Pakistan after the partition and independence of the Indian subcontinent, and twenty-five years later broke away from Pakistan to become Bangladesh. As an adult, I found myself, a Hindu Brahmin by birth, living for several years in Bangladesh where the majority is not only East Bengali, but also Muslim. Stereotypes and biases reared their heads at every turn and, even when allayed by humour, never lost their scorpion sting. Food, cooking styles, and eating habits of rival communities were the most common mediums for couching insults, jocular or vicious. But for me, in the course of life's journey, encountering and appreciating differing food habits and practices has served as a passport to unexpected enrichment.

East and West Bengalis use semi-derisive terms for each other—Ghotis for West Bengalis, Bangals for East Bengalis—that can be equally used as proud badges of identification and loaded terms of pejoration. People take refuge behind those terms to justify all kinds of closemindedness. My family was so Ghoti that, when marriages were arranged, one important question was whether the prospective bride or groom was also an unadulterated Ghoti. When one of my uncles went off and married a Bangal, it created far more commotion than when another married an American.

The Ghoti/Bangal divide was my first experience of the power of bias. With one exception, all the friends I made during my school years in Calcutta were from Bangal families. As a result, I was at the receiving end of much good-natured teasing about Ghotis, especially our eating habits. Food was big on our minds as we started the morning ride on the school bus. Since there was no organized school lunch, as there is in many western countries, we would carry something small—a sandwich, some fruit, something sweet—

for lunch. But the day's main meal of rice, lentils, vegetables, fish or meat, which is traditionally eaten in Bengal at lunchtime, was force-fed to us early in the morning to sustain us through the school day.

There we would be, a gaggle of girls in a school bus, chattering, whispering and giggling. What we had eaten was much on our minds. Many of us found getting ready in the morning a big hassle, often climbing into the bus with hair half-braided, belt untied, shoes unlaced—tasks to be finished during the ride. And so we sometimes resented the time taken up by having to eat all that our mothers insisted was necessary for good nutrition. Rice, of course, was the staple. But in the houses of my Bangal friends, there could be no meal without the obligatory fish stew, *maachher jhol*—no matter how early the departure.

For those who don't know much about Bengali food, this fish stew has traditionally been the centrepiece of the day's main meal. But in Ghoti households like ours, eating a meal without the fish stew was quite common if time was short, if the cook was late with the morning shopping. There were always plenty of things to accompany my rice—*daal* (lentils and other legumes made into thick soup), vegetables cooked in many ways, even a quick omelette to provide the protein. So doing without fish stew on some days was no great deprivation. But when I said this, my Bangal friends roared with laughter. To them it was unthinkable to start the day without the sacrosanct *maachher jhol*. One might as well not eat. With condescension and sarcasm, they would proffer portions of their midday snacks to me, the poor deprived Ghoti. As I spent more time at their homes, I began to realize how pivotal the *maachher jhol* was for the Bangals. When I mentioned this to my parents and relatives, they would laugh and shake their heads at the vagaries of the rustics from across the border. When I asked for an explanation, I sometimes got answers that made sense (they come from the eastern part of Bengal where there are many more rivers and fish is plentiful, so they think of fish as a staple) but more often sarcastic jibes about an unsophisticated lot that came from the hinterland, had the uncontrolled appetite of peasants, and needed potfuls of fish stew to mop up mountains of rice. A frequently quoted doggerel even referred to Bangals as sub-human!

My Bangal friends never missed the chance to laugh at the Ghoti habit of eating wheatflour chapatis at dinner which, I believe, came about because of the rice shortages in the 1960s. The Bangals were proud of pointing out that despite the costs, they still ate rice for both lunch and dinner. It was only the Ghotis, who were not true Bengalis, that could switch to eating chapatis like those Hindi-speaking louts from Bihar (West Bengal's neighbouring state).

Cooking styles were as varied between the two communities as food choice and priorities. The Ghoti trademark was the discernible sweet undertaste in the complex vegetable preparations that the Bengal region is famed for. To most Bangals, however, it was anathema. Ghotis, they said, were sissies, sweetening dishes that were meant to be hot, spicy, salty. If you want a sweet taste, why not eat dessert? In return, the Ghotis would sneer at the Bangals' predilection for chilis and rich, oily sauces that deadened the palate and left no room for subtle tastes. What do they know about food, I remember one of my great aunts saying, they put bitter gourds in their fish stew and make pudding out of white gourds!

Although I resented it bitterly when my Bangal peers ganged up on me and made fun of what we Ghotis ate and how we cooked, by the time I was finishing high school, I had reluctantly come to one conclusion that I knew would infuriate most Ghotis, particularly if they heard it from one of their own. There is a greater degree of adventurous inventiveness in the cooking of East Bengal. Perhaps it is related to the terrain, which is more untamed, crisscrossed with the great rivers of the Bengal delta—rivers that rage with floodwaters, erratically change course, blithely destroy human settlements, and throw up intensely fertile silt deposits that produce rich harvests for new settlers. Perhaps, under such a prevailing sense of uncertainty, you learn to make do with very little and yet turn it into something palatable to accompany the 'mountains of rice' needed for the voracious Bangal appetite. I say this knowing how dangerous it is, for it neatly echoes the stereotypes promoted by the Bangals themselves, of Ghotis being rigid, uninventive, locked in tradition!

Appreciation of Bangal cookery was reinforced during my late teens when my mother and I happened to embark on a parallel discovery (she was a champion cook who delighted in learning new dishes from her East Bengal colleagues) of how the culinary imagination rooted in a more rural or untamed landscape can create succulent dishes out of humble and ordinary ingredients. To take one example, most of us, in cooking a cauliflower, would use the florets and discard everything else. Not the Bangals. As one friend demonstrated, the leaves can be chopped fine and turned into a delicious stir-fry flavored with whole five-spice mix and dried red chilis. Potato and white gourd peel would also be treated the same way and taste ambrosial as a starter with rice. In traditional Ghoti homes like ours, a fish called *chitol* was only half enjoyed. It is an extraordinarily bony fish, and so only the rich, oily, front portion of the fish, where the bones are large and easier to pick out, was considered edible. It was only much later that my mother learnt from one of her Bangal friends the trick of scraping the flesh away from the fine bones of the back portion, combining it with spices and mashed potatoes, and frying it in little balls, the glorious Bangal dish of *muithya.* It was a discovery that silenced the anti-Bangal commentary in our household for quite a while.

Perhaps the most extraordinary instance of the transmutation of the humble into the extraordinary was something I learned from the visiting grandmother of a friend of mine. I happened to drop by at their home during the great autumn festival of Bengali Hindus—*Durga puja.* On the fourth day of the *puja,* Durga (goddess of deliverance) is given an elaborate send-off with many offerings, usually expensive sweets and rare fruits. I was amazed to hear this elderly visitor reminiscing about her youth in a remote East Bengal village where the married women would prepare a humble vegetarian dish—stems of the water lily in a hot and sour tamarind sauce—and offer it to the goddess, beseeching protection from the disastrous fate of widowhood. Women in Bengal are particularly fond of sour and tart preparations. Somehow, I felt, it was a supreme act of imagination and courage, to identify with the womanly aspect of this most powerful goddess, pushing aside the veil of divinity, and finding common ground in the appreciation of an inexpensive, lowbrow dish that would rarely be served to the males of the household, those mortal gods with immediate power to punish and reward. It created a new appreciation in my mind for those wild and untamed inhabitants of East Bengal.

I could go on for ever. But the point I wish to make is that by the time I was graduating from college, there was a wide and unpremeditated distance in my thinking about Bangal cookery and the attitudes of most Ghotis I knew.

The other element dividing Bengali people on either side of the border, east and west, is, of course, religion—Hinduism and Islam. The presence of a Muslim majority in East Bengal led to its becoming the eastern part of Pakistan, which was supposed to be the homeland for the subcontinent's Muslims. Although the religious commonality was not strong enough to keep the two wings of Pakistan together, the creation of Bangladesh (in 1971) did not increase the possibility of the two parts of Bengal finding any kind of political or social unity. When I went to live and work in Bangladesh I had no idea what to expect from Bengali Muslims, although dire predictions from family and friends rained down like hailstones.

I can truthfully say today that this was the most eye-opening experience of my life, much more so than coming to America as a student from India. Despite all the benefits of higher education, a substratum of prejudice, avoidance, and fear had kept a distance between Hindus like me and Muslims living in Calcutta. This would be reinforced by occasional pejorative references from neighbors, contemporaries, or distant relatives about Muslims and their backwardness, their fundamentalism, their dreadful habit of eating beef. Luckily, my immediate family, whatever they may have said about those Bangal Hindus from East Bengal, carefully refrained from expressing sectarian hatreds. The terrible memories of the bloody partition of India had taught them the wisdom of silence. As a result, Muslims were an unfamiliar community, but not the subject of any personal revulsion as far as I was concerned.

And so I went to Bangladesh, fancying myself a very open-minded, unprejudiced person. Full of curiosity, I eagerly accepted all invitations from Bangladeshi families. Immediately I found that although the basic ingredients, *daals,* vegetables, fish, meat (chicken and goat, not beef) were the familiar products of a similar geography, they tasted very different from what I was used to. I would ask my hostesses about what had gone into each dish, but never got very clear answers. Sometimes, when the occasion permitted, I even queried the servants. And they'd grin and say, 'Spices'. It took me a few weeks of tasting and observation to figure out that the one common ingredient in everything, apart from salt or oil, was the onion.

In Hindu cooking, especially among the Ghotis, onions are rare, used primarily in meat and only occasionally in fish or vegetable dishes. They have specific and unfortunate associations with Muslims—as demonstrated by the numerous literary references to those heathens reeking of onion and garlic. Orthodox Hindu Bengali widows never touch onions, nor do vegetarians—the onion being considered non-vegetarian because of its use in meat dishes. Worse, it is even supposed to arouse libidinous desires! But here I was in this unfamiliar land that once used to be part of my own country, eating everyday meals in which the allium reigned supreme. No vegetable—greens, gourds, potatoes, cauliflowers, cabbage—escaped the mingling with onions. Nor did any kind of fish. Although the food tasted delicious, one part of my mind shrugged with a twinge of superiority. How uninventive, I thought, how boring. Whatever happened to that lively imagination that was associated with this wild, untamed terrain?

But those were the early days. As time went by, I was amazed to discover the distinctiveness, delicacy, and variety of the food cooked by Bangladeshis. True to Muslim tradition, their preparations of chicken, *khashi* (castrated goat), duck, and beef were infinitely superior to anything I had tasted in Hindu homes. That was only to be expected. Muslims were supposed to be wizards with meat. But what served as a revelation was the conjunction of unthinkably unrelated elements, resulting in palatal experiences of unprecedented delight. Poppy seed paste, which I had grown up to consider a common and very appropriate accompaniment for delicate vegetables like *jhinge* (similar in taste and consistency to courgettes or marrows), was boldly added to chicken and lamb. The *khashi rezala,* a glorious Muslim invention which I had also tasted in restaurants in India, exploded with a sudden novel piquancy in my mouth as I tasted the sauce that included yogurt, lemon and extract of lily water—and was enhanced with the zestiness of ripened green chilis. The *koi,* a freshwater perch much prized in Bengal, was combined with oranges to become an eclectic pleasure.

On a winter evening, I found myself being the guest of honor in a rural homestead. My hostess and her daughters were busy tending the food that was being cooked over wood fires burning in deep pits dug into the earth. That meal of freshly caught carp seasoned with green chilis and coriander, duck meat nestling in a rich sauce flavored with coconut milk, and stacks of paper-thin chapatis made out of freshly ground rice flour was not only ambrosial for my tastebuds, but also a severe lesson in humility. No sense of preconceived superiority as an urban, educated, sophisticated or well-traveled person could survive in the face of such culinary perfection.

Those rice flour chapatis took on a very different aspect when I saw them being served in town during the great Islamic festival of *Shab-e-barat,* Night of Destiny. Custom in Bangladesh decrees that the occasion should be celebrated by eating rice flour chapatis with an array of *haluas.* Europeans and Americans know the term as halvah, a Middle Eastern concoction. In the Indian subcontinent it has come to mean a dessert made of finely ground grains or legumes sauteed in clarified butter, flavored with whole sweet spices like cinnamon or cardamom, and sweetened with sugar, not honey or molasses. The commonest variety is made with cream of wheat. But during my first *Shab-e-barat,* I was dumbfounded to see varieties of haluas, made not only with cream of wheat, but with ingredients like plain white flour, split pea flour, gluten, eggs, nuts, white gourd, carrots, and yes, even meat.

Perhaps the most memorable lesson in the power of food to upset preconceived ideas came to me through fish—the darling of the Bengali palate, whether the Bengali is a Ghoti or a Bangal, Hindu or Muslim. And of all the myriad species that the region is blessed with, the undisputed king is the hilsa. A large anadromous fish, like the American shad, the hilsa spawns during the monsoon in estuarine waters and then travels upstream through Bengal to northern India. Its unique flavour, soft, rich flesh, delicate roe, and graceful appearance have made Bengalis swoon with appreciation. Even its plentiful bones cannot detract from its appeal.

Before coming to Bangladesh, I had eaten hilsa cooked in a variety of ways, including the classic preparation of *ilish paturi* (pieces of fish coated in mustard oil and ground mustard, wrapped in banana leaves, and cooked in a slow oven). Over the centuries, Ghotis and Bangals have come up with many different ways to cook this delightful fish. Even the British in India made one of their few culinary contributions in the form of smoked hilsa. Two experiences with this fish have taught me about unity and diversity in Bengal's food practices.

Ghotis and Bangals in West Bengal have traditionally engaged in jocular rivalries about the taste and quality of hilsas from the two main rivers, Ganges (West Bengal) and Padma (East Bengal). Cooking styles have also been the source of friendly rivalry. But one of the things that we Ghotis always shuddered over was the strange pre-cooking practice of the Bangals. Since the fish is always bought whole, cleaning and cutting is mostly done at home. All other fish is carefully washed after it has been cut up into pieces. Blood and slime are repulsive to Bengalis and must be thoroughly removed. With the hilsa, however, the Hindus of East Bengal seem to have lost their heads. So eager are they to preserve the fish's unique flavour and taste, that they refuse to wash the blood from the pieces before cooking.

Had anybody asked me when I went to Bangladesh whether I would encounter a similar practice there (after all, this really *was* East Bengal, land of the Bangals), I would have given a definite no. For I knew that in Islam, blood is *haram,* an abomination. Observant Muslims will never eat meat unless it has been butchered properly so that all the blood has drained out of the carcass. And no fish can be eaten that has any perceptible blood clinging to it. Imagine my astonishment when I found the mother of a Bangladeshi Muslim friend, preparing to cook hilsa for our lunch and refusing to wash the blood off the pieces on the same grounds I had heard years ago in Calcutta—all the taste will be washed away. I admit I felt very queasy as I ate the fish, but I did relish discovering this commonality that had transcended religious barriers.

The second lesson from hilsa brings me back to the matter of preconceived notions and irrational prejudices. Fish in Bengal is always cooked with our preferred medium, mustard oil, which has a pungency that nicely balances fishy odors. In the absence of mustard oil, other vegetable oils, such as canola or soybean oil, are used. Hilsa lends itself particularly to the flavour of mustard. Not only the oil, but freshly ground mustard is frequently used in its preparation because the pungency cuts the fattiness of the hilsa. The fish can also be combined with sour tastes like that of tamarind or *karamcha* berries, or with spices like cumin, coriander and ground red chilis. But never could I imagine the union of hilsa with ghee (clarified butter), onions, coconut milk, lemon, and yes, even sugar. Never, that is, until a cook who worked in my house in Bangladesh declared he was going to treat me to a very special dish. When I heard what had gone into its preparation, I was dumbfounded. Hilsa and ghee—heresy! Hilsa with onions and coconut milk—blasphemy! But of course it is the tongue that is the ultimate arbiter, and one taste convinced me that my food universe would be singularly diminished if this did not become part of it. It has been many years since that revelation. I am happy to say that I have personally made this dish for family and friends in Calcutta and have been gratified by their incredulous appreciation.

Since I've mentioned onions so often, I can't resist using the onion one last time, as an image for both the decaying effect of hard-held prejudice and bigotry *and* the freshness of hope and openness. The great Bengali reformer, Swami Vivekananda, who electrified his audience at the world Parliament of Religions, held in Chicago on September 11, 1893, was someone who balanced his spiritual powers with an appreciation of good food. He not only loved to eat, but couched many of his moral and religious teachings in terms of food and cooking. He used to say that one prerequisite for good cooking was having an open mind. Knowledge or expertise are not enough if the mind is crowded with negative thoughts. Dump your baggage, wash your mind clean, he said, and you'll produce extraordinary creations with even the simplest of ingredients.

As creatures of our environment and historical circumstances, we tend to acquire the baggage of suspicion and prejudice about people and practices that are different from ours. The effect of such biases is to corrode the surface of our minds, much like the decay setting in on the top layers of an onion that's left unused for too long. But if we make an effort, peel away those layers, and reach the centre, most of us can still find a core that is fresh, eager, and untouched, waiting to be inscribed with new learning, new ideas, and new pleasures.

Cutting into the core of an onion is a sharp, awakening, vivifying experience that brings tears to the eyes. Could there be a better first step toward discovery?

The *Wedding* Feast of Caranus the Macedonian by Hippolochus

ANDREW DALBY

Andrew Dalby is the author of much the best book on food in classical Greece: Siren Feasts *(Routledge, 1996). He is also a highly valued member of INTERSPI, with a deep knowledge of obscure spices as well as those which have been in use since classical antiquity. In 2000, the British Museum Press published his book* Dangerous Tastes *which explores the story of spices and aromatics through more than two millennia and across both hemispheres. Andrew has made two important contributions to* PPC, *the earlier being a new translation of 'The Banquet of Philoxenus', in* PPC 26.

The somewhat hectic entertainment described here took place about 275 BC. We know of it thanks to the Greek writer on food, Athenaeus.[1] In his *Deipnosophists* Athenaeus liked to insert quotations, short and long, from earlier authors who had written of food and dining customs. Here he retails a letter by Hippolochus, one of the guests at Caranus' wedding feast. Athenaeus's introductory remarks, addressed to his friend Timocrates, conveniently set Hippolochus in his literary context and so have been included here.

Whether by intention or by inadvertence, the letter gives an impression of informality with its artless syntax and its repetitions. The repetitions have been silently copied in the translation. As for the grammatical errors, friends who kindly read the translation found some of them objectionable (this is a conformist age!) so I have had to justify these in footnotes.

The literary letter—addressed to a single person but intended for publication—had a history of at least a century by Hippolochus' time. It is a history that is now difficult to trace, unfortunately, because so many later writers liked to invent historical letters by 5th and 4th century BC notables. All the letters attributed to Phalaris, Themistocles, Socrates and others have long been known to be forgeries. Some of those attributed to Isocrates, Plato, Aristotle and Theophrastus are probably genuine, but which ones exactly? The uncertainties are so great that it is hard to say how much originality was being shown by Lynceus, Hippolochus and their friends in the early 3rd century in exchanging (and publishing) light, amusing letters about such topics as food.

A girl acrobat performing on a revolving stand spun by a clown, drawn by Soun from a photograph of a south Italian vase of the 4th century BC. This illustrates the banquet festivities described by Hippolochus.

The cultural background to Hippolochus' letter is this. After the conquests of Alexander, son of Philip, the kingdom of Macedon soon reverted to a size not much larger than it had been before. In the meanwhile, however, its upper class (a small, hereditary aristocracy) had become immoderately rich. The Macedonians were not originally Greek, but Philip's court had imbibed Greek culture. Alexander's, in turn, imbibed Persian.[2] The letter helps to show how these very different cultures had mingled with earlier Macedonian customs by the time of Caranus' wedding feast.

Given their shared interest in food, Hippolochus may naturally be supposed to have emphasised the details which would seem outlandish to his correspondent Lynceus, and probably they seemed so to himself: he appears to write as an outsider, and was perhaps Greek. Where necessary, I have highlighted in the footnotes the points of difference between this dinner and what we know of Greek ones of similar date: in working on ancient Greek food and dining customs it is the particularities, rather than the generalities, that I am searching for.

Nothing whatever is known of Hippolochus but what appears below. He has a sort of ex-directory status, having got himself omitted from the 49 volumes of Pauly's *Real-Enzyklopädie der classischen Altertumswissenschaft,* Stuttgart 1893–1972. This may be because once upon a time the German scholar Josef

Martin, wielding Occam's razor, suggested that Hippolochus and Caranus were fiction and the letter was written by Lynceus.[3] Lynceus, however, was a conscious stylist and would have found it next to impossible to write as carelessly as the author of this letter does.

Ancient Greek manuscripts have few paragraph divisions and are not normally punctuated to indicate the beginning and end of verbatim quotation. The layout of the following translation is therefore my responsibility. In the first two paragraphs Athenaeus introduces Hippolochus and appears to summarise the beginning of the letter. A sentence of what seems to be verbatim quotation (the third paragraph below) is followed by a further summary (the fourth paragraph). The remainder of the letter is then apparently quoted complete.

> Hippolochus the Macedonian, my dear Timocrates, was of the same generation as Lynceus and Duris of Samos, and was a student of Theophrastus of Eresus.[4] He had given a promise—so one may learn from his *Letters*—to tell Lynceus about any very sumptuous dinner he might attend, Lynceus having made him a similar pledge in return. And in fact letters about dinners by both of them survive: Lynceus describes the dinner that Lamia, the Attic flute-girl, gave at Athens for King Demetrius called Poliorcetes (Demetrius was Lamia's lover) while Hippolochus describes the wedding of Caranus the Macedonian.[5] We have come across other letters of Lynceus to this Hippolochus, too, telling him about King Antigonus' dinner at Athens to celebrate the Aphrodisia, and about King Ptolemy's. We shall give you these letters in due course;[6] but that by Hippolochus is seldom met with, so I shall run over its contents now for your amusement and diversion.
>
> It was in Macedonia, as I said, that Caranus' wedding was feasted; twenty was the number of men invited, and as soon as they lay down they were given each a silver cup, a present. Even before they came in each had been crowned with a gold circlet:[7] the value of these was five staters apiece. When they had emptied their cup[8] each was given, on a bronze plate of Corinthian make,[9] a plate-sized flat loaf, and chickens and ducks as well as pigeons and goose and plenty of other such things piled up; each took some on to his plate,[10] giving shares to the slaves behind.[11] Lots of other different things to eat were brought round; and next came another plate, of silver, again with a large loaf on it, and geese and hares and kids; and more loaves in fancy shapes, and woodpigeons and doves, partridges too and whatever other wildfowl was plentiful.[12]
>
> We gave the slaves shares of this, too (says Hippolochus); and when we had had enough eating we rinsed our hands; and lots of wreaths of all sorts of flowers were brought in, and gold circlets for all, equal in weight to the first.

Hippolochus goes on to say that Proteas, grandson of the other Proteas who was the son of King Alexander's nurse Lanice, drank more than anyone (he was a heavy drinker just like his grandfather, Alexander's comrade) and toasted everybody. He then writes:

We were already pleasantly far from sober when in rushed flute-girls and singers and some Rhodian harp-girls, I seem to think they were naked, only some have been saying they had tunics on;[13] they did their act and went away, and more girls trooped in each carrying a pair of half-pint flasks of perfume, one silver, one gold, yoked together with a golden strap, which they proferred to each of us.[14]

Next was served a treasure rather than a dinner! A silver dish (with quite a broad gold rim) big enough to take a whole roast porker, and a very large one, which lay on its back displaying all the good things its carcass was full of. Baked together inside it were thrushes and wombs and an infinite number of beccafici, and yolks of egg poured over them.[15] And barbecued oysters and scallops[16] were given to us, with a plate for each.

After this we had a drink and each received a stewed kid on another plate just like the others, with gold spoons.[17] Caranus saw the difficulty we were in and had them give us hampers and bread-baskets made of plaited ivory strips, at which we clapped the bridegroom for having helped us save our gifts. Then more wreaths and a pair of perfume-flasks, gold and silver, the same size as before.[18] When it was quiet, in came performers like the ones at the Pots at Athens; after them phallic dancers[19] and buffoons and some women acrobats, naked, who breathed fire and did somersaults over swords.[20]

When we were clear of them a hot[21] and fairly strong drink took our attention, the wines before us being Thasian, Mendaen and Lesbian,[22] offered to each in very large gold bowls. After the drink a glass tray three feet across,[23] resting in a silver receptacle, full of all kinds of grilled fish jumbled together, was proferred to everyone; so was a silver bread-basket of Cappadocian loaves,[24] some of which we ate, some we gave to the servants. Then, rinsing our hands, we put on wreaths and had gold circlets again, twice as heavy as the last ones, and another pair of perfume jars.

When it was quiet Proteas, leaping up from his couch, called for his six-pint bowl and filled it up with Thasian wine and just a trickle of water, saying as he drained it: 'He who drinks most shall have most happiness!'[25]

Caranus said: 'As first to drink up, you are first to be given your bowl as a present! And all others who do the same shall have the same reward.'

At this nine royal princes rose[26] and grabbed their bowls, trying to outdo one another; but one of the guests, poor fellow, could not drink up, and sat and cried at not getting his bowl until Caranus made him a present of an empty one.

Next a chorus of a hundred men came in to sing a tuneful wedding song, and then dancing-girls got up as Nereids, and some more as Nymphs.[27] The drinking continued, and as it began to get dark they drew back the white linen curtains all around the room; and as they were drawn, torches appeared (their hoods opened by a hidden mechanism) and so did the Eroses and Artemises and Pans and Hermeses and other such statuary that held aloft these torches in silver lanterns. As we were admiring this clever touch, proper Erymanthian boars,[28] spitted on silver spears, were served to each on square dishes with gold rims. And the amazing thing: tipsy and drowsy with drink as we were, at each new thing we saw we all sobered up again (start upright, as the poet said).[29]

So the slaves went on piling food into our lucky hampers[30] until a trumpet sounded the usual signal for the end of dinner (this, you know, is the Macedonian custom at big celebrations) and Caranus began the drinking in small cups,[31] telling the slaves to hurry round. We drank gently, this time, by way of antidote to the strong wine we had had before; while in came the clown Mandrogenes, a descendant of the Athenian one called Strato, and again and again made us burst out laughing. Eventually he did a dance with his wife, who is over eighty.

At last the second tables came in and fruit and nuts were offered to all in ivory baskets, and all sorts of cakes, Cretan and your very own Samian, my dear Lynceus,[32] and Attic,[33] with the receptacle proper to each.

Eventually we got up and came away, sobered (ye Gods) by fear for the treasure we carried. So you can stay in Athens and enjoy listening to the lectures of Theophrastus and eating thyme[34] and rocket[35] and those rolls you like[36] and watching the *Lénaia*[37] and the Pots; we at Caranus' wedding have been entertained to a whole fortune each, and now we are looking for houses or land or slaves to buy.

That is the end of Hippolochus' letter. Athenaeus then has a parting word for Timocrates:

Considering these details, my dear Timocrates, which Greek dinner can you possibly compare with a party like that?

Notes

1. Of the early 3rd century AD. See 'The Banquet of Philoxenus' (*PPC 26*) for some information on Athenaeus. The passage translated here is *Deipnosophists* 128a–130e. The Greek text is in print as *Athenaei Naucratitae Dipnosophistarum libri XV* recensuit G. Kaibel, vol. 1, Leipzig 1887, reprinted Stuttgart (Teubner) 1961, pp 291–6. For another English translation see Athenaeus: *The Deipnosophists* with an English translation by C. B. Gulick, vol 2, London (Heinemann) 1928, pp 90–101.

2. On Alexander's entertaining see E. N. Borza, 'The symposium at Alexander's court' in *Ancient Macedonia III,* Thessalonica 1983, pp 45–55.
3. J. Martin, *Symposion: die Geschichte einer literarischen Form,* Paderborn 1931, pp 159–160.
4. Theophrastus was Aristotle's successor as head of the Academy at Athens. His botanical writings had an enormous influence and tell us much of food plants in the Greek world. See Theophrastus, *Enquiry into plants* with an English translation by Sir Arthur Hort, 2 vols, London (Heinemann) 1916-26; Theophrastus, *De causis plantarum* with an English translation by B. Einarson and G. K. K. Link, vol 1, London (Heinemann) 1976. These editions are in print.

   Duris was a historian, his brother Lynceus a lighter author; only a few extracts from their works now survive. On Duris see L. A. Okin, *Studies on Duris of Samos* Ann Arbor (University Microfilms) 1974 [a dissertation submitted at the University of California at Los Angeles].
5. Very likely a descendant of the Caranus who fought with Alexander the Great and is several times mentioned in Arrian's *Campaigns of Alexander:* see the translation by A. de Sélincourt, new edn, Penguin 1971, pp 194, 205, 209–210.
6. Athenaeus did not keep the promise.
7. The circlets were presumably also gifts. See further note 14.
8. At Athens at this time one drank not at all before dinner, sparingly while eating, heavily afterwards. Evidence on this (as on other details of Athenian dinners) is collected by W. A. Becker, *Charikles.* New ed by H. Göll, Berlin 1877–8, vol 2, pp 335–6.
9. Made of an alloy of gold, silver and copper, tableware of Corinthian bronze was a costly luxury discussed at length by Pliny, *Natural History* 34.6-12. Pliny's statement that Corinthian bronze was discovered accidentally in the fire at the sack of Corinth in 146 BC is incorrect if the present passage really does refer to the alloy, since it was written more than a century earlier than that. Indeed connoisseurs could argue that 146 BC, when Corinth was for the time being deserted, was when Corinthian ware ceased to be made. That seems to be the point behind a joke by the character Trimalchio in Petronius' *Satyricon,* section 50 (p 64 in the translation by J. Sullivan, Penguin 1965): 'I am the only man who has real Corinthian . . . Why? . . . The maker I buy from is called Corinth. How can anything be Corinthian unless you've got a Corinth?'

   The emphasis on tableware, throughout the letter, points a contrast with Athens, where food was not always eaten from plates but placed directly on individual tables, which were scrubbed down before meals.
10. The meat circulated on a serving-dish; diners loaded a share for themselves and their attendants on to the bread on their individual plates. This apparently Macedonian way of eating bread with meat is not otherwise recorded in classical texts: an early Greek fashion was for hollowed-out bread spoons, *mystílai.* These are mentioned in Aristophanes' comedy *Knights,* lines 1168–9 (see Aristophanes, *The Knights* [and other plays] translated by D. Barrett and A. H. Somerstein, Penguin 1978, p 79): 'And I bring spoons, spooned by the goddess with her ivory hand.' The word is defined by the second-century AD lexicographer Pollux in his *Onomasticon* 6.87 (edited by E. Bethe, Leipzig 1900–37).
11. R. A. Tomlinson, 'Ancient Macedonian symposia' in *Ancient macedonia* [I], Thessalonica 1970, describes the couches as arranged along the walls of the dining room in Macedonian symposia. Where then did the slaves stand, and where (see below) did the

curtains run? Tomlinson drew his conclusions from religious architecture, which is not good evidence for Macedonian practice generally.

In the early Greek epics, slaves might eat with the mistress of the household (*Odyssey* 15.376–9: p 247 in E. V. Rieu's translation, Penguin 1945) while dependents of no standing (beggars in *Odyssey* book 19; orphaned children in *Iliad* 22.492–8, p 371 in M. Hammond's translation, Penguin 1987) waited at the edges of a banquet hoping for food or dared to approach the diners. In medieval western Europe food was distributed at dinner by the great to their subordinates, as by Caranus' guests to their slaves. In both periods dining took place in the main room or hall of the house, which tended to be large enough for everybody to be there at once, eating or not. It must have been so in Caranus' house too.

In imperial Rome, on the other hand, dining-rooms were purpose-built and of restricted size like those described by Tomlinson, and so any distributions of food to subordinates took place after dinner, outside: see for example Juvenal, *Satires* 1.94–6, p 68 in Peter Green's translation, Penguin 1967. A hint of classical Athenian practice, similar to Roman, is in the anecdote by Machon quoted below, note 30.

12. The kinds of food served so far would surprise a Greek observer, who would have begun a big dinner of his own with hors d'oeuvres and bread, followed by fish. Meat, in less lavish quantities, would follow, game in particular tending to arrive last. See for example 'The Banquet of Philoxenus', *PPC 26.* Lynceus, quoted by Athenaeus 131f–132b, criticises the Athenian fashion for dainty hors d'oeuvres, the forerunners of modern *meze.*
13. Any of these, but hardly so many on any one occasion, might entertain at an Athenian symposium. Vase paintings suggest that they might wear more or less transparent costumes (for example, J. Boardman, *Athenian red figure vases,* London (Thames and Hudson) 1975, figs 253, 317) if any (*ib* fig 265). The construction of the original sentence is not wholly grammatical.
14. It was an Athenian custom, of which some disapproved (such as the Socrates portrayed in Xenophon's *Symposium* 2.2–4: see Xenophon, *Memoirs of Socrates and The Symposium* translated by H. Tredennick, Penguin 1970, pp 235–6), to distribute perfume after meals or between the two courses; likewise to distribute wreaths, and water for washing the hands, before meals and between the courses. These practices appear here to have been grafted into a quite un-Greek kind of meal with far more courses, giving scope for lavish display and consumption.
15. The stuffing of whole carcasses with smaller delicacies was practised in imperial Rome (cf Petronius, *Satyricon* 49, p 63 of Sullivan's translation); it seems that Romans borrowed the idea from Macedonian cuisine. The Macedonians did not get it from the Greeks, nor, probably, from their own relatively undeveloped homeland: the classical Athenians did not roast whole large animals, and Greeks generally practised grilling or spit-roasting. The cuisine depicted here would require oven-roasting, which the Athenians at any rate considered to be a Persian practice. This is evident from Aristophanes' *Acharnians,* lines 85–9 (see Aristophanes: *The Acharnians, The clouds, Lysistrata* translated by A. H. Sommerstein, Penguin 1973, pp 52–3), and a fragment of Antiphanes' play *Oenomaus.* Both are quoted by Athenaeus, *Deipnosophists* 130e–131a, vol 2, p 101 of Gulick's translation.

It is surprising to find sow's womb here: no other offal is mentioned. Sliced sow's womb and yolk of egg are both included in a similar concoction, undoubtedly imitating this one, served to Athenaeus's fictional *Deipnosophists* at 376c. Womb was a delicacy to the Athenians in the 4th century BC (for evidence see the *Deipnosophists* 100c–3, vol 1, pp 431–3 of Gulick's translation). The one tiny surviving fragment of Lynceus's letter about King Ptolemy's dinner (*ib* 100f), roughly contemporary with Caranus, shows that womb was eaten there 'in vinegar and silphium', as the Romans, later, also liked to eat it: see Apicius, *On cookery* 7.1.1-4, pp 156–7 in Barbara Flower and Elisabeth Rosenbaum's *Roman cookery book*, London (Harrap) 1958.

16. The seafood appears to form a side-dish. There is something wrong with the text of the manuscript here, but no convincing emendation has been proposed.
17. Such things were not used in classical Greece, but silver gilt spoons were among valuables seized by the Macedonians in Persia, according to a document quoted in the *Deipnosophists* 784a (vol 5 p 53 of Gulick's translation).
18. These two sentences are too brief for clarity. 'The difficulty we were in' must be the problems of knowing what to do with an excess of food and gifts. The second sentence lacks a verb.
19. The Pots was the second day of the annual Anthesteria festival in early spring: participants wore wreaths of flowers and ivy and carried leafy branches. See G. van Hoorn, *Choes and Anthesteria,* Leiden 1951. Large phalluses were worn on stage in Athenian comedy, which was also part of a festival. These, then, are displays imitating or parodying religious observances: such things had never been a feature of Athenian dinners or symposia.
20. A girl acrobat (not a troupe) might perform at a symposium in 4th century BC Athens, where the sword-dance was already popular. See Plato, *Euthydemus* 294e (Plato, *Early Socratic dialogues* edited by T. J. Saunders, Penguin 1987, p 354); Xenophon, *Symposium* 2.11–14, 7.3, pp 237–8 and 266 in H. Tredennick's translation. For a vase painting of an acrobat and a dwarf clown see *The birth of Western civilization* ed M. Grant, London 1964, p 151; and the drawing on page 289.
21. 'No man would choose to drink wine hot,' said a character in the Athenian comedy *The Coolers,* by Strattis quoted in the *Deipnosophists* 124d. Perhaps the Macedonians disagreed. 'Hot' and 'rather strong' were the alternative suggestions, disputed by later Greeks, for the meaning of the obsolete adjective *zoróteros* used in the *Iliad* (9.203) of wine. Curiously, Plutarch in his *Symposium Questions* (5.4) includes a discussion of this word, and it is a Macedonian character who argues for 'hot' as against 'strong'. But four centuries separate Hippolochus from Plutarch. See *Plutarch's Moralia,* vol 8, translated by P. A. Clement and H. B. Hoffleit, London (Heinemann) 1969, pp 401–5.
22. These were good wines, all produced relatively close to Macedonia, and all known to be popular at this period. They are discussed, among others, in the *Deipnosophists* 28d–29e (vol 1 pp 125–131 in Gulick's translation).
23. Glassware had already a long history in the Aegean but remained a costly rarity.
24. 'In Greece there is bread called "soft", made with a little milk and oil and a proportion of salt. The dough must be slack. This bread is called Cappadocian, because that is where soft bread is mostly made. The Syrians call such bread *lakhm,* and it is found very serviceable in Syria because it is eaten very warm. It is like a flower': Chrysippus of Tyana, *Bread-making,* quoted in the *Deipnosophists* 113b–c. Cappadocia is in central Asia Minor.

25. A parody, it seems, of a pessimistic line from Euripides' *Oenomaus* (fragment 541 in A. Nauck's *Tragicorum Graecorum Fragmenta,* Leipzig 1889): 'He who does most, does the most wrong.'
26. *Iliad* 7.161: here and below I have borrowed from *The Iliads of Homer, prince of poets,* translated by George Chapman, London 1611.

    The competitive hard drinking of the Macedonian court probably contributed to Alexander's death (Arrian, *The campaigns of Alexander,* 7.24–7, pp 391–5 in de Sélincourt's translation). Greeks were particularly shocked by the fact that Macedonians and Scythians drank their wine neat; see the *Deipnosophists* 427a–c, vol 4 pp 433–5 in Gulick's translation.
27. At Athenian symposia, dancers (two or so) might mime scenes from mythology: such a ballet is suggested by the Socrates portrayed in Xenophon's *Symposium,* 7.5 and is performed at 9.2–7 (pp 266–7, 278–9 of Tredennick's translation). But the dance described here seems to be something between that and the *bakkheîon,* the drunken dance of religious ceremonial (not of the symposium) mentioned by Plato, *Laws* 815c; see T. J. Saunders's translation, Penguin 1970, p 308.

    This sentence is awkward and asymmetrical in the original text.
28. The capture of the Erymanthian boar was the fourth labour of Heracles in the standard narratives of Greek mythology.
29. A reminiscence of *Iliad* 24.11.
30. In Contemporary Greece one finds no hint that guests took surplus food home. On the contrary, hosts would save what leftovers they could. In book 13 of the *Deipnosophists* (vol 6 pp 119–145 of Gulick's translation) Athenaeus quotes at length from a collection of anecdotes by Machon on the *hetaírai,* the high-class prostitutes of 4th and 3rd century BC Athens, and includes (580c) this story about two of them: 'Gnathaena was once at dinner at Dexithea's, and Dexithea was putting almost all the dishes aside for her mother. "By Artemis, woman," said Gnathaena, "if I'd known this would happen I'd have had dinner with your mother, not with you!"' It must be understood that the highly privileged social position of a *hetaíra* did not extend to her relatives: Dexithea's mother would be eating later. Macho's verses have been edited in Greek with a commentary by A. S. F. Gow, Cambridge 1965.
31. A trumpet-call marked both the beginning and the end of dinner at the famous multiple wedding celebrations during Alexander's expedition; see Aelian, *Miscellanies* 8.7: *Claudii Aeliani varia historia,* ed M. R. Dilts, Leipzig 1974, p 95. At Alexander's other entertainments the trumpet was sounded when dinner ended and drinking began with a libation to the gods; see the *Deipnosophists* 538d, vol 5 p 435 of Gulick's translation. Athenaeus is quoting the historian Chares of Mytilene, and so, undoubtedly, is Aelian.
32. The *glykinas* is thus described in the *Deipnosophists* 645d: 'the cake made by the Cretans with sweet wine and olive oil.' Those of Samos were well known according to the comic author Sopater of Paphos, slightly earlier than Hippolochus, quoted *ib* 644c (vol 6 p 477 in Gulick's translation). Lynceus was born in Samos.
33. 'Accept a cake made in Athens,' said the 4th century gourmet Archestratus, quoted in the *Deipnosophists* 101d: Lynceus in his *Letter to Diagoras,* quoted *ib* 647b, also hints at their superiority. The Attic honey of Mount Hymettus improved them, Archestratus adds. Many quotations from Athenian comedies mentioning various cakes are given *ib* 643e–648c (vol 6 pp 475–503).

34. The thyme of Mount Hymettus was famous, according to Antiphanes, quoted in the *Deipnosophists* 28d, and among the cheapest of foods, *ib* 108f.

35. *Eruca sativa* is a salad vegetable and pot-herb mentioned by several Greek and Roman authors but never favourably. See for example Horace, *Satires* 2.8.51, p 124 in the translation by Niall Rudd, 2nd edn, Penguin 1979.

36. 'Even the loaves of the marketplace are exalted among them. They bring them in at the beginning of dinner and in the course of it till none is left,' wrote Lynceus in his *Letter to Diagoras,* quoted in the *Deipnosophists* 109d.

37. One of the two annual drama festivals of Athens.

A well-supplied drinker at a symposium, as depicted by Macron on an Attic drinking cup of c 490 BC. Redrawn from an illustration in G. Hagenow, Aus dem Weingarten der Antika, *Mainz, 1982.*

Elizabeth David, 1913–1992

ALAN DAVIDSON

Most readers of *PPC* will already know that Elizabeth David died in May of this year [1992], in her sleep. A number of moving tributes to her, and to her achievements, were paid in the press, both in the UK and abroad. Gerald Asher, who was with her on the day before her death and who had been her host on her frequent visits to San Francisco in the 1980s, wrote an especially good essay for the *Independent,* although, as he remarked at the simple funeral held at the village church of Folkington in Sussex, he was well aware that she disliked being written about.

This facet of her personality does indeed pose something of a problem for those who wish to celebrate her life. But it will be no invasion of her cherished privacy if I recall those acts of generosity on her part which had a most radical effect on me, and on this journal which you hold in your hand.

The first act caused me to change careers. I had been working for decades in the Diplomatic Service, and would no doubt have plodded on to the statutory retirement age, had ED not intervened. While working at the British Embassy in Tunis I had written a primitive booklet about *Seafish of Tunisia;* goodness, how primitive, cyclostyled on the Information Department's machine in the lunch hour, collated on the Ambassador's conference table while he was conveniently absent, crudely illustrated, furnished with but one virtue, enthusiasm. The Information Officer who so obligingly allowed his machine to be used had known ED in Cairo during the war, so he sent her a copy. In it she found information on a matter which had recently perplexed her considerably: the common and market names of Mediterranean fish in various languages. She broadcast (in the pages of the *Spectator*) her approval, and we became correspondents and then friends. What is more, when she heard some years later that I was wondering whether to reprint the booklet in its existing form, she said certainly not, that was a recipe for disaster, the booklet should be turned into a book and published by Penguin; she would speak to her editor there, Jill Norman.

Thus it came about that, a few years later, I was a Penguin author, and very happy to be one. And this was the necessary condition for what happened next, which was that I decided to retire early and become a writer. By her kind interest, and her quick perception of what needed to be done, ED had switched the points and changed my destination.

Next, when I was enjoying my new role, she added a new dimension to it. She played a principal part, one might say an essential one, in the birth of *PPC* and Prospect Books.

The early issues of *PPC* contained many contributions from her. Had it not been for the enthusiasm and generosity with which she offered essays for the first issue, the journal would probably have remained no more than an interesting idea. Without the stimulus of her continuing interest it would probably have had a short life. Her intellectual vitality (she had one of the quickest minds I have ever met), her amazing memory for detail, her passionate interest in getting everything right, her feeling for style in the larger sense—all these things made our close association with her in the early years of *PPC* an unforgettable experience. And they all left a stamp not just on *PPC* but also on various things which followed from *PPC 1,* including twelve years of publication of books by Prospect Books and, at one remove, the series of annual Oxford Symposia on food history, starting in 1981.

ED will of course be remembered primarily for her own books and for the leading role which they played in transforming British attitudes to food and cookery. But we can justly add that what she did for Prospect Books is one more part of the same story.

She was our Honorary President up to the day of her death, and she did not regard this position lightly. There were occasions when particular things done by Prospect Books were not done as she would have thought right; for every ten postcards or telephone calls to us expressing pleasure or congratulations over something we had done there would be one telling us that we had gone off the rails. However, all were welcome, for all were evidence of her feelings of involvement and interest; and her basic approval of the work being done by contributors to *PPC,* by our bibliographic team, by the authors of hundreds of essays for the Oxford Symposium, and by the authors of the new books we published, shone brightly and steadily throughout.

Now, it so happens that the last thing ED wrote for *PPC,* and probably the last piece of her writing to be published in her lifetime, was a Note on Anglo-American Tomato Ketchup in *PPC 40.* She had noticed, and wished to correct, what she regarded as an error on the part of one of our contributors. She did so with characteristic courtesy; but her Note would make a rather downbeat ending to the list of contributions which she made. So with the kind permission of those concerned we are providing a better 'last word'. This is an essay which she wrote many years ago for Terence Conran's *The Kitchen Book.* It will be less familiar to many *PPC* readers than her own books; and for this reason her nephew Johnny Grey chose passages from it to read at the funeral service. In reproducing the text here, we have added a slightly redrawn version of the plan which accompanied the text in the book (where it was also accompanied by a 'visitor's-eye' view of the kitchen in colour).

In case you wonder, ED never had this 'Dream Kitchen'. She did have a new one installed in her Chelsea home but the configuration of the house did not permit following her ideal plan—although Johnny Grey (whose profession is kitchen design) was able to go some way in the desired directions. (By the way, the Victorian ceiling light fitment which had hung over the kitchen table in her old kitchen became surplus; and ever since then it has hung over the big table in the one workroom which is all that Prospect Books can call its own. Continuing illumination for us!)

Elizabeth David's Dream Kitchen

So frequently do dream kitchens figure in the popular newspaper competitions, in the pages of shiny magazines and in department store advertising that one almost begins to believe women really do spend half their days dreaming about laminated work-tops, louvered cupboard doors and sheaves of gladioli standing on top of the dishwasher. Why of all rooms in the house does the kitchen have to be a dream? Is it because the in the past kitchens have mostly been so underprivileged, so dingy and inconvenient? We don't, for example, hear much of dream drawing-rooms, dream bedrooms, dream garages, dream box-rooms (I could do with a couple of those). No. It's a dream kitchen or nothing. My own kitchen is rather more of a nightmare than a dream, but I'm stuck with it. However, I'll stretch a point and make it a good dream for a change. Here goes.

This fantasy kitchen will be large, very light, very airy, calm and warm. There will be the minimum of paraphernalia in sight. It will start off and will remain rigorously orderly. That takes care of just a few desirable attributes my present kitchen doesn't have. Naturally there'll be, as now, a few of those implements in constant use—ladles, a sieve or two, whisks, tasting spoons—hanging by the cooker, essential knives accessible in a rack, and wooden spoons in a jar. But half a dozen would be enough, not thirty-five as there are now. Cookery writers are particularly vulnerable to the acquisition of unnecessary clutter. I'd love to rid myself of it.

The sink will be a double one, with a solid wooden draining-board on each side. It will be (in fact, is) set 760 mm (30 in) from the ground, about 152 mm (6 in) higher than usual. I'm tall, and I didn't want to be prematurely bent double as a result of leaning over a knee-high sink. Along the wall above the sink I envisage a continuous wooden plate rack designed to hold serving dishes as well as plates, cups and other crockery in normal use. This saves a great deal of space, and much time spent getting out and putting away. Talking of space, suspended from the ceiling would be a wooden rack or slatted shelves such as farmhouses and even quite small cottages in parts of Wales and the Midland counties used to have for storing bread or drying out oatcakes. Here would be the parking place for papers, notebooks, magazines—all the things that usually get piled on chairs when the table has to be cleared. The table itself is, of course, crucial. It's for writing at and for meals, as well as for kitchen tasks, so it has to have comfortable leg room. This time round I'd

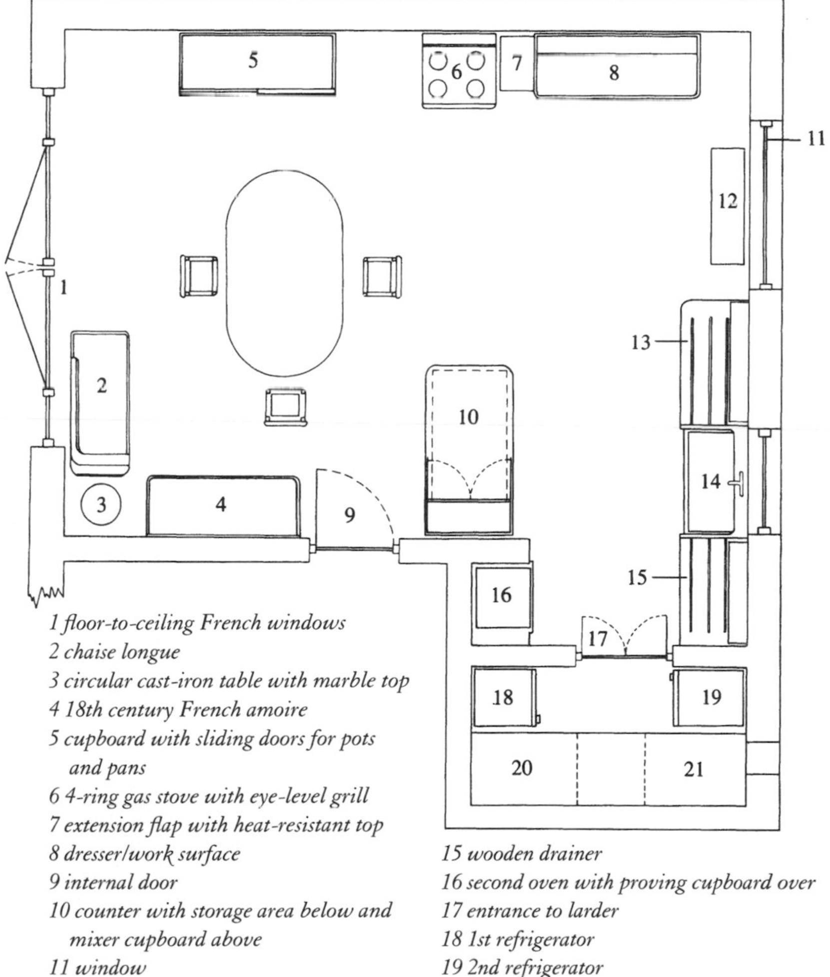

1 floor-to-ceiling French windows
2 chaise longue
3 circular cast-iron table with marble top
4 18th century French amoire
5 cupboard with sliding doors for pots and pans
6 4-ring gas stove with eye-level grill
7 extension flap with heat-resistant top
8 dresser/work surface
9 internal door
10 counter with storage area below and mixer cupboard above
11 window
12 low table
13 wooden plate rack
14 large porcelain sink
15 wooden drainer
16 second oven with proving cupboard over
17 entrance to larder
18 1st refrigerator
19 2nd refrigerator
20 marble slab
21 front-opening deep-freeze

like it to be oval, one massive piece of scrubbable wood, on a central pedestal. Like the sink, it has to be a little higher than the average.

Outside the kitchen is my refrigerator and there it will stay. I keep it at the lowest temperature, about 4°C (40°F). I'm still amazed at the way so-called model kitchens have refrigerators next to the cooking stove. This seems to me almost as mad as having a wine rack above it. Then, failing a separate larder—in a crammed London house that's carrying optimism a bit too far—there would be a second and fairly large refrigerator to be used for the cool storage of a variety of commodities such as coffee beans, spices, butter, cheese and eggs, which benefit from a constant temperature of say 10°C (50°F).

All the colours in the dream kitchen would be much as they are now, but fresher and cleaner—cool silver, grey-blue, aluminium, with the various browns of earthenware pots and a lot of white provided by the perfectly plain china. I recoil from coloured tiles and beflowered surfaces and I don't want a lot of things coloured avocado and tangerine. I'll just settle for the avocados and tangerines in a bowl on the dresser. In other words, if the food and the cooking pots don't provide enough visual interest and create their own changing patterns in a kitchen, then there's something wrong. And too much equipment is if anything worse than too little. I don't a bit covet the exotic gear dangling from hooks, the riot of clanking iron-mongery, the armouries of knives, or the serried ranks of sauté pans and all other carefully chosen symbols of culinary activity I see in so many photographs of chic kitchens. Pseuds corners, I'm afraid, many of them.

When it comes to the cookery I don't think I need anything very fancy. My cooking is mostly on a small scale and of the kind for intimate friends, so I'm happy enough with an ordinary four-burner gas stove. Its oven has to be a good size, though, and it has to have a drop-down door. Given the space I'd have a second, quite separate oven just for bread, and perhaps some sort of temperature-controlled cupboard for proving the dough. On the whole though it's probably best for cookery writers to use the same kind of domestic equipment as the majority of their readers. It doesn't do to get too far away from the problems of everyday household cooking or take the easy way out with expensive gadgetry.

What it all amounts to is that for me—and I stress that this is purely personal, because my requirements as a writing cook are rather different from those of one who cooks mainly for a succession of guests or for the daily meals of a big family—the perfect kitchen would really be more like a painter's studio furnished with cooking equipment than anything conventionally accepted as a kitchen.

M F K Fisher, 1908–1992

ALAN DAVIDSON

The death in June of America's foremost writer on food has prompted many a survey, not emulated here, of her books, but of them I will say this, that although food was the main theme of many of them it was at most the core and never the whole; indeed much of her writing was of a scope so broad that one could best describe it as being about life.

What I think must be her last book, *The Boss Dog,* published in 1991 by the late and lamented North Point Press (with which she had enjoyed such a happy relationship), belongs to the series of books about the time she spent in France. It is a delight. But then all her books were and are; and their span is so wide that Elgy Gillespie was absolutely right to say, in the *Independent,* that to label MFK as 'a cookery writer would be like calling Sir Richard Burton a travel writer'.

Indeed none of the labels which might occur to one fits. I once had occasion, writing about Elizabeth David, to say: 'she is eminently someone on whom it is not appropriate to stick any label, for her high renown is based firmly and precisely on the fact that she is different.' These words could just as well be applied to MFK; and it is noticeable that people who have written tributes to her often finish up by falling back on the adjective 'unique'.

One salient characteristic of her writing, and indeed of herself, was a highly developed and subtle sensuality. Another was wit. Both these have often been described and celebrated. So has her facility in handling words, in tumbling her phrases, sentences, paragraphs beside and on top of each other with the combined skills of architect, juggler and artist, and having the resultant structure always achieve a perfect balance, precarious only in the sense that if anyone else had tried to put it up it would have fallen down in ruins. She lived and wrote dangerously, right out there on the cutting edges of life and literature.

But I would add another feature, namely her uncanny power of looking intently, very intently, at a person or thing and seeing more therein, and more clearly, than others would see. Disconcerting, this could be; one felt that one was being unclothed, intellectually and emotionally, and rendered as transparent as a tadpole on a glass slide under a microscope. Yet her eyes were kind, and the verdict would be as charitable as could reasonably be expected.

I paid four visits to her in her home in Glen Ellen. In terms of intensity of experience and lasting memories they counted as much as would forty visits to other people.

What I remember most vividly of all was the first visit, when I was shown round the extraordinary house which had been designed to her own plan; not a 'dream house' in the usual sense, for this one patently and palpably existed, but a house in which one would surely dream exciting dreams. One end was a huge bedroom and writing room. The other end was equally huge, providing an all-in-one space for living and eating and cooking, with a wonderful view across the valley to hills whose constant and subtle changes of colouration delighted her.

Sandwiched between these great rooms was the entrance hall and the bathroom. The latter doubled as her private art gallery. As one went into it, and began to grasp its dual function, she would be watching the expression on one's face; what was the reaction? I hope that my unfeigned pleasure, and my being careful to ask before I left whether I could go back there and benefit from **both** its functions, passed muster. The bathroom, I figured, was a kind of touchstone for assaying the genuineness/phoniness of her visitors; something to tap them against to check whether they rang true.

Altogether she was just about the most unconventional, nonconformist and pleasantly surprising person one could hope to meet. It would be quite implausible to suppose that there is or will be another like her in our midst.

From Quarter-Deck to Cooking Pot

MICHAEL D COE AND ERNESTO VITETTI

We have already said something by way of introduction to this essay on page 262. Here we add that Professor Michael Coe (who enlisted his cousin, Count Vitetti, as co-author) is Charles J MacCurdy Professor of Anthropology, Emeritus, Yale University. In 1986 he was elected to the National Academy of Sciences, and in 1989 received the Tatiana Proskouriakoff Award from Harvard University for distinction in Mesoamerican Research. His books include Breaking the Maya Code; The Maya; *and* Mexico: From the Olmecs to the Aztecs. *It was Michael who, after the death of his wife, Sophie, set up by a generous benefaction the Sophie Coe Memorial Prize Fund to which, in acquiring the present book, our readers are making a welcome contribution.*

In large, extended families, memories—and memorabilia, including cherished recipes—tend to be pecuniotropic, that is, they generally cluster in that part of the family tree where there is the most money. Poor relations are soon forgotten, along with their foodways. This is definitely the case with the ancestry of our grandmother, Mary (Mai) Huttleston Rogers Coe. She was the daughter of Henry Huttleston Rogers, one of the founders of the Standard Oil Company and a legendary 'robber baron' of his time. Thomas H. Lawson, in his muckraking book *Frenzied Finance,* had this to say about our great-grandfather:

> Away from the spirit of dollar making, this remarkable man is one of the most charming and lovable human beings I have ever encountered; a man whom any man or woman would be proud to have for a brother; a man whom any father or mother would give thanks for as a son; a man whom any woman would be happy to know as her husband; and a man whom any boy or girl would rejoice to call her father.
>
> But once he passes under the baleful influence of the machine, he becomes relentless, ravenous, pitiless as a shark, knowing no law of God or man in the execution of his purpose.

He may have been called 'Hell Hound Rogers' by his enemies on Wall Street, but he was also a close friend of Mark Twain, whom he rescued from bankruptcy, and the patron and friend of Helen Keller and Booker T. Washington. Once he had achieved his riches, he showered his native town of Fairhaven, in southeastern Massachusetts, with benefactions, including a town hall, high school, library, Unitarian church, public park, paved streets, and water system.

Until the collapse of the whale-oil industry after the Civil War, Fairhaven was a typical Yankee whaling town, closely linked to the larger port of New Bedford on the western side of its harbor. Families like the Howlands, Giffords, Winslows, Tripps, and Delanos (ancestors of FDR) were heavily involved in the whale fishery. Henry Rogers' father Rowland had once shipped out on a whaler, and the Rogerses (an old Yankee family descended from two of the passengers on the *Mayflower*) were related to most of the whaling families. In 1862, Henry Rogers, just back from an initial foray into the newly-discovered oil fields of Titusville, Pennsylvania, married Abbie Palmer Gifford in the house of her father, Captain Peleg Winslow Gifford. The two returned to Titusville, where our great-grandfather began his meteoric rise to immense wealth. 'Rock oil' had replaced whale oil.

Surviving logbooks show that Captain Gifford had been master of several whaling barks (barks had two square-rigged masts and one rigged fore-and-aft); at various times between 1846 and 1866, he commanded the *Clarice,* the *Sea Fox,* and the *Sea Queen,* and at one time he was master of the *Niger.* Readers of *Moby-Dick* (published 1851) will recall Ishmael's encounter with Ahab's friend 'Old Captain Peleg'; the crew list of the actual whaler on which Melville sailed out of New Bedford in 1841 listed his place of residence as Fairhaven, and we have often wondered whether the author picked up this unusual biblical name from our great-great-grandfather (who would have been but 36 at the time). In all events, *our* Captain Peleg's moment in history came in 1861, when he was among the Yankee captains who sailed 24 ships laden with stones down to Charleston, South Carolina, and scuttled them to prevent blockade runners from entering the harbor. A wonderful group photograph of the 'Great Stone Fleet' captains shows our spade-bearded ancestor standing to the left.

Not surprisingly, a number of manuscript recipe books from the Rogerses, Giffords, and Huttlestons (the family of H. H. Rogers' mother) have survived, and some of these recipes have 18th and even 17th century dates. The copies which we have are typescripts prepared for our cousin Millicent Rogers (1904–1963), apparently some time in the 1940s. The oft-married Millicent was a remarkable woman, whose elegant beauty and outstanding taste in clothes established her as one of the fashion trendsetters of her day; she was also a talented designer of jewelry (Dame Edith Sitwell would wear her creations only), and the founder of an important Indian museum bearing her name, located in Taos, New Mexico. Beneath her sophisticated high style, Millicent was a warm and down-to-earth woman, who loved to cook, and the survival of these recipes should be credited to her.

[Editors' note: In gratitude for this benefaction, we commemorate Millicent below, in a drawing from a photograph.]

While many of the recipes in this collection date to the tycoon days of H. H. Rogers, when he would summer with his children and grandchildren on the family estate in Fairhaven, or entertain friends like Mark Twain on his fast steam yacht, the *Kanawha,* others are clearly early and more typical of Yankee life in the towns and villages of this part of New England. Those with the earliest dates are assigned to the Huttlestons, whose original home base was Little Compton, Rhode Island, about 17 miles southwest of Fairhaven; they include recipes for wild game like woodcock, quail, and duck, but also marine

Millicent Rogers, memorable for many reasons including the steps she took to preserve some 18th century chowder recipes which had come down from her forebears. The drawing, by Soun, is after a photograph by Louise Dahl-Wolfe for Harper's Bazaar, *1946: used by courtesy of the Millicent Rogers Museum, Taos, New Mexico.*

fish and shellfish. The fish chowders for which New England is famous are absent from this part of the collection (they make a notable appearance after 1800), but the Huttleston family recipe dated 1710, Little Compton, which is for pickling smelts, is of interest:

Pickled Smelts

24 Smelts
1 Oz. Ground White Pepper
5 Bay Leaves, broken
6 Ground Cloves
3 Blades Mace
1 Small Nutmeg, grated
1 Pt. Red Wine Vinegar
1 Oz. Salt
1 Oz. Powdered Allspice
1 Large Onion, chopped fine

Clean Fish, but leave Roes. Put Fish in earthenware jar in layers. Over each layer, sprinkle all of the above, well mixed, except the Vinegar. Boil Vinegar and when it is cold, pour over. Seal for 2 months.

Smelts could be netted in quantity along the coast during their runs, but cod were handlined by professional fishermen, and formed an integral part of the Yankee diet. We cannot tell if this 1747 recipe for boiled salt codfish was from Little Compton or Fairhaven, but it does show how a simple dish could be made from it, after it had been treated to remove the salt.

Boiled Salt Codfish

On previous day to eating at 4 P.M. put the Fish in a kettle of Cold Water and put it over the Stove so as to keep at about 100 deg. F. all night. At 10 A.M. next morning take it out and scrub it with a hard brush, put it again in a kettle of fresh cold water, to which a Gill of Molasses has been added and place it over the stove again; 20 minutes before serving boil it hard for 18 minutes, drain, cut in large pieces, wrap closely in a napkin and serve with Egg Sauce and Potatoes.

As befits a seaport, there are many chowder recipes from Fairhaven here, most of them not substantially different from those given by Sandra L. Oliver in her 1995 book *Saltwater Foodways*. We give two which are of some interest, for they include wine—a substance absent from almost all fish chowder recipes known to us, probably because of the temperance movement which was so strong in 19th century New England. Here is our favorite from the Millicent Rogers collection; it is one that we have actually made, and very good it is:

Quarter Deck Fish Chowder

Capt. P. W. Gifford 1830

2 Small Haddock or Cod, cut in chunks
1 Gill Stock made from Heads, Tailes and Bones of Fish
1 Pint Port Wine
1 Pint thin Cream or Milk
3/4 Lb. Salt Pork, diced
2 Large Onions, sliced
1 Tablespoon Parsley, chopped fine
4 Tablespoons Cracker Crumbs
2 Cloves
10 Pepper Corns
1/4 Teaspoon Salt
1/4 Teaspoon Paprika
1/2 Bay Leaf
1 Little Pinch Thyme
4 Pilot Biscuits broken

Clean and bone Haddock, put Heads, Tails, Fins, Bones and Skin in a pot with 1 Pt. of Water; reduce 1/2 and strain the Stock. Put Salt Pork in bottom of pot and try out until partly browned; then add the Onions and brown well but do not burn; add the Stock and Seasoning. Mix Port and Cream, and when Stew boils, add them with pieces of Haddock. Clap on the lid and cook 15 minutes. Add the Cracker Crumbs, Parsley and cook slowly for another 10 minutes. Put in Pilot bread, stir around pot once and cook another 5 minutes.

'Pilot Biscuits' are, of course, sea biscuits or hardtack. This is by far the richest chowder we have ever tasted, and is quite alcoholic! It was presumably enjoyed by Peleg and his fellow captains when in home port.

A truly historic chowder recipe appears in Millicent's collection, entitled DANIEL WEBSTER'S CHOWDER, and subtitled *Receipt given by him to my Grandmother Rogers.* Webster was a giant in the public life of the United States during the 19th century; born in New Hampshire in 1782, and dying at his home in Marshfield, Massachusetts, in 1852, he was a great orator, statesman, and outstanding constitutional lawyer. 'My grandmother Rogers' is somewhat of a mystery: it could have been Mary Eldredge Huttleston (1811–1899), the wife of Rowland Rogers, or, more likely, it was Henry Rogers' grandmother Judith Cushman, who married his grandfather Abisha Rogers in 1806.

Daniel Webster's Chowder

6 Lbs. Codfish in chunks
1 1/2 Lbs. Broken Sea Biscuit
5 Tablespoons Salt Pork diced
4 1/2 Tablespoons Sliced Onion
4 Cups Boiled Mashed Potatoes
5 Oysters
1 Teaspoon Thyme
1 Teaspoon Summer Savory
1/2 Bottle Mushroom Catsup
1 Bottle Claret
1/4 Nutmeg, grated
12 Cloves
1/4 Saltspoon Mace
1/4 Saltspoon Allspice
1 Teaspoon Salt
1/4 Teaspoon Black Pepper, freshly ground
1/2 Lemon, sliced

Crisp Pork in iron pot and fry in the Grease the Onions a golden brown. Put on these layers of Fish, Biscuits, Potatoes and Oysters. Sprinkle each layer with everything else. Cover over with 1" Cold Water and simmer slowly for 1 1/2 hours until done.

'Hell Hound Rogers' was always very proud of his New England roots, and if these recipes are considered, he had every right to be. Fish chowders were a unique Yankee contribution to the world's cuisines.

Mae Khloa Hoa Paa

('Head Cook from the Forest')

SU-MEI YU

The pleasant Thai custom of distributing to the mourners, at a funeral, a 'funeral cookbook' has not been much remarked upon outside Thailand, although Alan Davidson published a short piece on the subject in A Kipper with My Tea *(Macmillan, 1988 and North Point Press, 1990).*

The author of this essay made a wonderful find in Bangkok: a copy of a major example of the genre, which because of its age, is also a document of importance in the history of Thai cuisine. She very kindly agreed to allow PPC *to carry a substantial extract from this, with her own highly illuminating introduction. No further introduction is needed, except perhaps to highlight dates pertaining to the two leading ladies in the story. The funeral cookbook was written by Than Phuu Ying Prann at some point in the latter part of the 19th century; she died in 1900. Its publication in the form in which Su-Mei Yu happened upon it took place in 1971 for the funeral of her daughter, Jaou Jomm Phits, who had survived to the age of 95. Details of previous publication of its contents (probably in the 19th century) may eventually come to light but have not yet been established.*

Su-Mei Yu's book Cracking the Coconut: Classic Thai Home Cooking *(Morrow, 2000) became a modern culinary classic from the day when it first appeared in the book shops.*

It is a book with a simple white paper cover. At the top of the title page is a seal of Queen Sirikit followed by 'MAE KHLOA HOA PAA written by Than Phuu Ying [Her Ladyship] Prann Phasakhonvong'. Below, the title page states that: 'Her Royal Highness The Queen grants permission for the printing in honor of the funeral of Jaou Jomm [The Royal Consort] Phits from The Fifth Chakri Dynasty at Wat [temple] Prayuvongsawa on the 21st of February 2514 [1971].'

Wrapped in dusty cellophane paper, the book was tucked between hundreds of used books in one of the many stalls at the Sunday market in Bangkok, Thailand. It is brand new and in excellent condition, although some pages are yellow with age and some have been feasted on by insects. Having stumbled upon this treasure, I bought it for 150 Baht (US $3.00). As I carefully leafed through the book I could not contain my excitement. The pages reveal the odyssey of a remarkable family whose common thread over several generations was food and cooking. With more than 300 recipes, the book seems to be the earliest substantial document for the history of Thai food, dating back to the mid 19th century, and remarkably comprehensive.

It is a tradition in Thailand that when someone famous or wealthy passes away, a memorial or funeral book is published in their honor. The book is a written testimonial containing a biography and letters written by relatives and friends in remembrance of the person. For authors or poets, samples of their writing are included in the book. For renowned cooks, it is their recipes. These books are published as keepsakes for guests attending the cremation.

The book includes several black and white photographs of Jaou Jomm Phits and her family, three of which have been turned into drawings by the artist Soun Vannithone, for publication with this essay. The first, reproduced in a drawing below, was taken when Jaou Jomm Phits was in her forties. Her short cropped hair, a style popular among the women during the 19th century, is not only extremely unbecoming but made women look like men who shared the same hair style. Often, what distinguishes them is their clothing. In the picture, Jaou Jomm Phits wears a blouse, a Thai adaptation of an English Victorian fashion which swept through the Royal Court. She is heavily bejeweled with a diamond collar and several strands of pearls. Draped over her left shoulder is a jewel-encrusted sash covered with rows of ribbons and medals. Jaou Jomm Phits has a faint smile. Her deep-set eyes stare sadly into the distance.

The next photograph, a picture of Jaou Jomm Phits, her father and her younger sister, was taken at the same time. The drawing from this photograph is reproduced below. The father has a jovial face, he is slightly plump with a mop of white hair. He stands behind his two daughters with his arms around them. His affectionate gesture is out of step with traditional Thai etiquette, according to which affection should not be shown in public, and may perhaps have reflected new manners adopted from the West by members of the Royal Court. Jaou Jomm Phits is dressed in the formal Thai costume of a dignitary and is again covered with many strands of necklaces. Her young teenage sister is not married, as signified by her long, curly hair splayed wildly down her back. She is dressed in a foreign dress with a sailor collar and is equally bedecked with jewelry.

The next picture in the collection (not reproduced here) shows an aged Jaou Jomm Phits. She wears a simple white top over a plain sarong and is holding a baby. She still has the same unflattering hairdo. However, her demeanor has changed. She looks more relaxed, at ease and peaceful.

But the photograph which most captured my attention belonged to the mother, Than Phuu Ying Prann, the author of the cook book *Mae Khloa Hoa Paa.* She has a long manly looking face framed by the same short cropped hair cut, severely combed back. She is dressed in a light color lace blouse. Unlike her daughter, her only piece of jewelry is her belt. Draped over her left shoulder is a sash decorated with ribbons and medals. She has the look of someone with tremendous inner strength who has seen and experienced suffering. The drawing for this photograph comes on page 326 just after the end of the extract from the author's book.

The funeral book begins with obituaries written by Jaou Jomm Phits' relatives and friends from the Court. They present the portrait of a woman who was loved and respected for her generosity, kindness, fun-loving and warm personality. We learn that her skills in the Court ceremonies and rituals were unsurpassed. She apparently had a distinctive, musical, high pitched voice. She adored the theater and never missed a performance regardless of how exhausted she might have been. She was fond of animals. During her time, owning a pet was a new and exotic habit brought back from Europe by King Chulalongkhorn. He had dogs imported from England and bred them in the palace grounds. Members of the Court were considered very fortunate to be given one of the King's puppies. Jaou Jomm Phits was one of these people. Her puppy was noted for its devotion to Jaou Jomm Phits. It was trained to fetch sweets from vendors for her and never eat one.

She was a celebrated cook like her mother. There is an episode related by one of her nieces about her recipe for cooking a ham, the latest of many foreign foods introduced to the Royal kitchen by the King. Apparently, Jaou Jomm Phits could cure an imported ham, removing the saltines while retaining its texture and flavor, in a way unmatched by anyone else. When asked how she did it, she revealed only bits and pieces of information. The niece was determined to learn her secret technique. Appointments were made but they were always broken. Forty years later, Jaou Jomm Phits passed away, taking her secret recipe with her.

Jaou Jomm Phits was born on the 21st of August 2413 (1870), on a Saturday at nine o'clock in the evening in the Year of the Horse at her family's estate in Dhonburi (the former capital of Thailand, 1769–1782). She was the second daughter in the family of five children, two sons and three daughters. Both sides of the family descended from royal blood. Her mother's lineage went back to Queen of Rama The Second of Chakri Dynasty (1809–1824). The King was a celebrated poet who wrote a book of poetry praising the Queen's culinary skill.

Jaou Jomm Phits' father was a member of the honored Royal Cadets of King Rama the Fifth of Chakri Dynasty (King Chulalongkhorn, 1868–1910).

From an early age, Jaou Jomm Phits accompanied her father to the Royal Palace and was officially presented to the King as his Consort at the age of 13. She lived in the Royal Palace and served both King Chulalongkhorn and later his son, King Mongkut Klao, for 30 years. She had a rank of Middle Consort, an honor bestowed to Royal consorts who never consummated their relationship with the King. In addition, she was presented a special commendation elevating her to a rank equal with consorts who produced heirs. This was in recognition of her tireless work as an expert in Court protocol, presenter of ritual and ceremonial arrangements as well as her service to other members of the Royal Court. This honor was both rare and highly prestigious.

When her mother passed away, Jaou Jomm Phits asked permission to leave the Court to care for her aged father. She continued to serve the Court but remained on her family's estate until her death at the age of 95.

Mae Khloa Hoa Paa, originally published in five journals, constituted to the best of my knowledge, the first Thai cook book ever written. These journals were printed by Jaou Jomm Phits' mother, Than Phuu Ying Prann, but there is no record of this first printing. My guess, based on such relevant information as I have been able to gather, is that the journals were printed in the latter part of the 19th century, after 1868 but well before Than Phuu Ying Prann's death in 1900. By the way, the original preface to the journals is included in the funeral cook book.

Than Phuu Ying Prann was a brave and remarkable lady. During the conflict between Thailand and France (1883), with soldiers from both countries injured in battles, she established a social service center and infirmary, the first of its kind to care for soldiers regardless of their nationalities. She also raised funds to care for their families. Her writings characterize an educated woman with a strong conviction to perform duties beyond the traditional roles for women. Her book of cookery and social customs relating to food reflects her desire to leave a legacy for future generations.

During her time, the only printing press was in the Royal Palace. It was first set up by King Mongkut, Rama The Fourth of Chakri Dynasty, who was a self-taught scholar (1851–1868). It remained on the Palace grounds after his death and was used by his son, King Chulalongkorn, for his pleasure and official duties. Scholarly journals and historical records were written and printed by male members of the Royal family. Than Phuu Ying Prann's book was perhaps the first to be written and published by a Thai woman.

She named her book *Mae Khloa Hoa Paa,* a tribute to the origins of humankind, in recognition of our emergence from primitive life in the forest to the cultured and refined lifestyle of her day. To her, cookery represented the evolution of the human race from the primitive to the civilized. Cooking techniques and tools all reflected this continuing and progressive change in Thai history and culture.

The original five journals which constitute *Mae Khloa Hoa Paa* took two years to complete. When her daughter's funeral book was printed, long afterwards, this was so far as we know the first compilation of *Mae Khloa Hoa Paa* in its entirety, the earlier publications having been partial.

Than Phuu Ying Prann writes extensively about the difficulty of recording recipes, in particular the measurement of ingredients. During her time, the only measuring tool was the Chinese scale used in commerce. Skills were passed down from one generation to the next. One learned to cook by watching and helping experienced cooks. It was a part of Thai women's education. However, being renowned as a cook, she was frequently asked for recipes which she gave orally. Often a list of ingredients was the only information shared, leaving the recipients to figure out for themselves how to duplicate a dish. When a recipe failed, they would plead with her to be more precise in her directions. Hence, she resorted to a more scientific manner of recording her own techniques. Her measuring tools included not only the Chinese scale, but also household items such as a drinking glass, a porcelain tea cup, a soupspoon, an empty coconut shell or an empty can. Ironically, this range of measures was adopted and used as the standard for recipes until very recently when western measuring tools were introduced to modern Thai kitchens.

Another explanation she gives for her uneasiness in giving the exact measurements has to do with taste. She believed that taste is very individual. Her idea is central to Thai cuisine today. It is one of very few cuisines in the world that encourage the eater to doctor the taste of a dish to his/her preference by providing an array of seasonings with a meal: salt; white pepper powder; fish sauce; dried crushed chiles; fresh chiles preserved in distilled vinegar (or with fish sauce and fresh lime juice); soy sauce; sugar; and crushed peanuts are common at the table. To suggest that the dish should taste certain way is to suggest that other people's tastes are inferior. In her book, she apologizes for giving advice on amounts of seasonings, and goes out of her way to explain that the recipes reflect her preference and that others should feel free to add or subtract according to their choice.

Mae Khloa Hoa Paa chronicles the growing sophistication of Thai cuisine from as far back as the early the 18th century. There is no doubt that this creative achievement could not have come about were it not for the stability and peace Thailand enjoyed. This tranquil environment was the nest in which artistic expression was allowed to flourish. Unlike her neighboring countries who were being colonized by western powers, Thailand was able to maintain her freedom and her rulers spent their time cultivating the arts instead of making war.

This was especially true during the time of Rama The Second who was called 'the Artist'. It was during his reign that cooking became a highly praised skill for one simple reason: the King loved to eat and his wife, the Queen, was an outstanding cook. His patronage encouraged experimentation in the Royal Court. This continued to flourish and reached its zenith during the time of King Rama The Fifth (King Chulalongkhorn), again because the King not only loved to eat but was himself a great cook. He loved to picnic and was famous for arranging elaborate outings both by land and boat in which he planned the menu and often cooked himself. His enthusiasm and pride in his country's cuisine were evident as he traveled overseas on official duties.

In the Royal Court, competitive spirits thrived, resulting in the creative blending and balancing of varieties of fresh herbs and spices with regional vegetables, fruits, fish and meats. This became the signature of Thai cuisine as we know it today. Innovation was enhanced by Thailand's abundance of wild herbs and greens which grew profusely in her tropical climate. Nature's gifts were valued not only for their medicinal properties, but for adding a particular distinctive taste to a dish. One waited patiently for each season to yield its fruits. One savored the harvest. The hundreds of recipes in the book testify to Thai people's appreciation and enjoyment of, and obsession and fascination with, fine cooking.

The book can be read as a history, recording changes in Thai cuisine, in particular how foreign recipes and ingredients influenced Thai food. The Royal Court was where new foreign dishes were first introduced. Among favorites were white bread, macaroni, potatoes, apples, grapes, butter and mayonnaise, which both puzzled and intrigued members of the Court who had never traveled outside their country. Their attempts to duplicate or incorporate these new foods challenged Thai adaptability and ingenuity. The author points out simply: 'we are not people who eat bread, Roti [Indian bread] or Pang Chi [Chinese Fried Bread].' To cook foreign foods, she continues, is a lesson in trial and error and experimentation. It also was an opportunity to enlist foreign friends to lend a helping hand. This in itself was difficult, because the majority of foreigners living in Thailand during that time were men.

Mae Khloa Hoa Paa was written in Royal language interspersed with formal and common Thai language. Many words have since changed or are spelled differently. Words such as 'Paa' for forest was spelled in the ancient way while 'Kao' for rice was written in the ancient way, as well as the modern way. Often, a recipe contains both Royal language and common language to describe the same ingredient. This is particularly true for the word for pig: 'Sugon' formal or 'Moo' common. Names of ingredients change from the beginning of the book, where ancient words no longer in use occur, to the latter part with modern dialect in use today. For example, shrimp paste was once called 'Yeur Kur-uay' which means 'baby shrimps in fermentation'; today, it is called 'Krapi'. Sugar was once called 'Nam Tann Knew' or 'water of fan palm like glass'. Today it is called 'Nam Tann Sann' or 'water of fan palm like sand'.

The author loved poetry. Throughout the book, she often begins a chapter with a poem and always ends with one written by a famous poet including King Rama The Second. Her playfulness was evident in her inclusion of well-known rhymes. This charming Thai custom is a mechanism to help people remember names of dishes, fruits, vegetables and how to select, prepare and cook them through recitation of popular rhymes. She is very precise about the presentation of dishes giving minute details. She even suggests specific serving dishes, especially cut glass from Germany, on which to serve a particular kind of dessert. Her writing style is informal, resembling a conversation between friends. Mid-sentence, however, she suddenly, almost as though she wants to remind herself of a special secret, inserts an instruction on how to balance the right proportions among several ingredients for recipes completely unrelated to the subject at hand.

Than Phuu Ying Prann was expert in Court protocol, ceremonial and ritual presentations and menu planning. She was a fabulous cook. This is most evident in the first chapter of her book. It begins with instructions on how to cook dishes according to Thai tradition for providing alms to Buddhist monks; for special occasions such as the ceremony of initiation into monkhood; or for paying respects to a teacher or to royalty. Each menu is written in great detail with names of dishes, how to serve them on particular kinds of platters or bowls and how to arrange the dishes on the table. When a menu includes a whole cooked pig, especially in a ceremony honoring the teacher, the placement of the pig should be with the head pointing toward the audience and legs carefully tucked under. When presenting dishes to the monk, she specifies which groups of dishes are to be offered to the novice, to the monk and to the Buddha image.

The desserts for a ceremony not only have names such as 'gold nuggets', 'gold threads' and 'ruby', but they are color-coordinated to enhance the aesthetics of the occasion. Services for royalty are in meticulous detail beginning with the preparation of a recipe. Then comes an explanation of how to transfer the food to exactly what kinds of bowls and plates (including the correct and proper decoration on the china). Finally, how to wrap each dish in a cloth and seal with beeswax. Every menu includes 'Namm Prikk Pow' (roasted chile paste) which Than Phuu Ying Prann says is to be placed at the center of the table.

The second chapter is devoted to how to cook rice. It was during her era that a machine was introduced to process rice. It changed both the texture and color of the rice grains. It also affected the cooking process. 'Country rice' (hand-processed rice) was highly prized and preferred. This was the only kind served in the Royal Palace. The grains resembled golden nuggets. When cooked, according to Than Phuu Ying Prann, it tasted better, grains stayed intact and had a marvelous aroma. She praises hand-processed rice done by the farmer, cooked by the farmer's wife and eaten at the farm. This, to her, was the ultimate and perfect rice. She cautions readers to examine machine-processed rice or 'city rice' closely, and suggests readers get to know their rice sellers to avoid buying rice blends consisting of a mixture of both poor and good quality rice.

The recipes in this chapter include:

- how to cook rice for alms
- how to cook rice with 'regular changed' water
- how to cook rice without 'regular changed' water
- how to cook rice with oil
- how to cook rice 'Sudan' style
- how to make rice salad
- how to make rice and noodle dish
- how to make rice gruel
- how to make rice gruel with chicken
- how to make fried rice with ham

The instructions on how to cook rice for alms and how to cook rice with 'regular changed' water are basically the same, the only difference being a larger quantity of rice used for alms. 'Regular changed water', or the traditional way of cooking rice, consists of adding water all the way to the top of the pot. Until metal pots were introduced, terracotta pots were used. The common heat source was a charcoal brazier. Rice was brought to a vigorous boil until the grains softened. The pot was removed from the hot charcoal and placed on top of a 'Saweng' (a circular twine 'sling' the size of the pot with two semi-circle loops on each side; see below). The semi-circle loops were placed across the top to secure the lid and pot. While holding onto the loops at opposite ends, the pot

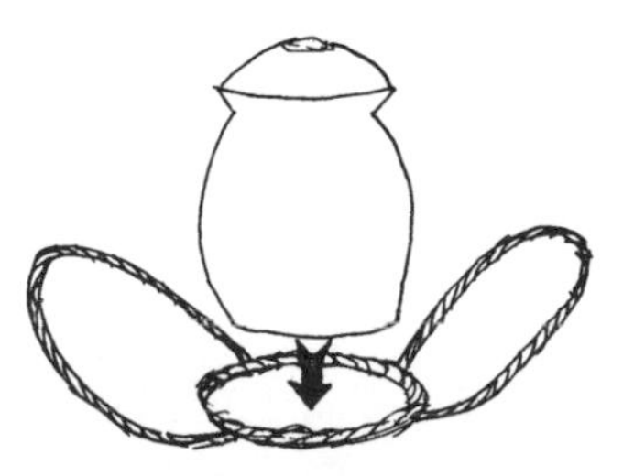

The author's sketch of a 'Saweng', showing how the sling holds the cooking pot.

was turned sideways to drain away the water. The rice was put back on the fire and cooked slowly. Once again, the 'Saweng' was used to secure the pot and lid together while the rice grains were shaken and loosened.

The recipe on how to cook rice without changing water is the technique described by the author as Canton style rice. It is the method we use today to boil-steam rice.

Here is Than Phuu Ying Prann's recipe on how to cook rice for alms.

How to Cook Rice for Alms

Ingredients

Long grain rice, five portions, enough for a pot (nowadays, there are different kinds of foreign imported pots made with yellow metal, red metal, silver or lightweight aluminum all over the market. You will have to learn how to pick the best one).

Technique

Put rice in the pot and fill it with water. Wash the rice two to three times. Pour in clean water up to the neck of the pot. Make certain it is not overflowing, to leave room for a lid. Cover with a lid.

Put the pot on top of the charcoal stove. Make certain the fire is very hot for the rice to boil very hard and fierce. Open the lid.

Use a wooden spoon to stir and separate the grains. Inspect the grains to be sure that the grains are not hard. If they are, stir, cover the pot and continue to cook.

Uncover the pot to check the grains. When they are soft, remove the pot from the fire.

Put the pot on a Saweng. Secure both sides very tight. Drain out the water.

Lower the heat from the charcoal. Put the pot back on the stove and use very weak fire. Be careful do not burn the rice.

Move the pot around several times and cook until the rice is dried. Remove and transfer to the Saweng. Swing the pot back and forth to scatter the rice about. Cover and put back on the stove. Move the pot around several times to dry it completely.

Remove and use for 'making alms'.

Caution: When you first learn how to cook rice, you need to be careful and pay attention. Do not let water dry too soon or stir too hard. This will make rice grains swell up too much. Rice will be too wet. This will ruin the taste. Do not stir too vigorously. This will break up the rice grains. Most of all be patient, do not daydream, the rice will burn.

Thirty-three chapters follow with the last, the thirty-fourth chapter, devoted to basic curry paste recipes. Each chapter has the same format, beginning with a traditional Thai menu of five 'Kubb Kao' (dishes to accompany rice), two desserts (one liquid and one dry) and two snacks (one liquid and one dry). 'Kubb Kao' consists of one spicy soup or curry, one mild soup, a salad, a condiment and a dipping sauce. A poem ends each chapter.

I have translated the list of 'Kubb Kao' from the first chapter, plus the recipes for the five items listed. These are dishes believed by Thai people to help one consume rice, considered the most nutritious part of the meal. Since eating rice alone is bland and tasteless, a bit of 'Kubb Kao' is spooned on top for flavor. Consequently, a dish of 'Kubb Kao' not only goes a long way, it is also highly seasoned.

I have not gone on to translate the recipes from the first chapter for two desserts and two snacks. However, readers may be interested to know what these are. The liquid dessert is 'Floating Lotus' made with rice flour; and the dry one is Kanum Koh, made with beans. The liquid snack is Indian Namya, boiled chicken with red noodles; and the dry one is Kanum 'Hough Pakk Gaud Ma-leang' (which means 'cabbage head reborn').

My translation is exactly the way the recipes are written in Thai, except that the Thai language does not include punctuation and I have added a little. Thus, the translation may seem odd. I do it on purpose to give a flavor for the language. Each recipe begins with my own observations to bring to light the historical changes in Thai cuisine, especially ingredients no longer used in modern Thai cookery.

List of 'Kubb Kao' (dishes to accompany rice)

1. Kaeng Som (Orange Soup) with fresh shrimp and pickled vegetables

2. Kaeng Ba Shaw (Minced Pork Soup) with cow meat (beef) and coconut cream

3. Chinese Water Chestnut Salad

4. Condiment—La Tieng ('making a bed')

5. Dipping sauce—Namm Prikk (chile sauce) Nakorn Bann ('in the style of the state or monarchy')

Kaeng Som (orange soup)
with fresh baby shrimp and pickled vegetables

Kaeng Som is one of the most basic, traditional and authentic Thai dishes. It is named Orange Soup because of the color. The ingredients for the soup depend on seasonal and regional vegetables. There are slight variations on the paste from different regions. Usually, it includes fish, shrimp or other shellfish. Sometimes, it is just soup with different vegetables. But the major characteristic of Kaeng Som is always the same. It is sweet-sour-spicy and pungent. This particular recipe uses wild greens which are seldom used today. They are all virtually unknown to modern Thai people (although they can be found in the excellent book *Plants from the Markets of Thailand* by Christiane Jacquat, 1990, Editions Duang Kamol, Bangkok). 'Phak' means vegetable. 'Phak Namm' (nettle, *Lasia heterophylla*) is difficult to clean because of the sharp needles on the stems. It was believed to cure earache. The leaves, pounded with water, were also used to cure feverish sunburned skin. 'Phak Sieo' (*Bauhinia* sp) is a wild herb used to treat dysentery. This recipe called shrimp paste ('Krapi') by its old name 'Yerh Kur-uay'.

INGREDIENTS AND THE WAY TO COOK:

10 fresh baby shrimps. Rinse with water 2–3 times. Chop off the long 'mustaches' and slit it down the center. Remove the black vein. Peel the shell from the flesh. Make small slits all over the flesh. Wash in water.
'Phak Namm'; pickled vegetables; mustard greens; 'Phak Sieo'. Slice or pull into small clumps to a reasonable amount.
Three large dried red chiles. Remove seeds and membranes. Wash in water 2–3 times. Remove as much water as you can.
Sliced garlic, 1 teaspoon.
Sliced shallot, 1 dessertspoon—pile high in a heap.
1/3 teaspoon shrimp paste—you do not have to use this since some people don't like the taste.
1/2 teaspoon salt—put in the mortar and grind.
Tamarind paste—made into thick paste 1 1/2 sugar spoons.
Palm sugar—2 sugar spoons.
Fish sauce—3 soupspoons.
Boiling water—2 teacups.

Dissolve the chile paste which has been pounded with boiling water and bring it to boil. Add the vegetables. Add fish sauce, sugar, tamarind paste. Taste. Some tamarind paste may be very sour. When you are satisfied with the taste, add shrimps. As soon as shrimps are cooked, remove the pot from heat. Do not leave it long before serving. Shrimps which are overcooked will be hard and destroy the taste.

Kaeng Ba Shaw (minced pork soup) with cow meat and coconut cream

The word Kaeng is originally a Mon word. (Mon are the ancestors of Lao, Khmer and Burmese people.) It means to boil. Before 1800, Thai people used terracotta pots and shallow pans. The cooking techniques consisted of boiling, simmering, steaming and dry roasting. Deep-frying was not introduced until the time of King Chulalongkhorn (1868–1910), who was given a metal wok by a Chinese. Consequently, Kaeng dominated ancient Thai dishes. This particular dish traditionally used minced pork. Cows were never slaughtered. When an animal was injured, it was killed and used in a variety of dishes. Beef was special and rare.

Ingredients and the way to cook:

1/4 kilo cow meat. Wash clean. Slice and mince until fine.
Garlic, Thai peppercorn, salt, coriander root and grind into fine paste. Mix with meat and make into meat balls.
Grate coconut 1/2 kilo. Make thick coconut cream and put in a separate container 1 teacup. The rest mix with water and make into coconut milk 2 teacups.
Good quality pumpkin flesh. Remove all the hard peel. Slice into 1/2 inch squares.
3 Red 'Prikk Youk' (New Mexico or Anaheim chiles). Slit in the centre and remove seeds and membranes and slice into chunks. Rinse with water and remove all the water.
Coriander, chop coarsely.
Good quality fish sauce.

Use the thin coconut milk. Bring it to boil. Add pumpkin chunks. When cooked, add meat balls. Add Prikk Youk and good quality fish sauce. Taste to see if it is salty, if not, add more salt. Add the coconut cream. When it boils, add coriander leaves.

Chinese Water Chestnut Salad

In the past, fish sauce was made by the family for their own use. Some became known for their product and people begged to buy from them. Throughout the book, recipes define good quality fish sauce as clear and odorless. Good fish sauce is made from fresh baby fish and has a 'sea' aroma.

At the end of this recipe, the author encourages the reader to carve water chestnuts into different shapes, while at the beginning, she instructs to slice them very thin. During the reign of King Chulalongkhorn, the art of vegetable carving was all the rage in the Royal Court. Water chestnuts, jicama and baby ginger were among favorites to be carved into flowers, leaves and animals for salads, soup and pickling.

Ingredients and the way to cook:

Water chestnuts, wash clean, peel and slice into thin slices. You can also use jicama, peel and slice into long thin slices.
One crab, boil and extract the meat.
Three fresh shrimps, wash and boil, slice into long thin slices.
Pork, boil and slice into long thin slices, 3 soupspoons.
Pork skin, boil until cooked and shredded, 3 soupspoons.
Shallot 7 cloves, peel and slice very thin—sauté until golden.
Palm sugar, 1 soupspoon.
Very good quality fish sauce, 1 1/2 tablespoons, dissolve with palm sugar.
Tamarind, very thick paste, 1 sugar spoon, mix with sugar and cook over fire until thickened.
Peanuts, roasted and chopped, 2 soupspoons.

Mix all the ingredients (except water chestnuts), stir-fry it together and taste. Add the water chestnuts. Mix well and put on a plate. Make it beautiful. You can carve the water chestnuts to look like flowers, leaves, stars or any shapes you like. Garnish with minced fresh red chiles and cilantro.

Condiment: La Tieng ('making a bed')

During King Chulalongkhorn's trip to France (1897), his correspondence with the Queen was full of observations on French cooking. He wrote of eating an omelette while traveling on a train. Later, in his collection of recipes, omelette was one of his favorites filled with meat with Thai seasonings. La Tieng is a distinctly Thai presentation of the French omelette.

Ingredients and the way to cook:

5 fresh and beautiful baby shrimps, wash, peel and remove the guts. Chop and mince shrimp.
Thai peppercorn, garlic, salt, coriander roots. Chop and pound together it becomes a paste.
Fresh red chiles, slice and remove the seeds. Chop until fine. Soak in water and drain in fine woven bamboo basket until all the water is extracted.
Coriander, pick out individual leaves.
Two duck eggs, wash clean. Crack and beat them together.

Stir-fry the paste with lard and add the shrimp. When shrimp is cooked, add good quality fish sauce. The taste should be slightly salty. Add more lard to the pan. When it is hot, put your hand in the egg mixture and fan it over the hot pan, this way and that way, until the pan is covered with lace in one sheet. Put the cooked egg lace on a banana leaf. Place the red chile on top of egg lace. Put coriander leaf on top of red chile. Spoon the shrimp about the right portion. Fold into a square about a bite size. Put on serving plate beautifully.

Dipping sauce: Namm Prikk (chile sauce) Nakorn Bann (meaning 'in the style of the state or monarchy')

This is a fabulous chile sauce made with several kinds of citrus such as Calamondin (*Citrus mitis*) and sour orange as well as slightly sour and bitter tasting fruits creating a citrus flavor and sour taste to counteract the spiciness of chile peppers. According to my Thai friend, Khun Pao, this was one of King Chulalongkhorn's favorite chile sauces and when he traveled, especially overseas, it went with him. There are several variations. Khun Pao makes this chile sauce for her best friend's birthday every year. She uses all these exotic ingredients, picked from her parents' garden, it being nearly impossible to find them today in the market. 'Ma Enk' (*Solanum stramonifolium*) is a hairy globose shaped fruit which looks somewhat like a round loquat. 'Rah Gum' (*Sallacca* sp) is an elongated pear shaped fruit which grows in a cluster. When ripe, the outer skin turns deep red. Its thorny, leather-like skin is hard. The fruit is white, firm and pulpy at the same time. The aroma is musty. It is sweet and sour. 'Ma Done' (*Garcinia schomburgkinia*) is an oblong shaped fruit resembling a large olive. It is pale green and tastes crispy and sour. 'Som Men' (bitter orange) was used in the past instead of lime. 'Som Sa' (*calamondin,* see above) was used in the same way as 'Som Men'. Three-color chile (chile from 'Suan Nork') is a very aromatic and spicy chile. It has pretty much disappeared from Thai cooking today.

Ingredients and the way to cook:

Dried shrimp powder 1 soupspoon.
Shrimp paste 1 sugar spoon, wrap in banana leaf and grill until it is cooked.
'Prikk Kee Noo' (Bird Seed chiles), remove the stems and wash clean, the amount is up to you.
7 Three-color chiles OR chiles from Suan Nork, wash clean.
5 Ma Enk—use raw and ripe ones.
Remove all the hair, wash clean and shred.
2 Rah Gum, peel and separate the petals and shred.
3 Ma Done, shred.

1 Som Men, slice along the fruit into long thin strands, then slice across into tiny squares.
1/2 fruit of Som Sa, slice same way as Som Men.

Slice lime into three or four slices [*the author never mentioned it in the list of ingredients, it suddenly appears in the instructions*]. If you have mango, raw and unripe star fruit, fresh tamarind, you can use a bit of everything.

Mix the ingredients together. Mix good quality fish sauce, palm sugar to your taste. Eat with deep-fried fish such as 'Pla Too' [Rastrelliger *sp, mackerel*] or grilled catfish. Vegetables should include eggplant, cucumber, tops of 'Phakk Bong' [*sometimes called swamp spinach, water spinach, water morning glory,* Ipomoea aquatica], young water mimosa [*which is Phakk krachet,* Neptunia oleracea]. Arrange beautifully.

This recipe belongs to his honor, Phra Ya [Lord] Poo Ra Pun.

Than Phuu Ying Prann, the author of the funeral cookbook from which the above extracts are taken. The drawing by the Lao artist Soun Vannithone is from a photograph taken in her old age; see page 314.

Jane Grigson: A Celebration in Three Parts

The first part is an introduction to a bibliography of Jane Grigson's books contributed by the compilers Isobel Holland, Lynette Hunter and Geraldine Stoneham, working from Yorkshire. (Professor Lynette Hunter belongs to the University of Leeds and was deeply involved, as coordinator, in the bibliographies of cookery books and household books of the 18th and late 19th century published by Prospect Books in the 1980s.) The second is a tribute by Alan Davidson which was originally published in the Independent. *The third is a review of* Jane Grigson's Fruit Book *by Jane Davidson, who had a general responsibility for Book Reviews in* PPC *for its first 21 years.*

An Introduction to a Bibliography of Jane Grigson's Books

from Isobel Holland, Lynette Hunter, Geraldine Stoneham

We took up compiling this bibliography because we wished to pay a tribute to the memory of Jane Grigson, whose work we so much admire. Throughout the 1970s and 1980s she was a familiar figure to an extensive public—writing in *The Observer,* producing books of which many became classics, appearing in television series, acting as adviser and consultant and campaigner (for better food and better cooking), and giving her support to a whole new generation of writers on food and cookery. Yet, for us, the sheer breadth and substance of her activity—the immense generosity of this woman who was able to collaborate on so many projects and work with so many people—only emerged fully when we set out on the bibliographic trail.

What follows takes up many pages of *PPC* and may look like a comprehensive catalogue of Jane Grigson's writings. But we should explain that it deals only with her books; only with the British editions of these; and only with some of their impressions (very numerous, especially in paperback). What we have tried to do is to describe all the books on food or cookery of which she was sole author, and a few others to which she made a really substantial contribution, whether as co-author or as contributing editor. A number of other books, including translations, collaborations with Geoffrey Grigson, and works for which she provided forewords and introductions, are listed briefly at the end of the bibliography.

If readers are able to supply additional information or to correct anything we have not got right, this will be very welcome. We regard the present effort as a first one, which may well reappear in an enlarged and corrected version later on.

When we started gathering information about these books, we naively assumed that there would not be many problems getting hold of them. However, surprisingly few public libraries, including the copyright libraries, have good collections; none are comprehensive. On asking at one national lending library why so few of the books were available, the reply came back that they were frequently borrowed and often 'nicked'. No one was stealing Plato.

Not only this, those people who had bought the books when they came out, were certainly not letting them go: secondhand bookshops had copies of books by most other food writers but not by Jane Grigson.

On the way we discovered interesting things about Penguin imprints since 1986 which are described here out of interest but also as a help in reading the bibliography: since 1986, instead of resetting the title-page verso of a reprinted text to say what impression it is, Penguin includes a line of digits 1 3 5 7 9 10 8 6 4 2 centered on the line below the edition information. Each time they produce an impression they simply knock off the lowest number, the resulting lowest number is that of the current impression. But no date is given.

Should you be curious, the International Standard Book Numbering Agency has a set of guidelines concerning the change of an ISBN number for a book which is in fact identical to an earlier edition: the most frequent change of ISBN occurs when a book moves to a different publisher, or when it enters a new series as several of Jane Grigson's books did when they went into the Penguin Cookery Library Series. And for those fascinated by the arcane world of bibliography, an apparently completely new catalogue descriptor has had to be invented for a Grigson book: 'sd' to describe the seeds attached to the backs of her books *Spinach* and *Carrots*.

The emergence of such intriguing minutiae is of course just an incidental feature of a bibliographical survey such as the present one, whose main purpose must be to illuminate the development of the author's work over the years, and to provide the scaffolding on which proper critical appraisals can be erected. Yet such surveys illuminate other things too: in this instance, the evolution in the design and production of cookery books in Britain over a span of nearly 25 years. Our choice of information to provide has been made with such considerations in mind.

There is more, much more, to the subject of food and cookery than just recipes. It is true that the writing of recipes is an art, of which Jane Grigson was a brilliantly clear practitioner; but she also explored, deeply and consistently, many of the wilder social and historical implications in her writing. Her books glow with a warm awareness of history, of the myriad tangled skeins of connection which link a kitchen of today with kitchens of the past, of the gradual evolution of recipes and customs, of how some things have got better and others, many others, worse. Her introductions comment pointedly on the poor quality of cookery teaching in England; and she deplores the effects on the quality of food of some manufacturers' undue concentration on profit and of insensitive government regulations. She emphasizes the need to husband our own agricultural heritage and to understand that of others. She was very serious about all these things. But her homilies are never oppressive; her readers are always aware of her enthusiasm, always charmed by the originality of her presentation and by her wit.

Jane Grigson: A Tribute — from Alan Davidson

Jane Grigson left to the English-speaking world a legacy of fine writing on food and cookery for which no exact parallel exists. The uniqueness of her contribution was buttressed from two sides.

On the one hand, her keen intellect, her education (including Newnham College, Cambridge), her early experience as a prize-winning translator from Italian, and her supremely happy and devoted partnership and marriage with the poet Geoffrey Grigson, combined to ensure the literary quality of all she wrote. (When one thinks of how much this couple had read between them, the phrase 'widely read' seems quite inadequate.)

On the other hand, her amiable, robust and unpretentious personality, and the fact that she so clearly derived great enjoyment from exercising her gifts for cookery, guaranteed a really comfortable intimacy with her readers: not only the numerous devotees of the cookery pages which she contributed to the *Observer* Magazine for the last 21 years, but also the readers of her 11 books. In all, this must amount to millions of people.

She won to herself this wide audience because she was above all a friendly writer, equipped by both frame of mind and style of writing to communicate easily with them.

However much more she knew about this or that than do the rest of us, she never seemed to be talking down to anyone. On the contrary, she is a most companionable presence in the kitchen; often catching the imagination with a deftly chosen fragment of history or poetry, but never failing to explain the 'why' as well as the 'how' of cookery. How often have I heard people declare that her recipes are not just a pleasure to read—they always 'work'!

It was in 1967 that her first book, plainly but informatively entitled *Charcuterie and French Pork Cookery,* was published by Michael Joseph. In the introduction she remarked that 'Nobody can produce a cookery book these days without a deep appreciation of Elizabeth David's work.' And it was Elizabeth David who proposed her to the *Observer,* where she began writing in the following year. Jane Grigson never ceased to draw inspiration from and pay tribute to Elizabeth David; but from the beginning she was steaming ahead under her own bright flag.

The introduction to the *charcuterie* book was subscribed: 'Broad Town and Trôo, 1966.' Broad Town is in Wiltshire, where Geoffrey's main roots were. Trôo is the French village to which she and he repaired once or twice a year, with their daughter Sophie, to live in what they described as a cave (and which basically was a cave, though with additions), until Geoffrey's death in 1985. Again, twin buttresses. Two country scenes, each rich in material for both cook and poet. A foot on both sides of the Channel.

Her next book (*Good Things,* 1971, a favourite of mine), and many of the subsequent books were based on, or partly reflected, her writing for the *Observer.* All provide delightful reading, but three, to my mind, stand out as the most important: *English Food* (1974), *Jane Grigson's Vegetable Book* (1978) and *Jane Grigson's Fruit Book* (1982). The latter two subjects gave full scope to her combination of literary skill, learning lightly worn, and practical, meticulous, recipe-writing.

Each book is the classic work in its field. When I was choosing, recently, items for an anthology of good writing on food and cookery, I reread both and was perplexed how to select, as I had to do, just two pearls from such long strings of perfectly composed essays. There could only be two because the ration was three and I was determined to include her offbeat essay on 'Caul Fat', delivered at one of the Oxford Symposia on Food History. She was generous, completely generous, towards other people, and equally so in giving time and effort to causes in which she believed, including the study of food history. However, the cause which she supported with maximum favour was encouragement to producers—often very small producers—of first-class food. She never forgot that the good cook needs good materials; and I am sure that her insistence on this is one thing by which she would wish to be remembered.

Rightly so. But causes come and causes go (sometimes because they have been won). What lasts is brilliantly good writing about the enduring and mainstream aspects of cookery; and limpidly clear recipes which later generations can use with as much ease and confidence as the three now with us. If this yardstick is used, the number of authors who measure up to it 50 or 100 or 150 years later becomes quite small. From the last century we have, perhaps, only one such left: Eliza Acton. For this century, marked by a great upsurge of writing on cookery, there will be more 'survivors'. It is clear that Jane Grigson will be eminent among them.

The last years of her life were clouded by Geoffrey's death and then, not long after her usual vitality and positive outlook had begun to reassert themselves, by the onset of cancer. She withstood the sore trials of the uncertainty, and of the treatment, which this entailed with a gallant spirit and a miraculously tenacious sense of humour. Happily, there came a period of remission and for the first part of this year, until last weekend, the sun seemed to be shining upon her again and she was happily making plans for at least the immediate future. She had a great capacity for happiness; and to see her daughter Sophie making her own incisive and distinctive way as a writer on cookery was one great source of joy to her.

'If I fall off the perch . . .' she said to my wife and myself on one occasion last year, and proceeded with characteristic equanimity to discuss various consequences. Well, she fell off the perch this week; and suddenly it is even more apparent than before what a splendid and commanding perch was hers, and how hard it is to imagine anyone else upon it.

Jane Grigson's Fruit Book **reviewed by Jane Davidson**

Brilliant . . .

A lovely cover evoking thoughts of idyllic summer ensures that the *Fruit Book* is rapidly picked up. Its contents ensure that it is not rapidly put down, although a normally courteous friend may succeed in snatching it away 'just to have a quick look'. All who have seen it at our house seem to find that a short peek is enough to send them off to the bookshop to acquire a personal copy.

Jane Grigson's style seems to get better and better. In her introduction she says that her feelings about fruit have made this book more fun to write than any of her others, and I think it is probably more fun to read also. This is basically a scholarly and encyclopaedic treatment of fruit, but its presentation is knowledgeable rather than omniscient and entertaining rather than solemn. Anecdotes, history, poetry and personal appreciation are all here as well as practical suggestions on how to use both the familiar and the less so.

Although the book is divided into 46 sections, well over that number of fruits are treated; for example the grapefruit, pomelo, ugli, citron come in one group, while in another the grape stands alone (or rather, in a bunch). And then a few fruits are mentioned, only to be dismissed regretfully by the author because she has been unable to taste them for herself. One such is the malodorous durian from South-East Asia.

But let me not suggest that this is a frighteningly esoteric book. Opening it at random (page 121), one finds this recipe:

Cherry Cream Tarts

For 24 little tarts, made with sweet shortcrust or oatmeal pastry, you will need:

1 kg (2 lb) large black cherries of acid or Duke varieties
1 egg white
200 ml (7 fl oz/ 3/4 cup) soured cream
2 eggs
1 egg yolks
125 g (4 oz/1/2 cup) caster sugar

Stone the cherries. Beat egg white to break it up a little and brush it over the pastry cases (this diminishes the risk of sogginess). Put the cherries into the pastry cases, closely together. Mix any cherry juice with the cream and remaining ingredients. Pour over the cherries, being careful not to fill the pastry brimful, as the filling will rise.

Bake at gas 7, 220°C (425°F) for 15 minutes. Check and leave a little longer until the filling is puffed up and nicely browned. The filling will collapse unless you serve the tarts straight from the oven. If you cannot do this, don't worry; many people will agree with me that such things are best eaten warm anyway, rather than hot. Compared with this, the puff doesn't matter.

Note You can use one large pastry case. If you do, scatter the base, after brushing with egg white, with a layer of crumbs—macaroons, boudoir biscuits, plain cake, bread, chopped raw pastry can all be used. The crumbs can be flavoured with cardamom seeds.

And do not be deceived into thinking that the recipes all relate to fruit as dessert. Fruit with meat, fruit with fish, fruit liqueurs, fruit in salads, jams, drinks, chutneys, candied fruit; all this is here. Last year our neighbour came to ask how to make dried apple rings at home. Now I could tell him exactly how to set about it.

An added dividend for me is the section concerning pastry in the useful appendix. Jane Grigson appears to have ESP and to have observed my pastry-making bloomers, which, being self taught, I had not been able to identify for myself. Her advice on how to improve matters may help others like me. Fruit pies, here we come, if not with complete confidence, at least with renewed hope.

The print is good, the layout clear, the line drawings attractive. Brilliant. In Michelin language, *four* stars and *six* place settings.

Quizzing Glasse

OR *Hannah Scrutinized*

JENNIFER STEAD

Why was *The Art of Cookery Made Plain and Easy* by Hannah Glasse the most successful English cookery book in the second half of the 18th century, going into no fewer than 17 editions between 1747 and 1803? What exactly was it that made Hannah Glasse stand out among her many rival cooks? I have been trying to answer the question by detailed study of the book itself.

Hannah Glasse certainly had a novel aim:

> I believe I have attempted a Branch of Cookery which Nobody has yet thought worth their while to write upon: But as I have both seen, and found by Experience that the Generality of Servants are greatly wanting in that Point, therefore I have taken upon me to instruct them in the best Manner I am capable; and I dare say, that every Servant who can but read will be capable of making a tolerable good Cook, and those who have the least Notion of Cookery can't miss of being very good ones.

Her aim is not only to improve the servant, and thereby to save the ladies a great deal of trouble, but also to cut down on extravagance, a sin particularly imputed to the fashionable French cooks, whom she (along with most other cookery book writers of her time) accuses of cheating their English employers by the over-lavish use of expensive ingredients: "So much is the blind Folly of this Age, and they would rather be impos'd on by a *French* Booby, than give Encouragement to a good *English* Cook!'

Did she succeed in her aims to instruct the ignorant and reduce expense? Does the reason for the book's phenomenal polarity lie only there; or did she introduce further originality in, say, the novelty of her recipes?

The shameless stealing of recipes, usually verbatim, by cookery writers throughout the 17th and 18th centuries (and earlier) was widespread,[1] and it is possible to open almost any book at any page and immediately recognize old friends. Hannah Glasse, however, does not give this familiar impression, and so I was intrigued by a remark of Dr Johnson, who, 50 years after its first appearance, averred that Hannah Glasse's book was the best, even though 'the greatest part of such a book is made by transcription'.[2] Such a remark had been made earlier by Ann Cook, a rival cookery book writer who vilified Hannah Glasse from personal animosity, and who wrote, as sour as verjuice, 'She steals from ev'ry Author'.[3]

Hannah Glasse's book must surely be more than mere transcription. I determined to try to find out whether she had indeed filched recipes; if so, how many and from what sources; and exactly where her originality lay. This was to attempt an exercise which probably no one else has had the folly, opportunity or stamina to sustain over several months.

Being fortunate enough to live within two miles of one of the best historical cookery book collections in the world, the John F. Preston and the Blanche L. Leigh Collections in the Brotherton Library, Leeds University, was a good start (indeed, this sort of exercise can't be done with tomes in far-flung libraries) and the Special Collections Librarian Mr P. S. Morrish and his assistant Mrs J. Cooksey helpfully kept my 19 or more volumes where I could have instant access to them throughout the whole period.

Confining myself to the first edition of Hannah Glasse (1747) for simplicity, I decided to compare her with all the 18th century volumes she could possibly have consulted. My heart sank, since there were at least 32 (though not all in the Leeds collections).[4] Eventually I chose the following 12: F. Massialot: *The Court and Country Cook:* translated into English, 1702; Patrick Lamb: *Royal Cookery; or, the Complete Court-Cook:* 1716 and 1726; Henry Howard: *England's Newest Way in All Sorts of Cookery,* 4th ed'n, 1717; Robert Smith: *Court Cookery,* 2nd ed'n, 1725; John Nott: *The Cook's and Confectioner's Dictionary,* 1726; Charles Carter: *The Compleat City and Country Cook,* 1732; Mary Eales: *The Compleat Confectioner,* 1733; John Middleton: *Five Hundred New Recipes in Cookery,* 1734; Vincent La Chapelle: *The Modern Cook,* vols 1 to 3, 2nd ed'n, 1736; Richard Bradley: *The Country Housewife and Lady's Director,* ed'n of 1736; Eliza Smith: *The Compleat Housewife,* 10th ed'n, 1741; Mary Kettilby: *A Collection of above Three Hundred Receipts,* 6th ed'n, 1746.

The question was, where to begin? I decided to ease myself into the work gradually, that is with the smallest and thinnest book, which happened to be Mrs Eales, and make my way finally to the biggest and fattest, which were Massialot, La Chapelle and John Nott. Accordingly, I began on Mrs Eales, page one, and immediately hit a problem. Hannah Glasse (1st ed'n) had no index, and her table of contents is so higgledy-piggledy in spite of her rough marshalling into chapters, that I saw there was nothing for it but to make my own index. This was to save an enormous amount of frustrated page-turning and consequent wear and tear on fragile volumes. [Editor's note: the index composed by Jennifer Stead figures in the Prospect Books reprint of Hannah Glasse's book, Devon, 1995.] Another difficulty was trying to keep five or six of these books all open at once at, say, 'Pickled Barberries'; many would not admit of being opened flat out and so even with the books in front of one, one needed either six hands or a photographic memory.

At a snail's pace, I compared every recipe in Mrs Eales with a corresponding one in Hannah Glasse, but with no positive results—and did the same with Henry Howard, finding at last 27 corresponding recipes. This was more encouraging. The recipes she had copied verbatim I marked with a tick √ in my tables, and the ones that appeared very slightly different with a crossed tick √. Eliza Smith was even better, where I found no less than 86 recipes, borrowed almost word for word by Hannah Glasse. However, progress was painfully slow and laboured; the difficulty lay, not so much in tracing recipes with idiosyncratic titles like 'Portuguese Rabbits', but in the mass of almost anonymous ones like 'Mutton Another Way' or 'A Good Cake'. There were moments when one becomes highly diverted by a piece of 18th century oatmeal stuck to the page, or overcome with compassion for a long-dead woodworm, whose bumbling labyrinthine tunnelings through the pages had so closely resembled mine.

It was at this point that C. Anne Wilson (author of the authoritative *Food and Drink in Britain*) said to me 'Did you know Hannah Glasse borrowed extensively from *The Whole Duty of a Woman*?' I did not. I am most grateful to Miss Wilson for pointing me in the right direction, for here indeed, was the true lens which was to throw a concentrated light onto Hannah Glasse's way of working and originality.

Hannah Glasse Compared with The Whole Duty of a Woman: *Her Innovations as a Writer*

I soon found that *The Whole Duty of a Woman* was an excellent point of reference since it was the latest, most up-to-date, and largest compendium of recipes pirated practically word for word from other books, including taking French leave with La Chapelle. (And as such, it gives me no confidence whatever that the compiler ever cooked these recipes.) *The Whole Duty of a Woman* lifts as many as ten or more recipes verbatim and in the same order from other writers, especially La Chapelle. However, it was soon apparent that Hannah Glasse had done nearly the same thing with *The Whole Duty of a Woman;* as many as 17 consecutive recipes in the meat section are the same, and appear in the same order. The same, but with an important difference, as explained below. Incidentally, in most instances it is clear that Hannah Glasse has borrowed from *The Whole Duty of a Woman* and not from *Whole Duty*'s original, for example Carter or La Chapelle, since Hannah Glasse will copy a stylistic quirk or minor alteration added by *Whole Duty.* (From now on I shall abbreviate *The Whole Duty of a Woman* to *Whole Duty*.)

Once *Whole Duty* was put next to Hannah Glasse, the latter came immediately into focus, because here at last was a substantial body of her source material with which to compare her finished product. The comparison showed much identity, but also revealed interesting differences. Take, for instance, these three bits of recipes:

A pig in jelly

Whole Duty 331 from Carter 49:

stove it gently two Hours, let stand till cold, and send it up in its Jelly.

Hannah Glasse 32:

stove it, or do it over a slow Fire two Hours, then take it up, lay the Pig into the Dish you intend it for, then strain the Liquor, and when the Jelly is cold, skim off the Fat, and leave the Settling at Bottom; warm the Jelly again, and pour over the Pig, and then serve it up cold in the Jelly.

Fritters Royal

Whole Duty 488 from Howard 71 (also Middleton and Nott):

Take a Pint of Sack, make Posset with new Milk . . .

Hannah Glasse 81:

Take Quart of new Milk, put it into a Skellet or Sauce-pan, and as the Milk boils up, pour in a Pint of Sack. Let it boil up, then take it off, and let it stand five or six Minutes, then skim off all the curd, and put it into a Bason . . .

To make a very fine sweet lamb or veal pye

Whole Duty 494 from E. Smith 133:

Make the Caudle of White Wine, Juice of Lemon and Sugar, thicken it up with the Yolks of two or three Eggs, and a bit of Butter . . .

Hannah Glasse 70:

Have ready against it comes out of the Oven a Caudle made thus: Take a Pint of White Wine, and mix in the Yolks of three Eggs, stir it well together over the Fire, one way all the time till it is thick; then take it off, stir in Sugar enough to sweeten it, and squeeze in the juice of a Lemon . . .

It will be seen at once that *Whole Duty*'s recipes are for experienced cooks who can fill out the meagre instructions, and that Hannah Glasse is indeed rendering them 'plain and easy', and thus fulfilling her claim 'to instruct the lower sort.' She seems to have a constant mental picture both of the ignorance of her pupils, and of the limitations of ordinary larders and kitchens, as further detailed comparison soon made clear, for example, she adds at the end of Chestnut Pudding 109/467 (the first number refers to the page in Hannah Glasse, and the second to the page in *Whole Duty*):

> When you can't get Cream, take three Pints of Milk, beat up the Yolks of four Eggs, and stir it into the Milk, set it over the Fire, stirring it all the time, till it is scalding hot, them mix it in the room of the Cream.

It was apparent from my study that no cookery writer had done this externalizing—suggesting adaptations to available commodities or individual tastes—so thoughtfully or so thoroughly before Hannah Glasse.

An absolutely essential part of her clarity is the precise measurement of quantities, where there were no quantities given in her originals, in a way which reveals she must have made all these recipes herself: Sheep Rumps with Rice 26/306; To dress a Pig the French Way 32/331; Pigeons in Compote with White Sauce 45/387; Bean Tansey 103/444; Green Peas with Cream 104/446; A Third Rice Pudding 108/464; Fritters Another Way 81/487; Fritters Royal 81/448; Skirret Fritters 81/488; Water Fritters 81/489; Syringed Fritters 82/490; Almond Cream 144/574 and others. She halves quantities, especially of wine in two syllabub recipes on p. 144, and increases them, notably in Potted Cheshire Cheese 128 where she has 3 lbs of cheese to ½ lb butter, and in Common Biskets 140 where she doubles the coriander seeds to one ounce.

Hannah Glasse rearranges badly worded recipes so that each stage in the method follows logically, for example in Pullets a la Sainte Menehout 37/367, *Whole Duty* opens, beats the birds, and then takes out the thigh bones; Hannah Glasse removes the bones *before* beating with a rolling pin. In A Pillaw of Veal 28 she butters the dish at a different, better point; and Lemon Cream 143/574 she rewords in a more logical order. In Stew'd Cod she puts the oysters in at the end where they won't lose their texture and flavour, rather than at the beginning.

It seems from her content then, that Hannah Glasse did indeed simplify and explicate. But did she simplify the style of cookery writing as she claims to do in her preface?

> If I have not wrote in the high, polite Stile, I hope I shall be forgiven; for my Intention is to instruct the lower Sort, and therefore must treat them in their own Way. For example; when I bid them lard a Fowl, if I should bid them lard with large Lardoons, they would not know what I meant. But when I say they must lard with little Pieces of Bacon, they know what I mean . . . the great Cooks have such a high way of expressing themselves that the poor Girls are a Loss to know what they mean.

The high polite style Hannah Glasse is referring to is used notably by men writers and not the women, and particularly by those trained French cooks who have cooked for decades at court or with the aristocracy. These are the men who have served an apprenticeship to a master chef and who tend to preserve the mystery of their craft by using special old-fashioned chef's jargon, which must have been quite opaque to a half-educated servant. Hannah

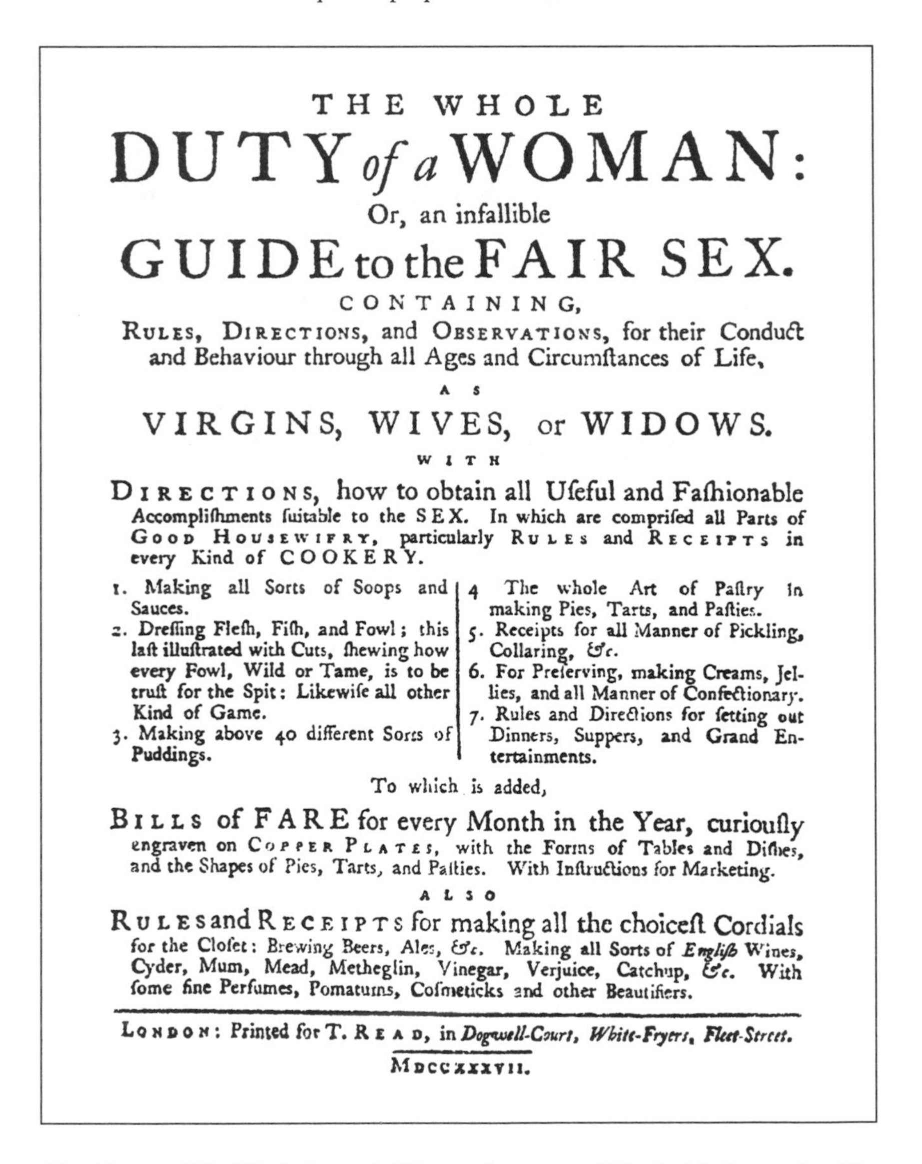

THE WHOLE
DUTY of a WOMAN:
Or, an infallible
GUIDE to the FAIR SEX.
CONTAINING,
RULES, DIRECTIONS, and OBSERVATIONS, for their Conduct and Behaviour through all Ages and Circumstances of Life,
AS
VIRGINS, WIVES, or WIDOWS.
WITH
DIRECTIONS, how to obtain all Useful and Fashionable Accomplishments suitable to the SEX. In which are comprised all Parts of GOOD HOUSEWIFRY, particularly RULES and RECEIPTS in every Kind of COOKERY.

1. Making all Sorts of Soops and Sauces.
2. Dressing Flesh, Fish, and Fowl; this last illustrated with Cuts, shewing how every Fowl, Wild or Tame, is to be trust for the Spit: Likewise all other Kind of Game.
3. Making above 40 different Sorts of Puddings.
4. The whole Art of Pastry in making Pies, Tarts, and Pasties.
5. Receipts for all Manner of Pickling, Collaring, &c.
6. For Preserving, making Creams, Jellies, and all Manner of Confectionary.
7. Rules and Directions for setting out Dinners, Suppers, and Grand Entertainments.

To which is added,
BILLS of FARE for every Month in the Year, curiously engraven on COPPER PLATES, with the Forms of Tables and Dishes, and the Shapes of Pies, Tarts, and Pasties. With Instructions for Marketing.
ALSO
RULES and RECEIPTS for making all the choicest Cordials for the Closet: Brewing Beers, Ales, &c. Making all Sorts of *English* Wines, Cyder, Mum, Mead, Metheglin, Vinegar, Verjuice, Catchup, &c. With some fine Perfumes, Pomatums, Cosmeticks and other Beautifiers.

LONDON: Printed for T. READ, in *Dogwell-Court, White-Fryers, Fleet-Street.*
MDCCXXXVII.

The title page of The Whole Duty of a Woman, *later renamed* The Lady's Companion. *The last recorded edition was the 6th (1753). See Maclean, pages 150–1.*

Glasse is at one with the women writers, who have not had the benefit of such an apprenticeship, and who write with a practical directness, in plain straightforward English. (Little wonder the women writers had notable success, they were more accessible.) Henry Howard, John Middleton, Charles Carter and Robert Smith are examples of such high style, which betrays its origins in royal or aristocratic establishments, so phrases like 'before you send it away' and 'send it up' imply a long distance between kitchen and dining room. Houses are smaller in Hannah Glasse's circle: when Carter says 'so serve away hot' Hannah Glasse has 'send it to table hot'.

Here is a typical example of the way in which Hannah Glasse modernizes the style of a recipe:

BEEF A LA MODE IN PIECES

Whole Duty 290 from Carter 17:

> You must take a Buttock, and cut it in two pound Lumps, lard them with gross lards seasoned; pass them off brown, and then Stove them in good Liquor or Broth of sweet herbs as will just cover the Meat; put in a faggot and season with cloves, mace, nutmeg and salt; and when tender, skim all well, and so serve away hot.

Hannah Glasse 20:

> You must take a Buttock of beef, cut it into two Pound Pieces, lard them with Bacon, fry them Brown, put them into a Pot that will just hold them, put in two Quarts of Broth or Gravy, a few Sweet Herbs, an Onion, some Mace, Cloves, Nutmeg, Pepper and Salt; when that is done, cover it close, and stew it till it is tender, skim off all the Fat, lay the Meat in the Dish, and strain the Sauce over it. You may serve it up hot or cold.

Hannah Glasse modernizes these old-fashioned phrases: 'Boil off your Ox tongues', 'Take two green Savoys and set them off' (boil), 'boil them off white', 'fry them off', 'pass off some butter' (melt). When the high phrase is 'pass it off brown', Hannah Glasse has 'fry it brown in some good butter'. When Howard says 'Take two right Seville oranges', she has 'two large Seville Oranges'; when R. Smith uses a 'porringer', she uses a 'bason'; when *Whole Duty* uses a faggot of sweet herbs, she uses a bundle; 'temper it with eggs' becomes 'add more egg'; 'stir that it may not clod or burn to' becomes 'stir that it may not clod or burn'; 'go on a thickening it' becomes 'go on to thicken it'; in dressing a pig 'draw him with parsley' becomes 'throw some parsley over him'; 'the tender ends of shiver'd Palates' becomes 'a Palate boiled tender and cut into Pieces'; when Middleton says 'lard them with small Lardoons' Hannah Glasse has 'lard them with little bits of Bacon', which brings us back to the preface.

'If I have not wrote in the high polite Stile'—Hannah Glasse is referring not only to this chef's jargon, but to the rhetorical flourishes and dedications in the prefaces of many cookery books, notably the royal and aristocratic ones. Hannah Glasse's patrons were her many upper middle class subscribers. The high polite style belonged to the previous century when conformity to rule and precedent prevailed. But the turn of the century saw a burgeoning of economic individualism, the growth of the middle classes in commerce and the professions, improved education among the lower orders, and a public at large avid to improve itself, to ape its betters. A spate of educational books, on gardening, medicine, spas, hygiene, geography, travel, marriage, children, etiquette, agriculture rolled off the presses and were eagerly snatched up. Even poetry stopped being divine or courtly and became didactic.

Hannah Glasse is firmly in this movement. But she is not the first cookery writer to claim ease and simplicity of instruction. As early as 1660 Robert May professes his book shows 'an easy and perfect method' in the art of cookery, intended both for 'Master Cooks' and 'young Practitioners', and Robert Smith, representative of more contemporary writers, says in 1725 that he has put his recipes 'in a plain *English* dress, endeavouring to have them understood by the meanest Capacity' (though he obviously does not succeed). For his lack of engraved table settings, usual in other books, he apologises in the same rational way that Hannah Glasse later does. Like her, Smith wishes cookery to flourish 'in a quicker and less expensive manner than hitherto'. Even so, he is still courtly in that he includes several recipes 'not unworthy the greatest prince'. Where Smith is still quite Palladian in his nobility, economy and plainness, Hannah Glasse hits you between the eyeballs with almost feminist ferocity.

The female cookery writers were notably successful in selling a lot of books—Mary Eales, Mary Kettilby, Eliza Smith, Elizabeth Moxon, Hannah Glasse (and later Mrs Raffald, Mrs Rundell and Eliza Acton). Reasons may be the plainness of their language as I have mentioned, and the practicality of their recipes which are suitable for ordinary cooks to make. So the women do not (as the men seem to enjoy doing) include the building of castles with salad or the making of hollow turrets in battalia pies to be filled with exotica. Just as in modern *haute couture,* the women design what is actually wearable, whilst the men design to some abstract ideal.

Mrs Glasse, being a thoroughly modern woman, throws out battalia pie altogether, even in its uncrenellated form, with its mish-mash of ingredients and conflicting flavours, an example of the 'odd Jumble of Things' beloved of high cooks that she so berates in her preface (though she is inconsistent, and does sometimes include recipes with gothic mixtures). But generally she simplifies the flavourings, ingredients and methods of many recipes in a similar way that medical receipts were being simplified at the same time—

a movement recommended by Culpeper and others in the mid-17th century which resulted in the 18th in the throwing out by the Pharmacopoeiae of many outdated and useless materia medica. She is also thoroughly modern in dispensing with the mass of household and medical recipes that were still usual in many recipe books not written by trained French cooks: 'I shall not take upon me to meddle in the physical Way.' She is not writing for leisured country gentlewomen on how to manage poultry, distill fragrant waters and make cosmetics and herbal medicines. Hannah Glasse is the thorough city woman, writing for a new busy professional level of society. Since standard medical treatment for most ailments was now largely mechanical (e. g. the rather dangerous practice of bleeding, and purging and vomiting often with new drugs) it needed to be in professional hands; traditionally the physicians', but after 1704, when apothecaries were allowed to prescribe as well as dispense, increasingly with the latter. Medicine was less and less doled out as an act of charity by the lady of the manor, and herbal medicines on the whole were left to the poor (though receipts continue to appear in many books).

A further innovation of Hannah Glasse is her special stressing of the need for cleanliness in all kitchen equipment, warning that using anything other than sand to clean spits will give off-flavours, and that wooden equipment is apt to do the same. Pudding cloths, pans and grid-irons must be scrupulously clean (7, 8, 10, 52, 68, 70). This tallies with the general rise in hygiene and living standards due largely to the increasing incidence of piped water. Foreign visitors of the time noticed that English servants generally looked remarkably clean.

Her style inspires confidence; she writes firmly about 'the best way' of doing things. I make a beeline for writers like her, who recommend especially good recipes: 'a good fat Neck of Mutton eats finely, done thus'. But her book is not as easy to use as it might have been.

Her Shortcomings as a Cookery Writer

I have mentioned Hannah Glasse's lack of index in her first edition. A cookery book without an index is like the catacombs without a candle—one has a reluctance to enter at all. The development of indexes in the 18th century is a subject by itself; some cookery books do have very good ones, others rudimentary ones, and yet others no index whatsoever. Massialot, Lamb and Nott attempted a dictionary-like alphabetical arrangement, which has its drawbacks, though Nott and Massialot have a helpful index as well. *The Whole Duty of a Woman* has no index, but it's easy to find one's way as the material is fairly well ordered under chapter headings and sub-headings (which I'm afraid makes me suspect it was compiled by a man—as does the insupportable advice to women in the first part). Hannah Glasse too has chapter headings, but two of these chapters are so huge and miscellaneous (Chapter II, Made Dishes, and Chapter IX, For A Fast Dinner, a Number of good Dishes, which you may make use of for a Table at any other Time) that it is very difficult to find the dish one is looking for. (Those modern recipe books with no index, which bunch recipes under 'Lunch Dishes' or 'Tea-time Specialities' are absolutely maddening, since one man's idea of lunch is another man's notion of supper.)

In spite of Hannah Glasse's many chapter headings, finding a particular recipe is very difficult. For example, the meats are not rigidly lumped together, though poultry and game-birds are; however, all kinds of mutton parts and a calf's liver creep into the fowl and game-bird section while the odd pigeon, chicken and large fowl come to roost in the red meat section, and a Calf's Head Surprise blinks at one among the veal. Soups are not all in the soup chapter—13 other soups appear elsewhere, and there are oat puddings in three different chapters. The cooks using this first edition of Hannah Glasse who may just come back from market with a plethora of cucumbers are going to find their bargains wilted into flaccidity while they raise the temperature searching for cucumber recipes (my own index reveals they are on pp. 38, 41; stewed 56, 100, 105; ragoo'd 56; forced 58, 104; and pickled 132). Such chaotic arrangement betokens an education or sensibility deficient in logic and orderliness. In her arrangement, Hannah Glasse has the instincts of the habit maker she later became, tacking things on here and there until the finished effect is one of impressive integrity.[5]

The appearance of Jumballs (sweet biskets) marooned in a sea of ragoo'd oysters, onions, and hashed mutton in the Side Dish chapter is not so strange when one knows that sweet biskets stayed on the table throughout the meal, along with the other little side dishes; nor is it odd that only ten puddings are in the pudding chapter, yet there are 84 throughout the book. The reason is that those ten use animal ingredients, whereas most of the others are meatless and in the Lent chapter. This Lent chapter is a headache, being a catch-all of 292 non-meat recipes. Soups, puddings, fritters, pancakes, fruit, fish, cheese, eggs, vegetables, pies and salads follow each other in bewildering profusion. I shall not comment further on this curious chapter IX except perhaps to mention that she may have got the idea from La Chapelle, who has a chapter on soups for Lent, and that there were Catholics in her family.[6] For Captains of Ships, Chapter XI may similarly be borrowed from La Chapelle who has a chapter called 'For the Sea Service'. 'For Captains of Ships' is a catchy title, but its contents seem to be of dubious utility to sea captains. This chapter is a mere flounce Hannah Glasse has tacked on.

Her Innovations as a Cook

The examples given here are based on a comparison with *Whole Duty,* as in the earlier section about Hannah Glasse's innovations as a cookery writer. The difference is that I am inviting attention here to differences of substance, not style.

Hannah Glasse improves the flavour of many dishes by using butter instead of suet. For example in Almond Pudding to boil 106/460 she uses 8 oz butter instead of 1 lb of suet, and she fries her fritters in butter, not lard though this is one of her inconsistencies, as I will show later.

She lightens the texture and flavour of other dishes by substituting milk or milk and eggs for some or all the cream; Chestnut Pudding 109/467; Bread Pudding 109/465; Boiled Rice Pudding 111/469. She gives a cleaner, lighter flavour to fish dishes by omitting the meat gravy and substituting water (To Stew Cod 89/228; To roast Fresh Sturgeon 92/271) or substituting fish liquor by boiling up fish-bones (as in A Soal Pye 115/517); and conversely a cleaner, more natural taste to poultry and game by discouraging the use of fish sauces with them (To roast Pheasants 48, 'A Frenchman would order Fish Sauce to them, but then you quite spoil your Pheasants'.) She does allow oyster sauce with turkey and chicken, but says to be sure to serve this 'in a Bason by itself, for everybody don't love Oyster Sauce', 34/413.

True to her Francophobia she omits the expensive and extravagant French cullis altogether for thickening and flavouring the sauces, using instead water or the boiling-liquor or good gravy where appropriate (though purely out of prejudice and economy—in fact cullis would give a superb flavour) and generally thickening with roux, beurre manié or egg yolks. She omits verjuice from To Stew beef Steaks 21/291 and Eggs à la Tripe 101/406; omits sugar from To dress a Pig like a Fat Lamb 33/334 and Peas Francaise 104/445; knows where to garnish with the right touch of crispness in A pretty Dish of Eggs 101/405; and stresses the cooking of vegetables until only just tender, 12, specific advice I have seen in none of her predecessors' books.

In Stewed Spinach with Eggs 99/452 *Whole Duty* adds gravy and butter to the boiled, chopped spinach before sliding the poached eggs on top. Hannah Glasse puts her poached eggs onto naked cooked spinach and hands melted butter in a cup, garnishing only with orange. This is a 'cleaner' version, aiming at a fresh green taste, for she insists one should stop cooking the spinach 'when it is just tender and whilst it is green'. The colours of the dish, unmuddied by gravy, would look superb.

Many times she starts word for word with *Whole Duty* then changes into her own invention, for example, To Pitchcock Eels 92/240, and A Calf's Head Surprise 30/319. Sometimes she elides two recipes; A Carrot Pudding is a hybrid of *Whole Duty*'s two versions 107/461 where she has put the first half of one with the second half of another. Thinking this was a transcription error, I decided to cook it. It came out with flying colours.

Her Shortcomings as a Cook

At first it struck me that Hannah Glasse did not fully understand or appreciate deep frying; she seems to shy away from it in all eleven of her fritter recipes, apparently shallow-frying in butter instead of deep-frying in lard or dripping. In Apple Fritters 81/487 using obviously the same basic recipe, where *Whole Duty* dips sliced apples in batter and deep fries in lard, Hannah Glasse chops her apples into the batter and fries, presumably dropped from a spoon, in butter; and in Vine Leaf Fritters 82/491 where *Whole Duty* (and La Chapelle) dip their vine leaves into batter and deep fry in 2 lbs dripping or lard, Hannah Glasse, using the same recipe, seems to shallow fry spoonfuls of batter in butter, then lays a vine leaf on each, which may look pretty, but sort of misses the point. Then she adds, rather oddly in view of her foregoing recipe, that all fritters 'should be fry'd in a good deal of Fat, therefore they are best fried in Beef-dripping or Hog's-lard, when it can be done'.

I was becoming convinced that she *never* deep-fried, especially when I discovered that one of Ann Cook's salvos seemed to reinforce the idea. According to Ann Cook, her instruction to put vinegar and sliced lemon into boiling fat 'would give a Crack like a Cannon; so there would be no need of the Chimney sweeping; for the Blast would bring down the Soot at once'.[7] But among the recipes which seem to be her own there are clear indications that Hannah Glasse *did* deep fry, for example (pp. 60–61) Fish in boiling Beef-dripping or Hog's-lard deep enough as to almost cover the Fish—that is how her fish in batter are done. And another remark among these recipes cleared up the fritter mystery; on p. 102 she writes 'Having a deep Frying-pan, and three Pints of clarified Butter, heat it as hot for Fritters'. So she *did* deep fry fritters, but in 3 lbs of very expensive butter! Not only that, this recipe on p. 102 is To Fry Eggs as round as Balls, where one drops raw eggs into 3 lbs of swirling deep hot butter; surely this is the equivalent to the Frenchman's crazily extravagant frying of twelve eggs in 6 lbs of butter that she refers to so disdainfully in her preface! The cost of butter in Hannah Glasse's day was twice that of meat, so that the cost of her fritter-frying butter, in today's terms, would be about £9! This is a prime example of her inconsistency (and her evident love of butter).

Whole Duty's pancakes are really French crêpes. Hannah Glasse, in taking over four of these recipes, 83/486–7, tends to anglicize them by introducing more butter than *Whole Duty* allows, i.e. more than enough to try the pan at the start. But her last pancake recipe, which comes from Mary Kettilby, has not been modified in this way, and really would produce something like French crêpes, although she does not draw attention to the difference. I wonder whether she knew what she was about in this section. Perhaps she did.

However, her one omelet recipe shows a total ignorance of what a French omelet should be. An Amulet of Beans 103/444 (from La Chapelle 1736 vol III 205) is very clearly in *Whole Duty* an omelet made with eggs and cream, and dressed on top with fried green beans: 'An Amulet is to be made with new laid Eggs and Cream [and salt], when it is enough, dress it on a Dish, thicken the beans with one or two Yolks, and turn them on your Amulet.' Hannah Glasse's version goes: 'have ready a Pint of Cream, thickened with the Yolks of four Eggs, season with a little Salt, pour it on your dish, and lay your Beans on the Amulet'. She has condemned herself with the word 'pour' for she has in effect made a custard! I feel she never made this dish at all. Indeed, there are other recipes which I think she has imaginatively re-written without ever having tried. If she was teaching herself 'high' or fancy French cooking from other people's inadequate books (not ever having had the benefit of instruction from a 'trained French cook', a point I will come to later) she should be given full marks for effort.

This note on Hannah Glasse's shortcomings as a cook would not be complete without further mention of her worst critic, Ann Cook, who devotes 66 pages of her 1755 *Professed Cookery,* to the minutest criticism of Hannah Glasse's recipes. This was in revenge for personal injury supposedly done her by Hannah's brother, Launcelot Allgood.[6] Much of the criticism is mere spiteful invective, but as a professional (very plain) cook herself, Ann Cook knew her onions, and some of her criticism seems justified.

For instance, Hannah Glasse (whom Ann Cook refers to as 'the Lady' or 'the Lady teacher') uses far too much butter in To Bake Lamb and Rice (14/50; the first number in this parenthetical series refers to the page in Ann Cook, the second to the page in later editions of Hannah Glasse, not the first edition). One pound of butter to only half a pound of rice would be 'a Surfeit to a hungry Plough-man'. Likewise in A French Barley Pudding (59/211) one pound of butter and a quart of cream is far too much for only six handfuls of barley: 'there will be a Well of Oil swimming upon the Barley'. To Fry Eggs as round as Balls (56/201) says Ann Cook would require six pounds of butter for the frying 'for three Pints of clarified Butter will require six *London* Butter Pounds'. She exaggerates, but her point about extravagance is taken.

The Lady has proportioned poorly in Another Way to make a Pellow (34/102) with the essence of 18 lbs of meat absorbed by only 1 lb of rice, which Ann Cook obviously thinks will be too glue-like, for 'who-ever gets the Rice in their Mouths, 'twill stick to their teeth like bird-lime'.

A common error of the Lady, according to her critic, is making a wasteful amount of forcemeat for stuffing. Thus in one of her recipes for beef-steaks Hannah Glasse has apparently made about 10 lbs of forcemeat to stuff four steaks, in To Stew Lamb or Calf's Head (14/52) she has made 5 or 6 lbs for one head, and to dress Turkey or Fowl to Perfection (20/70) suffers the same surfeit.

A too lavish hand with expensive ingredients comes in for most criticism. The two I thought justified were To Stew a Turkey Brown (20/70) and Farce Meagre Cabbage (65/204) where the humble cabbage worth ½d is dressed with luxury items worth 2/1d. My frugal nature sides with Ann Cook here, though my gastronomical one with the Lady!

The Lady is too generous with her salts in To Pot Beef like Venison (65/253)—8 lbs beef to 4 oz Salt-petre, 4 oz Peter-salt, a pint of Coarse salt, and 1 oz Sal-prunella. Says Ann Cook 'There are salts sufficient to colour a whole Beef red'.

The Teacher's cooking methods are ridiculed. Larded oysters (13/43) roasted on a spit will fall off. So will a fowl that has been boned and minced, with the flesh and bones put back in the skin to be spit-roasted (21/71).

A curious recipe demolished at length by Ann Cook is A Neck of Mutton, call'd the Hasty Dish (32/100) which is the subject of my next section.

Mystery of the 'Necromancer' Explained

Among the oddities my study spotlit was Hannah Glasse's note at the end of Beef Collops 20, which she has cooked in a stewpan: 'N.B. you may do this Dish between two pewter Dishes, hang them between two Chairs, take six sheets of white-brown Paper, tare them into slips, and burn them under the Dish one piece at a time.' One glance at *Whole Duty* 290 shows that the original never went near a stewpan, the raw sliced beef was indeed cooked in a little wine with seasoning in a dish, with another clapped on top, balanced on chair backs and cooked with six sheets of whited-brown paper whereupon 'your Stew will be enough, and full of Gravy'.

At first I thought this method was used, because I know, having cooked on the brick charcoal stove at the 17th century Clarke Hall at Wakefield (when the chafing-dish was being used by someone else) that it is sometimes difficult to get a gentle heat the minute you want it, for example for a sauce; if shoving the damping-brick in the air-hole doesn't do the trick, you either have to remove some of the charcoal, or else raise the trivet. Then a glance at Bradley Pt II 1732 p. 114 cleared up the mystery; here was the original of *Whole Duty*'s oddly cooked beef collups with a clue in its title as to its real origin, which I will shortly explain.

Hannah Glasse must have been so impressed with the novelty of the idea of this method of cooking that she applied it to six pounds of neck of mutton in the Hasty Dish 51, an infamous example of a rogue recipe that crept into her book, and rightly ridiculed by Ann Cook.

The Neck chops are supposedly cooked in a curious vessel called a Necromancer, an uncommon article, since Ann Cook goes on to describe it. Apparently it is a large pewter or silver dish a few inches deep with a hinged lid and a handle on top. Hannah Glasse's recipe is for six pounds of neck of mutton cut into chops, layered in the dish with onions, turnips, seasoning and bread slices. The dish is filled with boiling water, the lid fastened, the whole dish balanced by the rim on the backs of two chairs, then three sheets of brown paper are torn into 15 pieces and one by one burnt underneath the dish 15 minutes in all, and hey presto your dish is done! (My pressure cooker would not do it in 15 minutes.) Hannah Glasse claims this dish was first contrived by Mr Rich, and much admired by the nobility. Apparently John Rich, noted pantomine actor of Covent Garden theatre, was the founder of the Sublime Society of Steaks in 1735 as a result of cooking a dish of steak this way in his private room at the theatre, which delighted Lord Peterborough.[8]

I can now say, however, from my glance at Bradley Pt II p. 114 that Mr Rich was most probably not the inventor of this method of cooking (though he may have thought of putting a hinge and a handle to the two pewter dishes, thus inventing the Necromancer). For Bradley's recipe, pre-dating the Sublime Society of Steaks by three years, has as its title Thin beef-Collups Stew'd. From Oxford. So, can this be the origin? It is simply student bed-sitter makeshift cookery, also practised by the theatrical profession as a useful way of procuring a hot meal when no fire was available, for example, in summer?

Hannah Glasse's Ambivalence Towards French Cooking

This is an aspect of the work which comes regularly to notice as one works through *The Art of Cookery* in detail.

It is noticeable that Chapter I, Of Roasting, Boiling, etc, has nothing French in it whatsoever; it is instruction in good plain English cooking, and seems to be entirely Hannah Glasse's own composition (except for three lines at 10, beginning 'Boil all your Greens' which are taken from *Whole Duty* 691). However the lengthy Chapter II, Made Dishes, in spite of Hannah Glasse's invective against French tricks and extravagance in her preface, contains a very high proportion (nearly half) of French and foreign recipes, mostly French, which she has included, she says, because 'they are good'. This is a typical double-bind, which other English cookery writers share.

There was a widespread English prejudice against disguising the natural flavour of meat with foreign highly flavoured sauces. This seemed to obtain especially in the case of fowl and game-birds. (Most of the men of my acquaintance here in the north of England still exhibit this prejudice, abhor made dishes, and want plain meat, 'clean food' as one puts it.) It may be significant that only a third of the fowl and game-bird recipes in Chapter II are French or foreign, whereas of the red meat recipes in the same chapter there are about 52 French or foreign to 64 English.

The 'French Cook's Sauce' Chapter

Chapter III is very curious. Its full title is *'Read this Chapter, and you will find how expensive a* French Cook's *Sauce is'.* In it, Hannah Glasse has written out eight detailed recipes, five for French cullises, only to hold them up to ridicule. The expense of a French cook's sauce is easily demonstrated in the extravagant amounts of meat and flavourings which are boiled down to make a rich thick cullis, used for thickening and enriching.

This chapter is an example of Hannah Glasse's love-hate relationship with French cookery, scorn coupled with sneaking admiration. Ostensibly all the recipes are included only to be scoffed at. For example, Sauce for a Brace of Partridges 54 contains so many expensive fine ingredients that she says it is 'equal with boiling a Leg of Mutton in Champaign'. Another, The French Way of Dressing Partridges 53, is described as 'an odd Jumble of Trash'. And yet she has written these out in full detail, like her own recipes, as though she felt her book would not be complete without them. Anyone who doubts the ambivalence of her attitude need only reflect on the real give-away: the point to which Ann Cook (see opposite page) rightly drew attention.

Whence came these French recipes? Philip and Mary Hyman in Paris established that five of the eight could be found in the (English) first edition of La Chapelle (1733).[9] The others were not in La Chapelle, but did occur in Massialot (1698, 1712).[10] However, only two of these had appeared in the English translation of Massialot (1702). The question thus arose: did Hannah Glasse read Massialot in the original French (an exciting thought) or had the remaining recipe found its way into some other English book which she used? There was also a more general question: could it be shown that she had had recourse directly to Massialot and La Chapelle (in translation), or did she always pick up their recipes through the intermediary of another English book?

My study of the recipes had produced the following conclusions:

(1) The five La Chapelle recipes were all copied in *Whole Duty,* and it was from that book that Hannah Glasse took them. In at least two instances

she also consulted in La Chapelle (in English) directly; in others she almost certainly did not.

(2) She did not read Massialot in French. She took one of his three recipes from Lamb and the other two (probably) from Nott.

(3) She did not try out these recipes herself.

[Editors' note: The author gives much detailed internal evidence from Hannah Glasse's book to support her conclusions.]

Ann Cook, whose ill feeling towards Hannah Glasse was explained earlier in this article, naturally pounces on this French sauce chapter and exclaims that the Lady 'notwithstanding all her great Bravadoes of Thrift, . . . has tenfold more extravagant *French* cookery in her Book, than in the Chapter she bids you read'. For example the French way of dressing partridges so mocked by the lady is actually cheaper to make than her own Partridges a la Braise. But the real knock-out punch is the revelation that the mocked French Essence of Ham 53 is identical (but for the addition of a little basil) with Hannah Glasse's own Essence of Ham on the page before, 52! 'Therefore I see no reason why it should be a Mark of Infamy on the *French* Cook, and a Trophy of Honour to her.'[12] Tedious though Ann Cook's criticism can be, this one has the chill elegance of a rapier thrust through the heart.

Hannah's Motives in Writing Her Book

The whole business of French sauces and Hannah's attitude thereto as explained above may be relevant to this wider question. Part of her vigorous scorn of male practitioners of French cookery was possibly rooted in subconscious envy. Only the very rich could afford to be in the fashion and employ a trained French cook. By 1747 the very rich included not only the aristocracy and gentry, but prosperous merchants, bankers and lawyers. This was the class to which Hannah Glasse herself belonged, but it seems obvious to me that she could never had afforded to employ a French cook. Those who couldn't do so had to make do with a 'good plain cook', and contemporary newspaper advertisements for cooks show how unequal were the payments: a trained French cook (usually a man) around 1750 earned anything from £20 to £60 per annum, whereas a plain cook (usually a woman) earned from £6 to £10 per annum.[12]

May not Hannah Glasse's impatience with her own plain cooks have driven her into the kitchen to impress her guests with her own work? Was she suddenly delighted to find that she enjoyed cooking? She certainly writes with the enthusiasm and freshness of a convert. Perhaps, when her eyes were opened to the art of plain roasting and boiling and then more elaborate cooking, this gave her a desire to share her discoveries—and make some money, so that one day she could afford a French cook!

Yet we come back to the point that by birth she was a member of the gentry, a lady. As Ann Cook also queried, what *was* such a lady doing swinking and sweating over a hot stove? Was she really 'qualified' to write a cookery book? She certainly cannot claim, as does Eliza Smith, that her book is the result of 30 years' experience cooking for the best families. On the other hand, she may have learned a lot from the family cooks employed at the family homes in Hexham (Northumberland), London and Broomfield (Essex), and even if she was never under a *necessity* to cook she may have enjoyed doing so and putting into practice what she had learned.

Whether or not these speculations are right, there was a material reason for her turning to cookery writing: financial embarrassment. Having eloped at the age of sixteen with the impecunious adventurer John Glasse, she did run into financial problems. In 1744 it seems that she sought to set up in some sort of business, for in a letter of that year[13] she suggested she might market a patent medicine—that which achieved fame as Daffy's Elixir. Twelve months later she had begun *The Art of Cookery* and a year after that, in January 1746, it had already been sent to press. In the year of its publication, 1747, John Glasse died and Hannah's financial difficulties became worse. By 1749 she had set up as a successful dressmaker with her daughter Margaret as milliner. Her brother Launcelot, staying with her in Covent Garden when an M.P., wrote that: 'Hannah has so many coaches at her door that, to judge from appearances, she must succeed in her business . . . she has great visitors with her, no less than the Prince and Princess of Wales, to see her masquerade dresses.'[14] But, not being a good businesswoman ('she does not calculate well', her husband had complained), she went bankrupt in May 1754 to the tune of £10,000.[15]

One consequence of her bankruptcy was that she lost all that was left in her hands of the copyright of *The Art of Cookery.* The 5th edition of the book, which came out in 1755, had been prepared before the bankruptcy. The separate *Appendix to Mrs Glasse's Cookery,* a fairly extensive collection of additional recipes, was 'printed for the author' in 1758, and was later incorporated into the main book. Numerous further editions of the whole were published; but the extent of Hannah's involvement, after 1755, in a book which had ceased to be her property, seems quite unclear. Certainly, she can have had nothing to do with any changes made after her death in 1770.

These points are of some importance, since many comments on Hannah Glasse's work have been based on the later editions (especially that of 1796, the only one so far reprinted) and therefore risk being directed at recipes which she may neither have written nor even approved (by selecting them herself from other books).

All this should lead me to my conclusions, based on an assessment of the recipes which appeared in the first edition and up to 1755. But first, like a top which has been whirling round long enough to acquire its own mad momentum, I must spin off other material which is clinging in my mind.

[Editors' note: At this point Jennifer Stead included fascinating details, which we have reluctantly had to omit, about accidents to the text of Hannah Glasse's book; pertinent information about how ingredients in the 18th century differed from those current now; and some questions about measures which modern cooks should consider in interpreting Hannah's recipes.]

Conclusions

In my study I found that 263 out of 972 recipes had been taken from or based on other writers. I compared Hannah Glasse in detail to only these books: *The Whole Duty of a Woman,* Eliza Smith, Henry Howard, Charles Carter, Robert Smith, John Middleton, Mary Eales and Mary Kettilby (except her wines); and with the other authors mentioned in the article (including John Nott, whose compendium of recipes is the second largest after *Whole Duty*) I made only a partial comparison. That leaves 709 recipes thankfully unaccounted for.*

Hannah Glasse's number of foreign recipes is unusual—I have found an Indian curry nowhere else—and this might imply a number of merchants and sea-captains among her, what must have been numerous, acquaintance. Her husband's Irish connections, her mother-in-law's Scots ones and her own family's north of England ones may have furnished a substantial number of recipes. She probably badgered innkeepers, confectioners and bakers for theirs (Elizabeth David believes that her muffin recipe 151 came from a baker). The great number and variety of obviously original recipes and the novelty she brings to many of those she borrowed must indeed have been a large factor in her book's success.

And so, did Hannah Glasse succeed in her aims to instruct the ignorant and to reduce expense? It is difficult to see that she did the latter, except by her gesture of discouraging the French cullis. As for instructing the ignorant, her book is not a primer—it does not tell you how to case your hare—but she went a long way in the direction of making recipes more generally comprehensible and of creating an atmosphere of real communication between

*Editor's note: In her essay Jennifer Stead provided a detailed table (not printed here) of equivalences between Hannah Glasse's recipes and those of earlier authors.

writer and reader. The public response to her book bespeaks the effect of this, and reminds us that, in relation to the scale of her achievement, her occasional inconsistencies and mistakes are of no consequence. For, as I hope this, albeit imperfect, study had made clear, in *The Art of Cookery Made Plain and Easy* this resourceful woman did, in her own words, 'far exceed any Thing of the Kind ever yet Published'.

References

1. Why did cookery writers steal so shamelessly from each other? In the eighteenth century, recipes, as indeed other writings, were not considered the personal property of the writer (the first Copyright Act of 1709 had no effect on cookery books) and so the same recipes were duplicated time and again, and new ones immediately pirated. The same thing happens today of course, but not so overtly, since the precise wording of recipes, and even more, collections of them, *are* considered to be the property of the writer. (The Romantic Movement, with its stress on an individual's oeuvre being his own property, laid the foundations for modern stringent copyright laws.)
2. Boswell's *Life of Johnson* 1848, p. 592. He also implied that, because it was no good, a woman could not possibly have written it!
3. Regula Burnet, *Ann Cook and Friend,* London 1936, p. 2.
4. Virginia Maclean, *A Short-title Catalogue of Household and Cookery Books published in the English Tongue 1701–1800,* London 1981.
5. In her 4th edition 1751 Hannah Glasse describes herself as 'Habit Maker to Her Royal Highness the Princess of Wales in Tavistock Street, Covent Garden'.
6. Madeleine Hope Dods, 'The Rival Cooks: Hannah Glasse and Ann Cook', *Archaeologia Aeliana,* Series 4, vol. 15, pp. 43–68.
7. Regula Burnet, op. cit. p. xxxiii. Ann Cook *Professed Cookery* 1755 p. 42. She is criticizing Hannah Glasse's How to preserve Cocks-combs.
8. Regula Burnet, op. cit. p. xxxii.
9. Philip and Mary Hyman, private communication.
10. Of the three recipes which only occur in Massialot, those for Essence of Ham and A Cullis for all Sorts of Ragoo are to be found in the enlarged 2-volume edition which first came out in 1712; while that for Sauce for a Brace of Partridges is only present in the earlier 1-volume edition (current from 1691, version consulted for present purposes that of 1698). When the 1-volume edition was enlarged some recipes in it were dropped. The English translation of Massialot, 1702, was of course of the 1-volume edition.
11. Regula Burnet, *Ann Cook and Friend,* London 1936, p. xxi.
12. J. Jean Hecht, *The Domestic Servant in Eighteenth-century England,* London 1980, pp. 142–7.
13. Referred to by Ann Willan, *Great Cooks and Their Recipes,* McGraw Hill (UK) 1977, pp. 93–7.
14. Ibid.
15. Ibid.

5.
Exotica

There has been no lack of exotic subjects in *PPC*. In this section we exhibit a few, beginning with the notorious topic of medieval Arab condiments made from rotted barley. Notorious, certainly, to those who tasted this when Charles Perry brought some to the Oxford Symposium, for the first time in 1987. The two essays by him should be enough to satisfy the curiosity of any readers who wish to master this subject in depth or make some of the substance themselves.

At this point, for a reason which will become apparent, we introduce the one and only competition which has ever been set for *PPC* readers. It appeared under the title 'A Dubious Competition' and the puzzling menu which competitors were asked to elucidate was quite sufficiently bizarre to count as an exotic item. The competition was set by Jon Grossman, former head of publications at the FAO in Rome and a valued associate of ours. He also acted as judge for the competition and produced a witty judgement of several pages, which was itself an exotic item.

For many people snakes are repellent to such an extent that they would find it difficult to imagine eating them. Yet many are edible, and eaten. As happens suspiciously often with exotic flesh foods, the taste has been compared to that of chicken. In this instance, the comparison is generally appropriate, although the tastes of particular species do vary. Anyway, we here begin with a duo of pieces on the viper, from *PPC 50* and *51*. Simon Varey, who contributed the first, is an academic in the USA with a strong amateur interest in food history. His essay refers back to the Dubious Competition. What Simon wrote was supplemented by a note in *PPC 51*, supplied by Jennifer Stead and here reprinted to round off the story.

The rattlesnake is the second snake in our collection and was written by someone with real hands-on experience, to wit Sam'l P Arnold, owner and manager of the Red Fort restaurant near Denver. The paper here reprinted is a version of an address which the author prepared for the October 1994 conference of the Western Historical Association. Sam Arnold's previous contributions to *PPC* have likewise carried the flavour of what was and still is in some ways the Wild West. See, for example, his 'Food and Drink of the Mountain Men' in *PPC 25*.

After snakes, we step down in size to worms, also repellent to many people, although those who have read the whole worm sequence presented here (from *PPC 51* to *55*, including the last item, which is very much longer than the others) will now view them in a different light. The sequence was initiated by Anon, the device traditionally used to protect the anonymity of modest authors. There were so many subsequent contributors on this theme that for once we have to dispense with the separate introductions which we would normally supply.

One might think that by now we have enough of worms. However, they figure again in our next choice, ' "Snails", "Caterpillars" and "Worms" ' by Marjorie Cohn. As the quotation marks imply, the worms in this earlier article were not real ones, but seed pods so resembling worms in shape that persons eating salads in which they appeared would be greatly astonished. Marjorie Cohn explains at the outset of her essay by what strange route she was led into an investigation in the use of vegetable pseudo-animals as culinary jokes. Who would have thought that the Conservator of Works of Art on Paper at the Harvard University Art Museums would have strayed into this exotic field of study?

Now follow two meaty items, the first on eating udder, by Lynda Brown. As she explains, there are people for whom udder is not an exotic food; but for most of our readers it will be. Much the same applies to the examples chosen by Russell Harris of eating Raw Meat. Although he is a onetime would-be opera singer, from which it is a long way to his present professional interest in important collections of 19th century photographs, Russell's interest in food history has been a constant in his life. Johan Mathiesen, on the west coast of the USA, is not just a valued contributor to *PPC* but also its present agent in North America, an activity enhanced by his lively 'wah-to-yah' approach to all things.

Arthur French, in his study of mushroom-growing termites, surely the smallest farmers in the world, was a pioneer in this field. A separate introduction to his essay explains how he became involved and provides useful clues for anyone who might wish to delve even deeper into it.

Finally, to end on a fragrant note and to demonstrate that some exotic items are thoroughly pleasant, in contrast to those which are repellent, shocking or just plain bewildering, we reprint the essay on 'Candle-Scented Cakes and Sweets of Thailand' by Professor Richard Hosking, who is perhaps best known for his brilliant *A Dictionary of Japanese Food* (Charles Tuttle, Tokyo and Rutland, VT, 1996 and later editions). Let jasmine, roses and ylang ylang flowers be strewn before him to celebrate a charming contribution to our anthology.

A Nuanced Apology to Rotted Barley

CHARLES PERRY

An American scholar of Arabic and other languages, and of etymology with particular reference to food terms, Charles Perry has worked for the last 12 years as editor in the food section of the Los Angeles Times, *punctuated by research journeys in the Arab world and visits to the Oxford Symposia on Food (where he is generally accounted to have the driest wit of all the Symposiasts). He has a number of books on diverse subjects to his credit, the latest being the scholarly volume,* Medieval Arab Cookery, *for which he was contributing editor (see page 96).*

For the 1987 Oxford Symposium, I wrote about a family of medieval Arab condiments made from rotted barley—loaves of raw barley dough typically wrapped in fig leaves and allowed to rot 40 days. For the favorite sauce *murri,* the rotted barley would be ground up, mixed with salt, water and usually more flour, and rotted in a warm place 40 days longer.

I rotted some dough and, because Symposium papers were due shortly, made a condiment called *bunn* which required only a few days' rotting. But before tasting it, I asked a medical researcher whether it could be dangerous. He warned me that the dough was likely to have been infected with the mold *Aspergillus flavus* and therefore to contain carcinogenic aflatoxins. I dutifully included this warning in my paper, indeed emphasized it; and the paper was published in 1988, in *Taste: Oxford Symposium on Food and Cookery 1987* (Prospect Books) and in Paul Levy's anthology, *The Penguin Book of Food and Drink* (Viking Penguin, 1996).

I want to apologize to these probably blameless condiments. I have made a new batch of *murri* and had it analyzed by a laboratory, and yes, the product did contain aflatoxins, but at a level accepted as safe, 3.47 parts per billion. The United States Food and Drug Administration permits nuts to be sold with aflatoxin concentrations nearly six times as high. Since this quite salty sauce was not likely to be consumed in large quantities, it does not appear to have been a health danger.

Of course, there is no certainty that every batch of *murri* will show the same level of aflatoxins. Much depends on the stage at which *A. flavus* enters the rotting process, for instance. But on the whole, and astonishingly for anyone who has watched the gruesome rotting process from beginning to end, these products apparently deserve a clean bill of health. My sample did not even show significant levels of the common food-borne pathogens *E. coli* and *Staphylococcus,* and no *Listeria* or *Salmonella* at all.

In my first rotting experiment, I had been at a loss to know which of the samples I had rotted had come out right. I cautiously assumed it was a lightly rotted batch with a pleasant smell. I now see I should have rotted much more boldly. In my recent experiment, the most rotten sample—the one that was covered with a cloud of translucent mycelium by the third day, the one where every lump of dough was swollen and mottled black, white, charcoal and four shades of green by the end of the 40 days—turned out best.

In fact, it proved to be a condiment we already know. The highly rotted dough, when mixed with an equal amount of flour, salt in the amount of one quarter the total dry weight and enough water to make a paste, turned dark mahogany brown within a week and began smelling distinctly like soy sauce. The late Rudolf Grewe speculated that *murri* was something like soy sauce. I was skeptical, but now I am convinced he has been proven right.

With both *murri* and soy sauce, there are two stages of rotting, the first in damp conditions which permit only molds to flourish, the second in a wet, salty environment. For soy sauce, cooked rice is rotted with the molds *Aspergillus oryzae* and *A. sojae* and then introduced to steamed soybeans. When the beans are thoroughly afflicted with mold (three to seven days, depending on the temperature and the vigor of the molds), they are mixed with salt and water and aged in vats for months or even years, the equivalent of the second 40 days of rotting *murri.* In the first stage, the molds convert starches to sugars and proteins to amino acids (among other reactions). In the second stage, with yeasts and bacteria active, a myriad of chemical changes take place. More acids are created (including glutamic acid, which is related to monosodium glutamate). The yeasts excrete alcohol, which reacts with the various acids to produce the aromatic compounds called esters.

This process does not depend on beans; the same reactions should take place with any source of proteins and carbohydrates. In fact, the soybeans are often extended with wheat, rye, millet or even barley in East Asia. The typical Japanese recipe is 50% wheat.

Both soy sauce and *murri* are evidently descended from ancient brine sauces. As is well known, the Greeks and Romans used the brine from pickled fish, *garum,* as a sauce which was exactly parallel to the East Asian fish sauces, such as *nuoc mam.* Throughout the first millennium BC, the Chinese also used the brine from pickled pork and other meats as a sauce.

The Chinese have been great pioneers in mold technology. For three millennia, they have made black beans by culturing yellow soybeans with mold. And throughout the same period they have added a moldy rice starter (*qu*) to both meat and fish sauces to improve the flavor. By the first century BC, they had started making a brine sauce from soybeans that was virtually soy sauce (though it was apparently a paste, rather than a liquid).

Meanwhile, in the Middle East, *murri* probably arose from *garum.* Arab lexicographers suspected that *murri* was a foreign word and reported that the common people pronounced it with one r: *al-muri.* This could easily be the Greek *halmuris,* which is also the source of the Latin word for brine, *salmuria.* The words for the grain element come from Persian. The rotted barley was *bûdhaj,* which is the Persian *pudag,* 'rotten'; *bunn,* the paste from which *murri* was extracted, is *bon,* 'foundation'.

There are more parallels between *murri* and soy sauce. Most *murri* recipes say to wrap the raw dough in fig leaves. Leaves, particularly broad leaves, are a common landing place for mold spores, and in East Asia the rice is commonly wrapped in leaves to start it rotting: reed leaves in China, banana leaves in Vietnam, hibiscus leaves in Indonesia. (In my 1987 experiment, I assumed that any leaves would do and used bottled grape leaves; a grievous mistake, I now see, because there would have been no mold spores on them.)

However, I do not believe the *murri* technology came from China. Soy sauce is basically made from beans with an optional grain extender, but the Arab product was never made with legumes at all, though a lentil *murri* would have had a richer flavor because of the higher protein content. There is no definite evidence that the Chinese were extracting a liquid sauce from their soy paste until 1578 (by which time *murri* was already extinct in the West), but *murri* was always a liquid. All the Arab recipes describe making multiple extractions from the lees.

And the Chinese and Arab recipes seem to show roots in their respective cooking traditions. In China, where grains were cooked whole, the starter is boiled rice. In the Arab world, where grains were by preference made into bread, the starter is lumps of raw dough. *Murri* starts out as bread gone very, very wrong.

But not so wrong that we need shudder at it. I humbly apologize to the whole rotted grain clan.

More Rotted Barley

In *PPC 58,* I described rotting loaves of raw barley dough for 40 days and then adding water and salt and rotting them another 40. The result of this process, a medieval Arab condiment called *murri,* was virtually identical to soy sauce. Recently I essayed the other chief medieval rotted condiment, *kâmakh ahmar,* which is made by mixing rotted barley with milk, rather than water, and exposing it on one's rooftop in the middle of summer 'until it reddens'.

I started another batch of barley at the beginning of August 1998. The recipes in *Kitâb al-Tabîkh* (10th century) and *Kitâb Wasf al-At'ima al-Mu 'tâda* (13th or 14th century) say to wrap the raw dough in fig leaves, which are the source of the necessary mold spores. When I went to gather my fig leaves, however, I found that my neighbors had actually taken their fig tree with them when they moved, so I tried another source of broad, slightly hairy leaves, rose geranium. A few days later, I made a second batch using iris leaves. When the rotting was complete, I tried making both *murri* and *kâmakh ahmar* from the two batches (rotting them on my porch in Los Angles, rather than on a rooftop), and I have five observations to report.

First: As the Chinese have known for millennia, it is essential that the grain (and soybeans, in the Far East) be attacked by moulds of the genus *Aspergillus* (in Chinese, *qümei,* 'yeast mold; starter mold') if *murri*/soy sauce is the aim. Their presence is shown within two or three days by the cloud of translucent mycelium that mycologists refer to as an arachnoid mat and, when rotting is complete, by a smell like rotting leaves.

Second: It appears that not all leaves are equally good for *murri-* or soy sauce-making. Unless some other factor is at work, such as a higher moisture level in the first batch, the rose geranium leaves did not seem to harbor *Aspergillus* spores, because the arachnoid mat and rotted leaf smell did not result. Iris leaves worked fine in this regard.

Third: *Aspergillus* is not the principal mold at work in *kâmakh ahmar,* which turns out to rely on *Penicillium* spp. For this purpose, the essential is ordinary greenish bread mold.

Fourth: The canonical 40-day rotting period is unnecessarily long. Twenty days, or even two weeks, is enough. A layer of raw barley loaves should nearly fill the floor of the box, which should be covered for the first week or so to ensure moist conditions. Thereafter the lid should be removed so that the barley can dry. At the end, it will be generously covered with green spores and dry enough to pound into dust. I recommend using a food processor, rather than a mortar; otherwise the air will be unpleasantly filled with swirling spores.

Fifth: *Kâmakh ahmar* is, in its way, and despite its loathsome color, as much an old friend as *murri.* I followed the recipe given in *Kitâb Wasf al-At'ima al-Mu'tâda,* which uses five parts fresh milk to one part rotted barley and one part salt (all measurements by weight). Since *murri* is like soy sauce, I expected something like a sour 'yogurt cheese' with an added soy sauce flavor. But evidently the rotted barley contains so many spores of *Penicillium roqueforti* (and perhaps others of the same genus) that mold gets a head start on the yeasts and bacteria which would ordinarily monopolize milk cavalierly exposed on a porch or rooftop. The level of salt also inhibits some microbes. Instead of being a sort of yogurt, *ķâmaķh ahmar* has the sharp aroma of a blue cheese (in the beginning, of a very strong blue cheese; I have emptied rooms by opening a container of it).

Within a week, the drab green color from the mold spores becomes a reddish brown, justifying the recipe instruction to rot this product until it reddens (and its Arabic name, which means red *ķâmaķh*). After ten days, more subtle aromas develop which may be due to the same biochemical activities which produce soy sauce. I have not submitted this product to a laboratory and cannot say whether it contains significant levels of toxic contaminants such as kejoic acid, aflaxtoxin or b-nitropropionic acid.

The liquid also dries and thickens as it ages on one's porch or rooftop, making it a suitable condiment for bread, which was its medieval use. All the medieval recipes suggest flavoring *ķâmaķh ahmar* with herbs, spices, onion, garlic and so forth, evidently making it the medieval equivalent of flavored spreadable cheese products such as Boursin.

It has long been noted that Europe cultures dairy products with mold and East Asia does the same with beans and grain. The medieval Arab world was unique in mold-culturing both dairy products and grain.

A Dubious Competition

(SET BY THE EDITORS)

As a novelty, and in celebration of our fifth birthday, we propose the following competition.

The Whole Duty of a Woman (1737), to which frequent references were made by Jennifer Stead in her article in *PPC 13* and *14*, changed its title in later editions to *The Lady's Companion.* The two-volume edition of 1743 under that title, which we have recently been studying, contains a surprise. After the first 80 pages of admonitions constituting an 'Infallible Guide to the Fair Sex' and providing 'Observations for their Conduct thro' all Ages and Circumstances of Life'; and after the more than 2000 recipes, presented systematically and in a wholly serious manner, consonant with the aforesaid admonitions*; after all this come Bills of Fare, proposing dishes suitable for first and second courses for each month of the year. Nothing to raise an eyebrow or provoke a smile in these. But then, without warning, preamble, a change of typeface, or any other signal that the compiler's self-control has snapped or that an imp has taken over from the compositor, come the two pages reproduced overleaf.

Thereafter, all is normal again. Instructions follow on how to go marketing, how to make cosmetics and wines.

We are baffled, both by the very existence of these two rogue pages and by the nature of the jokes in the 'Oenigmatical Menu'. Jon Grossman has remarked in another context that we are slow to perceive a joke. We have spotted this one, thus doing something to redeem our reputation. But we don't understand it; and we have an uneasy feeling that this failure may lay us open again to Grossman's second charge, that we are not alert to obscene meanings. And yet . . . how could this book, of all cookery books, contain anything improper?

For the reader who sends in the most illuminating explanation of both the existence and the content of the OENIGMATICAL MENU (disregarding the Extraordinary Bill of Fare which follows it) there will be a prize of £100

*The author or compiler states in one passage that he does not expect women to foreswear laughing; a notable concession. But the general tenor of the advice leaves little room for laughter and suggests that any tendency in this direction should be indulged rarely and in a subdued fashion; and that it should of course be directed only at objects of innocent merriment.

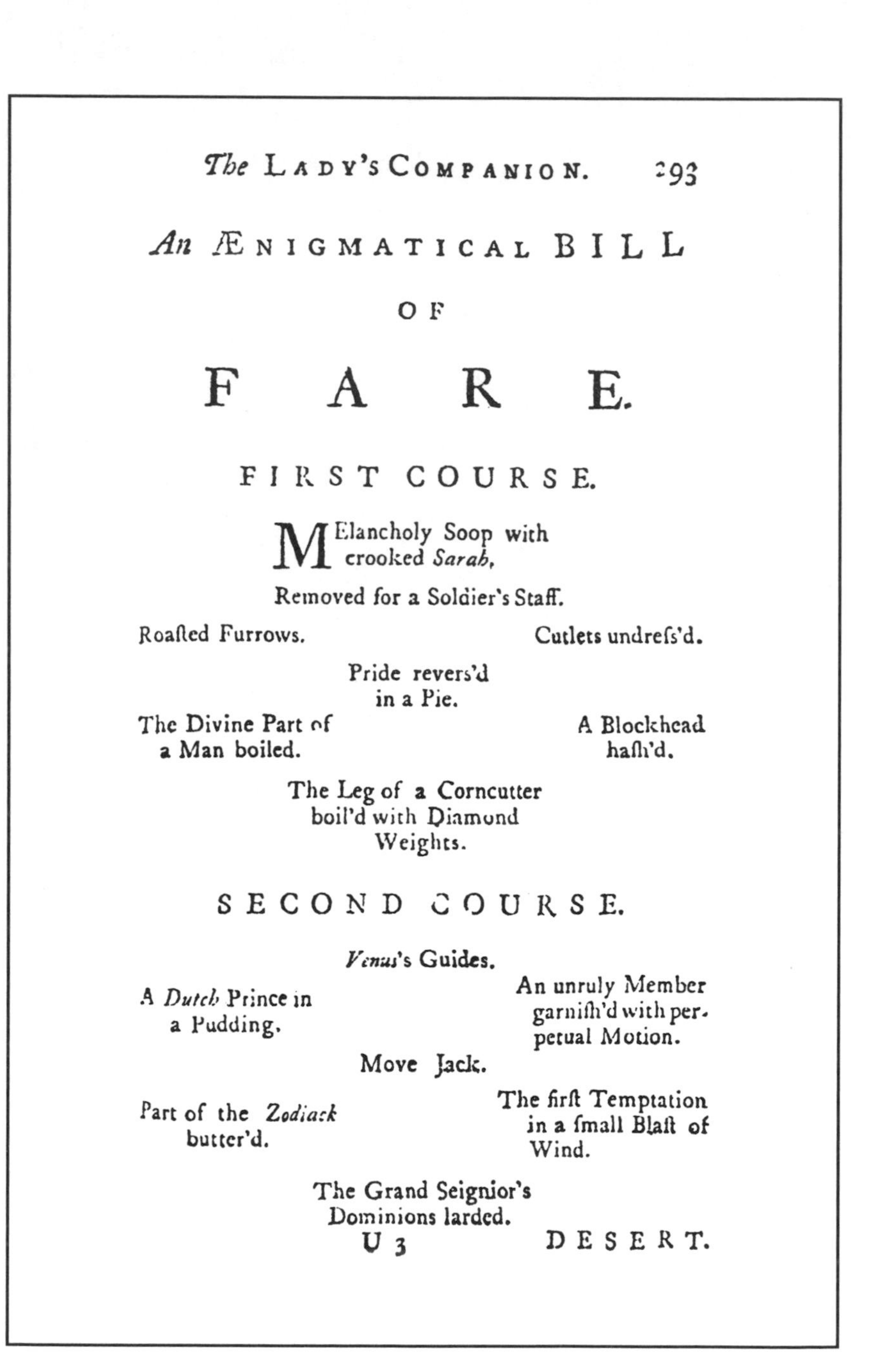

The LADY'S COMPANION. 293

An ÆNIGMATICAL BILL
OF
FARE.

FIRST COURSE.

MElancholy Soop with crooked *Sarah*,

Removed for a Soldier's Staff.

Roasted Furrows.

Cutlets undress'd.

Pride revers'd in a Pie.

The Divine Part of a Man boiled.

A Blockhead hash'd.

The Leg of a Corncutter boil'd with Diamond Weights.

SECOND COURSE.

Venus's Guides.

A *Dutch* Prince in a Pudding.

An unruly Member garnish'd with perpetual Motion.

Move Jack.

Part of the *Zodiack* butter'd.

The first Temptation in a small Blast of Wind.

The Grand Seignior's Dominions larded.

U 3 DESERT.

DESERT.

The Loſs of a Wiſe the Gain of a Huſband in Jelly.

Cow's Provender with Half Gooſeberries.

Some Hundred Thouſands.

Sorrowful Apples with bad Wives about them.

Buſy Bodies.

Couples.

The Reward of a Soldier in Cream.

LIQUORS.

The Joke of a Puppet-Shew made with Torture.
A Bottle of Hyp.
A Bottle of Bag.
A Bottle of *Torbay*.

A Bottle of Hill-Top.
A Soldier's Habitation with a pretty Girl in it.
A Side Grace Cup of lamentable Cloathing.

An Extraordinary BILL *of* FARE *in the High Goût.*

A Viper Soop.

Couple of roaſted Hedge-Hogs.

Fricaſey of Frogs.

Stewed Snails.

Badger's Ham and Cauliflowers.

worth of our books. It is not necessary to explain everything; only to do better than anyone else. The judge will be Jon Grossman himself and his decision will be final. He will have discretion to split the prize.

The Dubious Competition: The Judge's Report

'A knot!' said Alice. 'Oh, do let me help to undo it!'

[Editors' note: In this report *'LC4'* is the abbreviation used to refer to the 4th edition (1743) of *The Lady's Companion,* whence came the menu which was the subject of the competition.]

The competition proved to be a dubious one indeed. Most competitors addressed themselves only to decoding the clues; two furnished good analyses of the *nature* of the clues and how to decode them (one quite rightly compared them with the clues of the modern English crossword puzzle); but no one offered an explanation of what the Bill of Fare was doing in *LC4* in the first place.

Perhaps the answer was too self-evident. Riddles are as old as legend and folklore: the story of Oedipus and the Sphinx, one of the best known of the ancient riddle-stories, is far from being the first of them. And they have always been popular in England, the hilarious (and obscene) decoding scene of Malvolio in *Twelfth Night* being perhaps their most illustrious literary manifestation until the Mad Hatter asked, 'Why is a raven like a writing desk?' They had a tremendous fad during the first part of the 18th century, and at that time nearly every almanack and household-book featured them prominently. Presenting a riddling bill of fare after the 'normal' bills of fare in *LC4* was therefore catering to the popular taste, with the ingenious refinement of combining a number of riddles into a new (and, as one reader pointed out, perfectly plausible) menu.

Certainly the most curious entry came from Marian Brubaker (324 N. Duke Street, Lancaster, PA 17602, USA), who wrote as follows:

> The Bill of Fare and the attached 'Explanation' were found in the manuscript cookbook compiled by Sarah Yeates (Mrs Jasper) (1749–1829). The original book in Sarah's hand, and possibly that of a daughter, is in the collection of The Pennsylvania Farm Museum at Landis Valley, Lancaster, Pennsylvania. Sarah, who was the wife of a prominent Lancaster lawyer and judge, probably began her cookbook about the time of her marriage in 1767

[and therefore a quarter-century after the publication of *LC4*!]. Many of the receipts in her book are traceable to Hannah Glasse [and] Elizabeth Rundell, and it seems may have come from *The Lady's Companion*. . . . I confess I had imagined that Sarah herself had created the Enigmatic Bill of Fare. Now I content myself with the picture of Sarah and her friends working out the 'Explanation' around the tea table. The omissions from the explanation seem to indicate this rather than that Sarah found the key to it.

Allowing for minor editorial differences, Mrs Yeates' menu is the same as that in *LC4,* with one addition: 'Counterfeit Agony', explained as 'Champaign', Brubaker suggests that the addition was Sarah's. (Or perhaps it is a variant from a later edition of *LC*?)

Living in the heart of the Pennsylvania Dutch country, Sarah was geographically more remote from the origin of the riddles than we are, even if she lived a couple of centuries closer to it. As a result, a number of the clues puzzled her just as much as they puzzle us, and a few of her solutions have us sighing, with Byron, 'I wish she would explain her explanation!' Several of her answers differ from those of all other readers, but in only two of these is she clearly right, and in one she is very clearly wrong. She does however offer a useful starting point for examination of the replies.

The Answers Examined

Alice sighed wearily. 'I think you might do something better with the time,' she said, 'than waste it asking riddles with no answers.'

1. As a starter, 'Melancholy Soop with crooked Sarah' was a stopper. Mrs. Yeates guessed 'Brown Soup with Cel-e-ry'. One reader, a doctor, pointed out that melancholy, one of the four humours, traditionally resided in the kidneys, and therefore suggested kidney soup. Another entry, starting from 'sorry', reached 'sorrel soup with salad', a strange way to begin a meal. The best guess, and quite possibly the right one, was *'Mourning Soup with Sal-awry'*. The 'receipt' for 'A good savoury Broth for Mornings' in *LC4* specifies that 'you may add Cabbage, or Leeks, or Endive, or Parsley Roots, in the due Time . . . In the Summer you may put in Lettuce, Sorrel, Purslane, Borrage, and Bugloss, or what other pot-Herbs you like; but green herbs take away the Strength and Cream of the Pottage.' So celery is not absolutely ruled out.
2. Most competitors saw that 'A Soldier's Staff' was a *pike,* but
3. only Sarah and one *PPC* reader perceived that 'Furrows' *part ridges*!

4. 'Cutlets undress'd' puzzled Sarah and everyone else. One entry proposed 'cutlets au naturel', which is no way to eat cutlets in the civilized world. Another tried 'neck of lamb', arguing from the false premise that 'cutlets are usually dressed off a neck of lamb', so that 'undressed' they are still on the neck. In the unlikely event that bear was still to be found on 18th-century tables, my own guess would be 'bear cutlets'.
5. *Humble* ('umble', for us purists) *pie* for 'Pride revers'd in a Pie' troubled no one;
6. nor did *sole* for 'The Divine Part of a Man'.
7. There was however no such unanimity for 'A Blockhead hash'd'. Sarah Yeates went for 'A Calve's Head Hashed'; two readers suggested mutton-head; one entry pointed out that a woodcock, according to the *OED,* was a fool; another voted for 'turnip'; still another, for unavowed reasons, suggested Irish stew. (NO one proposed 'fool'.) Yet another possibility might be cock's comb, unhashed ingredient of two *LC4* Ragoos. Or coney?
8. All competitors agreed that the 'Diamond Weights' with which the 'Leg of a Corncutter' was boiled are *carrots,* but the leg itself gave them more trouble. Sarah Yeates says 'A Leg of Pork' but doesn't tell us why; a California reader agreed but was equally discreet. Another competitor proposed 'leg of beef' (imagine boiling a whole leg of beef!), advancing in its favour the following irrefutable but Dodgsonian reasoning: 'A corn-cutter is almost certainly a "bill" (short for billhook), but "bill" is also an old version of "bull" as in "papal bull".' (Strangely enough, neither the *OED* nor the first (and best) edition of *Webster's International Dictionary* lists 'corncutter' as meaning 'chiropodist', even though this is the most current household sense of the word. Could there have been a famous chiropodist named, for example, Lamb or Lamm?)
9. Three American readers defined 'Venus's Guides' as 'doves', but none told us why; Mrs Yeates was silent. In Europe at least, doves symbolize peace, or fidelity in love, traits neither of which is characteristic of Venus who, according to mythology, was as quarrelsome a harlot as they come.
10. Few competitors found it difficult to identify 'A Dutch Prince in a Pudding' as *Orange pudding.*
11. My own favourite riddle in the Bill of Fare is 'An unruly Member garnish'd with perpetual Motion'. Several competitors recalled the familiar mis-quotation 'The *tongue* is an unruly member' (*James,* iii, 8: 'The tongue is an unruly evil.'), but not all of these realized that only time (= *thyme*)

never stands still. One reader proposed 'Fidget pie garnished with Worcester apples,' arguing that 'an unruly member is a fidget, and fidget pie is an old Cheshire dish made with apples, onions and streaky bacon', while 'one of the heroic attempts to demonstrate perpetual motion was that of the Marquis of Worcester (ca. 1663), using a large wheel fitted with sliding weights. The reference to Worcester must be to Worcester pear-main apples, as Worcester sauce only dates from ca. 1845.' Any riddle that can generate a reply like that one can be proud of itself (which is more than one can say for an apple dish garnished with apples).

12. The same reader produced a brilliant explanation of 'Move Jack': 'The jack (in the game of bowls) is usually moved at the conclusion of one "end". Probably refers to changing finger bowls.' The other replies received were not much more convincing: Mrs Yeates says 'sturgeon' (but jack was another name for sturgeon, so that the riddle disappears; and jack is also the name of several varieties of pike, but we've already had pike in the first course); another entry suggested that a jack was a pulley (which it wasn't), whence 'pullet'; while still another proposed 'turned rabbit'. (But jackrabbit doesn't seem to pre-date the 19th century—Mencken says 1870).

13. There was general agreement that a *crab* is the 'Part of the Zodiak' most likely to be 'butter'd'. (The dish is included in the 'normal' bills of fare in *LC4*.) According to Marian Brubaker, Mrs Yeates proposed 'heart', but this is hard to understand, not only because a buttered heart doesn't sound appetizing but also because there is nothing like a heart in the zodiac.

14. All competitors knew that an *apple* was the 'First Temptation', and most of them also recognized a *puff* for 'a small Blast of Wind'.

15. Almost everyone knew that 'the Grand Seignior' (variously spelled) was the sultan of *Turkey.* One disciple of Humpty Dumpty ('When *I* use a word, it means just what I choose it to mean—neither more nor less.') found however that 'The Grand Seignor's Dominions larded' corresponded to 'fresh fruit steeped in liqueur', arguing that 'The Grand Seignor's dominions could refer to the island of Sark, which is divided into two parts connected by a ridge called the *coopée.* "Coupe" is a fresh fruit salad improved (or, in old English, larded) by the addition of liqueur.' ('When I make a word do a lot of work like that,' said Humpty Dumpty, 'I always pay it extra.')

16. 'The Loss of a Wife the Gain of a Husband in Jelly' stopped almost everyone. Sarah Yeates solved it, and so (I am proud to report) did I:

when a wife loses her heart, her husband gains horns—whence *hartshorn jelly.* (Note to *PPC* editors hunting out obscene meanings: this mild joke on cuckoldry is as far off-colour as the menu goes.) One ingenious reader proposed a rather nauseating 'junket in jelly', alleging that 'it is traditionally the men who go off "junketing", leaving the women-folk at home.' A tradition, I fear, more honour'd nowadays in the breach than the observance.

17. Most competitors offered 'strawberries' for 'Cow's Provender with Half Gooseberries', but I cannot agree. It is hay, not straw, that constitutes cow's provender, as any farmer can attest. (True, recent researchers such as Z. Müller, an FAO expert, have found that if you cook straw in a lye solution and then mix it with molasses and other goodies, you can get cattle to eat a little of it, but its food value, except as roughage, is about nil.) To obviate the difficulty, one contestant invented 'hayberries' which, he *said* he believes, is a local name for one of the wild edible berries. An interesting guess, if less creative, was 'stubble goose', but here again, cattle don't generally feed on stubble, and is this a proper dish for a dessert?

18. Dessert troubles continued with 'Some Hundred Thousands'. Sarah Yeates and a contemporary American reader said 'melons', but with no explanation: a particular variety? In England, in our day, 'hundreds and thousands', or 'vermicelli', are the nasty bits of coloured sugar used by some to decorate birthday cakes, but in the days of *LC4* these were 'vulgarly' called 'covering seeds' (recipe, volume II, p 281). My own theory, probably ruled out because of the position on the menu and for reasons of linguistic history, would otherwise be salmon, on the following reasoning: 100,000 = 1 lakh in India; 'some' hundred thousands = lakhs; lax (*OED*) = 'a salmon; in later use, some particular kind of salmon', but (still *OED)* obsolete, and 'revived as an alien word from the continent'.

19. 'Sorrowful Apples' inspired two readers to hypothesize—very tentatively—'crab-apples', and another 'apple dumplings', but the 'bad Wives about them' inspired almost no one. An interesting guess was 'Apple Shrewsbury' (whatever that is!), explained as 'Apples bury (therefore sorrowful) bad Wives (= shrews)?' But the bad Wives are 'about' the Apples, not vice versa; and if the Wives were bad, would the Apples be sorrowful? And if 'apples' are in the riddle, they probably shouldn't be in the answer. Sarah Yeates couldn't even make a guess. Reading 'false ribs' for 'bad Wives' is doubtful: the expression is more anatomical than culinary.

20. No credit is due for discovering that 'Busy Bodies' are *medlars;*

21. nor for observing that 'Couples' are *pears.*
22. Sarah Yeates was unable even to guess at 'The Reward of a Soldier in Cream', thus giving ground to all the other competitors, who at least guessed, but all differently: salary, trifle, pease, gages, ribbons . . . (MY own guess, based on bitter experience, was march-panes.) There was one creative guess: Blenheim apples in cream, on the grounds that 'the Duke of Marlborough was given Blenheim Palace for his soldiering during the War of the Spanish Succession.' There is indeed a variety of apple called 'Blenheim orange'; but what with apple puffs and possible crab-apples, I suggest that the menu might risk having too much of a good thing.
23. 'The Joke of a Puppet-Shew made with Torture' tortured everyone. Almost all saw that *punch* was involved, but made with what? Sarah Yeates says 'Ar-rack', and another American reader also favoured 'rack'. One entry called for champagne (why sham?); another proposed 'whipped punch', new to me; still another pointed out that there was an instrument of torture called the 'gin'. The offer of 'birch wine' cannot be taken very seriously (even if part of a recipe, probably based on *LC,* was included), because punch is clearly right, and birching, while painful (God wot), is not really torture.
24. The prudent silence of Sarah Yeates with regard to 'Hyp' was not shared by modern readers, who guessed variously at 'spirits', 'ale', 'hip-pocras', 'weak spirits' and 'bitter'. If there is any pattern to the replies to this competition, it lies in the fact that when there is a wide variety of guesses to a single riddle, *all* are likely to be wrong . . .
25. There was no such variety with 'Bag', identified by all as *sack* (= sherry),
26. and most competitors realized that there was a *port* at Torbay.
27. 'Hill-Top' puzzled most readers. Sarah Yeates favoured 'mountain', a Spanish wine mentioned in *LC4,* II, 306; while an American competitor specified 'English mountain' (called simply 'Raisin Wine' in *LC4,* II, 309), giving for it the following recipe from *The Farmer's Wife:* 'To make it. To each gallon of water put five pounds of raisins, with the stalks pulled clean off, and when they have steped a fortnight, let the liquor be squeezed into a barrel that has been well aired with brimstone burnt in a rag [the FDA being still happily uninvented]: when it has done working, let it be stopped close up, and in a month it will be ready to be bottled up for the use of the family.' *Mountain* is probably right, even if a mountain is not, properly speaking, a hill-*top.* (One reader guessed 'marc', on the grounds that 'hill-tops were often used as marks in surveying.')

28. A range of guesses, again, for 'A Soldier's Habitation with a pretty Girl in it', but here only Sarah Yeates is clearly right. One reader proposed Saragossa wine, arguing that Saragossa was 'a soldier's habitation' during the War of the Spanish Succession. Another tried 'barack with Angelica' (Who is Angelica? What is she, that all our swains commend her?). One modern reader got so far as recalling that *tent* is a sweet red Spanish wine, but he could find nothing better than a cherry to put in it. Unfortunately for him, and perhaps for her as well, Sarah lived in a time when they put *toast* in their wine, and a toast was a pretty girl as far back as the 17th century.

29. Only one competitor could even guess at the 'Side Grace Cup of Lamentable Cloathing', and his guess is an unconvincing one. 'Lamentable cloathing', he says, '(i.e. mourning clothes) would be most likely found near graves (a grace cup would be a sweet Graves from Bordeaux).' A grace-cup, the *OED* tells us, is 'the cup of liquor passed round after grace is said; the last cup drunk before retiring, a parting draught'. In short, the modern 'one for the road'. If 'lamentable Cloathing' is indeed weeds (and not rags or tatters or some such, as seems more likely), then a cigar might be a valid guess, tobacco being 'the weed' as far back as 1600.

Well, we will probably never have the entire Bill of Fare decypher'd.

The Winners

Much as I am tempted, I cannot resort to the Dodo's subterfuge that 'Everybody has won, and all must have prizes'. Two firsts and two seconds are the best I can do. Firsts, of £30 each, go to Marian Brubaker for Sarah Yeates, who got the greatest number of clearly or probably right answers, including some of the most difficult, and to Ann Arnold, of Berkeley, California, a close runner-up. Seconds of £20 each to Join C. Burruss, of Cambridge, Massachusetts—a consistently high standard—and to Dr J. C. Harrison, of Maidenhead, Berkshire, for a series of brilliant (albeit often erroneous in my view) diagnoses.

Hell upon Earth

OR *the Joys of Viper Soup*

SIMON VAREY

Back in 1984, *PPC* celebrated its fifth birthday by publishing its first (and last?) dubious competition, in *PPC 15:* the purpose was to identify the dishes lurking behind punning names given them in 'An Ænigmatical Bill of Fare', a two-page joke in *The Lady's Companion* (1737), a two-volume epitome of sobriety and composure. Interpretations were duly supplied by *PPC*'s assiduous and learned readers, and dubious prizes were awarded (see preceding article). However, there was another point to the contest, and that was to determine why a cookbook of this sort should suddenly plunge into the pages of jokes, and then, equally abruptly, plunge right back again into its seriousness without a word of explanation. Although D. Jon Grossman, the judge of the competition, had a go in delivering his judgment, no one really answered that one (neither can I).

Down in the bottom right corner of that mysterious two-page opening is 'An Extraordinary Bill of Fare in the High Gout', consisting of viper soup, a couple of roasted hedgehogs, a fricassee of frogs, stewed snails, the whole rounded off with badger's ham and cauliflowers. I can at least show where this dubious menu came from. In 1733 a pamphlet appeared in London, entitled *Hell upon Earth: Or, the Town in an Uproar.* The pamphlet remains obstinately anonymous. It is essentially a piece of catchpenny wit, an effort to have a little fun at the expense of fashionable London society, and in one particular passage the author aims for that society's desire to impress with ostentatious, exotic, or just rare and preferably foreign food.

Our anonymous pamphleteer tells a tale of his visit to a gentleman with pretensions. Rather oddly, the author slips off to the kitchen, where he meets a French cook preparing dishes whose principal ingredients will be unrecognizable: in the kitchen, the cook is pounding roast partridges 'in a Mortar, with all the Fat and the Inside of a Surloin of Beef; I ask'd him the Reason of this strange Havock, and he told me, it was to make a *Cullis* for a *Pupton'*. Readers are being invited to share the author's slack-jawed incomprehension, but this is also an example of cookery as trickery, only with overtones of ostentation and Gallicism: 'Legerdemain . . . Affectation and Folly.' This chef's bill of fare includes two soups, carp au court bouillon, pupton of partridge, beef à la tremblade, and cutlets à la maine; all this is followed by a fricassee of salamanders, huffle of chickens, pain perdu, oysters à la daube, blancmange, and stewed lion.

This menu is, for the most part, a collection of 'fancy' food, all of it supposedly French and absurdly adopted by fashionable Englishmen. The truly exotic dishes are salamanders, lion, and a huffle of chickens. 'Pupton' or 'poupeton' of partridge was at least to be found in English cookery books of the period, which still does not not make it a native, plain, or everyday dish, but I have never found any evidence of anyone in England in the 17th or 18th century consuming lion meat. (In fact, I know of only one restaurant of even vaguely Anglo-Saxon origin where it was ever possible to eat lion—the Parkway Grill in Pasadena, California—but maybe I have not travelled enough.)

In contrast to this supposedly ludicrous menu the pamphleteer then presents a 'natural' one chosen by a more robust Englishman with a healthy contempt for fanciful French frippery. The point about the viper soup menu is that it comes from the hedgerows, and thus, in a peculiar way, it confirms one of the normal rules of cooking that was reiterated implicitly and explicitly, in the books of the period: use ingredients that come to hand. In the English countryside in the 18th century, there was certainly no shortage of badgers, snails, frogs, and hedgehogs, which certainly do turn up, though not as popular favourites, in the period's cookbooks. Vipers were probably just as common, if more difficult to catch, and perhaps more likely to be boiled or grilled than put in soup. Ultimately, what is this little menu doing in *The Lady's Companion*? It is a joke in *Hell upon Earth,* but a joke with barely plausible roots in reality. Because it is placed next to the 'Ænigmatical Bill of Fare' in *The Lady's Companion,* nobody is expected to give it a moment's serious consideration, I would imagine. Could it be true that in ten short years from 1733 to 1743, viper soup and its companions had passed, already, into the realms of unmentionable cuisine?

Postscript from the Editors

While preparing the above for publication we observed in 'Jottings from the dean, issue 40' which constitutes the enclosure to (the recent) Catalogue 67 from Cooks Books (T. & M. McKirdy, 34 Marine Drive, Rottingdean, Sussex BN2 7HQ) that the McKirdys have been sent a similar puzzle. Theirs is called 'An Enigmatical Dinner' and it figures not in a cookery book but in *The Kaleidoscope, or the Spirit of the Periodicals,* Compiled and Published by Christopher Columbus Crosstree in Philadelphia in 1831. It features 14 first courses, 11 beverages, and 16 desserts. The McKirdys offer a small prize 'to the person who makes the *most* sense of it and will pass on the answers (or not) in the next Jottings'.

Viper Soup, Viper Broth, Viper Wine

Jennifer Stead

The author, a local historian in Leeds, has been a frequent contributor to PPC *and is one of those responsible for initiating the annual Leeds Symposia on matters to do with food history.*

I am delighted that Simon Varey has found the origin of the joke menu, 'An Extravagant Bill of Fare in the High Gout' which appeared so mysteriously in *The Lady's Companion* (1743). In it, viper soup, roasted hedgehogs, frog fricassee, stewed snails, badger's ham and cauliflowers are all held up for our ridicule. Simon Varey has discovered that the origin is a 1733 pamphlet: 'a piece of catchpenny wit, an effort to have a little fun at the expense of fashionable London society', aiming especially at 'that society's desire to impress with ostentatious, exotic, or just rare and preferably foreign food'. He wonders: 'Is it true that in ten short years, 1733 to 1743, viper soup and its companions had passed, already, into the realms of unmentionable cuisine?'

All the dishes sound unmentionable to most British ears (except cauliflowers!). However, the origin of most of the dishes lies in Richard Bradley's *The Country Housewife and Lady's Director Part II,* 1732, pp 143–6.[1] This collection of recipes includes many unusual ones from contributors overseas, including France, a Mr Ganeau[2] has contributed two frog fricassees, a white and a brown; two stewed snail recipes, one in white and one in brown sauce; and a viper-soup. From Mr R.T. of Leicestershire comes a gammon of badger roasted. But where are the hedgehogs? And what of the cauliflowers?[3] Bradley, a Fellow of the Royal Society, has dedicated this book to Sir Hans Sloane, President of that society. It is not beyond the bounds of possibility that Society members, who were constantly making experiments of all kinds, actually sat down to such a jokey dinner, partly for 'science', but mostly for fun. They would discover, for instance, as Mr R.T. said, that badger 'eats like the finest Pork, and is much sweeter than Pork'. In his introduction to Part II of *The Country Housewife and Lady's Director,* Bradley acknowledges the assistance of his contributors, who are 'Persons of Distinction, and good Oeconomy'. He goes on: 'Most of the Receipts I have been witness to, at some Meal or other.'[4] He had travelled widely on the Continent, and eaten frogs and snails in France.

Here is the recipe for Viper Soup, from Mr Ganeau:

> Take vipers, alive, and skin them, and cut off their Heads; then cut them in pieces, about two Inches in length, and boil them, with their Hearts, in about a Gallon of Water to eight Vipers, if they are pretty large. Put into the Liquor a little Pepper and Salt, and a Quart of White Wine to a Gallon of Liquor; then put in some Spice, to your mind, and chop the following Herbs, and put into it: Take some chervill, some white Beet-Cards or Leaves, some Hearts of Cabbage-Lettuce, a shallot, some Spinach-Leaves, and some Succory. Boil these, and let them be tender; then serve it up hot, with a French Roll in the Middle, and garnish with the raspings of Bread sifted, and slices of Lemon.

This viper soup is dinner-table fare, and must have been highly unusual, perhaps a short-lived wonder. However, viper broth, as a medicine, had a long vogue in England: it survived into the second half of the 19th century among country folk.

Only the heads of vipers are venomous—the heads were cut off and the gall was also avoided, but the flesh, liver and bones were all used. Pliny and Galen regarded viper flesh good for curing ulcers and elephantiasis, among other diseases. In 17th-century Italy, where vipers were plentiful, they were made by apothecaries into viper oil, salt, troches, powder, and essence: these were highly regarded medicines for a range of diseases. In Britain, viper jelly and viper wine could be made easily at home: the latter was made by simply drowning the viper in wine—unless small snakes were used, a large vessel was necessary as the full-grown British viper is over two feet in length, and fat.

Dr John Schroder, in *The Compleat Chymical Dispensatory in Five Books, Englished by William Rowland, Dr. of Physick,* London 1669, says: 'Vipers are stronger than other serpents in Virtue'. However, he also said, perhaps because of the paucity of vipers in some areas of Northern Europe: 'Some call all Serpents Vipers.' This was still true in England in the 19th century where vipers (adders) and other snakes were being caught with a cleft stick for use in medicines.

In 1732 John Arbuthnot in *Rules of Diet in Aliments* (I, 509) said: 'Viper-broth is both anti-acid and nourishing.' Viper preparations, like so much other physick labelled 'nutritive, restorative, strengthening, invigorating, vitalizing', were often taken in the belief that they would restore failing libido. In 1631 Francis Quarles wrote:

> Their Viper wines, to make old age presume
> To feele new lust, and youthfull flames agin.
>
> *The historie of Samson,* in *The Complete Works in prose and verse of Francis Quarles,* ed A.B. Grosart, 3 vols, 1880/81; II 149/2.

and also in 1631 Philip Massinger wrote:

> . . . viper wine,
> So much in practise with gray bearded gallants [is]
> But vappa to the nectar of her lippe
> *Believe as You List, a tragedy,* IV, I

In 1745 Eliza Haywood wrote in *The Female Spectator* No 12 (1748), II, 292, of 'Lady Frolick pouring a glass of viper wine down his throat'.

The Academy magazine of 1896, 28 Nov, 448/3, mentioned 'The legend that Lady Digby died of drinking viper-wine.'

Viper broth enjoyed its main popularity in the early 18th century. In gentry and aristocratic houses, it was made in the distilling room, generally by the lady of the house, whose special care it was to prepare medicines and invalid food. The method was that noted by C. Anne Wilson as being described in *A Closet for Ladies and Gentlemen,* 1611: in order to extract all the essence and supposed virtues out of animal flesh, a cock is stilled, not in the usual copper alembic, but in a stopped-up 'glassen pot'.[5] A jug or other vessel could also be used, so long as it was covered and sealed well with huff paste, and then immersed in a large pot of continuously boiling water for several hours. Sir Kenelm Digby noted how, in the 1620s, his mother and the Countess of Kent made broth for invalids 'In a close flagon *in bulliante Balneo*'. (*The Closet of Sir Kenelme Digbie, Kt., opened:* 1669, p 141, 1920 edition.)

I have just finished writing an introduction to a collection of MSS recipes from Dorset, dated in the 1780s, among which is a medicinal recipe for viper broth which uses a similar method:

To Make Viper Broth

Take a Viper and cut it very small, and then take a Vial that will hold nigh a pint put into it a half a pint of Water and the Viper cut in pieces will be careful in corking the bottle very close and tie it over the Cork with a piece of Cloth, then put the bottle into a pot that will hold water enough to cover it then put the pot over a gentle fire and let it boil four or five hours, the best method is to boil it in the evening and let it stand in the same till the Morning then put it over the fire again and let it boil till it is warm enough for drinking when you may strain it through a piece of Muslin or any thing that is thin in to the bason you drink out of.

Drink this four eight or ten Mornings fasting at least an hour after it, after resting four of five days you may repeat it again, and if it should happen to go against the Stomach or drink insipid you may add in the boiling one small blade of Mace, and after it is boiled a very little salt which will make it very pallatable.

This recipe was for a very small snake; the pint vessel held only 16 oz, and half its volume was filled with water.

In 1843 *The Penny Cyclopaedia* (XXVI, 349/1) said 'the lingering belief in the wonderfully invigorating qualities of "viper broth" is not yet quite extinct in some places.' Did it really invigorate those parts that other broths couldn't reach?

References

1. Richard Bradley, *The Country Housewife and Lady's Director,* Parts I and II, first published in 1727 and 1732 respectively; facsimile from the 1736 edition, with an introduction, a list of recipe contributors, a glossary and notes, and bibliography, by Caroline Davidson; Prospect Books, 1980.
2. Caroline Davidson noted that Mr Ganeau or Garneau of Brussels sent Bradley eight recipes, three of which are published in Part I.
3. Before I discovered the dishes in Bradley, I found the inclusion of cauliflowers odd and it made me wonder if this was not a satirical reference to some public personage, most likely a cleric—clerics were noted for their cauliflower wigs—and if the animals represented public figures too. However, Bradley's book rules this out.
4. There is no reference to the eating of unusual animals in vol VII, 1724–1734, of the *Abridged Philosophical Transactions of the Royal Society,* but there may be a reference in the Society archives in Burlington House.
5. C. Anne Wilson, 'A Cookery-Book and its Context: Elizabethan Cookery and Lady Fettiplace', *Petits Propos Culinaires 25,* p 22.

A Rattle in the Throat: The Unmentionable Cuisine

SAM ARNOLD

This is a version of an address which the author prepared for the October 1994 conference of the Western Historical Association.

Rattlesnake eating isn't all that difficult. It's just that lots of people have a problem with eating snake. Many people fear all snakes, and wouldn't touch 'em with a ten foot snake pole. Truth is, the meat is rather like chicken, and after being braised for 90 minutes, it comes away from the bones in flakes, not unlike lump crab. I guess it's the thought of it that turns people off, but surprisingly, it's number one of all the appetizers at my restaurant, The Fort, near Denver. We serve some 200 snake portions a week, and 1200 pounds of rattlesnake meat a year.

My first experience with cooking rattlesnake came in 1975 when Historic Denver held a three-day downtown festival called 'Night in Old Denver'. Somehow, my wife nodded yes at the wrong moment when they were looking for food booth operators, and I ended up preparing 4,000 buffalo burgers, 300 pounds of rocky mountain oysters and 120 pounds of rattlesnake. We bought the snake from west Texas where they'd caught them for use at the big San Antonio fiesta. We got the leftovers.

Today, rattlesnake catching is a much larger business. Citizens of small west Texas towns catch them in big communal rattlesnake roundups. Those who bring in the largest, or most, or highest weight, are the winners of trophies and cash awards. The snakes are put in a large box, and sent by air to Denver, where companies like Dale's Exotic Meats process them. They're poured out onto a cold-room floor. The temperature is lowered and the snakes go to sleep.

Next, a man enters the room, picks up the snakes and decapitates them. Then they are skinned, cleaned and packed in Cryovac and frozen. The heads are freeze-dried for use as hat decorations, or key 'tainers; the skins used as wallets, boots, cowboy hat bands, and other items.

Well, back in '75, this being my first snake venture, I found that all I could get from Texas was 120 pounds of snakes for the three-day event. So, I rationed them to 40 pounds a night, brought in two large deep fat friers, and offered the snake first thing in the evening when the event opened. We made a thin tempura type batter of flour, egg, salt and water. I went to cut the snakes, some long and thin, others short and fat, and a few over six feet in length . . . into four inch pieces. I cut down hard with a good Henckel French chef's knife. The blade broke, against the steel-like bones. I tried another knife, and broke another $40 blade. Rattlesnake bones are tough! Too tough for a good chef's knife. I went to a cleaver, and hacked the snake into pieces . . . shorter for the fat, full ones, and longer for the narrow ones. Then, after dipping them in the tempura batter, they were dropped into the hot fat. In a short time, they were golden brown, and delicious. We sold out each evening's 40 pound quota in the first hour of each night. That told me that there was indeed a BIG market for rattlesnake. The buyers at $2 for two pieces all said that it tasted like good fried chicken.

Now at The Fort, nightly we serve more than 30 cold rattlesnake cocktails . . . 2 ounces of cooked snake meat, on a bit of lettuce, with a dab of sweet chile sauce and a slice of lemon.

The price is $7.50 which isn't hard to understand when you realize that we pay between $11 and $12 a pound for the skinned, cleaned snakes which are more than 50% bone. The meat costs us $24 a pound, or $1 per half ounce.

We buy the snake coils, frozen, from the wholesaler, and let two or three snakes thaw at a time. One must be very careful of salmonella, just as with raw chicken. Gloves should be worn, and working surfaces sterilized with Clorox.

Then the snakes are braised in a pot with minced onions, bay leaf, and black peppercorns. When we began serving snake, we had a near riot in the kitchen, for some of the younger workers went to peek at the snakes as they were heating up. The snakes were writhing in the pot, and looked like they were alive! While it was just the dead snake's muscles flexing as they thawed in the heating water, it was scary, and several dishwashers took off.

After about 90 minutes of gentle cooking, the snake is done. We cool it, and then by hand, strip off the meat from the bones . . . mostly rib bones. Incidentally, one enterprising dishwasher collects the rib bones, cleans and bleaches them, then packs one to a glassine envelope, and staples these to a large card advertising 'mountain man toothpicks'. They are sturdy, and make a splendid toothpick. Sherrill Garramone, a senior waitress, collects the vertebrae and fashions beautiful necklaces from them. The extreme white and intricacies of the vertebrae make a handsome, high fashion choker, or necklace with a stone or gold pendant. The Fort buys them from her and resells them in our trade room.

We have, at the restaurant, a great big coiled, mouth-wide-open, beady-eyed, stuffed, 14-bead rattler named Fat George which I like to take to tables where they're really interested in the snakes. Most children don't seem nearly as offended by Fat George as adults. But one lady ordered six servings, saying that she'd been told by a rattler-bitten friend of hers from eastern Colorado, to 'please eat up as many of those nasty buzz-worms as you can'. The lady showed me pictures of her friend whose arm was swollen double and was hideously black. She'd really suffered from snake bite.

We have rattlers in the fields near The Fort, and likely in the big red rock which is adjacent to it. I have to say that although our staff has seen 'em, in owning the property for 35 years, I personally have never seen one on my land. The old farmer, the late Ott Sanger, who used to grow wheat in the fields below The Fort, once showed me a cigar box filled with big rattles which he'd taken from the snakes he'd met while raising his wheat.

Eating snake, including rattler, is common among Orientals who, during The Year of the Snake a few years ago, bought up all the whole snakes they could find. They wanted the entire snake, head, skin, gall bladders . . . all. The price which had been about $9 per lb. rose above $12, and for a year, rattlers, or any other kind of snake too, became almost unavailable.

Calvin Schwabe, in his book *Unmentionable Cuisine,* tells how a Chinese café owner in a small Montana town also ran a thriving business in rattlesnakes. He'd put the snakes in bourbon, drowning them and letting them age for four or five years in the bottle. The bourbon was filtered through a piece of bread, and then shipped to San Francisco's Chinatown where it was reported in great demand as a cure for rheumatism, arthritis, and impotency. A 'Chinese Montana rattlesnake recipe' from this same café owner has gutted, skinned and bite-sized pieces of snake marinated in a mix of soy sauce, garlic, ginger, and bourbon; then laid on partially cooked Chinese rice and cooked until both are done.

A soup of snake and cat meat is found in China, and last January, while in Singapore, I was offered snake in alcohol touted as an aphrodisiac.

In China I bought green snake bile wine, which was reputed to give one the lithe, slithery nature of a snake, and to alleviate symptoms of rheumatism and arthritis. It was sweet and weird in taste, clear green in color. I didn't have rheumatism, but I'll swear by it. (However, it made me neither lithe nor slithery.)

A Good Rattlesnake Soup

A good rattlesnake soup may be made by cutting the snake into 2" pieces, then flouring them with seasoned (red and black pepper, garlic salt) flour. Heat 1/3 cup oil with a bit of butter till quite hot, then sauté julienne (toothpick) shreds of fresh ginger, six diagonally sliced green onions, one minced serrano chile, and two smashed garlic cloves. When crisp, remove these from the oil, and cook the snake, browning all sides in the hot, flavored oil. Return the green onions and ginger and add a quart of delicate chicken broth. Simmer all, then top with a few cilantro sprigs, and some hardboiled peeled quail eggs.

Rattlesnake meat may be used for making meat balls, or better yet, rattlesnake crab cakes without crab, by adding French bread crumbs, an egg, minced onion, water chestnut, and some toasted sesame seeds. These are formed into patties about 3/4" thick by 3" wide, then pan-sauteed until brown on both sides.

What about the potential for over-using rattlesnakes and putting them on the endangered list? Not likely, say the west Texas rattlesnake producers. There are jillions of new snakes each year, and the known dens are not diminishing. They lay lots of eggs which hatch new snakes, and rattlers are found in a large part of the country. I have found that the mountain snakes here in Denver aren't very big, long or fat. But the largest skin I've seen was 76" long. A 7" diameter isn't unknown.

What's the future for rattlesnake meat cuisine? Ross Allen in Florida years ago used to sell canned rattler . . . but it didn't taste too wonderful. A good novelty. But we have people who come back again and again to have more, so there must be some future for farming these snakes for food. Ogden Nash put it well in his poem, 'Experiment Degustatory':

> A gourmet challenged me to eat
> A tiny bit of rattlesnake meat,
> Remarking, "Don't look horror-stricken,
> You'll find it tastes a lot like chicken."
> It did.
> Now chicken I cannot eat.
> Because it tastes like rattlesnake meat.

The Subject of Worms

ANON

This subject, once it had been raised by Anon, attracted surprisingly many comments.

Diet of Worms **from Anon**

I do not wish to be publicly associated with the eating of worms, if only because some of the those near and dear to me are excessively squeamish on this and other similar matters.

However, I had occasion recently to do a little research on this and was puzzled to find that it is not uncommon to come across references to the eating of earthworms, but it is quite difficult to locate first-hand reports. I am left thinking that maybe in a lot of cultures, past and perhaps present also, earthworms have been eaten as a matter of course. But I also speculate that this may be quite wrong, and the currency of undocumented reports about eating earthworms may simply reflect the fact that a lot of people find the idea quite sensationally repulsive, and it is the sensational aspect of the matter which has caused a few straws of evidence to be built up into myths which have acquired a life of their own.

In this situation, my curiosity strongly aroused but no definite conclusions drawn, I was alerted by Glen Baxter (acting in his capacity as a member of Interspi) to the fact that the current (December 1995) issue of *GamePro,* a periodical devoted to computer games, provides, sellotaped to its cover, a transparent lollipop in which is embedded a 'worm', which is identified inside as a larval form of *Tenebrio molitor,* the very item which is added in Mexico to Tequila. Again, first-hand information about consumption of these lollipops is not easy to obtain. However, I have three definite reports. The 10 year old son of another Interspi member consulted a school friend then went ahead and consumed the lolly, but reported later that it was 'disgusting'. The second report, which was actually published in a Yorkshire newspaper, reached me through yet another member of Interspi. It states that a girl called Joanne, aged 13, was only too keen to eat the creepy crawly, though she was not so happy with the lolly! However, it emerged from the report that she is known as 'a tough cookie', who plays with her brother's fishing maggots. The other 13 year old, Ben, lacked this promising background but nevertheless 'gritted his teeth' and tried the worm. 'It's warm and crunchy, it tastes all right,' he said.

I should be grateful for any comments, and also for any information which will assist me in my ongoing research programme into the children's verse which lives on in the memories of many adults but which is rarely found in print, the authoritative version seeming to be that given in *Puddings and Pies* compiled by Iris Grender. The text there given is:

> Nobody likes me, everybody hates me,
> Guess I'll go and eat worms,
> Long fat curly ones, short fat wriggly ones,
> Worms that squiggle and squirm.
> I bite their heads off,
> I suck their bodies out,
> I throw the skins away.
> Nobody knows how well I thrive,
> On worms three times a day.

However, I have heard several other versions and know that some people prefer, for example, to have the 5th, 6th and 7th lines in the imperative ('Bite their heads off . . .').

The fact that Interspi channels have been so productive in this whole affair deserves thought. On top of what I have already recorded, I had the probably unique experience of listening to the verse being sung to me by the (Californian) Chief Etymological Adviser to Interspi. I am sure that no one would wish to see the main thrust of Interspi's work on rare spices weakened by diversification into other areas of study. On the other hand such diversification could only be beneficial to these other fields of study, and it may be that the intrinsic dynamism of Interspi is so strong that it can safely spread its tentacles ever wider and wider.

Eating Worms — from Various Contributors

The query from Anon in *PPC 51* flushed out a number of experts on worm cookery or persons with vivid recollections of worm-eating incidents. Our thanks to **Lynda Brown**, who went off at a slight tangent to investigate, with the help of Charles Dickens, what the worms themselves like to eat (cabbage leaves are the top treat, but they also go for sugar and liquorice and have an occasional nibble on mint). **Maggie Black**, in a vein of personal reminiscence, writes: 'I remember vividly the disdain with which my cousin and I, then aged seven, treated my three-year-old brother when he was removed by Nanny from our garden's goldfish pond and up-ended to get at the worms he was swallowing. She did not seem to think them a suitable delicacy for the christening-party my parents were giving for our youngest sibling (who was screaming, purple-faced, at not being able to share the treat, being still "in arms"). Nanny just spanked us all impartially whether we had eaten worms or not.'

Fritz Blank, writing from the Deux Cheminées in Philadelphia, contributed snatches 'of another ditty about corpses which we children would sing whenever a funeral procession was encountered':

> The worms crawl in, the worms crawl out;
> The worms play pinochle on your snout.
> [then something about]
> They use your bones for telephones . . .

Nothing gastronomical here, but Fritz Blank then snaps into focus and points to chapter 20 of *Unmentionable Cuisine* by Calvin W. Schwabe. This book, which Anon had overlooked, contains a Chinese recipe for Earthworm Broth (*Tio in tin tan*). But the really startling information in it is that Gaddies North American Bait Farm, of Ontario CA, used to (and may still) sponsor earthworm recipe contests; and that these would produce about 500 recipes each year! Schwabe quotes Gaddie as saying: 'Worms [presumably dried] taste like shredded wheat. I like them best in oatmeal cookies, but I've eaten them with rice, sprinkled on top of salads . . . with scrambled eggs and with steak and gravy.' We learn that another enthusiast compared the taste of worms to that of jerky; and that worms reputedly consist of 72 percent protein and less than 1 percent fat.

Worms, Worms, Worms . . . — from Elise Fleming

Following Anon's revelations in *PPC 51* ('Diet of Worms'), readers may be interested in an historical use of worms. In *A Queen's Delight* by W.M., 1655 (reprinted by Prospect Books in 1984) there is a recipe on page 100 for 'The admirable and most famous Snail Water' which calls for a quart of worms. The recipe goes:

> Take a peck of garden shell snails, wash them well in small beer, and put them in a hot Oven till they have done making a noise, then take them out, and wipe them well from the green froth that is upon them, and bruise them shells and all in a stone Mortar, then take a quart of earth worms, scower them with salt, slit them & wash them well with water from their filth, and in a stone Motar [sic] beat them to pieces, then lay in the bottom of your distilled pot Angelica two handfuls [sic], and two handfuls of Celandine upon them, to which put two quarts of Rosemary flowers, Bears foot [stinking hellebore, the plant *Helleborus foetidus*], Agrimony, red Dock Roots, Bark of Barberries, Betony, Wood sorrel, of each two handfuls, Rue one handful, then lay the Snails and worms on the top of the Herbs and Flowers, then

> pour on three gallons of the strongest Ale, and let it stand all night, in the morning put in three ounces of Cloves beaten, six penniworth of beaten Saffron and on the top of them six ounces of shaved Harts-horn, then set on the Limbeck, and close it with paste, and so receive the water by pints, which will be nine in all, the first is the strongest, whereof take in the morning two spoonfuls in four spoonfuls of small Beer, and the like in the afternoon; you must keep a good Diet and use moderate exercise to warm the blood.
>
> This Water is good against all Obstructions whatsoever. It cureth Consumption and Dropsie, the stopping of the Stomach and Liver. It may be distilled with milk for weak people and children, with harts-tongue and Elecampance.

For delectability of ingredients this Snail Water is nearly the equal of Ann Blencowe's 'horse dunge water', recommended for women in labor and in childbed!

And More Worms — from Diana Bolsmann

Here is more information on Mopane worms, a local delicacy where I come from. They are seasonally available in their dried form in certain shops. I have never tried them!

Malcolm Funstor talks about the worms in *Bushveld Trees:* 'The insect most widely associated with the mopane tree . . . is the emperor moth, *Imbrasia belina,* for its voracious caterpillar—colourful, large and spiny—inundates the trees at certain times of the year and can denude large stands of their leaves . . . Today the mopane worm is the centre of a thriving industry and is even distributed canned in tomato or peri-peri sauce!'

In *Food in Africa: Roots of Traditional African Food Culture,* Renata Coetzee writes:

> Different caterpillars are eaten in different societies, depending on location. The method of preparation is usually to squeeze out the insides, wash them and either fry them in their own body fat in a cooking pot until they are brown, or cook them in a little water.
>
> The caterpillars are often dried to preserve them throughout the year. They are cleaned, boiled and then spread out in the sun to dry. To cook these, they are first boiled in a small amount of water and then fried in fat.
>
> The best known caterpillars are those feeding on the Mopani tree. They are called *masonja* and are relished by the Northern Sotho people.

Rather gruesomely, the editor of *The Shell Guide to the Common Trees of the Okavango Delta* describes the ingestion process: 'When the Mopani worms are gathered, their heads are squeezed off and then discarded. I have been witness to Bushmen consuming these raw, wriggling, headless creatures and deriving much pleasure from the squirming of onlookers.'

Rather them than me.

Yet More on Worms **from Anon**

Ove Fossa (joint winner of the 1995 Sophie Coe Memorial Prize—see page x) has demonstrated his versatility by switching attention from whales (which won him the prize) to insects. He has tactfully set me straight on the identity of the 'worm' which Glen Baxter introduced to me, thereby setting off this whole correspondence. He writes:

> The Tequila worm lollipops mentioned in *PPC 51* are advertised on the Internet by a company in Seattle along with crème de menthe flavoured cricket lollipops! I assumed at first, as was done in *PPC 51,* that *Tenebrio molitor* is the larvae in the tequila bottle, and maybe it occasionally is used for that purpose. *Tenebrio molitor* is not, however, the *gusano* or maguey worm, but the common mealworm. I quote from Sophie Coe, *PPC 20,* p 51–52: . . . *the notorious maguey worms, the white larvae of* Aegiale hesperiaris *and* Agathymus *spp and the pink larvae of* Xyleutes redtenbacher, *which still appear in bottles of mezcal (a form of tequila) to make tourists shudder . . .*

Ove also sent me a mass of interesting material on other aspects of insect-eating, much of it gleaned from the World Wide Web. Since insects have already invaded quite a few pages of *PPC,* I can hardly occupy another two dozen with this other material. Perhaps some of it, such as addresses for ordering your Tequila Worm Sucker lollipops (Archie McPhee, P O Box 30852, Seattle, WA 98103) can be accommodated in a later issue of *PPC.* Meanwhile I can't resist popping in a few choice extracts. Like the same Archie McPhee's Internet ad for another of his products, the crème de menthe item mentioned above:

> We have all experienced the social stigma of being caught eating bugs in public. Now with Cricket Lick-It you can ingest insects without shame. Nestled in the center of a sugar-free crème de menthe flavor sucker lies a crunchy cricket just asking to be eaten! Avoid scorn and ridicule, eat your insects in the nineties way.

I must add that Ove has been collecting insect recipes, as well as other information, from the Web, and that one of the resources he has tapped is at Iowa State University, whose recipes include Banana Worm Bread, calling for '1/4 cup dry-roasted **army worms**'. (They also offer Bug Blox and Chocolate Chirpie chip Cookies, this last item being where crickets finally meet their fate.)

Army Worms

The Editors

We recently received from Ian Jackson (for whose erudite essay about the history of the pear see *PPC 49*) a remarkable contribution to the literature on insects as human food. This is reproduced on the following pages, with the kind approval of the Lowie Museum of Anthropology at the University of California, Berkeley. Our purpose is to give to Samuel Barrett's remarkable research, so far only available in a volume of *Essays on Anthropology,* an additional lease of life in a food history context.

Samuel Barrett (1879–1965) had a long and distinguished career as anthropologist, ethnologist and museologist. He was at the Milwaukee Public Museum for thirty years, as Director from 1920 to 1940. It was during this period that he wrote about the army worm, drawing on fieldwork which he had conducted among various groups of Indians in the period 1903–7. Perhaps it was not a coincidence that during the Second World War he was called upon to serve as associate director of the Army Specialized Training Program on the Berkeley campus of the University of California.

We regret that we could not reproduce the plates which are referred to in the essay. However, they are not essential and the important drawing which Barrett included in his text is still present (see page 391). It has prompted the following comment from Ian Jackson:

> The careful drawing of the pits (and this not a permanent installment comparable to a town plan, but temporary battlements closer to choreography than surveying) surely foreshadows the installations that he is said to have been expert at in his museum career.

Barrett described his army worm very precisely but did not give it a scientific name. Seeking to discover what this is, we have found indications that the name is applied to different species in different places. Craigie and Hulbert (1938, *A Dictionary of American English*) give the following definition for army worm:

> The larva of the cotton-moth (*Leucania unipuncta*), a caterpillar very destructive to grass, grain, etc.

Among their numerous citations of use are several which seem to show that the 'worms' appeared in the mid-West of the USA (Illinois, Indiana, Michigan). One refers to the army worm attacking cranberry bogs in New England.

Among other reference works, *Insects* (Hamlyn, 1979) refers to 'the African Armyworm (*Spodoptera exempta*)' as owing its name to the way in which it descends like an army on crops of maize and sorghum in Africa.

THE ARMY WORM: A FOOD OF THE POMO INDIANS

By S. A. Barrett

Among the Pomo, as among most Californian tribes, practically everything in nature was called upon to furnish its quota of foods. Insects were not omitted from the dietary of this tribe, grasshoppers, angleworms, yellow-jacket grubs, and various others being esteemed.

Perhaps the most interesting insect used as food by the Pomo is the so-called army worm [lī' (C)]. Like certain other insects this worm has a cycle which causes it to appear in vast numbers once every several years. The exact periodicity is not known and could not be determined by questioning the Indians.

It happened to be the writer's good fortune to drop in at the Yokaia rancheria on the morning of May 15, 1904, only to find that the entire village was deserted except for two of the very aged. From these he learned that the entire population had moved down to a certain grove on the eastern bank of Russian river, where the army worms had suddenly appeared in hordes, the first time since 1898. Taking one of these old men along in the buggy, for he was too feeble to walk the several miles, the author immediately joined in the "hunt" and spent the entire day observing the gathering of this, the rarest, of all Pomo foods. The following statements are not, therefore, mere hearsay but direct personal observations confirmed by photographs, four of which are reproduced here in plates 1 and 2.

The army worm is a caterpillar which is almost hairless, having not to exceed half a dozen hairs on its entire body. It is about 2½ inches in length and is a general brownish color with Indian red stripes along the sides. The male [lī'baiya (C)] is distinguished, according to the Indians, from the female [lī'maṭa (C)] by the fact that it has a pinkish white belly, while the belly of the latter is always yellow in color.

According to the Indians' statements this worm comes only for at most a few days, in the early summer and only in years when there is a great deal of fog. It is said to belong to Thunder and to travel on the fog from the west. It feeds exclusively on the leaves of the ash [kala'm (C)], and when an army of these worms finishes with a grove of this species there is not a vestige of green to be seen. Plate 1, figure 1, shows some very small ash saplings at the edge of an opening and immediately adjacent to the larger ash trees of a grove. These had been completely stripped by the army worms so that they looked like the naked branches of deciduous bushes in the winter time.

It is an interesting fact that these worms move from tree to tree or from grove to grove chiefly in the afternoon. From observations made, this fact may be explained as due to the sun's heat. Eating during the night and early part of the day, the worms divest the trees of their leaves and the sun's rays pour in upon them, causing them to drop to the earth and seek the shelter of the leafy canopy of another ash which has not been disturbed. There is of course more or less movement of the worms all day long for, regardless of the hour, if a tree has been stripped of its leaves the worms descend to earth in search of a new food supply. However, by far the greatest number move in the afternoon. Their descent from the tree is as a rule most precipitate. They simply let go and drop, and this apparently without harm to themselves, regardless of the height. Almost never is one seen to descend the trunk of a tree. During the day the author spent in this ash grove, he was subjected to a continuous hail of falling army worms and a shower of leaf fragments dropped by the worms from their lofty dinner table.

The Indians know very well the route the worms will take when they do drop to the ground and move on to the next ash tree or grove. They prepare for this advance by digging large numbers of pits and trenches across the line of march of the worms and by encircling the bases of the ash trees toward which they are moving. These pits are of various sizes and shapes, circular, square, or rectangular. Each is about 6 inches in width and rarely more than 2½ feet in length. They are always from 4 to 6 inches in depth, and are vertical-walled little moats dug in the solid damp sand. As the worms race over the ground, with incredible rapidity, they fall into these little moats in large numbers. Yet seeing that they can ascend the vertical trunk of a tree, surely a vertical wall of solid damp sand proves no obstacle and they will climb out of this prison with the utmost ease. And so they would if it were not for the clever device employed to prevent just that kind of escape. When the little moats are dug the Indians bring over a quantity of fine, dry sand, with which they line the edges of the tops of these pits. The captive caterpillar finds no difficulty whatever in ascending the vertical wall of his prison, but when he reaches the edge of the pit his feet encounter the line of shifting, dry sand so that he loses his balance and topples over backward to the bottom of the pit again. Try as he may, he never can get out so long as the line of dry sand lasts at the edge of the pit. For this reason fresh dry sand is added from time to time. Also this line of dry sand serves another purpose. While it is true that these worms race along at great speed they are cautious to a certain extent. When they reach the edge of such a pit they could easily turn aside. They, however, are on the dry sand which shifts and rolls them headlong to the bottom of the pit.

There is one means of escape, however, which must be carefully watched. When a pit is fairly well filled with worms, the topmost ones can make their escape fairly easily. Therefore pits must be emptied quite frequently to prevent this.

In plate 1, figure 2, we have a very characteristic set of these sand-lined pits completely surrounding the base of a tree. In this particular instance, there were fourteen circular pits each about 6 inches in diameter and together making about 120 degrees of the circle. There were also six rectangular pits varying from 9 to 30 inches in length. These finished the line which completely encircled the base of this tree, and which formed a circle about 5½ feet in diameter. The spaces between successive pits is not to exceed an inch in each case, a space too small to allow a worm much chance to slip by on the dry rolling sand.

Another tree had a circle about 25 feet in diameter encircling its base and made by only eighteen pits varying in length from 1 to 3½ feet. Each had a width of about 6 inches and was 6 inches in depth.

Other such pits are arranged in straight or curved lines many feet in length across the general line of march of the army worms. One such set of

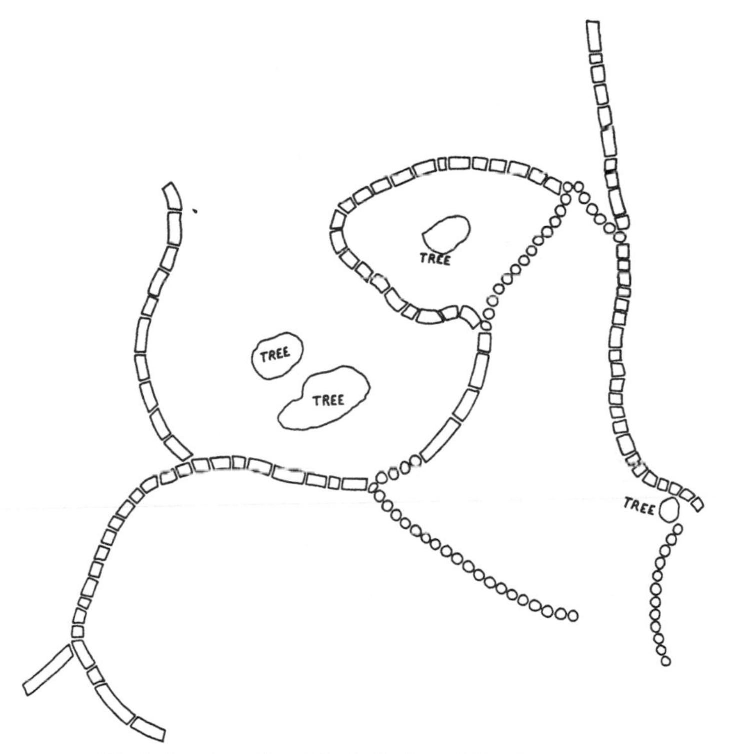

Fig. 1. A system of sand-lined pits for catching army worms.

pits numbered forty-two. They were rectangular and varied from 6 to 15 inches in length. Another line of thirty-seven pits measured nearly 50 feet in length. Another rather intricate pit system is shown in figure 1.

With all these deadly pitfalls we might think that no worms could possibly escape. However, some do, and to insure the fullest possible harvest, the Indians place girdles or collars [lī hubeu (C)] of ash leaves about the bases of the trees, 3 or 4 feet from the ground, as shown in plate 1, figure 2. The worms that do run the gauntlet and escape the pits start to ascend the tree, are arrested by the fresh ash leaves, and are easily collected by hand.

Other workers also obtain quite a harvest by hand-picking worms from the low young ash saplings.

When the worms are obtained, whether it be from the pits, from the collars, or from the saplings, they are immediately placed in a vessel of ordinary cold water, where they quickly drown.

They are then roasted in hot ashes or are boiled and are devoured in large quantities on the spot. When everyone has satisfied his appetite, the cooked worms are spread out in the sun to dry for winter use.

Plate 2, figure 1, shows some of the live worms crawling about on the inner surface of a basket before being placed in the water. Plate 2, figure 2, shows a Pomo woman sifting out some of the army worms. They are first placed, with live coals and hot ashes, in a tightly woven basket to roast, after which they are placed in an openwork sifting basket, to separate them from the ashes. This method of cooking turns the worms a reddish color and is said to produce a very excellent sweet flavor.

Custom requires that conversation shall be carried on in low tones and that no undue noise shall be made by those gathering the army worms, because it is said that the worms become alarmed and leave. If any noise is made the army worms in the immediate vicinity will stop eating, raise the forward half of their bodies at an angle of about 30 degrees and sway the elevated part of the body rapidly back and forth in agitation for some time.

No one may speak crossly to another under penalty of being bitten by a rattlesnake.

Loeb,[1] in speaking of the army worm, states that they are gathered with much ceremony and great solemnity. His information comes from the Northern Pomo and is undoubtedly merely a statement made by an informant. It does not correspond with the above direct observations among the Central Pomo. In our work we found no solemnity; on the contrary we found much joy, though not boisterous, for reasons already stated. There was no singing of ceremonial songs and no idea that this food must be kept and treated with special respect. It was eaten on the spot and handled in every way just as any other food might be.

Just as the army worm appears, so suddenly and mysteriously does he disappear. Without warning of any kind he is gone and does not reappear again for several years.

It was really a red-letter day in any Pomo community when this little caterpillar made his appearance, and the Indians made this the occasion not only of an immediate feast but they stored for winter use as large quantities as possible of the dried caterpillars. No opportunity presented itself to check the amount dried upon this particular occasion, but certainly several hundred pounds of the dried product were garnered by the inhabitants of this relatively small village.

[1] Pomo Folkways, UC-PAAE 19:164.

Milwaukee Public Museum,
Milwaukee, Wisconsin.

'Snails', 'Caterpillars' and 'Worms'

MARJORIE COHN

The coincidence of an old paddle tennis court turned into a vegetable patch and the acquisition of a 19th century guide to New England horticulture, which included tennis-ball lettuce, eventually led Marjorie Cohn into an investigation of the use of vegetable pseudo-animals as culinary jokes. This odd outcome could not have been predicted from the author's professional background: she is the Head Conservator and Philip and Lynn Straus Conservator of Works of Art on Paper at the Harvard University Art Museums, Cambridge, Massachusetts.

Like many suburban vegetable gardens, my tillage is restricted to one corner of a houselot. The property, less than one-quarter acre in the town of Arlington, an older, inner suburb of Boston, is largely occupied by the house and driveway, and the north half is heavily shaded. Only the southwest corner is flat and sunny enough for crops.

When we bought the property in 1972, this area was entirely paved over by an asphalt paddle-tennis court. The designer and first owner of the house had been, according to an elderly neighbor, a 'sport'. His inclinations were still betrayed not only by the court but also by a massive doghouse, wood-framed and stuccoed to match the house. I stored my garden tools there, and after eight years of tucking lettuce and tomato plants into flower borders, I decided to convert the court into a vegetable patch.

Eighteen inches of asphalt, crushed rock, and cinders were carted away. The boulders unearthed below were added to a nearby wall, more than doubling its height. The plot was refilled with twenty-six yards of loam enriched by rotted horse manure from a nearby police station. When the court was excavated, I left foot-wide paths still faced with the playing surface along its former base and service lines. The walkways would keep my shoes cleaner, I supposed, and the division of the plot into rectangles would be an aide-memoire for crop rotation over the years. Yet these were only rationalizations for my keeping at least a trace for archeologists of what must have been Arlington's first and only paddle-tennis court. Nor could I bring myself to pull up the net-stanchions. I planted a laundry tree in one and planned to run twine to the other to support cucumber vines.

The next event in my new garden's calendar, the mid-winter arrival of seed catalogues, coincided with the low point of the New England salad season, when supermarkets carry only tasteless, odorless iceberg lettuce. Their pale green pyramids are matched by pale red tomato mountains, corroborating testimony to the efficient rigidity of spheres bred for packing, shipping, and stacking. But the seed catalogues offered the prospect of vegetables that could not support dozens of their fellows, that could not even support themselves if imprudently set down counter to their own succulent structures. Brittle leaves that had to arch from their stalks, plump fruits that had to hang from their vines if they were to reach the salad bowl intact were promised not in a single variety but by dozens. Burpee, my favorite supplier (preferred because of faithful mailings to a penny-ante customer for so many years), did offer an iceberg lettuce and a 'winter storage' tomato, but it also offered fifteen other kinds of lettuce and thirty-four other tomatoes.

Such were my hopes for a prodigal spring, the first year of my garden I selected five different lettuces. Considering my life with lettuce over the past few years, I seem to be recapitulating the childhood formation of the sense of quantity and quality. First I had recognized only the difference between none and some (even if it was only iceberg). Then, after we bought our house but before I built my garden, I learned to insist upon either nothing or the best, for I had space to grow only a single kind. Now that I had the luxury to multiply my selections, I discovered that discrimination faltered above a certain number—one, two, three, more.

My ingenuous enthusiasm for more and more lettuces was put sharply into perspective by my acquisition at a local antiquarian book fair of a

Fearing Burr, Jr (1816–97), from an old photograph, courtesy of Mrs Merideth R. Abbey.

vegetable gardening manual, *The Field and Garden Vegetables of America* by Fearing Burr, Jr, first issued in 1963.[1] I bought it hoping that a book which antedated modern fertilizers, pesticides, and refrigeration would support my urges toward organic gardening without imposing the cultism inherent in the revival of extinct crafts: here would be honest gardening. Burr, a farmer from Hingham, Massachusetts, twenty-five miles southeast of Arlington, did not disappoint me; but it was not his hints for cultivation and storage that made his sections on lettuce, tomatoes, and salad plants in general so immediately marvellous to me. It was his enumeration of varieties.

Burr listed fifty-two lettuces, including, to my delight, the 'Tennis-ball', which he described as 'one of the oldest and most esteemed of the Cabbage [head] Lettuces'.[2] After months of searching, I would finally locate in a historical seed catalogue 'Tennis-ball' seeds, too late to plant in the cool spring weather they require. Next year!—the gardener's perennial comfort.

In 1863 the tomato was still a relative novelty. Burr not only gave as its alternate tag 'Love-apple'; he commented, incredibly, that 'to a majority of tastes, its flavor is not at first particularly agreeable'.[3] After detailing the plant's culture and propagation, with wood engravings of 'hoop' and 'trellis-training', he described no less than twenty-four varieties. Tomato nomenclature seemed less well developed in 1863 than that for lettuce, which surpassed 'Tennis-ball' with 'White Stone Cabbage' and 'Monstrous Brown Cos'. Tomato names were more subdued: 'Large Red', 'Round Yellow', 'Yellow-Pear-Shaped', though one kind, 'of a rich, deep color and remarkable solidity', received the encomium 'The Cook's Favorite'.

Although in his Preface Burr gave a terse epitome of the farmer's vocation—'to plant, to till, to watch, and wait an entire season'[4]—he was synopsizing his calendar to raise produce not for market but for his book, produce which included crops 'which have proved of little value either for the table or for agricultural purposes.' Burr did not intend to recommend only a selection to his reader. Rather, he wanted to inform him of everything, 'to give full descriptions of the vegetables common to the gardens of this country', 'the characteristics which distinguish the numerous varieties; their difference in size, form, color, quality, and season of perfection; their hardiness, productiveness, and comparative value for cultivation'.[5] From every indication one can learn from his writings and his few memorials, Burr's heart-of-hearts did not lie with vegetables; rather, he was a lover of lists. Among experts in any field, even one so mundane as the kitchen garden, a certain number will always revel in the exact identification of their ingredients or products. They will find their greatest pleasure in itemization, even above the items themselves, and Burr was one of these.

Fearing Burr, Jr, the fifth generation of his family native to Hingham, was born and died in a Federal mansion still standing on Main Street.

Brick-ended, hip-roofed, with quoined corners and dentilated eaves, the elegant home was nonetheless his family farmhouse. Its front windows overlook the Hingham Centre burying ground, where in 1897 at the age of eighty-one he joined his ancestors. Among them were the Fearings, from whom Burr gained his remarkable Christian name with its fortuitous intimations of Puritan gloom. He was named after his father, whose mother and mother-in-law were the first and tenth daughters of Hawke Fearing, an eighteenth-century Hingham farmer. Hingham was a long-settled town of few families (Burr's business partner was his first cousin Matthew Hawkes Burr, the grandson of Hawke Fearing's first and second daughters), and it was not surprising to discover that a listmaker such as Fearing Burr, Jr, would also have been drawn to 'geneological studies', as reported by his front-page obituary in the October 8, 1897, *Hingham Journal*.[6]

Though in business as a grain, produce, and seed dealer for twelve years until he took over his late father's Hingham Centre store, Burr was primarily a market gardener. He worked the family farm, a long, narrow plot which stretched almost two-fifths of a mile west of Main Street. There were rose and peony beds around the house and behind it a greenhouse filled with grapevines, which kept the cellar full of wine bottles.

Burr was a founder and active member of the Hingham Agricultural and Horticultural Society and a member of the Massachusetts Horticultural Society, where, according to his memorial in the society's *Transactions,* he served upon 'several of its important committees, including those on Fruits, Vegetables, etc.'[7] Burr alive would never have tolerated the indefinite 'et cetera'. At the annual fair of the Hingham Society, where others exhibited 'turban squashes' and 'peppers', Burr in 1867 won $1 (a significant prize) for 'Potatoes, sixteen varieties'. And in 1857 the Massachusetts Society awarded his seed firm a silver medal for its display of 'Sixty Varieties of Beans, all neatly and correctly labelled.'

Burr's local obituary characterized him as, 'in his early life . . . a faithful student, quick as an arithmetician, and an especially good grammarian,'[8] just the talents that in their most simplistic development, in what seems to have been a simpler time, would have led a Hingham farmer to count and describe vegetable varieties. Late in life they also led him to collaborate in the definitive three-volume *History of the Town of Hingham.*

Burr did not, however, write the chapter on farming or even the massive geneology of the town's families (where his earliest listed progenitor was the 1647 Hingham settler Simon Burr, 'farmer' and where Fearing Burr, his father, was described as 'distinguished through life for his practical knowledge of Horticulture'). Fearing, Jr, then seventy-eight, was 'a well-known author and horticulturist'. Burr was the author of the chapter titled 'Publications', a catalogue of books, pamphlets, articles, essays, and, most notably, printed sermons by Hingham natives. His listing is replete with technical descriptions such as 'royal octavo' and critical annotations such as 'long out of print and valuable'. Evidently Burr, whose education had like that of all his Hingham Burr relations stopped at the Centre school, was a bibliophile. His writings betray access to an excellent library, perhaps his own, which seems to have been dispersed after his death. Odd volumes with his signature or a personal dedication to him still turn up in the second-hand stores.

One obituary noted that 'Mr. Burr was a dilligent reader', another that 'Mr. Burr was a ready and efficient writer, and his pen was never long idle.' Such a literary bent sent to the service of the lowly kitchen garden offered an irony that Burr enjoyed, even in the parochial context of the local agricultural society where, presumably, the elite bred horses and their wives raised varietal roses. Burr began a lecture (titled with typical pleasure in verbal niceties 'Vegetable Gardens and Garden Vegetables'): 'It is true that there is a charm in the graceful motion of a noble horse, and there is sentiment in a collection of roses . . . But when you speak of potatoes and squashes, of beans and cabbages, . . . Poetry covers her face in mortification and disgust.' He went on to vindicate his cabbage patch: 'Possessing no beauty, dressed in the plainest garb, and forbidden the parlor, there is scarcely a class of the products of the earth that contributes more to human happiness and comfort.'[9]

Of course, the plant as food is always the vegetable gardener's muse, and in *Field and Garden Vegetables of America* Burr was almost eloquent when he referred to the actual consumption of, say, Persian melons: 'As a class they are not only prolific, but their flesh is extremely tender, rich, and sweet, and flows copiously with a cool juice, which renders them still more grateful.'[10] Yet despite his rhetorical disclaimer about some vegetables 'Possessing no beauty', by the account of his own book and his obituary Burr was also susceptible to the visual appeal of vegetables. In the *Hingham Journal*'s compliments upon his character, an appreciation for beauty was matched with utility: 'of spotless purity in the domestic walks of life, courteous, hospitable, kind, he found time and opportunity to embellish its routine with what was useful and beautiful as well as enduring.'

Though the obituary writer may simply have intended an allusion to the wine cellar and peony beds, Burr's book reveals a home-grown vegetable aesthetic as well developed and certainly more altruistic than that of commercial seed catalogues bursting with hyperbole and illustrations. He recommended even the attractive culture of vegetables, with, characteristically, order as the criterion of charm: 'The staking, or bushing [of peas] . . . should be of equal height, and all straggling side twigs should be removed, for appearance's sake.'[11]

But Burr's most constant emphasis was on the visual appeal of the produce itself, whether through its forms or colors: 'The large Purple Winter Radish is a beautiful variety . . . of a beautiful purple . . . the coat, when cut through, shows the purple very finely.' '[Varigated or Spotted Chicory is] distinguished by the color of its leaves, which are veined, and streaked with red. In blanching, the red is not changed, but retains its brilliancy; while the green becomes nearly pure white, the two colors blending in rich contrast. In this state they form a beautiful as well as tender and well-flavored salad.' ['Green Curled Lettuce is] one of the most beautiful of all the Lettuces . . . When in perfection, the plants have the form of a rosette, and make an excellent garnish.'[12]

In this aesthetic vein, Burr constantly reiterated the value of vegetable garnishes, extolling them grown to 'perfection': 'In some gardens [Dwarf Curled Parsley] is grown to such perfection as to resemble a tuft of finely curled green moss.' He specified the means to these verdant ends: 'The best curled Parsley is obtained by repeated transplantings . . . when thus treated, the plants become remarkably close, of a regular rosette-like form.'[13]

Lulled by his emphasis upon vegetable beauty and its acme in garnishes, it was a shock to discover, in Burr's chapter on salad greens, sections on 'Snails', 'Caterpillars', and 'Worms'. These it seemed, were vegetables whose seed pods 'so nearly resemble . . . caterpillars [or snails or worms] as to completely deceive the uninitiated or inexperienced.'[14] They 'are sometimes placed on dishes of salad to excite curiosity, or for pleasantly surprising the guests at table.'[15] Had the obituary writer who found Burr so 'hospitable' and 'kind' been a guest at that table?'

It is easy enough to imagine that in an age before the proliferation of insecticides little beasts would turn up as inadvertent garnishes even on the lettuces which, according to Burr, themselves 'furnish a beautiful garnish for either fish, flesh, or fowl'.[16] In fact, Mrs Beeton, a nineteenth-century cookbook author, cautioned that 'sufficient care is not . . . always bestowed upon cleansing [salad greens], and there is no doubt that parasitic animals are sometimes introduced into the human body through such negligence.'[17]

Yet nothing in Burr's writings or his memorials proves that he played the pranks he describes so amiably, and twentieth-century horticultural dictionaries may simply echo his manual and not reflect practice. They describe '*Scorpiurus* . . . Caterpillars . . . seed-pods being used as a salad-garnishing by those fond of practical jokes' and 'as surprises in salads and soups'. '*Astragalus hamosus* . . . worms [are] of a mediocre taste but [are] employed in Salads chiefly to cause an innocent surprise.' '*Medicago scutellata* [snails are] cultivated for the odd pods, which are sometimes used by Old World gardeners as surprises or jokes, and are occasionally grown in this country as oddities.' These eccentric garnishes, like the salads themselves, were for American writers sometimes slightly suspect as evidence of Continental sophistication.[18]

A quick survey of nineteenth-century cookbooks confirmed that for home cooking as well as haute-cuisine, garnishes were an essential ingredient of culinary success, although 'Snails', 'Caterpillars', and 'Worms' went unmentioned by name. Fashions in cooking are as subject to argument and revision as every other manifestation of good taste, and by 1923 deceptive practices were condemned in the *Book of Unusual Soups*: 'Some time ago we used to run to silly garnishings that violated both logic and good taste in the fact that though meant to stimulate appitite they could not be eaten.'[19] (According to the dictionaries, 'Snails', 'Caterpillars', and 'Worms' are edible, though it would be a strange appetite that they stimulated.)

The 1938 *Salads and Herbs* also rebuked urges toward prankish imitation which survived from earlier times, 'the monstrous period of food fantisies . . . which deceived and discouraged the appetite'. 'Undoubtedly food should look like what it is, with no attempt to play tricks on the expectant palatte.' With no mention of the 'Snails', 'Caterpillars', and 'Worms' which might have sparked such unequivocable condemnation, the authors went on to recommend violet salads to accompany Chateau d'Yquem sauterne and sauteed sunflower buds to honor the State of Kansas.[20]

Finding that none of the cookbooks advocated imitation insects in salads, I turned to early vegetable seed catalogues, hoping that in an analogy with modern-day full-page spreads for cheap revolvers, the availability of means would make practice obvious, even though the ends could not be explicitly recommended. In the catalogues I was delighted to discover that 'Tennis-ball' lettuce was as much a favourite as Burr had indicated, and Joseph Breck and Son even offered in 1902: 'Black Seeded Tennis-ball, Arlington strain. One of the most popular sorts'. A century ago my home town had been a national leader in horticultural practice. It had pioneered hothouse vegetable culture ('Tennis-ball' lettuce was recommended for forcing) and developed many new market-garden seed strains, including one, evidently, expressly suited for my made-over court.

With even greater delight I discovered that in 1868 the same company had offered among its lettuces not only 'Tennis-ball' but also 'Magnum Bonum Coss'. My fantasies, nurtured on science-fiction films of horrible man-eating plants, discovered the secret revealed by meaning and monogram: 'Magnum Bonum Coss' was the magic antidote to Burr's 'Monstrous

Brown Cos'. Their initials 'MBC' were my own, and I imagined myself waving my leafy personal charm above the invader predestined to attack Marjorie Benedict Cohn. I'd found the lettuce cross to hold before the lettuce vampire! But no 'Snails,' 'Caterpillars', or 'Worms' joined these more fanciful monsters in the standard listings of available seeds.

The catalogues did advertise many specialized collections, including 'Novelties', which always comprised not jokes but new varieties. They offered 'Miscellaneous Agricultural Seeds', which included sugar cane and peanuts, 'Assorted Seeds for Families', which did not indulge any childish taste for pranks, and in Brecks's 1949 catalogue even 'Seeds for West Indies . . . with names in French, English and Spanish'. Herb collections for cooking and medicinal purposes were fairly common, but they never included simulated bugs and beasts. And Kelway and Son, 'The Royal Seed and Nursery Establishment . . . under the distinguished patronage of Her Most Gracious Majesty the Queen,' even offered in 1886 a special section on 'Plants for Decorating and Garnishing'. But 'Kelway's Invincible Parsley' was not joined by 'Snails', 'Caterpillars' and 'Worms', and Queen Victoria would have had no occasion to exclaim over her salad that she was not amused.

In the end it was in a horticultural dictionary, *Description des plants potagères* of 1855,[21] exactly comparable to Burr's manual of eight years later, that I found the probable source of his texts on prankish garnishes. He cited the French book first among the published sources in his Acknowledgments. Burr must have read it assiduously as he imported seed 'both from England and France,' although it is hard to imagine that his command of a foreign language could have been well-polished at the Hingham Centre School.

Description des plants potagères, fore-runner of the well-known illustrated work *Les Plantes Potagères* (1883), seems to present the earliest reference to 'Snails', 'Caterpillars', and 'Worms' as salad jokes. Earlier botanical dictionaries, including Lamarck's great *Encyclopedie méthodique* of 1783, simply describe the plants and the mimicry of their pods. While Lamarck noted that in the late eighteenth century 'Snails' and 'Worms' grew in the Paris Jardin du Roi, he did not mention a role for them in the cuisine of the Milkmaid Queen Marie Antoinette. Presumably the gardens' earlier royal proprietor Louis XIV would have found such a use a bad joke indeed, for the Sun King suffered from real works, probably 'ascarids', according to his recent biographer, 'usually associated with eating improperly washed salad'.[22]

The French manual was not translated into English until 1885, when its 1883 edition's listing of 'Vers' was rendered: 'Salad Milk-vetch', or 'Worms'. Like the seed-vessels of Caterpillars, they are, as a harmless practical joke, sometimes put into Salads, to startle the unwary, but their flavour is poor'.[23]

Unfortunately, the nice distinction between poor taste and poor flavor essential to a discussion of 'Worms' as a garnish eluded the translator, for the French text 'des surprises innocents, mais d'un goût assez médiocre' can refer only to the taste of the chef and not his ingredients. Burr's laconic conclusion to his section on 'Worms'—'Though inoffensive, they are seldom eaten'[24]—is nearer to the French in spirit, although the conventional modern connotation of 'inoffensive' is as much a misunderstanding of a meaning altered over time as 'their flavour is poor' was a mistranslation of the foreign tongue. To Burr 'inoffensive' would have simply meant that the pods were harmless.

Though it seemed likely that Burr's acquaintance with 'Snails', 'Caterpillars', and 'Worms' was at first only a literary one, I was left wondering if he had imported their pods among those seeds he obtained from 'both England and France'. Would a 'courteous' and 'hospitable' farmer 'of spotless purity in the domestic walks of life' have slipped a 'Snail' into his salads?

According to his obituary, Burr's 'remarks were received with attention for their real merit and practical bearing', but surely this is too sober and utilitarian a characterization. A home-grown *literateur* and agrarian aesthete, he was surely not 'all business'. In fact, though a working farmer, he regretted the contemporary transformation of agriculture into an industry. 'As in manufacturing and the arts, so in the matter of raising our vegetables, there is an evident concentration of forces . . . the market garden is but a colossal manufactory, where roots of celery and asparagus are made by the acre, cabbages and melons, by thousands, squashes by tons.'[25] Only the lack of cross-continental refrigeration saved lettuces from his list.

'Regret the fact as we may, there is no power strong enough to turn . . . this setting tide . . . we are gradually losing what so long has been . . . in its ever varying attractions and wealth of wholesome, health-preserving products . . . an object of interest and source of truest enjoyment to those maturer years, who will search in vain for a substitute.'[26] In Burr's self-admittedly anachronistic kitchen garden there would always be room for yet another lettuce which, in his words, though not 'equal to many . . . as it is deficient in crispness, and tenderness of texture—qualities essential in all salad plants', still had its 'recommendations', 'particularly its beautiful appearance'.[27]

Burr would pick his crops for beauty; I'd choose mine for their names, like 'Tennis-ball' and 'Magnum Bonum Coss'. And perhaps both of us, if we could find the seeds, would plant 'Snails', 'Caterpillars', and 'Worms' in defiance of good taste and agribusiness together. A garnish for beauty or a bad joke would seem to be the ultimate luxury when multi-national corporations form yet people starve, but such garnishes may be the saving gracenote in such a world. Even a 'Monstrous Brown Cos' is welcome in my patch.

References

1. Fearing Burr, Jr, *The Field and Garden Vegetables of America,* J. E. Tilton & Co, Boston, 1865. The first printing was in 1863.
2. *Ibid,* p 359.
3. *Ibid,* p 628.
4. *Ibid,* p vii.
5. *Ibid,* p pp v–vi.
6. [George Lincoln], 'Fearing Burr', in *Hingham Journal* of 8 October, 1897, p 1. For general information on Hingham, the Burr family, etc, see: Fearing Burr and George Lincoln, *History of the Town of Hingham, Massachusetts,* 3 vols, Hingham, 1893.
7. *Transactions of the Massachusetts Historical Society,* 1899, p. 189.
8. Lincoln, 1897.
9. Fearing Burr, Jr, 'Vegetable Gardens and Garden Vegetables', in *Hingham Agricultural and Horticultural Society Transactions,* 1881, p. 66.
10. Burr, 1865, p. 178.
11. *Ibid,* p 506.
12. *Ibid,* pp 75–6, 324, 351.
13. *Ibid,* pp 417, 416.
14. *Ibid,* p 310. Burr lists four varieties of 'caterpillar': the common, furrowed, prickly, and villous or hairy.
15. *Ibid,* p 384, referring here to 'snails'.
16. *Ibid,* p 347.
17. Isabella Mary (Mayson) Beeton, *Mrs. Beeton's International Cookery,* Platt & Peck Co, New York, undated, pp 80–1.
18. See, for example: L. H. Bailey, *Cyclopaedia of American Horticulture,* 2nd edn, the Macmillan Co, New York, 1902, pp 116, 259, 997, 1990; E. Lewis Sturtevant, *Sturtevant's Notes on Edible Plants,* J. B. Lyon co, Albany, 1919, pp 75, 358, 528. Sturtevant dates the introduction of 'snails' into American gardens to '1863 or before', citing Burr.
19. Mary D. Chambers, *A Book of Unusual Soups,* Little Brown & Co, Boston, 1923, p 3.
20. Rose, Cora and Bob Brown, *Salads and Herbs,* J. B. Lippincott Co, Philadelphia, 1938, pp 262–3, 129.
21. Vilmorin, Andrieux, et Cie, *Description des plantes potagères,* Paris, 1855. This reprinted much information, including a description of 'caterpillars' as salad surprises, from: Poiteau et al, *Le bon jardinier, almanach pour l' année 1853,* Dusacq, Paris, 1853.
22. John B. Wolf, *Louis XIV,* W. W. Norton Co, New York, 1968, p 597.
23. Vilmorin-Andrieux, *The Vegetable Garden,* John Murray, London, 1885, p 511.
24. Burr, 1865, p 390.
25. Burr, 1881, pp 70–1.
26. *Ibid,* p 71.
27. Burr, 1865, p 352. Referring to Green Curled lettuce.

Elder: 'A Good Udder to Dinner'

LYNDA BROWN

When Lynda Brown first swam into the ken of PPC *readers she was active as a food historian in the north of England. Besides the essay presented here, her best known contribution was on oatcakes, as made by Stanley's crumpets in Barnoldswick, a town which had the unusual distinction of being in Yorkshire until 1974 and in Lancashire thereafter: one of the most vivid and detailed accounts ever written of traditional oatcake-making in that region. Since then she has written many books and has developed a particular interest in and knowledge of organic foods.*

Elder is a form of tripe; more precisely, boiled cow's udder. The term appears to be Middle Dutch, and was probably first recorded in Ray's *North Country Words* (1674). It was used in the north and north west of Britain, appearing in Scotland and Ireland, down the north west side of England from Lancashire almost as far as the Severn estuary, and stretched inland diagonally across to Lincolnshire and Yorkshire. It is still used in parts of Yorkshire and Lancashire. In virtually every case, the term refers to the udder of a cow or horse, occasionally even that of a woman—but, I am informed, only women in the lowest sections of society.[1]

Not surprisingly, little is known of its history. Though udder appears to be first mentioned as a food in 1474 (*OED*), its finest hour I suppose came on October 11th 1660, when Samuel Pepys in the company of his wife and Mr Creed, dining at the 'Leg' in King Street, thought sufficiently of their 'good udder to dinner' to record it in his diary. That at least assured a place for it in posterity and the *OED* and the *Encyclopedia of Gastronomy.*

Since then, for the most part, it's been downhill all the way. Though La Varenne (1654) and Charles Carter (1730), for example, give recipes, and Hannah Glasse (1747) recommends both a roast and *forced* udder, udder is more often conspicuous by its absence. Kettner, writing in 1877, notes that udder is no longer abundant in the market though it formerly had a recognised position in French cookery. Cassell's *Dictionary of Cookery* (1899) gives it, but of more recent authors I have been able to consult, only Escoffier and Prosper Montagné seem to include an entry of any note—confirming, perhaps, French affection over English apathy.

Long gone from the daily diet of most of us, udder is thus a vanishing food which no one particularly wants any more and which has escaped interest from everyone, except these days the old environmental health officer.[2] In all probability, therefore, we are witnessing a food in terminal decline. Newly introduced EEC regulations governing the handling of elder at the slaughterhouse, making it more economic and less trouble for the abattoir to sell elder to the pet food market than for human consumption, are helping to speed its general demise.[3]

To the best of my knowledge it survives almost exclusively in a small cluster of towns in industrial West Yorkshire—Keighley, Bradford (where, by the way, it's called udder), Halifax, Huddersfield, Dewbury, Wakefield and Castleford, and in East Lancashire, especially in the market halls of places like Accrington, Wigan, Burnley, Nelson, Colne, Bacup, Preston and Radcliffe on the outskirts of Manchester. I don't think, for example, you will find it in Leeds[4] (although you will find *maws,* pig's tripe) or Barnsley, or on the far west side of Lancashire. Liverpudlians, apparently, won't touch the stuff. I myself discovered it whilst wandering around Halifax market one day; many northern markets are often the last bastions of genuine traditional foods—the ones our working forefathers really ate, as opposed to those which flow from the pens of hard-pressed food writers or tourist boards desperate to find something other than roast beef and Yorkshire pudding to put in their brochures. That in turn led to a visit to a small tripery in Denholme, a craggy Pennine hill village above Bingley and Bradford.

The tripery is run by a father and son team with two staff, though, at 69, the father is now officially retired. The family have been tripe dressers for five generations and, like most tripe dressers, have their own retail outlets, in their case a stall in Keighley and Halifax markets. The tripery is a converted piggery: a small low building belching steam, with vast iron cauldrons to the left, gurgling steel tanks to the right, and a couple of antiquated tripe dressing machines down one end. It's like a sauna bath in there and the air reeks with the smell—actually not that bad—of tripe, tripe and more tripe. A sort of 'Bubble, bubble, toil and tripe . . .'

In here, they prepare dark and light tripe, cow heel, neat's foot oil (20p a small bottle, good for the chest), black pudding and elder. In true Yorkshire fashion nothing gets wasted. The copious quantities of fat produced as a by-product are sold by the bucketful to the fish and chip trade (West Yorkshire are still largely dripping men). About 240 lb of finished elder is prepared a week.

Devoid of teats and skin, raw elder looks like a large, pink, amorphous blob. Like women, explained my tripe dresser, somewhat embarrassed when pressed for information as to size and weight, they vary. He settled on 12 lb as a fair average, though they may go to 50 lb, and another tripe dresser thought 20 lb was nearer the mark.

Whatever the weight, the first job is to drain the udder of any remaining milk, otherwise the milk taints the flavour of the elder, making it too strong. This is not so important with very fresh elder which is boiled there and then, because the milk seeps out into the water, but if the elder is left in the cold room, draining must be thorough. At Denholme, they use a machine which gives it 'a bit of a bashing' to remove the excess liquid.

The elder is then gently simmered for a good six hours or longer until judged sufficiently tender. At Denholme it's cooked from 10 am to 4 pm. The heat is then turned off, the tank covered, and the elder left to continue cooking in the gently cooling liquid. Next morning, it's boiled again for another couple of hours until lunchtime. It is then rapidly cooled in very cold water, and 'dressed' by removing excess fat and any remaining skin with a stiff brush, followed by a final cosmetic trimming with a knife to remove any bruised bits or teat holes and to trim the shape.

During its lengthy cooking the elder will lose up to three quarters of its original weight. What emerges is a compact lump of light coloured, flesh-toned elder. The exact colour, difficult to describe, varies with the breed of the cow and may be either pink, yellow or brownish hued. It smells faintly of tongue and has something of the same softness, but is chewier. Indeed, early recipes usually group the two together. It has a bland, mildly offally taste, is very cheap (32p per quarter at current prices) and is sold by the slice on tripe stalls or butchers' stalls.

Nutritional analysis reveals that elder supplies 234 calories per 100 grams of edible portion. Sixty-five percent is moisture, 15% protein and 19% fat. It contains some B vitamins and some minerals (notably iron), no fibre and no carbohydrate.[5]

Like all offal, elder should be eaten fresh and kept cool. The best way to keep it (and tripe) is, apparently, under water, preferably at freezing point (a couple of ice cubes should do the trick), in a box in the refrigerator. Like this, it should keep for up to a week. You eat it as it is, northern style with salt and vinegar—which considerably improves it; or warmed through in fat—Jane Grigson, in her *British Cookery,* gives a rather nice recipe with young turnips cooked separately, and then finishing with a creamy sauce.

I speak here as if elder, or rather udder, was a peculiarly British phenomenon. It isn't, of course. In Belgium, at least one prestigious restaurant has served its honoured guests with smoked *pis de vache*[6], and the French connection has already been touched on. What mammarian dainties lurk elsewhere would be interesting to know about.

There remains, for me at least, the question of its unmentionable profile. Food taboos have been discussed at length by Calvin Schwabe in *Unmentionable*

Cuisine; Stephen Mennell in *All Manners of Food;* and Tom Jaine in *Cooking in the Country,* who analysed his own response on being presented with Brough the Badger. For my own part, my reluctance to embrace elder lay less in its taste and texture and more in the fact that I couldn't stomach boiled tits. Far too close for comfort—but whether this is a personal taboo, social 'refining', or something more fundamental, I leave for others to judge.

Instead, I shall endeavour to end on a lighter, more appetising note, kindly supplied by Betty Saville, chef/proprietor of the Weavers Shed restaurant in Golcar, just outside Huddersfield, who, succeeding where I failed, came up with the following three suggestions for would be elderites to try.

BETTY SAVILLE'S RECIPES

(1) Dice the elder into 1/2" cubes. Marinate for 30 minutes in a well-seasoned vinaigrette with finely chopped parsley and spring onions. Serve as pre-dinner nibbles. 'Pâté,' declared one unsuspecting diner.

(2) Cube the elder slightly larger, dip into well-seasoned flour, egg and breadcrumb, and deep fry for one minute only. 'A lovely crisp coat with a soft inside resembling sweetbreads.' Serve with a mustard, tomato or onion sauce.

(3) From Peter Saville. Sweat button mushrooms in butter, add cream and reduce slightly, season, add strips of elder to heat through and serve with toast sprinkled with finely chopped parsley. 'Delicious.'

Notes

1. For this information I am indebted to both Peter Brears of Leeds City Museum and Stanley Ellis, who was principal collector for the Survey of English Dialects directed by Professor Orton, from which the maps in the *Word Geography of England,* Seminar Press, 1974, were based. Elder appears on map 50A. Mr Ellis has provided this information also.
2. There has been a recent case of one tripe dresser in Bradford being prevented from preparing elder, as his was found to contain salmonella. This has led to some concern, not least by reputable tripe dressers who explain that, as with all offal, and in all cases where food is being prepared, especially when cooked and uncooked foods are likely to come into contact with each other, the risk of salmonella contamination must be guarded against at all times. Strict hygiene and thorough cooking are the best safeguards.
3. It may be appropriate here to mention something of tripe. Since the war the market has contracted severely, with membership of the Tripe Dressers' Association falling from over 500 to a mere 17. Nonetheless, of those that are left, tripe dressers that I spoke to report brisk business. Certainly pioneer tripe men like Chris Hey of Dewsbury (who

supplies Langan's Brasserie in London with tripe and who has just produced a little book of tripe recipes, available free of charge) and the current chairman, Roger Taubman in Brighton, are doing their best to promote tripe to a wider audience. In this case, then, the reverse may be true, and we may see a modest revival. Whether Langan's will start serving 'a good udder to dinner' remains to be seen, though.

4. Chris Hey reports that up until a few years ago, raw udder was sold in Bradford market. Recently he was asked by a Leeds butcher for raw udder for one of his Afro-Caribbean customers.
5. From information supplied by the Ministry of Agriculture, Fisheries and Food. Interestingly, the Ministry has no official figures for the nutritional composition of cow's udder. A review of their foreign food tables yielded a table from the INCAP-ICNND Food Composition Tables for use in Latin America, from which I drew my information. The full (impressive) reference is: Institute of Nutrition of Central America & Panama, Guatemala City, C.A., and the Interdepartmental Committee on Nutrition for National Defence, National Institutes of Health, Bethesda, Maryland, U.S.A., June 1961, Woot-Tsuen Wu Leung (Author). It made me wonder about chili con elder.
6. See Christopher Driver, *European Wine and Food,* June 1986.

Acknowledgments

I should like particularly to thank Peter Brears and Stanley Ellis for their much appreciated help in providing some of the answers to elder. Thanks are due, too, to the many tripe dressers, all of whom were most forthcoming. Long may they prosper! I mention here only Roger Taubman, Chris Hey, Ernest Hoyle and R. Schiach. I should also like to express my gratitude to Tom Jackson, of Jackson's Books Ilkley; Marjorie Houlihan; Betty Saville; and the *Guardian* newspaper, for allowing me to use some material from an article prepared for them.

* * * *

Lynda Brown's essay evoked two interesting comments in PPC *which are reproduced below. The first of these was accompanied by two recipes, one for udder and one for ox penis, from which we have chosen the former to include here. The second contribution provided half a dozen summary recipes which included veal teats, and from these we selected for presentation here Cima Ripiena Alla Genovese.*

Udder and Other Extremities: Recipes from the Jews of Yemen
from Barbara Kirshenblatt-Gimblett

Lynda Brown's interesting essay on udder (*PPC 26:* 60–64) brought to mind the resourceful culinary practices of Yemenite Jews, who cooked not only the udder, but also the penis.

In his pioneering ethnography of Yemenite Jews, Erich Brauer reported (on pp 105–7) that meat was a luxury, particularly among Jews in rural areas. Even in the city, where Jews could buy their meat from the slaughterer, they ate it almost exclusively on the Sabbath and holidays. In the countryside, where Jews had to slaughter the animals themselves, several families would share an animal to provide meat for a Sabbath or festival meal. If, however, after ritually slaughtering the animal, they discovered it was unfit according to Jewish dietary laws, Yemenite Jews in the countryside simply did without meat on that occasion.

According to the requirements of *kashruth,* meat must be soaked in water, salted, and rinsed. However, parts such as udder and liver are separated from the other cuts of meat and kashered differently, because of the nature of the flesh. Brauer explains that udder is broiled before being cooked, in order to eliminate the milk.* (Liver is also broiled, but because it is too bloody to soak.) Udder, like other meats, would then be stewed with a mixture of hot and aromatic spices, onion and garlic, and eaten with bread that would take up the sauce.

The recipe for udder appears on page 22 of *Yemenite and Sabra Cookery,* and reads as follows (quantities for 4).

Kahal (udder)

500 grams udder
1 tomato, chopped
*hawayij***
salt

Wash the meat well. Grill over the fire until the milk oozes out. Rinse and dice. Place in a pot with onion, chopped onion [onion is omitted from the list of ingredients], chopped tomato, hawayij, and salt. Cover with water and boil. Transfer to small fire for 3–4 hours until meat is tender. Serve hot.

References

Brauer, Erich: *Ethnologie der jemenitischen Juden.* Carl Winters Universitätsbuch-handlung, Heidelberg, 1934.

Ganzfried, Solomon: *Code of Jewish Law.* Hebrew Publishing Company, New York, 1961. Translated from the Hebrew by Hyman E. Goldin.

Tzabar, Naomi and Shimon: *Yemenite and Sabra Cookery.* Sadan Publishing House, Tel-Aviv, 1963. Translated from the Hebrew by Gerald Sevel.

* The Code of Jewish Law (p 118) makes provision for animal organs that contain milk: 'The milk contained at times in the stomach of a calf must be spilled out before soaking the stomach in water, and it is treated like ordinary meat.'

***Hawayij,* a recipe for which appears on page 9 of the book, is a mixture of ground spices: 2 tbsp black pepper, 2 tbsp caraway seed, 1 tsp cardamom, 1 tsp saffron, 2 tsp tumeric.

On Udder **from Audris d'Aragona**

I was interested to read Lynda Brown's query on udder in *PPC 26*. Here in Italy I have not (yet) come across udder recipes, which I find surprising because everything is eaten once an animal has been slaughtered. Thus there are numerous recipes for tripe, heart, lungs, intestines etc, but not udder, although we know that pig's udder was considered a great delicacy in ancient Roman times. *De Re Coquinaria* gives two recipes for *sumen* (pork udder) and although we have heard about *zinna* (Roman dialect for pork udder), we have never come across it in a trattoria or seen a recipe for it.

However, we find a lot of delicious preparations using veal teats in Liguria and one cannot help wondering what happens to the udders. (Waverley Root, in his book *Food,* claims that udders go into little tins marked 'mousse de fois gras'!) The teats are sold cleaned and prepared in the same way as tripe.

A New Zealand food expert, Annabel Langbein, told me that she was served a huge piece of udder prepared in a tomato sauce in Bolivia just recently.

Cima Ripiena Alla Genoevese

A veal 'pocket' stuffed with a mixture of minced veal, brain, sweetbreads, veal teats, veal testicles, beef marrow, eggs, Parmesan cheese, pistachio nuts, peas, breadcrumbs, hardboiled eggs, various flavourings etc. The bag is sewn up, tied, boiled in broth and served cold, sliced fairly thinly.

Feasts of Raw Meat

Russell Harris

It was while cataloguing a group of photographs of Ras Makonnen for the Victoria and Albert Museum that Russell Harris happened upon the early reports of Abyssinian culinary habits which had horrified readers in the past. He decided to investigate these, and here exposes some misconceptions which in his view flawed the reports and exaggerated the barbaric aspects of the practices.

When the 18th-century Scottish explorer, James Bruce, published his book of travels in Abyssinia (now Ethiopia) in search of the source of the Nile,[1] there were two incidents which his readers took with rather a large pinch of salt and which inspired almost as much curiosity as the location of the source of the Nile. As a later compiler-cum-author, John Hotten, wrote: 'Indeed several subsequent travellers appear to have visited that country more with a view to criticise Bruce's statements than to add to our knowledge of the country.'[2]

Earlier travellers to Abyssinia had written of the fashion for raw flesh. The Portuguese friar, Francisco Alvarez, during his visit in 1520, had seen the Governor of Massowah and his ladies eagerly devouring pieces of raw flesh and warm blood. In 1589, Peter Paez, another traveller, wrote of how pieces of raw and warm flesh were wrapped in bread by servants and forced into their masters' mouths 'as if they were stuffing a goose for a feast.'[3] These appalling tales of feasts of raw flesh and blood were echoed in Bruce's book by his description of two incidents.

Incident I

This took place when Bruce was travelling with a group of soldiers. He relates how some travellers they overtook dealt with a cow.

> The drives suddenly tript up the cow, and gave the poor animal a very rude fall upon the ground . . . One of them sat across her neck, holding down her head by the horns, the other twisted the halter about her forefeet, while the third, who had a knife in his hand, to my very great surprise, in place of taking her by the throat, got astride upon her belly before her hindlegs, and gave her a very deep wound in the upper part of her buttock.

Bruce had supposed that the travellers were going to kill the cow and assuage his hunger and that of his men by selling them a part of the flesh.

Bruce had already averted his eyes, not wishing to see the beast's last breath. However, after the appearance of two pieces, 'thicker, and longer than our ordinary beef steaks, cut out of the higher part of the buttock of the beast.' Bruce brought himself to look upon the group and saw that

> one of them continued holding the head, while the other two were busied in curing the wound. This too was done not in an ordinary manner; the skin which had covered the flesh that was taken away was left entire, and flapped over the wound, and was fastened to the corresponding part by two or more small skewers, or pins. Whether they had put any thing under the skin, between that and the wounded flesh, I know not; but at the river side where they were, they had prepared a cataplasm of clay, with which they covered the wound, they then forced the animal to rise, and drove it on before them, to furnish them with a fuller meal when they should meet their companions in the evening.[4]

Incident II

This is a description which only appeared in the first edition of Bruce's *Travels*. He claimed that the following was a custom both in the capital and in the villages and country.

> A cow or bull . . . is brought close to the door, and his feet strongly tied. The skin that hangs down under his chin and throat, which would be called the dew-lap in England, is cut only so deep as to arrive at the fat, of which it totally consists, and, by the separation of a few small blood-vessels, six or seven drops of blood only fall upon the ground. They have no stone, bench, nor altar, upon which these cruel assassins lay the animal's head in this operation. We should beg his pardon indeed for calling him an assassin, as he is not so merciful as to aim at the life, but, on the contrary, to keep the beast alive till he be totally eat up. Having satisfied the Mosaical law, according to his conception, by pouring these six or seven drops upon the ground, two or more of them fall to work; on the back of the beast, and on each side of the spine, they cut skin-deep; then, putting their fingers between the flesh and the skin, they begin to strip the hide off the animal halfway down his ribs, and so on to the buttock, cutting the skin wherever it hinders them commodiously to strip the poor animal bare. All the flesh on the buttocks is cut off then, and in solid, square pieces, without bones, or much effusion of blood; and the prodigious noise the animal makes is a signal for the company to sit down to table . . . the man with his long knife cuts a thin piece, which would be thought a good beef-steak in England, while you see the motion of

This illustration from Hotten's book, of which part is reproduced here, bears the caption: AN ABYSSINIAN DEVOURING RAW BEEF—*from a sketch by M Vignaud—'Seizing one end of the strip of meat with his teeth, and holding the other end in his left hand, he cuts a bit off close to his lips by an upward stroke of his sword, only just avoiding the tip of his nose, and so on until he has finished the whole strip.'*

> the fibres yet perfectly distinct, and alive in the flesh . . . All this time the unfortunate victim at the door is bleeding indeed, but bleeding little. As long as they can cut off the flesh from his bones, they do not meddle with the thighs, or the parts where the great arteries are. At last they fall upon the thighs likewise; and soon after the animal, bleeding to death, becomes so tough, that the cannibals, who have the rest of it to eat, find very hard work to separate the flesh from the bones with their teeth like dogs . . .[5]

It is interesting that in the second edition of his *Travels,* Bruce's editor felt obliged to add a note after *Incident I:*

> This story, which has been the cause of much ridicule and doubt, among persons of different descriptions, requires no other commentary than the following: Raw flesh has been eaten in the country from time immemorial. It is esteemed best, when newly cut from the animal. The author does not say how far they were able to drive the cow, after the operation; he only adds, in a humorous manner, that they reserved her, alive or dead, for a fuller meal in the evening. These men were Abyssinian soldiers, robbers, savages of a description unknown in this part of Europe. Those who are best informed with regard to the natives, will readily believe the account in its full description.[6]

Incident I is corroborated by Henry Salt, who was Consul-General in Egypt and during a trip to Abyssinia in 1810 witnessed 'two pieces of flesh, weighing about a pound cut from the animal's buttock, and devoured, still quivering, by the soldiers . . . the wounds were sewn up, plastered over with cowdung, and the animal driven forward.'[7] Henry Dufton, writing some fifty years later about Bruce and 'the case of live-ox eating, which so affected his fame at home',[8] was also ready to believe Bruce's description, although he himself had only eaten the warm and quivering flesh from a slaughtered animal, and repeated the story told him by a native, how it was 'common for shepherds to cut a sheep's tail while alive and suck the fat out, filling the wound with salt for another occasion.'[9]

Perhaps the most authoritative source for the eating habits of the Abyssinians in the last century is Mansfield Parkyns, who lived in Abyssinia for three years and married an Abyssinian noble lady. He obviously developed a taste for raw meat and takes the time to recommend the warm and quivering meat to his English readers as 'very superior in taste to when cold' and 'far tenderer than the most tender joint that has been hung a week in England'.[10] As regards *Incident I,* Parkyns questioned a soldier who told him a similar story. 'On inquiry he said that such a practice was not uncommon among the Gallas . . . when, as in the case Bruce relates, a cow had been stolen or taken in foray. The men who drive her being hungry have no alternative but to go on fasting, kill the cow, or act as described. The first they will not do; the second would imply the necessity of leaving it to the jackals . . . so the third is adopted . . .'[11]

Another visitor, August Wylde, who was Vice-Consul for the Red Sea, carried on the debate as late as 1900. He complained: 'I have seen exactly the same thing as [Bruce] saw, but I should not describe it in the same manner, and it only shows how observant people should be of every little detail.'[12] Wylde cannot be contradicted for his criticism of the accuracy of Bruce's account, particularly since the latter admitted that he looked the other way during the operation. However, Wylde claims that the procedure was actually an operation carried out to remove the 'long tumour [which] forms under the hide, and between it and the flesh . . . This tumour or sack must be entirely removed before the back will heal up properly, so a long incision is made alongside it parallel to the back bone, and the hide cut into a flap and lifted up, and the red tumour is removed; the hide is then put back in its place again and the wound bandaged.'[13] This was apparently a common affair, and although Wylde often saw his men eating raw meat, it was never 'the filth and matter taken away from the animal'.

An explanation for *Incident II* can be ascribed to the Abyssinians' literal acceptance of Old Testament precepts. In fact, Bruce, who states that the butcher, or 'assassin' satisfied the 'Mosaical law according to his conception', then contradicts himself by claiming that the aim was to keep the animal alive as long as possible. The essence of the biblical law on the slaughter of animals was to assure that the animal was in fact killed. This point was neglected by the Israelites, who after battling the Philistines from Michmash to Aijalon, were faint with hunger:

> And the people flew upon the spoil, and took sheep, and oxen, and calves, and slew them on the ground: and the people did eat them with the blood. Then they told Saul, saying, Behold, the people sin against the Lord in that they eat with the blood. And he said, Ye have transgressed: roll a great stone unto me this day.[14]

Saul called for this 'great stone' in order that he could teach the people how to slaughter an animal correctly by laying its head on a stone, passing the knife over its neck, and draining out its life-blood. When that had taken place, it could be assumed that the animal was dead and could then be dismembered and eaten.

In Bruce's account, the blood-letting from the animal's dewlap appears to be the Abyssinians' method of slaughter. Having seen these drops of blood, the animal could be considered 'dead' and butchering could start. Thus, the intention was not to keep the animal alive at all, but purely a misconception by the Abyssinians of when 'alive' stopped and 'dead' started. That the Abyssinians had no intention of eating meat from the live animal is stressed by Wylde, who repeated Bruce's story to many locals, who became 'very indignant at the idea of being accused of eating meat that has not been killed in the orthodox manner, that is, with a short prayer repeated when the animal's throat is cut.'[15]

Parkyns, perhaps the authority in whom we should place the greatest credence, further explains how this misunderstanding over the eating of live animals could have arisen. 'The animal is thrown down with its head to the east, and the knife passed across its throat while the words, "In the name of the Father, Son, and Holy Ghost," are pronounced by the butcher. Almost before the death struggle is over persons are ready to flay the carcase, and pieces of the raw meat are cut off and served up before this operation is completed; in fact, as each part presents itself it is cut off, and eaten while yet warm and quivering.'[16] We can hardly be surprised that the early travellers deemed the animal to be still living!

In fact, the eating of raw meat, or '*brundo*', continued to be reported throughout this century. James Baum, on an expedition into Abyssinia, mentioned in 1928 that 'raw meat is the preferred dish and our caravan men ate pounds of it[17] at a sitting.'[18] A year later, the Georgian personal physician of Menilek II, Dr. Mérab, gave a particularly Euro-centric explanation for the Abyssinians' love of raw meat. He accepted a peasant's words ('c'est plus commode de manger la viande crue que cuite!'[19]) and drew an analogy with

Proverbs, chapter XII, verse 27: 'The slothful man roasteth not that which he took in hunting . . .' In 1962, George Lipsky, in his handbook on Ethiopia, was able to inform us that 'a favorite food on special holidays is raw minced beef called *berando* . . . much importance is attached to its consumption since according to popular belief *berando* lends more strength than any other food.'[20] The final word on the matter of raw meat came from a Brahmin acquaintance of mine who was posted in Ethiopia in the 1960s. Upon hearing of my findings on this subject he related to me that he had been invited by a group of officers to an officer's club, just outside the centre of Addis Ababa. They sat around drinking *tej*[21] while the animal was slaughtered. Hunks of flesh dripping in blood were immediately brought to the table and were eaten with a *berbera*[22] sauce.

No discourse on a people's eating habits would be complete without a 'recipe section'. In this case, as we are speaking of raw meat, mention should be made of a 'dish' which was observed with different degrees of aversion by the various travellers. The first mention I have found is a reference to an early traveller, Jerome Lobo, who erroneously claimed that the Galla natives 'adorn themselves with the entrails of cows.'[23] Dufton explained further that the natives like 'to eat the raw paunch and liver, with the gall-juice of the goat.'[24] A slight variation on this sickened Baum, after he had killed some roebucks. His men set about the animal and 'as the entrails came out there was a scramble for the stomach of each animal. These were cut open, and, as we were far from water, the contents were simply shaken out and the tripe, or inner lining of the stomach, was peeled off, wiped on the grass and devoured raw.'[25]

However, the most detailed account, complete with a word of warning to the fair sex, is to be found in Parkyns:

> The dish of *'mantay hàmot,'* or *'chogera'* is a dish prepared of the tripe and liver cut into small pieces. The contents of the gall-bladder are then squeezed over it, as also a part of the half-digested green matter found in the intestines of the animal. This dish, after having been duly seasoned with pepper, salt &c., and a little warmed, till it acquires the natural heat of the animal, is eaten with the greatest gusto, not only by the poor, but even by the greatest chiefs in the country. This preparation is also much esteemed all over Nubia, Sennaar, and Kordofan, only with a trifling variation in these countries, where they dispense with the 'green matter' and warming, but add raw onions chopped and chilis instead of capsicums. My description will, no doubt, have already sufficed to disgust many of my readers especially those of the fair sex; so that I dare not presume to request them to try a dish of this same *chogera.* Still it is an eatable dish; nay, verily, a palatable dish; and it hath, moreover, a quality for inducing men to partake freely of the cup which always accompanies it.[26]

Notes

1. Bruce, James, *Travels to Discover the Source of the Nile in the Years 1768, 1769, 1770, 1771, 1772 & 1773,* Longman, London, 1804.
2. Hotten, John Camden (ed)., *Abyssinia and Its People; or, Life in the Land of Prester John,* London, 1868, p 23.
3. Quoted in Hotten, *op cit,* p 22.
4. Bruce, *op cit,* vol 4, pp 332–5.
5. Quoted in Hotten, *op cit,* pp 38-40.
6. Bruce, *op cit,* vol 4, p 335.
7. Quoted in Hotten, *op cit,* pp 44–5.
8. Dufton, Henry, *Narrative of a Journey through Abyssinia in 1862–3,* Chapman & Hall, London, 1867, p 205.
9. *Ibid,* p 206
10. Parkyns, Mansfield, *Life in Abyssinia: Being Notes Collected during Three Years' Residence and Travels in that Country,* John Murray, London, 1868, p 202.
11. *Ibid,* p 204.
12. Wylde, August B., *Modern Abyssinia,* Methuen, London, 1900, p 153.
13. *Ibid,* p 153.
14. *I Samuel,* chapter 14, verses 32–34.
15. *Ibid,* p 153.
16. Parkyns, *op cit,* p 202.
17. In fact, many reports claim that a man can eat much more raw meat than he can cooked. There are various tales of a hungry Abyssinian eating a whole sheep weighing 96 lb in one sitting, although this is dubious, as other reports state categorically that mutton was never eaten raw.
18. Baum, James E, *Savage Abyssinia,* Cassell and Company, London, 1928, p 52.
19. Mérab, Le Docteur., *Impressions d'Éthiopie (L'Abyssinie sous Ménélik II),* Ernest Leroux, Paris, 1929, p 465.
20. Lipsky, George A, *Ethiopia—its people, its society, its culture,* HRAF Press, New Haven, 1962, p 9.
21. A fermented honey drink, similar to our mead.
22. A pepper sauce reputed to be so hot that it cooks the raw meat inside the diner's stomach.
23. Quoted in Hotten, *op cit,* p 22.
24. Dufton, *op cit,* p 206.
25. Baum, *op cit,* p 52.
26. Parkyns, *op cit,* pp 206–7.

'Wah-to-Yah': A Teenager's Reports about Food on the Taos Trail, 1846–7

JOHAN MATHIESEN

The author tells us: 'After reading PPC 40, *I happened to pick up Lewis H Garrard's* Wah-to-yah and the Taos Trail; Or Prairie Travel and Scalp Dances, With a Look at Los Rancheros from Muleback and the Rocky Mountain Campfire. *This contained passages remarkably similar to some of the reports in Russell Harris' 'Feasts of Raw Meat' (see previous article). Garrard went on to say even more of culinary interest, enough so that I thought you and your readers might be interested in a summary of them.'*

Lewis Garrard was seventeen when he set out on the trail from Independence, Missouri, to Taos, New Mexico, in 1846 for a year of fun and adventure among the Indians and mountaineers. He thought it perfectly sensible to go off and fight Indians, hang revolutionaries, bury the weak who have died from scurvy, go better than a month without a bath or change of clothes, have no shelter other than a blanket or a robe; and if it rains or snows, by God, then it rains or snows. Pray it's not raining the next day so you can dry out. He also said he went 'for [his] health,' from which A. B. Guthrie concluded that he lacked 'a stout constitution'. Constitutions presumably were different back then.

Garrard firmed up his constitution living primarily among the mountaineers and muleskinners who plied their trades on the early trails west, but he also spent some time living among the Cheyenne; and, while in Taos for the hanging of the insurrectionists, he had a close look at the people and customs of New Mexico. If Garrard's constitution was weak, his libido appears to have been sufficiently healthy for a seventeen year old boy, and he speaks lovingly of both Indian and New Mexican women, something he was not always inclined to do about the men, though on the whole he liked the Indian braves well enough. Garrard is reticent about any potentially incriminating liaisons, but the broad impression is given that he was welcome company among the young women of the West. Perhaps it was this delight in the presence of the ladies that encouraged Garrard to take special note of eating habits. Perhaps Garrard spent more time than was absolutely necessary around the cooking fires. On the other hand, the eating habits of the campfire were unique enough in themselves to warrant comment.

The 1840s were the last great days of the mountain men. By then the endless wagon trains had already begun their invasion of the West. What began with a few iconoclastic renegades striking out to live with 'the savages', trade a few hides, and sire some mixed-breed children, became a vast horde sweeping over the land pushing aside anyone who came before. The Indians they exterminated; the mountaineers just became useless. Within a few decades, the wilderness was gone. In a few more the remnants would be declared 'parks'. The mountaineers were not a civilized lot. They, like all their neighbors, native or otherwise, literally owned only the clothes on their backs. A change of clothes was just that much more to carry. Likewise, culinary equipment was often reduced to a knife. If it couldn't be roasted, it was eaten raw. Sometimes even if it could be roasted, it was eaten raw. Garrard comments that, 'in the total absence of plates, the leg doubled up, served, except when the meat was too hot; then a rock, chip, or anything handy, interposed. Indeed, we *have* used dry buffalo chips on the plain, instead of the more agreeable delft.' Luxuries that we take for granted were often a matter of some difficulty far out on the plains hundreds of miles from civilization. Roasted coffee, for instance, was not something one carried with one. Garrard continues:

> That night parched coffee gave out. We had nothing in which to burn more; but, as necessity is, ever, the mother of invention, we selected two flat stones from the channel at hand, twenty-five to thirty inches in diameter, which we placed on the fire till heated; then one was taken off, the coffee poured on, and stirred with a stick. The stones served alternately as they became cool. When the coffee was sufficiently burned, a piece of skin was laid on the ground, and a clean stone, a foot in diameter, rested on the knees of the grinder, with one edge on the skin. A smaller stone, held in the hand, reduced the grains between it and the larger one to powder by a rotary motion.

It's important to remember that often by the time a hunter brought down any game he was beyond merely hungry. This being a perpetual state of affairs, hunters soon develop a connoisseurship as to which parts of the animal taste best fresh. It's not surprising that Garrard's evaluations accord with Dufton's assertion in *Narrative of a Journey through Abyssinia in 1862–3* (quoted in Harris's 'Feast of Raw Meat' *PPC 40)* that the natives liked 'to eat the raw paunch and liver with the gall juice of the goat'. Garrard's account from seventeen years earlier on the prairies of the American West could be dropped with hardly a ripple into Dufton. 'The men ate the raw liver, with a slight dash of gall by way of zest, which served *à la Indian,* was not very tempting to cloyed appetites; but to hungry men, not at all squeamish, raw, warm liver, with raw marrow, was quite palatable. Before the buffalo range was half traversed, I liked the novel dish pretty well.' What is surprising is not that this dish was so universally popular, but that it has been so thoroughly forgotten.

Garrard's notes about the diet of the New Mexicans are brief save for frequent mention of *atloe* (the thin, gruel drink) and *biscoche,* which he describes as a 'hard bread . . . light, porous, and sweet', which I take to be a relative of the biscotti. He goes on to say that the New Mexicans use 'a mud oven, in shape like a cupping glass, in which is baked the whitest bread it has ever been my fortune to taste. No bolting cloths are here used; and those wanting white bread sift for themselves.' Other than that, although he spends considerable time describing the New Mexican women with their dark eyes, long tresses, trailing rebozas, and off the shoulder blouses, Garrard's only culinary observations of the New Mexicans was to mention their 'national dish *chile colorado*— a compound of red-pepper pods and other spicy ingredients; a hot mess at first; but, with the aid of *tortillas* (a thin, soft cake of flour and water, baked on a griddle), of which we consumed a great number—a new taste was soon acquired.' Garrard substantiates that the cuisine of the Southwest is essentially the same as it was a hundred and fifty years ago; but he might be surprised that chile colorado is now available in Boston as well as Saint Louis, MO.

Garrard heaps great praise on the buffalo as a source of meat, and readily prefers it to beef, spurring further concern as to the wisdom of filling the Plains with ill-adapted cattle in place of the ecologically adapted buffalo; but much as he appreciates buffalo, Garrard really gets worked up about dog. He devotes considerable space to discussions about eating dog prior to even doing it and then spends another couple of pages on how he was tricked into eating dog by being told it was really terrapin cooked in its entirety in the shell, in itself something I might be a little squeamish about. In the end he avows 'that "dog" was next in order to buffalo', and goes on for yet another page describing just how dog was prepared by the Cheyenne to taste so delicious. The editors of *PPC* tell me that they are reluctant to upset dog-loving readers by printing his description (though they could send a photocopy to anyone with a really serious interest).

The Cheyenne were indeed the real exotica for which Garrard travelled west. Even then he must have known he was witnessing their swan song, and it is for the Cheyenne he reserves the greatest culinary detail. Most likely he felt he had to preserve what he could. Garrard was no visionary, but he was careful with what he saw.

The Cheyenne, for all their nomadism and their flexible life-style, were a formal people, and Garrard gives a precise account of the ritual followed when they welcomed a white man into their dwelling. He goes on for a whole further page describing typical Cheyenne victuals.

> The Cheyenne have quite a variety of dishes, some hard to stomach—others quite palatable. Among them, a favorite of wild cherries, gathered in the mountains in the summer and pounded (stone and all) to a jelly, which, when dried, is put away for the winter, when the buffalo marrow is good—the time for a reunion of the small bands, to trade, feast, smoke, and deliberate. These cherries, incorporated by much manipulation at the hands of the not particularly clean matrons with marrow and pounded meat, and patted in balls, form a principal portion of the feasts.
>
> A buffalo skin is quite thick, which, to make pliable, is stretched to its utmost on the ground (the hair side down), as soon as it is brought in from the hunt, by means of wooden pegs. When it dries, the squaws take the adze-shaped instrument, fitted to the angle of an elk's horn . . . , and, with repeated blows, chip off small shavings of the raw hide until it is the required thinness. The shavings are carefully preserved, and, when a nice feast is wished, these 'chips' are put in a wooden bowl and boiling water poured over them, which cooks and reduces the whole to a pulpy mass immediately. This dish tastes similar to boiled Irish potatoes to which, with the addition of cherries, a fancy flavor is added.
>
> The fungus growing on the sides of decaying logs is gathered by the squaws and boiled with meat for several hours; on tasting the poisonous stuff, as I previously supposed it to be, my thoughts instantly traveled to Galveston Bay and its fine oysters. It was first rate, but the appetite soon cloys.
>
> A root growing in the bottoms is much eaten, raw or cooked, partaking both of the flavor of the potato and Jerusalem artichoke.

The cooking of buffalo hide scraping smacks of a dish born out of necessity as does that of the 'fungus growing on the side of decaying logs', which is not to say that those dishes so sired are not delicacies in and of themselves; but the cherries and bone marrow is obviously a reference to what was for the Indian nations all across Turtle Island a dish of high culinary refinement: the honored pemmican. Pemmican is likely not what the Cheyenne called it, that being a Cree word from the Canadian north, but it surely was that dish. Even more so than fresh liver and bile it's surprising a form of pemmican didn't survive the transition to a European dominated cuisine. After all, pemmican doesn't seem that far away from the French rillettes.

One could wish more from Garrard than what we got, but what we got was probably substantially what he got. One can date many of the dishes of the Southwest to historical and even recent times; the classic emergence, diffusion, and establishment of the chimichanga within recent decades is a good case in point. Even though there are antecedents elsewhere, it is their adoption by the Southwest that is of recent vintage. Furthermore, the diet Garrard ate was probably much more primitive than either that of the Cheyenne or New Mexicans. I doubt mountaineers and army personnel were known for their cooking. Still and all, what we got from Garrard was valuable and enjoyable. In a voice bordering on lyrical, Garrard takes us to a now distant world riding down a trail I'm glad I didn't have to ride down myself.

The Mushroom-Growing Termites of Uganda

ARTHUR FRENCH

When the author went to Makerere University College, Uganda, in 1955 (as a mathematician, lecturing in Education), he had no particular interest in termites, but he had for many years in England collected (and, where appropriate, eaten) the larger fungi. He was very disappointed to find that there was hardly anything on tropical fungi in the College library, and what there was was useless for identifying specimens. Left to his own devices, he made enquiries and conducted research with results which appeared subsequently in the Exotic Entomology Group Newsletter. *This paper, virtually complete, constitutes the first section of what follows. The second section contains additional notes, about the use of the termites as food. The third section is another note, giving further information about the fungi.*

Since there is relatively little published information available about fungi in Africa, we particularly welcome the opportunity to place on record the information which Arthur French has put together. For those wishing to pursue the subject further, we should mention an interesting paper in the Kew Bulletin *(vol 35 [3] [1980]) on 'The Edible Mushrooms of Zambia' by D N Pegler and G D Piearce; this contains much information on* Termitomyces *spp, including* T titanicus, *which has a huge cap—it may be almost one metre in diameter—and is regarded by Dr Pegler as one of the finest edible fungi in the world.*

1. Problems of Identification

I started learning the local language (Luganda), and asking what mushrooms the local people ate, or otherwise knew about. It soon became clear that most of the favourite edible species were associated with termites (which are also eaten). Moreover, there seemed to be a one-to-one correspondence between mushrooms species and termite species. This was represented in the language, thus:

TERMITES	MUSHROOMS
entunda	obutundatunda
ensejjere	obusejjeresejjere
ennaka	obunakanaka
embaala	obubaala

By November 1956, I had found out, from Kew, that there was indeed no literature in English, but that Professor Roger Heim, of the Natural History Museum in Paris, had published a monograph on termite mushrooms, and had set up a new genus—*Termitomyces*—for them (thereby calling into question the whole traditional system of mycological taxonomy, which would have assigned them to different genera!).

Unfortunately, Professor Heim was not an entomologist, so he could not usually say what kind of termite was associated with each *Termitomyces* sp. I decided I would have to study the termites myself. From the local Agricultural Research Station I found that the basic books for the identification of termites were still *Monographie der Termiten Afrikas,* vols 1–3, by Y. Sjöstedt (Stockholm, 1900–25). I persuaded the College to buy copies—they were still in print! Although written in German (by a Swede), they were not too difficult, with pictures, numbers and technical terms, to refer to. Sjöstedt says that some termites grow fungi but, alas, he was not a mycologist and could not name them. It was obviously desirable for me to try to work out the relationships, combining the scientific and traditional knowledge.

There were still problems. The traditional knowledge is in danger of being lost—if it isn't written down and translated into English, it isn't taught in schools. As a cash economy develops, people have less time for gathering 'wild' foods. I found that 'educated' people were ignorant and unreliable in their own tradition: it was necessary to ask old peasant women. I soon learned the specialised words needed to talk in their own language about alates, workers, queens, termitaria and mushrooms, etc.

There were also problems with the reference books. The first collecting of termites in East Africa had been done around the turn of the century. For the first 25 years, two related species (*Macrotermes bellicosus* and *M natalensis*) had been completely confused. Yet they had separate names in the vernacular, and the Africans knew that their local distribution was different, their mounds had a different structure, they swarmed at different times of the night and had different mushrooms, as well as the small differences in size already recognised by scientists in West Africa. A check with the local tradition would have shown at once that both species were present and widespread. Was the rest of the 'scientific' information reliable? Not entirely, as we shall see.

By 1959, I knew enough about the local termites to make a film-strip for schools, with my own drawings of local material. I took a copy of it, and some specimens, to W. Victor Harris at the 'Colonial' Termite Research Unit at the Natural History Museum. (The 'Colonial' was dropped later.) I corresponded with him intermittently over the next ten years, and he gradually put together my evidence with his own (he had been in Uganda, too) and everything else he could find. He was particularly interested in the genus *Pseudacanthotermes,* with three species in Uganda, all used as food (they swarm by day) and all growing edible mushrooms. A letter he wrote to me in 1968 illustrates some of the difficulties:

> The confusion has arisen mainly from the large range of variation in size of the soldier *militaris,* the fact that *grandiceps* was described from a single specimen collected at Kisumu and which was particularly large, and to the lumping together of all the specimens he had from Uganda into *militaris* by the American, Emerson (whose work we have only recently come to question) . . . In Snyder's catalogue you will find *P piceus* recorded from Uganda, but this is due to Emerson equating 'nnaka' alates with *piceus* from Salisbury, where as they are, in fact, alates of *grandiceps,* while the Salisbury materials is just a dark form of *militaris.*

Let those who work in exotic places beware of putting too much trust in the published material!

The actual physiological function of the fungi in the life of the termites does not seem to have been fully worked out. It has been proved for one species that 'their' fungus is an essential part of their food supply, and although the fungus can, with difficulty, be kept alive in a culture, it cannot live naturally except in association with termites. It helps, presumably, with the digestion of cellulose, but the extent to which these termite eat wood is probably exaggerated—they eat lots of other plant material, and they use some of the wood they collect in growing the fungus.

The relationships that were fairly well established by the time I left Uganda were:

TERMITE SPECIES	CORRESPONDING FUNGUS SPECIES
Pseudacanthotermes spiniger (Sjöstedt) (entunda)	*Termitomyces mammiformis* (obutundatunda)
P grandiceps (Sjöstedt) (ennaka)	*T striatus* (obunakanaka)
P militaris (Hagen) (emboobya)	*T letestui* (eggudu)
Odontotermes badius (Haviland) (embaala)	*T microcarpus* (obubaala)

There is still probably some confusion with closely related species of both termite and mushroom. Indeed there must be a lot more to be worked out. As the mushrooms occur only once or twice a year, and are promptly gathered for food, it's slow work accumulating facts.

One final warning for anyone else trying to work on local knowledge: although most of the tribes around Lake Victoria eat (and, therefore, name) termites and mushrooms, there are tribes in Kenya and Tanzania (eg the Kikuyu) among whom only the children eat termites or mushrooms (and other wild foods such as grasshoppers). After initiation at puberty, they completely suppress all memory of this childhood culture and it is impossible to talk to adults about the actual specimens eaten—they have 'put away childish things'. This must be a great handicap to Kikuyu biology teachers!

2. Collecting Termites for Food in Buganda*

This passage, as far as the foot of the next page, is based on an account written in the Luganda language some 30 years ago by J S Kasiyre.

There is an eager market for termites in Buganda: everyone looks forward to the season and rejoices when it comes.

The most popular species are: ntunda (*Pseudacanthotermes spiniger*); nnaka (*P grandiceps*); mpawu (*Microtermes natalensis*); nsejjere (*M bellicosus*); and mbaala (*Odontotermes badius*).

People know when the termites are about to fly, because the workers start building afresh on the top of their mounds. The men go to the big mounds of nsejjere and mpawu, out in the bush, and clear them of weeds; the women collect reeds and make torches of them, to attract these night-flying termites in the dark. When the watchers notice that the insects have cut exit-holes, collection can start. Nsejjere fly about midnight (which is called 'killing-nsejjere') while mpawu fly about the second time the bottle-bird calls (3am). In the old days, people would have left the goats in the hut, and 'left the house to the cobwebs' (as the saying goes), while the whole family joined in the fun. After nsejjere, they might wait for mpawu, but, in most seasons, those fly a day or two later.

The winged termites fly towards the light, so a hollow is made in the ground and the torch is held over it. The termites fall into the hollow, and can be scooped up. A very big mound may need two traps like that, and it is then called 'Mother of Twins'.

Collecting termites is considered a great sport, and people chat and laugh, nibbling the occasional termites, raw, if they like. As people look around in the dark they see lights burning here and there as other families

* Buganda is the area of Uganda occupied by the Ganda tribe (after whom Uganda is named), comprising roughly one sixth of the country, in the southern part of Uganda, centred on Kampala.

work at 'their' termite mounds. All kinds of wild creatures come to get a share of the feast—even leopard—but they, too, are busy with the termites, and don't attack humans if they are left to get on with it. A family will get a bag, or two or three pots, full of insects from a night's work.

There are songs about termites, especially nsejjere. One goes: 'What kind of termites? Nsejjere! Hit them! We shall feed on them!' Another says: 'How good nsejjere taste! Look, they are flying! We are delighted!'

An adaptation by Soun of what was originally a painting by a Ugandan schoolboy entitled 'Catching Nsejjere at Night'. Note that the full moon would really have been much higher in the sky, since catching takes place between midnight and 3 am; and that the monkey in the tree is planning to take a share of the termites for himself. Soun has commented that in his own country, Laos, people trap termites in exactly this way.

There is another way of collecting. A framework of flexible sticks is built round the mound, and this is thatched, with bark-cloth, banana leaves, or grass, with an exit and a trap at one side. This isn't usually done with the big mounds of the night-flying termites, but it's the common method for ntunda and nnaka, which fly before sunset. These, too, can be eaten raw, and have a stringent, savoury taste. Birds hover above, also catching termites, and people are usually strict about not eating the first termites to fly, which is considered unlucky.

Some people bring the termites to the surface artificially by drumming on a billet of wood on the ground. The idea seems to be to kid the termites that the rainy season has started! Anyway, it works. In some areas they build tubes out of damp clay, loading up from each exit hole and curving over into the mouth of a pot.

Cooked and dried termites are on sale in many African markets, in season. One sample was analysed and found to contain 27% protein. But they probably taste better fresh (alive). One European acquaintance said that they tasted

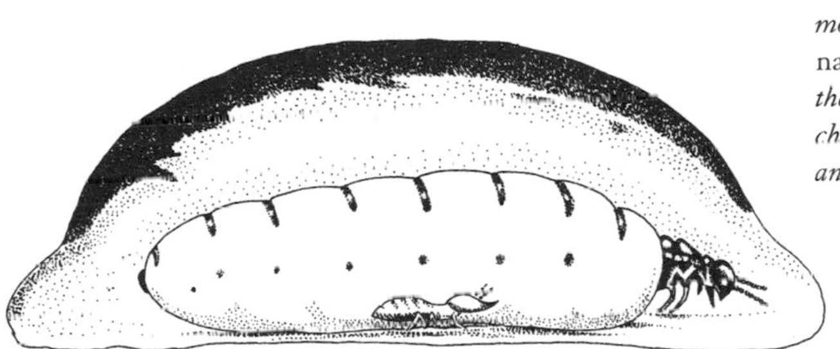

*Section of a termite mound (*Microtermes natalensis*), showing the queen in her chamber with a soldier ant alongside her.*

'somewhere between whitebait and hazelnuts'. The queens can also be eaten: they can be 3 or 4 inches long in the larger species, rather like a soft roe. The Nilotic tries are said to eat the soldiers, too, and even the coral-like 'fungus-gardens' from inside the mound, but this isn't commonly done in Buganda.

3. More about Mushrooms in Buganda

The size of any species of termite mushroom seems to depend on the depth at which its mycelium grows. *Termitomyces microcarpus* (obubaala), as you might expect from its Latin name, is very small. The termites throw out the 'fungus gardens' from their nest, and the mushrooms develop on the surface. They are white, and perhaps 1/2" across, but there are lots of them! They are very popular and can be dried for keeping. They are an essential dish for bride and bridegroom at weddings, and for some reason must be cooked without salt. (Are they aphrodisiac?) A proverb says: 'Katiko nnantabula ku mbaga.' This means: 'Mushroom is an essential guest at the feast.' It was also customary to mark the end of a period of formal mourning by serving a mushroom meal.

In Buganda there is a Mushroom clan, and their totem is this little white mushroom. They are not allowed to eat it. Three other clans have mushrooms as secondary totems.

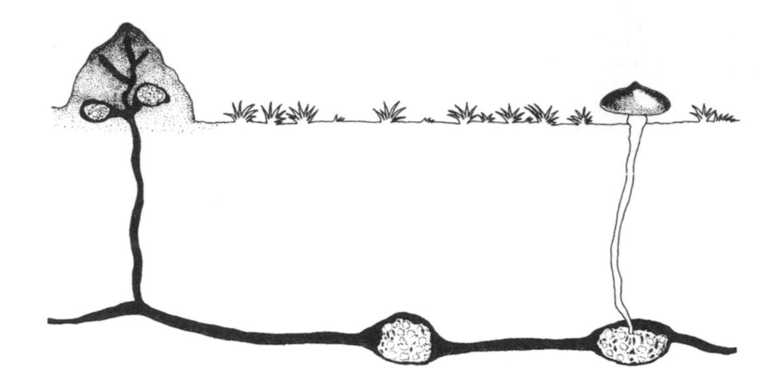

A mound of Pseudocanthotermines spiniger *with underground 'fungus gardens' and* Termitomyces mammiformis *growing up through the soil.*

A middle-sized mushroom is *T mammiformis* (akatundatunda). The fungus gardens are in galleries a foot or more deep, and the mushroom forces its way up through the soil, forming a long tapering 'root'. It is 3 or 4 inches across, with a central umbo or 'nipple', and a ring.

T letestui (eggudu) is enormous. It can be anything from 8 or 9 inches to two feet across, again with a long tapering pseudo-root, because it comes up from two or three feet underground where 'its' termites live. I could occasionally buy one in the market.

The usual way of cooking mushrooms would be as a relish for one of the staple starchy foods like plantains or sweet potatoes.

Apart from the termite mushrooms, there are about 30 other species named in Luganda. Some with black spores, similar to the 'English' mushroom, are eaten. The very poisonous Amanitas, which cause most of the fatalities from mushroom poisoning in Europe, don't seem to occur in East Africa, but there is one species of mushroom which causes gastro-enteritis, and at least one that is hallucinogenic. One victim who had a stomach pump applied (probably unnecessarily) had the illusion of being inside the tube of the pump; another saw everything in shades of pink. The termite mushrooms all seem to be safe, however!

The Candle-Scented Cakes and Sweets of Thailand

Richard Hosking

Highly scented cakes and sweets are very popular in Thailand and scented flower-waters such as jasmine water are extensively used as a flavouring ingredient. Sugar scented with flowers is also used, but perhaps the most remarkable way of perfuming Thai cakes and sweets is the use of aromatic candles. Before describing that procedure in detail, I should like to give an account of the other Thai methods of transferring the aroma of flowers to cakes and sweets.

1. *Aromatic Sugar*

This is the same process as making vanilla sugar or geranium sugar. Aromatic flowers are mixed with sugar and kept in an airtight container. The strength of the scent of the flowers used in Thailand is such that they only need to be left in the sugar overnight for it to be adequately perfumed. Here is a recipe from Princess Sibpan Sonakul's *Everyday Siamese Dishes*. Khanom is a category of Thai dishes corresponding to desserts and sweets.

Khanom Tom

Choose dry palm sugar, the drier the sugar is, the better the *khanom* will be. Cut into cubes about the size of the end of your finger. Put into a closed jar with sweet-scented flowers. To get the full fragrance, let the flowers and sugar stand all night.

Knead glutinous-rice flour well with scented water until a smooth paste is formed. Divide into balls of even size, and with your fingers, flatten each ball into a thin wafer, and close this wafer over a piece of sugar as evenly as possible. Care must be taken not to make a hole in the paste, which must cover the entire piece of sugar. Drop into boiling water. When it floats to the surface, lift it out of the water. Serve the balls coated with fresh coconut.

Some varieties may be made by using different scents and colours in the water with which the flour is kneaded—green colour is made from pounded *toey* leaves [*Pandanus amaryllifolius* (formerly *odorus*)], while pink is made by adding pink lime to the dough. For a dark colour, use flour made of black glutinous-rice instead of the ordinary white rice flour.

To obtain better results, keep the dough in the refrigerator some time before dividing it into balls.

2. Scented Water

Scented flower-waters are made by floating certain aromatic flowers on water overnight. Above all jasmine is used for this purpose, but it must be unsprayed jasmine to get the desired aroma. Commercially grown jasmine bought from the market will not do. Another flower used is that of *Cananga odorata* (Thai kadannga, English ylang ylang).

Scented water is used either directly as an ingredient for mixing a dough or for preparing aromatic coconut milk or scented syrup. The recipe on the previous page is an example of the direct use in making a dough. The scented coconut milk can be used when making *Sankhaya,* a very popular kind of custard. Here is Sibpan Sonakul's recipe:

SANKHAYA

1 cup thick coconut milk made with scented water
1 cup palm sugar
3 eggs
1 pumpkin or squash or 3 green young coconuts

Dissolve palm sugar in the coconut milk, add the beaten eggs and mix well.

Scoop out all undesirable parts inside the pumpkin, or if coconuts are used, peel off the outer husks, and scrape the shells well. Cut open on top as evenly as possible.

Pour the custard through a thin cloth into the prepared pumpkin set on a tin or enamel dish of the same size as the pumpkin, to keep it from breaking. Steam till well cooked. For the coconuts no dish is needed.

Serve hot or cold.

If preferred less sugar may be used.

3. Aromatic Candles—The T'ien Ob

So far, the recipes have shown us how the Thais transfer the scent of flowers to sweetmeats by perfuming sugar, by mixing doughs with scented flower-waters and by using scented flower-water to make coconut milk. However the use of candles is much more interesting and unusual, even if the results don't particularly commend themselves. The method has been referred to in Thai cookery books in English, particularly those bilingual with Thai, but nowhere have I found a detailed description of the method. Jennifer Brennan (p 47) notes: 'The Thai have traditionally flavoured their sweets and desserts with blossoms or the smoke of scented candles.' Vatcharin Bhumichitr (*Thai Vegetarian Cooking,* p 144) writes:

The commonest way of perfuming a dessert is to include flowers such as jasmine in the recipe; more unusual is the practice of placing tiny cakes (*kanom*) in an earthenware pot with a little cup of burning incense which will suffuse them with its aroma. The art of perfuming sweetmeats is as tricky as making *Look Choob* [imitation vegetables and fruit made from mung bean 'marzipan']; too much incense or too many fresh flowers in a dish results in a bad smell!

The special candles used for this method of flavouring are so readily available in Thailand that the method must be fairly commonly practised. The candle is called *t'ien ob*. It has a thick wick rather like that of a spirit lamp and the surrounding wax is a light brown colour and is heavily impregnated with aromatics that would qualify as incense. There are various qualities and sizes and the more refined the aroma, the more expensive the candle.

Drawings by Soun Vannithone.

The lidded container required by the method is usually a large, beautiful porcelain jar, decorated in rich colours with much gilding. Here are two methods of setting the candle in the jar. The *t'ien ob* is either horseshoe shaped or wound into a loop, and the traditionally 'correct' way of setting it in the container is to soften the bottom of it over a flame and press it upside down into the lid of the jar. The danger of this method is that if it comes unstuck, it will fall into the cakes in the bottom of the jar and damage them. To obviate this, the *t'ien ob* can be set in a little cup, right way up, in the middle of the cakes. In either case, the wick at both ends of the candle is lit and blown out immediately before the lid is put on. It is then left 'a long time', at least for a day, for the aromatic smoke to penetrate the cakes. Jasmine, roses or ylang ylang flowers are usually put in the jar along with the candle. Here is a recipe, again from Sonakul.

Khanom Phing

> For cream made from a kilo of grated coconut use 2 cups of granulated sugar; beanflour, well ground and sifted; unbeaten egg yolks.
>
> Boil together the sugar and coconut cream over a low heat, stirring from time to time just to be sure that the sugar does not get burnt at the bottom of the pan. When a thick syrup (238° F) is obtained, take from fire. Cool down a little, then stir with a wooden spoon till thick and smooth. Cover closely and keep in a cool place.
>
> To obtain about 100 little cakes, put 8 tablespoons of the above fondant in a bowl. Mix in gradually 10 tablespoons of beanflour. Add 4 egg yolks one by one, alternately with the flour. Beat with a wooden spoon until the mixture begins to bubble.
>
> Heat the oven to 350° F.
>
> Drop the mixture half a teaspoon at a time onto an ungreased cookie sheet dusted with flour, leaving a space of about an inch between. Bake till well browned (10–15 minutes) in a moderate oven with heat coming only from above. Increase the heat a little during the last five minutes.
>
> Remove from pan, cool on a rack, then put in a closed receptacle in which they are to absorb aroma from the smoke of a perfumed candle just extinguished, as well as from certain specified flowers such as *mali* [jasmine] and *kadannga* [ylang ylang].
>
> This is the most difficult *khanom* I have ever tried to make, including foreign cakes. Good results depend very much upon experience, especially in baking.
>
> There are some other methods, but this, I think, is the best.

In all, Sonakul gives six recipes for cakes scented by means of the *t'ien ob*. She also describes another use of the *t'ien ob* in the Glossary of her book:

> Scented Water: obtained by floating certain edible aromatic flowers in water overnight. The *mali* (jasmine) and *kadannga* (ylang ylang) flowers preferred. The latter is prepared by being smoked over the flame of a perfumed candle, made for the purpose and known as the *t'ien ob*. The smoke of the *t'ien ob* is often added to the aroma of the water by adhering the candle, duly blown out, to the inner cover of the receptacle containing the water.

Thus we find that there is not only the scented flower-water, but also one that has the addition of the aromatic smoke of the *t'ien ob*.

4. The Aromatic Flower

The principal aromatic flowers so far mentioned are roses, jasmine and ylang ylang. Another one mentioned by Sonakul, but much better known from Indian sweetmaking, is the screw-pine, *Pandanus tectorius*. This should not be confused with the pandanus which is used for its green colour and musty aroma, *Pandanus amaryllifolius* (formerly *odorus*) (Thai *toey*). *Pandanus tectorius* is called *lamciak*. This is the bewitching *kewra* of Indian perfumery and sweetmaking. Sonakul gives a recipe for *Kanom Kesorn Lamciak* and, although *lamciak* nowhere appears in the recipe as an ingredient (unless it is assumed to be the aromatic of the scented water required), she gives an interesting note on *lamciak* at the end of the recipe:

> Lamciak (*Pandanus tectorius*) is a considerably branched screw pine, common on the sea coast. The leaves are used for making mats, bags etc. The scent of the flowers is very strong. Half a century ago, when perfumes were not so plentifully imported, we kept the lamciak inflorescence with our clothes in a closed box for the perfume.

The Indian *kewra* (see above), is sold in India as an essential oil, an essence and a scented water (usually the only form available in England). It is used to flavour *Ras Malai* and various sorts of burfi and halwa, etc.

In conclusion, I should like to observe that the use of aromatic candles to flavour cakes and sweets seems to be unique to Thailand. The *t'ien ob* on the one hand seems to be truly exotic, and on the other, very much part of a living tradition in Thailand.

Bibliography

Brennan, J., *Thai Cooking,* Jill Norman and Hobhouse, London, 1981.

Sibpan Sonakul, *Everyday Siamese Dishes,* The Prachandra Press, Bangkok, 5th printing, 1969.

Taw Kritikara and Pimsai Amranand, *Modern Thai Cooking,* Editions Duang Kamol, Bangkok, 1977.

Vandee Na Songkla, *Thai Foods from Thai Literature Book II. The Royal Favourite Dishes.*

Vatcharin Bhumichitr, *Thai Vegetarian Cooking,* Asia Books, Bangkok, 1991.

6.
Recipes

Our collection of recipes begins, as is fitting, with the one which can be said to have been the genesis of *PPC*. It is the recipe for Aubergine Gratin which Richard Olney (here disguising himself as Nathan d'Aulnay) simply had to get into print—and how else than by creating a new food history journal to be the vehicle for it? The story is related in the box following his recipe—our farewell to him from *PPC 62*.

Some of the other recipes in the collection are free-standing, while others are integral parts of articles. They appear in chronological sequence and each has its own mini-introduction.

Now for Nathan d'Aulnay . . .

Aubergine Gratin

NATHAN D'AULNAY

Nathan d'Aulnay, the painter, here leaves his studio to claim our attention for the parallel artistry which he exercises in the kitchen. Erudite in the classical cuisine of France, passionately interested in the technical and practical details of culinary operations, he communicates his knowledge with panache and precision. There are few dishes which he enjoys making more than a gratin such as the one which he has chosen to present below.

Peel about a pound and a half of firm aubergines and slice them lengthwise into 1/2 inch thicknesses; fry in olive oil over medium heat until golden and the stem ends, which take longer to cook than the rest of the aubergine, lend no resistance to the point of a knife. This will have to be done in several batches with more oil being added as needed. As each slice is ready, remove it and put to drain on kitchen toweling, adding the uncooked slices as space in the pan is available.

Put an onion and a clove of garlic, both finely chopped, to cook in a bit of olive oil and, when yellowed, toss in about a pound of peeled, seeded and coarsely cut-up tomatoes. Season with a pinch of sugar, cayenne to taste, and salt. Toss over high heat and cook over medium heat until the tomatoes' liquid has largely disappeared.

Reduce 1/4 pound of brousse or ricotta, preferably sheeps' milk, and an egg to a smooth mixture with a fork, incorporate enough parmesan to form a stiff paste, then loosen the paste to the consistency of a thick, but easily pourable cream, by the addition of double cream, tasting for salt.

Arrange half the aubergine slices in the bottom of a gratin dish, salt lightly, grind over a mixture of pepper and allspice berries, spread with the sautéed tomatoes, sprinkle over a small handful of torn-up basil leaves and budding flowers, more pepper, another layer of the remaining aubergine, salt and pepper lightly and pour the cheese and cream mixture over the lot. Sprinkle with a handful of parmesan and bake for about 1/2 hour, first in a hot oven, lowering the thermostat to medium after 10 minutes. The gratin is ready to serve when the surface is golden brown, swelled to a dome and firm to the touch at the center.

Adieu, Nathan d'Aulnay!
Adieu, Tante Ursule!

We lament the death, announced just as we go to press, of Richard Olney, the famous American writer on food and drink, who was one of the founding partners of *PPC*. Indeed, for reasons explained in *PPC 47*, he was the proximate cause of *PPC* coming into being.

To abbreviate what was a long story, his work as master-mind of the huge Time-Life 'Good Cook' series in the 1970s and '80s brought him into conflict with the Time-Life bureaucracy on more than one occasion. There was one tremendous row over the 'rule' that no recipe could be published in any of the 30 or so volumes unless it had already been published. Two of Richard's favourite recipes, which he was determined to include, had not previously appeared in print. The solution was to bring *PPC* into being and to have him put the two recipes in our first issue, where Aubergine Gratin appeared as the work of Nathan d'Aulnay and Crayfish à la Bordelaise as a contribution from Tante Ursule. The Time-Life bureaucrats could then accept the recipes; and, so far as we know, they never became aware of the deception.

It has been said that a true genius will not only pursue his own pioneering work but will also, perhaps inadvertently, spark off—from the creative flames raging within him—other pioneering activities. That seems to be what happened to us. We look back with particular affection to the contributions which Tante Ursule made to our early issues. Her essay on custard tarts and the quiches which had become ubiquitous by the late 1970s, was brilliant—concise, vivid, informative and inspirational. The world mourns a famous book author; and we mourn a favourite aunt.

Kibbeh Nayyeh

Suad Aljure

Suad Aljure's parents were Lebanese and, although she now has Colombian nationality, Suad has retained a keen interest in the food and cookery of the Near East.

When I was a little child I knew it was Sunday when my mother took over the kitchen. Sunday was kibbeh day and no hands were allowed to touch the kibbeh except Mama's (which, now that I think about it, must have been rather humiliating for our cook). That was my father's rule; only Mama's touch was right for kneading the kibbeh, and he claimed he could tell when strange hands had prepared the mixture.

As I watched my mother prepare the kibbeh I had dreams of one day being able to make it myself without Papa knowing. He would then eat it with delight, smile and thank Mama. So I watched intently as she first measured the burghul (7 fistfuls per pound of meat after trimming) into a large bowl and filled it with water. While the burghul was soaking, she would start, carefully almost lovingly, to trim the meat, separating the muscles and scraping the red flesh from the white tissues. Every now and then she would ask the cook to sharpen the knife. What has always amazed me is that she would, without fail, wind up with the right amount of scraped meat to mix with the burghul she had measured beforehand. How did she know before trimming the meat what the gristle would weigh?

By the time the meat was trimmed, the burghul was *al dente* and the cook had already peeled the onions, cut them up in small pieces and washed the mint leaves. Meat, onions and mint were put in the mortar and the cook, with a resigned look on her face, would start to pound the ingredients with the pestle. Meanwhile, Mama scooped out handfuls of burghul from the bowl and squeezed them dry. As the meat, onions and mint became a paste the burghul would be added to the mortar and the pounding continued. (Sometimes, when making large quantities of kibbeh, Mama would allow the cook to put the meat, onions and mint through the finer disc of a meat grinder—twice. Then, after kneading in the burghul the mixture was passed, twice again, through a grain grinder.) When the pounding stopped (the mixture was again a paste), my older brothers and sister would casually appear in the kitchen: it was tasting time. The mixture was then transferred to a large bowl and Mama added salt, pepper and a dribble of olive oil. The kneading started and we all waited. A bit more oil. More kneading. It still feels dry. More oil, more kneading. And, finally, we would see Mama's hand rolling a large pinch of kibbeh into a ball. Five mouths would open at the same time and the ball was placed delicately in the mouth nearest her hand. Four more balls were made very quickly and placed in the other mouths. 'Could have used a bit more mint.' This was inevitably my sister. 'More pepper.' That was my oldest brother. 'A bit dry.' 'Needs salt.' Mama would add more salt, pepper and oil and knead the mixture again. After the second tasting round everyone as pleased, except my sister. It was too late to add more mint. If she liked the taste of it that much she could still munch on a leaf while eating her kibbeh. I still don't agree with her. The taste of mint should not overwhelm the other ingredients. Six to eight leaves per pound of meat are enough. The other ingredients are:

1 lb of shoulder of lamb, trimmed of all fat and membranes
5 oz fine burghul (cracked wheat) available in Middle Eastern or health food shops
1 medium-sized onion, peeled and cut up in 1" pieces
salt and pepper to taste
1/2 cup olive oil in all
a few more mint leaves for decoration

After Mama herself had proved and approved the kibbeh, she'd make a big ball of it, set it on the chopping board and slash it across, repeatedly, with a big knife, hoping that bits of white tissue would cling to the edge of the knife . . . as if she had not trimmed the meat ever so carefully to start with. With that last exercise out of the way, she'd feel satisfied that her kibbeh was perfect. All that was left to do now was to mound the kibbeh on a serving platter and flatten and smooth the mound with the palm of one hand moistened with olive oil. Then the traditional sliding and pressing down of a spoon handle around the edge of the flattened mound of kibbeh to make wells that would be filled with a few drops of oil as a finishing touch along with the decoration of mint leaves.

Mole Poblano and Turkey

Elisabeth Lambert Ortiz

Elisabeth Lambert Oritz's authoritative books on food and cookery range over a wide area, but Mexico, Central America and Latin America have always been the region of greatest interest for her. Here, in a characteristic essay, she discusses, and gives a recipe for, an important festival dish of Mexico.

I have always thought of the 17th century legends of the colonial origin of Mexico's festival dish, *Mole Poblano de Guajolote* (Turkey in Chili Pepper and Chocolate Sauce), as charming, but thoroughly silly.

One legend has it that Sor Andrea de la Ascunción, a Dominican nun, invented the *mole* on the spur of the moment in the kitchen of the Convent of Santa Rosa in Puebla de Los Angeles, Puebla, City of the Angels. I've visited the kitchen, a lovely tiled one with plenty of work space, but remain unconvinced that anyone could put together such a complicated list of unfamiliar ingredients as Sor Andrea is credited with; three kinds of dried peppers, one sweet, one pungent, one hot, soaked and ground, all of them unknown to the western world until after the Spanish Conquest (1521), as well as that strange fruit, the tomato, and the equally strange chocolate. The Convent is credited with passing the recipe to other Convents in the city and each is supposed to have worked out minor variations, creating its own version of the dish.

Another legend has it that the Mother Superior of the Convent, expecting a visit from the bishop, started off by making a turkey stew, and wanting to change it into something a little more special set one of the nuns to grinding chili peppers, almonds, raisins, cinnamon, chocolate and so on, in a mortar. Much later, on finding the nun still at work, she is said to have remarked: "You poor soul, grinding and grinding." The Spanish word for grind is *moler,* so according to this story the dish was called *mole* (pronounced MOlay) from the verb *moler. Mole* however comes from the Nahautl word *molli* meaning a sauce made with peppers, any one of the Capsicums, that large assemblage of fruits so diverse in form, color, dimension and flavor that we think of and use as a vegetable, and which we owe to the New World, specifically the Valley of Mexico where it was first cultivated in about 7,000 B.C. Nahautl was the language of the Indians of the region, and in Spanish *molli* became *mole.*

Yet another legend, surely the least probable, claims that a holy father, Fray Pascual, preparing a feast at a convent in Puebla for the visiting Viceroy, came back into his kitchen after a brief absence to find that an errant wind had blown a miscellaneous assortment of spices left out on a tray into the *cazuelas,* the earthenware cooking pots simmering on the charcoal stoves where the main dish was being prepared. The result was *Mole Poblano.*

The most plausible version of the story is that Sor Andrea, wishing to thank the Archbishop for having had a convent constructed for her Order, combined the ingredients of the Old and New Worlds to create a dish in his honor and in honor of the Viceroy, visiting with him. In so doing, she willy-nilly created *Mole Poblano.* Two things do seem clear. All this activity took place in Puebla, and the name of the Viceroy was Don Juan de Palafox y Mendoza.

I believe the origin of the dish to be far less romantic than any of the legends. I am sure it existed before the Conquest, and since it contained chocolate was a royal dish. Chocolate was forbidden to women and among men was reserved for royalty, the military nobility, the higher ranks of the clergy and the most prominent of the merchants. The Aztec girls in the Convent would not have mentioned the dish since they lived in a world of women. I like to imagine that when the visit of Don Juan and the Archbishop was announced, the Convent was in a simmer of excitement, eager to give the distinguished guests a very splendid meal. There were many Aztec girls in the Convents in addition to Indian servants, and it must surely have seemed to them that this was the occasion for a royal dish—the Viceroy being equated with their Emperor, and the Archbishop with their High Priest. What else but a dish with turkey, a native bird that the Aztecs had long domesticated, forbidden chocolate, chilis, with which they were entirely familiar, and tomatoes, another commonplace, but exotic to the nuns. Pooling memories, they could have pieced the recipe together with the nuns making their own contribution. I think perhaps instead of cloves and cinnamon, so recently brought by Spain from the Far East and at that time immensely popular in cooking, the original dish used allspice, native to the region; and *epazote,* a favourite local herb instead of coriander; and peanuts instead of almonds. Onions and garlic were common to both the Old World and the New, and would naturally be included. I cannot prove the authenticity of my version of this early post-Conquest serving of the famous *mole,* but at least it presents a logical solution to the problem of where the dish came from.

There is no doubt that after the Conquest the richly imaginative and varied kitchen of Indian Mexico fell into decline, so that even if the nuns did not invent the turkey *mole* they certainly saved the recipe from oblivion. I am grateful to them. Despite its long list of ingredients it is not difficult to make, and with the help of a food processor or blender not even very time consuming. It is marvellous party food and there are as many versions of it as there are cooks in the State of Puebla. Richard Condon, writing with his daughter Wendy Bennett in their book *The Mexican Stove,* has the highest praise. He calls it "the oldest surviving evolved recipe of cooked food of any system of cooking of any of the ancient civilizations of the world". He believes that the dish is older than the Aztecs, going back to the Mayas who had an older and perhaps higher civilisation than the Aztecs, and claims it to be 9000 years old. This could be. After all, chocolate originated in what is now the Mexican State of Chiapas, once part of the Maya Empire, and both Aztecs and Maya had domesticated turkeys.

The turkey, central to the *Mole Poblano,* is itself a misunderstood bird. Turkey farmers will tell you that it is the stupidest of fowl. That it will drown in a rainstorm because it is too silly to come in out of the rain. It seems that when the ancient Mexicans domesticated the wild and wily turkey, it lost its

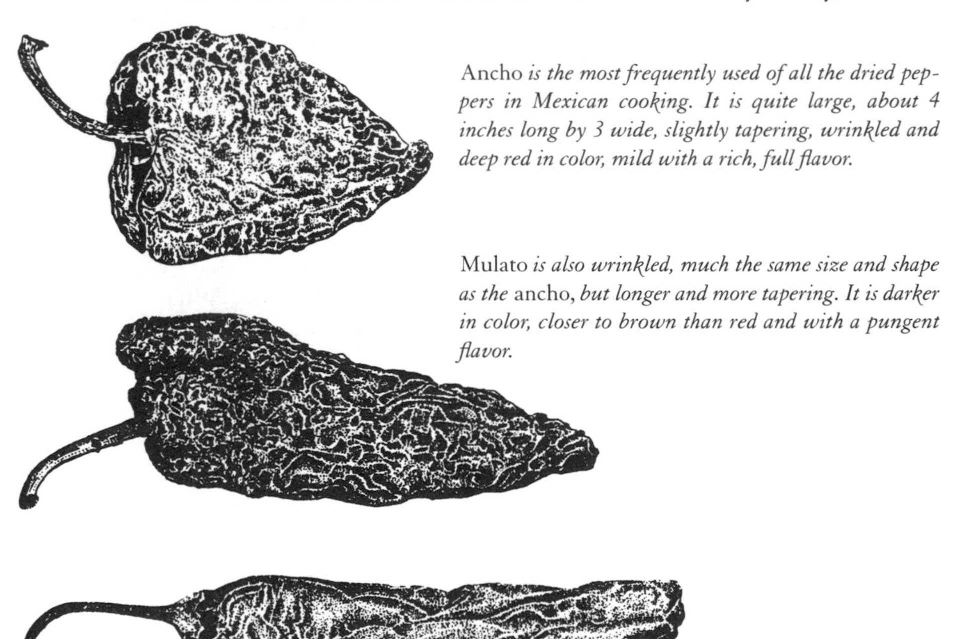

Ancho *is the most frequently used of all the dried peppers in Mexican cooking. It is quite large, about 4 inches long by 3 wide, slightly tapering, wrinkled and deep red in color, mild with a rich, full flavor.*

Mulato *is also wrinkled, much the same size and shape as the* ancho, *but longer and more tapering. It is darker in color, closer to brown than red and with a pungent flavor.*

Pasilla *is a long, slender, wrinkled chili 6 to 9 inches long and an inch or so wide. It is dark in color, almost black and is sometimes sold as* chile negro *(black chili). It is hot and well flavored.*

The three chilis are often used in combination, especially for Mole Poblano. *All are native to Mexico and belong to the genus* Capsicum annuum *of the* Solanaceae *family.*

wits. But wily or not, the wild turkeys did not survive the superior cunning of the Pilgrim Fathers and other early settlers on the Eastern seaboard of the United States who hunted them very nearly to extinction. They have been saved by conservationists and there are probably more wild turkeys in the U.S. right now than at any time since 1620 when the Pilgrims landed.

The turkey that we buy in butcher shops and supermarkets today is not a descendant of that wild bird, *Meleagris gallopavo silvestris*. It is a descendant of *Meleagris gallopavo gallopavo,* the turkey domesticated by the Aztecs and taken to Spain by the conquistadors. From Spain it reached England, and about a century ago crossed the Atlantic about the time when the wild bird had become very nearly extinct in New England. Why ever it was called a turkey remains a mystery. The French called it *poulet d'Inde* (chicken of the Indies) which in time became *dinde* or *dindon;* in Spain it is *pavo,* a sort of poor relation of the *pavo real,* the peacock; in Brazil it is a *peru;* in Peru, as in other Spanish-speaking countries of Latin America, it is *pavo.* Only in Mexico does its original name *guajolote* survive, though used interchangeably with *pavo.* I think it splendid that the wild turkey has survived and also, despite equal hazards, the recipe for its cultivated cousin.

Prepared *mole* can be bought in powder form in tins. It is very good but the *mole* made at home is better. This is one of my own preferred recipes:

Mole Poblano de Guajolote (Turkey in Chili and Chocolate Sauce)

Serves 10

5 to 6 tablespoons lard
8 lb turkey, cut into serving pieces
1 medium onion, coarsely chopped
2 cloves garlic, chopped
salt

for the sauce:
8 ancho chilies
6 mulato chilies
4 pasilla chilies
1 cup blanched almonds
1/2 cup peanuts
1/2 cup pumpkin seeds
1/2 teaspoon coriander seeds
1/4 teaspoon anise
2 cloves

1/2 inch piece of cinnamon, broken up
2 medium onions, coarsely chopped
2 cloves garlic, chopped
1/2 cup raisins
lard
1 1/2 ounces unsweetened chocolate, broken in bits
1 tablespoon sugar (optional)
salt
2 tablespoons sesame seeds

Heat about two thirds of the lard in a heavy frying pan and sauté the turkey pieces, a few at a time, until lightly browned all over. Add more lard if necessary. Put the turkey pieces into a large casserole or heavy saucepan with the onions, garlic and salt to taste and enough water barely to cover. Bring to the boil, reduce the heat and simmer, covered, for 1 hour, or until the turkey is almost tender. Lift out the turkey pieces and set them aside. Strain and reserve the stock. Return the turkey pieces to the casserole.

To make the sauce, remove the stems and seeds from the chilies and tear the chilies into pieces. Put them into a bowl with warm water barely to cover, 1 1/2 to 2 cups. Let them stand for 30 minutes, turning them from time to time. Meanwhile grind the almonds, peanuts, pumpkin seeds, coriander seeds, anise, cloves and cinnamon in a blender, food processor or small coffee grinder and set aside. Drain the chilies and reserve the water in which they have soaked. Put them into a blender or food processor with the onions, garlic, tomatoes and raisins and reduce to a paste using the soaking water as needed. Add the nut mixture and a little more of the liquid and blend to mix.

Measure the lard left in the frying pan and add enough to bring up the quantity to 4 tablespoons. Add the chili paste and sauté over moderate heat, stirring for 5 minutes. Stir in 2 cups of the reserved turkey stock, the chocolate, salt to taste and the sugar, if liked. Cook the mixture over low heat, stirring until the chocolate is melted and adding more turkey stock if necessary to make the sauce coating consistency. Pour the sauce over the turkey pieces and simmer over low heat for 30 minutes. Toast the sesame seeds in a small frying pan. Arrange the turkey and the sauce on a warmed serving platter and sprinkle with the sesame seeds.

Traditionally this *mole* is served with either tortillas or plain, unstuffed tamales, white rice, beans and *guacamole* (avocado sauce).

In Pescod Time...I Went to Gather Strawberries

Elizabeth David

We have already explained the pivotal role which Elizabeth David played in the setting up and subsequent history of PPC. *Most of the essays she wrote during her long career, including a number of those which first appeared in* PPC, *have been reprinted in two volumes:* An Omelette and a Glass of Wine *(1984) and* Is There a Nutmeg in the House? *(2000).*

Looking for an essay which was a good example of her lucid and charming prose style and which included attractive recipes, we chose this item, which we reprint by kind permission of Jill Norman, her literary executor.

Speaking for myself, I seldom have enough strawberries to do adventurous dishes with them. Strawberry sorbets, fools and ices are so delicious that it seems unnecessary to look further, but so many people now go on pick-it-yourself fruit expeditions that I think the following collection of old, unusual and beautiful strawberry recipes will be of interest, at any rate to those who don't feel like consigning the whole load they've so painstakingly gathered straight to the deep freeze.

My title, by the way, comes from a poem called *The Sheepheards slumber* published in *England's Helicon* in 1600, over the name of Ignotus, said to have been a pseudonym used by Sir Walter Raleigh. That may well be wishful thinking, but at least the tenuous connection makes it appropriate that I should start with Sir Walter's recipe for strawberry cordial.

A Cordial Water of Sir Walter Raleigh

Take a Gallon of Strawberries, and put them into a pint of *Aqua vitæ,* let them stand so for four or five days, strain them gently out, and sweeten the water as you please with fine sugar; or else with perfume.

A Queen's Delight: or, The Art of Preserving, Conserving and Candying; As also A right Knowledge of making Perfumes, and Distilling the most Excellent Waters. Never before Published. Printed by R. Wood for Nath. Brooks, at the Angel in Cornhill, 1658.

Notes: Sir Walter Raleigh's strawberry cordial is a recipe worth following up, although eight pints of strawberries to one pint of spirit does seem rather a lot. I tried it one year, using vodka and allowing a pint to two pounds of fruit. After two or three days of steeping the strawberries had given all their colour and scent to the vodka. Having strained them out, it was necessary to filter the vodka, using a coffee paper filter and a glass jug. The filtering was a very slow process, but the result was good, although I think I was wrong in not adding any sugar. A little would have been an improvement.

I think we can accept that the receipt for the cordial really did come from Raleigh, or at any rate that it could have done so. We know that during his imprisonment in the Tower Sir Walter had access to a still and other apparatus necessary for the concoction of cordial spirits, that he availed himself of this welcome diversion and that he communicated the receipts and the 'virtues' of various of his inventions to companions who were with him in the Tower.[1] The 'virtues' of cordials were regarded as medical rather than as purely stimulant. Spirit of strawberries for example was 'excellent good to purifie and cleanse the blood; it preserveth from, and also cureth the yellow Jaundies, and deoppilateth the obstruction of the Spleen; it keepeth the body in a sweet temperateness, and refresheth the spirits. The dose is a spoonful at a time when need requireth any of those helps for the aforesaid diseases.'[2]

1. *Home Life under the Stuarts 1603-1649.* Elizabeth Godfrey, London 1925. P. 231. *A Choice Manual, or Rare Secrets in Physick and Chirurgery: Collected and practised by the Right Honourable the Countess of Kent, late deceased.* Nineteenth edition 1687. (First published 1653) Opp. P. 190.
2. *A Choice Manual,* p. 195.

Composta di Fragole al Latte di Mandorle
(compote of strawberries with almond milk)

I adapted the recipe for this lovely dish from one given in a book published in Turin in 1846, when that city was still the royal capital of the House of Savoy.

For 500 g or 1 lb of strawberries, make the almond milk with 200 g or 6 oz of shelled almonds—preferably bought in their skins—3 or 4 bitter almonds (or about 4 drops of pure extract of almonds) and just over 1/4 pint of water. Sugar.

Blanch the almonds, slip them out of their skins, put them to steep in cold water for a couple of hours. Pound them to a paste, adding a few drops of water, or rosewater if you have it, to prevent the almonds oiling. Mix very thoroughly with the water. (The blender can be used for these operations.)

The mixture now has to be wrung twice through a finely woven cloth. This isn't really as daunting as it sounds, but it does take a little time. What should—and does—eventually emerge is a smooth white milk. The residue of almonds is kept for some other dish. Almonds are far too expensive to waste. (A saving can be made—a saving of time too—by simply stirring a couple of tablespoons of very finely ground almonds into half a pint of thin cream. Leave an hour or two and strain.)

Hull the strawberries. Arrange them in a glass or white china compote dish or bowl (or, perhaps easier to serve, individual goblets or bowls), strew them with sugar. Just before serving—on no account in advance—pour the almond milk over and round the fruit.

Francesco Chapusot. *La Cucina sana, economica ed elegante, secondo le stagioni.* Torino 1841.

Notes: Chapusot was a former head chef to the English ambassador to the Court of Savoy. In spite of his French surname he seems to have been a true Piedmontese by birth, although Piedmont and particularly its capital are close enough to France to seem in some respects very Frenchified. Chapusot's work, published in four slender volumes, each one giving recipes and menus for one season of the year—the strawberry and almond milk compote appears in the Spring volume—represents a school of cooking which is indeed rather franco-italian, although in an unusually delicate way. The ambassadorial style is also unexpectedly restrained, the illustrations of decorative and decorated dishes light and curiously graceful—we have reproduced two of them in *PPC*s—the menus quite simple for the period. All in all, Chapusot seems to have fulfilled the promise in his title of 'healthy, economical and elegant cooking according to the season'.

The strawberry and almond milk dish figures in a menu for a *pranzo di cacciatore,* a shooting lunch, in the Spring volume of Chapusot's work. The other dishes, in the order given, are fried spring chickens with small onions, cold roast beef, timbale of tunny fish, asparagus in salad, and scrambled eggs with ham. Not entirely a cold picnic, so presumably the lunch was to take place in a hunting lodge, with somebody to fry the chickens and make the scrambled eggs, a dish for which few chefs would think it necessary or worthwhile to give a recipe. Chapusot does.

Crème de Fraises

Take about one half-setier (8 oz) of hulled strawberries, washed and drained, which you pound in a mortar, boil three half-setiers of cream with a half-setier of milk and some sugar, let them boil and reduce by half, leave to cool a little and put in your strawberries, so mix them to together; dilute also a piece of rennet the size of a coffee bean and put it to the cream when it is no more than tepid, at once pass all through a tammy and turn it into a compotier which may be put straight upon the coals without breaking, so put your compotier upon a few hot coals, cover it with a cover and some hot coals on the top; when it has set you are to put it in a cool place or on ice until you serve it.

[Menon] *La Cuisinière bourgeoise de l'office* etc.
Nouvelle Edition, p. 381. A Bruxelles chez François Foppens,
Imprimeur-Libraire, 1781. (First published 1745).

Notes: I find this strawberry cream or rather strawberry junket a recipe of great interest, foreshadowing as it does the fruit-flavoured yogurts so commercially successful today. It is also a most unusual recipe for the period. But the technique of warming the cream with heat below and above is one we have lost with the disappearance of charcoal and coal burning stoves, and consequently of the utensils with special covers upon which hot coals were placed. It was this top heat which was so important to the successful cooking of a great many creams, open flans, custards and so on. The oven doesn't replace the old *tourtière,* or *testo* as it was called in Italy. So having put the rennet to the tepid strawberry cream I would simply transfer it to a warm place and leave it, as for any other junket, until set. Then into the refrigerator.

To Make Snow Cream

Take a large deep dish, strew the bottom with fine sugar beat to powder; then fill it with strawberries; take some sprigs of rosemary, stick a large one in the middle, and several roundabout to resemble a tree; then take a quart of the thickest cream you can get, and the whites of eight or ten eggs; then whisk it up for half an hour, till you have made the froth very strong; let it stand ten minutes, and with a proper thing take off the froth, throw it over your tree and cover your dish well with it; If you do it well, it makes a grand pile in a dessert.

The Court and Country Confectioner: or the Housekeepers Guide: a new edition. By Mr. Borella, now head confectioner to the Spanish Ambassador in England. London 1772.

Notes: Mr. Borella's charming snow cream is a survival from the seventeenth century, when rosemary sprigs were so frequently used in the manner he describes that Cotgrave in his French-English Dictionary of 1611 gives an entry to the French term *neige en rosmarin* meaning 'the besprinkling of a rosmarie branch'.

To Make Strawberry Jam

Richard Olney

By a happy coincidence PPC 5 *contained not only Elizabeth David's strawberry recipes but also this one for strawberry jam by Richard Olney.*

To make a strawberry jam that is not too sweet, with a deep ruby cast and an astonishing density of flavour, in which each berry remains intact, count no more than a pound or two of sugar to ten or twelve pounds of fruit, choose small, perfectly ripened strawberries at the height of the season, use an untinned copper preserving pan or, lacking that, a heavy copper basin, normally destined to receive egg whites, and do not be troubled about the relatively small proportion of sugar to that of berries; the final weight of solid fruit will be radically diminished through the repeated reductions of the juices at the same time that the berries' natural sugars are concentrated.

Before hulling the berries, wash them by plunging them into a large basin of water, swirling them rapidly and removing them immediately with wide-spread hands, fingers splayed, to a colander. Do this in several batches, changing the water for each new batch. Hull them and spread them loosely on a tray to avoid crushing them.

In the copper preserving pan, prepare a syrup with the sugar and a pint or somewhat more of water, stirring over heat until the sugar is dissolved. Boil for a minute over high heat and throw in as many strawberries as you can hold piled up in joined hands—about a pound. Leave them in the syrup for a minute or so after it has returned to the boil and, with a spider, remove them to a colander placed on a tray or over a large bowl. Boil the syrup until it has reduced to approximately its original volume and throw in another batch of strawberries. Continue in this manner, removing each batch of strawberries to the colander after a minute or so at the full boil and reducing the syrup back to its original amount after the removal of each batch. From time to time drain the juices that collect beneath the colander back into the preserving pan. When the last batch has been removed, reduce the syrup once again and return all of the strawberries at once, along with any more juices that have collected, to the pan. Cook at a light boil for about ten minutes, stirring gently from time to time to displace the berries in the syrup. Cool partially before ladling the jam into the jars, filling each half full at first and then returning to fill them completely in order to distribute equally the whole berries and the thick, enrobing liquid.

The fresh berries lose their juice and their colour rapidly to the syrup when first plunged in and are pathetic, grey, flabby carcasses when skimmed out but, when returned to the reduced syrup, the concentrated juices and the rich colour are magically drawn back into the flesh with sumptuous result. It is the best jam I have ever tasted. Because it is so rapidly consumed, I have never been able to keep it for more than six months; it is possible that a five-minute sterilization would be wise for longer periods.

Strawberry Illustrations. *These two and that on page 445 are from the* Dictionnaire Encyclopédique de l'Épicerie *by Albert Seigneurie, Paris 1898, and Edition Nouvelle, Paris 1904.*

A Mussel-Feast in the Charente-Maritime

ROSEMARY HANSON

In sending us this recipe, the author asked whether it is unique in that the mussels are cooked without any liquid. She also wondered whether anyone had come across it elsewhere, for example along the coast of Norfolk (England) where both pine forests and mussels are found . . . 'it is such a felicitous way of using local materials and a particularly good holiday dish as there's no washing up, not even a cooking pot'. So far as we know no one came up with the sort of information she was seeking.

We stayed one August in Ronce-les-Bains with friends who own a dilapidated old villa where at high tide you can walk across the spiky grass of the terrasse and dive off the wall into the water, and, at low tide, walk out several miles across the sands in the direction of the oyster parcs. It was the year of the drought, 1976, and as a result the local oysters, to be had at every café or ordered by the basket from the fishermen, were small and salty—not worth bothering with, said our hostess. The mussels were a different story, small but sweet. We ate them in copious amounts in *mouclade,* as *moules marinières,* and, best of all, in *la terrée,* the local dish also known as *éclade.*

La Terrée is by definition a party or feast. A *terrée* for one or two is unimaginable. What you do is this: first of all the mussels must be gathered, and while most of the party are out doing this the rest are harvesting dried pine needles. Next you must have a thick plank. The family we stayed with had one ready that had been used before and would be re-used until it was too charred and fell to bits. This is placed on two piles of stones or bricks in an open space in the garden or on the beach. In the middle you put a round stone—you can use a pile of sand or a large potato instead—to steady the first mussels which are put round it in ever larger circles, standing on their pointed ends.

When the buckets have been emptied and all the mussels arranged, they are covered with the pine needles which are set alight. The needles smoulder, giving off a pleasant smell and cooking the mussels which emerge, the shells charred and the flesh exquisite. They are eaten, taking care not to burn the fingers, with plenty of fresh bread and local Charentais butter and lots of white wine.

I recently came across a reference to something rather similar in Guernsey. It is described by Sir Edgar MacCullock in *Guernsey Folk-lore* (1903) and quoted by A.R. Wright in *British Calendar Customs,* a Folklore Society publication of 1936, thus:

> 'In Guernsey, it is the custom of young people to collect limpets on Good Friday, place them in their shells, on a flat rock-surface, cover them with furze and ignite it. The limpets, carefully cooked in the ashes of the furze fire, form an item in a picnic.'

I have not come across any other account of this way of cooking limpets and wonder whether it is unique to Guernsey and still practised there. Alan Davidson (*North Atlantic Seafood,* Macmillan London 1979, Viking Press New York 1980, Penguin Books 1980 [and now Ten Speed Press 2003]) refers to a similar technique recorded from Eastbourne in England and from Normandy, but this involved straw rather than furze.

Elderflower

JENNY KENRICK

There are three elderflower recipes here. The elderflower cordial, which comes first, frequently refreshed the editors of PPC *while at work in the summer months. Jenny Kenrick was and still is our neighbour just across the road.*

I first discovered the versatility of the elder (*Sambucus nigra*) at the age of 10. I used to sit with my friends round a camp fire at the far end of the garden behind the compost heap. After a meal of ash-blackened potatoes we would reach out to the scruffy shrub nearby, cut a length of twig, blow out the insects in the hollow stem and, having lit one end in the fire, we would puff and cough away—to our infinite satisfaction.

Many years later on a summer's day in a friend's garden I was introduced to elderflower cordial. Cool and refreshing, it could be preserved only as long as summer lasted, I was told. I suspect that this family had always drunk its supply before summer ended; I have succeeded in keeping it well into the next spring. Although some moulds appear they can be strained out and have never yet affected the taste of the cordial. Sometimes it has fermented slightly; but as the drink is a cordial and has to be diluted to taste it has been regularly drunk by young and old in great quantity, and without ill effect.

The recipe as given to me by my friend is as follows:

ELDERFLOWER CORDIAL

Pick 40 large heads of elderflower at the end of a dry summer's day. (This is very important. After the sun has shone on the flowers the pollen and nectar are more fully flavoured and scented, and the flavour of the cordial is thereby enhanced.) Place 4 lb of white sugar, 3 oz citric acid (for flavour), and the juice and rind of 2 lemons in a large preserving pan. Pour 3 pints [U.K.—nearly 4 pints U.S.] of boiling water over into the pan and stir until the sugar is dissolved. Add the whole heads of elderflower and stir them in the liquid. Cover and leave in a cool place for 5 days. Strain the concentrate into strong screw-capped bottles. To use, dilute with water to taste, and serve with lots of ice.

I have used the cordial to complement the flavour of gooseberries. For example, in a gooseberry tart baked with custard or with a crème patissière I add cordial to the cream until the scent of elderflower is quite strong. It can also be used when making Hannah Glasse's Gooseberry Cream (quoted from *The Whole Art of Cookery Made Plain and Easy,* 7th edition, 1760). Add the cordial with or instead of the orange-flower water/sack.

Gooseberry Cream

> Take two quarts of gooseberries, put to them as much water as will cover them, scald them, and then run them thro' a sieve with a spoon: to a quart of the pulp you must have six eggs well beaten; and when the pulp is hot, put in an ounce of fresh butter, sweeten it to your taste, put in your eggs, and stir them over a gentle fire till they grow thick, then set it by; and when it is almost cold, put into it two spoonfuls of juice of spinach, and a spoonful of orange-flower water or sack; stir it well together, and put it into your bason. When it is cold, serve it to the table.

It was adapting this recipe which led me to wonder how early a reference to elderflower I could find in English cookery books. Going right back to the mediaevel herbals I found that Albertus Magnus, whose 13th century anthology of material on herbs and much else besides was first published in English in about 1550 as *The Book of Secrets of Albertus Magnus,* had a 'recipe' which involved blood and elder oil and the head of a green frog. But this was not for eating or drinking; it was to produce a concoction to be burned in a green lamp through the glass of which would be seen the likeness of a black man! In some 17th century books, and many later ones, I found rather unappetising recipes for pickling elder buds, which I have not tried. These were soon accompanied and later supplanted by the more familiar recipes for making wine from elder berries and flowers. The berries were also used for 'elder rob', a syrup potion, which seems almost always to have been alcoholic. Recipes for elder wine are still with us. And on the herbal side, I know that many country people still use elderflowers in lard-based ointments and salves.

But I was looking for something edible or potable and non-alcoholic, based on the elderflower. The first such reference which I have found is a recipe in Richard Bradley's *The Country Housewife and Lady's Director* (1727) for elderflower vinegar. Interestingly, he says that the flowers should be gathered in May. In Southern England I would expect to find them at their most fully scented in late June. The difference, which applies also to many other fruits which he mentions (all of them a month earlier than nowadays) cannot be explained by the change from the Julian to the Gregorian calendar, since Bradley was already using the latter, although it was not officially introduced until 1752. (See page 23 and 30 of Caroline Davidson's Introduction to the facsimile reprint of Bradley's work, Prospect Books, 1980.)

Bradley's recipe for this vinegar is pleasant enough, but the most charming version I have found in the 18th century books is that of Elizabeth Raffald (*The Experienced Housekeeper*—I quote from the 8th edition, 1782).

To Make Elder Flower Vinegar

> To every peck of the peeps of elder flowers put two gallons of strong ale allegar [presumably vinegar]; and set it in the sun in a stone jug for a fortnight, then filter it through a flannel bag; when you bottle it, put it in small bottles, it keeps the flavour much better than large ones.—Be careful you do not drop any stalks among the peeps.—It makes a pretty mixture on a side table, with tarragon vinegar, lemon pickle, &c.

There is also an English tradition of giving additional flavour to jellies and jams by drawing bunches of elderflowers through them before they set.

On the other side of the Atlantic there are references to elderflower (*Sambucus canadensis, S. melanocarpa, S. mexicana*) in compilations of the recipes of American Indians. Here we find infusions of elderflowers, to be drunk hot or cold and recommended for a queasy stomach. There are also recipes for elderflower fritters and muffins; but I wonder whether these—especially the elderflower muffins—are really Indian dishes or ones which have been developed more recently in well-accountred North American kitchens. The fritters, whatever their real origin, are delicious. This recipe is based on that in Carolyn Niethammer's excellent book *American Indian Food and Lore* (Collier Books, New York, 1974).

Elderblow Fritters

elderblow in sufficient quantity
1 (U.S.) cup flour
1 tsp baking powder
a pinch of salt
2 eggs
1/2 (U.S.) cup fresh orange juice
oil for deep-frying

Elderblow is the attractive name for the elderflowers. For this recipe it is best to shake them loose from the sprigs (although some people deep-fry whole sprigs).

Mix the flour and baking powder and salt together. Separate the eggs and beat yolks lightly. Mix the yolks and the orange juice with the dry ingredients.

Beat the egg whites and fold the prepared mixture into them, together with the elderblow. (The quantity of elderblow can be varied, but you should certainly have enough to fill 1 U.S. cup.)

Heat the oil to deep-frying temperature, then drop the batter into it, a tablespoonful at a time. Turn them as they fry and take them out when they are golden-brown.

You can sprinkle them lightly with sugar before serving them.

One great advantage of the elderflower is that it is easily found even by the city-dweller; it grows luxuriantly on building sites and tow paths. One can pick the flowering heads without too bad a conscience—but selectively, without stripping a bush or feeling that one has deprived others.

Filets de Sole à La Marguery

JAMES M ANDREWS

The amazing story of the exploit which led to the original version of this recipe being brought across the Atlantic to 'Diamond Jim' Brady is here complemented by the testimony of someone who took down the recipe in the Café Marguery 50 years ago.

Before the First World War of 1914–18 every well-informed person who strolled along the grands Boulevards of Paris knew that the Café Marguery, at No 34 on the Boulevard de Bonne Nouvelle, served the most delicious Filets de Sole to be found anywhere in the world. They were imitated by the Chefs of London, Berlin, St Petersburg, and New York, but everyone knew that the original was far better than any of the imitations and that its recipe was a closely held secret.

'Diamond Jim' Brady, who started out as a bellboy in New York and became a millionaire, was famous for two things: his love of diamonds, and his love of good food. He wore more and bigger diamonds than any dozen other men, and he ate so much that Charles Rector, proprietor of a famous Broadway restaurant, said that Diamond Jim was the 'best 25 customers' he had. *The People's Almanac* (Wallechinsky and Wallace, Doubleday, 1975) tells what happened when Diamond Jim learned about Filets de Sole Marguery.

> One day, '. . . Brady was dining at Rector's when a member of his party began talking rapturously about the splendors of Filet de Sole Marguery—as prepared only at the Café Marguery in Paris from a secret recipe.
>
> 'This new dish immediately became an obsession with Big Jim, and he refused to rest until he could enjoy the fabled fish on a regular basis in New York. He threatened to take his business elsewhere unless Charles Rector was able to come up with the secret recipe.
>
> 'The next day, Rector's son George was pulled out of Cornell and prepared for a difficult undercover mission. Under an assumed name young Rector began by washing pots at the Café Marguery, and slowly worked his way up to the position of apprentice chef. After months spent under the watchful eyes of his masters, Rector was finally admitted into the inner circle which knew the secrets of the special sole and its priceless sauce. After more than two years in Paris he was able to sail for New York with the knowledge demanded by Diamond Jim.

> 'Brady was at the dock to meet young Rector when he arrived. "Have you got the sauce?" Diamond Jim bellowed while the vessel was still out in the river. That night Jim fully indulged himself after his long wait, finishing 9 portions of the sole and sopping up the last bit of sauce with a piece of bread held between 2 bejewelled fingers. When he went back to the kitchen to congratulate the chef he said he guessed that: "If you poured some of the sauce over a Turkish towel, I believe I could eat all of it." '

The Café Marguery was still in existence when my family took me to Paris in 1922 to spend a year learning French, and we enjoyed the famous Filets de Sole many times. My memory of them is still very clear, and I know that the recipes published in even the best French cookbooks are wrong. Some even call for cream and flour in the sauce, and it is certain that the Café Marguery did not use either with its Filets. Once I mentioned this in a letter to my friend Nina Lobanov, and this led to a most extraordinary COINCIDENCE! Nina was then living in San Francisco, and she showed my letter to her charming old landlady who reacted immediately:

> 'But I was in Paris in 1926, and my father took me often to the Café Marguery because he was a friend of Monsieur Mangin, the Maître Chef of the Marguery for more than 30 years! We had dinner there the night before we left Paris to come home, and I asked M. Mangin if he wouldn't please tell me the recipe if I promised not to reveal it to anyone else. He did so very graciously, and I wrote it down. I think I still must have it among my old letters and souvenirs, and I'll look for it.'

Mrs Burmister did in fact find the recipe which she had written down 50 years before, while sitting at a table in the Café Marguery with M. Mangin and her father. She made a copy for Nina and me, and I enclose one for you.

The famous café disappeared from the scene many years ago, and its wonderful Filets de Sole are no longer to be had in Paris. The last time I ordered them I was served a dish with the sole completely embalmed in a cream sauce almost as thick as Cream of Wheat. Abominable! One can get in Paris Filets de Sole Dieppoise which are reminiscent of sole Marguery, but not in the same class.

Now that I have a friend who is himself a Maître Chef, it gives me great pleasure to pass along to him all the information on an important culinary subject.

Café Marguery
34 boulevard de Bonne Nouvelle

Filets de Sole Marguery

1. Use bones and trimmings of 2 Soles to make a white wine fumet flavored with 2 or 3 shallots, a sprig of thyme, 1/4 bayleaf, a little parsley, salt and white pepper.

Simmer 15 minutes.

Add to this fumet (after straining and concentrating) the strained cooking liquor of a quart of mussels cooked the usual way in white wine.

2. Place the sole fillets, seasoned and flattened, on a buttered baking dish. Put several tablespoons of the fumet around them. Cover with buttered greaseproof paper and poach gently.

Drain fillets well. Set in oval dish. Surround them with doubled row of shelled mussels and shrimp.

Keep hot and cover while making sauce.

3. Strain the fumet, to which have been added the cooking juices of the sole. Boil down to one-third the quantity.

Remove from heat, allow to cool a little, then add 6 egg yolks.

Whisk sauce over a gently heat, like a hollandaise, incorporating about 3/4 pound of best butter, slightly melted. Season sauce, and strain.

4. Coat the fillets and the garnish with the sauce, and glaze in a hot oven.

Note. When available, bigorneaux (little periwinkles) are added to the garnish of mussels and shrimp.

* * * *

This recipe was given to me in 1926 by M. Mangin, who was head Chef of Marguery for 30 years. Anne Burmister, 1976.

Kulich

Sophie Coe

Sophie Coe, whose Memorial Fund benefits from publication of this book, contributed to PPC *a series of important and pioneering essays on pre-Columbian (Aztec, Maya and Inca) cuisines. These later became the basis of her book* America's First Cuisines *(University of Texas Press, 1994). Here we reprint a shorter essay on a Russian Easter speciality. Sophie's father was the eminent Russian-American geneticist, Theodosius Dobzhansky, who was teaching in the USA during the 1930s when she was born.*

This article was inspired by J Peter Maher's notes in PPC 9 *on the etymology and shape of the 'baba'. The kulic, and the baba have many points of resemblance.*

Perhaps it was to disguise the phallic contours of the kulich that my mother always used another method of decoration. She claimed it was invented by a Siberian pastry cook, but who he was, or when and where, remain unknown to me.

Originally this method must have used a linen napkin, but we always used paper. Several paper napkins were unfolded and placed on one another so that the folds matched. Then they were placed on top of the baked kulich to make sure the napkin was of a proper length. There is no reason why the edges could not be cut into fancy scallops, but we never did anything but shorten. Confectioners' sugar was then mixed with lemon juice to a fairly thick yet spreadable consistency and a tablespoon of this mixture put in the center of the trimmed napkin, now lying flat on the table. The icing is spread from the center to the margins. When the napkins are all covered they are deftly put on top of the kulich and the folds arranged. Now the white expanse can be suitably decorated with whatever suits your fancy: nuts, flowers and leaves made from candied cherries and citron, candy sprinkles, silver shot, or jelly beans and flabby yellow marshmallow chicks.

The sugared napkin will soon harden, and the whole affair can be lifted off the kulich when it comes time to slice it. This method has two advantages, it keeps the kulich fresh, and it does not mess up the top, the tastiest portion for some of us, with great quantities of sugar. While the method can be accused of wastefulness the very young have been known to snap off the corners and eat them, paper and all.

This recipe for kulich is one evolved by my mother, who firmly believed that the olive oil, honey, and sour cream add some dimension that could not be achieved by butter, sugar, and milk alone.

Kulich

10 cups flour
12 egg yolks and one whole egg
2 cups sugar
1/4 pound butter
1/3 cup olive oil
3 tsp salt
1/3 cup honey
2 pkg yeast in 1/2 cup warm water
3/4 cup sour cream
2 cups milk

Mix 1 cup flour, the egg, the sour cream, honey and salt. Pour in 3/4 cup boiling milk. Let cool, add yeast, and let rise. Mix butter with two cups of sugar, then add the egg yolks. Add flour, salt and yeast mixture, olive oil, and remaining milk and mix thoroughly.

At this point one can flavor the kulich with any number of things. Personal favorites are saffron, vanilla beans and raisins, but candied fruit, grated lemon peel, cardamom or chopped almonds are also used.

It is best to do this first mixing of the dough in the late afternoon or evening, so that the very rich and heavy dough can have its first rising overnight. In the morning punch it down and let it rise a second time. Old Russian cookbooks say that men clumping about in heavy boots should not be allowed in the house while the kulich is rising. The dough is then put into molds, which are tin cans of the size used for some institutional food, six inches in diameter and seven to eight inches high. The molds are prepared by being buttered, and then bread crumbs rolled around to cover the buttered inside and discs of paper cut out and put in the bottom of the mold.

The prepared mold is filled half full and the last rising is allowed to take place after which the kulich is slipped in to a 325 degree oven with the greatest of care and baked for about an hour. It must be watched carefully, as the top likes to burn and may need a protective cap of aluminum foil. Test with a long broom straw. Once out of the oven they should be allowed to stand for a few minutes and then carefully eased out of their molds and placed on their sides on the family down pillows which are assembled in the kitchen for this occasion and covered with clean dish towels. It makes the pillows smell delicious.

The molds are treasured from year to year to the great astonishment of movers, should one chance to change houses. One has to explain that these objects, darkened from long use (dark ones bake better than new shiny ones), are not old tin cans that belong on the dump but part of an ancient tradition and something very valuable indeed.

'Aubergines Dursun'

Osman Mardin

In editing the early issues of PPC, *and indeed the later ones too, we were always pleased to find a contribution which was informal and lively, thus guarding against any risk that* PPC *would seem to be too uniformly serious. This article is a good example of the sort of thing we had in mind. It was contributed to* PPC 14 *by a gastronomically minded Turk at a time when he was working in Brussels.*

Good restaurants are few in Istanbul. Occasional gastronomic treasures can be found, but only after much searching.

I found one such delight entirely by chance. I had started work one grey day in autumn 1982 in a Turkish industrial company. My manager was a soft-spoken but shrewd ex-civil servant. After spending the morning chatting about his days in the finance ministry, he offered to show me where company employees had lunch.

The place itself looked very ordinary: a small, bustling restaurant full of private sector functionaries, with busy waiters dressed in ill-fitting dinner suits, and a television set in one corner giving live coverage of the Turkey-Bulgaria football match (two-nil to Bulgaria). A typically earthy, middle-class, Istanbul atmosphere.

We found two places next to some colleagues, one of whom devoured a 'pirzola' (lamb chop) with relish, then waved it to us in lieu of greeting.

An authoritative 'Garson!' immediately produced results: one of the Moss Bros Misfits was with us in a second. No menu; the waiter describes what's on today.

The first choice was a menu fixe: 'düğün corbası' (wedding soup—a particular favourite of mine made with yoghurt and mint) followed by 'Karnıyarık' (a type of aubergine dish) with 'tomato-rice', and as dessert 'ayva tatlısı' (quince-sweet).

My manager looked embarrassed—'what other sort of lovely "kebabs" do you have, son, for our honoured new guest from England?' I was, however, determined on experiencing the Turkish working man's life in full, and plumped for the menu fixe.

My choice was brilliant. The gastronomic benefits of this job obviously outshone the commercial ones. As the various dishes arrived, Mr Moss Bros Misfit received more and more compliments from me, something he obviously found rather unusual in a customer. . . .

The food was unquestionably delicious, though. Probably the most exotic thing worth describing is the aubergine dish 'karnıyarık', for which my parents' cook, Dursun, also has a special recipe. For want of a better expression (the literal translation is rather unappetizing: 'stomach—ripped—out') I shall christen it 'Aubergines Dursun'.

Aubergines Dursun

Supplies for six people

12 medium-sized aubergines
3 onions
2 lbs minced beef
1 soupspoon of sugar
2 soupspoons tomato paste
1/2 lb chili peppers, cut in half lengthwise
1 lb tomatoes, sliced quite thinly
1 cup olive oil
1/4 lb margarine
1 quart water

Equipment

Three frying pans, two small and one large (radius slightly greater than the length of one aubergine).

First, the aubergines have to be prepared. Begin this by peeling each one, *not* cutting off the stem. Now comes the 'stomach-ripped-out' stage, shown in the diagram: use a teaspoon to scoop out an oval section in the middle of the aubergine, burrowing about three quarters of the depth of the aubergine, i.e. *not* boring a hole straight through. . . . The scooped out bits are of no more use, but can be made into aubergine salad, of which more some other time.

Place the peeled and hollowed aubergines into a basin of salt water, leave for half an hour, then take them out and wrap them individually in a cloth or paper towel.

While the aubergines are still in the water, you can start thinking about how to prepare the meat. This stage begins by mincing the onions quite finely, and frying them over moderate heat in the 1/4 lb of butter, in one of the small frying pans. When they are slightly pink, add the mincemeat and continue frying until most of the butter is absorbed.

Now add the water, tomato paste and sugar, mix with a fork, and continue to simmer for another ten minutes. Next pass the mincemeat through a sieve, keep the remaining water in a beaker or cup, and place the mincemeat in a bowl or plate.

You have probably taken your aubergines out of the water by now, and wrapped them in paper towels. You can unwrap them when they are dry.

At the next stage we need the other small pan. Heat the cup of olive oil here, and fry the aubergines in it until they are a slightly yellow colour. This can be done in threes or fours, depending on how many aubergines fit into the pan.

After the whole lot are ready, place the fried aubergines in the large pan, so that their stems face inwards, as shown below.

We have reached the last stage! Use a teaspoon to fill the hollows of the aubergines with the mincemeat, and place a slice of tomato and half a chili pepper on each aubergine. Pour the water in which the mincemeat was cooked (kept in a beaker or cup), into the pan, from the side (i.e. not directly onto the aubergines).

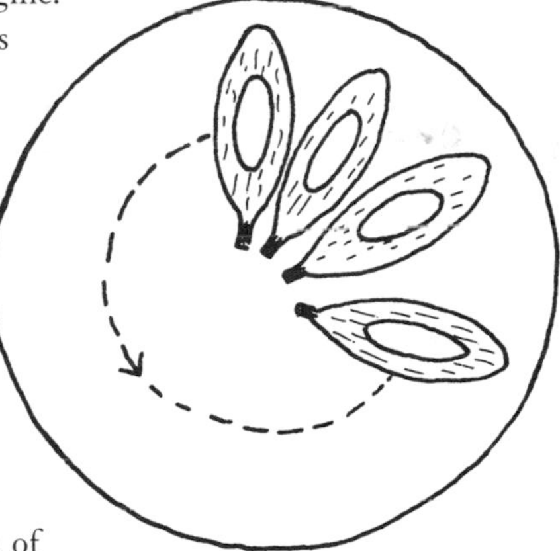

Cook over moderate heat on a ring for 15 minutes, then place in the oven until the surface of the peppers and tomatoes looks cooked.

Two months, many delicious Anatolian dishes (and about a stone) later, I am recognized as the resident curious tourist at 'Bizim Lokanta' restaurant. My impression of the place as a no-glamour but superb quality restaurant, serving a surprising variety of dishes is unchanged, they even seem to be consistent—a rare quality in the Middle East.

Photographer's Cheesecake

B A HENISCH

The first book by Bridget Anne Henisch which we came across was Medieval Armchair Travels *which addressed a subject previously neglected by food historians, namely how did Noah provision his ark with a sufficiency of food for all the heterogeneous voyagers. Later, Prospect Books was privileged to publish* Cakes and Characters, *a charming piece of embroidery on the theme of Twelfth Night cakes and associated customs. A similar combination of deep research, beautiful prose and a penchant for the quaint or surprising can be found in this essay. Much of it is concerned with the problems facing early photographers (Bridget and her husband Heinz being eminent among historians of photography) but there is a recipe, right at the end, and it does work!*

Brillat-Savarin once shook his head sadly over the fate of Adam and Eve: 'Parents of the human race, you lost everything for an apple. What would you not have done for a truffled turkey?"[1] Despite the devoted labours of enthusiasts, a mist hides long stretches of the road which winds through history from the first simple apple to the glories of that complex masterpiece. The origins of most cooking techniques, the acceptance of new ingredients, the slow process of trial and error in their choice and combination, all these remain in large part matters for ingenious speculation built on inconclusive evidence. Some recipes, like Chicken Marengo or Malakovtorte, have come down to us with their identification papers in good order, but the vast majority have slipped into the record books without even the shred of an acceptable birth certificate. Photographer's Cheesecake is one of the lucky few with impeccable credentials and an indisputable pedigree.

William Henry Fox Talbot introduced the art of photography on paper in 1839, but in solving one old problem for the world posed several small new ones. To be able to receive a photographic image, the sheet of paper must be prepared for its role. Fox Talbot had discovered that, by treating paper first with a solution of common household salt and then with silver nitrate, he could make it sensitive, so that it grew dark when exposed to light. It was thus possible to lay a leaf on this 'photogenic drawing paper' and obtain a fine negative, with the delicate, perfect impression of the leaf standing out bright and clear against the darkened expanse of paper around it. When the next step was taken, to obtain positive images, these too were printed onto salted paper.

The salt process had several advantages, of which the most important were the simplicity of the method and the cheapness of the main ingredient. The disadvantage was that it did nothing to hide the fibre and texture of the paper itself. When a paper print was laid beside the smooth silver surface of a daguerreotype it seemed unpleasantly coarse and irregular. The albumen alternative, made public by a Frenchman, L. D. Blanquart-Evrard, in 1850, was hailed as a distinct improvement because it closed the pores of the paper and covered its surface with a thin, shining coat which retained the minute, sharp details of the photograph.

To make up the albumen mixture, egg whites were separated from the yolks, added to a salt solution and then beaten to a froth (Fig. 1). The beating was necessary to break down the different protein structures and create a uniform liquid. Although much emphasis was laid on the importance of using fresh eggs, the albumen mixture itself had to be left to age for one week. After that it could be stored for some time longer, and used until even the most dedicated dark-room fanatic began to have misgivings. As one French writer bluntly put it: 'A ce moment, elle exhalera une forte odeur animale.'[2] No wonder that Lydid Bonfils, wife and mother of two famous photographers in Lebanon, was heard to exclaim: 'I never want to smell another egg again,' after forty years spent in whisking up solutions.[3]

Cooking and chemistry have strong family ties; in the flurry of suggestions on ways to improve the basic albumen recipe they seem to be twin sisters, bending over the solution and each throwing in a pinch of this or that as inspiration strikes. M. Blanquart-Evrard himself thought that the egg whites should be whisked up with the whey separated from curdled milk: 'Beat up

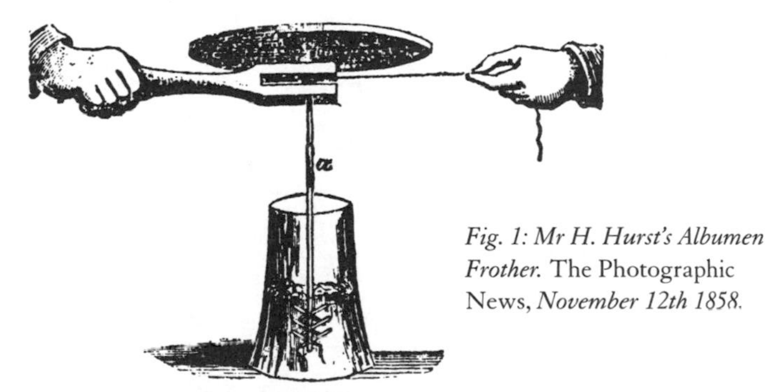

Fig. 1: Mr H. Hurst's Albumen Frother. The Photographic News, *November 12th 1858.*

DEAR SIR,—I have used the above apparatus to froth albumen rapidly, and found it answer very well; at *a* can be placed a ferrule, so that the lower part can be taken off. The lower stick is cut into four portions, quills are slid in crosswise, and then tied in position. H. HURST.

with about three-fourths of a pint of this serum the white of one egg; this solution is then to be boiled, and again filtered, after which five grains per. cent. of iodide of potassium is to be dissolved in it.' In the same issue of *The Art Journal,* M. Niépce de Saint Victor recommended the addition of a touch of honey from Narbonne.[4] When it had been found that not only paper but glass negative plates could be prepared for photography by coating with albumen, Sir William de Wiveleslie Abney offered a recipe containing albumen, water and ammonium hydrate, 'mixed immediately before use with an equal quantity of beer or stout.'[5]

The albumen process dominated the world of photography from the mid-1850s to the 1890s. As that world expanded, with the endless discovery and development of new applications for the art, so the demand for commercially-prepared, ready-to-use albumenized paper grew ever more insistent amongst amateurs and professionals alike. It was realized quite quickly that the albumen paper process works best on a thin, smooth paper of exceptionally high quality, made in mineral-free water. Inferior grades of paper derived from rags were not suitable for this process owing to the presence therein of metal from buttons. Only two paper-mills achieved this high quality consistently, one established at Rives, in France, and one whose product was made in Malmedy (then part of Germany) and known as 'Saxe' paper (Fig. 2).

For a variety of social and economical reasons, it was the German city of Dresden which became the capital of the albumen empire. Several factories flourished there, and the scale of manufacture can be gauged from the output of just one. In 1888 the Dresdener Albuminfabriken A.G. produced 18,674

Fig. 2: 1885 advertisement for albumen paper, marketed by the company of A. Rivot and made from 'Rives' and 'Saxe' raw stock.

Fig. 3: separating the eggs in a Dresden albumen factory, circa 1890.

reams of albumen paper. To make the coating for each of these reams, twenty-seven dozen egg-whites were needed, and so in the course of one year this factory alone used over six million eggs (Fig. 3). As all the factories in the city believed in encouraging the albumen to ferment for several days before it was made up into a solution, the atmosphere must have been overwhelming, and it is hardly surprising to learn that a Dresden paper could be instantly identified by smell alone.[6]

Although albumen was an exceedingly useful substance as a transparent glue, its weaknesses showed themselves unmistakably as time wore on; albumen prints had an unfortunate tendency to turn yellow and to fade away. Criticism mounted, and new gelatin and collodion emulsion-type papers were introduced in the late 1880s, with triumphant claims to permanence, using an immortal phoenix in their advertisements, to displace albumen's emblems, the sturdy cock and hen (Fig. 4). The old process soon fell from favour. As an enthusiast wrote in 1887:

> . . . soon may all follow
> A 'Permanent way',
> And from out of our albums
> No prints fade away.
> For when Albumen's yellow,
> And Chloride is flown,
> Platino and Carbon
> Shall still hold their own.[7]

While albumen was king, its manufacture presented both problems and opportunities. What was to be done with all those egg yolks? Large commercial enterprises could make a profit from them; in Dresden they were preserved with salt and sold to bakers, or to tanners who used them in the finishing of their kid leathers. No outlet on so grand a scale was needed by the amateur, and yet it was not to be expected that a conscientious cook could bear to stand by and see that golden hoard thrown away and wasted. On September 2nd 1861, the *British Journal of Photography* suggested a solution:

> A HINT TO ALBUMENIZERS. What can you do with the yolks of your eggs? Make them into cheesecakes that will be pronounced unrivalled. . . . This is one of the pleasantest 'bye-products' we are acquainted with in the economics of manufacturing photography. Try it!

The idea must have proved popular, for the recipe was published again in the Journal's *Photographic Almanac for 1862:*

The Photographer's Cheesecake

> To convert the yolks of eggs used for albumenizing to useful purposes: Dissolve a quarter of a pound of butter in a basin placed on the hob, stir in a quarter of a pound of pounded sugar, and beat well together; then add the yolks of three eggs that have been previously well-beaten; beat up altogether thoroughly; throw in half a grated nutmeg and a pinch of salt; stir, and *lastly* add the juice of two fine-flavoured lemons, and the rind of one lemon that has been peeled very thin; beat all up together thoroughly, and pour into a dish lined with puff-paste, and bake for about twenty minutes. This is a most delicious dish.[8]

Cooks today will find the recipe works very well, with one or two small modifications for modern conditions. It makes a very piquant filling (indeed, one lemon many prove sufficient), and a short-crust pastry seems even better as a partner for it than the puff pastry recommended. The unfilled base should be pricked all over with a fork and baked for ten minutes at 375°F (gas mark 5). Once the mixture has been poured in, the tart is cooked for another twenty-five minutes at 400°F (gas mark 6). True enthusiasts will naturally wish to serve it accompanied by a glass of white burgundy from the vineyard owned by a descendant of Nicéphore Niépce, the father of photography.

References

1. J.-A. Brillat-Savarin, *The Philosopher in the Kitchen,* trs. Anne Drayton (Penguin Books, 1970, 1981), chap. 27, p. 378.
2. Frédéric Dillaye, *La Pratique en Photographie* (Paris: A la Librairie Illustrée, n.d., c. 1876), p. 249.

3. Will H. Rockett, 'The Bonfils Story', in *Aramco World Magazine,* vol. 34, no. 6 (November-December 1983), p. 13.
4. *The Art Journal* (1850), pp. 329–30.
5. Sir William de Wiveleslie Abney, *A Treatise on Photography* (London: Longmans, Green, and Co., tenth edition, 1901), p. 171.
6. James M. Reilly, *The Albumen and Salted Paper Book* (Rochester, New York: Light Impressions, 1980), pp. 29, 33–4.
7. *Ibid.,* p. 101.
8. The recipe is reprinted in D. B. Thomas, *The Science Museum Photography Collection* (London: Her Majesty's Stationery Office, 1969), p. 70.

Fig. 4: an 1889 advertisement for one of the new photographic papers which were replacing albumen paper.

Cocido

Alicia Rios

Alicia Rios has already contributed an illuminating historical/sociological/philosophical essay on one important aspect of food in Spain; see page 217 for her reflections, from PPC 27, *on tapas. A long essay in similar style, devoted this time to Cocido, had already appeared in* PPC 18, *and it is from that essay that we reprint the following recipe.*

Cocido Madrileno Deluxe

1/4 kg chickpeas
1/2 kg shoulder beef
half of a hen
100 g bacon fat
100 g ham
100 g chorizo
one black pudding
one salted pig's trotter
1 kg greens (cabbage, spinach, broad beans, thistles, etc)
3/4 kg potatoes
70 g soup noodles
50 ml oil
1/2 kg tomatoes
spices: garlic, salt

A large, broad-based pot is needed. In this the meat, bacon fat, hen, and ham are put—with enough cold water to cover them—on the fire. When foam begins to form, skim it off. When the mixture begins to boil, add the chickpeas and pig's trotter (which have been previously soaking together for at least ten hours). When the pot boils again it is taken off the flame and left on the side of the fire to cook as slowly as possible, but without interruption, for three hours (or more, if necessary). When it begins to cook add the required salt and half a small onion with a clove stuck in it. The greens are cooked in a separate pot, together with the chorizo and black pudding, taking care that all is cooked at the right moment and seasoning well. A quarter of an hour before serving, six small peeled potatoes are added.

At the right moment, the broth for preparing the soup is extracted, filtered through a cloth, and noodles added. The soup constitutes the first course of the whole dish.

The chickpeas are thoroughly drained and put on a platter; on them is put the beef, cut in small pieces and then decorated with the ham, hen, bacon fat and pig's trotter—all cut into morsels and arranged as artistically as possible.

The greens, well drained, are lightly fried in oil, where a chopped garlic clove will have been frying. It is then put on another platter along with the chorizo and black pudding, cut into slices with the potatoes.

The two platters are served together and are often accompanied by a sauce of the tomatoes fried in small pieces and presented in a jug.

Saunders

Rita O'Brien

A charming reminiscence and a wonderful recipe. If read in the summer, it could serve as a timely reminder that it is high time to be making Christmas Pudding for December—or indeed December of the following year.

It wasn't her real name; she was actually 'Sanders' which is rhymed with 'danders', but she and my grandmother were too shy to arrive at the right pronunciation. They were both eighteen. My grandmother had been wedded to a man she scarcely knew and was landed with a large house in Hampstead together with a staff she knew not at all, and of whom she was terrified. Saunders, freshly recruited from the country, was amid strangers in a totally strange environment. How the two got together I don't know; it was not usual for the mistress of the house, in those days, to have direct contact with her kitchenmaid. But the shared terror and the shared youth led to a deep and mutually respectful friendship, and Saunders stayed with my grandmother, first as Head Cook and then as sole cook, until she died of diabetes when she was in her sixties. I don't think my grandmother ever ceased missing her for the remaining years of her life.

I remember Saunders most vividly: a tiny thin autocrat, sparse grey hair scraped into a severely tidy and minuscule bun. 'Her' children were always addressed as 'Miss Norah', 'Miss Stella', and 'Master Frank' regardless of the fact that the first two were matrons and the last was a tycoon. We 'grandchildren' were also always addressed as 'Master' and "Miss'.

In the London of the late nineteenth century it was thought that the best house servants, and certainly the best cooks, came from Bedfordshire. That was why, I have been told, Saunders was recruited into my grandmother's household. She certainly came from a country family in Bedfordshire, and brought with her some of that county's recipes and much of its tradition. This Christmas pudding, a true Plum Pudding, is one such. Saunders would never serve a Christmas Pudding that had not been kept for over a year. We always make them in our family, but sometimes they are youngsters of a mere five months old when eaten. They still taste excellent and rather different from most other Christmas Puds. The quantities given are enough to cater for a very large household plus donations to various offspring. I make up a half quantity and still have enough to give a couple of the puddings to my children. Stored in a cool place they keep for 2 years.

Saunders' Plum Pudding

2 lb prunes
2 lb currants
1 lb sultanas
1 lb chopped peel
juice and grated rind of 2 lemons
2 lb chopped suet
2 oz blanched and chopped bitter almonds
1/2 lb blanched and chopped sweet almonds
1/2 lb plain flour
1/2 teaspoon mixed spice } mixed together and sieved
1 lb brown sugar
5 well beaten eggs
1 gill rum
1/4 pint brandy
1 pint strong old ale

Stone and cut up the prunes. Add to, and mix well with the other dry ingredients. Add the eggs and the liquids and stir very well indeed. Turn into greased pudding basins. Cover with greaseproof paper and pudding cloths. Steam for eight hours, or according to pressure cooker timings, or (as I do) steam for one hour and then cook overnight in the simmering oven of an Aga stove or a very slow oven. Cool, then remove old pudding cloths and re-tie with fresh ones before storing.

7. Notes and Queries

Ever since issue number one, *PPC* has included a feature called Notes and Queries, the name being taken from the journal of that name which was founded in the 19th century. Our own Notes and Queries has accumulated a truly vast collection of miscellaneous pieces of knowledge, plus questions from readers. A selection is given here, in something like chronological sequence but starting with one of the longest running items, which was set going in *PPC 11* by the Editors and continued through *PPC 12*, *13*, *14* and *21*. Not all the items appeared under the heading Notes and Queries, but the one which did not is fitted in here because it was contributed in a similar spirit.

Poubelles de Table **from Alan and Jane Davidson in PPC 11**

When touring the Languedoc and the Pays Basque recently we found that kitchen equipment and gift shops were all displaying 'poubelles de table'. These are pottery recipients with lids, average capacity about 2 litres. They invariably have 'poubelle de table' written on them. But there is a rare sub-species, much smaller, which is inscribed 'poubelle d'apéritif'. We never witnessed the purchase of either, but inferred from their ubiquity that sales must occur.

Buying a bottle of wine at a remote farmhouse in the Minervois region, the urge suddenly overtook us to pose in this back-of-beyond locale the question which we had felt shy of putting to busier urban people. 'Permit us, Madame, to ask you something unconnected with our purchase. Do you possess a poubelle de table?'

Oh yes, came the answer, they had become quite the fashion since 1980 or so. Daughter-in-law had presented one to her last Christmas. See, she would show it to us. So she did, lifting the lid off and displaying a few olive pits inside. Très pratique it was, according to her.

Can any readers tell us whether this item of equipment is really new in France, or a revival of something which used to be common; and whether there are similar things to be bought in other countries? Our address is 45 Lamont Road, London SW10 0HU.

Poubelles de Table **from Various Correspondents in PPC 12**

The Note on this subject in *PPC 11* elicited many comments, of which we print the following:

Pamela Vandyke Price writes: '. . . . I first saw these things in 1977, when I had been staying in the Lot and, on returning to Bordeaux, my hosts and I walked round Condom after lunch. After that I was vaguely aware of them in many shops—usually of the "craft and gift" type, although there were some very smart ones in Bordeaux. I should imagine, therefore, that the things may have been introduced to Paris and the other cities—where I seldom go—somewhere earlier.

'It occurs to me that they may have originated because, in regions where fish and its subsequent debris is often served, the smaller tables in modern flats and many inexpensive restaurants simply cannot easily accommodate a large bowl for the bones and bits which otherwise is set in the middle of the table. Certainly my Bordeaux friends found the things somewhat unusual at that time so I suppose they may have been the latest gift idea. I do not recall ever seeing anything of the sort in any of the museums of displays of former table settings and therefore I assume that they are a fairly recent item; most of those that I have seen have been either pottery or at least the sort of china that is "peasanty" in style, and I have a theory that one manufacturer got left with thousands of gherkin pots that he couldn't sell, so had an inspiration! (Like the one who invented the "Tom n' Jerry" to shift the quantity of mugs he was stuck with!)'

Peter Lewis says: 'I can trace my first sighting to 1976: it was then as always in one of those smart shops in small French towns which advertise their "listes de mariage". I suspect that is the market they are made for, since they are generally en suite with pots for cornichons and olives and trays for cochonailles, sometimes even sangria sets. Functionally they must be inferior to the "brush and crumb tray" which many English couples got as a wedding present in the twenties. Their giant size alone makes them quite unputtable on the table. I suspect they are a gimmick (apparently hugely successful) of the ceramic gifts industry. The poubelle apéritif (which surely cannot be a *revival* of anything) seems to confirm this.'

D Jon Grossman has these comments: 'No self-respecting French housewife would ever, before recently,* have dreamed of having a "poubelle" on her table. The scraps are pushed aside on your plate, and plates are changed after every course, . . . My modern son reports that poubelles de table are showing up on the tables of "clever, modern" females, "chez qui", he says, "on ne mange pas très bien". Now you know.

'The thing is new, nor can its name possibly be very old. "Poubelle" comes from the name of Eugène Poubelle, Prefect of the Seine from 1883 to 1896, who at the beginning of his administration established the requirement that Parisian housewives use the things. Dauzat (*Dictionnaire étymologique de la langue française,* 1938) informs me that Poubelle's ordinance was dated 15 January 1884. The word is therefore just under a century old, happy birthday to it. Littré died in 1881 (birth year of Picasso), so could not have known the thing (nor the word).

*'I should really reword this. "Before recently" implies that a "self-respecting French housewife" *would* now love one of these things. Which is of course ridiculous. The dinner table is no place for cuteness. Eating is not a solemn enterprise, but it is a serious one. I also draw the line at paper bibs for eating lobster, which I place in the same category as poubelles de table.'

Caroline Davidson reports sightings in another country: 'Poubelles de table have become very common in German hotels at the breakfast table. They are used as waste bins for egg shell, jam wrappers, ham fat, salami rind and bits of leftover bread and roll—the debris, in short, of a large German breakfast. There are two types, both made out of plastic: an orange one, labelled "Breakfast Things" (in English) and decorated with pictures of a coffee pot, coffee mug, a boiled egg in a cup etc., and a light brown variety labelled "Für Fische Abfälle" (for fish debris) and decorated with an apple, pear, strawberry, gooseberry and daisies set against a trellis background. The orange type doesn't say where it was made, but the brown is clearly marked "Made in Germany". There is no sign that these poubelles de table are used at other meals, although the reference to fish debris is suggestive in this connection, or that they have been adopted in German homes. I certainly didn't see any in kitchen equipment and gift shops and, inspired by your account of them in France, I did look quite hard.'

Poubelles de Table **from Various Correspondents in PPC 13**

Cathy Salzman writes: '. . . when I was in a shop in Bruges last month I saw not only a "poubelle de table" but also a "tafel emmer". The shopkeeper told me that the poubelle de table appeared about two years ago. The tafel emmer came shortly thereafter, in response to demands by Flemish speaking patriots.'

Edward Schneider offers the first North American contribution to the subject. 'Wylie's restaurant on First Avenue and 50th Street [in New York] does a roaring trade in broiled pork ribs (nice to eat, but nothing to do with barbecued ribs, which is what they are billed as) and broiled and fried chicken. Clearly, unless you adopt the Spanish *tapas*-bar practice of tossing detritus onto the floor, a poubelle de table is a required item at a place like Wylie's. The management has found the perfect article: an aluminium wine-cooler. They have scores of them. There are nests of them in piles in the kitchen. There is one on every table whose occupants are eating things with bones in them. The white wine is served in carafes simply placed on the table, sans wine-cooler, sans ice. But the fried onions are divinely greasy.

Your Editors close the matter for the time being with the following further report from what appears to be the heartland of the poubelle de table, the South of France.

'On a recent visit to the region of Toulouse/Périgord/Bordeaux, we had two illuminating conversations, and a number of eye-opening experiences. The proprietor of the shop "Cadeaux St. Jacques" in Montauban talked to us about his sales of poubelles de table. They had started about five or six years ago, mainly for wedding present lists, but had recently become especially lively on the occasion of Mothers' Day. His record sales figure for one day was approximately 40. He offered a wide variety, but nothing of a startlingly novel design. We did notice that some of the objects were inscribed "table nette" rather than "poubelle de table".

'In Agen we found our first unlabelled p de t: a creation of astonishing purity. Imagine a tall octagonal vase with two handles and a lid, all in white faience, and with no decoration or inscription on it except for "made in Italy" on the bottom. The lady in the shop seemed to be unaware of the rarity of this item. In answer to our breathless enquiries she said merely that the "grossiste" had chosen it for her. She agreed that most p de t were inscribed, and that this was something of an exception, but remained resolutely calm about the whole affair. In the same town we found a p de t in the form of a WC. The same series, all marked "création Céramiques à main", included a "table nette", which—and this is significant—was of normal shape. A purchaser was clearly expected to take one or the other, not both, and his or her choice (most purchasers are male, incidentally) would be dictated by either aesthetic values or a certain sense of humour.

'Finally, taking lunch in a hotel in a small market square, we asked our companion at the communal table what he did. He was a commercial traveller catering for gift shops. Ah, did he know about p de t? But of course, a very popular line. He had explored the possibility of importing some from Britain, but the difficulties were formidable and he had to continue obtaining supplies of cheap ones from Taiwan and China and more expensive pottery ones from a craft factory at Lourdes. He confirmed that there is a trend towards labelling the things "table nette", and said that this refined version now accounted for about a third of his sales. Reverting to Britain, a country high in his esteem, he enquired whether any form of p de t was available there. We assured him that the market was wide open!'

Voiders — from Mary Wondrausch in PPC 14

A propos the [discontinued correspondence on] poubelles de table—Hugh Rhodes in 'The Booke of Nurture 1568' talks at some length on this subject—but here, of course, it was the servant who placed the 'rubbish' in a vessel.

> Also see ye have voiders in readiness to avoid the morsels they do leave on their trenchers. Then with your trencher knife take off such fragments, and put them in your voider, and set them clean again . . .

He goes on at some length on this subject—I cannot imagine what the 'voider' look'd like, probably earthenware, rather than a sort of medieval crumb tray. The reference is to be found in a very interesting little Pelican paper back by John Dover Wilson entitled 'Life in Shakespeare's England'.

Poubelles de Table — from the Editors in PPC 21

This subject (*PPC 11–14* and *16*) has been laid to rest for some time, but an extraordinary discovery compels us to give it one more airing.

Contemplating a miscellany of unsold goods in a household goods shop, closed down for ever, on the King's Road in Chelsea only a hundred yards from our editorial desk, we beheld a dusty carton which bore the astonishing inscription reproduced on the following page.

We traced the owner of the former shop, had it opened up, and found within the carton a silver-plated object which was, unmistakeably, a biscuit container with a hinged lid, as shown in the drawing. The makers are identified as a company called Mayell, and the product is certified 'made in

England'. We bought it, and are left wondering whether any French tourists in England may have acquired specimens and put them to use in accordance with the French name. Ours works thus quite well.

The next item, of a fishy nature, also ran in several issues.

Why Huss? Or Uss? **from Dawn and Douglas Nelson in PPC 6**

The English common names of the small sharks known as dogfish are confusing. Living in Kent and having the opportunity to talk with old French fishermen, we think that we have a little light to shed on the matter, so far as the mysterious name 'huss' is concerned. In his book on *North Atlantic Seafood* (Macmillan 1979 [reissued by Ten Speed Press in 2003]), Alan Davidson links it with the larger-spotted dogfish, *Scyliorhinus stellaris.* In our examination of Kent catches over the years we have concluded that both *S. stellaris* and *S. caniculus* (the lesser-spotted dogfish) were simply called 'dogs', but that the 'spurdog', *Squalus acanthius,* was known because of its viviparous habits as a 'nurse dog'. This was shortened to 'a Nurse', which was pronounced in the markets as 'a Nuss', which the fishmongers thought was 'an Uss', with the result that they labelled the fish simply 'Uss'. When these fish got to London the highly educated Billingsgate porters assumed that the ignorant Kentish men had dropped an 'h', which they restored by changing 'Uss' to "Huss'. We think that this is the origin of the name. In the last 20 years or so, however, we have noted that, while most of the dogfish sold in the market at Folkestone are still labelled 'Uss', and later, when sold in the shops, 'Huss', these are often lesser-spotted dogs (*S. caniculus*) and not spurdogs. So the name may have been moving from one species to another as their abundance in the catch changes.

Davidson refers to another name, 'hurse'. We have never come across this and would like to know whether any reader can tell us where it is used.

Huss **from Jane Grigson in PPC 8**

I like huss, which is a very underrated fish, but really there is no mystery about the name (*PPC 6*, page 67), except one of its remote origin. As a name for kinds of dog-fish 'huss' wasn't overlooked by the *OED,* which quotes 'husse' (1530), along with the form 'huske' (c. 1440), saying the name was then obsolete (1933). The Dictionary didn't refer to Frank Buckland's mention of huss in one of his books—huss dried and salted outside fishermen's homes at Folkestone (other names he picked up were 'rig' and 'Folkestone beef'). The *OED Supplement,* vol. 2 (1976), deletes obsolete, and adds later examples of 'huss' from 1963 onwards. Alan Davidson's 'hurse' (remember the typewriter proximity of h and n) looks to me like an error for 'nurse', another dog-fish name going back to the 15th century, in the earlier form 'nusse', which is likely (*OED* again) to have arisen from 'an husse'. ['Hurse' was not a misprint, but an alternative version of 'huss'. Ed.] Certainly it has nothing to do with the nursing-mother or viviparous nature of any species. The upshot of this etymological flurry is how sensible modern fish authorities were to fix on the time-honoured name 'huss' instead of 'dog-fish' for upgrading this good fish which has been despised as poverty food. What about upgrading tripe with another name?

Huss and Uss **from Dawn and Douglas Nelson in PPC 9**

The fishermen with whom we talked about the name of this fish (*PPC 6*) were 'old Kent' not 'old French' fishermen (a misprint which may have weakened faith in our findings).

As regards the comments by Jane Grigson in *PPC 8* (page 73), we were aware of the *OED* explanation of the name, but we think that this, like many derivations in the *OED,* fails to fit the known facts.

The word has always been spelled in Kent without an 'H'. The word 'uss' certainly occurs in the 18th century, if not earlier. That this should come from 'huske' seems improbable.

The *OED* definition of 'huss' (not quoted by Jane Grigson) is: 'The dog-fish, the skin of which was much used by fletchers for smoothing and polishing arrows.' The *OED* adds: 'Also *attrib.,* as *huss skin* (*huskyn, hurse-skin*).' Our information is that the production of archery implements was not an industry of coastal Kent, and that the use of fish skin in it was not likely to influence a fish name. It would also be a backward type of derivation. That a fletcher might be called an usser would be the right way round, if there was a right way round, which we dispute.

Some years ago we had exchanges with the *OED* on the derivation of the Kentish (and other counties) word 'gratton' and its various spellings. We ended with the impression that their authority for what they said was usually their own earlier editions which were presumably delivered personally by Moses!

But at least we agree with Jane Grigson that the fish authorities have done well to retain the name 'huss' for this fish instead of insisting that it be officially dubbed 'dogfish'.

Jim Peterson's contribution reflects the interest of a number of PPC *readers in making culinary contrivances at home. (Another example was a home-made coffee roaster, designed by Ralph Hancock, sales of which—through a retired postman from Laos—were actually organised by Prospect Books.)*

A Home-made 'Truffler' — from Jim Peterson in PPC 13

I am often frustrated by instructions in old French cookbooks for the larding of meats with truffles. Requests to 'piquer aux truffes' or 'clouer aux truffes' result invariably in the brittle allumettes of truffle falling to pieces in my hand. I recently was asked to truffle a capon breast for a special dinner and, in order to do so, I invented a little device that I think may be of interest to *PPC* readers.

It requires only a length of metal coat hanger, a piece of copper tubing and a plastic drinking straw. The piece of copper tubing is crimped or glued to the length of coat hanger. This forms a kind of plunger. This plunger is then inserted into the straw.

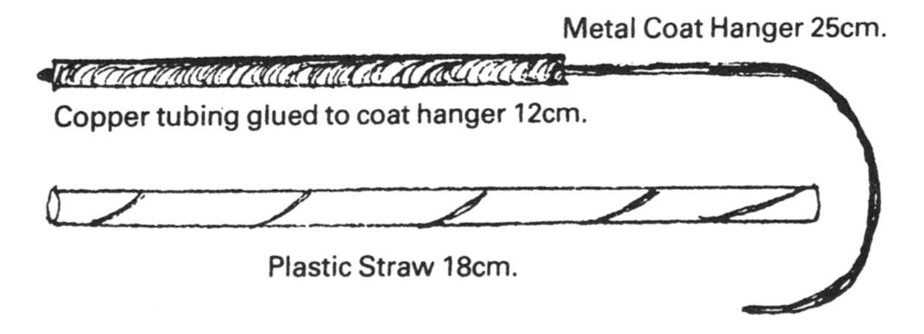

Truffler, 1/2 actual size.

To use the 'truffler', a hole is started in the piece of meat with a larding needle (an aiguille à piquer, not a lardoir). The larding needle is followed directly behind by the truffler. When the truffler has penetrated the meat and come out the other end, the plunger is pulled back and the piece of truffle inserted into the straw. The truffler is then pulled back into the piece of meat, and the straw is then slid out over the plunger, leaving the piece of truffle embedded in the meat. Larding a piece of meat this way is admittedly a time consuming process, but, when I finally cut into my roast breast of capon, there was a stunning chequerboard pattern of truffles.

I have not as yet experimented further, but I imagine that the same principle might apply for larding with other things—pieces of marrow, foie gras, strips of vegetable, etc. Please see the diagram.

Among the 'hands-on' contributors to PPC, *the potter Mary Wondrausch has an outstanding record. Her book* Mary Wondrausch on Slipware *contains much of interest on the relationship between food and pottery vessels.*

A Potter's Beans — from Mary Wondrausch in PPC 25

I am a vegetarian, and, although from a historical point of view Joop Witteveen's article in *PPC 24* was enormously interesting, it was hard work to detach myself from the Swan—if you see what I mean, particularly as at the moment I am enjoying making some large one-handled supper bowls that have a swan swimming in them.

These bowls are for eating a 'mess of beans' in front of the open fire, particularly appropriate in our family as my daughter and her children live in a Tipi (wigwam). When they are here, they do their same thing in the house, which is absolutely maddening—blackened pans and everyone naked on sheepskins by the ashy fire—but her cooking is superlative. This leads up to your lady (Lynda Brown, *PPC 24*), who sounds a bit naïve to those of us who have farted our way through hundreds of bowls of every type of bean stew.

For the last 10 years I've had solid fuel cookers—not, sadly, Agas, but Danish and now a large Rayburn, and these and the open fire replicate, I'm sure, earlier ways of cooking using both heavy pans and earthenware dishes.

As I get older and seem to work even harder and longer hours in the pottery, and basically live on my own, the simpler the food the better, and the less time doing it also the better. I buy the best and freshest ingredients in season, bake all my own bread with marvellous Loseley flour bought by the sack straight from the mill. Each baking is different from the last, with additions of rye or barley or white flour, and with or without seeds or nuts, and sometimes a wicked treat of *pain briochée,* gold with butter and eggs.

What a digression! Cooking beans—beans of the day (dry), cover with water, 2 large garlic cloves, branch of thyme and perhaps a few juniper berries, put in a cool oven at 6pm, adjust water before bed, and next morning put in a top oven. I scoop out some beans for pâté, salad, or 'rissoles'. Have soup for lunch, shared with workers, and beans for supper. Next day there is the little bowl of beans in the fridge to make another meal.

My daughter (Clio) does this sort of thing on the open fire in a big black pot, often with layered contents (like the gipsies). I will try this year to take some notes, for her food is extraordinary, from the huge blackened 'chappatti' (their bread) to the wild weeds and fungus and mirabelle jam—they make all of it smoky and strong with flavour.

This is an example of a question in Notes and Queries receiving an illuminating response from another reader—exactly what was supposed to happen.

Pie Crust Decorations **from Geraldine Killoran in PPC 26**

Does anyone have any information about the pie crust ornament depicted in the accompanying sketch? It is made by cutting and scoring the flat rolled crust, and no cut-out crust appliqués are used.

My mother taught me to make the design (which also serves as steam vent) and she learned it from her mother. Since this side of my family are all English in nationality, I can only assume that the pattern originated in Britain. Also, when I was about ten years old, I saw this design in the illustrations of pies in what I now believe was an English edition of a Mother Goose book. This suggests to me that the design may have been commonly used in England at one time.

Also, does any reader know of any book or article which treats the history of pie crust decorations?

Pie Crust Decorations in Early American Cookery
from William Woys Weaver in PPC 28

In response to Geraldine Killoran's question in *PPC 26* about pie crust decorations, I should like to offer some material to expand upon her theme.

First, pie crust ornamentation by scoring or cutting the crust is an area of historical research that is largely ignored, most obviously because the evidence is destroyed in the eating. Yet, and I repeat *yet,* this aspect of folk or popular cookery is a very important one in British and American culture. I say this because pies once formed a large if not conspicuous segment of everyday diet, and because decorative motifs of this kind may have a regional dimension: cooks in certain localities may have used particular decorative patterns. This is the kind of fascinating material that leads itself to food maps of the type European ethnologists have been compiling over the past 60 years—no better place for us to begin than with pies.

I am personally unfamiliar with the composite pattern as drawn by Killoran, but I have seen the various parts of it used in other ways. The middle pattern, which to my eyes resembles a stylized sprig of rosemary, goes by the name of 'bird tracks' in some south-eastern Pennsylvania households. In fact, I believe that it is also known by this name in parts of New Jersey and Delaware.

Several years ago I interviewed an elderly cook (then in her 80s) who made a green tomato or 'summer mincemeat' pie after the manner of her grandmother, Rachel Cook Hallowell (1814–94), whom she knew as a child.[1] I photographed the pie because the 'bird tracks' in the crust fascinated me. 'Bird tracks' were one of the most common decorative motifs used in rural Pennsylvania, New Jersey and Delaware for what our old cookbooks would call fruit tarts—shallow fruit pies covered with an upper crust (a lower crust always implied). The upper crust on these fruit pies was generally fashioned like a lid so that it would be removable by lifting with a spatula or broad knife. It was general practice before baking to brush this crust with cold water and scatter grated loaf sugar or vanilla sugar over it. Then the 'bird tracks' do indeed look like tracks in snow.

The 'bird track' design was also used on the top crust of pot pies, that is, the rich crust used to seal the thing in its iron pot. This upper crust, like that of the fruit tarts, generally bakes flat and therefore lends itself to such scoring and incising.

Fruit pies with lattice-work top crusts, where the lattice-work (strips of dough) is laid at angles to form diamond-shaped openings, were called 'window pies' locally.[2] This term, as well as 'bird tracks', was in common use in the Delaware Valley during the 18th century, and one must suppose that the terms were also known in Britain.

Although they represented about 40% of the population, the Pennsylvania Germans did not traditionally make fruit tarts like those of Anglo-Americans during the 18th century. Furthermore, they did not have a word for such tarts in their vocabulary, aside from the non-dialect term *Pastete,* which is more correctly a term for a pie with a standing crust. *Pastete,* however, was used as the equivalent of 'pie'

in Kantner's *Book of Objects* (Reading, PA, 1887), a book published in German and English for the use of Pennsylvania-German school children.[3] I have reproduced Kantner's pie illustration (see previous page) because it obviously shows a fruit pie, its top crust decorated with 'bird tracks'.

Historical juvenile literature is doubtless one of the richest sources for pie crust iconography, and I do believe that very little has been done with this material by food historians. Research should be linked with field-work: interviews with as many elderly cooks as possible, to record what they remember about family and regional patterns. Geraldine Killoran's tentative question about her mother's crusts is an excellent starting point for such a project. I am very glad she took the time to ask the question.

References

1. Interview with Mary Larkin Thomas, February 1975. Rachel Hallowell was a recorded minister in the Society of Friends (Quakers) at New Garden in Chester County, Pennsylvania. Her cookbook, compiled between 1860 and 1889, is now in my possession.
2. See Cornelius Weygandt's *Philadelphia Folks. Ways and Institutions in and about the Quaker City,* Appleton-Century, New York and London, 1938. Weygandt devotes fully a chapter to reminiscences on this subject.
3. W. C. Kantner, *Kantner's Illustrated Book of Objects,* E. H. Rhoads, Reading, PA, 1887: p 10.

William Woys Weaver, already quoted on pie crust decoration (page 486), is a food historian of longstanding, who has tended to focus on subjects such as 'Pennsylvania Dutch Cookery' (he lives in Pennsylvania and contributed a brilliant essay on 'Shad Cookery in Old Philadelphia' to PPC 11*), but his interests and expertise range much further afield. His essay on the 'Patent Conjuror' attracted some footnotes from other* PPC *readers, but essentially stands on its own as the locus classicus for this subject.*

Lifting the Lid on the Patent Conjurer

from William Woys Weaver in PPC 26

The mystery of Hannah Glasse's necromancer or conjurer has recently precipitated a lively round-robin among several food historians on both sides of the Atlantic. While Jennifer Stead has already explored the matter at some length,[1] and Eliza Acton has provided us with an illustration—gratefully reproduced in the Prospect Books facsimile of Glasse in 1983,[2] a happy discovery has brought to light new material on the subject. I should like to share it with readers of *PPC.*

There seems to be general agreement that the necromancer was distinct from the conjurer, older in form, yet functioning along similar principles. Jennifer Stead concluded that John Rich (an 18th-century actor) was not its inventor, although there seems to me no confirming evidence that Mr Rich the actor and Mr Rich the inventor according to Glasse were actually the same man. The invention lore in fact may be apocryphal, because pictures of necromancers can be found in continental sources dating from the 16th century. It is clear, however, that the English conjurer—the conjurer of Acton, was an 'improved' necromancer that was patented during the 18th century. The original owner of that patent is not presently known.

References to conjurers in the 18th-century American newspapers are not common, to say the least, but where they do appear, they refer consistently to the conjurer's *patented* design and to arrangements made with unnamed patentees for special manufacturing rights. The patent appears to be English, although no definite proof of that has yet surfaced in patent archives, American or British.

One of the most extensive and informative American references to the conjurer appeared in the January 26, 1797, issue of *New World,* a Philadelphia commercial newspaper with national circulation.[3] Thomas Passmore, a Quaker tin manufacturer in the city, claimed to have obtained exclusive American rights to the conjurer. The text of his advertisement ran as follows.

THE PATENT CONJURER
THE SUBSCRIBER

> Having obtained an exclusive right of making a very useful and valuable Machine, called the CONJURER; begs leave to recommend to the public as a cheaper, and more expeditious way of cooking and boiling water, than any before invented, he flatters himself that a person to be convinced of its utility, needs but to see it. It is very convenient for masters of vessels, as it will enable them to cook in the cabin, when the weather will not permit them to be on deck. Its great saving of fuel makes it useful to those families, or persons who wish to lessen the expence of that necessary article, while for convenience it is useful to all—as a kettle of water for tea may be boiled in six minutes, with a sheet of paper, a few shavings or any combustible. It will cook a steak very nicely in three minutes, also veal cutlets, mutton chops, hash meats of any kind, boil eggs & c. & c. It is very convenient for gentleman [sic] in chambers, as it quite precludes the necessity of lighting a fire: it is likewise very convenient on fishing parties, as the fish may be boiled immediately as they are taken out of the water.—Come and see the Conjurer, it is perfectly innocent and harmless.

N.B. Orders from any part of the United States will be attended to. The Conjurer is small, not more than twelve inches diameter.

Thomas Passmore

No. 228 Market Street.

January 7

Not only does Passmore describe how to use the conjurer, he gives its dimensions and makes a very pointed reference to its usefulness for shipboard cookery. There is supporting evidence to suggest that in America, conjurers were used mostly by the shipping industry, particularly with the growth of East Indian and China trade after 1787. The fuel-saving feature is one obvious benefit.

Nothing more is heard of the Passmore conjurers until 1804, when S.H. Williams established a tin manufactury at Passmore's old address.[4] It is quite likely that Passmore and Williams were in some way related by marriage, because Passmore appears to have gone into retirement soon after Williams took over the firm's location. Isaac Williams, a son, established the company as one of the leading suppliers of culinary equipment in the United States, and as a sideline, continued to manufacture conjurers well into the 1880s.[5]

The Williams conjurer was somewhat different from the model illustrated by Acton. It was redesigned a bit so that it could serve both as a conjurer and chafing dish or warming pan. This made it useful for cooking on steamboats and in canal boat kitchens, as well as for general hotel applications. The Williams model was heated with an oil lamp rather than strips of paper. It is illustrated on one of the firm's trade labels found in the Chew Family Papers

at the Historical Society of Pennsylvania.[6] This is the same identifying label Williams attached to all his conjurers and other large kitchen utensils. It was applied with gum and could be removed easily with water. It is illustrated on the facing page.

The presumed date of the Williams label is 1855, although it is no different from somewhat earlier examples. A complete Williams conjurer, identical to that shown on the label, is presently on display in the culinary exhibit at Philadelphia.[7] It is constructed of sheet tin and Britannia ware (an alloy similar to pewter). Having given that conjurer a trial according to directions provided by Glasse, Acton and Thomas Passmore, I can confirm that Williams's conjurer, while somewhat larger than Acton's model, works with remarkable efficiency. It is not competition for the microwave, let that be clearly understood. And it will not cook six pounds of mutton in fifteen minutes as Hannah Glasse would have us believe. In fact, six pounds of meat will fill a standard twelve-inch conjurer fairly solid and will thus scorch on the bottom before the top part has begun to cook. If Hannah Glasse's cooker were 24–30 inches across, then it would be possible to cook the meat in 15 minutes, but the heat must be constant and evenly distributed on the bottom of the apparatus, and that is no easy task with strips of paper.

Notes

1. Jennifer Stead, 'Quizzing Glasse: or Hannah Scrutinized,' Part I, *PPC 13* (March 1983): pp 22–23. [See page 333 of the present book.]
2. Hannah Glasse, *The Art of Cookery* (1747), London, Prospect Books. 1983: p 192.
3. Copies of *The New World* are in the collection of the Library Company of Philadelphia.
4. James Robinson, *The Philadelphia Directory for 1804,* Philadelphia, John H. Oswald, 1804, p 178, lists Passmore as a tin manufacturer at 15 North 7th Street. Williams is not actually listed in the city directory until 1805, by which time Passmore had moved to 172 High Street. All of the Williams trade literature clearly states that the firm established itself at 228 High Street in 1804, presumably between printings of the city directories.
5. They are even advertised under 'Chafing Dishes' in Charles S. Archer's *The Latest and Best Cook Book,* New York, Edgewood Publishing Co, 1884, p 290.
6. The Chew Family Papers, Box 282 'Advertisements', Manuscript Division, Historical Society of Pennsylvania, Philadelphia.
7. 'The Larder Invaded: Reflections on Three Centuries of Philadelphia Food and Drink', jointly sponsored by the Historical Society of Pennsylvania and the Library Company of Philadelphia. Complete label copy for all items in the exhibition, including the conjurer, are available with the catalogue on microfisc.

Next we have a controversial question, discussion of which was initiated by David Karp (whose detailed essays on various fruits for the Los Angeles Times *have attracted much interest and admiration) and Cara De Silva (a well known food writer in New York). A contrary point of view was put forward, with eloquence, by Sri Owen, who has for long been writing authoritatively about the food and cookery of Indonesia, her native country and other parts of South-east Asia. This attracted a vigorous riposte from Karen Hess and comments by myself (Alan Davidson) which sought to clear me of any suspicion that the term might first have appeared in a book of mine, while leaving open the question of the first recorded use in print, on which we did, as promised, have discussions with the* OED. *The outcome of their further investigations is not yet known. Meanwhile, contacts in South Africa who were helping with research for* The Oxford Companion to Food, *have confirmed that the expression is very definitely an offensive one in that country.*

Infidel Lime **from David Karp and Cara De Silva in PPC 58**

What's in a name? A lot, when it comes to the politically problematic nomenclature of the kaffir lime. Native to southeastern Asia, from Sri Lanka to Indonesia, this green, golf ball sized citrus (*Citrus hystrix*) has become available in Western countries only in the last two decades. Its bumpy, wrinkled rind and double leaves add distinctive pungency to soups, salads and curries.

'Kaffir' (also spelled kafir) means infidel in Arabic, from *kafara,* to be skeptical in religious matters. G. C. Whitworth's *Anglo-Indian Dictionary* (1885) states that not only was the term applied by Muslims to unbelievers, but 'in Western India the word is a common term of abuse'. When Arab slavers first came to the east coast of Africa they applied the word to the inhabitants, and it is best known today as a derogatory term used by South African whites for blacks. According to *A Dictionary of South African English* (Oxford, 1991) this 'term of contempt' is 'now an actionable insult'.

Although we have not found an authoritative etymology for kaffir lime, reference works list more than a dozen compound names with kaffir: kaffir chestnut, corn, melon, orange, plum, etc, all southern African products. But surely 'kaffir lime' derives from Asian rather than South African usage. We propose this explanation: Indian Muslims most likely encountered the fruit as an import from lands such as Thailand and Sri Lanka, where Buddhists and other non-Muslims predominated. (True, both kaffir limes and Muslims abound in Malaysia and Indonesia, but the main point holds.) From this Indian usage, intended to convey otherness and exotic provenance, the term passed into English. CAN ANYONE CONFIRM THIS SUPPOSITION?

Although the name is not directly linked to South African usage, it is understandable that South African and other blacks find it offensive. The problem then arises, what to substitute for a term that has only recently become familiar? Many authors are unaware that this is an issue, and most cookbooks and publications do use 'kaffir lime'; otherwise, notes Charles Perry of the *Los Angeles Times:* 'no one would know what you're talking about.' However, Nancie McDermott, in her excellent *Real Thai* and *Real Vegetarian Thai,* opts for 'wild lime'. Alas, in Australia this term refers to an entirely unrelated citrus. In fact, Cherry Ripe, food columnist for *The Australian,* uses the Thai word, *makrut,* though she hedges her bets with a phrase such as 'also known as kaffir lime'. Can anyone suggest a better solution?

Incidentally, *hystrix,* in the kaffir lime's Latin name, means 'porcupine', and according to Charmaine Solomon's recent *Encyclopedia of Asian Food,* one of the fruit's common names is 'porcupine orange'. Indonesians call it *jeruk purut.* Cambodians refer to it by a name meaning 'funny lime', but *Bruce Costs's Asian Ingredients* lists as alternate names 'ghost's lime' and 'lime of an evil spirit'. James Saunt's *Citrus Varieties of the World: An Illustrated Guide* says the fruit is called *combava* in France. Most amusingly, he relates that Malaysians liken its appearance to that of a crocodile's eyebrows.

On 'Infidel Lime' **from Sri Owen in PPC 59**

I cannot resist the urge to reply to David Karp's and Cara De Silva's comments (in *PPC 58*) on the name 'kaffir lime', although I gave David my opinion on the subject when we met earlier this year.

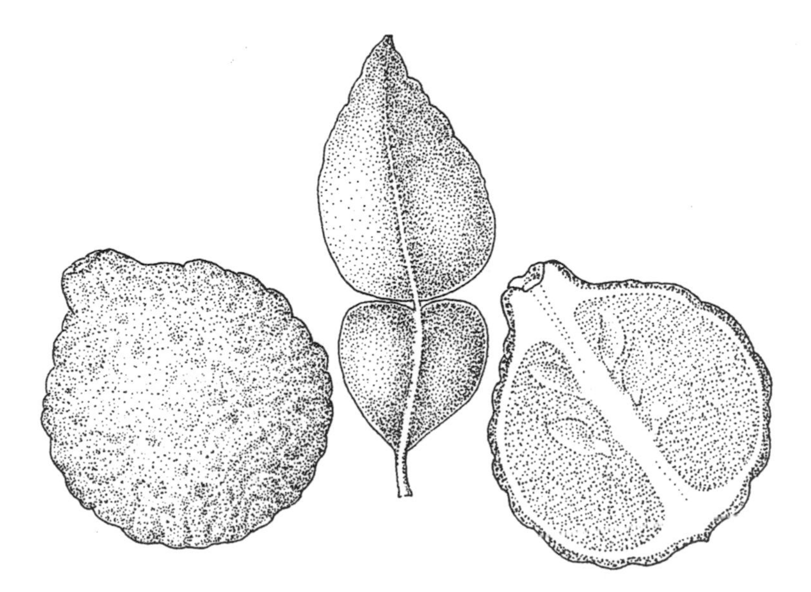

I admit to being among the cookery writers he mentions, who 'are unaware that this is an issue'. The only reason for avoiding the term 'kaffir lime' is that it gives offence to certain groups of people. Fine. If I receive a reasonable number of complaints from individuals who say they have been hurt, upset, or otherwise disadvantaged by my using the word 'kaffir' as part of the name of an ingredient in any recipe or cookbook, I promise to follow Cherry Ripe's example and refer to this knobbly lime as *makrut.* Or I may prefer to revert to my own language and call it *limau purut* (*jeruk* is Javanese). In any case, as Charles Perry points out, I shall still have to explain that I really mean 'kaffir lime'.

However, I don't believe I ever shall get a complaint from an upset kaffir. Why? Because there is no group of people to whom the description *kaffir* is regularly applied with a derogatory meaning. South Africa may be a special case, but even there the word is apparently only actionable if it is used as a calculated insult. The word is, as David and Cara say, Arabic for 'non-Moslem' or 'unbeliever'. But the South Africans who use it as an insult are whites and presumably call themselves Christians; they have simply borrowed *kaffir* because it was originally used by Moslem traders in East Africa to refer to non-Moslem natives. Such borrowings can lead to the devaluing of a word and its eventual adoption as an insult, but that does not mean that the word loses its proper meaning and usage in the world at large.

In Indonesia, the world's largest Moslem nation, *kafir* (with one *f,* or very often a *p*) is a non-judgmental word that carries no bad overtones whatever. A Moslem can say to a Christian or Hindu friend: 'Ah, well, you don't have to fast in Ramadan, or course—you're *kapir.*' The friend will not bat an eyelid at this, it is simply a statement of fact. If you want to insult an Indonesian, you can call him 'kaffir-lime face', but this simply means that his face is knobbly and rough like the rind of the fruit. True, in colonial days, if a party of Dutch soldiers visited a Javanese village and started to misbehave, the villagers would drive them out with shouts of *'Orang kapir!'* But the Moslem villagers did not regard unbelievers or infidels as objectionable in themselves.

Meanwhile, across the Straits in Malaya, Henry Burkill was compiling his incomparable *Dictionary of the Economic Products of the Malay Peninsula.* Under *Citrus hystrix* he lists its local names, including those I have mentioned above. But he does not give any English name, because in his time—the 1920s and 30s—it was not imported to the West. So how did it get its English name? Probably in the way David and Cara suggest, if (for instance) Moslems in East Africa thought of it as originating in Thailand. I think I have said enough already to show that the name did not imply the slightest disrespect for either the fruit or the people who exported it.

In short, I don't think there is an issue here at all. And there is more than enough political correctness in the modern world already, don't you think?

Infidel Lime **from Karen Hess in PPC 60**

The letter from David Karp and Cara De Silva (*PPC 58*) concerning the popular name 'kaffir lime' when referring to *Citrus hystrix* should give pause to any thoughtful person. It is true that many writers do not realize that it is an offensive term, but once it is pointed out to them, that should suffice, *pace* Sri Owen (*PPC 59*). She writes: 'And there is more than enough political correctness in the modern world already, don't you think?' An offense to one is an offense to all, is what I say.

Karp and De Silva asked about parallel examples. The popular name of *Brazil nut* in the United States was long *Niggertoe,* this documented in Sturtevant's *Notes on Edible Plants* (1919). It was still common in the 1920s, at least in St Louis, where I lived at the time. I have reason to remember it, because when my father heard me use the term, he threatened punishment if ever again I used the word in any form. I also remember the term *nigger melon* used to designate watermelon. A licorice confection was called *nigger baby* well into the twentieth century, and various pastries containing raisins or blackberries are still known as *niggers-in-a-blanket* in some of our more benighted areas.

There must be any number of such offensive popular terms designating various foods, *dago red,* just for instance.

Kaffir Lime **from Alan Davidson in PPC 60**

Prompted by the debate on this matter, initiated by David Karp and Cara De Silva (*PPC 58*) I have been trying to find out when and where this name came into use, partly from fear that I might turn out to have been one of the first authors writing in English to have used it (in *Fish and Fish Dishes of Laos,* Vientiane, 1974). Looking back in my own archives, I realise that I took it from a pleasant little book, in English, on the *Resources and Products of Thailand.* The author was Suraphong Kanchananaga and the book was published in 1973 by Siam Communications in Bangkok. So, someone else had used it before me. But whether he was the first is, surprisingly, an open question. I have looked in a lot of obvious publications without finding any trace of an earlier use of the term. If anyone can help here, I would be grateful. So, I think, would the *OED,* whose entry for 'kaffir' does not at present include any reference to 'kaffir lime' although it cites many other examples of the adjectival use of kaffir.

I remember that when I first encountered the term I found it puzzling and, to my shame, neither knew what 'kaffir' meant nor took any steps to find out. Now that I am beginning to form a reasonably full picture of how the term has been used in the English language, I am fairly well convinced that it should be avoided. In my own next book I am recommending that for English language purposes the Thai name *makrut,* which has quite wide currency, should be used: thus, 'makrut lime'. I see that Saunt, author of the authoritative book *Citrus Varieties of the World* (1990) adopts this course. Incidentally, McFarland's excellent *Thai-English Dictionary* (1944) explains that in the word 'ma-gkroot' (as he transcribes it) the 'ma' part is a common prefix to the names of fruits of various kinds; thus the durian is *ma-thurian.*

However, I intend to have further discussions with the *OED* on the basis of the bulky dossier which I have now compiled, and will report again if appropriate.

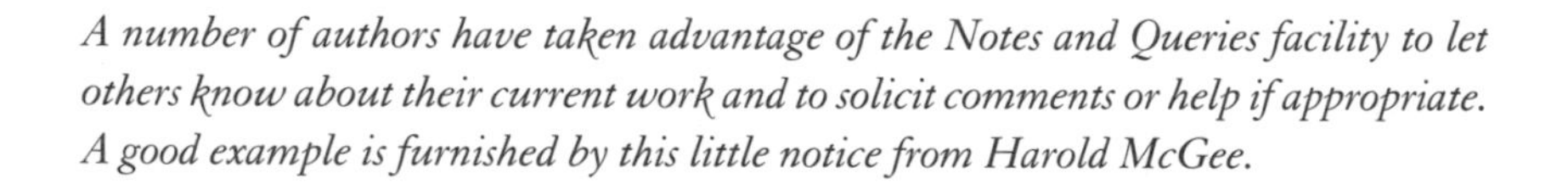

A number of authors have taken advantage of the Notes and Queries facility to let others know about their current work and to solicit comments or help if appropriate. A good example is furnished by this little notice from Harold McGee.

Revision of On Food and Cooking — from Harold McGee in PPC 48

Having recently reached an agreement with my publisher to produce a second, revised edition of *On Food & Cooking*—the first is now ten years old—I have begun to gather the materials, and to seek advice. In the revising I intend not only to correct errors and bring the culinary biology, physics, and chemistry up to date, but also to repair significant omissions, and to open the book's perspective beyond its current American and west-European limits. Toward these ends, and especially the last two, I would like to solicit suggestions from the broadly read, widely fed readers of *PPC.*

One large suggestion has been looming on the back burner even longer than *On Food & Cooking* has been sitting on bookshelves. At our very first meeting, a month or two before the official publication date, Alan Davidson asked whether seafood in all its variety and peculiarity might possibly warrant more than an occasional paragraph in the chapter on meat. I've been waiting a long time for the chance to fix that one! As other examples, less drastic and less direct, I would mention Helen Saberi's recent investigation into the chemistry of Afghan tea theatrics (transforming green tea into black), Charles Perry's exploration of the rationale for couscous (also at an Oxford Symposium), and Yan-Kit So's query about the surprising texture of salted duck eggs (liquid white surrounding a solid yolk): each highlighted an important technique or ingredient to which *On Food & Cooking* pays insufficient attention, or none at all.

I will be most grateful to hear of any corrections, excisions, adumbrations, or other alterations that *PPC* readers would advise for the new improved *On Food & Cooking*. Early replies are appreciated, but this is a long-term project and my request is an open-ended one. I would always like to know better.

[Harold McGee can be contacted by email at: mcgee@curiouscook.com]

Pineapple Tart

The Editors

> **To make a Tart of the** Ananas, **or** Pine-Apple. **From** Barbadoes.
>
> TAKE a Pine-Apple, and twiſt off its Crown: then pare it free from the Knots, and cut it in Slices about half an Inch thick; then ſtew it with a little Canary Wine, or Madera Wine, and ſome Sugar, till it is thoroughly hot, and it will diſtribute its Flavour to the Wine much better than any thing we can add to it. When it is as one would have it, take it from the Fire; and when it is cool, put it into a ſweet Paſte, with its Liquor, and bake it gently, a little while, and when it comes from the Oven, pour Cream over it, (if you have it) and ſerve it either hot or cold.

That heaven helps the reckless is here illustrated by a reminiscence about an incident in the early days of Prospect Books. The late Mike McKirdy, who was then building up with his wife Tessa the business known as Cook's Books, had seen the two volumes of Richard Bradley's The Country Housewife and Lady's Director *(1736), on another bookseller's shelves, classified as agriculture. Realising that they were essentially cookery books, and very interesting ones too, he bought them and suggested to us that we might like to consider a facsimile reprint. The idea appealed to us greatly, all the more so since it seemed to be a genuinely original work (rare in the 18th century) and partly because it seemed that Richard Bradley, the first Professor of Botany at Cambridge, had been unjustly vilified by his successor in that chair and deserved a belated rehabilitation. Our daughter Caroline, a historian, willingly undertook the task of editing the books to become a single volume.*

This was the first occasion on which we really had to think very hard about the size of the print run. We settled on 780, accepting what any other publisher would have regarded as a grotesquely tight ratio between unit production cost and retail price and hoping for the best. After the first flurry of sales it looked as though we had been too optimistic. However, a lucky break in the USA saved the day. James Beard, one of the triumvirate of the best-known cookery writers in the States, set eyes on the book and in his own words had 'an immediate love affair' with it. A focal point of the love affair was Bradley's recipe for Pineapple Tart, the earliest such recipe in England and one which Caroline had tried and found wonderfully good. (It seemed that a recipe which combined historical interest and delicious results was an irresistible lure; Jane Grigson wrote about it too, picking it out as her favourite.) The recipe is given above.

Beard was then at the end of his illustrious career and indeed at the end of his long life; the piece on Bradley which appeared under his familiar by-line was in fact the last of his syndicated columns, and it had a dramatic effect on our fortunes. Instead of trickle-sales lasting for ten years or more, as we expected, Bradley was suddenly out of print. Happy end of story and happy note on which to conclude this book.

INDEX OF ARTICLES

Following is a list of the issue numbers of Petits Propos Culinaires *in which the articles in the present anthology first appeared.*

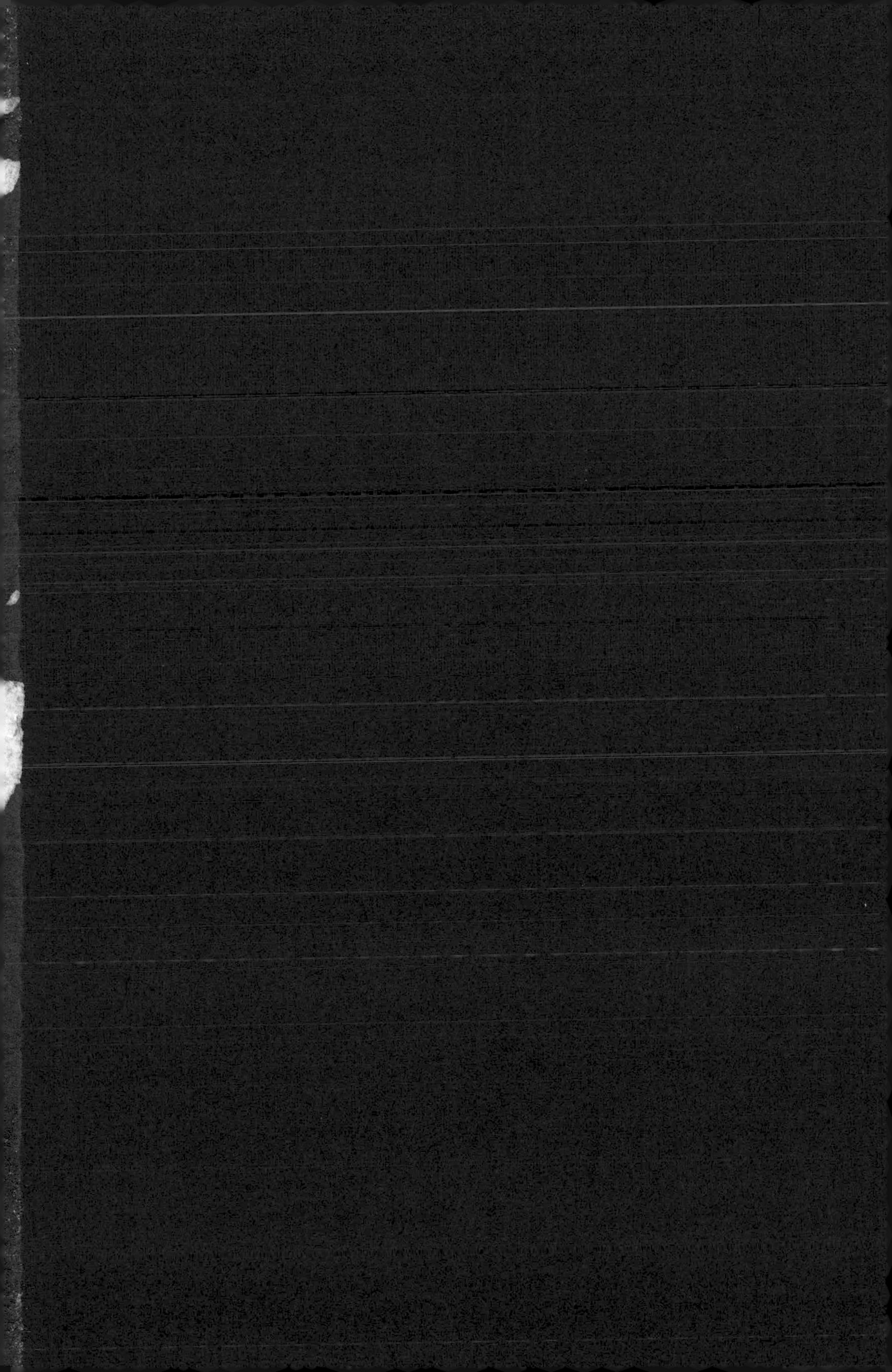